Diagrammatic Rea

Diagrammatic Reasoning

Cognitive and Computational Perspectives

B. Chandrasekaran
Janice Glasgow
N. Hari Narayanan
editors

AAAI Press / The MIT Press

Menlo Park, California
Cambridge, Massachusetts
London, England

445 Burgess Drive
Menlo Park, California 94025

Library of Congress Cataloging-in-Publication Data

Diagrammatic reasoning : cognitive and computational perspective /
Janice Glasgow. N. Nari Narayanan, B. Chandrasekaran, editors.
p. cm.
Includes bibliographical references and index.
ISBN 0-262-57112-9
1. Automatic theorem proving. 2. Artificial intelligence. 3. Image processing. 4. Problem solving. I. Glasgow, Janics. II. Narayanan, N. Hari. III. Chandrasekaran, B., 1942– .
QA76.9.A96D53 1995
006.3'3–dc20 95-14683
CIP

Copublished and distributed by The MIT Press,
Massachusetts Institute of Technology,
Cambridge, Massachusetts and London, England.

Manufactured in the United States of America

Contents

II Theoretical Foundations

III Cognitive and Computational Models

Acknowledgments

The editors owe thanks to a number of individuals. First, and foremost, to the authors who wrote papers or who allowed us to reprint previously published papers for the volume. We are also grateful to Herb Simon for penning an inspiring foreword to the book, and to the section coordinators (Aaron Sloman, Patrick Hayes, David Waltz and Yumi Iwasaki) for volunteering their time toward reviewing papers and writing section introductions. As well, we would like to acknowledge all of the participants of the 1992 AAAI Spring Symposium on Reasoning with Diagrammatic Representations—the enthusiasm of this group of high-quality researchers provided the inspiration for this volume. We thank Herb Simon and Yumi Iwasaki for their role in the organization of this meeting.

The American Association for Artificial Intelligence was supportive in sponsoring the symposium, and Editor-in-Chief Ken Ford was supportive in the publication of this book. David Mike Hamilton of the AAAI Press, in particular, has provided us with ongoing assistance and advice in the preparation and organization of the collection.

Janice Glasgow would like to acknowledge the Natural Sciences and Engineering Council of Canada for their ongoing financial support of her research in imagery and spatial reasoning. She would also like to thank her parents, John and Dorothy, her son, Kyle, and her best friend, Tim, for their continual love, understanding and emotional support.

Hari Narayanan would like to thank Yumi Iwasaki and the Knowledge Systems Laboratory at Stanford University for providing a conducive environment for his editorial endeavors during his stay there. He also wishes to acknowledge similar support from Janet Kolodner and the EduTech Institute at the Georgia Institute of Technology. Most invaluable of all, however, has been the unwavering faith of Nancy, his wife, in his efforts.

Chandrasekaran wishes to acknowledge his on-going conversations with John and Susan Josephson on issues related to cognitive architectures. He is also grateful to ARPA and AFOSR for long-term support for his various research projects in AI, out of which his interest in diagrammatic reasoning grew.

Previously Published Papers

Chapter 2, "Problem Solving with Diagrammatic Representations" by Brian Funt first appeared in *Artificial Intelligence* 13 (1980), pp. 201–230. It is reprinted with the permission of Elsevier Science, North-Holland Publishers, Amsterdam.

Chapter 3, "Why a Diagram Is (Sometimes) Worth Ten Thousand Words" by Jill H. Larkin and Herbert A. Simon first appeared in *Cognitive Science* 11 (1987), pp. 65–99. It is reprinted with the permission of Ablex Publishing Corporation.

Chapter 4, "Images and Inference" by Robert K. Lindsay first appeared in *Cognition* 29 (1988), pp. 229–250. It is reprinted with the permission of Elsevier Science, North Holland Publishers.

Chapter 5, "Capturing the Dynamics of Conceptual Change in Science" by Nancy J. Nersessian, first appeared in *Cognitive Models of Science,* Minneapolis: University of Minnesota Press, 1992, pp. 3–45. It is reprinted with the permission of the University of Minnesota Press.

Chapter 8, "On Visual Formalisms" by David Harel first appeared in *Communications of the ACM* 13 (5) (May 1988), pp. 514–530. It is reprinted with the permission of the Association for Computing Machinery.

Portions of Chapter 9, "Principles of Knowledge Representation and Reasoning" appeared in *Principles of Knowledge Representation and Reasoning: Proceedings of the Third International Conference (KR–92).* San Francisco: Morgan Kaufmann, 1992, pp. 189–200. Those portions are reprinted with the permission of Morgan Kaufmann Publishers.

Portions of Chapter 11, "Visual Reasoning: Its Formal Semantics and Applications" by Dejuan Wang and John Lee first appeared in *Journal of Visual Languages and Computing* 4 (1993), pp. 327–356. Those portions are reprinted with the permission of Academic Press.

Chapter 13, "Computational Imagery" by Janice Glasgow first appeared in *Cognitive Science* 16 (3) (1992), pp. 355-394. It is reprinted with the permission of Ablex Publishing Corporation.

Chapter 16 "Mental Animation: Inferring Motion from Static Displays of Mechanical Systems" by Mary Hegarty first appeared in *Journal of Experimental Psychology: Learning, Memory, and Cognition* 18 (5) 1084–1102. It is reprinted with the permission of the American Psychological Association.

Chapter 17, "Abstract Planning and Perceptual Chunks: Elements of Expertise in Geometry" first appeared in *Cognitive Science* 14 (4) (1992), pp. 511–550. It is reprinted with the permission of Ablex Publishing Corporation.

Chapter 19, "Analogical Representations of Naive Physics" by Francesco Gardin & Bernard Meltzer, first appeared in *Artificial Intelligence* 38 (1989), pp. 139–159. It is reprinted with the permission of Elsevier Science, North-Holland Publishers, Amsterdam.

Foreword

Herbert Simon
Carnegie Mellon University

Human beings have been curious since ancient times about how they draw inferences that extend their information beyond what they already know. Aristotelean logic and Euclidean geometry were major and abiding contributions of the Greeks to this question, dealing, respectively, with two of its major aspects: reasoning in language (natural or formal) and drawing inferences from diagrams or other pictorial sources.

That reasoning using language and using diagrams were different, at least in important respects, was brought home by the Pythagorean discovery of irrational numbers. Although irrationals found no place among the integers or fractions, they were essential for representing the lengths of lines in geometric diagrams: for example, the ratio of the diagonal to the side of the square and of the circumference to the diameter of the circle. It has even been suggested that this ability of diagrams to represent irrationals that arithmetic could not handle was a main motive for Euclid's developing his scheme of geometrical reasoning.

Linguistic (algebraic) and diagrammatic representations found common ground for a time with Descartes' invention of analytic geometry. And, with the legitimation of the irrational (real) numbers in the 19th Century by Dedekind, symbolic mathematics threatened to swallow up geometry, especially its diagrams. In fact, because certain paradoxes could be derived from cleverly (or carelessly) constructed diagrams, the use of diagrams to carry out proofs, even in geometry, became increasingly unfashionable. Rigor, it was believed, called for reasoning to be formalized in symbols arranged in sentences or equations. Even natural language was insufficient, and around the turn of this Century, logic and mathematics were wedded by the work of Frege and of Whitehead and Russell. Rigorous reasoning came to mean reasoning in the formal languages of logic and mathematics.

Justice Oliver Wendell Holmes declared that "rigor is not the life of the law." It is equally the case that rigor is not the life of thought. Most thinking in which human beings engage, even in highly mathematical fields like physics or economics, is not rigorous in the sense in which logicians and pure mathematicians use that term. Words, equations, and diagrams are not just a machinery to guarantee that our conclusions follow from their premises. In their everyday use, their real importance lies in the aid they give us in reaching the conclusions in the first place.

Noting how radically our reasoning differs from the standards of formal logic, we call it "intuitive." Sometimes we even say that it requires "insight" or (in our less modest moments) "creativity." The inference processes we use are heuristic processes that aid search and discovery. They often reach the desired end, relatively seldom deceive us, but are fallible enough so that it is usually worth while to check them, at least qualitatively, by more formal methods or against factual evidence.

For example: *I notice a balance beam, with a weight hanging from a two-foot arm. The other arm is one foot long. How much force must I apply to it to balance the weight?* Do we know what kind of reasoning we use to answer this question? Is it verbal reasoning? If so, what are its axioms and rules of inference, and where do they come from? Are the axioms logical, or do they embody laws of physics? Do we make use of the diagram of the balance that we (most of us) can see in our Minds' Eyes? If so, what processes do we use to conclude that, as the one arm of the balance is twice as long as the other, the force on the short arm must be twice as great as the weight?

Whatever processes we use in solving problems like these, they are processes for *finding* answers, and the *assurance* they give that the answers are correct, while important, is only secondary. Until we find answers, their correctness is hardly in contention.

However much, thanks to Descartes and Dedekind and others, we can see the logical identity (knowledge equivalence) of symbolic and diagrammatic representations of a given problem, that identity does not imply that it is equally easy to reason in both kinds of representations, or that we will be able to draw the same inferences from both. Representations may be equivalent in the knowledge embedded in them without being equivalent in the power and speed of the inference processes they enable. They may be informationally equivalent without being computationally equivalent.

This book reports nearly two dozen recent investigations into the logical, and especially the computational, characteristics of diagrammatic representations and the reasoning that can be done with them. Its chapters provide a view of the recent history of the subject, survey and extend the underlying theory of diagrammatic representation, and provide numerous examples of diagrammatic reasoning, human and mechanical, that illustrate its powers (and limitations).

Research in diagrammatic reasoning has two goals, beyond the fundamental goal of understanding the phenomena and their processes. The first is to deepen our understanding of ourselves and the ways in which we think. That deeper understanding is already beginning to enhance our sophistication and effectiveness in using visual displays, in books and on computer screens, to communicate and teach. The second goal is to provide an essential scientific base for constructing representations of diagrammatic information that can be stored and processed by computers, enabling computers to achieve some of the computational efficiencies in their thinking that diagrams now provide to human beings.

As we progress toward these two goals, understanding diagrammatic thinking will be of special importance to those who design human-computer interfaces, where the diagrams presented on computer screens must find their way to the Mind's Eye, there to be processed and reasoned about. In a society that is preoccupied with "Information Superhighways," a deep understanding of diagrammatic reasoning will be essential to keep the traffic moving on those highways, and even more, to give us tools to help cope with, and even make constructive use of, the mass of information that we now know how to generate.

Introduction

B. Chandrasekaran, Janice Glasgow, and N. Hari Narayanan

The subject matter of this book is how diagrammatic (or pictorial) representations can be used in problem solving and reasoning. The issues are not about how the raw sensory information in the visual modality is processed to form percepts; that is the subject of theories of image processing and perception. Rather, the issues relate to representations of diagrams and mental images and the functions played by them in problem solving. Research in this area involves a large, diverse and multidisciplinary effort: philosophers, cognitive psychologists, design theorists, logicians and AI researchers are among those studying diagrammatic reasoning. Philosophers have been interested in the nature of mental imagery for a very long time, and debates about the reality and nature of mental images and visual representations have also raged in psychology. Design theorists have always been interested in the role of sketches and diagrams as design aids. Logicians have, however, traditionally disdained diagrams as merely "heuristic" aids to be discarded once the correct path to the real proof is obtained. And AI, while it flirted with diagrams in its early decades, especially in the early work on geometric theorem proving, has been carried on the wave of the so-called "discrete symbol processing" view or the logic view, and representation and use of diagrams have not been anywhere near the center of its attention in the last couple of decades.

Lately there has been a groundswell of interest in AI on working with different types of representations, and in seeing how perceptual and motor components of intelligence can be integrated with the explicitly cognitive components. Correspondingly there has also been an interest in treating the external world itself as a representation and in the multiplicity of types of representations available in it for an agent working in the world. Figure 0.1 shows the emerging picture of these concerns in AI. Since visual modality is one which seems so rich in its participation in problem solving and reasoning, diagrammatic representation has been one of the subjects of interest in this emerging milieu of research interests.

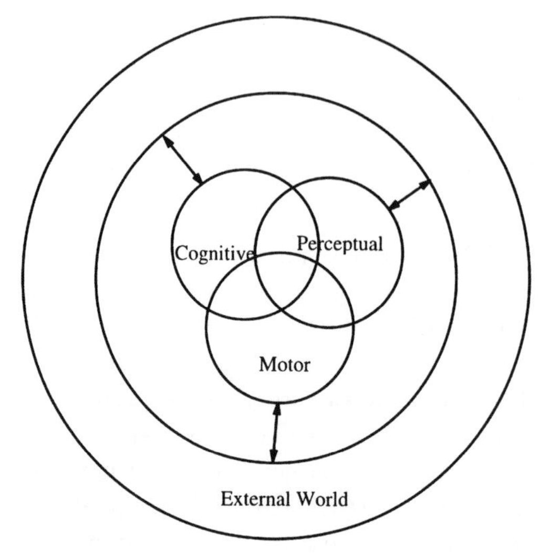

Figure 0.1
Multiple Types of Representations for a Situated Agent

Despite indications of early enthusiasm, research on diagrammatic reasoning has largely been sporadic at best during the eighties. The 1992 AAAI Spring Symposium on Reasoning with Diagrammatic Representations, organized by B. Chandrasekaran, Yumi Iwasaki, N. Hari Narayanan, and Herbert Simon, acted as a catalyst for the recent resurgence of research interest in this area. More than seventy researchers from nine countries participated in this meeting. This symposium revealed an emerging consensus on the need to expand AI's representational repertoire to include diagrammatic representations and integrate their use with traditional representations. Furthermore, it highlighted contributions that research in other disciplines can make to this endeavor[1]. The publication of this book was originally motivated by the success of the symposium, and many of the chapters in this volume are contributions from researchers who participated in it.

Following, we introduce the subject of diagrammatic reasoning by discussing some of the fundamental and ongoing issues in the area. We also present ideas on the role of diagrams and images in problem solving.

[1]Papers presented at the symposium are now available as a technical report – N. H. Narayanan (Ed.), Reasoning with Diagrammatic Representations, Technical Report SS-92-02, Menlo Park, CA: AAAI Press.

We conclude with a brief overview of the structure of the book.

Fundamental Issues in Diagrammatic Reasoning

In this section, we introduce some of the fundamental issues in the field of diagrammatic reasoning as we see it.

Internal Versus External Diagrammatic Representations

In discussing the issue of the role of diagrams in reasoning we find it useful to make the following distinction about where the representations reside:

- *External world:* This is the world in all its detail and form as sensed in various modalities.
- *External diagrammatic representations:* These are constructed by the agent in a medium in the external world (paper, etc), but are meant as representations by the agent.
- *Internal diagrams or images:* These comprise the (controversial) internal representations that are posited to have some pictorial properties.

Questions that arise in this context include: Are there any continuities in the mechanisms of processing and use regarding the above representations? What are their common functional roles in problem solving and reasoning?

Mental Images and Their Status

There has been a tradition in psychology and philosophy that dismisses mental images as epiphenomenal, i.e., they do not causally participate in reasoning or problem solving. There are even some who dismiss claims of mental imagery with the assertion that people who think they have mental images are just imagining things! Obviously this is the heart of the imagery debate. But the discussion in the field about this issue has been stymied by a lack of consensus on what various terms mean. We hope the following discussion is helpful in clarifying the relevant issues.

Let us refer to whatever it is that people have when they say they have a mental image as the "phenomenal image," and denote it by I. The agent can describe its content as propositions, but phenomenally it is an image for the agent. Let R refer to the pattern of activation in the neural structure in long-term memory that contained information which gave rise to I. Let P refer to the pattern of activation in the neural structure when the agent reports having I. The neural pattern P occurs in the part of the cognitive architecture that corresponds to current awareness or deliberation.

What is the appropriate way to talk about R? We can talk abstractly about the content of R. We can certainly have a debate about which is the best type of language to talk about or describe the contents of visual memory. We can draw pictures to describe the content; after all, we are talking about information that directly gave rise to the phenomenal image. Logicists in AI have argued that predicate logic can describe the content pretty well also, and there is no need to assign a privileged and unique role to images as a language for describing this content. On the other hand, other logicians argue that there is something fundamentally different about pictures as representational categories. Whatever the resolution of this debate, our point here is that the debate is about the appropriate descriptive language. It makes no sense to ask if R is a picture or a set of propositions: R is neural pattern. It does make sense to ask if there is a consistent interpretation of R's content as an image, but such an interpretation is not in opposition to R having a consistent interpretation as a set of propositions. In this sense, "image" versus "propositions" is a false opposition about the contents of R. With advances in neuroscience, we might discover that the neural pattern R has a preferred interpretation as the content of a picture, but still talking about R as a picture would be a category error.

How about the "picture-likeness" of P? P is the neural activation which corresponds to the agent having a phenomenal image. All the points that we made about the content of R are applicable about the content of P as well, but we can also ask what it is about P that gives the agent the experience of the phenomenal image. One hypothesis is that the activation pattern of P has commonalities both in shape and location with the activation patterns with some part of the architecture that is involved in seeing. Specifically, in the architecture that is involved is the final stages of perception, having the activation pattern P would correspond to the experience of image I. So far, there is nothing specifically picture-like about P other than that it gave rise to I. However, as we discuss in the next section, there are image-processing theories which propose that the neural activation patterns corresponding to seeing have a systematic spatial array character. To the extent P shared the patterns with those that occur in perception, there would be a sense in which P would be picture-like.

There is another dimension to how mental images arise, and that is about the degree to which typical mental images are the result of composition and construction operations at run-time, as opposed to retrieval of complete images. When people are asked to recall images of objects that they are familiar with (for example, the map of South America), they often produce images in which different parts were moved and rotated to "standard" positions in relation to each other. This provides support for the constructivist hypothesis. However, this leaves open the issue of how the elementary pieces are represented (i.e., how far down does the constructivist hypothesis go? Are there any visual primitives in representation?).

The World, Diagrams and Mental Images: Some Distinctions

We will use the term "visual information" to refer to information that humans can extract by inspection from an image or from the world by directing visual attention to it. What can be extracted visually by inspection varies somewhat from person to person due to training and other personal factors and hence an exhaustive list cannot be given of what this information consists of, but shapes, certain simple spatial relations, color, texture, etc, are the kind of information we have in mind for this term.

It is useful to make a number of distinctions so that the issue of mental images, their representation and use are not conflated with the issue of diagrammatic reasoning in general.

1. *Seeing:* perceiving the 3-dimensional reality of the visual world "out there." As we mentioned, most of this is in the realm of image processing from sensory information in the retina to the construction of, say, 3-d shape descriptions.
2. *Problem solving by using vision on the world:* As the problem-solving process sets up subgoals that require visually obtainable information from the world, visual attention can be shifted to the relevant part of the world and information extracted.
3. *Drawing:* An external representation is constructed, often from mem-

ory, of relevant aspects of some visual domain, possibly imaginary. There are interesting issues about how the pieces of the drawing are conceived, related, annotated or otherwise modified and so on.
4. *Using drawings for problem solving:* Some aspects of this are similar to the use of the world around for problem solving (scanning by attention-driven mechanisms, using perception for extracting needed information, and so on), but the drawings are generally simplified, preserving only the visual information about the world that is necessary for problem solving. Also, many drawings are abstract and are not meant as veridical visual representations of the real world, but are used to represent information about some problem in a form that can be visually easily extracted.
5. *Imaging:* Making a mental image of some aspect of a real or imaginary visual world. Here some of the issues are similar to drawing, but there are open issues about how the images are generated and processed (e.g., what mechanisms are shared between processing an external diagram and internal one).
6. *Using mental images for problem solving:* Some of the issues are similar to the ones in 4 above, but it is not clear what "scanning" really means here, or what role perception plays.

A point that repeatedly comes up in discussions on imaging is the degree to which the "hardware" is shared between seeing and imaging. Previously we talked about the location and shape of activation patterns being shared between mental images and perception. It is unlikely that early visual processing (i.e., to use Marr's language, extraction of the primal sketch, 2 1/2-d sketch, etc., from the retinal array) is being performed on a mental image. (To suppose that the full range of image processing operations that are performed during seeing objects in the world or external diagrams is done on mental images is truly to fall into the vortex of infinite regress!) However, a repeatedly proposed hypothesis is that there is a visual buffer in which the final stage of visual perception resides, and this visual buffer is shared between imaging and seeing. In the Marr view, one can think of image processing as taking place in layers. Each layer preserves some aspects of the "pictorialness" of the visual world, the lower layers corresponding to the results of early image processing operations, while the final layer is the visual buffer whose elements are perceptually interpreted elements of the scene. The buffer preserves the spatial relations between the elements, each of which is already in some sense "interpreted," not requiring low- level visual processing. Only the elements of the visual buffer are available to the agent for access (in perception) or construction (in imaging).

Similarly, some of the motor and perceptual mechanisms are shared between seeing the world, seeing a drawing (which is a representation of some possible world), or using an image during problem solving. Extraction of certain classes of visual predicates seems to be shared by all these processes. Scanning is also generally thought of as an activity that can be performed on the world, the drawing, or the mental image, though it is doubtful that an agent has to engage the same muscular actions in scanning a mental image as he would in scanning an external image or the world. It is possible that "scanning" a mental image is scanning only in a metaphorical sense, but instead what really happens is the reconstruction of the image to correspond to the results of scanning.

In the constructivist view, images are constructed in the visual buffer from pieces that are set in a certain relation. The pieces themselves tend to be stereotypical in character, often resulting in relations between the elements of the image which violate verisimilitude. In this sense imaging is partly like drawing, with all the errors and biases that are features of most peoples' drawings. The constructivist view still leaves open the issue of how the elementary pieces of the image are stored.

A persistent issue about images is the degree to which additional direct work is done on the images by visual modality-specific operations to yield further information. This issue can be illustrated by considering two examples, one due to R. Lindsay and the other attributed to Z. Pylyshyn:

- Take one step north, one step east, and one step south. How do you get back to the starting point?
- Imagine a vat of blue paint, and imagine pouring yellow paint into it and stirring it. What do you see happening to the paint in the blue vat?

To the extent that articulations of cognitive strategies that people consciously adopt for solving a given problem can be relied upon, it seems that a common strategy for the first problem is to construct a mental map, and extract from it by inspection the relation of the starting point to the ending point. It is also possible to use prior factual knowledge directly to conclude that the starting point will be to the west of the ending point. A deliberative syllogistic reasoning account, distinct from both the image-based strategy and the direct application of factual knowledge, is theoretically possible, but rarely reported. On the other hand, in the paint example, a strong argument can be made that the conclusion that one sees the paint in the blue vat turning green is not given by the image, but rather retrieved from one's store of factual knowledge and imparted to the image.

Representational Issues

What kinds of representations can support the range of behaviors associated with the use of images and diagrams? Proposals for representation include perceptual primitives for mental images a well as approaches that distinguish between spatial and visual representations as a basis for computational imagery. Two-dimensional pixel representations and pixel-pattern to pixel-pattern inference rules have been presented as components of a deductive system that uses only picture-like representations.

Diagrams and Images in Problem Solving

The chapters in this volume provide rich evidence that images and diagrams are used extensively in reasoning and problem solving in all sorts of domains. In the following we will use the word "diagram" to stand both for mental images and externally drawn diagrams. (We have already provided some arguments for the hypothesis that there are important commonalities in the processes involved in extracting visual information from diagrams and images. At any rate, this is a working hypothesis for the rest of the discussion in this section.) The following argument suggests why and under what conditions diagrammatic representations may be helpful.

Diagrams preserve, or represent directly, locality information. A number of visual predicates are efficiently computed by the visual architecture from the above information, e.g., neighborhood relations, relative size, intersections, and so on. This ability makes certain types of inferences easy or relatively direct. (It should be emphasized that only some visual predicates are particularly easily computed by the visual architecture. There exist numerous inferences for which there is information directly available in the diagram, but the visual system is not necessarily good at making them. For example, given a large circle and a smaller circle, the visual system can directly tell that one is smaller than the other, but given two complicated shapes, where one of the shapes has a smaller area than the other, the visual architecture cannot compare them directly or easily without additional measurements and calculation.)

This ability to get some of the needed information visually explains the role of diagrams in problems that are essentially spatial, such as geometry problems. Even here, there are interesting strategies by which the diagram is additionally manipulated. Additional constructions are made on the diagram which enable the detection of new visual information (or emergent properties) in the next cycles of inspection. Also, symbolic annotations can be made on the diagram, which enable a new round of inferences to be made, not by the visual architecture but by use of information in the conceptual modality. The result of this inference may be represented in the diagram, which may then enable extraction of additional visual information. This highly interlaced sequence of extraction of visual information and symbolic inference-making is what gives this whole approach its power: each modality obtains information it is best suited for, and then sets up additional information which makes it possible for the other modality to arrive at additional information for which it is best suited.

Now, the above explains the role diagrams play in problems which have an intrinsic spatial content. How about problems that are not spatial? What explains the ubiquity of diagrams in such problems as well? The key is the existence of mappings with the property shown in Figure 0.2.

Suppose R is some (non-visual) representation and P is a predicate that we are interested in computing about that representation. Suppose there is available a mapping such that R goes to VR, a visual representation. And suppose that some visual predicate PR can be extracted from VR efficiently by the visual architecture, and that P can be obtained from PR by the reverse of the mapping from R to VR. If these conditions are satisfied, then one can effectively use the visual representation

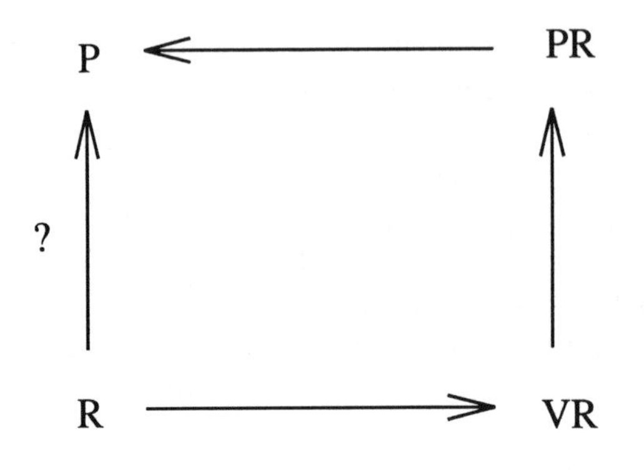

Figure 0.2
Mapping from a Nonvisual to a Visual Problem. R is a nonvisual representation from which it is desired to compute a predicate P. VR is a visual representation of R such that PR and, hence, P can quickly be computed by the visual architecture.

for the original problem.

All the assumptions in the above scenario might make it sound as if it is a rare event for such mappings to be found, and it would only be relatively infrequently that a non-visual problem might be aided by such visual analogs. In fact, however, for commonsense reasoning phenomena, we learn, over a period of time, a whole repertoire of such analogs constructed by the culture. Think of how common are mappings from temporal phenomena to spatial phenomena. We often represent time as a line and reason with lengths of lines when we want to compare durations.

In general, mapping to visual representations is a possible option for nonvisual problems whose properties can be mapped to spatial properties which are easy to recognize visually. "Easily visually recognizable" is important here because there are many properties that are spatial but not easily visually recognizable. Easily visually recognizable properties include such things as "larger and smaller," "longer and shorter," "more to the right (left, above, below)," "thinner and thicker," "brighter and darker," etc. In these types of properties, what is important seems to be the notion of (total) ordering in the one or two dimensions in which the properties of interest vary. Another type of spatial property that is often used to represent nonvisual properties is containment as in the case of Venn Diagrams. Spatial containment of the sort used in Venn Diagrams is also easily visually recognized. However, containment does not necessarily impose a total ordering among represented objects.

There is another important role played by diagrammatic representations. In this role diagrams help not so much in making immediate inferences as in the selection of methods to solve a problem. That is, diagrams aid in the organization of cognitive activity.

But there are also limitations to the diagrammatic form of reasoning. Since diagrams are concrete representations (i.e., they are models in the sense of Johnson-Laird's mental models), when inferences can be made they are fast and direct. This concreteness enables such representations to avoid some of the problems associated with the frame problem in inference. But unless special techniques are employed, they cannot be used, *per se,* to perform reasoning involving universal quantification. Disjunctive reasoning (especially when the numbers of disjunctions are large) becomes hard in a purely visual mode. These limitations of a purely diagrammatic reasoning are why most nontrivial problems involve integration of both visual and nonvisual modes of reasoning.

One form of diagrammatic reasoning is exemplified by the use of sketches in the task of design. Sketches have a significant component of "vagueness" to them—but this vagueness plays a functional role in that it helps the designer avoid overcommitment to those aspects of the design to which she is not yet ready to make a precise commitment, but at the same time still take advantage of the visual mode for organizing problem solving activity and inference-making. In fact what makes sketches especially useful is the fact that a sketch is not so much vague as something that stands for a family of precise models[2].

The role of images and diagrams in qualitative reasoning about the physical world is an important issue covered in this book. It has been suggested that much of our commonsense knowledge about how objects in the world behave under various forces and collisions is actually in the form of abstract perceptual chunks that direct the reasoning activity. Representation of object configuration diagrams and predictive knowledge indexed by shapes as well as visual events are emphasized as central problems in this work. This is to be contrasted with much of the current research in qualitative physics, which emphasizes symbolic and axiomatic reasoning in this task.

As mentioned earlier, normative logic (i.e., logic as an approach for

[2]This has been suggested by Boi Faltings in a paper presented at the symposium.

deriving sound conclusions) has long treated diagrams as mere heuristic aids in the organization of thought, and as objects that should not appear in the proofs that are finally produced. Chapters appearing in this volume challenge this tradition in logic: they suggest that it is possible to devise logical systems which take diagrams seriously and which have their inference rules organized partly as diagrams with symbolic annotations.

Book Organization

This book is more than a mere collection of papers. It is meant to be a foundational publication that provides both a coherent introduction to the area of diagrammatic reasoning and an overview of current research. It is organized into four sections, each which is introduced by a section coordinator. These section introductions discuss important and sometimes controversial issues as well as set the context for understanding the chapters in each section. Section I provides an historical and philosophical introduction to the topic of diagrammatic reasoning. The second section presents some of the theoretical foundations for the area. Work on the cognitive and computational studies of imagery and diagrammatic reasoning is covered in Section III. The volume concludes with Section IV, which contains chapters on the role of diagrammatic reasoning in problem solving and qualitative reasoning.

The papers chosen for this book offer a sampling of research in the area of diagrammatic reasoning, an exciting and rapidly growing research discipline. Although the subtitle of the book mentions only cognitive and computational aspects of reasoning with diagrams, papers that provide historical, philosophical, and theoretical perspectives have also been included to provide a comprehensive treatment of the topic. The chapters are of two types: papers that have been previously published in journals and are reprinted as they are, and papers describing recent research that have been reviewed by the editors and section coordinators. The organization, structure and contents of the book were carefully designed to serve several purposes:

1. to provide an introduction to the topic of diagrammatic reasoning,
2. to expose readers to the theoretical underpinnings of the area, and

3. to serve as an archival publication of the latest research on the topic.

I HISTORICAL AND PHILOSOPHICAL BACKGROUND

Introduction to Section I
Historical and Philosophical Background

Aaron Sloman
The University of Birmingham

This book provides readers with pointers into the literature on diagrammatic reasoning, along with introductions to a variety of topics, including:

- theoretical analysis of the nature of different sorts of representations and their strengths and weaknesses,
- demonstrations and analyses of the use of diagrammatic reasoning in humans,
- examples of the use of diagrammatic reasoning in machines.

This section on historical and philosophical issues provides a background to the remainder of the book. The older papers have already been influential in AI and cognitive science, and the newer ones are all relevant to the recent revival of interest in diagrammatic reasoning.

When the editors originally asked me to write the introduction to this section they intended my 1971 paper (Sloman 1971) to be included, partly because it was one of the earliest critiques of logicist AI, partly because it included some theoretical analysis of the differences between Fregean (applicative) and analogical (iconic, pictorial) representations, and partly because, along with its 1975 sequel, it had had some influence. However, the first draft of my introductory musings turned out far too long to be a section introduction. Moreover, at about the same time it became clear that the whole book was growing too long. So I built a mental model of the book, visualized the removal of my 1971 paper, saw that that would shorten the whole book, and proposed that the paper be excluded, since it has already been published in three different places. Instead, my draft introduction became a separate paper, and this revised introduction therefore had to be very short.

Funt's chapter reports some of the earliest work on the use of transformations of images to solve problems. He showed that there are some problems where translation and rotation of images enables predictions to be made regarding the effects of physical processes. This technique is equally effective whether the objects involved have simple and regular shapes that are amenable to algebraic analysis or have very complex shapes that would make prediction of points of collision by algebraic or logical means very messy and time-consuming. His work combined theoretical analysis with demonstration in a working program. This relatively early proof of possibility helped to substantiate some of the claims in Sloman 1971 and also influenced further exploration of diagrammatic reasoning.

The influential chapter of Larkin and Simon is one of several addressing cognitive processes involving manipulation of spatial structures that play a role in scientific reasoning. In particular they explain how the use of spatial structure can sometimes help scientists control the search for a solution to a problem.

Lindsay was the author of one of the earliest programs that reasoned by manipulating networks of relationships (Lindsay 1963). His chapter in this volume combines theoretical analysis with a description of a collection of mechanisms for constructing and transforming diagrams, which could be useful for a wide range of non-logical inferences. His main claim is not that diagrams can express anything that logical assertions cannot, but that they are sometimes more efficient for reasoning or solving problems. I.e. they have heuristic rather than epistemological power (McCarthy and Hayes 1969): a theme found in several other papers on visual or spatial representations. (My chapter in this volume adds a note of caution to this claim.)

Nersessian's chapter does not discuss mechanisms. Instead, it looks at the role of diagrammatic reasoning in the development of scientific theories. Although it says nothing about the underlying mechanisms of perception and reasoning it provides evidence that spatial reasoning sometimes plays a significant role in the thinking of scientists. To that extent it helps to identify phenomena that need to be explained by cognitive mechanisms.

The chapter by Forbus, an expanded version of (Forbus 1992), is part of a growing body of literature reporting on the development of computer systems that reason or make predictions using diagrams or images. Forbus makes some interesting claims about the differences between representations that are qualitative, in the sense of using information about relative ordering rather than exact values, and representations that have exact numerical measures, which he assumed was characteristic of visual systems. Reading about this in an early draft of his chapter provoked some of the musings about animal vision reported in my chapter, below.

All the chapters address complex and subtle issues to do with the nature of intelligence. Forbus lists a set of six "grand challenge" problems concerned with spatial reasoning. Perhaps we should also address the meta-challenge of trying to collect a comprehensive list of examples of spatial or visual reasoning capabilities found in humans and other animals and try to analyze the types of mechanisms that would or would not be able to explain them. The list might include, for example, the nest-building abilities of many birds and other animals, and at another extreme the ability of human mathematicians to reason about infinite sets with the aid of spatial models (discussed in my chapter).

My own guess is that the problems are more difficult than most people think, and in particular that human and animal visual systems use an extremely powerful representation of spatial structure and motion that is quite unlike anything researchers in AI or cognitive science, or computer graphics, or computer aided design, have yet dreamed up. I speculated about some of the requirements for such representations in Sloman 1989, but I shall not be surprised if many years pass before those requirements are met.

References

Brachman, R. J. and Levesque, H. J. (eds). 1985 *Readings in Knowledge Representation.* Los Altos, Calif.: Morgan Kaufmann.

Feigenbaum, E. A. and Feldman, J., eds. 1963 *Computers and Thought.* New York: McGraw Hill.

Forbus, K. 1992. Qualitative Spatial Reasoning: Framework and Frontiers. Presented at the 1992 AAAI Spring Symposium on Reasoning with Diagrammatic Representations, Stanford University.

Funt, B. V. 1980. Problem-Solving with Diagrammatic Representations. *Artificial Intelligence* 13(3): 201–230.

Lindsay, R. K. 1963. Inferential Memory as the Basis of Machines Which Understand Natural Language. In *Computers and Thought* ed. E. A. Feigenbaum and J. Feldman. New York: McGraw Hill.

McCarthy, J. and Hayes, P. J.. 1969. Some Philosophical Problems from the

Standpoint Of Artificial Intelligence. *Machine Intelligence 4*, ed, B. Meltzer and D. Michie. Edinburgh: Edinburgh University Press.

Nicholas, J. M., ed. 1977. *Images, Perception, and Knowledge.* Dordrecht-Holland: Reidel.

Sloman, A. 1971. Interactions Between Philosophy And AI: The Role Of Intuition And Non-logical Reasoning In Intelligence. In Proceedings Second International Joint Conference on Artificial Intelligence, London. San Francisco: Morgan Kaufmann.

Sloman, A. 1975. Afterthoughts on Analogical Representation. In *Readings in Knowledge Representation* ed. R. J. Brachman and H. J. Levesque. Los Altos, Calif.: Morgan Kaufmann.

Sloman, A. 1989. On Designing a Visual System: Towards a Gibsonian Computational Model of Vision. *Journal of Experimental and Theoretical AI* 1(4): 289–337.

1 Musings on the Roles of Logical and Nonlogical Representations in Intelligence

Aaron Sloman
The University of Birmingham

1.1 Introduction

Discussion of how to represent and manipulate knowledge intelligently has a very long history, going back to ancient times, as evidenced by the systematic codification of mathematical knowledge in Euclid, and Aristotle's invention of a formal approach to reasoning. An important later development was Kant's discussion in his *Critique of Pure Reason* regarding the non-analytic nature of some mathematical knowledge. Although his concepts lacked clear definition, and his understanding of logic was apparently restricted to what could be learned from Aristotle, Kant attempted to show (roughly speaking) that some mathematical knowledge was 'synthetic', i.e. it went beyond what could be derived from definitions using only logic. Important ideas about how to represent and manipulate information were also contributed by Descartes, Boole, Frege, Peirce, Russell and many more. Scientists and mathematicians have often had to invent new specialized forms of representation, with associated manipulative techniques, in order to deal with new problems. The invention of the arabic numeral notation was a major landmark. Another was the invention of notations and techniques of differential calculus by Newton and Leibniz.—inxxLeibniz

Perhaps the greatest logicist of all time was Gottlob Frege. A century ago he attempted to demonstrate that all arithmetical concepts could be defined in logical terms and all arithmetical knowledge could be derived entirely from those definitions and logical axioms. He thereby claimed to show that in a very precise sense arithmetical knowledge was analytic, not synthetic as claimed by Kant. In the process, Frege invented predicate calculus after generalizing the concept of a function to allow non-arithmetical arguments and values and demonstrating the possibility of higher order functions, thereby providing a deep foundation for much of what followed in computer science (including the lambda calculus and Lisp).

But even Frege, while attempting to show that Kant was wrong about arithmetical knowledge, conceded that geometrical knowledge could not be derived from logic, though as far as I know he had nothing positive to say about how we obtain or use geometrical knowledge. Later, Bertrand Russell dealt Frege a body-blow by showing that the logical system on which he had tried to base arithmetic was inconsistent, as it led to the paradox of the set of all sets that do not contain themselves (or the predicate 'heterological' which describes all and only those predicates that do not describe themselves), sowing the seeds that later led to Gödel's incompleteness results.

The development of computers in the middle of this century added enormous momentum to studies in software engineering, cognitive modeling and AI, as shown by the 47 page size of Minsky's annotated bibliography produced as early as 1963 for the Feigenbaum and Feldman volume. Much of this work raised new issues about representations and their dynamics, as illustrated by some of the articles reprinted in that collection, for instance Gelerntner 1959, Lindsay 1963 and Minsky 1961. The latter includes a discussion of some complexity issues in problem solving, and claims that structured, computed descriptions will be needed: "To be useful, these should reflect some of the structure of the things they designate, abstracted in a manner relevant to the problem area." (p. 413 in Feigenbaum and Feldman). There's nothing new under the sun.

2.2 Logicism in Artificial Intelligence

Many people have been bemused by the logicist claim, put forward by some extremely intelligent AI folk, that systems built solely on logical representations and general logical forms of inference might exhibit human-like intelligence. The logic-based approach in AI was pioneered by John McCarthy during the 1950s and 1960s. For instance, in McCarthy 1968 he argued that not only the facts used by an intelligent agent but also the rules and heuristics for processing them could be expressed using logic, an idea which was subsequently embodied in the programming language Prolog and its successors, and to some extent in rule-based expert system formalisms. Some of the logicist ideas were developed further in the influential paper by McCarthy & Hayes 1969, which included a list of criteria for assessing forms of representations, including metaphysical adequacy, epistemological adequacy and heuristic adequacy.

At the second International Joint Conference on AI at Imperial College London, I challenged the assumption that logic could suffice for AI, in Sloman 1971. That paper led to an unscheduled inconclusive debate with McCarthy, Hayes and others, following the formal sessions at the conference. My 1971 paper was in turn criticised by Hayes 1974, to which there was a partial response in Sloman 1975 and in my later papers. (Some of the arguments on both sides are regularly re-invented.)

Disagreement persisted throughout the 1970s between those who sought totally general, logic-based, means of representation and inference (mainly people in the AI laboratory at Stanford) and those who argued for special purpose domain-oriented or problem-oriented representations and mechanisms (mainly people at MIT). There are relevant articles in Bobrow and Collins 1975, including the influential article by Woods, and further relevant discussion can be found in the collection of reprints edited by Brachman and Levesque 1985, especially Hayes 1974, Hayes 1985, Funt 1980, and my 1975 article.

Alongside the theoretical debates, designers and developers in AI and software engineering continued to use whatever forms of representation seemed best suited to their problem, some in ignorance of the theoretical debates and some explicitly taking sides, e.g. Bundy 1973 (though he later claimed that his diagrams could have been replaced by purely logical derivations). For instance, AI vision researchers used 2-D arrays, histograms, semantic nets, or logical databases for different stages in the interpretation of images and many of them would simply have laughed at any suggestion that they do it all using logic. (In fact such an interaction occurred around 1974 between an early Prolog proselyte in Edinburgh and a group of vision researchers at Sussex and Essex universities in the UK.)

I remember some of the debates being very muddled on account of confusion over definitions: for example there were some who treated the semantic nets used by Winston 1975 in his concept learning program as instances of analogical (pictorial, iconic) representations, because the topology of the net corresponded closely to the topology of the physical structures represented, while others regarded them as instances of symbolic or logical representations, because the use of explicit labels for relationships ensured translatability between the nets and logical formulae, a point developed further in connection with "frame" representations by Hayes 1979.

What is not always noticed is that two formalisms with similar expressive power and the ability to validate the same derivations, may differ in their heuristic power, for example in facilitating searches for solutions to problems: that was one of the main points in Sloman 1971, and before that in Lindsay 1963.

Parallel debates raged in psychology, e.g. see the volume edited by Nicholas in 1977 (especially Pylyshyn 1973, reprinted therein), and still continue. Although some of the experimental results (e.g. such as time taken to perform 'mental rotation' tasks being proportional to the amount of rotation required) are open to alternative interpretations, it does seem well established by neurophysiological research that a significant portion of the brain concerned with visual processing uses representations that preserve some aspects of retinal relationships (especially neighborhood relationships), though not much is known about how those representations are used, nor how the higher-level tasks of vision are achieved, nor how tactile and motor representations concerned with spatial structure and motion integrate with visual representations. (I'll return to animal vision below.)

Since the 1970s the debate has continued in AI; for instance, an extreme logicist position was taken by Kowalski 1980 and elaborated in his later publications, to which my 1985 paper arguing for multiple knowledge representation formalisms was, in part, a response. However, during the 1980s the debate came to be dwarfed by other issues, for instance the clash between connectionist and symbolic AI, and a host of extremely difficult technical problems faced by the logicists, such as the problems of accounting for human abilities to reason with incomplete information which could later be extended or corrected, and the problems of efficiency in theorem provers.

In the last few years (since about 1990) there appears to have been a revival of interest in the debate, as shown by symposia on diagrammatic or spatial reasoning at AI conferences, a special issue of *Computational Intelligence* (Narayanan 1993), this volume and a volume being edited in parallel with it by Peterson, forthcoming. Work on multi-media interfaces has also led some (e.g. Wahlster 1994) to study the relationship between verbal and diagrammatic forms of communication and good ways of integrating them: an area that is bound to attract increasing attention as the use of computers becomes more widespread and dissatisfaction with their communicative limitations grows.

2.3 What's Wrong with Logicism?

There are several different bases for attacking logicist AI. One that is popular with some philosophers uses Gödel's incompleteness theorem, or similar metamathematical 'limit' theorems, in an attempt to demonstrate that human beings (or at least human mathematicians!) have capabilities that cannot be replicated in a logic-based formal system or any mathematically equivalent system (including all computing systems that are in principle implementable as Turing machines). There is a considerable philosophical literature on whether Turing-equivalent machines could ever implement mental states and processes, much of which hinges on Gödel's theorem and related results. The best known recent attack of this form is Penrose 1989, discussed at length in the commentaries following Penrose 1990 and criticised at length in Sloman 1992. I shall say no more about this line of argument, which essentially assumes that if logicist AI fails then AI fails. There is a broader conception of AI as the study of principles for designing or explaining (actual or possible, natural or artificial) intelligent systems, which is not committed to any particular restriction of formalisms or mechanisms (Sloman 1994a).

The main basis of my criticism of logicists in 1971 was the oft-noted fact that human beings fruitfully use many different forms of representation (Hayes 1974 calls them 'schemes'), including natural languages, gestures, maps, musical notation, dance notation, Venn diagrams, Euler diagrams (often confused with Venn diagrams!), dress-making patterns, programming languages, blueprints, flow-charts, 3-D models of molecules, many types of data-structures used in computing systems, and a host of special-purpose mathematical notations (including, for instance, the number notation in which concatenation of digits stands for the combination of multiplication by 10 and addition).

More recently, connectionist representations have also added to the variety. For instance, a neural net may include information about many instances of some category superimposed and distributed over a collection of synaptic weights.

My claim was and is that this proliferation of types of representation is not simply a quirk of human nature but a profound and universal requirement for intelligence. In part my views had been shaped by reading Kant's (somewhat confused and unclear) argument that some forms of mathematical discovery extend our knowledge in ways that seem distinct from logical inference: this matched my own experience of doing mathematics.

Whether they are aware of these debates or not, many computer programmers, both inside and outside AI, naturally use different sorts of representations carefully crafted to meet the requirements of particular problems. Often this is done without reflection on the variety of forms of representation available and the reasons for selecting some rather than others. A good, experienced programmer, like good, experienced mathematician, intuitively adopts a fruitful approach, without necessarily knowing how or why.

The chapters in this volume discuss the issue explicitly. The main point is not what can be expressed in various formalisms, but how they compare in *heuristic* power, e.g. how the syntax of specialized representations facilitates control of search for a solution to a problem. Sometimes the improvement results from the way the syntax restricts what can be represented, thereby reducing branching in search spaces. Sometimes it results from the 'indexing' power of analogical or pictorial representations, which allows good candidates to be found first, because the syntax encodes a heuristic evaluation function to guide the search. (Both points are frequently re-discovered, so they must be important!)

An example of the first point is the difficulty of drawing an object that is both round and square (except when viewed end on!), compared with the ease of construction of the assertion **round(obj)&square(obj)**. An example of the second point is the use of direction in tracing a good route from A to B on a road map: roads going off in completely the wrong direction can usually (but not always) be ignored.

2.4 Confusions About Efficiency

One thing that emerges from close analysis of the chapters in this volume and other publications, including the papers in the special issue of the journal *Computational Intelligence* on computational imagery (Volume 9, Number 4, 1993), is that there is still no clear consensus as to what the options are, how they differ, and what criteria there are for choosing between them in building working systems, either for engineering purposes or for the purpose of modeling human or animal capabilities.

In particular it is too easy when arguing about the relative efficiency of different representations to forget that *actual* efficiency depends not only on the abstract properties of representing structures and processes manipulating them (usually implemented in software in virtual machines), but also on the properties of the underlying engines that implement those processes. For example, visual or spatial reasoning processes that introspectively seem very simple and efficient for the human brain may actually make use of enormously 'expensive' computations performed by vast numbers of neurons working in parallel. Attempting to replicate those processes on computers might be far less efficient than using different representations whose manipulations fit more directly onto computers.

For example, in some cases it may be cheaper and easier to add indexing and constraint mechanisms to a logical representation in a computer than to give the computer human-like map-reading capabilities.

Confusion on these points will probably reign for some time, and often leads to debates at cross-purposes. I'll mention a few of the common confusions before moving on to discuss some ways in which different forms of representations interact.

2.5 Misconceptions about Logical and Analogical Representations

My 1971 paper defined analogical representations as those that used properties and relationships in the representing medium, rather than explicit symbols, to represent properties and relationships in the situation depicted. This was misinterpreted by some readers as the claim that analogical representations are always isomorphic with what they represent, even though the paper presented a counter-example in the form of a 2-D picture of a 3-D scene.

The paper argued that in *some* cases analogical representations were more efficient, e.g. in controlling search. This was often misinterpreted as saying what some people actually believe, namely that logical representations are always inferior to pictures or diagrams, or that there are only two sorts of representations, logical (Fregean, applicative, symbolic, verbal) and analogical (pictorial, iconic, 'direct').

All of these are mistakes. I have never denied that logic remains the most powerful and general form of representation available, which, because of its applicability across domains and across problems, supports powerful forms of analogy-making and learning. Analogical representations (e.g. pictures and diagrams) can be very powerful in some cases, for reasons discussed in several chapters in this volume, but in other cases logic wins, especially where disjunctive, negative, conditional, or quantified information is involved. In yet other cases more specialized representations, tailored to the needs of the domain, may be best, e.g. the use of arabic numerals in long multiplication and division. Most programming languages fit neither the logical nor the analogical models, though they often contain elements of both. (Even Prolog uses analogical representations of lists, and to some extent the order of processing is depicted by order of symbols, though backtracking complicates this mapping.)

However, a logical system can be self-sufficient in the sense that in principle it is possible to have a completely logic-based (virtual) machine, whereas pictorial representations need to be embodied in a machine that also uses non-pictorial representations to control the use of the pictures. For an example see Funt 1980. I've explained some of these points in more detail in Sloman 1985. (These comments about logic being more self-sufficient might be refuted by producing a purely pictorial general purpose programming language.)

It is a mistake to suppose that there are just *two* forms of representation: besides logical and analogical representation there are all sorts of other types, including those mentioned above. In Sloman 1993a, 1993b, 1994b, 1994c, I have begun to develop the notion of a mind as a self-modifying, self-monitoring, control system, and to generalize the concept of 'representation' to cover a host of different types of information-bearing, causally effective, control states. These control states can exist in virtual machines at different levels of abstraction, like function definitions in a Lisp virtual machine or rules in a Prolog virtual machine or OPS-5 virtual machine. From this general viewpoint, all sorts of different types of representations, internal and external, can be seen as having syntax, semantics, pragmatics and inference methods. Syntax is a matter of the available structures and forms of variation. Semantics is concerned with one thing representing (depicting or denoting) another. Pragmatics is concerned with the functional roles of various sub-systems in a larger whole. Inference methods are simply the pragmatically useful syntactic transformations.

I suspect that there are still many new forms of representation waiting to be discovered, all with their own syntax and forms of transformation suited to particular subject domains and types of problems. In particular I believe that attempts to understand and replicate human-like *visual* capabilities will not succeed without some radically new forms of representation that integrate information about spatial structure and motion with information about possible changes, causal relations, and functional roles in a deep way (Sloman 1989). The fact that we don't yet know how to give machines visual capabilities that even begin to match the sophistication of human vision, or even squirrel vision, is one reason why it has been hard for research in AI to make use of the obvious fact that visual representations play a powerful role in human (and animal) intelligence.

2.6 Confusions Regarding the Syntax of Analogical Representations

Besides the confusions already mentioned, there are many common errors that are made about analogical representations, such as that they need to be continuous (not so, for a discrete ordered list can be an analogical representation of a sequence of events) and that they obey the same principles of compositionality as sentences or logical formulas (some diagrams do, but not all pictures, for there are no unique ways of decomposing typical photographs or paintings into parts, or replacing parts with other items without ruining another part of the picture or leaving empty spaces).

Related to the mistake that pictures always have a unique decomposition on which a formal semantics can be based is the erroneous but common assumption (e.g. Hayes 1974) that analogical or pictorial representations are necessarily isomorphic with what they represent, in that parts, properties and relations in the representation correspond unambiguously and systematically with parts properties and relations in what is depicted. This is a common misinterpretation of Sloman

1971, which merely stated that analogical representations use properties and relations in the representing medium to represent properties and relations in the represented domain. This does not imply isomorphism. Although we agreed on many points, Hayes was partly at cross-purposes with me as he apparently thought that I meant by 'analogical' what he meant by 'direct', whereas I regarded his direct (and isomorphic) representations as merely a special case of analogical representations.

Anyone who works on 3-D machine vision knows that pictures are typically not isomorphic with what they depict. The scene depicted by a picture will necessarily include things, like the far side of a cube, that do not correspond to any component of the picture. Likewise a line drawing of a wire-frame cube will typically contain several junctions that do not correspond to junctions in the cube, namely where projections of edges cross in the picture. Deciding which image junctions do and which do not depict scene junctions may include a search for a globally optimal interpretation. Insofar as I can make sense of what Hayes meant by 'direct', many images are not direct representations, which is one of the reasons why vision is so hard to explain and replicate.

The lack of isomorphism, the lack of a unique context-free segmentation and the presence of much local ambiguity are the sorts of things that add up to make computer vision extremely hard, or even *impossible* without a sophisticated mixture of top-down and bottom-up, or knowledge-based and data-driven, processing. Very often working out the interpretation is not a matter of applying a semantic interpretation function but of solving a problem. Sometimes, in the presence of noise or occlusion, there is no unique solution, merely a collection of candidates requiring a selection based on extraneous considerations (e.g. interpreting on the basis of what you were expecting to see, or optimizing some function).

Most AI work on the use of pictorial or diagrammatic representations in reasoning or planning by-passes the problems of visual interpretation, by using special-purpose analogical representations that simplify the problem, e.g. Funt 1980, Glasgow 1983, and chapters in this volume. It is possible that the brain does the same: why create an ambiguous representation to manipulate when you *start* by knowing what it is a representation of? However, we sometimes use what we *see* as a basis for reasoning or problem solving, e.g. looking at the shape of an armchair and its relationship to a door, in order to work out how to get it through the door by rotating it. In such cases we do not choose the representation: the environment presents us with it, and all the hard problems of vision are there.

2.7 Symbiosis Between Logical and Analogical Representations

In human thinking there often seems to be a rich interplay between different forms of representation. For example, one can reason about numbers by manipulating algebraic expressions, expressed in a notation that is equivalent to a logical formalism. This sort of process now pervades science and engineering. However we often find it useful to think of numbers as forming a spatially ordered series, along which something can move in either direction. Thus it is sometimes helpful, especially for a child learning to understand numbers, to think of subtraction as moving backwards a fixed number of steps. Multiplication of integers is definable logically using a recursive definition, but it can also be thought of in terms of replication of spatial groups, usually producing a rectangular array of objects. Replacing arrays of objects with areas gives an interpretation for multiplication of non-integers (fractions and reals). It is more common to teach such arithmetical operations in terms of their spatial analogues than in terms of direct logical definitions. (How many primary school children, or their teachers, would be able to cope with the latter?)

Similarly, although many functions from numbers to numbers can be defined and discussed in a purely logical (or algebraic) way, people often find it very useful to think of them in terms of a 2-D graph which can be drawn on paper. Thus the exponentiation function can be pictured in terms of a curve whose steepness continually increases at an ever increasing rate.

There are many well known proofs of properties of numbers and operations on numbers that use diagrams, such as the proof that the sum of the first N odd numbers is always a perfect square, which can be seen by carving up an N by N square of dots appropriately. Start in the top left corner, where there is one dot. Consider all the immediate neighbors of that dot as the next number, namely 3, then all the immediate neighbors to the right and below as the next number, namely 5, and so on. A little reflection shows that each new set of neighbors (to the right of and below the previous set) contains exactly two more dots than the previous set, so only the odd numbers are involved, and they add up to form the square. Notice that I have used verbal descriptions of a class of pictures to help the reader grasp the pictorial proof of a theorem of arithmetic, which could be expressed logically. I.e. words *describe* a picture *which proves* an arithmetical theorem. This sort of interplay between different types of representation is typical of the use of pictures and diagrams in reasoning.

Here's another example: given a pair of numbers we can describe their parity as 1 or 0 depending on whether their sum is odd or even. Consider a set of transformations of such pairs all of the form of increasing or decreasing each number by 1. Thus the four possible transformations are (+1, +1), (+1, -1), (-1, +1), (-1, -1). Is it possible to start with a pair of numbers of odd parity and change it to a pair of even parity by repeatedly applying transformations from that set? Some readers will find that easy to answer whereas others will have to think quite hard. However, everyone finds it obvious that a bishop in chess, allowed only diagonal moves, can never change the color of the square it is on. Seeing the isomorphism between these two problems makes the answer to the first one obvious (though seeing the isomorphism is not trivial).

Good mathematicians, scientists and engineers seem to switch rapidly between different ways of thinking and reasoning about numbers and numerical functions and relationships. They also use spatial and diagrammatic reasoning in many other contexts. For instance category theorists use diagrams to represent morphisms and operations on morphisms. It is commonplace to use diagrams to represent set-theoretic relations (e.g. Euler circles, Venn diagrams). What is not always noticed is that finite spatial structures can play a powerful role in thinking about infinite sets. For example many students first learn that infinite sets permit one-to-one mappings (bijections) from the whole set to a proper subset by being presented with a picture something like the figure below, demonstrating the bijection between the set of positive integers and its even subset.

$$\begin{array}{ccccccccc} \mathbf{1} & \mathbf{2} & \mathbf{3} & \mathbf{4} & \mathbf{5} & \mathbf{6} & . & . & . \\ | & | & | & | & | & | & | & | & | \\ \mathbf{2} & \mathbf{4} & \mathbf{6} & \mathbf{8} & \mathbf{10} & \mathbf{12} & . & . & . \end{array}$$

How do we see that the picture can be continued indefinitely?

More interesting is the theorem that if **S1** and **S2** are two sets and there exists a bijection between **S1** and a subset of **S2** and a bijection between **S2** and a subset of **S1** then there exists a bijection between **S1** and **S2**. This is very easy to express logically and a proof can be formulated logically, but most people I have talked to find it almost impossible to think about the problem without using some sort of spatial image of the two sets and the mappings between them.

Another example, first drawn to my attention by Alan Bundy, is the difficulty of using logic to solve the equation:

$$\mathbf{sin(x) = x}$$

for which people can quite easily find at least one solution by thinking of the definition of **sin** in terms of ratio of opposite to hypotenuse in a right-angled triangle, and then doing 'qualitative' reasoning by visualizing the graph for $\mathbf{y = sin(x)}$ superimposed on that for $\mathbf{y = x}$, and noticing that there is an intersection point at the origin. (There may be more than one intersection point, depending on the unit of measurement for angles.)

This ability to combine different forms of representation, including static and dynamic spatial representations, is a characteristic feature of human intelligence. Perhaps it is an essential feature of intelligence in general. We don't yet know much about how to implement it or explain how it works.

2.8 Efficiency of Representations May Depend on Underlying Machines

One of the important points made in Hayes 1974 is that a working system may have different levels of description. At one level a software system may use 2-D arrays to represent spatial information. At a lower level the array might be implemented as a set of logical assertions about the contents of the locations of the array. E.g. the following might represent the fact that at the location (3,7) the color is blue.

value(3, 7, "blue")

It might turn out that on a machine designed for very fast logical operations this would be more efficient than a more conventional array representation where slices in the array are mapped into contiguous portions of memory, usually at the cost of symmetry with respect to rows and columns. Thus, it is wrong to state without qualification that analogical representations are more efficient for a given problem than logical representations: it all depends on what runs fastest on a given machine. From this viewpoint, if brains don't use a logical engine that is merely a quirk of evolution.

This tempting relativistic compromise view misses an important point, namely that whatever the properties of the low level machine being used, for certain problems it may still be useful to ensure that there is a higher level virtual machine that uses representations suited to the problem. Software engineers do that all the time.

For example suppose there are many thousands of events recorded in a temporal sequence. It would be possible to store an unordered list of assertions of the following form in a logical database:

event(label, features, time)

If one had information about two events, with labels A, and B, and wished to know whether any other event occurred between them, then if the information were unordered it would be necessary to search the whole list to ensure that no other event had a time between those of A and B. If the items were ordered in the list according to time, then having found event A we would need to look only at its immediate predecessor and successor in order to see if any other event came between it and B. The time this saves on average compared with the unordered list will be roughly a linear function of the size of the list. For some problems a change from one representation to another can make a very dramatic difference to the type of function mapping database size to time required. For example, a switch from an exponential complexity function to a polynomial function may turn a totally useless system into one that delivers results in a reasonable time.

For some problems the speed-up gained by using the right representation in a high level virtual machine can, as the problem size grows, dwarf the potential speed-up gained by re-implementing on a different sort of physical computer (which usually gains at most a constant factor). For example, if a switch of representation replaces an exponential function with a linear function, this will, for large enough databases, dwarf any gain obtained by engineering advances or even highly parallel implementation on a fixed number of processors, which produces only a constant speed-up compared with an optimal serial implementation.

Thus discussion of efficiency of representations must include the representations used in virtual machines, and not only the physical or electronic structures. Newell and Simon (Newell 1980) caused some confusion by referring to 'physical' symbol systems when they were actually talking about symbols that could occur in non-physical, abstract, *virtual* machines. Instead of talking about 'physical symbol systems' they should have talked about 'physically implementable symbol systems.'

2.9 Simultaneous Multiple Representations

The example of an ordered list of events described logically shows that a representation can simultaneously be of more than one form. The individual information items use only a logical notation in which predicates are applied to arguments. At the same time, the *ordering* of those logical formulae in a list allows a new semantic relation to be used, in which the collection of items functions as an 'analogical' representation, in the terminology of Sloman 1971. (Note that from a logical point of view the information in the ordering is strictly redundant since it can be derived from the time values of the events.)

In other cases logical assertions can be organized in the form of a 2-D array (e.g. Glasgow 1993), or in the nodes of a network. Instead of simply using a data-structure whose locations have useful relationships, the items in the database may make use of a sophisticated indexing scheme which enables the neighbors of an event to be found quickly without scanning the whole database. Clever indexing schemes may implicitly implement orderings or other useful relationships just as well as storing assertions in a list, though perhaps with small (constant) differences in efficiency. An example would be an efficient index that mapped each event label onto an integer giving its location in the ordering (not the time: the listed events might have intervals of varying length). Then checking whether A and B were neighbors would be a matter of checking whether they mapped onto integers that differed by 1. Here one would be locating events not in contiguous bits of memory in the computer but in locations in an abstract space: the space of positive integers. The inverse mapping, from integers to stored assertions, would be needed for some applications (e.g. answering "What comes after B?"). Properties and relations in that space could provide just as good a medium for implementing analogical relations as relationships in physical memory, or on a sheet of paper.

All this shows that in the very same system different forms of representation may be used which interact in a deep way, including both logical (applicative, Fregean) representations and analogical (pictorial) relationships.

2.10 What Defines a Form of Representation?

What defines a form of representation is the combination of syntax, pragmatics, semantics, and inference strategies supported by the form (see Sloman 1993a, 1994b). We can now see that there may be several different syntaxes and forms of inference at different levels in the same representational system. The use of resolution and logical inference when dealing with individual stored facts may be compatible with quite different modes of inference that make use of the structure in which items are stored, or the indexing schemes used to control access.

A system that uses a neighborhood relation in the representing medium to represent some kind of neighborhood relationship in the domain represented, is a special case of an analogical representation, even where the representing medium uses logical expressions. It would not be an analogical representation if the neighborhood relation were represented by an explicit symbol, e.g. a function symbol or predicate such as '**next_to(x, y)**,' instead of a relation in the medium. However, neighborhood relations implicit in one virtual machine could be based on explicit relations in a lower-level machine, like 2-D arrays implemented as logical assertions about values corresponding to different array coordinates.

2.11 Mixing Modes of Representation

We have so far discussed ways in which the implementation of a particular set of representations may simultaneously use different formalisms at different levels in an implementation hierarchy. A subtly different point is that there may be *co-existing* systems some of which are used to *control* or *reason about* others. In these cases one sort of formalism F1 is used for some purpose and another sort F2 is used to refer to F1, for purposes of reasoning about F1 or in order to control manipulations of instances of F1. F2 may or may not be of the same general type as F1. Similarly yet another formalism F3 may be used to refer to F2. It is also possible for two different formalisms, F2a and F2b, to be used to refer to or manipulate F1 in different contexts, or for different purposes. And one or more formalisms may be used to manipulate F2a and F2b, and so on. The fact that such chains of reference (and control) can coexist with chains of implementation can be very confusing when thinking about how representations work. I'll now try to illustrate these points, in connection with representation of logical expressions and representations of list structures.

In several programming languages lists are used as a data-structure for many different purposes. For example, logical assertions could be implemented using lists (which in turn are implemented using lower level facilities for managing memory in the machine). If we use square brackets to denote lists, then the following three element list might represent the assertion that john is the parent of fred:

[**parent john fred**]

And the following might represent information about an event, of the sort described above:

[**event E2367 collision lorry car Thursday 0952**]

This use of lists to implement a logical form of representation (applying a predicate **event** to 6 arguments) could coexist with the use of lists to implement analogical forms of representation, where order in a list represents temporal or spatial order. I.e. a large list functioning as an analogical representation might contain many logical representations.

However, this analogical form of representation has properties that we (or a program) might need to talk about in deciding when and how to use lists. One way to talk about the properties of lists and operations on them is to use a list-processing programming language. Another is to use logic. In general a non-logical form of representation, such as lists or diagrams, may have properties that can be represented logically and reasoned about logically. An intelligent hybrid system might use logic for this purpose.

Consider the use of lists to represent analogically what happens when people stand in a queue. We might occasionally need to represent a process in which the person at the head of the queue moves to the back of the queue. We could represent this process by defining an operation called 'rotate' which takes a list and a number and moves that number of items from the front to the back, in order.

It is possible to define such operations recursively using logic, and then to use logic to reason about them, as I'll shortly illustrate. However, it turns out that such logical reasoning may sometimes compete with or be supplemented by spatial or some other form of non-logical reasoning, which I'll also illustrate.

2.12 Logical Reasoning About Lists

Lists are used a great deal in AI programming, both as a basis for logical formulas and also as a basis for analogical trees, networks, or other representing structures. (See Woods 1975 for further discussion.)

Understanding how such programs work depends on being able to reason about the properties of operations on lists. An example is the operation **rotate(List, Num)** which takes a list and an integer, and and moves the first **Num** elements of the list (if there are any) to the end of the list. It can be defined recursively as follows, where [] is the empty list, sometimes called 'nil', **cons** is a binary operator that creates a new list from a new element and an old list, and <> represents the list concatenator operator, (sometimes called 'append'):

rotate([], N) = []
rotate(cons(X, L), 1) = L <> cons(X, [])
rotate(L, N + 1) = rotate(rotate(L, N), 1)

Note that <> can also be defined recursively:

[] <> L = L
cons(X, L1) <> L2 = cons(X, L1 <> L2)

Another operation on lists returns an integer giving the length of the list, and can be defined recursively thus:

length([]) = 0
length(cons(X, L)) = 1 + length(L)

On the basis of all this it can be proved by induction that if a list L has length N, then rotating it N times produces an equivalent list:

Theorem: list(L) -> rotate(L, length(L)) = L

A system capable of automated logical proof of this and other theorems about list processing is described in Ireland and Bundy, forthcoming. In order to prove this logically it is necessary to have an explicit logical definition of what a list is. This can be done by inductively defining lists as things that can be created by repeated application of the binary list constructor **cons**, starting from the empty list []. The predicate **list** can be defined inductively to say that [] is a list, and anything constructed by applying **cons** to an item and a list is a list, thus:

1. list([])
2. list(L) & item(X) -> list(cons(X, L))
3. Nothing is a list unless it can be proved to be a list on the basis of the preceding axioms in a finite number of steps.

(If updating the head or tail of a list were to be allowed, as in Lisp and Pop-11, the definitions would need to be made more complicated.)

On the basis of such recursive definitions, using structural induction, it is possible to prove many interesting theorems about lists and operations on lists, such as the rotate theorem. (Readers are invited to try proving it by induction.) So a form of representation that is used in analogical representations and in non-logical forms of reasoning (e.g. traversing a list to answer a question about ordering) may be reasoned *about* using logical representations and logical inference techniques. This is an illustration of the power and generality of logic.

2.13 Logic Is Not the Only Way To Reason About Lists

However, these logical proofs are quite hard for people to think of and to follow unless they are experienced logicians familiar with structural induction. Quite sophisticated logical apparatus is required to control the search for a proof. Nevertheless, even without having seen or understood the proof, many programmers (and non-programmers) can intuitively grasp the truth of (some of) the theorems, and confidently and justifiably use their intuitions in designing good programs. How?

Discussion with such people suggests that instead of always interpreting lists as recursively defined binary trees, they often think of them as spatial one-dimensional, totally ordered structures, for which iterative rather than recursive concepts are naturally applicable. They use their deep understanding of the properties of space and of spatial transformations to see that, for example, if you move an item at one end of a row to the other end, shifting everything else along to make space, and continue doing so until all items have been moved, then you will end up with exactly the same row of items, as illustrated here:

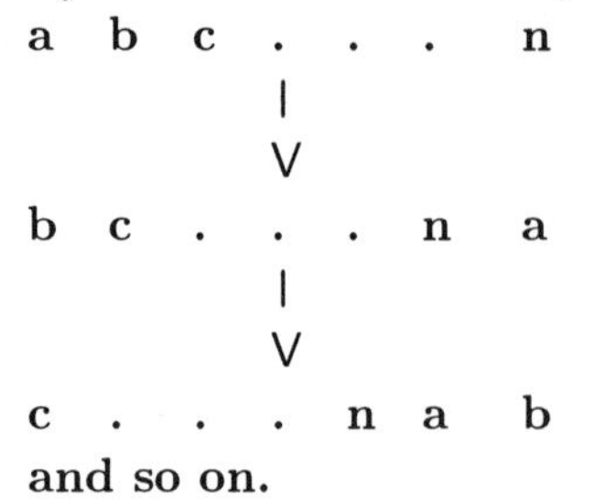

Similar spatial intuitions can be used in reasoning about operators that treat a list as a stack, or as a queue, i.e. operators which, like **rotate**, can be defined and reasoned about logically.

Informal experiments with seminar audiences suggest that such 'spatial' proofs of the **rotate** theorem and similar theorems, are far easier for most people to discover and to understand than the logical proofs using structural induction. This appears to be true even of people who understand the logical modes of reasoning. However, little is known about what sorts of internal processes actually correspond to what people describe on the basis of introspection as 'spatial' reasoning. When we have machines that also find the spatial proof easier we may be a little closer to understanding human intelligence. (Whatever the mechanisms are we may still find it helpful to reason about them in part using logic, and in part using other means!)

This human ability to reason spatially about list structures depends on construing lists not as algebraic structures recursively built up by successive applications of a binary operator (cons) but rather as a flat, linear, spatially ordered structure. Because human programmers use this intuitive grasp of lists all the time in their programming, the list-processing syntax of the language Pop-11 (See Anderson 1989) was extended to include notations for list processing (including list construction syntax and a pattern matcher with segment variables) that supported this spatial view of lists, since for many problems this is of great help for both experts and beginners learning about list processing and AI. For example, the structure that might, from the Fregean viewpoint, be denoted thus:

append(append(L1, cons(X, L2)), L3)

or as

```
L1 <> cons(X, L2) <> L3
```

could be represented in Pop-11 as

```
[ ^^L1  ^X  ^^L2  ^^L3 ]
```

where “^^” represents splicing in the elements of a list, and “^” represents insertion of only one element. In Common Lisp, this would be:

```
'( ,@L1  ,X  ,@L2  ,@L3)
```

Similarly, picture-like patterns of a list structure can also be used with a pattern matcher to extract information from lists. This makes many list processing operations much easier to get right in Pop-11 than in Prolog or Lisp without a pattern matcher, at least for beginners.

However, like many spatially based representations this is less general than the logical format. There are problems that require recursing both along ‘tails’ of a list and down the ‘heads’, for which this particular spatial view can be very limiting. Moreover, I am not claiming that it is impossible to use logic to characterize this spatial view of lists. After all, one can express many of the key ideas of Euclidean geometry in a logical form. All I claim is that the human brain finds the spatial representation easier to use for certain sorts of problems, and I suggest that this is because for those problems a spatial representation (possibly occurring in a high level virtual machine that could be implemented using quite different representations) *intrinsically* has more heuristic power. Defending that claim would require a lengthy discussion for which there is no space here, though several chapters in this volume address the topic.

2.14 Precision and Spatial Representations

To finish, I'd like to raise some questions about the nature of spatial representations in animal vision, provoked by reading an early draft of the chapter by Ken Forbus in this volume.

Forbus discusses representations and forms of reasoning that use not only exact numerical values but also assertions about relative magnitudes in some cases where exact values are not known. The latter is often called “qualitative” reasoning in the AI literature (which can be confusing for those who are used to reserving “qualitative” for non-numerical information, e.g. information in family trees). As I understand him, he claims that natural visual systems, like artificial visual systems that capture TV images in regular 2-D arrays, start from *exact* metric information rather than being restricted to "qualitative" information. On reflection I do not find this claim about natural vision obvious: it is not clear how best to describe visual processes in animals.

One can assume that because visual information is projected in a precise way onto the retina and to some extent processed there, exact information about location of features on the retina is available to the visual system. However, if retinal receptive fields vary in precision, as is the case with many animals, the information available to the brain about certain features may actually have considerable imprecision, especially near the periphery of the visual field. This makes the visual system very unlike a computer that projects an image directly into a uniform resolution 2-D array.

Many researchers have taken it for granted that visual systems use 'exact' coordinate representations for image structures, and this is indeed commonplace in machine vision using 2-D arrays to represent images. But it is not obvious that location on an animal's retina is treated that way by the animal's brain. It may be, for example, that receptive fields are represented by neurons that fire when those receptive fields are suitably stimulated, and that 'links' between neurons represent neighborhood relations between receptive fields without representing absolute distances. Then relations between remote portions of the image would be represented by chains of neighborhood relationships between receptive fields of varying sizes (the fields are much smaller near the fovea than further out), as described in Young 1989. Such chains of relationships would not correspond to exact measures of distance.

Such a system would directly map images onto structures that are more like so-called semantic nets (networks of nodes and links) than like 2-D arrays. Of course, it is clear that somehow our visual system computes very precise metrical relationships (required for accurate throwing for example), but it may do so by making complex inferences from very imprecise ('qualitative') topological relationships which are constantly recalibrated according to context. One reason for doing things this way may be that a collection of receptive fields of varying sizes arranged in concentric circles is more useful than a regular rectangular grid for supporting certain transformations such as rotation, expansion or contraction, as shown in Funt 1980.

Another reason for not attempting to make direct use of exact metrical information regarding image structure could be that although within the visual subsystem there are many transformations from one part of the brain to another that preserve retinal ordering and neighborhood relations, it is very difficult to arrange for metrical properties to be preserved. Further, such preservation may be pointless because constant saccadic motion causes the geometry of the projected images of a particular object to be constantly changing.

Insofar as precise metrical information is required (e.g. for judging time to contact) it is not image measurements, but measurements in the 3-D environment that are needed. Thus it is possible that the brain largely ignores transient and irrelevant exact geometric measurements in the *2-D image* and instead computes exact geometrical relationships in the *3-D scene* as and when needed, using the inexact image relationships found in several views.

A possible objection to this might be that our visual system uses precise measures of binocular disparity to compute depth information, as shown by random dot stereograms (e.g. in Frisby 1979). However, it is interesting that some of the more difficult random dot stereograms (e.g. those depicting scenes with gradually changing depth rather than large discontinuities) do not fuse properly at first; and only after several seconds, or even minutes, during which the image does not need to be fixated on the retina, does the depth information emerge. This suggests that there is not a simple computation of disparities between two retinal images, since saccadic motion ensures that the images are constantly changing while the perceiver waits for the 3-D structure to appear.

The point of all this is first of all to show that there is much we don't know about spatial representations in animal brains, and secondly to show that the fact that some physical structure (e.g. the precise pattern of intensity of illumination on the retina) exists in sensory stimulation does not imply that all the information it contains is used directly. The brain moves in mysterious ways its wonders to perform.

2.15 Conclusion

I have tried to show that the study of forms of representation goes back a long way, and that some of the very oldest controversies in philosophy (e.g. about the nature of mathematical knowledge) remain unresolved by developments in AI. Perhaps the time is ripe for new attempts to investigate and simulate how human mathematicians think about infinite sets and continuous shapes and transformations in Euclidean spaces, and how we use these spatial capabilities in reasoning about abstract and discrete algebraic or logical spaces.

Work done so far on diagrammatic reasoning identifies some of the problems, and provides fragments of evidence about how people work, and how some of their capabilities might be modeled on computers, yet there is still much to be done to understand the variety of forms in which information can stored and manipulated in intelligent control systems, natural or artificial. We may be better able to understand the full range of possibilities and the trade-offs between different design decisions if we keep an open mind in our exploration of design space.

References

Anderson, J. A. D .W. ed. 1989. *POP-11 Comes of Age: The Advancement of an AI Programming Language.* Chichester: Ellis Horwood.

Bobrow D. G. and Collins A. M. eds. 1975. *Representation and Understanding: Studies in Cognitive Science.* New York: Academic Press.

Brachman, R. J. and Levesque, H. J. (eds). 1985. *Readings in Knowledge Representation.* Los Altos, Calif.: Morgan Kaufmann.

Bundy, A. 1973. Doing Arithmetic with Diagrams, in *Proceedings of the Third International Joint Conference on Artificial Intelligence.* San Francisco: Morgan Kaufmann.

Feigenbaum, E. A. and Feldman, J., eds. 1963. *Computers and Thought.* New York: McGraw Hill.

Forbus, K. 1995. Qualitative Spatial Reasoning: Framework and Frontiers. In *Diagrammatic Reasoning* ed. J. Glasgow et. al. Menlo Park, Calif.: AAAI.

Frisby, J. P. 1979. *Seeing: Illusion, Brain and Mind.* Oxford: Oxford University Press.

Funt, B. V. 1980. Problem-Solving with Diagrammatic Representations. *Artificial Intelligence* 13(3): 201–230.

Gelerntner, H. 1959. Realization of a Geometry-Theorem Proving Machine. In Proceedings of an International Conference on Information Processing, 273-282. Paris: UNESCO House.

Glasgow, J. I. 1993, The Imagery Debate Revisited: A Computational Perspective. *Computational Intelligence: Special Issue on Computational Imagery* 9(4): 309–333.

Hayes, P. J. 1974. Some Problems and Non-problems in Representation Theory. In Proceedings, 1974 AISB Summer Conference, Univ. of Sussex.

Hayes, P. J. 1979. The Logic of Frames. In *Frame Conceptions and Text Understanding*, 46–61, ed. D. Metzing. Berlin: Walter de Gruyter & Co.

Hayes, P. J. 1985. The Second Naive Physics Manifesto. In *Formal Theories of the Commonsense World,* ed. J. R. Hobbs and R. C. Moore, 1–36. Norwood, NJ: Ablex.

Ireland, A. and Bundy, A. 1994 Productive Use of Failure in Inductive Proof. Tech. Rep., Dept. of Artificial Intelligence, Edinburgh University.

Kowalski, R. A. 1980. Contribution to a Survey on Knowledge Representation In *Special Issue on Knowledge Representation, SIGART Newsletter* No. 70, ed. R. J. Brachman and B. C. Smith.

Lindsay, R .K. 1963. Inferential Memory as the Basis of Machines Which Understand Natural Language. In *Computers and Thought,* ed. E. A. Feigenbaum and J. Feldman. New York: McGraw Hill.

McCarthy, J. 1968. Programs with Common Sense. In *Semantic Information Processing,* ed. M. L. Minsky, 403–418. Cambridge Mass: The MIT Press.

McCarthy, J. and Hayes, P. J. 1969. Some Philosophical Problems from the Standpoint of Artificial Intelligence. *Machine Intelligence 4*, ed. B. Meltzer and D. Michie. Edinburgh: Edinburgh University Press.

Minsky, M. L. 1961. Steps Towards Artificial Intelligence. In *Proceedings of the Institute of Radio Engineers* 49: 8–30.

Newell, A. 1980. Physical Symbol Systems. *Cognitive Science* 4(2): 135–183.

Narayanan, N. H., ed. 1993. Taking Issue/Forum: The Imagery Debate Revisited. *Computational Intelligence* 9(4): 303–435

J. M. Nicholas, ed. 1977. *Images, Perception, and Knowledge.* Dordrecht-Holland: Reidel.

Penrose, R. 1989. *The Emperor's New Mind: Concerning Computers, Minds and the Laws of Physics.* Oxford: Oxford University Press.

Penrose, R. 1990. Precis of *The Emperor's New Mind: Concerning Computers, Minds, and the Laws of Physics. The Behavioral and Brain Sciences* 13(4): 643–705.

Peterson, D.M., ed. 1995. *Forms of Representation* Oxford: Intellect Press.

Pylyshyn, Z.W. 1973 What the Mind's Eye Tells the Mind's Brain: A Critique of Mental Imagery. *Psychological Bulletin* 80: 1–24.

Sloman, A. 1971. Interactions Between Philosophy And AI: The Role of Intuition and Non-Logical Reasoning In Intelligence. In Proceedings Second

International Joint Conference on Artificial Intelligence, London. San Francisco: Morgan Kaufmann.

Sloman, A. 1975. Afterthoughts on Analogical Representation. In *Theoretical Issues in Natural Language Processing*, ed. R. Schank and B. Nash-Webber. Association for Computational Linguistics.

Sloman, A. 1985. Why We Need Many Knowledge Representation Formalisms. In *Research and Development in Expert Systems,* ed. M Bramer, 163–183. New York: Cambridge University Press.

Sloman, A. 1989. On Designing a Visual System: Towards a Gibsonian Computational Model of Vision. *Journal of Experimental and Theoretical AI* 1(4): 289–337.

Sloman, A. 1992. The Emperor's Real Mind: Critical Discussion of Penrose 1989. *Artificial Intelligence* 56: 355–396.

Sloman, A. 1993a. Varieties of Formalisms for Knowledge Representation. *Computational Intelligence, Special issue on Computational Imagery* 9(4): 413–423

Sloman, A. 1993b. The Mind as a Control System. In *Philosophy and the Cognitive Sciences,* ed. C. Hookway and D. Peterson, 69–110. Cambridge: Cambridge University Press,

Sloman, A. 1994a. Explorations in Design Space. In Proceedings Eleventh European Conference on Artificial Intelligence, ed. A. G.Cohn, 578–582. Chichester: John Wiley.

Sloman, A. 1994b. Towards a General Theory of Representations. In *Forms of Representation* ed. D. M. Peterson. Intellect Press.

Sloman, A. 1994c Semantics in an Intelligent Control System. In Proceedings British Academy and Royal Society Conference, Artificial Intelligence and The Mind: New Breakthroughs Or Dead Ends? *Philosophical Transactions of the Royal Society.*

Winston, P. H. 1975. Learning Structural Descriptions from Examples. In *The Psychology of Computer Vision* ed. P. H. Winston, 157–209. New York: McGraw-Hill

Woods, W. A. 1975. What's In A Link?. In *Representation and Understanding: Studies in Cognitive Science,* ed. D. G. Bobrow and A. M.Collins, 35–82. New York: Academic Press.

Wahlster, W. 1994. Computational Models of Multimodal Communication. Invited Address to Eleventh European Conference on AI, *ECAI94*. Amsterdam.

Young, D. S. 1989. Logarithmic Sampling of Images for Computer Vision. In *AISB89: Proceedings Seventh Conference of Society for the Study of Artificial Intelligence and Simulation of Behaviour*, ed. A. G. Cohn, 145–150. London: Pitman & Morgan Kaufmann.

2 Problem-Solving with Diagrammatic Representations[1]

Brian V. Funt
Simon Fraser University

2.1 Introduction

Diagrams are very important tools which we use daily in communication, information storage, planning and problem-solving. Their utility is, however, dependent upon the existence of the human eye and its perceptual abilities. Since human perception involves a very sophisticated information processing system, it can be argued that a diagram's usefulness results from its suitability as an input to this powerful visual system. Alternatively, diagrams can be viewed as containing information similar to that contained in the real visual world, the canonical entity the human visual system was presumably designed through evolution to interpret. From this latter perspective, diagrams are a natural representation of certain types of primarily visual information, and the perceptual system simply provides an appropriate set of database accessing functions. Both these viewpoints underlie the work described in this chapter. The role of diagrams is explored in a computer problem-solving program, named WHISPER, which refers to diagrams during its processing. WHISPER'S high-level reasoning component (HLR), built along the lines of traditional procedural AI problem-solving programs, has the additional option of requesting observations in a diagram. It does this by asking its "perceptual system" to "look at" the diagram with its parallel processing "retina." The questions that the perceptual system can answer are called *perceptual primitives.* If necessary, the HLR can also make changes to the current diagram. Figure 2.1 shows WHISPER'S overall structure.

Upon receiving a diagram of a blocks world structure, WHISPER outputs a set of diagrams representing the sequence of events which occur as the structure collapses. The HLR contains knowledge about stability and the motion of falling objects. Using the retina to locate objects and their supports, it checks the stability of each object shown in the diagram. Unstable objects may either rotate or slide. In cases where one is rotationally unstable, the HLR asks the retina to "visualize" it rotating and thereby determine at what point it will hit some other object.

[1] Originally appeared in *Artificial Intelligence* 13. Copyright, 1980, North Holland. Reprinted with permission.

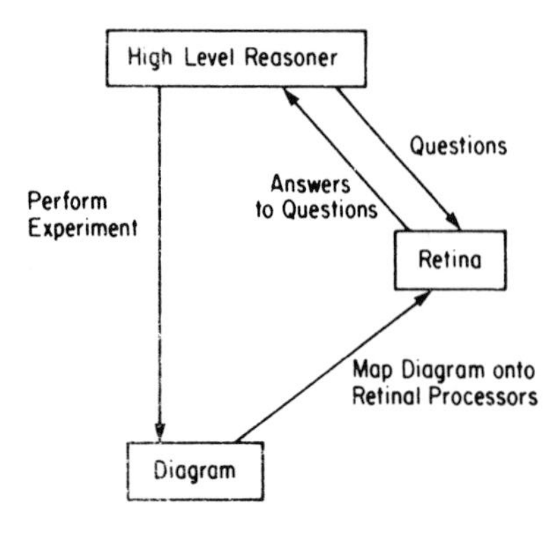

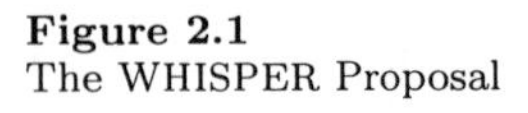
Figure 2.1
The WHISPER Proposal

Using this information WHISPER outputs an updated diagram showing the object rotated into its new position. Then with this new diagram, it restarts the problem-solving process from the beginning—rechecking the stability of each object, moving one of them, outputting another diagram, and restarting again. The process terminates when either all the objects are stable or the problem becomes too complex for the stability tester. A detailed discussion of the HLR will be postponed until Section 2.3.

2.1.1 Motivation

A strong case for computer use of diagrams as models for geometry has been made by Gelernter (1963), and as general analogical representations by Sloman (1971). Networks with nodes representing "ideal integers" and arcs representing relationships between them were used as models for statements in arithmetic by Bundy (1973). Hayes (1974) and Bobrow (1975) comment on the theoretical nature of analogical representations; Hesse (1969) and Nagel (1961) discuss analogical reasoning.

There is a variety of reasons for using diagrams in computer problem-solving. Diagrams such as maps, architectural plans, and circuit diagrams routinely facilitate human problem-solving. Perhaps diagrams function not merely to extend memory capacity, but rather present the important information in a particularly usable form. If they do, then the human visual system provides a paradigmatic example of a system for accessing these representations. Since it exploits a high degree of parallelism, it leads us into the realm of a different type of hardware. This is an exciting step, however, because we can see how much hardware characteristics influence our thinking about the difficulty of various problems and the feasibility of their solution. For example, we know we could compute with Turing Machines—but would we? Because WHISPER'S retina harnesses parallelism, it in effect extends the available machine instruction set with special ones for diagram feature recognition. WHISPER is primarily an exploration of the question: to what extent can problem-solving be simplified through experiment and observation with diagrams? This is in contrast (but not in opposition) to the usual method of deduction within a formal theory as explained in the next section.

2.1.2 Theoretical Framework

Any problem-solving system needs a representation of the problem situation. The standard approach in AI is to formalize the domain. We choose a language and write down a set of statements (axioms, productions, assertions, or a semantic network) describing the world. So that the problem-solver can generate new statements from this initial set, we provide a general deductive mechanism (theorem prover, programming language control structure, network algorithm). In terms of the predicate calculus the axioms define a theory, T, and so long as it is not self-contradictory there will be at least one model M (an assignment of predicates to the predicate symbols, functions to the function symbols, and individuals to the constant symbols) which satisfies it. Since our intention in axiomatizing the world was to accurately describe it, we expect it to be one of the models satisfying T.

We may find a second model M' satisfying T (in general there will be many such models). Now—and this is the main thrust of WHISPER—in some cases we can use M' to provide information about M without deriving it from T. What is required is that some of the predicates, functions and individuals of M' correspond to some of the predicates, functions and individuals of M in such a way that it is possible to translate the results obtained when these predicates and functions are applied to individuals in M' into the results that would be obtained if the corresponding predicates and functions were to be applied to the corresponding individuals in M. The similarity between M and M' means that

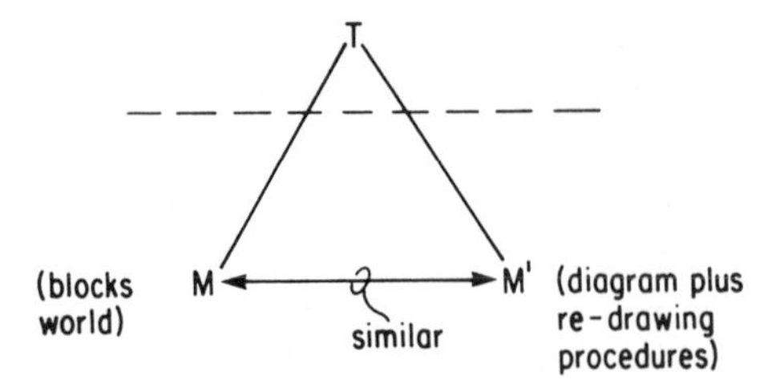

Figure 2.2

experiments and observations made in M' yield results similar to those that would be obtained in M. As shown in Figure 2.2, for WHISPER M' is the combination of its diagram and diagram redrawing procedures. WHISPER obtains information about the blocks world by using its retina to observe the results of experimental changes made to its diagrams by the re-drawing procedures.

WHISPER is a prototype system designed to explore the extent to which problem solving can be carried out below the dashed line of Figure 2.2; however, it does do some reasoning above the line. WHISPER'S success argues for working below the line, but not against working above the line. WHISPER'S HLR is an above-the-line component.

A natural question is why use M' instead of M? If M is readily accessible then there is no reason not to use it; but, frequently it will not be. For example if we want to determine the stability of a pile of blocks on the surface of the moon, then we could construct a similar pile of blocks on earth and determine the result by experiment. In this case M, the pile of blocks on the moon is inaccessible. We can see that a lot can be learned from the blocks on earth, but some above-the-line inference must be done to handle the discrepancies arising as a result of the difference in gravity.[1]

2.2 Mechanisms for Diagram Interaction

The retina and perceptual primitives are designed to provide WHISPER with a new set of operations whose execution times are of the same

[1] I am grateful to Raymond Reiter for many of the ideas in Section 2.1.2.

order of magnitude as conventional machine instructions. To achieve this a high degree of parallelism has been incorporated into the system. The retina is a parallel processor, and the perceptual primitives are the algorithms it executes. (Do not be misled by the term "retina;" it refers to a general system of receptors and processors for the early stages of perceptual processing, rather than implying any close resemblance to the human retina.) Each perceptual primitive, when executed by the retina, determines whether some particular feature is present in the diagram. WHISPER'S retina mixes parallel and sequential computation, so the features it can recognize are not subject to the same theoretical limitations as perceptrons (Minsky and Papert 1969).

2.2.1 The Retina

WHISPER'S retina is a software simulation of hardware which, given the rapidly advancing state of LSI technology, should soon be possible to build. It consists of a collection of processors, each processor having its own input device called a *receptor*. There is a fixed number of processors, and they are all identical. As with the human eye, WHISPER'S retina can be shifted to fixate at a new diagram location (also a feature of a program by Dunlavey [1975]), so that each processor's receptor receives a different input from the diagram. This fixation facility is important because the resolution of the retina decreases from its center to its periphery. Without being able to fixate, it would be impossible for WHISPER to examine the whole diagram in detail. Economy of receptors and processors dictates the use of decreasing resolution. (A declining resolution is also a characteristic of the human eye.) Each receptor covers a separate segment of the diagram and transmits a single value denoting the color of that region. The geometrical arrangement of the receptors and the area each covers is shown in Figure 2.3.[2]

The "circles" in the figure are called *bubbles,* and they are arranged in *wedges* (rays emanating from the center) and *rings* (concentric circles of bubbles). The resolution varies across the retina because a larger portion of the underlying diagram is mapped onto a bubble depicted by a larger circle. Since the complete group of receptors is assumed to sense

[2]There are more receptors filling the central blank area of Figure 2.3; however, there is still one special case receptor in the very center which must be handled separately. In order to speed up the retinal simulation the bubbles lying in the blank central area can be fixated separately so they are mapped onto only when they are needed.

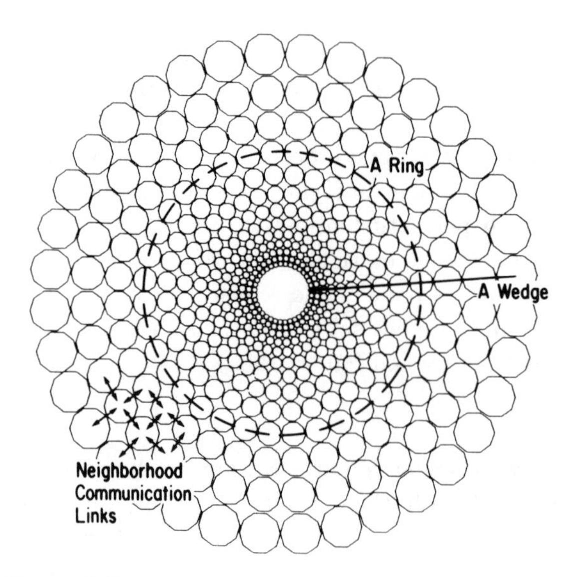

Figure 2.3
WHISPER's Retina.

and transmit all signals in parallel, fixations are fast.

Each retinal processor has direct communication links to its nearest neighbors plus one additional link via a common databus connecting all the processors to a supervisory processor called the *retinal supervisor*. The communication topology has been restricted in this simple way to ensure a feasible future hardware implementation.

The bubble processors are each small computers with independent memory. They all simultaneously execute the same procedure; however, each bubble does not necessarily execute the same instruction at the same time. In the current implementation, a call to the Lisp evaluator simulates a processor; and Lisp MAPping functions simulate the parallel control structure.

Although the bulk of the processing of the perceptual primitives is done in parallel, there is also a small amount of sequential processing which is performed by the retinal supervisor. The retinal supervisor also directs the parallel processing by choosing which procedure the bubbles should execute next and broadcasting this common procedure to them.

2.2.2 The Perceptual Primitives.

Each perceptual primitive detects a *problem domain independent diagram* feature. The HLR assigns these features interpretations pertinent to the problem it is solving. The current set of implemented perceptual primitives include ones to: find the center of area of a shape; find the points of contact between a shape of one color and a shape of another; examine curves for abrupt slope changes; test a shape for symmetry; test the similarity of shapes; and visualize the rotation of a shape while watching for a collision with another shape.

The CENTER-OF-AREA perceptual primitive is an illustrative example of the general operation of the perceptual primitives. It computes the center of area of a shape relative to the origin defined by the center of the retina. For each piece, δA, of the total area we need to compute the x and y components of its contribution to the total area. Dividing the vector sum of these contributions by the total area yields the coordinates of the center of area. Since each retinal bubble receives its input from a fixed sized area of the diagram and is at a fixed location relative to the retina's center, each bubble can independently compute the components of its contribution to the total area. The bubbles whose receptors do not lie over any part of the shape simply do not contribute. The retinal supervisor performs the summation and the division by the total area. A separate primitive computes the total area. It simply totals the area of all the contributing bubbles. If the computed center of area is far from the retina's center its accuracy can be improved by fixating the retina on the estimated center of area and then recomputing. The decision to iterate is made by the retinal supervisor. The accuracy improves because more of the central, high-resolution portion of the retina is used.

It is possible that systematic errors might lead to a discrepancy between the center of area as seen by the retina and the actual center of area of the object in the diagram. This is the case because the diagram-to-retina mapping does not take into account what fraction of a bubble's picture region is covered by an object. The bubble is simply marked whenever any portion of its region is covered. In practice, the accuracy of the center of area test was more than adequate for WHISPER; if necessary the accuracy could always be improved by adding more bubbles to the retina, increasing its resolution.

The center of area is used for more than simply providing the center of gravity of the objects in WHISPER'S problem domain. Other primitives (symmetry, similarity, and contact finding) fixate on a shape's center of area before beginning their calculations. For example, if a shape is symmetrical its center of area will be on its axis of symmetry.

Another important primitive is RETINAL-VISUALIZATION. What is "visualized" is the rigid rotation of a shape about the retinal center. While the shape is rotating the collision detection primitive can be called as a demon to watch whether the rotation causes the shape to overlap with another stationary shape. This is useful both in "blocks world" environments involving moving objects and in testing whether two shapes are equivalent under rotation. The process is termed *visualization* because it does not involve modifying the diagram, but instead is totally internal to the retina itself. It simply entails an organized and uniform exchange of information amongst neighboring bubbles.

The geometrical arrangement of the bubble receptors facilitates the visualization of rotations. From Figure 2.3 it can be seen that aligning the bubble centers along wedges results in a constant angular separation between bubbles of the same ring when they are from neighboring wedges, and that this constant is independent of the ring chosen. Thus, to rotate a shape clockwise each bubble marked by the shape simply sends a message to its clockwise ring neighbor asking it to mark itself. The sender then erases its own mark. A collision is detected if a bubble receives a message to mark when it is already marked by a shape other than the rotating one. Although the shape is rotated in sequential steps, the time required is still short because

1. there are, as a maximum, only as many steps to be made as there are wedges on the retina (currently 36); and
2. all the message passing and collision checking occurs in parallel during each step.

The coarse retinal resolution means that the visualization process is much faster than the alternative of rotating the object by small increments directly in the diagram. However, the coarse resolution also means that the collision test may falsely predict a collision. Although the collision test may occasionally generate such "false alarms," it will never fail to correctly predict a true collision. The reason for this is that during the diagram-to-retina mapping a point in the diagram is blurred to fill a whole bubble on the retina with the result that the objects in the diagram appear slightly enlarged on the retina. To check out a possible false alarm the HLR

1. calls the re-drawing procedures to rotate the object in the diagram to the point where the collision is expected,
2. fixates the retina at the predicted collision point,
3. asks the retina (now with its high resolution center) to see if the colliding objects are touching.

The CONTACT-FINDER primitive establishes the points at which an object touches other objects. The retina is first fixated on the center of area of the object and then the retinal supervisor directs each retinal bubble to execute the following steps:

1. If the bubble value is not the color of the object then stop.
2. For each of its neighboring bubbles do Step (3).
3. If neighbor's value is the color of a different object send a "contact-found" message to the retinal supervisor.
4. Stop.

The retinal supervisor may receive quite a number of messages from bubbles in the contact regions. It must sort these into groups—one for each distinct area of contact. To do this the retinal supervisor sequentially follows the chain of neighborhood links from one contact bubble to another. Each bubble in the chain is put in the same contact group. If no neighboring bubble is a contact bubble, then the chain is broken. Long chains indicate that the objects touch along a surface while short ones indicate that they touch only at a point. The bubble coordinates of the endpoints of the chain represent the extremities of a contact surface, and the average of the coordinates of all the bubbles in the group is a good place at which to fixate the retina for a more detailed analysis of the contact.

When two objects touch there is a good chance that one supports the other unless they are just sitting side by side. To determine which object is the supporter and which the supported the coordinates of the touching bubbles are compared to find which is "above" the other in the diagram. The assignment of "up" is problem domain dependent and so is made by the HLR.

Another perceptual primitive, FIND-NEAREST, finds the bubble closest to the retinal center satisfying a given condition. For example, to find the object nearest to point P in the diagram the retina is fixated at P and then asked for the nearest marked bubble. The organization of the retina into rings, each an increasing distance from the center, facilitates the search for the required nearest bubble. To find the nearest bubble to the center of the retina satisfying condition C, the retinal supervisor executes the following algorithm:

1. Direct each bubble to test C and save the result (either 'true' or 'false').
2. For $n = 1$ to the number of rings on the retina do Steps 3 and 4.
3. Direct each bubble to report its wedge and ring coordinates as a message to the retinal supervisor if the following hold: (a) it belongs to ring n, (b) its saved value is 'true.'
4. If there is a message pending for the retinal supervisor from step (3), return the coordinates specified in that message (if there is more than one message pick any one of them—all bubbles in a ring are equidistant from the retinal center) to the calling procedure.

This algorithm is a good example of the difference between efficiency in sequential and parallel computation. Since testing C could be a lengthy computation, it is more efficient in terms of elapsed time to simultaneously test C on all bubbles as in Step 1, than to test it for only those bubbles in the scanned rings of Step 3. On a sequential processor it would be best to test C as few times as possible; whereas, on a parallel processor the total number of times C is tested is irrelevant (assuming the time to compute $C(x)$ is independent of x). It is the number of times C is tested sequentially which is important.

The SYMMETRY primitive tests for symmetry about a designated vertical axis by comparing the values of symmetrically positioned bubbles. An object is symmetrical (WHISPER tests for vertical and horizontal reflective symmetry), if each bubble having its "color" value has a symmetrically located bubble with the same value. If when testing the vertical reflective symmetry of a blue object, say, the bubble in the third wedge clockwise from the vertical axis and in the fourth ring from the center has the value 'blue,' then the value of the bubble in the third wedge counterclockwise from the vertical axis and in the fourth ring must be checked to see if it is also 'blue.' If it is not, then possibly the discrepancy can be ruled out as insignificant; otherwise, the object is asymmetrical. Neighborhood message passing is used to bring together the values from bubbles on opposite sides of the proposed axis. The technique is to cause whole wedges to shift in a manner perhaps best described as analogous to the closing of an Oriental hand fan. All the bubbles to the left of the axis send their values clockwise, while all those to the right send theirs counterclockwise. Messages which meet at the axis are compared and will be equal if the object is symmetrical.

The symmetry test must be supplied a proposed axis of symmetry. The center of area offers partial information on determining this axis since it must lie on it if the object is symmetrical. This does not, however, provide the orientation of the axis. Although the simplest solution may be to test the object in all of the wedge orientations by using the rotational visualization, if one more point on the axis of symmetry could be found the axis would be uniquely determined. Such a point is the center of the circumscribing circle of the object. The only problem is that thus far I have not managed to devise a quick parallel algorithm for finding this center. Although in some cases they may coincide, in general I expect the center of area and the center of the circumscribing circle to be distinct for objects with only a single axis of symmetry.

An unexpected and interesting property of WHISPER'S retinal geometry leads to a simple method, employing neighborhood communication, for scaling the retinal 'image' of an object. The primitive is RETINAL-SCALING. An object is scaled correctly (i.e. without distorting its shape) if each bubble having its value, sends this value to a bubble in the same wedge, but a fixed number of rings away. As long as each value is moved the same number of rings either inwards or outwards from the bubble which originally holds it, the size of the 'image' of the object is changed but its shape is preserved (Figure 2.4). This is the case because the constraint of aligning the bubbles into wedges such that each bubble touches all of its immediate neighbors is satisfied by increasing the bubble diameters by a constant factor from ring to ring. For a proof of this see Funt (1976). Scaling an object by neighborhood communication is implemented by having each bubble simultaneously send its value as a message to its neighbor in the same wedge in either the appropriate

Figure 2.4

inwards or outwards direction, and repeating this message passing process sequentially as many times as necessary to bring about the required scaling.

The SIMILARITY PRIMITIVE determines whether two objects A and B are similar under some combination of translation, rotation and scaling, and if so returns the angle of rotation, direction and distance of translation, and the scale factor. It works by taking one object, say A, and translating, scaling and rotating it so it can be matched with the other. Since the center of area of an object is unique the centers of area of A and B must be aligned if they are to match. Thus the first step is to find the centers of area, and then to translate A. Rather than call the re-drawing transformations to move A in the diagram, its translation can be accomplished entirely on the retina by:

1. fixating on the center of area of A,
2. asking all bubbles not containing A to mark themselves as empty space,
3. fixating on the center of area of B while superimposing this new image on the old one.

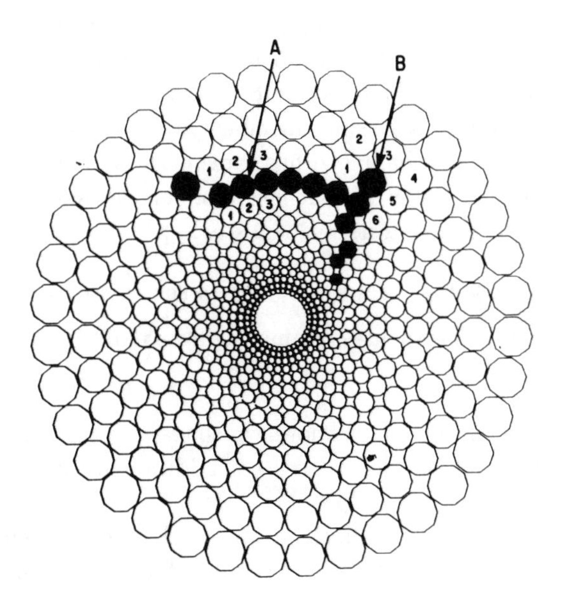

Figure 2.5

After translation A must be scaled. If A and B are to match, then their areas will need to be the same; therefore, we must scale A by a factor equal to the square root of the ratio of the areas of the two objects (i.e. scalefactor = squareroot(area(B)/area(A)). The areas of A and B are available as a by-product of the center of area calculation. Now that the objects are aligned and the same size, A is rotated about its center of area using retinal visualization to see if there is any orientation at which it matches B.

CURVE-FEATURES analyses curves. In order to begin, it must first find the retinal bubbles on the curve. Given one bubble on the curve, the others can be found by following the chain of bubbles each having the same value. In WHISPER'S diagrams the contours of objects are "colored" a different shade from their interiors, and this helps prevent the curve following process from getting lost tracing chains of bubbles which are part of an object's interior. It is not strictly necessary to color code the object contours, since a contour bubble can be determined by the type of neighbors surrounding it, but coding is cheaper and easier.

Once the set of bubbles on the curve is found, each bubble in the set can individually test for the occurrence of a particular feature; therefore, the whole curve is tested in parallel. A bubble detects a sharp bend in the curve if there is an imbalance in the number of its neighbors on opposite sides of the curve which are themselves not members of the curve. This is illustrated by Fig. 2.5 in which bubble A has three neighbors on each side of the curve, whereas bubble B has six neighbors on one side and none on the other. Thus, a bubble tests for bends by:

1. asking its neighbors whether or not they are on the curve, and
2. comparing the number of responses originating from opposite sides of the curve.

For a simple closed curve, if the bubble knows which responding neighbors are interior and which are exterior, then it can additionally classify the bend as convex or concave.

The slope of a curve at any curve bubble is determined as the perpendicular to the bisector of the angle between the centers of its neighboring bubbles on the curve. This yields a rough approximation to the actual slope, but it is sufficient for quickly testing whether any drastic slope change occurs over the length of the curve. To more accurately determine the slope at a particular point, the retina is fixated on it for higher resolution. The curve tangent is then the perpendicular to the bisector of the angle between wedges with the most bubbles on the curve. The angle between wedges can be used because they emanate directly from the center of the retina, just as the curve must when the retina is centered on it. This method is more accurate than measuring the angle between neighboring bubbles because there are more wedges than neighbors. The HLR mainly uses this test to measure the slope of surfaces at contact points to decide whether or not an object will slide.

2.2.3 The Underlying Diagram

We began with the view that the retina is a special purpose parallel processor designed to detect diagrammatic features without saying anything about the precise nature of the diagrams themselves. With the retinal processor in hand, we can now see that the representation of the diagrams is unimportant as long as each bubble receives its correct input. This is analogous to a program which issues a READ command without caring whether the input is coming from a card reader, a file, or a terminal. The method of mapping from the diagram to the retinal bubbles' input must be fast, however, because the retina is re-filled every time it is fixated at a new diagram location.

There are at least two different types of representing media for the underlying diagram. The first is the conventional medium of visible marks on a two-dimensional surface, usually paper. The map from diagram to human retina is accomplished by the lens of the eye focusing the incoming light. Since there is simultaneous stimulation of the receptors, it is a very fast process.

The second possible type of diagram representation is similar to that used in generating computer graphics. The diagram is specified as a list of primitive elements (in graphics applications, usually line segment equations). In a similar vein, Kosslyn (1975) proposes that human visual imagery is in some ways analogous to the storage and display of graphics images. The parallel processing capacity of WHISPER'S retina can be used to quickly map each primitive element into the proper bubble inputs. To mark all bubbles lying on line segment, S, the retinal supervisor directs every bubble to determine independently if it is on S and if so, to mark itself. Since this simple test—do a circle and a line segment intersect?—is performed by all bubbles simultaneously, the time required is independent of the length of S. The same method can mark all bubbles within any simple shape such as a circle, square or triangle in time independent of its area. Regardless of the type of primitive element, the time taken to "draw" the diagram on the retina is, however, proportional to the number of primitives in its description. They must be processed sequentially.

Due to the lack of true parallel processing, neither of the above two types of diagram representations is used in WHISPER. Instead, the diagram is implemented as a square array. Each array cell denotes a point on a real world, pencil and paper diagram.

2.2.4 The Re-Drawing Transformations

The re-drawing transformations are the procedures the HLR can call to change the underlying diagram. In WHISPER there are transformations for adding and removing lines, and for rigidly translating and rotating shapes. Other non-linear transformations could be added if required. These re-drawing procedures are of course dependent upon the representation of the diagram they modify, and the ease and efficiency with which they can be implemented could affect the choice of diagram representation.

2.3 WHISPER in Operation

With the basic mechanisms for interaction with the diagram now understood, it is appropriate to see how they are used in the course of solving a problem. We will consider problems of the type: predict the sequence of events occurring during the collapse of a "blocks world" structure. The structure will be a piled group of *arbitrarily* shaped objects of uniform density and thickness. If the structure is stable, there are no events to describe; if it is unstable, then the events involve rotations, slides, falls, and collisions. WHISPER accepts a diagram of the initial problem state, and produces a sequence of diagrams, called snapshots, as its qualitative solution. A quantitative solution specifying precise locations, velocities, and times is not found; however, deriving one from a qualitative solution should not be too difficult (deKleer 1975).

Figure 2.6 is a typical example of WHISPER'S input diagrams. They all depict a side view of the structure. Each object is shaded a different "color" (alphanumeric value) so it can be easily distinguished and identified. Objects' boundaries are also distinctly colored. The diagram depicts a problem, called the "chain-reaction problem," which is particularly interesting because the causal connection between objects B and D must be discovered.

2.3.1 The Qualitative HLR

The HLR is the top level of the WHISPER system. It is solely responsible for solving each problem; the diagram and retina are simply tools at its disposal. It consists of procedural specialists which know about stability, about the outcome of different varieties of instability, how to interpret each perceptual primitive, and how to call the transformation procedures to produce the solution snapshots. There are two types of instabilities—rotational and sliding. For clarity, sliding instabilities will not be discussed for the present. Operation of the system follows the steps:

1. Determine all instabilities.
2. Pick the dominant instability.

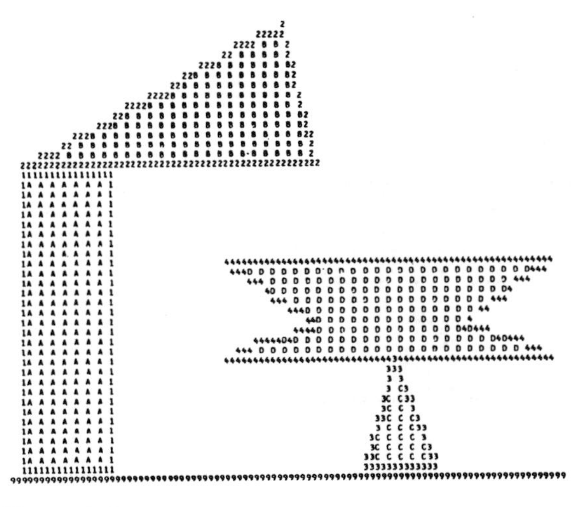

Figure 2.6
The Chain Reaction Problem

3. Find pivot point for rotation of unstable object.
4. Find termination condition of rotation using retinal visualization.
5. Call transformation procedure to modify diagram as determined in Step 4.
6. Output modified diagram as a solution snapshot.
7. Use snapshot from Step 6 as input and restart from Step 1. In what follows we elaborate on each of these steps.

The diagram and retina are an invaluable aid to the HLR in discovering what stops an object's motion, and in accomplishing the necessary state change. The chain reaction problem demonstrates this. The stability specialist directs the retina to fixate at numerous locations while perusing the diagram, and from an analysis (discussed below) of the visible support relationships determines that B is the only unstable object. B will pivot about the support point closest to its center of gravity. The retina is fixated there (the top right corner of A), so B's rotation can be visualized. As the object rotates, two events are possible. It may collide with another object, or it may begin to fall freely. The conditions under which either of these occur are monitored during the visualization. From this simulation of B's rotation, its collision with D is discovered, and its

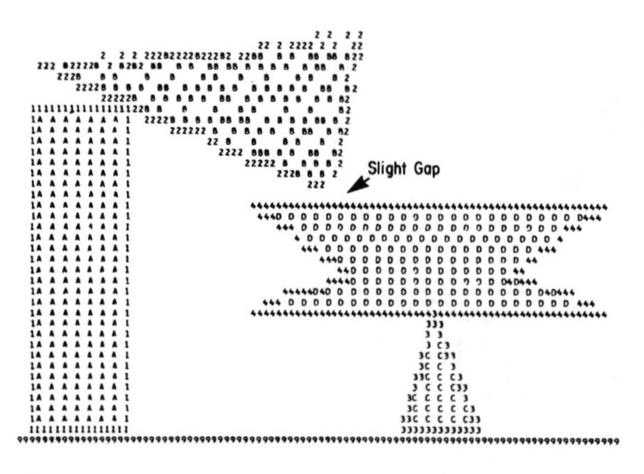

Figure 2.7

angle of rotation and location of first contact with D are found. Because of the coarseness of the retinal resolution, this angle of rotation is only approximate. This approximate value is used in conjunction with feedback from the diagram to refine the angle of rotation as follows. First the redrawing transformations are called to produce a new diagram (Figure 2.7) in which B is rotated by slightly less than the estimated value. The rotation is made on the short side so that B will not overshoot. The retina is then fixated on the anticipated point of collision so that the gap between the two objects can be examined. If there is none, then the update is complete; however, if there is, then B is rotated again until the gap is closed. The resulting diagram (Figure 2.8) is output as WHISPER'S first snapshot of the solution sequence.

2.3.2 Motion Discontinuities and Experimental Feedback

There are several important observations to be made at this point. One is that discovering the reason for the interruption of an object's motion, accomplished so simply here for B through visualization, is generally found to be a very difficult problem. Physics provides equations for object motions, but these equations describe a condition which theoretically lasts indefinitely. They do not indicate when new boundary conditions should take effect. Certainly it is possible to design a set of special heuristics specifying when and where collisions are most likely to occur (e.g. below the rotating object). However, it is quite probable that the collision occurring in Figure 2.9 would be overlooked, whereas

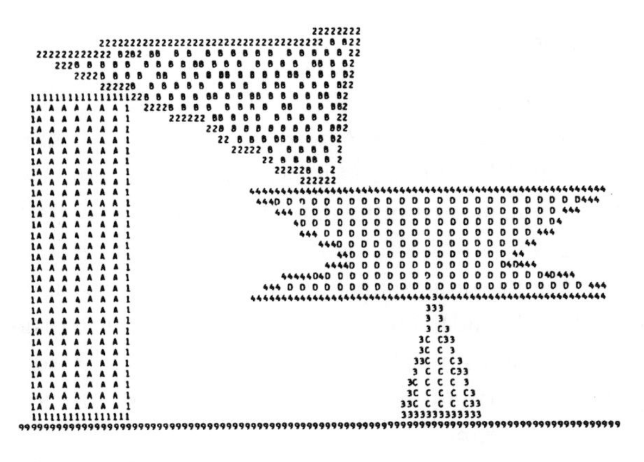

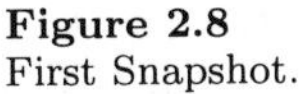

Figure 2.8
First Snapshot.

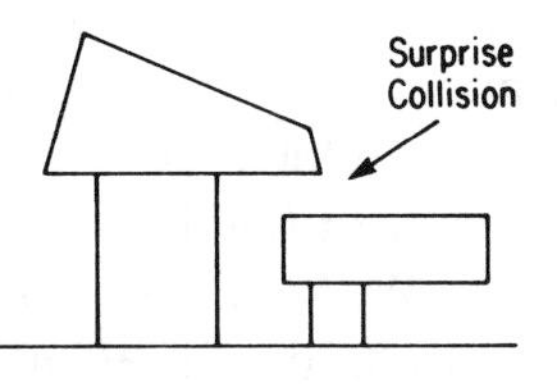

Figure 2.9

WHISPER'S visualization process would detect it as a matter of course.

WHISPER relies on *experimental feedback* to successfully update its diagram in its method of visualization followed by gap closure. This method is basically a pragmatic equivalent to the unfeasible experiment of rotating the object in the diagram by very small increments until a collision occurs. Usually feedback is thought of in terms of a robot immersed in a real world environment. In WHISPER'S case, however, the feedback is from a situation analogous to that in the real world—the diagram and diagram transformations—rather than from observation of actual falling objects. Alternatively, we can say that WHISPER is using M' to derive results about M. Using this feedback WHISPER is able to find when and where discontinuous changes in an object's motion occur without being forced to use sophisticated, "number-crunching" algorithms for touch tests (see Fahlman 1973) for arbitrary shapes.

2.3.3 The Frame Problem

Once WHISPER has produced the first snapshot, it is ready to compute the next one. All the information the HLR needs for this is contained in the first snapshot diagram. Thus to produce the next snapshot, the HLR takes its last output snapshot as input, and begins processing exactly as if it were working on a fresh problem. Although some results derived while working on the previous snapshot remain valid (e.g. some contact relationships will still hold), many will be inapplicable to the new problem. It is easier to disregard this old information than to sort it out and update it, since the retina provides a fast and efficient method of fetching it from the new diagram.

The problem of updating a system's representation of the state of the world to reflect the effects of actions performed in the world is the frame problem. Raphael (1971) and Hayes (1971, 1976) discuss it in detail. The transition between WHISPER'S snapshots is exactly the type of situation in which we expect the frame problem to arise. It involves the representation of action, the effects of action, and the discovery of chains of causal connection. However, because WHISPER relies on a diagram as a representation of the state of the world, it remains under control. For WHISPER the state of the world is represented by the state of the diagram, and action in the world is represented by corresponding action in the diagram. The corresponding action is the application of the appropriate transformation, and the effects of the action are correctly represented by the resulting state of the diagram.

In WHISPER'S current problem, the HLR knows that the action of B's rotation is represented by calling the rotation transformation procedure to re-draw B at its new location in the diagram. Almost all of the information that it needs to continue its problem solving is correctly represented by the updated diagram. It can proceed just as if the new snapshot (the updated diagram) were its original input and it were starting a brand new problem. The most important information which has changed in the transition between the states as a result of the rotation is: the position and orientation of object B; the position of its center of area; the contacts it makes with other objects; and the shape of the areas of empty space. There are also a multitude of things that will not have changed in the world and are correctly left unchanged by the rotational transformation, such as the position of all the other objects, the

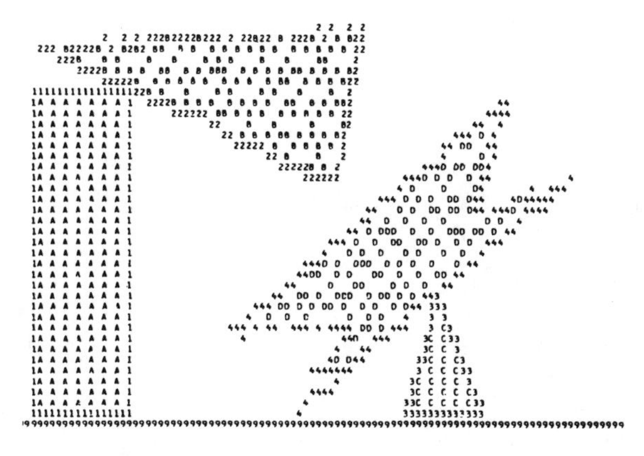

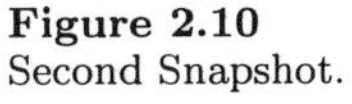

Figure 2.10
Second Snapshot.

shape of all objects, the area of all objects, and the contact relationships of other objects not involving *B*. All of these things work out correctly without the need of any deduction or inference on WHISPER's part. All that it need do is to use its retina to look at the diagram and extract whatever information it needs from the updated diagram.

An expanded WHISPER system could not completely avoid the pitfalls of the frame problem because not all of the information about the current state of the world (e.g. velocities) can be represented by the state of the diagram.

2.3.4 Subsequent Snapshots of the Chain Reaction Problem

The analysis producing the second and third snapshots is very similar to that for the first. In Figure 2.8, *B*'s weight on *D* causes *D* to be unstable. Its rotation is visualized with the retina fixated at the peak of *C* leading to the discovery of its collision with the table. The diagram is updated to produce the second snapshot, Figure 2.10, which is again input for further analysis. *B* now lacks sufficient support, and topples to hit *D* again as shown in Figure 2.11. The complexity of the problem rises sharply at this point, and WHISPER'S analysis ends, as, I believe, would most peoples'.

B and *D* could be shown to fall simultaneously (WHISPER currently does not) by rotating *D* only part of the way to the table before allowing *B* to catch up, and then iterating this process a few times until *D* reaches

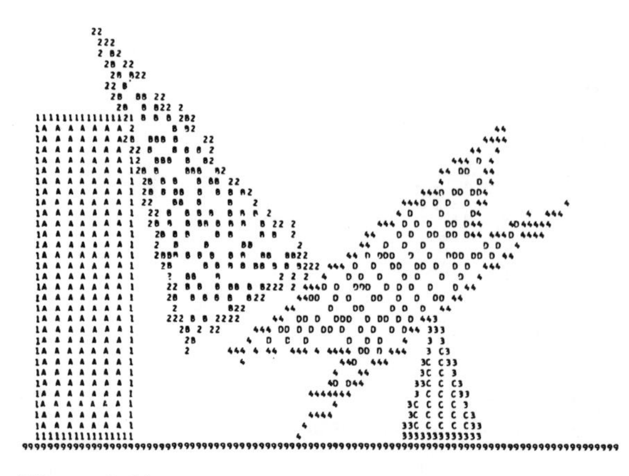

Figure 2.11
Final Snapshot.

the table.

2.3.5 Some Limitations of WHISPER's Qualitative Knowledge

WHISPER'S knowledge of physics is far from comprehensive. As mentioned above, one obvious limitation is that a snapshot by its very nature portrays all objects as stationary, whereas some may be moving. To take velocities into account requires the addition of a quantitative reasoning component to the HLR's qualitative knowledge. Knowledge of velocity, acceleration, momentum and moments of inertia would have to be represented in terms of equations. The HLR's current qualitative predictions can be used to guide the application of these equations in the search for a quantitative solution.

Another limitation is that WHISPER approximates simultaneity by moving objects one after another. This process works for problems like the one discussed above; but this approximation is insufficient in some cases where two or more objects move at a time. In Figure 2.12, for example, if B is moved after A is moved, then they will not collide; however, if they are moved simultaneously they will collide. Again we can make use of the diagram by shading the areas each object will sweep through. If no two shaded areas overlap then there will not be a collision; wherever they do overlap a collision might occur and further quantitative analysis of the angular velocities of the objects is required.

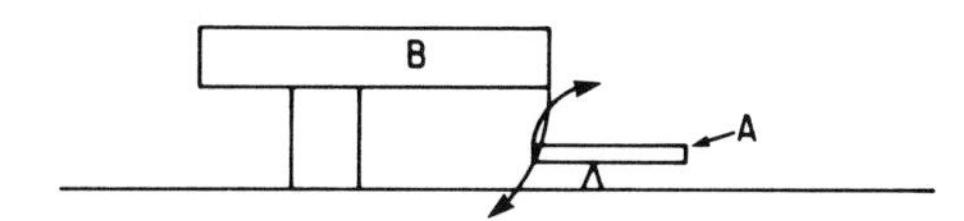

Figure 2.12

2.3.6 Slide Problems

Unstable objects may also slide. When Figure 2.13 is given to WHISPER its reasoning up to the point where it generates the first snapshot, Figure 2.14, is the same as for the chain reaction problem. At this point it is faced with a problem involving a sliding object. Although the basic outline of the solution process for slide problems—test stability, find termination point of motion, update diagram, output snapshot, restart with the output as input—is the same, there are some essential differences in handling sliding objects. The most important arises because it is not possible to visualize the slide of an object down an arbitrary curve. What WHISPER does instead is examine the curve itself with its retina.

A variety of conditions can terminate an object's slide. For example, there may be a sharp rise (a bump), a sharp fall (a cliff), or a hill which is higher than the starting point. Also the object may slide into another object resting on or near the surface.

These conditions are illustrated in Figure 2.15. In the current implementation WHISPER fixates only once (at the starting point of the slide) to test for these conditions. Multiple fixations at regular intervals along the curve would improve the accuracy of the tests.

The case shown in Figure 2.15(e) of a "surprise collision" is one which requires multiple fixations. Although WHISPER does not yet handle this situation, it is clear how it easily could as illustrated in Figure 2.16. In the figure an x indicates a fixation point, a semi-circle indicates the area of the diagram to be checked by the retina at each fixation (checking a circular region is easy because of the retina's ring structure), and the space between the dashed line and the surface indicates a clear "corridor" for the object. The radius of the semi-circle is a function of the object's size and the fixation interval. The same sized corridor can be examined with fewer fixations by using a larger radius. The only disadvantage is that the probability of false alarms is increased because the distance

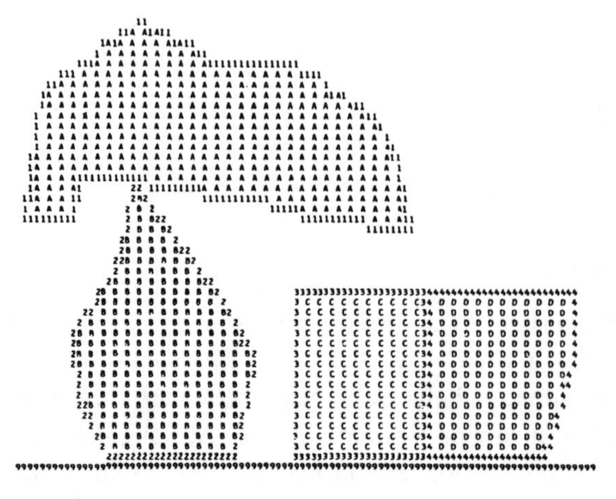

Figure 2.13
A Problem with a Sliding Object.

between the dashed line and the circumference of the semi-circles is greater. A false alarm can be investigated by making more fixations in the region where it occurs. This method of detecting collisions is good for two reasons:

1. because the retina can check large segments of space in a single glance, the number of fixations required to examine the space near the surface is relatively small;
2. a collision will never be missed.

The HLR, in addition to specifying which conditions the retina should look for, must specify which curve segments it should look at. There are two kinds of curves to test:

1. those representing surfaces on the moving object (its underside) which will slide past a point on a stationary object, and
2. those representing surfaces of stationary objects (their topsides) which will have a point on the moving object ride over them.

Thus in the current example (Figure 2.14) the HLR directs the retina to examine the surface of *A* from *C1* to the left, and the surface of *C*, possibly continuing over to the surface of *D*, from *C2* to the right. If there is more than one reason why the object's slide will end, then

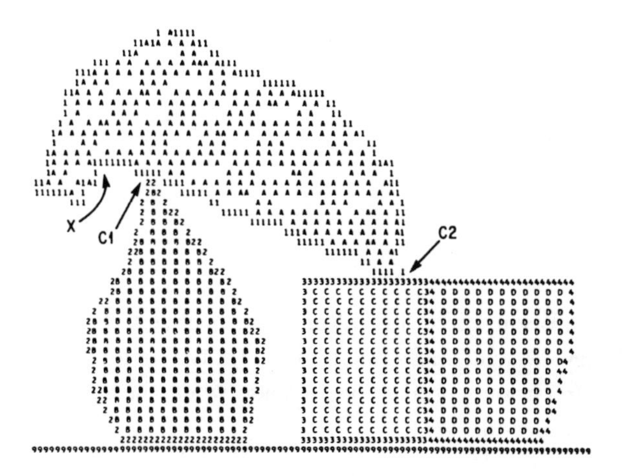

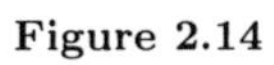
Figure 2.14

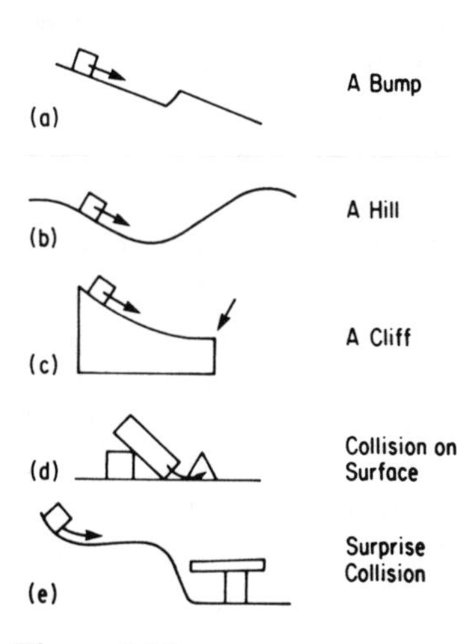

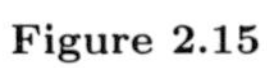
Figure 2.15

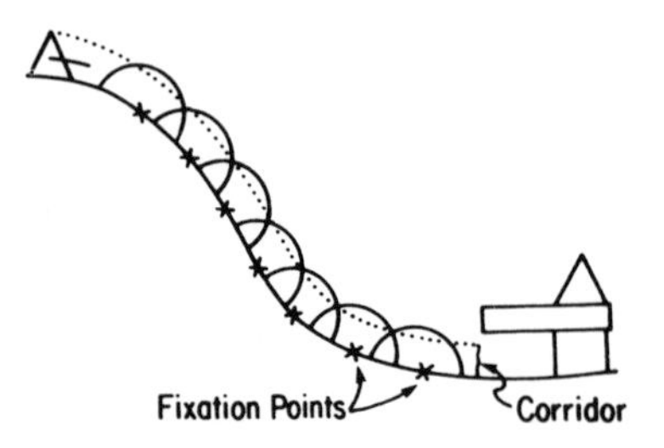

Figure 2.16

only the condition which occurs first (i.e. after the object has slid the shortest distance) is relevant. One more fine point is that tests for some conditions, for example collisions, need only be made when the surface is a topside and not an underside.

2.3.7 Updating the Diagram to Reflect a Slide

After the curve examination is complete and the spot where the object's slide will end is known, the next step is to update the diagram so that it will show the object at its new location. First the HLR calls the re-drawing procedures to translate the object. This is shown in the change from Figure 2.14 to Figure 2.17 in which point X is aligned with *C1*. This does not complete the diagram update however, since the object's orientation will most likely change during its slide. The contacts between the object and the surface it slides along should be the same when the slide ends as when it began. Knowing this the HLR can determine the object's correct orientation using retinal visualization. It directs the retina to fixate at the object's new location and then visualize its rotation while watching for the original contact relationships to be re-established. The angle of rotation is returned to the HLR which then calls the re-drawing procedures to rotate the object by that amount in the diagram. As before, the angle returned by the retina is only approximate so the HLR directs the retina to fixate on the expected point of contact and check for any remaining gap. If there is, a second corrective rotation is made. The resulting snapshot is Figure 2.18. This two-step method—translation followed by a corrective rotation—works for curved as well as straight surfaces.

What we can see from all this is how experimental feedback combined

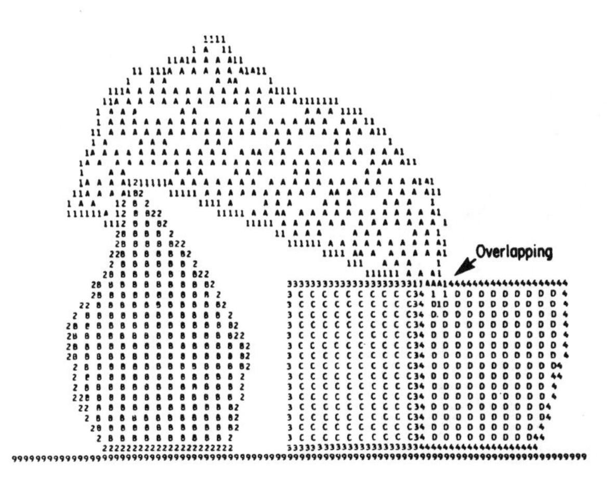

Figure 2.17

with a first order theory of sliding motions results in a very natural form of qualitative reasoning.

2.3.8 Benefit of the Diagram During Slide Analysis

In the curve examination and diagram update process, the diagram is very useful to the HLR in the course of curve following, and it also provides feedback as it did in the case of rotations. The main pitfall in curve following is the possibility that two objects will coincidentally align so that a smooth curve is formed across them both. An object could then begin its slide on one object and continue sliding along the other as A did when it slid across C and onto D. This emergent property of the curve must be noticed, and the two curve segments appended. In a system relying on an independent description of each object, this would pose a significant problem because one would require:

1. that it have a built in expectation that the situation might arise;
2. that it continually check for the situation;
3. that its check involve testing whether the first object touches any other object in the universe; and
4. that it know how to amalgamate the two separate curve segment descriptions into a new curve description.

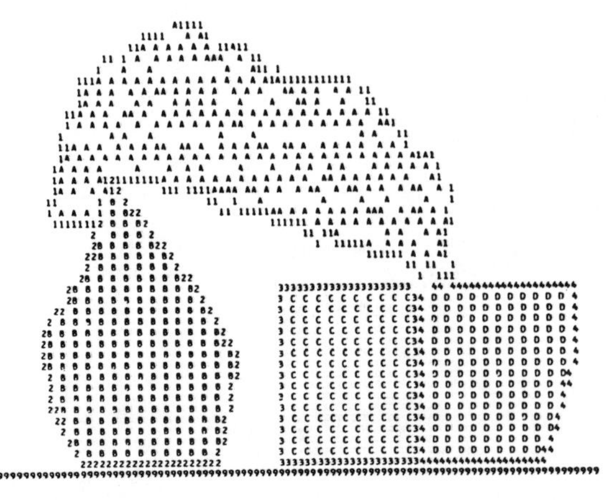

Figure 2.18
Final Snapshot of the Sliding-Object Problem.

For WHISPER it does not create a problem because two aligned surfaces of neighboring objects form a continuous curve in the diagram; WHISPER only has to look at this curve, rather than, in a sense, discover or construct it.

2.4 The Stability Test

Rather than solve the stability problem with a sophisticated general method, as Fahlman (1973) did in his BUILD system, WHISPER seeks qualitative solutions using rules corresponding to those a person untrained in Physics might apply. The HLR has specialists which express rules like: "If an object hangs over too far, it will topple;" and 'If an object and one of its supporters make contact along a surface (rather than at a single point) and if this surface is not horizontal, then the object will slide." A frictionless environment is assumed.

2.4.1 Sub-Structuring

Overall organization of the stability test is based on the observation that a complete structure is stable if each of its independent subparts is stable whenever their supporters are stable. Thus the initial structure is broken down into smaller substructures whose stability as individual units is easier to test than the stability of the structure as a whole. To

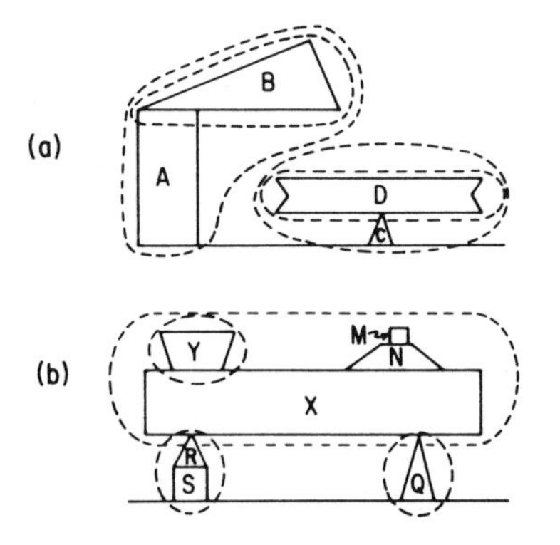

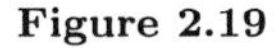
Figure 2.19

perform the stability test the HLR first asks the retina for a list of the names of all objects in the scene. Each object, O, is then handled in turn. The retina is used to find whether or not O supports any other object(s). If it does not, then its stability is tested by SINGLE-STABLE, a specialist in individual object stability. At this point the assumption is that O's supporters are themselves stable. If O supports other objects then its stability is not tested, but rather it is amalgamated with its supportees as if it and they were all glued together to form a single conglomerate object, C. If C does not support anything, then its stability is tested by SINGLE-STABLE; if it does support something, then recursively it is combined with its supportees to form a new conglomerate, C', which is then also checked for supportees.

There is an important exception to the above description. When an object is a cosupporter, as one pillar in an arch for example, then it is not amalgamated with its supportee. In this case the object is sent to SINGLE-STABLE for testing with an addendum specifying the point of contact between it and the supportee.

The dotted curves in Figure 2.19 encircle the sub-structures which are passed to SINGLE-STABLE. In (b), Q and RS are cosupporters of X, so they are not combined with it.

Incidentally, treating two objects such as A and B as a single object AB is another example of a situation in which two descriptions must be amalgamated. It is a trivial task for WHISPER to amalgamate two object descriptions, since all it need do is interpret their two color codings as

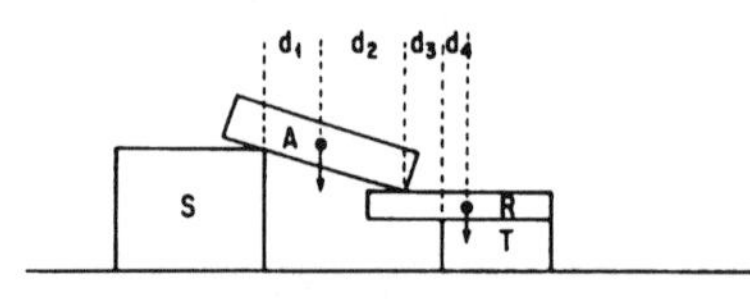

R is stable if $(d_4/d_3)w_R \geqslant (d_1/(d_1+d_2))w_A$
where: w_A is the weight of A
w_R is the weight of R
↓ is an object's center of gravity

Figure 2.20
The WHISPER Proposal

the same color.

2.4.2 Single Object Stability

As we have seen, the problem of determining the stability of a complete structure is reduced at each stage to the determination of the stability of individual objects. For a single object there are only three basic types of instability. It can either rotate about some support point (rotational instability), slide along a surface (translational instability), or simply fall freely (free fall instability).

SINGLE-STABLE considers the relative positions of an object's center of gravity and its supporting contacts to decide on rotational stability. Consider first the case of an object with nothing on top of it. One with a single support must have its center of gravity positioned directly above the contact region. One with multiple supports must be positioned so that a vertical dropped from its center of gravity passes through either a contact region or the space between two contact regions. The restrictions of uniform density and thickness of objects mean that an object's center of area can be substituted for its center of gravity. SINGLE-STABLE thus sees that an object "hangs over too far" when its center of area falls outside its supports.

The stability of an object with something on top of it will be affected by the extra weight. Because of the way in which objects are formed into conglomerates before they are passed to SINGLE-STABLE, if one supports something then it must in fact be one of two or more cosupporters. Let us say SINGLE-STABLE is testing the stability of an object R which, along with cosupporter S, supports A. First it checks the easy cases:

1. if ignoring A, R is already rotationally unstable and A's weight will only add to this instability, then R rotates;
2. if ignoring A, R is already rotationally unstable, but A's weight might counteract its rotation, then this is a counterbalancing type problem which is too difficult to handle without further quantitative investigation;
3. if A, no matter how heavy it is, will not topple R (i.e. test R's stability under the assumption that its center of gravity is located at the contact point between it and A) and R ignoring A is stable, then R remains stable.

The most difficult case is when ignoring A, R by itself is stable, but A may or may not be heavy enough to cause it to rotate. In this situation the location of A's center of gravity relative to its support must be considered. These distances are shown in Figure 2.20. If $w_R(d_4/d_3) \geq w_A d_1/(d_1 + d_2)$ then R is stable; otherwise, it will rotate. SINGLE-STABLE cannot handle objects which participate in two or more cosupport relationships. Figure 2.21 shows two problems the stability test does not handle.

Objects, such as D in Figure 2.6, which are balancing in an unstable equilibrium provide a special problem. Since the slightest deviation in the location of D's center of gravity would upset the balance, it must be known precisely. The CENTER-OF-AREA's estimation is not sufficiently accurate. We expect D to balance because it is symmetrical. Using the retina's symmetry test, WHISPER draws the same conclusion. For it to balance, D must be symmetrical about a vertical axis through its support point. Since D is, the stability test reports it as stable; if it were not, then the stability test would have to report that it was unable to decide.

2.4.3 The Eye Movement Protocol for the Chain Reaction Problem

During the problem-solving process the retina is constantly moving from place to place in the diagram. A trace of the eye movements is given by the circled numbers in Figure 2.22 and Figure 2.7. Each circle represents a fixation of the retina. The numbers give the order in which the fixations occurred. The retina was split so that its central and peripheral portions could be fixated separately. For some fixations in Figure 2.22

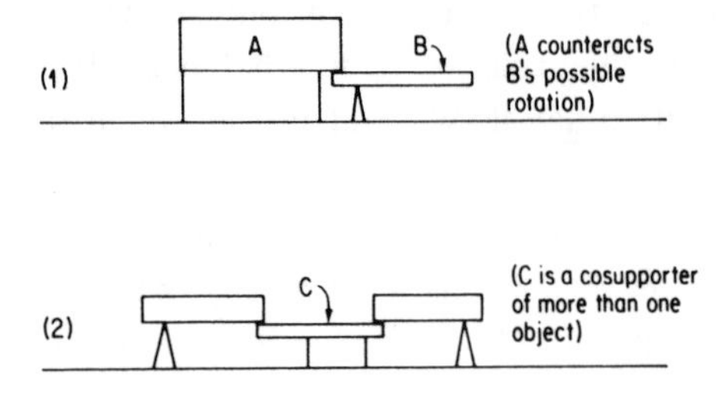

Figure 2.21
Stability Problems WHISPER Cannot Handle.

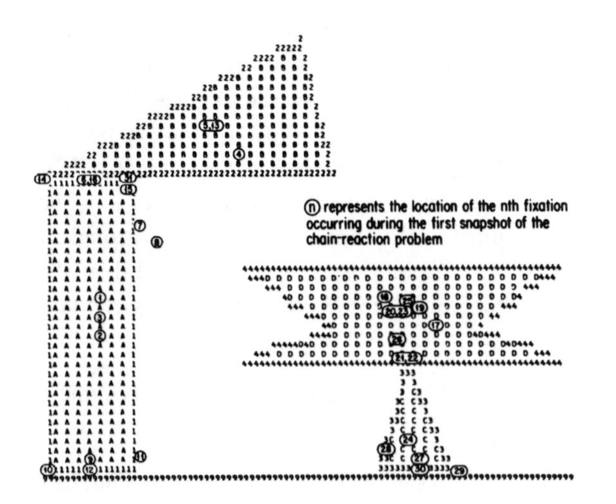

Figure 2.22

only the center of the retina was used, while for others only the periphery. Although moving the two parts of the retina separately would be unnecessary if there actually were many processors operating in parallel, it saves a considerable amount of computation in the pseudo-parallel simulation. What follows is a list of the plotted fixations accompanied by the HLR's reasons for requesting them.

(1) Move to center of diagram; return names of all the objects in the scene.

(2–3) Find the center of gravity of A; find supportees of A.

(4–5) Find the center of gravity of B; find supportees and supporters of B.

(6) Move central section of retina; find exact contact point of A and B.

(7–8) Find center of gravity of AB; find supporters of AB.

(9) Move central section; find exact contact point of AB with table.

(10–11) Move central section; find extremities of contact surface.

(12) Find the slope of the contact surface.

(13) Move to center of gravity of B and look at contact between A and B.

(14–15) Move central section; find extremities of contact surface between A and B; (5, 72) and (19, 72) are returned.

(16) Determine the slope of the contact surface.

(17–20) Find center of gravity of D; look for supporters and supportees.

(21–22) Move both the central section and the periphery; find the exact point of contact with C. Discovers that support is a point not a surface indicating possible equilibrium situation.

(23) Move back to center of gravity of D to check for symmetry of D; equilibrium is found to be OK.

(24) Finding center of gravity of C; look for supportees of C.

(25–26) Finding center of gravity of CD; find supporters of CD; finds the table.

(27) Move central section; find exact point of contact of CD with table.

(28–29) Move central section; find extremities of contact surface; returns (64, 22) and (76, 21).

(30) Determine the type of contact and its slope.

(31) Move to the pivot point of the rotation of B to visualize the rotation. The rotation is then carried out in the diagram, see Figure 2.7.

(32) Move central section to estimated point of collision between B and A to see if they touch; the gap is seen; the amount of the next rotation is estimated. Another rotation is carried out in the diagram, see Figure 2.8.

(33) Move central section to estimated point of collision between B and A (the same as (32)); now they are seen to touch.

Although it would be rash to claim that WHISPER accurately models human problem solving, the eye-movement protocol provides an unusual possibility for testing such a conjecture. An eye-tracking system could be used to record the eye movements of a human subject while he solves one of WHISPER'S problems. This record could then be compared with WHISPER'S protocol.

2.4.4 Translational Stability

WHISPER decides translational stability by examining the object's contacts. There are three types of contact that are considered: surface-to-surface, surface-to-point, and point-to-surface. The stability criterion for a particular contact is whether or not the tangent to the surface involved in the contact is horizontal at the point of contact. (Tangents are found by the CURVE-FEATURES perceptual primitive.) If the tangent is not horizontal, then the direction of downward tilt is taken as the resultant direction of motion of the object. If a conflict in the direction arises—one contact indicating leftward motion and another indicating rightward motion—then WHISPER reports that it is unable to decide what the motion will be. In these situations a quantitative investigation is needed in order to resolve the qualitative ambiguity. (Resolving qualitative ambiguities by quantitative reasoning is discussed by deKleer (1975).) There is, of course, no conflict between a horizontal contact slope and a non-horizontal contact slope, the former simply does not contribute to the motion. After A rotates to hit C (Figure 2.14), the HLR asks the retina to find and classify all the contacts. The A-to-B contact is classified as surface-to-point, with the rightward tilt of the surface of A at the contact noted as contributing to a rightward motion for A. Similarly, the A-to-C contact is classified as point-to-surface with no contribution to the motion of A because the slope of C is horizontal at the contact point. Thus WHISPER concludes that A will slide to the right along the surface of B.

2.5 Conclusion

WHISPER demonstrates the advantages and feasibility of using diagrams as an aid in problem-solving. We see from a theoretical standpoint that their role is one of a model M' which is similar to the model M—a blocks world structure in the problem domain. More simply stated, WHISPER'S diagrams and diagram re-drawing procedures, M', are analogous to blocks world situations, M. A fundamental component of the system is the retina which blends sequential and parallel processing while limiting the quantity of processors and processor interconnections to a fixed, not too large number. By asking questions of the retina, the HLR is able to obtain experimental feedback from M', and hence results about M—information it would otherwise have to deductively infer from general principles and assertions describing M.

Acknowledgments

I have benefited from the inspiration and assistance of Raymond Reiter, Alan K. Macworth, Richard S. Rosenberg, Gordon McCalla, Peter Rowat, Jim Davidson and Stuart C. Shapiro. I have also received valuable criticism from Zenon Pylyshyn and E. W. Elcock.

References

Bobrow, D. 1975. Dimensions of Representation. In *Representation and Understanding,* ed. D. G. Bobrow and A. Collins, 1–35. New York: Academic Press.

deKleer, J. 1975. Qualitative and Quantitative Knowledge in Classical Mechanics, M.Sc. Thesis, Massachusetts Institute of Technology, Cambridge, Mass.

Dunlavey, M.1975. An Hypothesis-Driven Vision System. In *Advance Papers of the Fourth International Conference on Artificial Intelligence*, 616–619. Tibilisi, Georgia, USSR.

Fahlman, S. 1973. A Planning System for Robot Construction Tasks. AI Technical Report 283, Massachusetts Institute of Technology.

Funt, B. 1976. WHISPER: A Computer Implementation Using Analogues in Reasoning, Technical Report 76-9, Department of Computer Science, University of British Columbia.

Funt, B. 1977. WHISPER: A Problem-Solving System Utilizing Diagrams and a Parallel Processing Retina. In *Advance Papers of the Fifth International Joint Conference on Artificial Intelligence.* Cambridge, Mass.: Massachusetts Institute of Technology.

Gelernter, H. 1963. Realization of a Geometry-Theorem Proving Machine. In *Computers and Thought,* ed. E. A. Feigenbaum and J. Feldman, 134–152. New York: McGraw-Hill.

Hayes, P. 1971. A Logic of Actions. In *Machine Intelligence 6,* ed. B. Meltzer and D. Michie, 495–520. New York: Elsevier.

Hayes, P. 1974. Some Problems and Non-Problems in Representation Theory. In *AISB Summer Conference Proceedings,* 63–79.

Hesse, Mary. 1966. *Models and Analogies in Science.* Notre Dame, Indiana: University of Notre Dame Press.

Kosslyn, S. M. 1975. Information Representation in Visual Images. *Cognitive Psychology* 7: 341–370.

Minsky, M. and Papert, S. 1969. *Perceptrons: An Introduction to Computational Geometry* Cambridge, Mass.: The MIT Press.

Nagel, E.1961. *The Structure of Science* New York: Harcourt, Brace and World.

Sloman, A. 1971. Interactions Between Philosophy and Artificial Intelligence: The Role of Intuition and Non-Logical Reasoning in Intelligence. *Artificial Intelligence* 2: 209–225.

Raphael, B. 1971. The Frame Problem in Problem-Solving Systems. In *Artificial Intelligence and Heuristic Programming,* ed. N. V. Findler and B. Meltzer, 159–169. Edinburgh: Edinburgh University Press.

3 Why a Diagram Is (Sometimes) Worth Ten Thousand Words

Jill H. Larkin & Herbert A. Simon
Carnegie Mellon University

3.1 Introduction

According to *Bartlett's Quotations,* "a picture is worth 10,000 words" is a Chinese proverb. On inquiry, we find that the Chinese seem not to have heard of it, but the proverb is certainly widely known and widely believed in our culture. In particular, problem solvers in domains like physics and engineering make extensive use of diagrams, a form of pictures, in problem solving, and many distinguished scientists and mathematicians (e.g., Einstein, Hadamard) have denied that they "think in words." To understand why it is advantageous to use diagrams—and when it is—we must find some way to contrast diagrammatic and non-diagrammatic representations in an information-processing system.

When they are solving problems, human beings use both internal representations, stored in their brains, and external representations, recorded on a paper, on a blackboard, or on some other medium. Some investigators (e.g., Pylyshyn 1973) have argued that all internal representations are propositional, while others (e.g., Anderson 1978) have argued that there is no operational way in which an internal propositional representation can be distinguished from a diagrammatic one. Although our discussion may be relevant to this current controversy about the distinguishability of different internal representations, our analysis explicitly concerns external representations.

We consider external problem representations of two kinds, both of which use a set of symbolic expressions to define the problem.

- In a *sentential* representation, the expressions form a sequence corresponding, on a one-to-one basis, to the sentences in a natural-language description of the problem. Each expression is a direct translation into a simple formal language of the corresponding natural language sentence.
- In a *diagrammatic* representation, the expressions correspond, on a one-to-one basis, to the components of a diagram describing the problem. Each expression contains the information that is stored

at one particular locus in the diagram, including information about relations with the adjacent loci.

The fundamental difference between our diagrammatic and sentential representations is that the diagrammatic representation preserves explicitly the information about the topological and geometric relations among the components of the problem, while the sentential representation does not. A sentential representation may, of course, preserve other kinds of relations, for example, temporal or logical sequence. An outline may reflect hierarchical relations.

We consider problems presented in these two representations and ask about the relative difficulty of solution. We start with the assumption that the problem is solved using the given representation (sentential or diagrammatic). In fact, of course, one way to solve a problem in a poor representation is to translate it into a better one. One may be able to use the information in a verbal description to draw or image a diagram or use a diagram to infer verbal statements. But in order to understand what makes a good representation, we ask what is required for solution without such translation.

3.2 Formalizing the Question

To compare diagrams with sentences, we need to define what we mean by representation and by a "better" representation.

3.2.1 What Does a "Better" Representation Mean?

Informational and Computational Efficiency. At the core of our analysis lie the wholly distinct concepts of *informational* and *computational* equivalence of representations (Simon 1978). Two representations are informationally equivalent if all of the information in the one is also inferable from the other, and vice versa. Each could be constructed from the information in the other. Two representations are computationally equivalent if they are informationally equivalent and, in addition, any inference that can be drawn easily and quickly from the information given explicitly in the one can also be drawn easily and quickly from the information given explicitly in the other, and vice versa.

"Easily" and "quickly" are not precise terms. The ease and rapidity of inference depends upon what operators are available for modifying and augmenting data structures, and upon the speed of these operators. When we compare two representations for computational equivalence, we need to compare both data and operators. The respective value of sentences and diagrams depends on how these are organized into data structures and on the nature of the processes that operate upon them.

Representations. A representation consists of both data structures and programs operating on them to make new inferences. The data structures we consider are node-link structures that include schemas employing attribute-value pairs. (Such structures have been called variously list structures, colored directed graphs, scripts, and frames. The differences, when there are any, are inconsequential for our purposes.) We can think of these structures as being represented in a list-processing language like Lisp. Programs are represented as production systems. Each instruction has the form: $C \rightarrow A$, conditions C with associated actions A. The conditions are tests on some parts of the data structures; whenever such tests are satisfied by the appropriate data structures, the actions of the production are executed. Actions modify data structures, that is, they make and record inferences. Although the data structures we shall postulate are stored externally, on paper, the productions that operate on them are in the problem solver's memory.

Since data structures for a problem are complex, we must also provide for an attention management system that determines what portion of the data structure is currently attended to and can trigger the productions of the program. The nature of attention management depends crucially on the linkages provided in the data structure since this is the only information available for guiding shifts in attention.

Later we describe systems for solving physics and geometry problems. In these systems the productions contain knowledge of the laws and principles of physics or geometry, while the data structures contain knowledge about the particular problem being solved. This separation corresponds to the usual division of labor between the knowledge a problem solver holds in memory and the knowledge he or she commits to paper. In both cases we will also need to consider how attention is managed in keeping with the data structure.

In general the computational efficiency of a representation depends on all three of these factors (data structure, program, attention management) and on how well they work together. Whether a diagram (or any other representation) is worth 10,000 words depends on what productions are available for searching the data structure, for recognizing relevant information and for drawing inferences from that information (Simon 1978). This point has been made again recently by Anderson (1984) in arguing that the distinction between representations is not rooted in the notations used to write them, but in the operations used on them.

3.2.2 Diagrams and Sentences

We are concerned with contrasting the operation of an inference program, human or computer, when using two different data structures with the same informational content. To assure informational equivalence, we start with a problem stated in natural language, translate it first into a sequence of more formal sentences, and then translate it into a diagram.

Data Structures. Producing a formal sentential representation from a verbal problem statement is relatively straightforward, using simple analogs of propositional coding like that of (Kintsch and Van Dijk 1978). But how can we produce data structures that capture important features of diagrammatic problem representations? Consider a situation described by a sequence of ordinary English sentences (e.g., a verbal problem statement). Associate with each sentence a location (perhaps x and y coordinates in a two-dimensional reference frame). Now sentences are indexed by location—a program using this data structure can choose to "look" at a particular location and thereby access all information present there (i.e., all information elements indexed by that location). In short we make the following definitions:

- A data structure in which elements appear in a single sequence is what we will call a *sentential representation.*
- A data structure in which information is indexed by two-dimensional location is what we call a *diagrammatic representation.*

Of course, when a sentence or diagram is analyzed internally it may acquire different linkages, (e.g., a person may form a "mental picture" upon reading a sequence of sentences), but here we are concerned with the external representations.

Programs. The program operating on the data structure employs the following kinds of processes: (1) *Search* operates on the node-link data structures, seeking to locate sets of elements that satisfy the conditions of one or more productions. This process requires attention management. (2) *Recognition* matches the condition elements of a production to data elements located through search. Recognition depends on a match between the elements in the data structure and the conditions of the productions in the program. (3) *Inference* executes the associated action to add new (inferred) elements to the data structure.

How do sentential and diagrammatic representations, respectively, affect the three components of information processing mentioned above: search, recognition, and inference?

Search. Consider first the sentential data structure consisting of a simple list of items. Unless an index is manufactured and added explicitly to this list, finding elements matching the conditions of any inference rule requires searching linearly down the data structure. Furthermore, the several elements needed to match conditions for any given rule may be widely separated in the list. Search times in such a system depend sensitively upon the size of the data structure.

Search in a diagram can be quite different. In this representation an item has a location. If the conditions of an inference rule are only satisfied by structures at or near a single location, then the tests for satisfaction can all be performed on the limited set of structures that belong to the current location, and no search is required through the remaining data. Often part of the search process involves identifying multiple attributes of the same items, for example, that a rabbit is both white and furry. Therefore one computational cost of search is the ease with which such attributes can be collected. Of course, some search may be required to find the right location. (As an example of such a system, see the model of chess perception constructed by Simon and Barenfeld 1969).

The two systems just described are not, in general, computationally equivalent. As we have described them, we would expect the second to exhibit efficiencies in search that would be absent from the first. Differences in search strategies associated with different representations are one major source of computational inequivalence.

Recognition. The effects of different representations on search are at least equaled by their effects on recognition. Human abilities to recognize information are highly sensitive to the exact form (representation) in which the information is presented to the senses (or to memory). For example, consider a set of points presented either in a table of x and y coordinates or as geometric points on a graph. Visual entities such as smooth curves, maxima and discontinuities are readily recognized in the latter representation, but not in the former.

Ease of recognition may be strongly affected by what information is explicit in a representation, and what is only implicit. For example, a geometry problem may state that a pair of parallel lines is cut by a transversal. Eight angles, four exterior and four interior, are thereby created but not mentioned explicitly. Moreover, without drawing a diagram it is not easy to identify which pairs of angles are alternate interior angles—information that may be needed to match the conditions of an inference rule. All of these entities are readily identified from a diagram by simple processes, once the three lines are drawn. The process of drawing the diagram makes these new inferences which are then displayed explicitly in the diagram itself. We will see later how this explicitness facilitates geometry proofs when a diagrammatic representation is used. Of course, the same information can also be inferred from the sentential representation, but these latter inference processes may require substantial computation, and the cost of this computation must be included in any assessment of the relative efficiency of the two representations.

Although our focus here is the contrast between diagrammatic and sentential representations, the human recognition process can often be specific to particular representations within these broad categories. For example, although the Roman, Cyrillic, and Greek alphabets are nearly isomorphic, a person who can read fluently in one of these alphabets cannot generally read the same information readily when it is transcribed into one of the others. The oral Serbian and Croatian languages are essentially identical, no farther apart than the English and American dialects of the English language. Serbian is written in the Cyrillic alphabet, while Croatian is written in the Roman alphabet. As a consequence, Serbs and Croats can read each other's newspapers only with the greatest difficulty.

The difficulty does not disappear for a person who knows both alphabets well, but each only the context of particular languages. For example, someone who reads Russian fluently when it is written in the Cyrillic alphabet and English in the Roman alphabet will have great difficulty in reading Russian transcribed to the Roman alphabet or English to the Cyrillic. (For similar effects of chess notation, see Chase and Simon [1973]).

It follows that we will be unable to recognize knowledge that is relevant to a situation and retrieve it from long-term memory if the situation is not presented in a representation matching the form of existing productions. This specificity of access is presumably remediable by training, but only at the cost of acquiring whole new sets of productions with condition sides adapted to the specific representation that is employed. While the specificity favors no particular form of representation, it does severely limit the immediate substitutability of one representation for another.

Because a representation is useful only if one has the productions that can use it, we can readily understand the common complaint of physics professors that students "refuse to draw diagrams" or "don't appreciate their value." If the students lack productions for making physics inferences from diagrams, they may not only fail to "appreciate" the value of diagrams, but will find them largely useless.

Inference. In view of the dramatic effects that alternative representations may produce on search and recognition processes, it may seem surprising that the differential effects on inference appear to be less strong. Inference is largely independent of representation *if* the information content of the two sets of inference rules is equivalent—i.e., the two sets are isomorphs as they are in our examples. But it is certainly possible to make inference rules that are more or less powerful, independently of representation.

Examples of this phenomena are suggested by the everyday use of the verb "see" when no explicit visual processes are present. What is this metaphorical "seeing" and how might it connect to information-processing differences between sentential and diagrammatic representations? We speculate that this metaphor refers to inferences that are qualitatively like perceptually "seeing" in that they come about through productions with great computational efficiency. This efficiency might arise from low search and recognition costs, or from very powerful inference rules or from both.

Consider, for example, a physical chessboard which we would represent as a set of squares, each with an (x, y) location and connections to adjacent squares. With each square is associated the name of any piece on it. Any person can "see" on what squares the pieces lie and locate adjacent or nearby squares. These inferences come from primitive production rules that everyone has. But a chess expert may "see" things in the board not evident to the non-expert observer. For example, an important feature of a chess position is an open file: a sequence of squares that are vacant, running from the player's side of the board toward the opponent's side. In what sense is this "seeing" if everyone cannot see it? This recognition could be accomplished by a production that, upon noticing an open square in the first row, would trace this square to the "North" until a piece was encountered, then store this feature in memory, indexed to its location on the board. For the chess player who has such a production in his or her repertory, an open file is "seen," meaning that it is easily recognized. But for a person without such a set of productions only the individual unoccupied squares may be visible, when attended to, but not the open file. In exactly the same sense, a logician, presented with symbol structures for A and $A \rightarrow B$ may "see" the conclusion: B.

3.3 A Simple Example

To make concrete our comments about differences in computational efficiency for two problem representations containing identical information, we work here a simple example from physics. In this example we will see, for the diagrammatic representation, considerable computational advantages in search, plus a subtle advantage due to different needs for labeling. We leave to a second example the more complex, but probably more important, utility of diagrams in aiding recognition.

We begin our comparison of representations by analyzing a simple pulley problem from elementary mechanics. After stating the problem verbally, we provide a formal sentential encoding of the problem statement. Then we write, in a semi-formal notation, inference rules (productions) that embody the laws of statics relevant to solving the problem. Next we construct a diagrammatic interpretation of the system consisting of the problem data structure and the rules. Finally, we

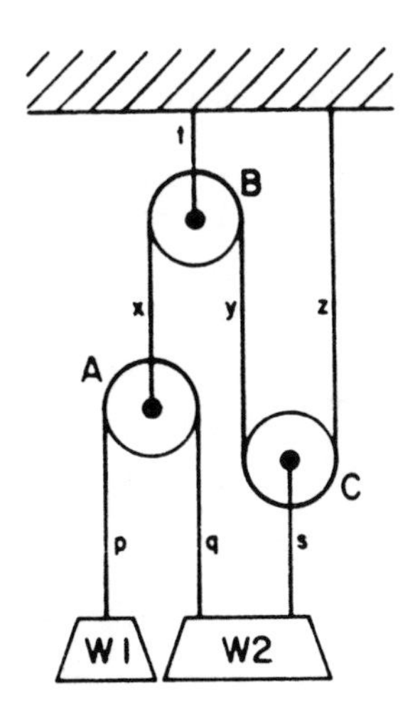

Figure 3.1
Diagram of the Pulley Problem.

compare the computational efficiency of the sentential and diagrammatic representations. In this example, the principal differences between the representations derive from the amounts of search they demand, rather than from differences in recognition or inference.

3.3.1 The Given Data Structure and Program

Consider a problem given in the following natural language statements. We have three pulleys, two weights, and some ropes, arranged as follows:

1. The first weight is suspended from the left end of a rope over Pulley A. The right end of this rope is attached to, and partially supports, the second weight.
2. Pulley A is suspended from the left end of a rope that runs over Pulley B, and under Pulley C. Pulley B is suspended from the ceiling. The right end of the rope that runs under Pulley C is attached to the ceiling.
3. Pulley C is attached to the second weight, supporting it jointly with the right end of the first rope.

The pulleys and ropes are weightless; the pulleys are frictionless; and the rope segments are all vertical, except where they run over or under

Table 3.1
Formal (a) Data Structure and (b) Program for the Pulley Problem.

(a)

```
          (Weight W1) (Rope Rp) (Rope Rq) (Pulley Pa)
(1a.1)    (hangs W1 from Rp)
(1a.2)    (pulley-system Rp Pa Rq)

          (Weight W2)
(1b.1)    (hangs W2 from Rq)

          (Rope Rx) (Pulley Pb) (Rope Ry) (Pulley Pc) (Rope Rz)
          (Rope Rt) (Rope Rs) (Ceiling c)
(2a.1)    (hangs Pa from Rx)
(2a.2)    (pulley-system Rx Pb Ry)
(2a.3)    (pulley-system Ry Pc Rz)
(2b.1)    (hangs Pb from Rt)
(2b.2)    (hangs Rt from c)

(3a.1)    (hangs Rx from c)
(3a.2)    (hangs Rs from Pc)
(3b.3)    (hangs W2 from Rs)

(4.1)     (value W1 1)
```

(b)

```
P1. Single-string support. (weight <Wx>) (rope <Ry>)
    (value <Wx> <n>) (hangs <Wx> <Ry>)
    ~(hangs <Wx> <Rx>)
    → (value <Ry> <W-number>)
P2. Ropes over pulley. (pulley <P>) (rope <R1>) (rope <R2>)
    (pulley-system <R1> <P> <R2>) (value <R1> <n1>)
    → (value <R2> <n1>)
P3. Rope hangs from or supports pulley. (pulley <R1>) (rope <R1>) (rope R2>)
    (pulley-system <R1> <P> <R2>) { (hangs <R3> from <P>) or (hangs <P>
    from <R3>) } (value <R1> <n1>) (value <R2> <n2>)
    → (value <R3> <n1 + <n2>)
P4. Weight and multiple supporting ropes. (weight <W1>) (rope <R1>) (rope
    R2>) (hangs <W1> <R1>) (hangs <W1> <R2>) ~(hangs <W1> <R3>)
    (value <R1> <n1>) (value <R2> <n2>)
    → (value <W1> <n1> + <n2>)
```

the pulley wheels. Find the ratio of the second to the first weight, if the system is in equilibrium.

Presented with the pulley problem, everyone we've observed reaches for pencil and paper, and draws a sketch of the situation somewhat like Figure 3.1. However, for the moment, we ignore the sketch, and proceed directly from the natural language statement of the problem.

We formalize and simplify the natural language sentences in this problem to produce the elements listed in Table 3.1. The labels 1a, 1b, and so forth, refer to the sentence numbers above, with the decimal numbers labeling successively elements produced from a single sentence.

The first propositions in each sentence associate labels with appropriate objects. We read subsequent propositions, for example, (1a.1) as: the weight *W1* is suspended from the rope *Rp*. We read proposition (1a.2) as: The rope, consisting of the left-hand segment *Rp* and the right-hand segment *Rq*, runs over (or under) the wheel of the pulley *Pa*. Sentences 2 through 3 are similarly translated. At the end, we add element (4.1) giving a specific simple value to the weight *W1* which can then be related to the value of weight *W2* in order to answer the question. We have captured the original problem statement, accurately we believe, in these formal elements that use the relations of *hangs, pulley-system,* and *value*.

In this data structure the various object labels (e.g., *W1,Rx*) are essential. It is only through these labels that one can infer that two different elements (e.g., 1b.1 and 3b.3) both refer to the weight *W2*. In the original problem statement these connections were provided (somewhat obscurely) by a combination of labels and anaphoric, numeric, and locational references (e.g., "supporting it jointly with the right end of the first rope").

We now turn from the given data structure to the program, composed of physics knowledge, that will act on it to solve the problem. This program consists of the following inference (or production) rules based on a few principles of statics. Pointed brackets (<>) indicate variables that refer to particular objects (e.g., ropes, pulleys).

P1. Single-string support. Given a weight of known value <*n*> and a rope <*R*> from which it hangs, if there is no other rope from which it hangs (indicated by the symbol ~), then the supporting rope also have value (tension) <*n*> associated with it.

P2. Ropes over pulley. If a pulley system <*P*> has two ropes <*R1*> and <*R2*> over it, and the value (tension) associated with <*R1*> is <*n1*>, then <*n1*> is also the value associated with rope <*R1*>.

P3. Rope hangs from or supports pulley. If there is a pulley system with ropes <*R1*> and <*R2*> over it, and the pulley system hangs from a rope <*R3*>, and <*R1*> and <*R2*> have the values (tensions) <*n1*> and <*n2*> associated with them, then the value (tension) associated with <*R3*> is the sum of <*n1*> plus <*n2*>.

P4. Weight and multiple supporting ropes. If a weight <*W1*> hangs from both ropes <*R1*> and <*R2*>, but hangs from no other ropes, and the values <*n1*> and <*n2*> are associated with <*R1*> and <*R2*>, then the value associated with <*W1*> is the sum of <*n1*> plus <*n2*>.

Table 3.2 shows these rules, stated then in a formal notation matching that used for the data structure in Table 3.1a. In this notation symbols with pointed brackets can be matched to any symbol. A "~" indicates an element that may not appear in the current data structure if the conditions of the rule are to be satisfied.

These inference rules are based on two physics principles. (1) The total force on an object at rest is zero. (2) The tensions are equal in all parts of an ideal (massless, frictionless) rope, even if this rope passes over ideal (massless, frictionless) pulleys. The productions are directions for applying these principles in several specific situations relevant to our problem. Principles must be rewritten as active inference rules for any problem solving system. (Indeed students may well be unable to solve problems in part because they learn principles, and do *not* translate them into inference rules.) We might have made the list of productions shorter, but at the cost of more complex explanations.

Our system, now includes a data structure and a program (rules of inference). It remains to consider how the data structure is searched to find information the inference rules can use, how such information is recognized, and how the inferences are made.

3.3.2 Sentential Representation

If we consider the data structure in Table 3.1a as a sequential list of elements, then, by our earlier definition, this is a sentential definition of the pulley problem. Using the program in Table 3.1b, the problem can be solved by a simple non-algebraic procedure. Applying our physics inference rules, we develop sequentially values associated with objects in the problem, ultimately finding the desired value associated with weight *W2*. In English, the steps of this solution are:

1. Because weight *W1* (value 1) hangs from rope *Rp* and no other rope, the value associated with *Rp* is 1.
2. Because *Rp* (value 1) and *Rq* pass over the same pulley, the value of *Rq* is 1.

3. Because Rp and Rq have values 1, and the pulley Pa over which they pass is supported by Rx, the value associated with Rx is $1 + 1 = 2$.
4. Because Rx (value 2) and Ry pass over the same pulley, the value of Ry is 2.
5. Because Ry (value 2) and Rz pass under the same pulley, the value of Rz is 2.
6. Because Ry and Rz have values 2, and the pulley Pc under which they pass is supported by Rs, the value associated with Rs is $2 + 2 = 4$.
7. Because weight $W2$ is supported by rope Rq (value 1) and rope Rs (value 4) and by no other ropes, its value is $1 + 4 = 5$.

This sequence of inferences is not logically complex, yet the reader has probably already discovered its psychological complexity. The major difficulty is that each inference requires locating simultaneously one or more recently developed values, together with sentences in the original data structure supporting the next inference. For example, consider the inference that the value associated with pulley Pa is 2 (see Figure 3.1 for relief). In the sentential representation, making this inference requires holding in memory the value associated with rope Rp (and perhaps also Rq), locating in the original data structure the relation (pulley-system $RpPaRq$), and perhaps also sentences identifying these objects appropriately as ropes and pulleys. Throughout the solution there is this continual need to hold on to values while searching for relational information. The search is particularly difficult for step 7 using production $P4$.

Weight and Multiple Supporting Ropes. If a weight <*W1*> hangs from both ropes <*R1*> and <*R2*>, but hangs from no other ropes, and the values <*n1*> and <*n2*> are associated with <*R1*> and <*R2*>, then the value associated with <*W1*> is the sum of <*n1*> plus <<*n2*>.

The reason is that information about two ropes, one mentioned much earlier, must be held in memory or recorded and then discovered by search; and then it must be verified that no other ropes support the weight.

To make these observations quantitative, we assume the following simple linear attention-control mechanism: Attention is initially at the first sentence. After each inference is made, the attention pointer is left at the beginning of the last sentence in which relevant information was found. New elements, added to the data structure are searched first, and in reverse order of their addition. Finally, if a production specifies that some element may *not* appear, then all data-structure elements must be searched to make sure this is the case.

Table 3.2 shows the seven steps of the solution using the formal representation developed earlier. The original elements of the data structure are listed at the left, and the seven steps, with the production applied, across the top. At the bottom are the new elements added to the data structure in that step. In each column, an x indicates an element that must be present for the inference rule to apply, and an o indicates an element that must be searched (assuming the simple linear search strategy outlined above) in order to verify that the production applies.

In step 1, for example, rule P1, **Single-string support,** is matched by the four x'd elements to conclude that the value associated with rope segment *Rp* is 1. All other elements must also be searched, however, to assure that weight *W1* is not supported by any rope other than *Rp*, one of the conditions of this inference rule. This kind of difficulty arises in using any inference rule based on finding all instances of a particular class, and examples in physics are common. (The net force is the sum of *all* forces acting on the system; energy is conserved if there are *no* dissipative processes.)

3.3.3 Diagrammatic Representation

A diagrammatic representation permits information at or near one locality to be accessed and processed simultaneously. Table 3.3 shows our pulley problem with such an indexing system. Each element contains one or more locations (labeled *a-m*).

To use this indexing by location, we need an attentional control mechanism with the following properties: (1) When one location is attended to, all information at that location is automatically available. (2) The system can switch attention to any location mentioned by the elements currently attended to. The attention switching can be handled by a simple inference rule of the form:

Table 3.2
Solution to the Pulley Problem Using the Sentential Representation.

Original Element	Steps		1	2	3	4	5	6
	Productions	P1	P2	P3	P2	P2	P3	P4
2. (Weight W1)		x	o	o	o			o
(Rope Rp)		x	x	x	o			o
(Rope Rq)		o	x	x	o			x
(Pulley Pa)		o	x	x	o			o
(hangs W1 from Rp)		x	o	o	o			o
(pulley-system Rp Pa Rq)		o	x	x	o		o	o
(Weight W2)		o		o	o	o	o	x
(hangs W2 from Rq)		o		o	o	o	o	x
2. (Rope Rx)		o		x	x	o	o	o
(Pulley Pb)		o		o	x	o	o	o
(Rope Ry)		o		o	x	x	x	o
(Pulley Pc)		o		o	o	x	x	o
(Rope Rz)		o		o	o	x	x	o
(Rope Rt)		o		o	o	o	o	o
(Rope Rs)		o		o	o	o	x	x
(Ceiling c)		o		o	o	o	o	o
(hangs Pa from Rx)		o		x	o	o	o	o
(pulley-system Rx Pb Ry)		o			x	o	o	o
(pulley-system Ry Pc Rz)		o				x	x	o
(hangs Pb from Rt)		o					o	o
(hangs Rt from c)		o					o	o
3. (hangs Rz from c)		o					o	o
(hangs Rs from Pc)		o					x	o
(hangs W2 from Rs)		o					o	x
(value W1 1)		x					o	o
New Elements								
1. (value Rp 1)			x	x				x
2. (value Rq 1)				x				o
3. (value Ry 2)					x			o
4. (value Rx 2)						x	x	o
5. (value Rz 2)							x	o
6. (value Rs 4)								x
7. (value W2 5)								o
Total Elements Searched: 138		25	7	20	19	14	22	31

(< anyobject> <location1> <location2>) (current-attention <location1>)

→

(change the last element to read: current-attention <location2>)

This mechanism is analogous to that proposed for the sentential representation, in which attention switched from one sentence to an adjacent one in the data structure. We define "adjacent" to mean that the two locations are mentioned in a single element of the data structure.

To aid in interpreting Table 3.3 and the solution based on it, Figure 3.2 shows the locations *a* through *m* roughly as they would appear in a diagram. The lines connect locations that are adjacent because they

Table 3.3
Data Structure for the Pulley Problem, with Locations Indicated by Lower Case Labels a, b, and c.

	(Weight a) (Rope b) (Rope c) (Pulley d)
(1a.1)	(hangs a from b)
(1a.2	(pulley-system b d c)
	(Weight e)
(1b.1)	(hangs e from c)
	(Rope f) (Pulley g) (Rope h) (Pulley i) (Rope j)
	(Rope k) (Rope l) (Ceiling m)
(2a.1)	(hangs d from f)
(2a.2)	(pulley-system f g h)
(2a.3)	(pulley-system h i j)
(2b.1)	(hangs g from k)
(2b.2)	(hangs k from m)
(3a.1)	(hangs j from m)
(3a.2)	(hangs l from i)
(3b)	(hangs e from l)
(4.1)	(value a 1)

appear in the same element in the data structure. Attention moves from one location to another. At most there are two possible adjacent locations, and search is limited to these locations.

Based on this data structure, and using the same physics program as before, the solution to the pulley problem is as follows:

1. A weight at *a*, with associated value 1, hangs from something at *b*, which is a rope. Therefore the rope at *b* has associated value 1. (**Single-string support,** No search, Attention now at *b*.)
2. The rope at *b* is in the pulley-system at *d* which also contains the thing at *c* which is a rope. Therefore the rope at *c* has associated value 1. (**Ropes over pulley.** Possible to make false attempt to apply **Rope hangs from or supports pulley** to (b c d f). Will fail because value at *c* is unknown. Attention now at *c*.)
3. The rope at *c* (value 1) is in the pulley-system at *d* which hangs from the thing at *f* which is a rope. The pulley-system at d also contains the thing at *b* which is a rope with value 1. Therefore the value associated with the rope at *f* is 2. (**Rope hangs from or supports pulley** Possible alternative step: Apply **Weight and multiple supporting ropes** to (c e 1). Will fail because value at *l* is unknown. Attention now at *f*.)
4. The rope at *f* (value 2) is the pulley system at *g* which also contains

the thing at h which is a rope. Therefore the value associated with the thing at h is 2. (**Ropes over pulley.** Attention now at h.)

5. The rope at h is in the pulley-system at i which also contains the thing at j which is a rope. Therefore the value associated with the rope at j is 2. (**Ropes over pulley.** Possible alternative step: Apply **Rope hangs from or supports pulley** to (h i j). Fails because value at j is unknown. Attention now at j.)
6. The rope at j (value 2) is in the pulley-system at i which also contains the thing at h (a rope, value 2) and suspends the thing at l which is also a rope. Therefore the value associated with rope l is 4. (**Rope hangs from or supports pulley.** No search alternatives. Attention at l.)
7. The thing at l (a rope, value 4) suspends the thing at e which is a weight, also suspended from the thing at c which is a rope with associated value 1. Therefore the value of the weight at e is 5. (**Weight and multiple supporting ropes.** No search alternatives. Attention at e.)

We assume that change of attention to an adjacent location is a computationally easy process. Therefore, the searches and inferences indicated above comprise essentially all of the work of solving this problem. There are instances where a false effort may be made. These efforts all fail immediately, leaving the solver with only the correct possibilities. Compared with the 138 considerations of elements for the sentential representation (see Table 3.2), the diagrammatic representation provides a large saving.

Note also that the object labels in the sentential data structure (e.g., *W1,PA*) have been replaced by locations. Thus in addition to cutting search, a diagrammatic representation eliminates the overhead of keeping track of object labels.

Finally, this example illustrates that the program used with the sentential data structure is not immediately applicable to the diagrammatic data structure. The later assumes additional location-based changes in attention.

3.3.4 Computational Power in Inference Rules

Inference rules can be more or less powerful, whatever the representation (diagrammatic or sentential) on which they operate. In the example con-

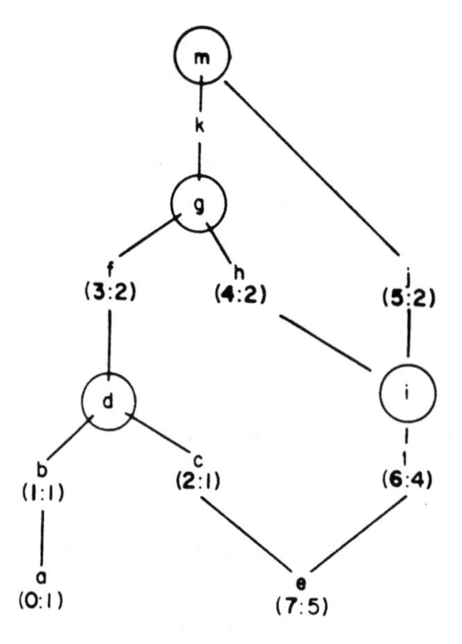

Figure 3.2
Schematic Diagram of Locations in the Diagramatic Representation. "Adjacent" (see text) locations are connected. Steps in the solution are shown in bold, with the value added to the location following the relevant step.)

sidered here, the physics inference rules (used in both representations) are far more powerful computationally than the physics principles on which they are based. For example, when **Single-string support** is used to infer the tension on *Rp* from the weight of *W1*, Newton's Third Law is being assumed implicitly: if the rope is in equilibrium, then the downward pull of *W1* must be exactly balanced by the tension in the rope. Also when **Rope hangs from or supports pulley** is used to infer the tension on *Rq* from the tension on *Rp*, Newton's Third Law is also being assumed implicitly: each small part of the rope is being pulled by a force exerted by the segment adjoining it on one side, which must be exactly balanced by the opposite force exerted by the segment adjoining it on the other side.

Thus, each production represents a "theorem" which could itself be derived by reasoning from the Laws of Motion. But the expert problem solver does not re-create this derivation each time. He or she simply incorporates it in a powerful operator. The analog in theorem-proving systems is a process for storing theorems that have been proved and using them directly as premises in subsequent proofs (Newell and Simon 1956). In systems like the ones described here, instead of representing these theorems sententially, we embed them in operators represented as productions. When we say that reasoning is carried out "intuitively," we are often referring to just these kinds of procedural replacements of declarative knowledge. Information processing schemes for making such replacements are largely based on the formalism of adaptive production systems (Waterman 1970). An early example of a program capable of converting declarative statements defining a problem into processes is UNDERSTAND (Hayes and Simon 1974). This idea has subsequently been developed extensively by Neves and Anderson (1981) and others.

The benefits of more powerful inference rules are, of course, not limited to physics. For example, in the most austere forms of logic, where propositions are viewed as sentences in the predicate calculus (or other formal system), new information is obtained by applying truth-maintaining rules of inference (perhaps in the form of productions) to these sentences, and adding to the store the new sentences that are thus produced. This is the basic representation of all systems that accomplish problem solving by theorem proving. If the rules of inference are very limited in number and power (say, consisting of *modus ponens* alone), the system is likely to be highly inefficient from a computational standpoint. If other knowledge (e.g., physics) is also incorporated in the system in propositional form (as axioms), without addition of inference rules, the inefficiency is compounded.

A simple example will make the point clear. Suppose we have a system whose only inference rule is modus ponens:

If A, and (A *implies* B) $\rightarrow B$.

Suppose, further, that the system contains an axiom stating that xy is commutative; i.e., (xy implies yx). Now if (xy is true, then a search will reveal a match of xy and (xy implies yx) with the conditions of modus ponens, and yx will be produced.

On the other hand if the system contains the inference rule:

If $xy \rightarrow yx$,

then in the presence of xy, the condition of this rule is matched without further search, and xy will be produced immediately. Similarly, a system that has productions allowing it to assign the same tension to all segments of a rope will proceed more expeditiously than one that has to reach this result from general reasoning based on Newton's Third Law.

In general, powerful inference rules will contain information that is specific to a particular task domain: they will be task dependent. A good deal of skill acquisition in any domain can be attributed to the gradual acquisition of domain-specific inference procedures, specifically, acquisition of the corresponding productions, including both actions and the conditions that cause them to be evoked when relevant.

3.4 A More Demanding Example

We now apply the analysis procedure illustrated in the previous problem to one that is more complex and interesting. Here we will see not only advantages to the diagram in search and labeling, but also a large and important role in facilitating recognition.

As in the preceding section, we will introduce an example, this time from geometry, and consider how it might be solved using a sentential and then a diagrammatic problem representation. In this case, again we find that the diagrammatic representation dramatically reduces search and removes considerable need for labeling. But we will find that, in contrast to the pulley example, the given data structure does not match the given program. Therefore to solve the problem at all, the problem solver must enhance the data structure in ways that prove considerably easier with diagrams than with sentences.

We first introduced the *given data structure and given program.* We then develop an enhanced sentential data structure and corresponding program that allow solution of the problem. Then we alter the data structure and program to see how the solution would proceed with a diagrammatic representation.

3.4.1 The Given Problem Representation

The given problem representation consists, as stated below, of a verbal statement of the problem (the given data structure), together with textbook statements of the definitions and axioms needed to solve the problem (the given program).

1. Two transversals intersect two parallel lines and intersect with each other at a point x between the two parallel lines.

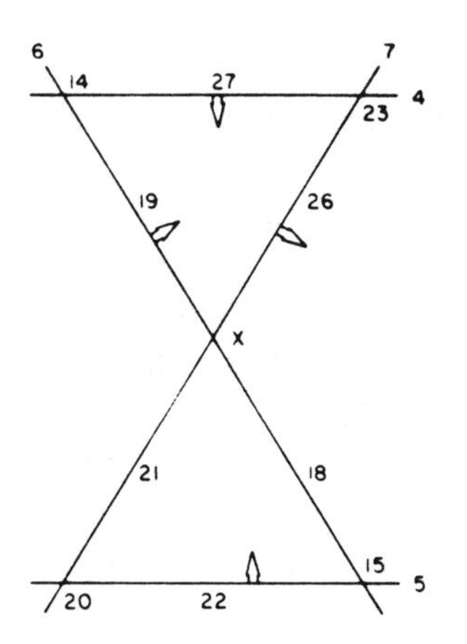

Figure 3.3
Diagram for the Geometry Problem. Labels correspond to Table 3.5.

2. One of the transversals bisects the segment of the other that is between the two parallel lines.
3. Prove that the two triangles formed by the transversals are congruent.

Figure 3.3 provides a diagram for this statement, but for now we will concentrate on the sentential representation.

The given program consists of the following axioms and theorems from geometry.

P1. Definition of Bisector. If something is a bisector, then it divides a line segment into two congruent segments.

P2. Alternate Interior Angles. If two angles are alternate interior angles, then they are congruent.

P3. Vertical Angles. If two angles are vertical angles then they are congruent.

P4. ASA. If two angles and the included side of one triangle are congruent to the corresponding two angles and included side of another triangle, then the triangles are congruent.

As in the pulley example, we rewrite the preceding natural-language statements into a sequence of propositions and a set of production rules, each using a limited set of predicates.

Formalizing the initial statement of the problem is straightforward and is given in Table 3.4a. For sentence 1 we use the element (transversal t1 l1 l2) to mean that line t1 is a transversal cutting parallel lines l1 and l2. Sentence 2 introduces a segment that is part of one of the transversals (t1), between the parallel lines and bisected by the other transversal t2. But then we are asked to prove congruent two triangles that have not been mentioned. This situation already contrasts with that of the pulley problem, where every necessary element was specified in the problem statement. In just interpreting the problem statement we already have significant difficulty in recognizing all mentioned elements.

The given program can also be formalized straightforwardly as shown in Table 3.4. When we compare the given program to the given data structure, however, we see further recognition problems. The condition elements in the program mention many terms (e.g., alternative interior, vertical, sides) for which there is no mention in the given data structure. Therefore neither a sentential nor a diagrammatic representation of this problem can be successful until we enhance the data structure and modify the program so that the elements in one can be recognized and operated on by the other. In short, while *search* was the major difficulty in the pulley example, we will find that *recognition* of appropriate elements for inference is the major difficulty here.

3.4.2 Sentential Representation

Starting with the given data structure, we first develop an enhanced data structure, and then add conditions to the given program so that it can use this data structure.

The Perceptually Enhanced Data Structure We call this new data structure "perceptually" enhanced because it includes exactly those elements that a person looking at a diagram like that in Figure 3.3 could immediately recognize. This enhanced data structure includes explicitly the points, segments, angles, and triangles implied by the given problem statement, and evident in the diagram in Figure 3.3. Although this data structure includes perceptually obvious elements, we initially represent it sententially, as the sequence of elements listed in Table 3.5. For simplicity we have omitted elements [e.g., (line 4)] that simply assert the existence of an object.

The initial elements shown in part (a) of Table 3.5 are those from

Table 3.4
The (a) Given Data Structure and (b) Program in Semi-Formal Notation.

(a)

```
                (line l1) (line l2) (line t1) (line t2)
(1a.1)          (parallel l1 l2)
(1a.2)          (transversal t1 l1 l2)
(1a.3)          (transversal t2 l1 l2)
(1a.4)          (intersect t1 t2 x)
(1a.5)          (between x l1 l2)

(2a.1)          (segment s1 of t1) (between s1 l1 l2)
(2a.2)          (bisector t2 s1)

(3a.1)          Prove: (congruent tr1 tr2)
```

(b)

```
(p  bisector
    (bisector <b> segment <s>)
    (forms-subsegments <b> <s> <s1> <s2>)
→
    (congruent <s1> <s2>)

(p  vertical
    (vertical <a1> <a2>) (angle <a1>) (angle <a2>)
→
    (congruent <a1> <a2>))

(p  alt-int
    (alternate-interior <a1> <a2>)
    (angle <a1> <a2>)
→
    (congruent <a1> <a2>))

(p  asa
    (triangle <t1> haspart <s1>) (side <s1>)
    (triangle <t2> haspart <s2>) (side <s2>)

    (triangle <t1> haspart <aa>) (angle <aa>)
    (triangle <t1> haspart <ab>) (angle <ab>)

    (triangle <t2> haspart <ac>) (angle <ac>)
    (triangle <t2> haspart <ad>) (angle <ad>)

    (congruent objects <ac> <aa>)
    (congruent objects <ad> <ab>)
    (congruent objects <s2> <s1>)
→
    (congruent <t1> <t2>))
```

the given problem. Parts (a) and (b) together form the perceptually-enhanced data structure and include all the points, segments, angles, and triangles that a human could readily identify in Figure 3.3.

This data structure is produced by a set of "perceptual" inference rules that operate on the given data structure to produce the elements of the perceptually enhanced data structure. The first set of these interpret various given data elements in terms of points and segments. Specifically, four productions make the following inferences that interpret the elements described at the left (given problem elements) by adding the elements described at the right. These latter elements interpret the former in terms of perceptually obvious items (segments, points, and lines).

Given element	Segment and line elements added
Segment between two lines:	a segment with endpoints that are intersection points with the two lines.
Point between two lines, lying on a line intersecting two lines	the point lies on the segment with endpoints at the intersection points.
Two lines intersect:	There is a point that lies on both lines.

A second set of perceptual productions identify segments, angles, and triangles, elements that are readily seen by a human and that appear in the given program of geometry theorems and definitions. The production inferring segments simply creates a segment with endpoints at any two points that lie on the same line. In order to define an angle, however, we need a way of distinguishing the two sides of a line. Each pair of intersecting lines makes four angles depending on which sides of the lines are considered. Therefore three productions define "regions" on the two sides of a line. Initially one point (not on the line) is arbitrarily assigned to lie in region 1 (for that line), and the other to region 2. Thereafter, any point not lying on a line is assigned to one region or the other depending on whether or not a segment joining it to the original point crosses the line. (A segment "crossing" a line means the segment has a point in common with the line) The double arrows in Figure 3.3 point to region 1 for each line.

With regions defined, four unique angles can be defined for each intersection, although, in order to make the program run faster, we restricted it to angles lying in the two triangles. With angles and segments defined, a final perceptual production collects appropriate triples and identifies

Table 3.5
Original Elements in the Final Perceptually Enhanced Data Structure, Including (a) Original Elements, (b) Elements Added by Perceptual Productions, and (c) Elements Added by the Geometry Program.

(a)

(parallel lines 4 and 5)
(transversal 6 of 4 and 5)
(transversal 7 of 4 and 5)
(intersect 6 and 7 in x)
(between x lines 4 5)
(segment 16 of 6)
(segment 16 between 4 and 5)
(bisector 7 of 6)

(b)

(point x on lines 6 and 7)
(point 14 on lines 6 and 4)
(point 15 on lines 6 and 5)
(segment 16 from 14 to 15)
(point x on segment 16)
(segment 18 joining x and 15)
(segment 19 joining x and 14)
(point 20 on lines 5 and 7)
(segment 21 joining 20 and x)
(segment 22 joining 20 and 15)
(point 23 on 4 and 7)
(segment 24 joining 23 and 20)
(point x on segment 24)
(x is between 20 and 23)
(segment 26 joining 23 and x)
(segment 27 joining 23 and 14)
(point 23 in line 6 region 1)
(point 20 in line 6 region 2)
(point 23 in line 5 region 1)
(point 14 in line 5 region 1)
(point x in line 5 region 1)
(point 20 in line 4 region 1)
(point 15 in line 4 region 1)
(point x in line 4 region 1)
(point 15 in line 7 region 1)
(point 14 in line 7 region 2)
(angle 38: vertex 14 line 6 region 1 line 4 region 1)
(angle 39: vertex x line 7 region 2 line 6 region 1)
(angle 40: vertex 23 line 7 region 2 line 4 region 1)
(triangle 41 is: 23 x 14)
(segment 27 is in triangle 41)
(segment 26 is in triangle 41)
(segment 19 is in triangle 41)
(angle 42: vertex 15 line 6 region 2 line 5 region 1)
(angle 43: vertex x 7 line 1 region 6 line 2 region)
(angle 44: vertex 20 line 7 region 1 line 5 region 1)
(triangle 45 is: 20 x 15)
(segment 22 is in triangle 45)
(segment 21 is in triangle 45)
(segment 18 is in triangle 45)

(continued)

Table 3.5
Continued.

```
                              (c)
(alternate interior angles 44 40
  angle vertex 20 line 7 region 1 line 5 region 1
  angle vertex 23 line 7 region 2 line 4 region 1)
(vertical angles 39 43
  vertex x line 6 region 1 line 7 region 2
  vertex x line 6 region 2 line 7 region 1)
(alternate interior angles 42 38
  angle vertex 15 line 6 region 2 line 5 region 1
  angle vertex 14 line 6 region 1 line 4 region 1)
(sements 15 x and 14 x are congruent
  definition of bisector)
(congruent triangles
  segments 15 x and 14 x
  angles vertex 15 line 5 region 1 line vertex 14 line 4 region 1
  angles vertex x line 6 region 2 vertex x line 6 region 1)
```

the two triangles.

The result is the perceptually enhanced data structure, including the original elements together with the elements shown in part (b) Table 3.5. Because (for good reason, as we shall see) Table 3.5 is hard to understand, Figure 3.3 is labeled to show in diagrammatic form most of the elements of Table 3.5.

In Table 3.5, explicit labels are necessary for each element, as they were for the sentential representation of the pulley problem. For example, we have a (triangle 41). It must be labeled, because that label, 41, provides the only connection to other elements concerning it (e.g., segment 27 is in triangle 41).

Looking again at the given program (theorems and definitions) described in Table 3.4b we find that many of the conditions on the left side of these inference rules still have no corresponding elements in our perceptually enhanced data structure. For example, there are no "alternate interior" or "vertical" angles. We therefore have a choice. We could further enhance the representation to include elements like "alternate interior" used by the program. Alternatively, we can leave the data structure as it is and make changes in the program so that it can recognize elements in the existing data structure. We choose the latter to make a conservative distinction between perceptually obvious elements and elements that must be developed by reasoning. We argue that all elements currently in the perceptually enhanced representation (including points, segments, angles, and triangles) are perceptually obvious to any educated person looking at a diagram like that in Figure 3.3. Although we could add patterns like alternate interior angles, it is not clear that such patterns are obvious to everyone, and we will develop our program to reason about them explicitly.

In summary, we now have a data structure including all the primitive, visually obvious elements in the problem situation. It remains (a) to modify the given program so that it can interact with this data structure, and (b) to see how these modified inference rules solve the problem.

The Program. Table 3.6 lists the four inference rules, corresponding to the original given program, but replacing elements undefined in the existing data structure with their definitions in terms of elements already defined. For example, in the alternate-interior-angles rule, the single predicate "alternate-interior" has been replaced by a set of elements that state explicitly what alternate interior means in the current data representation in terms of "parallel," "between," "region," "side," and so on.

Thus, the angles have different regions with respect to the transversal (they are "alternate"). The angles have overlapping regions with respect to the parallel lines (they are "interior" to these lines). Similar additions are needed for the other inference rules as given in Table 3.6. These inference rules add to the data structure in Table 3.5 the final five elements in part (c) which include the desired conclusion that the triangles are congruent.

In summary, Table 3.5 shows the data structure after the problem is solved. This structure includes the original problem elements (part a), those added by perceptual inference rules (part b), and those added by geometric inference rules (part c), the latter modified to refer to primitive elements like points and segments rather than constructs like alternate interior angles.

Costs of Recognition and Search. The perceptual elements in part (b) of Table 3.5 and the modified conditions of the geometry inference rules in Table 3.6 capture what is necessary to allow the given geometry program to interact with the given data structure. Producing this data structure and program is the cost of being able to *recognize* useful elements in the data structure. Neglecting the costs of modifying the program (probably a considerable cost to students of geometry), the costs of developing the perceptual elements are evident in Table 3.5 which includes 40 elements in part (b) (compared with just 5 in part (c) added by the geometry program). The computer-implemented production system language (Ops5, see Brownston, et al. 1985) used to produce this table uses a slightly different system of elements. In this form the given data structure has 15 elements, the perceptual productions add 78 more in 41 steps, and the geometry productions just 10 more in five steps. The overt costs of recognition are clearly large.

Even with a data structure adequate for recognition, *search* is still problematic. If we imagine a sentential representation consisting of the list of elements in Table 3.5, then to match each element in an inference rule, we must search through the entire list until we find it, an average of $48/2 = 24$ tests. In short, in this simple geometry problem, recognition of the conditions for an inference rule, and search for matching conditions are both significant problems in a sentential representation. We discuss now how these difficulties are diminished by using a diagrammatic representation.

3.4.3 Diagrammatic Representation

In contrast to the pulley problem considered earlier, the major efficiency difference between the sentential and diagrammatic representations in this problem arises from differences in *recognition* rather than from differences in *search* (although here search is also important). The reason is that the original given statement (and its corresponding formal representation) does not include elements that can be recognized by the inference rules in the given program (i.e., in the theorems and definitions of geometry). Therefore, to solve the problem in the sentential representation, we must first do a great deal of perceptual enhancement of the data structure (addition of points, lines, segments, etc.). We chose to limit this enhancement to just those elements that a human viewer can obviously detect unambiguously on a diagram. To make the program work with this data structure required also enhancing the inference rules so that high-level elements like "alternate interior angles" were replaced (using the definition of alternate interior) by sets of elements that appear in the data structure. When we turn to the diagrammatic representation, the perceptual enhancement of the given representation is done by processes that are computationally very cheap, i.e., the processes of drawing and viewing the diagram. Since this phase comprises most of the work in

Table 3.6
Formal Geometry Program in Terms of Primitive Elements (points, lines, and segments).

```
(p bisector
   (bisector by <b> segment <s>)                          ;original condition
     ;<s> bisected by <b>

   (line <b>)                                             ;definition of bisector
   (point <p> on <b>)
     ;line <b> with <p> on it

   (segment <s>)
   (point <p> on <s>)
     ;segment <s> with <p> on it

   (segment <s> endpoints <p1> <p2>)
     ;endpoints of <s>
   (segment <s1> endpoints <p1> <p>)
   (segment <s2> endpoints <p2> <p>)
     ;subsegments of <s> formed by <p>

   - (congruent <s1> <s2>)
     ; this inference hasn't already been made
-->
   (congruent <s1> <s2>)

(p vertical
   (angle <a1> vertex <v> line <l1> region <n1>
                           line <l2> region <n2>)
   (angle { <a2> <> <a1> } vertex <v>
               line <l1> region { <n3> <> <n1> }
               line <l2> region { <n3> <> <n1> })
   - (congruent object <a1> <a2>)
-->
   (make congruent> objects <a1> <a2>))

(p alt-int
   (parallel <l2> <l3>)

   (between> point <x> <l2> <l3>)
   (region side <n1> ofline <l2> containspoint <x>)
   (region side <n3> ofline <l3> containspoint <x>)
     ;these are interior angles

   (angle <a1> vertex <v1> line <l2> side <n2>)
         line <l1> side <n1x>)
   (angle { <a2> <> <a1> } vertex { <v2> <> <v1> }
         line <l3> side <n3>)
         line <l1> side { <n1y> <> <n1x> } )
     ;these are alternate angles

   - (congruent object <a1> other <a2>)
-->
   (congruent> objects <a1> <a2>))
```

(continued)

Table 3.6
Continued.

```
(p asa
   (triangle <t1> object <s1>)
   (segment <s1> point <pa> other <pb>)
   (triangle { <t2> <> <t1> } object <s2>)
   (segment <s2> point <pc> other <pd>)
     ;corresponding sides

   (triangle <t1> object <aa>)
   (angle <aa> vertex <pa> line <la> side <na>)
   (triangle <t1> object <ab>)
   (angle <ab> vertex <pb> line <lb> side <nb>)
     ;corresponding angles

   (triangle <t2> object <ac>)
   (angle <ac> vertex <pc> line <lc> side <nc>)
   (triangle <t2> object <ad>)
   (angle <ad> vertex <pd> line <ld> side <nd>)
     ;corresponding angles

   (congruent object <ac> other <aa>)
   (congruent object <ad> other <ab>)
   (congruent object <s2> other <s1>)
   - (congruent object <t1> other <t2>)
     ;congruences
 →
   (make congruent objects <t1> <t2>))
```

the sentential representation, we already have a major saving, but there are two other advantages for the diagrammatic representation.

The first is a computational difference in *recognition.* With the perceptual work done, the (enhanced) geometry rules can readily recognize their conditions. In the sentential representation, the perceptual work of recognition is explicit and extensive; in the diagrammatic representation, it is automatic and easy.

In addition to these large differences in recognition, however, there are also considerable search differences. How can we take the data structure in Table 3.5 and the program in Table 3.6 and interpret it as a diagrammatic representation? As in the case of the pulley problem, let us assume that we have a perceptual control mechanism that allows the system to have instant access to all information at a given location; specifically, we assume that if two elements refer to the same point, then they are at the same location. The spacing in Table 3.6 groups together (for the first three rules) elements at a single location. For these rules, information is always present at just one or two locations. If we make the primitive assumption that there is no guidance for locating the first object in a group, then search will be required through an average of $(48/2) = 24$

elements. But thereafter no further search is required for any elements in a location group. The number of elements that must be checked to satisfy a production referring to n locations is therefore $n^*(48/2)$, assuming also that each group is found independently of the last. In contrast, the number of elements checked in the sentential representation is $N^*(48/2)$ where N is the number of elements in the production. Therefore the grouping of about 10 elements per production in Table 3.6 into one or two location groups reflects the search advantage of a diagrammatic representation. The fourth rule (ASA) contains two location groups, each corresponding to one triangle, and each related to three point locations joined by segments. The rule is written to emphasize the pairs of congruent parts, rather than the locations. By our criterion that "same location" means "contains a common point," this rule covers four locations in two adjacent pairs. Furthermore, the points in the two locations are related in perceptually predictable ways (although this organization is not captured by our formal representation).

These estimates of relative search difficulty are extremely conservative. If a person can search for two or three things simultaneously, one search can find the conditions of a production with spatial groupings. Furthermore, two separate location groups in a production are often at predictably related locations (e.g., at opposite ends of a transversal).

3.4.4 Summary and Comparison of Representations

The major difference in a diagrammatic representation, we believe, is difference in recognition processes. We have seen that formally producing perceptual elements does most of the work of solving the geometry problem. But we have a mechanism—the eye and the diagram—that produces exactly these "perceptual" results with little effort. We believe the right assumption is that diagrams and the human visual system provide, at essentially zero cost, all of the inferences we have called "perceptual." As shown above, this is a huge benefit. If the geometry problem is given verbally, without a diagram, all of these elements must be constructed explicitly (or perhaps in part by some internal imaging process). It is exactly because a diagram "produces" all the elements "for free" that it is so useful.

In this problem, as in the pulley problem, using a diagram removed the need for labelling the objects. Because there are so many objects in the geometry problem, this is a considerable saving. In the formal

OPS5 system, all objects are defined in terms of points, that is, in terms of their locations. Informally, it is common to construct a geometry proof simply by making corresponding congruent elements in a diagram that need not include any labels at all. The labels are needed only when a conventional proof is written—and that is, in fact, a sentential representation.

Finally the inference rules contain information that can be used to guide attention when the desired information is not at the current location. For example, suppose the system is attending to one segment on a line while applying the definition of bisector. Within the inference rule is the information that the second segment can be found on the same line and at one end or the other of the currently attended segment.

Although in the geometry problem there are large differences in the recognition and search processes required by the sentential and diagrammatic representations, there are no differences in inference processes. In each case four geometric inferences are required to solve the problem.

We can, however, imagine at least two ways in which geometric inference rules can be more or less powerful. First, these rules might incorporate powerful recognition capabilities, so that in one step, without any need for search, an entire high-level pattern could be recognized. Examples of such patterns include alternate interior angles, vertical angles, and ASA patterns for triangles. Second, the textbook theorems and definitions could be broken down into special cases that apply recognition. This has already been done for our definition of bisector. The original definition states that a line or segment bisects a segment *if* and *only if* the subsegments produced are congruent. We have divided this single statement into two parts, one of which we have used to make the inference that if there is a bisector, then the segments produced are congruent. In other cases, the traditional inference-rule statements are quite specific. For example, rules for alternate interior and alternate exterior angles could readily be stated as a single general inference rule, but most geometry texts separate them. In all cases, the special-case rules require less search and recognition for their application.

Second, as was also illustrated with the pulley problem, we can imagine inference rules that make more powerful inferences. For example, one rule might apply the alternate-interior-angle theorem twice and also conclude that two sets angles are therefore congruent, eliminating the need for applying the vertical-angles theorem. As observed earlier, independent of representation, such powerful inference rules would increase computational efficiency in either a diagrammatic or a sentential representation.

3.5 "Artificial" Diagrams

The examples considered so far describe systems in real spaces (the pulley system) or ideal space (the geometry problem). Diagrams often, however, do not describe an actual spatial arrangement. Examples include graphs and vector diagrams. These "artificial" diagrams provide a test of the properties we have argued are central to the utility of diagrams. Are these simply properties of the spatial world that are then portrayed in diagrams of that world? Or are they properties having psychological utility in problem solving? If the latter is true, then they should also be seen in the diagrams depicting relations among nonspatial variables that people use in solving problems. To explore this issue, we consider briefly three further examples.

3.5.1 Graphs in Economics

Diagrams were the principal tool for reasoning in economics throughout much of its modern history. In the preface to the first edition of his famous *Principles of Economics,* which dominated the scene for 60 years after 1890, Alfred Marshall had this to say:

> It is not easy to get a full view of continuity in this aspect without the use of mathematical symbols or diagrams. The use of the latter requires no special knowledge, and they often express the conditions of economic life more accurately, as well as more easily, than do mathematical symbols. ... [E]xperience seems to show that they give a firmer grasp of many important principles than can be got without their aid; and that there are many problems of pure theory, which no one who has once learned to use diagrams will willingly handle in any other way. (Marshall, 1890)

The following is a simple and typical example of their use (see Figure 3.4):

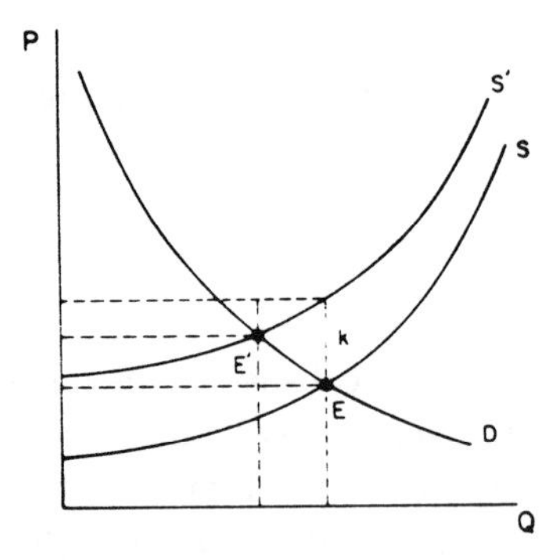

Figure 3.4
Graph Used in an Argument from Economics.

The abcissa of the diagram represents the quantity of a commodity that is produced or demanded, and the ordinate, the price at which that quantity will be supplied or purchased.

The line D is a demand curve, indicating the quantity that would be purchased at each price. It slopes downward to express the assumption that the lower the price, the larger the quantity that will be demanded.

The lines S and S' are supply curves, indicating the quantities that would be offered on the market at each price. They slope upward to express the assumption that the higher the price, the larger the quantity that will be offered. Notice that perceptually obvious features (e.g., slope) are used to represent important information.

We can immediately read off from the diagram the equilibrium price and quantity, as the ordinate and abcissa, respectively, of the intersection, E, of S and D (or E', of S' and D). At this price, supply and demand are equal. The information needed to make this inference is located together and again uses perceptually obvious features (e.g., intersections).

Next, we ask what the effect on the equilibrium will be of imposing a manufacturer's tax of k dollars on a unit of the commodity if the initial supply curve is S and the initial equilibrium E. The price at which any given quantity will be supplied will now be k dollars higher than the price at which it would have been supplied before, moving the supply curve from S to S', and the equilibrium from E to E'.

Again, we see immediately that the equilibrium price will increase, but by less than the amount of the tax, while the quantity exchanged will decrease. By considering demand curves of different slopes in the neighborhood of the equilibrium we would also see directly that the increase in price would be less, and the decline in quantity greater, the flatter the demand curve (the more "elastic" the demand). As in our other examples, the great utility of the diagram arises from *perceptual enhancement,* the fact that it makes explicit the relative positions of the equilibrium points, so that the conclusions can be read off with the help of simple, direct perceptual operations. It would be a useful exercise for the reader to undertake to reach the same conclusions from the problem statement using either a sentential representation or an algebraic one.

3.5.2 Free Body Diagrams in Physics

Figure 3.5a shows a physical situation commonly studied in elementary physics. The solver might be asked to relate the masses of A and B. Figure 3.5b shows the artificial "free-body" diagrams that are always recommended for solution of such problems (Halliday and Resnick 1970, Sears, Zemansky and Young 1981, Heller and Reif 1984). There are two diagrams, one for car A and one for car B. $\mathbf{F}_{\mathrm{AB}}$ is the force on car A due to car B. and $\mathbf{F}_{\mathrm{BA}}$ is the force on B due to A. These forces have equal magnitude, but opposite directions. Does this conventionally used, artificial diagram have the properties we have argued are important in our earlier examples?

1. *Localization.* Below each of the free-body diagrams in Figure 3.5b are the equations central to solving this problem. Each equation comes from one free-body diagram. Information used together is grouped together in the free-body diagrams. This localization is achieved by the conventional rule for free-body diagrams—they include all the forces *on* a particular system. This need not have been the case. Indeed novices often draw their version of "free-body" diagram that places, for example, the force F_{BA}, the force on B due to A, in the A diagram rather than in the B diagram, thus violating the locality property for the free-body diagram.

2. *Minimal labeling.* The only important functions of labels in Figure 3.5 is to relate parts of the real-world diagram unambiguously to the force diagram. Even this relation is often made unnecessary by experts who simply draw the force diagrams on top of the objects in the original picture.

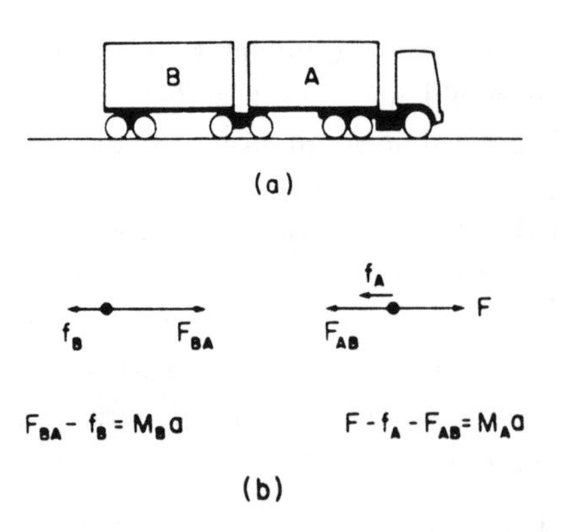

Figure 3.5
(a) Two cars (masses m_A and m_B) attached to an engine that exerts a force F. (b) Corresponding free-body diagrams and equations of motion for the cars.

3. *Use of perceptual enhancement.* In this example, the acceleration of the train is towards the right. Note that the skilled solver has drawn the first force diagram with the right-directed force larger than the left-directed force. This allows a quick, probably perceptual, check of whether the force diagram is consistent with the physical situation. In the vertical direction, the forces are of equal magnitude, and so there is no acceleration. In the horizontal direction, the left-directed forces are shorter or non-existent, and so acceleration is towards the right. Such quick checks can be important, especially in more complex problems.

3.5.3 Energy-Level Diagram

Figure 3.6 shows the energy E for a hydrogen atom as a function of the strength B of a magnetic field surrounding it. When the magnetic field is 0, there are just two possible energies for the atom. But when a field is applied, these levels "split" into four. One can readily see that, for large values of B levels I and III, and levels II and IV have a constant separation, but this is not the case for levels III and II. The horizontal lines represent various possible "energy states" of the atom for the field strength indicated by the dotted line. Consider the properties of this diagram using the following criteria for utility of diagrams developed earlier.

1. *Locality.* This diagram is used to guide computation of the energy released when there is a transition of an electron from one energy state to another. Various possible transitions are indicated in Figure 3.6 by vertical arrows between the states. As the atom makes this transition, its energy is reduced by the amount *E1-E2,* where *E1* is the energy of the higher state and *E2* the energy of the lower state. This then is the amount of energy released (as a photon). Again we find that all information needed to make this calculation is readily available in predictable locations with the lines representing the two energy levels.

2. *Minimizing labeling.* The labels in Figure 3.6 serve only to let us talk about the elements there. They are not essential to any of the inferences made.

3. *Use of perceptual enhancement.* The diagram represents perceptually the qualitative knowledge of the relative sizes of the energy levels. It is also drawn at least roughly to scale, so that the relative size of energies released by transition can be checked against the diagram. For example, transition *a* clearly releases more energy than does transition b.[1]

3.5.4 A Comment on Mental Imagery

In this chapter we have limited ourselves to the use of diagrams as a form of external memory. Our only references to psychological processes (other than the subject-matter inference rules) have been to rather obvious phenomena of perception: that people can focus attention on part of a diagram, and that they can detect cues there (e.g., simple objects like pulleys or angles), and use them to retrieve problem-relevant inference operators from memory. These assumptions agree with everything that has been learned in the past two decades about expert performance.

We cannot end our discussion however, without a few comments on mental imagery—the uses of diagrams and other pictorial representations that are not stored on paper but are held in human memory. We have no new evidence to offer, but we do offer the speculation that mental images play a role in problem solving quite analogous to the role played by external diagrams (and that this role is also played in

[1] Figure redrawn from Feynman et al. (1966).

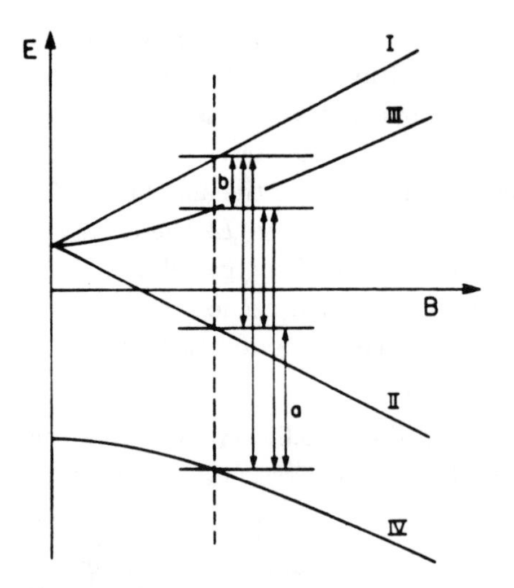

Figure 3.6
Graph showing energy levels in a hydrogen atom.

the two memories, internal and external, in concert). By this we mean that mental images, while containing substantially less detail than can be stored in external diagrams, have similar properties of localization of information and can be accessed by the same inference operators as the external diagrams. This implies also that the creation of a mental imagine (for instance, from a verbal description) employs inference processes like those that make information explicit in the course of drawing a diagram.

Thus, when we draw a rectangle and its two diagonals, the existence of the point of intersection of the diagonals is inferred automatically—the point is created on the paper, accessible to perception. In exactly the same way, when we imagine a rectangle with its two diagonals, we imagine ("see") the point of intersection in memory.

In this chapter, we have represented external diagrams symbolically as list structures, and the inference processes as list processes in a production system language. These representations and processes could equally well be interpreted as denoting mental images and imagery processes in the brain. But much difficult psychological research, the exact character of which we can only dimly perceive, will be required to test this hypothesis. Until then it must remain a speculation, albeit one that appears consistent with such psychological evidence as exists.

3.6 Conclusion

For external problem representations, we have provided a simple distinction between sentential representations, in which the data structure is indexed by position in a list, with each element "adjacent" only to the next element in the list, and diagrammatic representations, in which information is indexed by location in a plane, many elements may share the same location, and each element may be "adjacent" to any number of other elements. While certainly not the complete story on this important representational issue, this simple distinction lets us demonstrate the following reasons why a diagram can be superior to a verbal description for solving problems:

- Diagrams can group together all information that is used together, thus avoiding large amounts of search for the elements needed to make a problem-solving inference.
- Diagrams typically use location to group information about a single element, avoiding the need to match symbolic labels.
- Diagrams automatically support a large number of perceptual inferences, which are extremely easy for humans.

None of these points insure that an arbitrary diagram is worth 10,000 of any set of words. To be useful a diagram must be constructed to take advantage of these features. The possibility of placing several elements at the same or adjacent locations means that information needed for future inference can be grouped together. It does not ensure that a particular diagram does group such information together. Similarly, although every diagram supports some easy perceptual inferences, nothing ensures that these inferences must be useful in the problem-solving process. Failing to use these features is probably part of the reason why some diagrams seem not to help solvers, while others do provide significant help (Paige and Simon 1966, Larkin 1983). The advantages of diagrams, in our view, are computational. That is diagrams can be better representations not because they contain more information, but because the indexing of this information can support extremely useful and efficient computational processes. But this means that diagrams are useful only to those who know the appropriate computational processes for taking advantage of them. Furthermore, a problem solver often also needs the knowledge of how to construct a "good" diagram that lets him take advantage of the virtues we have discussed. In short, the ideas we have presented, not only provide an explanation of why diagrams can be so useful, but also provide a framework for further study of the knowledge required for effective diagram use.

References

Anderson, J. R. 1978. Arguments Concerning Representations for Mental Imagery. *Psychological Review* 85, 249–277.

Anderson, J. R. 1984. Representational Types: A Tricode Proposal, Technical Report #82-1. Office of Naval Research, Washington, D.C.

Brownston, L., Farrell, R., Kant, E., and Martin, N. 1985. *Addison-Wesley Series in Artificial Intelligence. Programming Expert Systems in OPS5.* Reading, Mass: Addison Wesley.

Chase, W. G., and Simon, H. A. 1973. The Mind's Eye in Chess. In *Visual Information Processing,* ed. W. G. Chase, 11–12. New York: Academic Press.

Feynman, R. P., Leighton, R. B., and Sands, M. 1966). *The Feynman Lectures on Physics,* 11–12. Reading, Mass: Addison Wesley.

Hadamard, J. 1945. *The Psychology of Invention in the Mathematical Field.* Princeton, NJ: Princeton University Press.

Halliday, D., and Resnick, R. 1970. *Fundamentals of Physics.* New York: John Wiley and Sons.

Hayes, J. R., and Simon, H. A. 1974. Understanding Written Task Instructions. In *Knowledge and Cognition,* ed. L. W. Gregg. Hillsdale, NJ: Erlbaum.

Heller, J., and Reif, F. 1984. Prescribing Effective Human Problem-Solving Processes: Problem Description in Physics. *Cognition and Instruction* 1: 177–216.

Kintsch, W., and Van Dijk, T. A. 1978. Toward a Model of Text Comprehension and Production. *Psychological Review* 85, 363–394.

Larkin, J. H. 1983. Mechanisms of Effective Problem Representation in Physics (C.I.P. 434). Department of Psychology, Carnegie-Mellon University, Pittsburgh, Penn.

Marshall, A. 1890. *Principles of Economics.* New York: Macmillan.

Neves, D., and Anderson, J. R. 1981. Knowledge Compilation: Mechanisms for the Automatization of Cognitive Skills. In *Cognitive Skills and Their Acquisition*, ed. J. R. Anderson. Hillsdale, NJ: Erlbaum.

Newell, A., Shaw, J. C., and Simon, H. A. 1959. Empirical Explorations of the Logic Theory Machine. In Proceedings of the Western Joint Conference on Artificial Intelligence.

Paige, G., and Simon, H. A. 1966. Cognitive Processes in Solving Algebra Word Problems. In *Problem Solving,* ed. B. Kleinmuntz. New York: John Wiley and Sons.

Pylyshyn, Z. W. 1973. What the Mind's Eye Tells the Mind's Brain: A Critique of Mental Imagery. *Psychological Bulletin* 80, 1–24.

Sears, F. W., Zemansky, M. W., and Young, H. D. 1981. *Physics.* Reading, Mass: Addison-Wesley.

Simon, H. A. 1978. On the Forms of Mental Representation. In *Minnesota Studies in the Philosophy Of Science. Vol. IX: Perception and Cognition: Issues in the Foundations of Psychology,* ed. C. W. Savage. Minneapolis: University of Minnesota Press.

Simon, H. A., and Barenfeld, M. 1969. Information Processing Analysis of Perceptual Processes in Problem Solving. *Psychological Review* 76, 473–483.

Waterman, D. 1970. Generalization Learning Techniques for Automating the Learning of Heuristics. *Artificial Intelligence* 1, 121–170.

Wertheimer, M. 1959). *Productive Thinking.* New York: Harper and Brothers.

4 Images and Inference

Robert K. Lindsay
University of Michigan

4.1 Introduction

The notion that mental imagery plays an important and distinct role in cognition has a long history. Indeed, there was once an extended debate as to whether *any* thought was possible without *imagery* (Woodworth 1938). Today the pendulum has swung the other way (to invoke an image-based metaphor), and there is debate as to whether imagery, *as a distinct form of representation,* plays *any* role in cognition (Dennett 1981a, 1981b; Fodor 1981; Kosslyn 1975, 1980; Kosslyn, Pinker, Smith, and Schwartz 1979; Kosslyn and Pomerantz 1977; Pylyshyn 1980; Shepard 1973, 1978).

Advocates of a distinct role of imagery in cognition have emphasized a variety of functions that imagery might serve. These include memory (Bower 1972; Paivio, 1971), navigation (Evans 1980), and perceptual recognition (Posner and Keele 1967). A recent review of empirical studies of mental imagery and its functional similarities to visual perception may be found in Finke and Shepard (1986). In this chapter I focus on imagery's function in inference. Inference is an important component of most if not all other cognitive processes, including perception (Rock 1983; but see also Gibson 1979), language (Lindsay 1963), navigation (Gladwin 1970), memory (Bartlett 1932; Chase and Simon 1973) and problem solving (Larkin and Simon 1987).

Any cognitive system, natural or artificial, must draw inferences from its knowledge. If its environment is changing, as would be the normal case, the inference problem becomes acute, because a change in even a single item of knowledge might have widespread effects on many others. The problem of determining which items are affected and how they are affected has been called the "frame problem" in artificial intelligence (Haugeland 1985; McCarthy and Hayes, 1969; Raphael 1971). The inferences in question need not involve long chains of deduction (although they may); the frame problem is difficult because of the sheer number of inferences possible in the face of large quantities of knowledge whose mutual dependencies must somehow be specified or derived. Obviously the frame problem is one to which any theory of human cognition must supply an answer.

The major theme of research attacking the frame problem has been the search for appropriate modifications and extensions of first order predicate logic (FOL) that will permit the description of world knowledge and situations and the formulation of rules of deduction that describe how situations change over time (a so-called situational calculus). One requirement of such a calculus is that conclusions must be retractable in the face of additional information; that is, unlike FOL where conclusions only accumulate, the logic must be "nonmonotonic." There is an extensive literature on these topics (for a review, see Reiter, 1987).

In this chapter I propose a different approach to the frame problem in which images are employed as inference-making representations. Specifically, I propose a model for representing geometric diagrams in a way that permits the drawing of inferences without the explicit use of rules of deduction. The kernel of this idea was present in an early artificial intelligence program (Lindsay 1961, 1963) which extracted kinship facts from linguistic inputs and used a family tree representation to make explicit some inferences that were only implicit in the inputs. Visual imagery, in addition to whatever other characteristics it has, provides a much more general and ubiquitous application of this idea. Haugeland (1985, p. 229), in commenting on the frame problem and imagery, puts the essential idea succinctly: "The beauty of images is that (spatial) side effects take care of themselves." Here I attempt to spell out for the case of geometric diagrams (which illustrates the more complex case of spatial imagery in general) just what is required for the "side effects (inferences) to take care of themselves."

One might well ask why inference is not adequately accounted for by predicative knowledge representations employing logic, since inference is a task for which logic was explicitly devised and for which there is a well-developed theory. My answer is that visual images possess properties (to be described shortly) not possessed by *deductive* propositional representation, and these properties help avoid the combinatorial explosion of correct but trivial inferences that must be explicitly represented in a propositional system. Accordingly, an important role of imagery in cognition is as a constructive inferential knowledge representation system that efficiently makes inferences based on one's beliefs (including one's accurate knowledge) of how real-world situations behave. It is one's beliefs, perhaps describable as predicative knowledge, that are used to construct images; inferences are retrieved from these images. The crucial property that distinguishes images from other knowledge representations is that they are nondeductive, that is nonproof procedure based. In order to explain this view it is necessary to take a more careful look at what a knowledge representation system is.

4.2 Knowledge Representation Systems

Although a general theory of knowledge representation is not at hand, the past two decades have seen a large number of computer implementations of methods for storing and processing knowledge. From this work have emerged certain limited generalizations in the form of programming systems for expressing procedural and factual knowledge of various sorts, and several authors (e.g., Bobrow 1975; Palmer 1978; see also Brachman and Levesque 1985) have offered analyses of the representation problem that have clarified several important issues.

To avoid the endless regress of the homunculus fallacy, it is now generally recognized that it is necessary to specify not only the structure of the representation but also how it is constructed, and how it is accessed and used. A completely specified knowledge representation system therefore consists of at least three parts: a set of *construction processes,* a set of *representation structures,* and a set of *retrieval processes.* A specification of the form of the representation structures alone has no explanatory power; however, a representation system with unspecified construction processes could still model those functions that use *externally* provided representations. The work here presented, however, addresses issues of the selective construction of *internal* representations and how construction and retrieval processes interact. Thus a full model of imagery-based abilities must prescribe all three components of the representation system.

A knowledge representation system should be described in the context of a task or purpose that it will serve: different tasks or purposes often, though perhaps not always, are better served by different representation systems. Thus even if a single representation system can in principle serve all purposes, it often serves one of them *better* (e.g., Amarel 1968). Since a knowledge representation system is not just a passive repository of facts, but includes methods for applying and retrieving information as well, issues of efficiency arise and may be criterial for judging theoretical adequacy. However, I am making no claim that the proposed representation system for images can make inferences that are *in principle* beyond, say, predicate logic representation systems.

Any knowledge representation system must record some information, that is, make it available at a later time. This may be thought of as a special, limited form of inference even if what is available at a later time is exactly what was entered explicitly. (The frame problem is nontrivial simply because it is not always correct to conclude that facts do not change over time, hence static memory often makes incorrect "inferences.") However, I wish to reserve the term *inference* for its more customary use: *making explicit* information that was *implicit* in sets of inputs (Lindsay 1961). Thus I will restrict the term *inference-making knowledge representation systems* (IKRs) to representation systems whose three components jointly yield information that was not directly provided to it. For example, a device that translates English text into predicate logic formulas and then back to English would be a knowledge representation system, but not an IKR. If it *also* applied a proof procedure to the formulas to generate other formulas, which could then be translated into English, it would be an IKR.

A knowledge representation system that did English-logic and logic-English translation and was able to retrieve inferences from inputs, but *did not embody a separate proof procedure,* may seem paradoxical. If the representation structure is FOL, that is indeed the case, for logic *requires* a proof procedure for making inferences: that is built into the concept of logic. However, there can be knowledge representation systems that make inferences without the use of explicit rules of deduction but simply by virtue of the properties of the knowledge representation system alone.

To illustrate this, consider a simple case consisting of a discrete grid, each cell of which could be occupied by a single point labeled by a letter. Consider the input *b is one grid point due right of a, c is directly above b, and d is one grid point due left of c.* From this we may conclude that *d is directly above a.* This inference could be supported by a calculus based system with appropriate rules of deduction; such a system would be *deductive.* Alternatively, the inference would be supported by a system of construction and retrieval routines that placed letters on the described grid and read off relationships by scanning the grid; such a system would be *nondeductive.* The nondeductive system requires no separate computational inference-making stage: the operation of the construction process entails the "making" of the inferences.

Similar tasks have been studied experimentally, attempting to establish that human subjects employ visual imagery in their performance. Huttenlocher (1968) and others have examined performance in solving problems requiring inferences from statements such as *Tom is taller than Sam* and *John is shorter than Sam;* the evidence (from errors and response times) supports the hypothesis that subjects image tokens of Tom, and so forth, translating height relations into spatial relations in the image. In this example, the imaging processes may be construed as "implementing" certain properties of a *simple ordering* relation (transitivity, anti-symmetry, and irreflexivity); Elliott (1965) provides examples of other classes of relations that can be treated with similar methods. Clearly, such a knowledge representation can make some inferences, and yet the inferences inhere in the knowledge representation, including the construction and retrieval processes, and do not require a separate proof procedure. The construction and retrieval processes are exactly the same whether the retrieved knowledge was given explicitly or inferred.

These examples are illustrations of nonproof-procedure methods of inference that represent a substantially different approach to inference from the standard view of logic, and that may provide a connection between inference and mind that does not rely on computationally opaque and inefficient methods. The suggestion is not without precedent. Lindsay (1963) proposed "inferential memory" as a nonrule-based form of deduction. Quillian's (1968) "semantic nets" and later elaborations permit nonproof-procedural deduction. Clearly "inheritance of properties" in semantic nets (Brachman 1979; Fahlman 1979, 1984) employs such a method. However, a more fundamental and general connection to cognition exists: imagery.

The basic hypothesis of this chapter is that *visual imagery employs nonproof procedural knowledge representations that support inference by a constraint satisfaction mechanism built into the processes that construct and access them.* A representation that possesses this quality may remain symbolic, and even digital, but is not based on predicate logic. This hypothesis is elaborated below for computer-based knowledge representation; I suggest that it is also true for human (mental) knowledge representation, though at present I can offer no empirical support for that hypothesis.

Nondeductive inference should not be *equated* with visual imagery, for then some "images" would have no specific spatial properties. For example, inheritance of properties in semantic nets is nondeductive but not explicitly spatial. On the other hand, there is a natural translation of such inheritance (which is based on the set-inclusion relation) into spatial terms, namely Euler/Venn diagrams. Indeed such translations are customary and powerful methods of problem solving by analogy and frequently are suggested as heuristic devices in mathematical texts. Haugeland (1985) attributes such methods, perhaps over generously, to Galileo, who used spatial metaphors to prove results concerning non-spatial propositions. Perhaps it is the case that all nondeductive representations that are available to human thought could be translated into spatial analogies. This is not a claim, however, that I am prepared to make, and thus I leave open the possibility that imagery does not tap all such methods.

Conversely I do not claim that nondeductive inference is *all* there is to imagery. Finke and Shepard (1986, p. 37) conclude from their recent review of experimental studies of imagery that "... the functional equivalence hypothesis [that the internal processes are essentially the same in perceptual and imagery tasks] provides the *single best* overall explanation for the results reviewed in the several sections." Many aspects of the percept-like character of imagery (e.g., color, texture, depth, and so forth) are not addressed in the model to be presented, and some of them may serve important functions other than inference (e.g., simple recall, emotional impact, aesthetic judgment, and so forth).

4.3 A Knowledge Representation for Diagrams

For purposes of illustration, in the remaining discussion the category of visual images will be restricted to *diagrams;* informally, these are drawings that can be made with paper and pencil with a straight-edge and compass, but without color or continuous grey-scale shading. A more precise definition of diagrams is given below (in the form of construction processes). Basically, diagrams include those things that can be drawn on a black and white computer terminal by "graphics software." Diagrams *are* expressible as a set of propositions, as witnessed by their representation with such software. However, such propositional representations are not in general perspicuous, for reasons later addressed.

I now present a more precise model of nondeductive inference (NDI), restricted to that subset of diagrams composed of points, straight lines, circular arcs, and symbolic labels for these components. The omission of many important qualities of actual drawings, such as colors, textures, widths of lines, and so forth, may well limit the range of inferences that can be supported by this model, but what remains to be addressed is an important and ubiquitous set of mental activities. The following are the basic functions of the proposed representation for these two-dimensional diagrams.

4.3.1 Representation Structure

The elements of a representation structure are symbolic names for points, line segments, and circular arcs, combined into expressions that relate these symbols to their locations on a two-dimensional, bounded flat *tablet*. A representation structure R for a diagram D is a specific set of such symbols and expressions.

Four things must be kept distinct:

1. the diagram which is represented
2. that which the diagram denotes
3. the representation structure for the diagram
4. the class of potential representation structures for diagrams in general

For example, we might wish to represent a specific diagram, such as a floor plan (1) of the White House. That floor plan denotes the layout of the building at 1600 Pennsylvania Avenue (2) in Washington. The representation structure (3) is a set of coordinates of pairs of tablet points (corresponding to the end points of the line segments in the floor plan) plus names for each of these points, plus several sets of points (corresponding to a sample of points on each line segment and curve of the floor plan), plus names of these line segments and curves. All points that are part of the representation structure are "marked," that is, they are distinguished from the other points on the tablet.

The class of representation structures (4) could be defined by a grammar specifying the set of real numbers that may serve as coordinates on the tablet, the classes of coordinate combinations (e.g., pairs) that form permissible expressions, what symbols may serve as labels, and so forth. In fact, however, the usual forms of immediate constituent rule grammars are not perspicuous descriptions of the nonlinear structures here employed. Consequently, the class of representation structures will merely be specified implicitly by the construction processes themselves. These processes implicitly obey a grammar of representations, but are not identical to it, just as a program that generates English might obey a grammar of English, but not *be* a grammar of English itself.

The implicit grammar of the representation structure defines specific classes of objects (points, lines, circles, etc.) that consist of sets of coordinates that lie within the bounded rectangular tablet. The tablet points are dense in the usual sense that, for any two given points reference can be made to a point between them. Points on the tablet may be labeled with symbolic names, and may be either *marked* or *unmarked.*

4.3.2 Construction Processes

The set of construction processes is formed from the following *primitive construction processes:*

Mark a given point on the tablet.

Erase a given point; that is, unmark it.

Label a given point with a specified name.

Construct due right/left point relative to a given point.

Construct due above/below point relative to a given point.

Construct a line segment between two given points (i.e., mark a covering set of points between the end points).

Select the midpoint on a given line segment and return its coordinates.

Construct a perpendicular to a given line segment (perhaps extended) from a given point (i.e., mark a covering set of the perpendicular).

Construct a parallel to a given line segment through a given point.

Parallel-translate a given line segment (i.e., mark its extension along itself) until a given *condition predicate* (see below) is true.

Pass a circle through three given points (i.e., mark a covering set of the circle).

Construct a circle with a given point as center and passing through a second given point (i.e., mark a covering set of the circle).

Select a point on the tablet meeting a specified ordered list of condition predicates (see below).

Extend a given line segment until a given ordered list of condition predicates is met.

Perpendicular-translate a line segment until a given ordered list of condition predicates is met.

Rotate a given line segment about a given point until a given ordered list of *condition predicates* is met (i.e., unmark its covering set and mark the covering set of the line segment that would result after a rotation meeting the condition).

In the above construction processes, *condition predicates* are statements that are either true or false and can be verified by compositions of the retrieval processes, enumerated below.

4.3.3 Retrieval Processes

The set of retrieval processes are formed from the following *primitive retrieval processes:*

Right/left order: Given two points determine which one is rightmost or that neither is.

Above/below order: Given two points determine which one is above or that neither is.

Point-line relation: Determine if a given point is on a given line segment, and if not determine which side of the line it is on.

Point-circle relation: Determine if a given point is inside, on, or outside a given circle.

Closure: Determine if a given set of line segments form a continuous, closed curve; this process returns *true* or *false.*

Comparative length: Determine which of two given line segments is longer, or whether they are of equal length within stated resolution; returns the longer segment, or *false* if they are of equal length.

Comparative angle: Determine which of two given angles is greater, or whether they are equal to within stated resolution.

Intersection: Determine if and where two given line segments intersect; returns the point of intersection, or *false.*

Angle metric quality: Determine if two given line segments are parallel and if not determine if the (directed) angle from the first to the second is zero, acute, right, obtuse, straight, oblique, a negative right angle, or reflex; returns *zero, acute, right, oblique,* and so forth.

Mirror symmetry: Determine if the entire representation structure exhibits mirror symmetry about a given line.

Some of the retrieval processes are predicative statements; those that are not can be converted into one or more predicative statements. For example, *closure* can be used directly as a condition predicate, and *angle metric quality* yields eight condition predicates. Similarly, the composite retrieval processes, such as those illustrated below, may yield additional condition predicates.

The condition predicates are the heart of the inferential power of the knowledge representation system. Consequently, their efficient implementation is extremely important to the problem solving power of the model. In this chapter, however, I discuss only their functional requirements and present what is hoped to be a *sufficient* set of processes to accomplish the purposes described in Section 4.4. It is not claimed that the set is unique, nor that the processes correspond in any direct way to neural or mental processes of humans.

From the primitive construction and retrieval processes, more complex construction and retrieval processes can be formed. For example:

Line-circle relation: Determine which points on a given line segment are outside, on, or inside the circle: returns three lists of coordinates representing the endpoints of these sets of points. (Uses *point-circle relation.*)

Parity: Determine if two given points are on the same or opposite sides of a given line segment (extended), or neither (that is, one or both lie on the line segment); returns *same, opposite,* or *false.* (Uses *point-line relation*).

Colinearity: Determine if three given points lie on the same line. (Uses *point-line relation* and *parallel-translate.*)

Construct rectangle: Given two parallel line segments, move one along itself until the two line segments form opposite sides of a rectangle. (Uses *parallel-translate, construct-perpendicular, comparative length,* and *angle metric quality*).

Due right: Given two points, determine if the first is due right of the second. (Uses *right/left order* and *above/below order*).

Note that many of these processes have no knowledge of metric properties; exceptions are midpoint construction, the two circle constructions, comparative length, comparative angle, and angle metric quality. The metric information in these processes, however, is "qualitative" (in the sense of de Kleer and Brown 1984 and Forbus 1984); the distinct values are limited to a small, ordered set, and distance measures are only comparative. These qualitative metric properties are necessary for dealing with direction and relative length, and these suffice for a wide class of inferences, though not all conceivable ones that might be supported by diagrams.

With this knowledge representation system it is possible to have nondeductive inference. The construction processes employ methods that impose constraints on what can be constructed, and these constraints preclude the construction of representation structures that embody (make available to the retrieval processes) invalid inferences. In some cases, enough invalid inferences are eliminated to leave some unambiguous, true conclusions.

No claim is made that NDI methods can in principle do things that logic cannot. It is likely, however, that they can do some things *more efficiently,* and that is the crux of the matter. The efficiency edge need not always be on the side of NDI knowledge representations, and yet humans, and machines, may use them more widely than would be prudent simply because the machinery is already in place, just as one might pound in screws with a nearby hammer rather than fetching a distant screwdriver. Note that this model of imagery is indeed computational since it may be implemented on a digital computer with standard (serial, digital) computational techniques. However, to achieve an efficiency advantage may require the use of nonconventional computers, including analog and parallel methods. Regardless of implementation, the model differs conceptually from proof-procedure and production-rule based inference schemes. The next section illustrates how the sorts of inference mechanisms this method provides may be used in geometric problem solving and thinking.

4.4 Uses of NDI Knowledge Representation in Cognition

There is, of course, more to cognition than the making of inferences. In this section I discuss how diagrammatic representations can be used in the service of goal-directed processes such as theorem proving and problem solving.

In the Geometry Machine (Gelernter 1959), an early artificial intelligence program, the inferences were made by a calculus that generated a problem-subproblem tree and sought to discover a nonrigorous but formal deductive proof of a given theorem. An important feature of this program was its use of a diagram as a mechanism for rejecting implausible subproblems. For example, if the calculus proposed proving that two triangles were congruent, the program first consulted its diagram to see if these two triangles had the same perimeter length; if not the subgoal was abandoned. Here the diagram is of service precisely because it is not possible to construct a diagram that depicts two triangles of unequal perimeter while remaining consistent with premises that imply that the triangles are congruent. It is of course possible for the diagram to err in the other direction: the premises may not imply congruency, but the chosen diagram may represent equal perimeter triangles, since geometry diagrams are in general under-determined. The Geometry Machine strategy is thus conservative: it may not reject all false paths, but those paths rejected are indeed false. Gelernter, Hansen, and Loveland (1960) estimated from their experiments that the amount of search was reduced by a factor of at least 200 by this method.

It is interesting to note that the use of the diagram as heuristic device in this way does not require that a sketch be "shown" to the computer. In fact, that would not work since the Geometry Machine did not have any vision programs. Instead, the functional equivalent of a diagram is required. In actuality, the programmers supplied "diagrams" that consisted of a list of numerical coordinates of the points referred to by the premises. Nonetheless, from our viewpoint, the list of coordinates functioned diagrammatically for the computer.

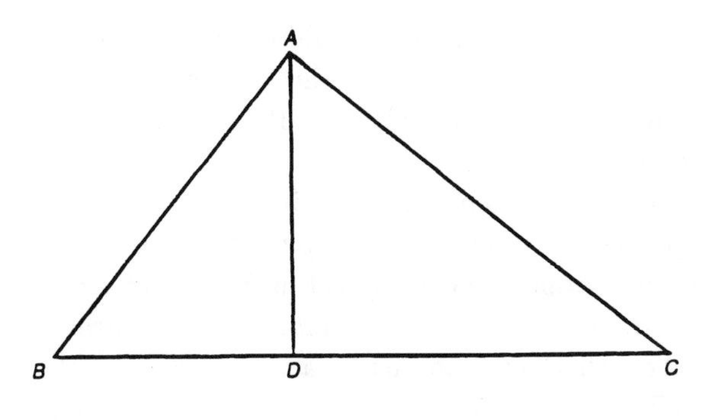

Figure 4.1

The Geometry Machine used diagrams to *dispose of* conjectures. Diagrams may also be used to *propose* conjectures. For example, attempting to draw diagrams consistent with a set of premises may force the construction of, say, an isosceles triangle rather than a scalene triangle; this may be taken to suggest that the forced feature follows from the premises. The Geometry Machine could not do this since it did not construct diagrams, but Lenat's (1976) AM program used essentially this method of conjecturing (but not with diagrams) when its generation of examples turned up "interesting" features.

Similarly, an NDI model does not always eliminate search, but aids search by the use of constraint satisfaction heuristics that can either propose or dispose of putative inferences.

Next consider Figure 4.1. ABC is a right triangle; a perpendicular from the right angle to the opposite side has been constructed, forming the two triangles DAB and DCA.

Inference 1: Area of ABC = area of DAB + area of DCA.

Inference 2: DAB is similar to DCA.

Inference 1 is direct, immediate, and compelling simply from an examination of the diagram; Inference 2 requires study but nonetheless results in conviction that its proof (in a formal calculus) could be readily obtained. How can the diagram serve these functions, and why are such conclusions more "direct" than the formal textbook proofs employing propositional statements?

Inference 1 of course is an instance of the whole being equal to the sum of its parts. The conclusion does not depend on the fact that ABC is a triangle, or even that the diagram consists solely of linear elements; an arbitrary shape containing a dividing contour would yield the analogous conclusion. A process that spreads "activation" through bounded areas (such as the "coloring" method proposed by Ullman 1984) could discover the validity of Inference 1.

On the other hand, proving Inference 1 deductively for the general case is a complicated procedure. Figure 4.1 is a planar graph (Harary 1969) that can be specified propositionally by listing the nodes *(A, B, C, D)* and the edges *(AB, BD, DC, CA, AD)*. From this specification alone it is possible to show that the graph has exactly three *meshes*[1]—*ABDA*, *DCAD*, and *ABDCA*—of which only *ABDCA* would remain if the edge *AD* were removed. This is the nonmetric analog of the addition of areas property, yet, to extract the mesh structure from the list of nodes and edges by serial computation is neither straightforward nor perspicuous. The algorithm of Tarjan (1971) for (essentially) this task, which he proved to be within a constant factor of optimal in efficiency, is expressed as some 500 lines of high-level code and more than 130 pages of explanation.[2]

In contrast to Inference 1, Inference 2 does depend on certain metric properties of the diagram, such as the recognition of right angles and the ratios of lengths of sides. For the human observer, the precision of the drawing does not need to be great. As noted earlier, the metric precision in the specification of our construction and retrieval processes has been limited to "qualitative" values; they need to be able to distinguish right angles from nonright angles, identify equivalent lengths of line segments, and make a few other distinctions. This seems to be appropriate as a model of human use of metric information here and in other problem solving tasks (de Kleer and Brown 1984). A slight sloppiness in drawing the perpendicular *AD* so that the angle *BD*A is, say, 87 degrees, does not interfere with a human's use of a diagram, and a similar coarseness of measurement is all that is available in our model. Similarly, a person does not need to know the actual values of the lengths of segments, or even of their ratios, they merely must "look" appropriate. We notice "by inspection," and our model would "notice" by process *comparative*

[1]A *mesh* of a planar graph is defined as a closed, connected sequence of edges, in which no edge appears more than once and no node is visited more than once except to return to the starting node, and which constitutes the boundary of a region of the plane that contains no other edges (Harary 1969). A mesh can equivalently be defined in terms of its nodes.

[2]This was called to my attention by David West.

length, that the order of the sides of DCA by length is $AD < DC < CA$, and the order of the sides of DAB by length is $BD < DA < AB$. We can then notice "by inspection," and our model would "notice" by systematic search, that the corresponding pairs of sides have the same ordering by length: AD is longer than BD, DC is longer than DA, and CA longer than AB. Why are these the things that we focus on, rather than any of a number of other facts, such as that AB is shorter than CA? One possibility is that the process is one of exhaustive search over all possible comparisons of certain primitive types (such as line segment length comparisons), with uninteresting observations filtered out as they are generated. Another possibility is that heuristics are used to prune such a search.

4.5 Relation of the Model to Other Proposals

Johnson-Laird (1983) described a method for making inferences without recourse to a rule-based proof procedure. His method uses what he calls *mental models.* These are finite representations of the content of propositions, and are similar to *models* in the sense used in logic, as introduced by Tarski, except for the finiteness restriction. From propositions are constructed finite sets of individuals that are true interpretations of the propositional content. The result of the construction of such a model is a structure which is a true interpretation of other propositions that could be validly inferred from the original propositions by rule-based deduction. Johnson-Laird presents evidence that humans use such finitary models as a vehicle for inference. The "images" employed in the work presented here are similar in function to Johnson-Laird's "mental models" (rather than what he calls "images"), but employ more elaborate constraints that reflect the structure of two-dimensional space rather than just the logical connectives and quantifiers.

Kosslyn and Shwartz (1977) devised a model of imagery that bears some similarity to our proposal, in that it employed a "surface representation" of images that is consistent with our definition of drawing. Their model and ours differ in several ways, however. The major difference is that we have restricted our consideration to the use of a few primitive object types (lines, etc.), combined into larger types by construction processes. Kosslyn and Shwartz deal with more complex objects, such as representations of chairs and cars, that are defined as specific arrays of pixels that can be scaled and translated. A second difference is our explicit consideration of mechanisms of spatial inference methods, and their role in proposing and disposing of hypotheses. Finally, our model is not motivated by specific psychological facts. Theirs, however, attempted to incorporate many features, such as loss of resolution toward the boundaries, that have not been addressed here.

Funt (1977 1981) constructed a model that reasons with "images." In that system, two dimensional objects were represented as on/off patterns of "cells" on a "retina." Processes were able to detect instabilities of balance and perform a systematic modification of the images that represented movement of the objects, for example by rotating them about a point. Collisions could be detected as the result of movements and from these and ancillary assumptions new instabilities could arise. Inferences were then made by playing out a simulation of the movements of the objects represented on the retina. In our terminology, this method is a nonproof-procedural IKR that operates by propagation of constraints. Rather than derive an analytic expression for trajectories, or construct a proof that given initial conditions would lead to certain results, local rules of geometric relations were used to propagate constraints and these constraints then forced the display of conclusions.

Larkin and Simon (1987) describe methods that use "diagrammatic representations" in a problem-solving situation. They illustrate the method with a mechanics problem (involving weights and pulleys) and a geometry problem (involving congruent triangles). They contrast the diagrammatic representation and associated processes with a "sentential representation" of the same problems, showing how the former enjoys decided computational advantages over the latter. The task set for their system is the discovery of a derivation, in the form of an appropriate sequence of production rule applications, of an unknown force ratio, in the mechanics problem case, and of a proof of congruency in the geometry case. The diagrams are used as heuristics in the search for derivations, in the spirit of the Geometry Machine, as discussed above in Section 4.4. In the context of this task, the value of the diagrammatic representation follows from its significant reduction, in comparison to the sentential representation, of the amount of search required to find a derivation. For example, in diagrammatic representations objects are indexed by location and attention moves from one object to adjacent objects; the search order turns out to be substantially better than the essentially exhaustive, unguided order which is all that is offered by the sentential representation. In addition, diagrammatic representations were found to simplify the matching of production rule antecedents to problem features because the diagrams coded the features directly whereas sentential representations hid these features. Since they were requiring the discovery of derivations, rather than simply the "observation" of correct conclusions, Larkin and Simon characterized the major advantages of diagrams as reduction of search and speedup of recognition, stating (p. 71) "...the differential effects on inference appear to be less strong." However, much of what I have been calling inference takes place in their model in the step of producing their "perceptually enhanced data structure," which is a representation that makes "explicit" certain perceptually salient elements, such as alternate interior angles, that are only implicit in the original sentential problem description. Thus their analysis is essentially in agreement with mine and our models have complementary strengths: mine generalizes the methods of diagram construction and retrieval, and theirs interfaces diagrams with rule-based inference.

Related suggestions have been made in the context of knowledge representations that are not explicitly image inspired. I have mentioned the inheritance of properties inference mechanism that is employed in frame-based representation schemes, and acknowledged the relation to our concept of nonproof-procedure inference methods, Elliot (1965), Brown (1970), and Lindsay (1973), employed generalizations of this notion that used properties other than the transitivity of set inclusion. Constraint propagation methods of problem solving have been employed extensively in artificial intelligence, for example, de Kleer (1979) and Steele and Sussman (1978). The truth maintenance system proposal of Doyle (de Kleer, 1984; Doyle 1979) addresses related issues from a different perspective (maintaining a consistent set of beliefs), but one that is related to our suggested mechanisms for proposing and disposing of conjectures. These and other proposals are compatible with the model outlined in this chapter, and offer possible avenues for integrating imagery and more traditional views of knowledge representation in fruitful ways.

There is an extensive literature on machine vision (Brady 1982; Rosenfeld and Kak 1976) that deals with systems that attempt to transform digitized physical images into propositional descriptions of "scenes" so that deductions may be made about the *content* of the original images.

The output from such "scene analysis" is typically expressed in propositional form: *there is a tank at coordinates (3, 5), this is a view of a 3/8 inch hex nut from 45 degree perspective,* and so forth. This is the form of knowledge needed for search and rule-based deduction by artificial intelligence programs that plan (Wilkins, 1984) or problem solve (Nilsson 1980), for example. Scene analysis, including object recognition, is the process of constructing complex retrieval processes and using them in goal-directed contexts, as discussed in Section 4.4. Ullman (1984) has called such processes *visual routines* and envisions a model of perceptual recognition that constructs complex visual routines from a set of elementary ones. My primitive retrieval processes would presumably comprise a proper subset of the elementary visual routines that Ullman seeks.

4.6 Discussion

The conventional lay wisdom is that knowledge representations can be divided into two distinct types. The two are imagery and language, corresponding to two phenomenologically distinct objects of introspection. Various suggestions have been put forth in the scientific literature to clarify this fundamental distinction. Often, visual imagery is identified with pictorial representations, and language with descriptional representations. Descriptionalists such as Pylyshyn (1980) hold specifically that all knowledge can be represented descriptionally. Apparently no one holds that the pictorial subsumes the descriptional; that battle has been conceded. Thus the question usually addressed is whether visual imagery employs pictorial representations that cannot be fully reduced to descriptions (see Block 1981, pp. 1-16).

The distinction between pictorial and descriptional representations has proven to be difficult to characterize. One popular approach is to identify pictorial with analog and descriptional with digital (see Kosslyn et al. 1979; also Pylyshyn, 1981). The analog/digital contrast is often in turn taken to be a contrast between continuous and discrete representations. Some writers, myself included, feel that this fails to capture the original imagery/propositional distinction.

Dretske (1981) suggests retaining the "analog-digital" terminology, but glosses it differently: a signal (representational element or notation) carries information that "property s has value F" in *digital* form if and only if the signal carries no additional information about property s; if the signal carries additional information, then by definition it carries information in *analog* form. Under these definitions, knowledge represented propositionally, e.g., as a statement in first-order logic, represents *only* what is stated explicitly; all other information must be derived by use of a separate set of structural relations among FOL statements, usually in the form of axioms, variable bindings, and rules of inference. On the other hand, a picture of a situation conveys additional information since the representation *must* make some additional things explicit in order to be a picture. To use Dretske's example (p. 137), "The cup has coffee in it" carries no information about how much coffee, how dark it is, or the shape of the cup's handle, whereas a picture of the situation must contain some such additional information. As in my discussion, Dretske's analysis and the intuitions on which it is based emphasize inference as the essential distinction between pictorial and descriptional representations.

A second influential analysis of knowledge representation issues comes to what I take to be the same conclusion. Palmer (1978) proposes a hierarchy of types of "isomorphism" between representation and that which is represented. Physical isomorphisms preserve information by virtue of representing relations that are *identical* to the relations represented. Thus a physical model of a natural terrain preserves the spatial relations of the represented terrain with the very same relations, including for example elevation, but on a smaller scale. Functional isomorphisms, on the other hand, preserve information by representing relations that have the same (algebraic) structure as the relations represented. Thus the elevations of a natural terrain may be represented as colors on a map of the terrain, provided the colors are interpreted appropriately (as an ordered set) and mapped so as to preserve the order of the physical elevations of the terrain. Thus physical models are a proper subset of functional models. Palmer proposes introducing a class of isomorphisms between physical and functional, which he calls natural isomorphisms. In a natural isomorphism, the representation of preserved relations need not be by means of *identical* relations, as in physical isomorphism, hence not all natural isomorphisms are physical isomorphisms. On the other hand, not just any identically structured set of relations qualify. In a natural isomorphism, the representing constructs have *inherent constraints* (Palmer's term); that is, there is a structure imposed on the representing objects that limits the ways in which they may relate. If these inherent constraints preserve the relations of the represented world, we have a natural isomorphism.

Palmer identifies natural (including physical) isomorphisms with analog (including pictorial) representations, and functional but nonnatural isomorphisms with propositional representations. Propositional representations are thus less restricted, as we normally suppose, because the structure of the representing world is extrinsic to it, that is it may be arbitrarily imposed, say in the form of rules of deduction. However, analog (including pictorial) representations employ representations that have inherent (nonarbitrary, unalterable) structure ("inherent constraints") that allow us to do away with deduction rules. This limits their applicability, but at the same time increases their power by reducing the computational complexity of inference (and easing the frame problem). The analysis in this chapter, I believe, illustrates how this can be done with a limited class of representation problems, and captures what is common to the Dretske and Palmer definitions.

4.7 Conclusion: Toward a Functional Theory of Imagery

This chapter has proposed a characterization of mental visual imagery that distinguishes that class of knowledge representations from representations based on logical calculi, which are the common currency of artificial intelligence problem-solving programs and expert systems. The proposed knowledge representations may be descriptional and discrete or they may not; they are specified in terms of the mechanism of inference they support. Even in-principle wholly descriptional knowledge representations such as diagrams have important inference support roles that transcend proposition-plus-proof procedure representations.

The theory defines a set of primitively recognizable features of the class of representation structures, rules for construction that maintain specified values of specified features, and strategies for searching the representation structure for feature values. An example of such a theory has been presented. Each of its components could acquire independent empirical and logical support. The theory does not depend upon knowing whether the substrate of images is neural or electronic.

There are many properties of drawings that are not encompassed by this model; some of them may prove amenable to generalizations of its methods. For example, no use was made of area information. By adding retrieval processes that could compute this metric property, conclusions about equality of area would be possible. Thus certain proofs of the Pythagorean Theorem could be represented and "understood," perhaps even discovered, with such an extension. Textured and colored regions could also be represented by allowing regions to be filled with points of various "colors" or qualities (in addition to "marks") at various settings of the covering resolution. Inferences about intersections of regions would then be available in a nondeductive, constraint generated manner. Inferences about, say, the effects of combining colors would require altogether new sorts of construction and retrieval processes. While I have suggested that the model discussed captures the essential method of the inferential work of imagery, the model presented is limited to very simple, though important, instances—diagrams. Images of more customary experience have not been addressed here. Obviously, extending these notions to percepts/images of complex familiar objects such as faces, animals, and scenes is not straightforward, but the processes dealing with spatial relations here outlined should remain intact and unaffected by the addition of other abilities.

Finally, a word about the status of this work as a psychological model is in order. None of this work has made use of or been tested by experimental methods; it is empirical only in the broad sense of being guided by obvious facts of common sense psychology. It is of relevance to psychological theory, however, in that it addresses a general problem, the frame problem, and an important psychological phenomenon, imagery, for which any theory of natural intelligence must offer some account. One may view perception as offering a solution to the frame problem by allowing "the world" to make appropriate inferences which are then "read" by the brain/mind. If imagery is conceived as a percept-like representation that is evoked in the absence of appropriate sensory input, as the functional equivalence hypothesis of Finke and Shepard has it, then the present model offers an account of how the natural constraints of world situations may be employed to solve the frame problem cognitively.

Acknowledgments

The author wishes to thank Manfred Kochen, David West, and Paul Resnick for their discussions of the ideas presented here and for their valuable comments on this chapter.

References

Amarel, S. 1968. On the Representation of Problems of Reasoning about Actions. In *Machine Intelligence 3,* ed. D. Michie, 131–171. New York: Elsevier.

Bartlett, F. C. 1932. *Remembering: A Study In Experimental and Social Psychology.* London: Cambridge University Press.

Block, N. 1981. *Imagery.* Cambridge, Mass.: The MIT Press.

Bobrow, D. G. 1975. Dimensions of Representation. In *Representation and Understanding,* ed. D. G. Bobrow and A. Collins, 1–34. New York: Academic Press.

Bower, G. H. 1972. Mental Imagery and Associative Learning. In *Cognition Learning and Memory,* ed. L. W. Gregg. New York: Wiley.

Brachman, R. J. 1979. On the Epistemological Status of Semantic Networks. In *Associative Frameworks—the Representation and Use of Knowledge in Computers,* ed. N. V. Findler. New York: Academic Press.

Brachman, R. J. and Levesque. H.. 1985. *Readings in Knowledge Representation.* Los Altos. Calif.: Morgan Kaufmann.

Brady, M. 1982. Computational Approaches to Image Understanding. *Computing Surveys* 14: 3–71.

Brown, J. S. 1970. A Symbiotic Theory Formation System. Ph.D. diss., The University of Michigan, Ann Arbor.

Chase, W. G., and Simon, H. A. 1973. Perception in Chess. *Cognitive Psychology* 4: 55–81.

de Kleer, J. 1979. Causal and Teleological Reasoning in Circuit Recognition. Technical Report No. Al-TR-529, Massachusetts Institute of Technology Artificial Intelligence Laboratory, Cambridge, Mass.

de Kleer, J. 1984. Choices without Backtracking. In *Proceedings of the Third National Conference on Artificial Intelligence,* 79–85. Menlo Park, Calif.: American Association for Artificial Intelligence.

de Kleer, J., and Brown, J. S. 1984. A Qualitative Physics Based on Confluences. In *Qualitative Reasoning About Physical Systems,* ed. D. G. Bobrow, 743. Amsterdam: Elsevier.

Dennett, D. C. 1981a. The Nature of Images and the Introspective Trap. In *Imagery,* ed. N. Block, 51–61. Cambridge. Mass.: The MIT Press.

Dennett, D. C. 1981b. Two Approaches To Mental Imagery. In *Imagery,* 87-107, ed. N. Block. Cambridge. Mass.: The MIT Press.

Doyle, J. 1979. A Truth Maintenance System. *Artificial Intelligence* 12: 231–272.

Dretske, F. L. 1981. *Knowledge and the Flow of Information.* Cambridge, Mass.: The MIT Press.

Elliott, R. W. 1965. A Model for A Fact Retrieval System. Ph.D. diss., The University of Texas, Austin, Tex.

Evans, G. W. 1980. Environmental Cognition. *Psychological Bulletin,* 259–285.

Fahlman, S. E. 1979. *NETL: A System For Representing and Using Real World Knowledge.* Cambridge. Mass.: The MIT Press.

Fahlman, S. E. 1984. Representing Implicit Knowledge. In *Parallel Models of Associative Memory,* ed. G. E. Hinton and J. A. Anderson, 145–159. Hillsdale, N.J.: Lawrence Erlbaum.

Finke, R. A. and Shepard, R. N. 1986. Visual Functions of Mental Imagery. In *Handbook of Perception and Human Performance,* Volume 11, ed. K. R. Boff, L. Kaufman, and J. P. Thomas. New York: John Wiley and Sons.

Fodor, J. A. 1981. Imagistic Representation. In *Imagery,* ed. N. Block, 63–86. Cambridge, Mass.: The MIT Press.

Forbus, K. 1984. Qualitative Process Theory. In *Qualitative Reasoning about Physical Systems,* ed. D. G. Bobrow, 85–168. Amsterdam: Elsevier.

Funt, B. V. 1977. Whisper: a Problem-Solving System Utilizing Diagrams and a Parallel Processing Retina. In Proceedings of the Fifth International Joint Conference on Artificial Intelligence, 459–464. Pittsburgh: Carnegie Mellon University.

Gelernter, H. 1959. Realization of a Geometry Theorem-Proving Machine. In *Computers and Thought,* ed. E. A. Feigenbaum and J. Feldman, 134–152. New York: McGraw Hill.

Gelernter, H., Hansen, J. R., and Loveland, D. W. 1960. Empirical Explorations of the Geometry Theorem Proving Machine. In *Computers and Thought,* ed. E. A. Feigenbaum and J. Feldman, 153–163. New York: McGraw Hill.

Gibson, J. 1979. *The Ecological Approach to Visual Perception.* Boston: Houghton Mifflin.

Gladwin, T. 1970. *East Is a Big Bird.* Cambridge, Mass: Harvard University Press.

Harary, F. 1969. *Graph Theory.* Reading, Mass.: Addison-Wesley.

Haugeland, J. 1985. *Artificial Intelligence: The Very Idea.* Cambridge, Mass.: The MIT Press.

Huttenlocher, J. 1968. Constructing Spatial Images: a Strategy In Reasoning. *Psychological Review* 75: 550–560.

Johnson-Laird, P. N. 1983. *Mental Models: Toward a Cognitive Science of Language, Inference, and Consciousness.* Cambridge, Mass: Harvard University Press.

Kosslyn, S. M. 1975. Information Representation in Visual Images. *Cognitive Psychology* 7: 341–370.

Kosslyn, S. M. 1980. *Images and Mind.* Cambridge, Mass: Harvard University Press.

Kosslyn, S. M. , Pinker, S., Smith, G. E., and Shwantz, S. P. 1979. On the Demystification Of Mental Imagery. In *Imagery,* ed. N. Block, 131–150. Cambridge. Mass.: The MIT Press.

Kosslyn, S. M. , and Pomerantz. I.R. 1977. Imagery. Propositions. and the Form of Internal Representations. *Cognitive Psychology* 9: 52–76.

Kosslyn, S. M. , and Shwanz. S. P. 1977. A Simulation Of Visual Imagery. *Cognitive Science* 1: 265–295.

Larkin, J., and Simon, H.A. 1987. Why A Diagram Is Sometimes Worth Ten Thousand Words. *Cognitive Science* 10: 65–100.

Lenat, D. 1976. An Artificial Intelligence Approach to Discovery in Mathematics as Heuristic Search. Technical Report CS-76-57, Department of Computer Science, Stanford Univ., Stanford, Calif.

Lindsay, R. K. 1961. Toward the Development of Machines Which Comprehend. Ph.D. diss., Carnegie-Mellon University, Pittsburgh, Penn.

Lindsay, R. K. 1963. Inferential Memory as the Basis of Machines Which Understand Natural Language. In *Computers and Thought,* ed. E A. Feigenbaum and J. Feldman, 217–233. New York: McGraw-Hill.

Lindsay, R. K. 1973. In Defense of Ad Hoc Systems. In *Computer Models of Thought and Language,* ed. R. Schank and K. Colby, 372–395. San Francisco: W. H. Freeman.

McCarthy, J. and Hayes, P. 1969. Some Philosophical Problems from the Standpoint of Artificial Intelligence. In *Machine Intelligence.* Volume 4, ed. B. Melzer and D. Michie. Edinburgh: Edinburgh University Press.

Nilsson, N. 1980. *Principles of Artificial Intelligence.* Palo Alto, Calif.: Tioga Press.

Paivio, A. 1971. *Imagery and Verbal Processes.* New York: Holt.

Palmer, S. 1978. Aspects of Representation. In *Computing and Categorization,* ed. E. Rosch and B. B. Lloyd, 259–303. Hillsdale, NJ: Earlbaum.

Posner, M. I. and Keele, S. W. 1967. Decay of Visual Information from a Single Letter. *Science* 158: 137–139.

Pylyshyn, Z. W. 1980. Computation and Cognition: Issues in the Foundations of Cognitive Science. *The Behavioral and Brain Sciences* 3: 111–133.

Pylyshyn, Z. W. 1981. The Imagery Debate: Analogue Media Versus Tacit Knowledge. *Psychological Review* 88: 16–45.

Quillian, R. 1968. Semantic Memory. In *Semantic Information Processing,* ed. M. Minsky, 227–270. Cambridge. Mass.: The MIT Press.

Raphael, B. 1971. The Frame Problem in Problem-Solving Systems. In *Artificial Intelligence and Heuristic Programming,* ed. N. V. Findler and B. Meltzer. Edinburgh: Edinburgh University Press.

Reiter, R. 1987. Nonmonotonic Reasoning. In *Annual Review of Computer Science.* Palo Alto, Calif.: Annual Reviews. Inc.

Rock, I. 1983. *The Logic of Perception.* Cambridge, Mass: The MIT Press.

Rosenfeld, A. and Kak, A. C. 1976. *Digital Picture Processing.* New York: Academic Press.

Shepard, R. N. 1973. Form, Formation, and Transformation of Internal Representations. In *Contemporary Issues in Cognitive Psychology: The Loyola Symposium,* ed. R. L. Solso. Washington. D.C.: V. H. Winston and Sons.

Shepard, R. N. 1978. The Mental Image. *American Psychologist* 3: 123–137.

Steele, G. L., and Sussman. G. L. 1978. *Constraints.* Cambridge, Mass.: Massachusetts Institute of Technology Artificial Intelligence Laboratory. AIM-502.

Tarjan, R. E. 1971. An Efficient Planarity Algorithm. Technical Report STAN-CS-244-71, Stanford University, Stanford, Calif.

Ullman, S. 1984. Visual Routines. *Cognition* 18: 97–159.

Wilkins, D. E. 1984. Domain-Independent Planning: Representation and Plan Generation. *Artificial Intelligence* 22: 69–301.

Woodworth, R. S. 1938. *Experimental Psychology.* New York: Holt.

5 Capturing the Dynamics of Conceptual Change in Science

Nancy J. Nersessian
Georgia Institute of Technology

The Scene: August 19, 1861, a cottage in Galloway, Scotland

The young Clerk Maxwell is sitting in a garden deep in thought. On the table before him there is a sheet of paper on which he sketches various pictures of lines and circles and writes equations.

The Question

What is he thinking? Is he trying to cook up a model to go with the equations he has derived already by induction from the experimental data and electrical considerations alone? Is he concerned that his mathematical results are not quite right and so is thinking how to fudge his analysis to make it look right in terms of the model? Is he searching for a way to make the notion of continuous transmission of actions in an electromagnetic 'field' meaningful? And if so, what resources is he drawing upon? What is he doing?

The Problem

Do we have the means to understand what Maxwell is doing? What scientists like him are doing when they are creating new conceptions? Can we hope to fathom the creative processes through which scientists articulate something quite new from the record they leave behind? Or are these processes so mysterious that we are wasting our time by trying to understand them? And if we could, what possible profit could such understanding yield for the philosopher of science? The historian of science? Others?

The Path to Solution

What I hope to persuade the reader is that we can formulate a more rigorous analysis of the creative processes of scientific discovery and give more satisfactory answers to long-standing, unresolved puzzles about the nature of conceptual change in science than we have now by combining two things that are usually kept apart. One is fine-structure examinations of the theoretical and experimental practices of scientists who have created major changes in scientific theory. The other is what we have been learning about the cognitive abilities and limitations of human beings generally. Creative processes are extended and dynamical, and as such we can never hope to capture them fully. But by expanding the scope of the data and techniques allowed into the analysis we can understand more than traditional approaches have permitted so far.

Recent developments in psychology have opened the possibility of understanding what philosophers and historians have been calling "conceptual change" in a different and deeper way. Through a combination of new experimental techniques and computer modeling, new theories about human cognitive functioning have emerged in the areas of representation, problem solving, and judgment. An interdisciplinary field of cognitive science has recently formed—a loose confederation of cognitive psychology, artificial intelligence, cognitive neurology, linguistics, and philosophy. It offers analyses and techniques which, if used with proper respect for their scope and their limitations, can help us develop and test models of how conceptual change takes place in science.

In this chapter I set myself the following aims:

- to propose a fresh method of analysis
- to recast the requirements of a theory of conceptual change in science
- to draw on new material from a heuristically fertile case study of major conceptual change in science
- to analyze some processes of conceptual change—analogical and imagistic reasoning and thought experiments and limiting case analyses
- to examine these in light of some work in cognitive science
- to argue, finally, and more generally, for what philosophers and historians of science and cognitive scientists might gain from further application of the proposed method of analysis.

5.1 What Is "Cognitive-Historical" Analysis

"Cognitive-historical" analysis in the sense employed here is not quite the same as what historians of science do in their fine-structure historical examinations of the representational and problem-solving practices scientists have employed to create new scientific representations of phenomena Rather, it attempts to enrich these further by means of investigations of ordinary human representational and problem-solving practices carried out by the sciences of cognition. The underlying presupposition is that the problem-solving strategies scientists have invented and the representational practices they have developed over the course of the history of science are very sophisticated and refined outgrowths of ordinary reasoning and representational processes. Thus, the method combines case studies of actual scientific practices with the analytical tools and theories of the cognitive sciences to create a new, comprehensive theory of how conceptual structures are constructed and changed in science. The historical dimension of the method has its origins in the belief that to understand scientific change the philosophy of science must come to grips with the historical processes of knowledge development and change. This is the main lesson we should have learned from the "historicist" critics of positivism. Equally as important as problems concerning the rationality of acceptance—which occupy most philosophers concerned with scientific change—are problems about the construction and the communication of new representational structures. The challenging methodological problem is: how can we find a way to use the history of scientific knowledge practices as the basis from which to develop a theory of scientific change?

The cognitive dimension of the method reflects the view that our understanding of scientific knowledge practices needs to be psychologically realistic. Putting it baldly, creative scientists are not only exceptionally gifted human beings— they are also human beings with a biological and social make-up like all of us. In a fundamental sense, science is one product of the interaction of the human mind with the world and with other humans. We need to find out how human cognitive abilities and limitations constrain scientific theorizing and this cannot be determined a priori. This point is not completely foreign to philosophers. It fits into a tradition of psychological epistemology beginning with Locke and Hume and making its most recent appearance with the call of Quine for a "naturalized epistemology." Why did earlier "psychologizing" endeavors fail to succeed? The main reason was their reliance on inadequate empiricist/behaviorist psychological theories. The development of cognitive psychology has paved the way for a much more fruitful synthesis of psychology and epistemology. Suggestions for how to frame such a synthesis are to be found, for example, in the work of Alvin Goldman (1986). Insights from cognitive psychology are beginning to make their way into investigations of scientific reasoning (See, e.g., Giere 1988; Gooding 1990; Gorman and Carlson 1989; Langley et al. 1987; Thagard 1988; and Tweney 1985) What is needed now is to integrate these with the historical findings about the representational and problem-solving practices that have actually brought about major scientific changes.[1]

Philosophers this century have mostly been working under the assumption that analysis of science takes place with two contexts: justification and discovery. The former is traditionally within the province of philosophers; the latter, of historians and psychologists. Cognitive-historical analysis takes place in a new context—that of development—which is the province of all three. The context of development[2] is the domain for inquiry into the processes through which a vague speculation gets articulated into a new scientific theory, gets communicated to other scientists, and comes to replace existing representations of a domain. These processes take place over long periods of time, are dynamical in nature, and are embedded in social contexts.

This new context of development, in actuality, was opened up by the work of Hanson, Kuhn, and Feyerabend nearly 30 years ago, but they lacked the analytical tools to pursue it in depth. True, they attempted to integrate insights from psychology into their analyses. However, cognitive psychology, in the form of the "new look" psychology of Bruner and others, was in its infancy, whereas Gestalt psychology offered no understanding of the processes underlying the "gestalt switch." Since their vision predated the kind of psychological theory that would have helped them better express it, it would be unfair to fault them for not completing what they had begun. It is, however, important to see the continuing repercussions of the inadequate insights they did use.

First, drawing from these psychological theories led to an unfortunate identification of knowledge change with hypothesized aspects of visual

[1]Giere (1988) argues against a role for history of science in a cognitive theory of science. His main point is that historians of science have - by and large - not done the kind of analysis of the scientific record that a cognitive theory requires. While there are notable exceptions, such as Holmes (1985), he is correct on this point. What I am arguing here is that the historical record, itself, does contain material of great importance to a cognitive theory of science. It contains much information on about the cognitive activity of scientists over the history of science.

[2]I owe the name, "context of development," to Richard Grandy.

perception. Second, and, more importantly, the metaphor of the "gestalt switch" led them astray in a way that has had deeper and more lasting consequences. The metaphor does not support the extended nature of the conceptual changes that have actually taken place in science.[3] Thus, while calling for an historicized epistemology, Kuhn's and Feyerabend's own historical analyses offered in support of the "incommensurability" hypothesis were decidedly nonhistorical in the following sense. By emphasizing the endpoints of a conceptual change, e.g., Newtonian mechanics and relativistic mechanics, the change of gestalt was made to appear artificially abrupt and discontinuous. However, historically we did not get to relativity without at least passing through electromagnetism and the theory of electrons; and this developmental process is central to understanding such questions as the nature of the relationship—or reason for lack of relationship—between, e.g., the different concepts called by the name "mass" in each theory. My earlier study of the construction of the concept of electromagnetic field, *Faraday to Einstein: Constructing Meaning in Scientific Theories* (Nersessian 1984), was an attempt to show how incorporating the dimension of development into the analysis gives a quite different picture of the nature of meaning change in science.

Significantly, although Kuhn does talk about discovery as an "extended process" (Kuhn 1965, p. 45ff) and, in his role as historian of science, has provided detailed examinations of such processes, in his role as philosopher of science he identifies conceptual change with "the last act," when "the pieces fall together" (Kuhn 1987).[4] Thus portrayed, conceptual change appears to be something that happens to scientists rather than the outcome of an extended period of construction by scientists. A "change of gestalt" may be an apt way of characterizing this last point in the process, but focusing exclusively on that point has—contrary to Kuhn's aim—provided a misleading portrayal of conceptual change; has reinforced the widespread view that the processes of change are mysterious and unanalyzable; and has blocked the very possibility of investigating how precisely the new gestalt is related to its predecessors. In short, the metaphor has blocked development of the historicized epistemology being advocated.

[3]Holmes (1985, pp. 119–120) argues in a similar vein.

[4]Cohen (1990) contains an interesting discussion of the "two Kuhns–the philosopher of science and the historian of science and of the repercussions of the split for his analysis of the Scientific Revolution of the 17th century.

The ultimate goal of the cognitive-historical method is to be able to reconstruct scientific thinking by means of cognitive theories. When, and if, we reach that point, we may decide to call the method "cognitive analysis of science." However, at present, cognitive theories are largely uninformed by scientific representational and problem-solving practices, making the fit between cognitive theories and scientific practices something that still needs to be determined.[5] Cognitive-historical analysis is reflexive. It uses cognitive theories to the extent that they help interpret the historical cases—at the same time it tests to what extent current theories of cognitive processes can be applied to scientific thinking and indicates along what lines these theories need extension, refinement, and revision. In other words, the method is a type of bootstrapping procedure commonly used in science.

5.2 What Would a Cognitive Theory of Conceptual Change in Science Look Like?

5.2.1 Background

Much philosophical energy this century has been spent on the problem of conceptual change in science. The major changes in physical theory early in the century thrust the problem of how to understand the seemingly radical reconceptualizations they offered into the spotlight for scientists, historians, and philosophers alike. As we all know, the comforting picture of conceptual change as continuous and cumulative offered by logical positivism itself suffered a revolutionary upheaval in the mid-1960s. The critics of positivism argued that major changes in science are best characterized as "revolutions": they involve overthrow and replacement of the reigning conceptual system with one that is "incommensurable" with it. The infamous "problem of incommensurability of meaning" dominated the literature for over a decade. Philosophers have by and large abandoned this topic. Those who work on scientific change tend now to focus on the problem of rational choice between competing theories. This shift in focus did not, however, come from a sense of having a satisfactory solution to the infamous problem, but more from a sense of frustration that the discussion and arguments had

[5] Notable exceptions are Clement (1983), Langley et al. (1987), McCloskey (1983), Qin and Simon (1990), and Wiser and Carey (1983).

become increasingly sterile.

The crux of the original problem, however, is still with us. How, if in any manner at all, are successive scientific conceptualizations of a domain related to one another? The instinctive response of critics of incommensurability has always been that even though they are not simply extensions, the new conceptual structures must somehow grow out of the old. The view of knowledge change as a series of unconnected gestalt switches has a high intuitive implausibility. In recasting the problem of conceptual change. the cognitive-historical method furnishes the means through which to turn these intuitions into solid analyses.

In cognitive-historical analysis the problem of conceptual change appears as follows. It is the problem of understanding how it is that scientists combine their human cognitive abilities with the conceptual resources available to them as members of scientific communities and wider social contexts to create and communicate new scientific representations of a domain. For example, the problem posed in the opening scene becomes that of understanding how Maxwell joins his human cognitive endowment with the conceptual resources of a Cambridge mathematical physicist living in Victorian England to construct and communicate a field representation of electromagnetic forces. Admittedly, this is a quite complex problem and we are only beginning to have the means to attack it. Nevertheless, I shall show in some detail that the cognitive-historical approach offers more possibility of achieving a solution than any we have yet considered.

Where the traditional philosophical approach views conceptual change as static and a historical, cognitive-historical analysis is able to handle the dynamic and historical process that it is. Customarily, conceptual change is taken to consist of the replacement of one linguistic system by another, and understanding conceptual change requires analyzing the logical relationships between propositions in the two systems. In a cognitive theory conceptual change is to be understood in terms of the people who create and change their representations of nature and the practices they employ to do so. This opens the possibility of understanding how it is that scientists build on existing structures while creating genuine novelty. That is to say, a route is opened towards explaining the continuous and non-cumulative character of conceptual change that is amply supported by results of individual studies of scientific creativity undertaken by historians of science.

5.2.2 Outline of a Cognitive Theory of Conceptual Change

Further on in this chapter I will turn to an examination of the some of the processes of conceptual change. However, we need first to have some sense of how a full theory would look.

A scientific theory is a kind of representational system. Several forms of representation have been proposed by cognitive scientists. Although it is a point of some controversy as to whether there is any form of representation other than strings of symbols, I will be following an authoritative account by Johnson-Laird (1983) in assuming the existence of at least three: (1) "propositional" (strings of symbols such as "the cat is on the mat"), (2) "mental models" (structural analogs of real-world or imagined situations, such as a cat being on a mat or a unicorn being in the forest), and (3) "images" (a mental model from a specific perspective, such as looking down on the cat on the mat from above). I will also be assuming with him that even if at the level of encoding all representations are propositional, in reasoning and understanding people construct mental models of real and imaginary phenomena, events, situations, processes, etc. One value of having a mental models form of representation is that it can do considerable inferential work without the person having to actually compute inferences and can also narrow the scope of possible inferences. For example, moving an object immediately changes all of its spatial relationships and makes only specific ones possible. The hypothesis that we do such inferencing via mental models gains plausibility when we consider that, as biological organisms, we have had to adapt to a changing environment. In fact, AI researches have run into considerable problems handling the widespread effects of even small changes in knowledge representational systems that are represented propositionally.

To continue, in a cognitive theory of conceptual change, a scientific theory will, itself, be construed as a structure that picks out classes of models, which accords better with the semantic view of theories (van Fraassen 1980), than with the Carnapian view of a theory as linguistic framework. Thinking about and in terms of a theory necessitates the construction of mental models. While scientific concepts may be encoded propositionally, understanding them involves interpretation, i.e., the construction of a mental model of the entities or processes they represent. Thus, what philosophers have been calling "meaning" and "reference," i.e., the interplay between words, minds, and the world, are, on this view, mediated by the construction of mental models that relate to the world in specified ways.

Like science itself, a theory of conceptual change in science needs to provide both descriptive and explanatory accounts of the phenomena. These dimensions of the theory will here be called, respectively, the "kinematics" and "dynamics" of conceptual change. Kinematics is concerned with problems of how to represent change, and dynamics with the processes through which change is created.

The Kinematics of Change Any analysis of how to represent conceptual change in science must be solidly informed by the actual representational practices scientists use in developing and changing conceptual systems. Examinations of the conceptual changes that have been part of "scientific revolutions" yield the following insights. New concepts are created, such as "spin" in quantum mechanics and existing ones disappear, such as "phlogiston" from chemistry. Some concepts in the new system, e.g., "mass" and "field" in relativity, are what can only be called "conceptual descendants" of existing ones. And, finally, some. such as "aether," while appearing to be eliminated, have significant aspects absorbed by other concepts, in this case "field" and "space-time."

If the situations of creation and disappearance were all we had to handle the problems would be far less complex. In that case, "conceptual change" could be characterized as the replacement of one concept or structure by another. Given the reality of descendants and absorption, though, in addition to representing change of conceptual systems, we need to be able to represent conceptual change at the level of individual concepts. Some philosopher have trouble countenancing what it could possibly mean for a concept to change its meaning. As I have argued in my book (Nersessian 1984), the failure of existing theories of meaning and meaning change even to allow for this possibility has led to many of the various conundrums associated with the so-called "problem of incommensurability of meaning." If, as has been traditionally held, concepts are represented by neatly bundled and individuated units, i.e., sets of necessary and sufficient conditions, only replacement, not change, is possible. Therefore, a different form of representation is needed to accommodate the data of change.

Psychological research on categorization supports the view that in many instances people do not represent concepts by means of sets of necessary and sufficient conditions (See, e.g., Rosch and Mervis 1978: Smith and Medin 1981; and Murphy and Cohen 1984). Examination of cases from the history of science also substantiates the view that for numerous scientific concepts it is not possible to specify a set of necessary and sufficient conditions that will take in all their historical usages—or even for a concept within a single theory. For example, I have shown in my book how there is no set of necessary and sufficient conditions defining electromagnetic field. Yet there is a traceable line of descent between the Faradayan and the Einsteinian concepts and a significant overlap in salient features between successive field concepts.

The question now is, can we assume that how scientists structure mental representations is reflected in their external representations? That is, does what they write give a clue to how they think? Psychological studies all start from the assumption that how people represent mentally is reflected in their use of language, and there is good reason to make the same assumption here. Since I have dealt with the kinematics of conceptual change extensively, though far from exhaustively, in my book and in a number of articles (Nersessian 1985, 1986, and in press(a)), I want the focus of this chapter to be its dynamics. We need to keep in mind, though, that the two problems are connected. In order to be complete a cognitive theory will have to determine how the historical data on the individual units of change—concepts—mesh with those from psychology and also with attempts at constructing psychologically realistic representational systems in artificial intelligence.

The Dynamics of Change By what processes are new scientific representations constructed? The prevailing view among philosophers is that the discovery processes are too mysterious to be understood. This view receives support from numerous stories of discovery through flashes of insight of geniuses, such a Kekulean dreams and Archimedean Eureka-experiences. What is omitted from such renderings are the periods of intense and often arduous thinking and, in some cases, experimental activity that precede such instantaneous discoveries. There again, the rendering of conceptual changes as "gestalt switches" reinforces the prevailing prejudice. Even Kuhn substitutes the phrase "exploitation by genius" for analysis of actual constructive processes when discussing how Galileo formed his concept of *pendulum* (Kuhn 1965, p.119). However, there is no inherent conflict between the view that discovery processes are creative and the view that they are reasoned. We need to give up the notion that creativity is an *act* and try to fathom it as a *process.*

Historical evidence supports the conviction that conceptual change in science is at heart a problem-solving process. While pragmatist philosophers, such as Dewey and Mead, and Popper have strongly defended this view of science, conceptual change has not been included in their analyses. Laudan (1977) does introduce conceptual problems into the realm of the scientist's concerns, but offers no account of the specific processes of conceptual change. I want to extend the conception of science as a problem-solving enterprise to include what has traditionally been called Conceptual change. New representations do not emerge fully grown from the heads of scientists but are constructed in response to specific problems by systematic use of heuristic procedures. Problem solving in science does differ from much of ordinary problem solving in that scientific problems are more complex, often less well-defined, and the solution not know in advance to anyone. A cognitive theory of conceptual change assumes the position long advocated by Herbert Simon that "the component processes, which when assembled make the mosaic of scientific discovery, are not qualitatively distinct from the processes that have been observed in simpler problem-solving situations" (Langley et al. 1981, p. 2). The fact that the computer Discovery programs implemented by Simon and his coworkers to model these processes thus far have tackled only the simplest of problem-solving heuristics, does not diminish the plausibility of this assumption. While the ability to model the problem-solving techniques that have brought about major conceptual changes seems a long way off, the type of cognitive analysis advocated here is within our grasp and is also a necessary preliminary to more realistic computer modeling.

The next section of this chapter will be devoted to examination of how a selection of problem-solving heuristics create new representations in science. Like in my earlier work, I will draw largely, though not exclusively, on historical data from the construction of the field representation of forces from Faraday to Einstein. These are very rich data and as yet have been far from exhausted in their fertility for our purposes. Extending my earlier work, I subject mostly novel data to fresh layers of analysis.

Throughout the history of scientific change we find recurrent use of

(1) analogical reasoning, (2) imagistic reasoning, (3) thought experiment, and (4) limiting case analysis. These are all modeling activities and, although they constitute a substantial portion of scientific method, none except analogy has received more than scant attention in the philosophical literature. The main problems philosophers have had in countenancing these as methods are that they are non-algorithmic and, even if used correctly, may lead to the wrong solution or to no solution. This very feature, however, makes them much more realistic from a historical point of view.

Limiting scientific method to the construction of inductive or deductive arguments has needlessly blocked our ability to make sense of many of the actual constructive practices of scientists. I call the particular subset of practices I will be discussing abstraction techniques. As we will see, they are strongly implicated in the explanation of how existing conceptual structures play a role in constructing new, and sometimes radically different, structures.

5.3 Abstraction Techniques and Conceptual Change

5.3.1 Background

There are numerous cases where analogy has played a central role in the construction of a new scientific concept: Newton's analogy between projectiles and the moon (universal gravitation), Darwin's analogy between selective breeding and reproduction in nature (natural selection), and the Rutherford-Bohr analogy between the structure of the solar system and that of the configuration of subatomic particles (atom) are among the more widely known. Also, although less well known, there are numerous cases that establish the prominence of reasoning from pictorial representations in the constructive practices of scientists who were struggling to articulate new conceptualizations. Such imagisitic representations have often been used in conjunction with analogical reasoning in science.

The major problem, as was noted above, is that while amply documented, these constructive practices have received scant attention from analysts of scientific method. Analogy has received the most attention, but the thrust of those analyses has been to conceive of it as a weak form of inductive argument. Following Campbell's (1920) lead, Hesse (1966) broke some ground in stressing the importance of analogy in giving meaning to new theoretical terms and in trying to formulate how it could be an inductive method without being a *logic,* i.e., algorithmic. Sellars (1965; See also, Brown, H. 1986) argued that, in general, analogical reasoning creates a bridge from existing to new conceptual frameworks through the mapping of relational structures from the old to the new.

What I intend to show here is that the insights of those who have recognized the importance and power of analogical reasoning in concept formation and change can be furthered by cognitive historical analysis. To do this I will go beyond my earlier analysis of the construction of the field representation of forces to discuss how it is that imagistic and analogical reasoning were used by Faraday and Maxwell in their constructive efforts and draw from current cognitive theories to show how it is possible that such reasoning generates new representations from existing ones.

Case Study: Faraday, Maxwell, and the Field This analysis will focus on Maxwell as we find him in our opening scene. Naturally, like all scientists Maxwell was working in a context. His analysis depends heavily, among other things, on a method he claims to have "poached" from William Thomson, on specific representations he takes from Faraday, and on a certain mathematical approach to analyzing continuum phenomena being developed at the time by Cambridge mathematical physicists.

The field representation of electromagnetic forces had its origin in vague speculations that there might be physical processes in the regions surrounding bodies and charges that could account for the apparent action of one body on another at some distance from it. Faraday was the first to attempt to construct a unified representation for the continuous transmission and interconversion of electric and magnetic actions. His formulation is primarily in qualitative form and reasoning from a specific imagistic representation figures predominantly in its construction. He constructed his field concept by reasoning from representations of the Lines of force such as those that form when iron filings are sprinkled around a magnetic source (See, Figure 5.1). Many line-like features are incorporated into his representation. He characterized the lines as expanding, collapsing, bending, vibrating, being cut, and turning corners, and attempted to devise experiments to capture the diverse motions of

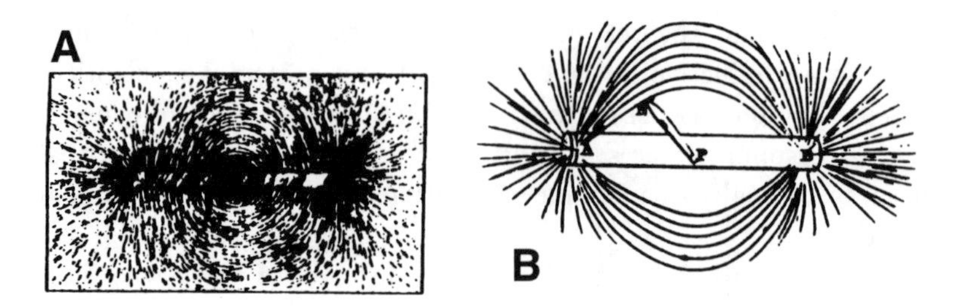

Figure 5.1
A: Actual Pattern of Lines of Force Surrounding a Bar Magnet (from Faraday 1938–55, vol. 3); *B:* Schematic Representation of Lines of Force Surrounding a Bar Magnet (vol. 1).

the lines. Thus, he transformed the static visual representation of the lines into a qualitative dynamical model for the transmission and interconversion of electric and magnetic forces, and, ultimately, for all the forces of nature and matter. As Maxwell (1890b) remarked, although this model is qualitative, it embodies within it a great deal of mathematical understanding, which Maxwell himself was able to extract from it.

In the most complete formulation of Faraday's field representation nothing exists but a sea of lines of force: all the forces of nature are unified and interconvertible through various motions of the lines, with matter, itself, being nothing but point centers of converging lines of force. The centrality of the image in his reasoning can also be seen in the only quantitative relationship he formulated explicitly: that between the number of lines cut and the intensity of the induced force. This relationship is incorrect because number of is an integer, while "field intensity" is a continuous function. With our hindsight we can trace the "mistake" directly to the fact that lines are discrete entities and the image represents the filings as such, whereas, except in rare cases, the actual lines of force spiral indefinitely in a closed volume.

Near the end of his research Faraday introduced another image that was to play a key role in Maxwell's construction of a quantitative field representation. That image was of interlocking curves that represent the dynamical balance between electricity and magnetism (See, Figure 5.2(a))—what Faraday called "the oneness of condition of that which is apparently two powers or forms of power" (Faraday 1839-55, 3, para-

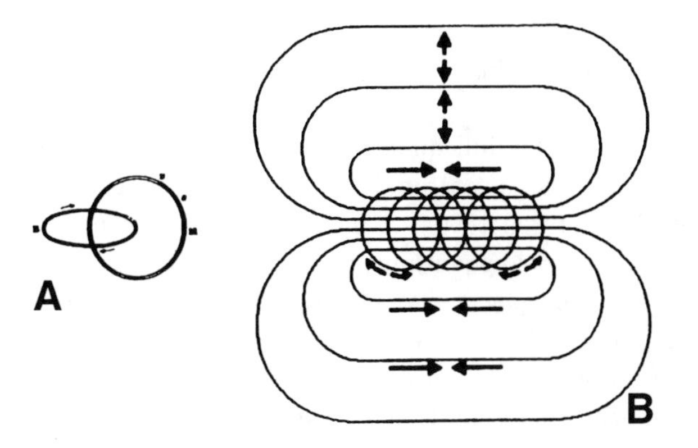

Figure 5.2
A: Faraday's Representation of the Interconnectedness of Electrical Currents and Magnetic Force (from Faraday 1938–55, vol. 3); *B:* My Schematic Representation of the Reciprocal Relationship between Magnetic Lines of Force and Electric Current Lines

graph 3268). The image represents the structural relations between the electric and magnetic lines of force and is, thus, itself abstracted from the lines of force image. We can see this from Figure 5.2(b). Here the outer lines represent magnetism and the inner lines, current electricity. The lateral repulsion of the magnetic lines has the same effect as a longitudinal expansion of the electric current lines and the lateral attraction of the current lines, the same as a longitudinal contraction of the magnetic lines. This dynamical balance is captured in the image of interlocking curves.

Maxwell called the reciprocal dynamical relations embodied in the image "mutually embracing curves" (Maxwell 1890a, 1, p. 194n.). While he does not include a drawing of this visual representation in the paper, Maxwell does describe it while referring the reader to the appropriate section of Faraday's Experimental Researches. Wise (1979) offers a convincing account of exactly how the image plays a role in the mathematical representation Maxwell constructed in his first paper on electromagnetism (Maxwell 1890, 1, pp. 155–229) and throughout his work in his complicated use of two fields each for electric and magnetic forces: one for intensity, a longitudinal measure of power, and one for quantity, a lateral measure. Wise further provides a plausible argument that the image could even have provided a model for propagation of electromagnetic actions through the aether. If we expand Figure 5.2(a) into a chain, then summations of the quantities and intensities associated with the electric and magnetic fields would be propagated link-by-link through interlocking curves.

While Maxwell constructed his full quantitative representation over the course of three papers, his central analysis is in the second, "On Physical Lines of Force" (Maxwell 1890a, 1, pp. 451–513). It is in this paper that he first derived the field equations, i.e., gave a unified mathematical representation of the propagation of electric and magnetic forces with a time delay, and calculated the velocity of the propagation of these actions. He achieved this by using a method he called "physical analogy" to exploit the powerful representational capabilities of continuum mechanics in his analysis. According to Maxwell, a physical analogy provides both a set of mathematical relationships and an imagistic representation of the structure of those relationships drawn from a source domain to be applied in analyzing a target domain about which there is only partial knowledge. In this case the method worked as follows.

Maxwell began by transforming the problem of analyzing the production and transmission of electric and magnetic forces into that of analyzing the potential stresses and strains in a mechanical electromagnetic medium (target domain) and then constructed an analogy between these and well-formulated relationships between known continuum mechanical phenomena (source domain). The process of application of the method of physical analogy comprised identifying the electromagnetic quantities with properties of the continuum mechanical medium; equating the forces in the electromagnetic aether with mechanical stresses and strains; abstracting what seemed to be appropriate relationships from the source domain and fitting them to the constraints of the target domain. In all this Maxwell explicitly provided imagistic representations to accompany the mathematical analysis.

Maxwell first constructed a simple representation consistent with a set of four constraints: the physical observations that (1) electric and magnetic actions are at right angles to one another and (2) the plane of polarized light is rotated by magnetic action, plus Faraday's speculative notions that (3) there is a tension along the lines of force and (4) there is a lateral repulsion between them. A mechanical analogy consistent with these constraints is a fluid medium, composed of vortices and under stress (See, Figure 5.3(b)). With this form of the analogy Maxwell was able to provide a mathematical representation for various magnetic phenomena.

The problem of how to construe the relationship between electric current and magnetism led to an elaboration of the analogy. As we can see from Figure 5.3(a), the vortices are all rotating in the same direction, which means that if they touch, they will stop. Maxwell argued that mechanical consistency requires the introduction of "idle wheels" to keep the mechanism going. He thus enhanced the source by surrounding the vortices with small spherical particles revolving in the direction opposite to them. There is a tangential pressure between the particles and the vortices, and for purposes of calculation Maxwell now had to consider the fluid vortices to be rigid pseudospheres. Maxwell's own imagistic representation of this enhanced source is seen in Figure 5.3(b). He represented the dynamical relationships between current and magnetism mathematically by expressing them in terms of those between the particles and the vortices.

At this point Maxwell submitted the paper for publication. It took him several months to figure out the last—and most critical—piece of the representation: electrostatic actions. This is the point at which we joined him in the garden in Galloway. He found that if he made the vortices elastic and identified electrostatic polarization with elastic displacement he could calculate a wave of distortion produced by the polarization, i.e., what he called the "displacement current." He now had a unified, quantified representation of the continuous transmission of electromagnetic actions with a time delay. A testable consequence followed: electromagnetic actions are propagated at approximately the speed of light.

Cognitive Analysis: Analogical and Imagistic Reasoning Analogical problem solving has been the subject of much recent work in cognitive psychology and artificial intelligence. It is widely recognized that analogy is a primary means through which we transfer knowledge from one domain to another. Knowing how this process works is essential for understanding learning and for developing expert systems. While still undergoing formulation, most cognitive theories of analogy agree that the creative heart of analogical reasoning is a modeling process in which relational structures from existing modes of representation and problem solutions are abstracted from a source domain and are fitted to the constraints of the new problem domain. A complete theory must give an

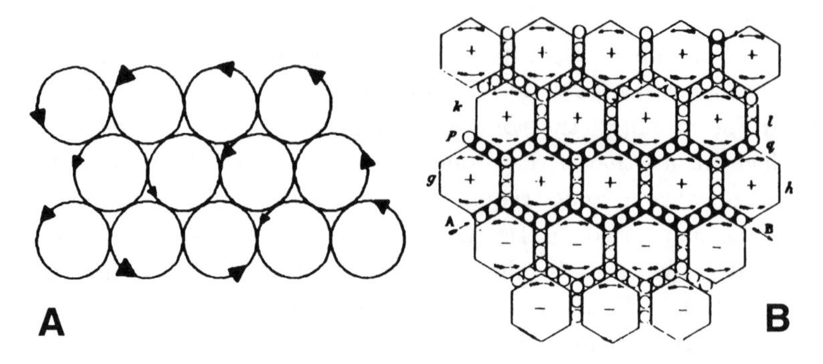

Figure 5.3
A: My Schematic Representation of Initial Crude Source Retrieved by Maxwell; *B:* Maxwell's Representation of His Fully Elaborated Physical Analogy (from Maxwell 1890, vol. 1).

account of the processes of retrieval, elaboration, mapping, transfer, and learning and of the syntactic, semantic, and pragmatic constraints that operate on these processes. Further, these processes need to be hooked up with other cognitive functions, such as memory. Most computational proposals are variants of three major theories of analogical problem solving: structure mapping (Gentner 1989), constraint satisfaction (Holyoak and Thagard 1989), derivational analogy (Carbonell 1986).

Since my purpose is to show how we might conceive of what scientists like Faraday and Maxwell were doing with their images and analogies, I will not give detailed descriptions and evaluations of these theories. Rather, I will note some pertinent results from the empirical studies that inform them. Many psychological studies have been undertaken to understand how analogy functions in problem-solving, especially in learning science. The results most germane to the issues of this chapter are as follows. First, productive problem solving has the following features: (1) structural focus: preserves relational systems; (2) structural consistency: isomorphic mapping of objects and relationships; and (3) systematicity: maps systems of interconnected relationships, especially causal and mathematical relationships. Additionally, the analogical reasoning process often creates an abstraction, or schema, common to both domains that can be used in further problem solving. Finally, in investigations of analogies used as mental models of a domain, it has been demonstrated that inferences made in problem-solving depend significantly upon the specific analogy in terms of which the domain has been represented. For example, in one study where subjects constructed a mental model of electricity in terms of either an analogy with flowing water or with swarming objects, specific inferences—sometimes erroneous could be traced directly to the analogy (Gentner and Gentner 1983). This result gives support to the view that analogies are not merely guides to thinking, with logical inferencing actually solving the problem, but that *analogies, themselves, do the inferential work and generate the problem solution.*

Do these findings lend support to the interpretation I gave the case study, i.e., that analogical and imagistic reasoning are generating the respective field representations of Faraday and Maxwell? Can we model Maxwell's use of physical analogy in cognitive terms? And what about the imagistic representations used by both him and Faraday?

While no current cognitive theory is comprehensive enough even to pretend to be able to handle all of the complexity of this case study, using what we believe we understand, cognitively, thus far, does enhance our understanding of it. It enables us, e.g., to fathom better what Maxwell was doing that summer day in Galloway and why he presented the physical analogy to his peers. Furthermore, this case points to areas of needed investigation in the cognitive sciences as well. I will first outline a cognitive analysis of Maxwell's generation of the field equations via the method of physical analogy and will then discuss the role of the imagistic dimension of that analogy along with the function of Faraday's imagistic representations.

Figure 5.4(a) provides a chart of Maxwell's modeling activities. His overall goal was to produce a unified mathematical representation of the production and continuous transmission of electromagnetic forces in a mechanical aether. The obvious source domain lay within continuum mechanics, a domain Maxwell was expert in continuous-action phenomena, such as fluid flow, heat, and elasticity, had all recently been given a dynamical analysis consistent with Newtonian mechanics and it was quite plausible to assume that the stresses and strains in an electromagnetic aether could be expressed in terms of continuum mechanical relationships. Using this source domain—if the analogy worked—he could presume to get (1) assurance that the underlying forces are Newtonian; (2) continuity of transmission with the time delay necessary for a field theory; and (3) unification through finding the mathematical expression for the dynamical relations through which one action gives rise to another. He got all three, but (1) was a false assurance. As we will discuss, the electromagnetic field equations represent a non-Newtonian dynamical system.

Maxwell retrieved a crude source from this domain by applying the four constraints we discussed above. He broke the overall goal down into sub-problems, viz., representing magnetic induction, electricity, electromagnetic induction, and electrostatic induction. He then produced mappings between the electromagnetic quantities and mechanical properties of the fluid vortex medium and between the presumed stresses and strains and those known to take place in fluid medium under stress. The mappings are isomorphic and maintain causal interconnectedness. He re-iterated the process twice, altering and enhancing the source to fit the constraints of the target domain. In the process he made mistakes, most of which can be explained in terms of the model. For example, he takes the "displacement currents to be in the direction opposite from the field intensity, and not—as is now customary and as he later held—in the same direction as the field intensity. In terms of the analogy, the equation is correct as it stands, i.e., in an elastic medium the restoring force and the displacement would have opposite orientation.

Through this process he abstracted a schema, i.e., a set of general dynamical (Lagrangian) relations, that could then be applied back to the target domain directly, without the need for any specific analogy. That is, at the end of the process he knew how to represent velocity, momentum, potential energy, and kinetic energy. With this knowledge he could re-derive the field equations using solely electromagnetic considerations, which is what he went on to do in his next paper on electrodynamics, "A Dynamical Theory of the Electromagnetic Field" (Maxwell 1890a, 1, pp. 526–597). But he only obtained this knowledge—the necessary general dynamical relations—by abstracting it from the analogy he constructed with continuum mechanics. This interpretation of what he actually did is consistent with what we have been learning about analogical reasoning in general. The physical analogy was generative and the process consistent with what are thought to be good analogical problem-solving techniques. But it also points to an area in need of investigation by cognitive theorists. None of the current theories addresses the kind of re-iteration process Maxwell carried out: the modification and enhancement of the analogy to fit the constraints of the target domain. Yet one

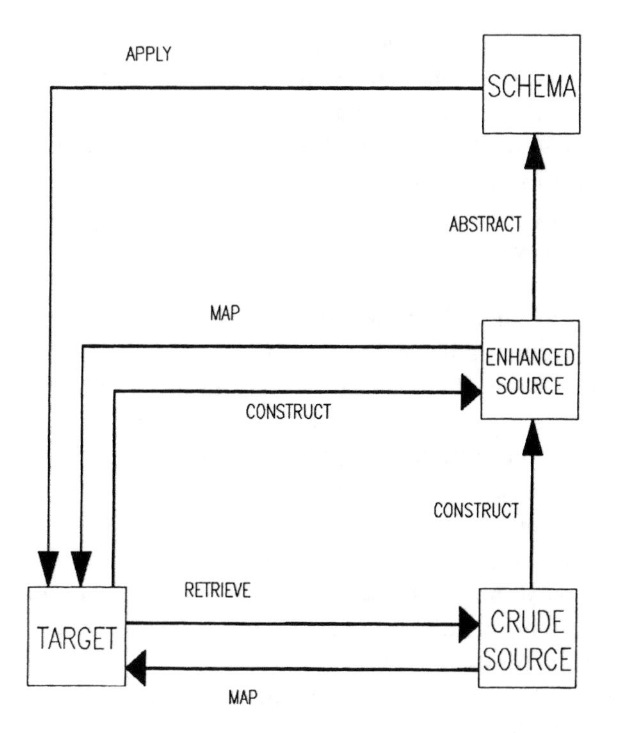

Figure 5.4
Maxwell's Use of the Method of Physical Analogy.

would expect such re-representation to be common in ordinary problem-solving as well.

I want to underscore the point of my message by returning briefly to the historical story. In Maxwell's eyes his problem solution was never complete. To be so he would have to give an account of the actual underlying forces in the aether. The real power of analogical reasoning in creating new representations is driven home quite forcefully when we realize that he could never have done this: Maxwell's laws are those of a non-Newtonian system. How could it have turned out this way? That is, how could he have created a representation for a non-Newtonian system using a Newtonian system as the source of his analogy?

Maxwell did not take an existing physical system and plug the electromagnetic parameters into the equations for that system to solve the problem, as Thomson had done in finding a potential field representation for electrostatics in terms of Fourier's analysis of heat. Rather, he used various aspects of continuum mechanics and constraints from electromagnetism to put together a system, which in its entirety even he maintained did not exist—possibly could not exist—in nature. And by drawing inferences from this abstracted model he was able to extract a mathematical structure of greater generality than Newtonian mechanics. Contrary to what was believed at the time, Newtonian mechanics and general dynamics are not coextensive. This belief made Maxwell think that by giving a general dynamical formulation of electromagnetism he had shown the underlying forces to be Newtonian in nature. We now know that many different kinds of dynamical system can be formulated in general dynamical terms, e.g., relativity and quantum mechanics.

Interpreted in the way I have been proposing, concept formation by analogical reasoning can, thus, be characterized as a process of abstraction from existing representations with increasing constraint satisfaction. This interpretation leads to a novel interpretation of continuity and commensurability between representations in cases like the one we just analyzed: these are to be found in the abstracted relationships common to the source and the target structures.

What about the imagistic representation of Maxwell's analogy and Faraday's earlier ones? While there are differences between the kinds of mappings made by Maxwell and those made by Faraday, both treated the imagistic representations as embodiments of an analogical source. I suggest that we construe this kind of imagistic reasoning as a species of analogical reasoning. In the early, qualitative phase, i.e., Faraday's work, the imagistic representation was taken as more nearly identical with what it represents than in Maxwell's quantitative analysis. That is, the schematic lines were identified with the physical lines they were to represent, and too many aspects of the specific image were incorporated into the field representation. A possible interpretation for this is that when there are insufficient constraints from the target domain to guide the process analogies can be too generative. In the quantitative phase, i.e., in Maxwell's work, the function of the image is more abstract. It serves primarily to make certain structural relationships visualizable, and, thus, it is possible that any imagistic representation that embodied these relationships would serve the same purposes.

What further cognitive purposes might these physical embodiments serve? There is very little in the cognitive science literature on the possible role of imagistic representations like these in problem solving. I will offer some speculations by putting together recent work by Larkin and Simon (1987) on diagrams, and James Greeno and myself (1990) and Roschelle and Greeno (1987) on abstracted models in the hope of opening some avenues for research into possible roles these representations on paper play in constructing and reasoning with mental models, especially in the process of constructing a mathematical representation.

The main idea centers on the fact that perceptual inferences are easy for humans to make. By clustering connected information and making visual a chain of interconnected inferences the imagistic representations support a large number of immediate perceptual inferences. The representations on paper are presented in a form that already focuses on and abstracts specific aspects of phenomena. A great deal of mathematical information is implicit in such representations. By embodying structural relations thought to underlie phenomena they could facilitate access to the quantifiable aspects of the phenomena. As such, they provide an intermediate level of abstraction between phenomena and mathematical forms of representation (formulae). Additionally, they stabilize the image for the reasoner and make various versions accessible for direct comparison, in a way not available for internal images, and may thus take some of the load off memory in problem-solving. Finally, they potentially play an important role in communicating new representations by providing a stable embodiment that is public. The imagisitic representation could make it easier for others to grasp parts of the new representation than text and formulae alone. For example, Maxwell did not comprehend all the subtleties of the field concept Faraday articulated, but he did grasp the mathematical structures inherent in the lines of force representation and in the dynamical balance embodied in the interlocking curves. And Maxwell, in trying to communicate his new field representation to his colleagues, felt it necessary to provide them with the physical, i.e., embodied, analogy, and extensive commentary on how to understand the method, in addition to leading them through the reasoning and rather than just presenting the mathematical arguments.

5.3.2 Thought Experiments and Limiting Case Analysis

Background Another heuristic that occurs frequently in cases of major conceptual change is thought experimentation. The notion that an experiment can take place in thought seems paradoxical. Earlier scholarship presented two poles of interpretation of their role in creating conceptual change. Duhem dismissed them as bogus precisely because they are "not only not realized but incapable of being realized" (Duhem 1914, p.202), i.e., they are not experimental in the customary sense. Koyré (1939, 1968), on the other hand, argued that their logical force is so compelling that they supplant real experimentation in the construction of new representations for phenomena. The thought part of the experiment predominates and shows the synthetic a priori nature of scientific knowledge.

Contemporary historians and philosophers of science by and large reject both the extreme empiricism and rationalism of their forefathers. They acknowledge that thought experiment, while not eliminating the need for real experiment, is an important heuristic for creating conceptual change in science. Despite the consensus, based on ample historical documentation, there has been little theoretical analysis of just how such experiments function. As with the heuristics of analogy and imagery, I will attempt a cognitive-historical analysis of thought experiment, subsuming limiting case analysis as a species of this form of reasoning.

There have been a few recent attempts to analyze the function of thought experiments. While these are sketchy and limited, some do yield useful insights. Kuhn's analysis provides the starting point for most of these discussions. Kuhn claims:

> "Thought experiment is one of the essential analytical tools which are deployed during crises and which then help to promote basic conceptual reform" (Kuhn, 1964, p. 263).

The importance of his analysis is that it is the first to try to come to grips with both the experimental and the thought dimensions of thought experiments. He argues that thought experiments show that there is no consistent way, in actual practice, of using accepted existing conceptions. That is, the thought experiment reveals that it is not possible to apply our conceptions consistently to real world phenomena and this practical impossibility translates into a logical requirement for conceptual reform. Gooding (1990) in his analysis of Faraday's experimental practices, picks up on Kuhn's analysis, rendering the empirical force of thought experiments in terms of their demonstration of what he calls the "impracticability of doing." Gooding is concerned to show how the real world experimenter's knowledge of practical skill is utilized in the construction and manipulation of thought experiments.

My point will be that cognitive-historical analysis, by placing thought experiments within the framework of mental models theory, offers the possibility of explaining how it is that an experiment made in thought can have both the logical and empirical force Kuhn and Gooding argue for. In unpublished work Manukian (1987) has begun a cognitive-historical analysis of Galileo's thought experiments focusing on thought experiment as a species processing that employs mental models. He is the only one thus far to attempt to understand thought experiments as a form of world modeling, as he calls constructing idealizations. However, since his attention is directed towards concerns in the field of artificial intelligence he restricts his analysis to what I sees as only a special case of thought experiment, the limiting case analysis.

Two other analyses need mentioning for the contrast in approach they provide. First, Brown (Brown, J. 1987) claims that thought experiments are a species of a priori reasoning and that they get at something that cannot be derived from logical argumentation. His positive suggestion is that they provide a special window through which the mind grasps universals. The most cogent rendering I can give this claim is that Brown is trying to capture the idealizing function of thought experiments. However, unlike Manukian, his approach through linguistic analysis does not afford the possibility of understanding their experimental nature. Second, Norton's (1986) view that thought experiments can, in essence, be reconstructed as and replaced by arguments is the most sympathetic for philosophers who wish to restrict reasoning to logical argumentation—whether deductive or inductive. Certainly thought experiments contain an argument. However, as Norton himself acknowledges, the argument can only be constructed after the fact, i.e., it is not evident until after the thought experiment has been executed. By concentrating exclusively on this aspect he misses the importance of their experimental dimension. Additionally, while his claim that the presentation contains particulars irrelevant to the generality of the conclusion is correct, this emphasis reveals that he has also failed to see the constructive function of the narrative form in which thought experiments are customarily presented.

Both of these analyses take the traditional philosophical route of construing thought experiments in terms of propositional representations. My contention is that propositional representations cannot do the trick. Mental simulation is required for a thought experiment to be both thought and experimental. The original thought experiment is the construction of a mental model by the scientist who imagines a sequence of events. She then uses a narrative form to describe the sequence in order to communicate the experiment to others. Considerations of space will not permit here an analysis of comparable depth with that on analogical and imagistic reasoning. However, I do want to put an analysis of a different heuristic before the reader to underscore the power of cognitive-historical analysis and to show that its utility is not restricted to what it offers for understanding the constructive practices of 19th century British field theorists!

Case Studies: Galileo and Einstein Although thought experiment occurs repeatedly in conceptual change, the thought experimenters who have attracted the most attention are Galileo and Einstein. I will give a brief presentation of a couple of their thought experiments to convey some sense of the variety such experiments display and to elicit some common features for further analysis.

Galileo's importance as a pivotal figure in the transition from the qualitative categories of aristotelian and medieval theories of motion to the quantitative representation of motion provided by Newton's mechanics is widely recognized. As shown in analyses by Koyré (1939) and Clavelin (1968), among others, Galileo drastically transformed the problem of how to go about constructing a mathematical representation of the phenomena of motion. That process, which Koyré called "mathematization," required constructing an idealized representation, quantifying this representation, and mapping the quantified representation back onto the real world. While it is now clear that Galileo must have performed many more real-world experiments than Koyré would have liked (See, e.g., Drake 1973: Naylor 1976; and Settle 1961), no one would deny the importance of thought experiment and limiting case analysis in the mathematization process. Take, as example, his analysis of falling bodies (Galilei 1683, pp. 62–86).

According to the aristotelian theory heavier bodies fall faster than lighter ones. This belief rests on a purely qualitative analysis of the concepts of heaviness and lightness. Galileo argued against this belief and constructed a new, quantifiable representation through a sustained analysis using several thought experiments and limiting case analyses. The outline of his use of these procedures is as follows. He calls on us to imagine we drop a heavy body and a light one, made of the same material, at the same time. We would customarily say that the heavy body falls faster and the light body more slowly. Now suppose we tie the two bodies together with a very thin—almost immaterial—string. The combined body should both fall faster and more slowly. It should fall faster because a combined body should be heavier than two separate bodies and should fall more slowly because the slower body should retard the motion of the faster one. Clearly something has gone amiss in our understanding of heavier and lighter. Having pinpointed the problem area, Galileo then goes on to show that it is a mistake to extrapolate from what is true at rest to what happens when bodies are in motion. That is, he has us consider that when the two bodies are at rest, the lighter will press on the heavier, and therefore the combined body is heavier. But when we imagine the two bodies are in motion, we can see the lighter does not press on the heavier and thus does not increase its weight. What Galileo has done up to this point is use the thought experiment to reveal the inconsistencies in the medieval belief, the ambiguities in the concepts, and the need to separate the heaviness of a body from its effect on speed in order to analyze free fall. He then goes on, using the methods of thought experiment and limiting case analysis in tandem to show that the apparent difference in the speed of falling bodies is due to the effect of the medium and not to the difference in heaviness between bodies.

As Clavelin has pointed out, it is crucial for quantifying the motion of falling bodies that heaviness not be the cause of the difference in speed because then we could not be sure that motion would be the same for all bodies. Galileo again used a thought experiment to demonstrate that the observed differences in speed should be understood as being caused by the unequal way media lift bodies. He asks us to suppose, e.g., that the density of air is 1, that of water 800, of wood 600 and of lead 10,000. In water the wood would be deprived of 800/600th of its weight, while lead would be deprived of 800/10,000th's. Thus, the wood would actuary not fad (i.e., would float) and the lead would fall more slowly than it would in a less dense medium, such as air. If we extrapolate to a less dense medium, such as air, we see that the differential lifting effect is much less significant (e.g., 1/600 to 1/10,000 in air). The next move is to consider what would happen in the case of no medium, i.e., in extrapolating to the limiting case. With this move, Galileo says "I came to the opinion that if one were to remove entirely the resistance of the medium, all materials would descend with equal speed." (Galilei 1638, p. 75). Having performed the extrapolation in this way we can quantify this idealized representation of the motion of a falling body and know that it is relevant to actual physical situations; we need only add back in the effects of a medium.

Galileo repeatedly used thought experiments and limiting case analyses in tandem as shown by this example both in constructing a quantifiable representation of bodies in motion and in attempting to convey this new representation to others. Later I will propose the cognitive function of thought experiments and of limiting case analysis are much the same. Before getting to the cognitive analysis, though, I want to lay out somewhat different thought experiments used by Einstein in the development of the special and general theories of relativity.

Einstein began his paper, "On the Electrodynamics of Moving Bodies" (1905), with the following thought experiment. Consider the case of a magnet and a conductor in relative motion. There are two possibilities. In the first case, the magnet is at absolute rest and the conductor moving. According to electromagnetic theory, the motion of the conductor through the magnetic field produces an electromotive force that creates a current in the conductor. In the second case, the conductor is at rest and the magnet moving. In this case, again according to electromagnetic theory, the motion of the magnet creates a changing magnetic field which induces an electric field that in turn induces a current in the conductor. However, with respect to the relative motions, it makes no difference whether it is the magnet or the conductor that is considered to be in motion. But according to the Maxwell-Lorentz electromagnetic theory, the absolute motions create a difference in how we would explain the production of a current in the conductor. Since the explanatory asymmetry could not, in principle or in practice, be accounted for by the observable phenomena—the measurable current in the conductor—Einstein argued that this supported his conclusion that "the phenomena of electrodynamics as well as of mechanics possess no properties corresponding to the idea of absolute rest" (p.37).

Although we will not discuss them at any length, two more thought experiments figure crucially in this analysis. The second thought experiment in the chapter is the most famous one in which Einstein constructed an operational definition for the concept of simultaneity. According to

Newtonian theory it is possible for distant events to occur simultaneously. Indeed this is necessary for there to be action at a distance. The thought experiment shows that we can only define simultaneity and thus what is meant by time for a particular reference system, and not in general. This experiment feeds into the next in which Einstein established the relativity of length, i.e., that the Newtonian assumption that a body in motion over a specific time interval may be represented by the same body at rest in a definite location is incorrect.

In a similar manner many thought experiments figured in Einstein's constructing and communicating the general theory of relativity, i.e., the field representation of gravitational action. We will just consider one he presented in various formats but claims to have first conceived in 1907. Einstein (1917, pp.66–70) asks us to imagine that a large opaque chest, the interior of which resembles a room, is located in space far removed from all matter. Inside there is an observer with some apparatus. In this state, the observer would not experience the force of gravity and would have to tie himself with strings to keep from floating to the ceiling. Now imagine that a rope is connected to the outer lid of the chest and a being pulls upward with a constant force, producing uniform acceleration. The observer and any bodies inside the chest would now experience the very same effects, such as a pull towards the floor, as in a gravitational field. The experiment demonstrates that the behavior of a body in a homogeneous gravitational field and one in a uniformly accelerated frame of reference would be identical. Once we see that there is no way of distinguishing these two cases we can understand the importance of the Newtonian law that the gravitational mass of a body equals its inertial mass: these are just two manifestations of the same property of bodies. That is, we have a different interpretation for something we already knew.

Cognitive Analysis: Thought Experiments as Mental Modeling Will rendering thought experiments as a species of mental modeling support the interpretation that when they are employed in conceptual change, they are essential analytical tools in the process? We can only speculate about what goes on in the mind of the scientist in the original thought experiment. Scientists have rarely been asked to discuss the details of how they went about setting up and running such experiments. As stated previously, it is quite possible that the original experiment involves direct construction, without recourse to language. However, reports of thought experiments are always presented in the form of narratives that call upon the reader or listener to simulate a situation in his or her imagination. Thus, drawing on what we think we know both about the processes through which we imagine or picture in general, and through which we comprehend any narrative, may help us to answer that most perplexing question about thought experiments: how can an experiment carried out in thought have such powerful empirical force? As was the case in the analysis of analogy and imagistic reasoning above, much research and development needs to be done in this area, but I hope the sketch I present will persuade the reader that following this direction does offer good prospects of accounting for both the thought and the experiment aspects of thought experiments.

The most pertinent aspect of mental models theory for this analysis is the hypothesis that understanding language involves the construction of a mental model. In the case of thought experiments we need to understand how: (1) a narrative facilitates the construction of an experimental situation in thought and (2) thinking through the experimental situation has real-world consequences. Framed in mental models theory, the thought dimension would include constructing a mental model and running a mental simulation of the situation depicted by the model, while the experimental dimension comprises the latter and the connection between the simulation and the world.

Briefly, the mental models thesis about text comprehension is that understanding involves relating linguistic expressions to models; i.e., the relationship between words and the world is mediated by the construction of a structural analog to the situations, processes, objects, events, etc. depicted by a text (Franklin and Tversky 1990; Mani and Johnson-Laird 1982; Johnson-Laird 1983; McNamara and Sternberg 1983; Morrow et al. 1989; and Tversky 1990). What it means for a mental model to be a structural analog is that it embodies a representation of the spatial and temporal relationships between, and the causal structure connecting, the events and entities of the narrative. In constructing and updating a representation, the reader would call upon a combination of conceptual and real-world knowledge and would employ the tacit and recursive inferencing mechanisms of her cognitive apparatus.

That the situation is represented by a mental model rather than by an argument in terms of propositions is thought to facilitate inferencing. We can actually generate conclusions without having to carry out the extensive computations needed to process the same amount of background information propositionally. The conclusions drawn are limited to those that are directly relevant to the situation depicted. The ease with which one can make inferences in such simulative reasoning has suggested to some that mechanisms either used in—or similar to those used in perception may be involved. As we saw in the discussion of the function of imagistic representations in problem solving, if we do employ perception-like mechanisms here many inferences would be immediate.

To date, most empirical investigations of the hypothesis have focused on the representation of spatial information by means of mental models. The main disagreement has been over whether the representation involves a perception-like image or is spatial, i.e., allows different perspectives and differential access to locations. Although there is some research investigating the use of knowledge of causal structure in updating, on the whole there is little research investigating how knowledge and inferencing mechanisms are employed in running and revising the simulation.

Before beginning to sketch a way of understanding thought experiments and their role in conceptual change in terms of mental models theory, we need first to glean some common features of thought experiments Tom the narratives presented above. While there is great variety among thought experiments, in general, they do share important salient features. The Galileo and Einstein examples help us to see some of these. First, as noted, by the time a thought experiment is public it is in the form of a narrative. The narrative has the character of a simulation. It calls upon the reader/ listener to imagine a dynamic scene–one that unfolds in time. The invitation is to follow through a sequence of events or processes as one would in the real world. That is, even if the situation my seem bizarre or fantastic, such as being in a chest in outer space, there is nothing bizarre in the unfolding: objects float as they would in the real world in the absence of gravity. The assumption is that if the experiment could be performed, the chain of events would unfold according to the way things usually take place in the real world.

Second, a thought experiment embodies specific assumptions either explicit or tacit—of the representation under investigation. It usually exposes inconsistencies or exhibits paradoxes that arise when we try to apply certain parts of that representation to a specific situation, such as heavy and light to falling rocks. The paradox can take the form of a contradiction in the representation, e.g. it requires that an object be both heavy and light, or of something being not physically possible. e.g., observing the asymmetry electromagnetic theory requires.

Third, by the time a thought experiment is presented it always works and is often more compelling than most real-world experiments. We rarely, if ever, get a glimpse of failed thought experiments or avenues explored in the construction of the one presented to us.[6] Some experiments, such as Galileo's second, could potentially be carried out—at least until the analysis extrapolates to the limit. Others, such as Einstein's first, underscore that doing a real-world experiment could not provide the data the theory requires. While others, such as Einstein's chest in space, are impossible to carry out in practice, either in principle or because we do not yet have the requisite level of technological achievement. However, once understood, a thought experiment is usually so compelling in itself that even where it would be possible to carry it out, the reader feels no need to do so. The constructed situation is apprehended as pertinent to the real world either by revealing something in our experience that we did not see the import of before—e.g., the measurable current in the stationary and in the moving conductor is the same, so on what basis can we support the difference in theoretical explanation?—or by generating new data e.g., in the case of no medium lead and wood would fall at the same speed—or by making us see the empirical consequences of something in our existing representation—e.g., the attributes called gravitational mass and inertial mass are the same property of bodies.

Finally, the narrative presentation has already made some abstraction from the real-world phenomena. For example, certain features of objects that would be present in a real experiments are eliminated, such as the color of the rocks and the physical characteristics of the observers. That is, there has been a prior selection of the pertinent dimensions on which to focus, which evidently derives from our experience in the world. We know, e.g., that the color of a rock does not effect its rate of fall. This feature strengthens our understanding of the depiction as that of a prototypical situation of which there could be many specific instances.

[6] An analysis of some of Faraday's explorations of thought experiments is to be found in Gooding (1990).

In more colorful narratives there may be more irrelevant features in the exposition, but these most often serve to reinforce crucial aspects of the experiment. For example, Einstein's characterization, in one version of the chest—or elevator—experiment, of a physicist as being drugged and then waking up in a box served to reinforce the point that the observer could not know beforehand if he were falling in outer space or sitting in a gravitational field. In the version discussed above, the opacity of the chest is to prevent the observer from seeing if there are gravitational sources around.

We can outline the function of thought experiments in terms of mental models theory as follows. The first performance of a thought experiment is a direct mental simulation. This hypothesis gains plausibility when we realize the likelihood that direct mental simulation precedes even real-world experiments, i.e., the scientist envisions and unfolds a sequence of steps to be carried out in the experiment.[7] The cognitive function of the narrative form of presentation of a thought experiment to others is to guide the construction of a structural analog of the prototypical situation depicted in it. Over the course of the narrative, we are led to run a simulation that unfolds the events and processes by constructing, isolating, and manipulating the pertinent dimensions of the analog phenomena. The process of constructing and running the model gives the thought experiment its applicability to the world. The constructed situation inherits empirical force by being abstracted from both our experiences and activities in, and our knowledge, conceptualizations, and assumptions of, the world. In running the experiment, we make use of various inferencing mechanisms, existing representations, and general world knowledge to make realistic transformations from one possible physical state to the next. In this way, the data that derive from a thought experiment, while constructed in the mind, are empirical consequences that at the same time pinpoint the locus of the needed representational change.

Limiting case analysis can be construed as a species of thought experiment. In this species the simulation consists of abstracting specific physical dimensions to create an idealized representation, such as of a body falling in a vacuum. The isolation of the physical system in thought allows us to manipulate variables beyond what is physically possible.

[7]See, Gooding 1990 for a fuller discussion of this point with respect to Faraday's experiments.

Just what dimensions produce the variation and how to extrapolate from these may be something we determine initially in real-world experimentation, but the last step can only be made in the imagination. In physics, it is the idealized representation that is quantifiable. However, the idealized representation is rooted in and relevant to the real world because it has been created by controlled extrapolation from it. We get from imagination to the real world by adding in some of the dimensions we have abstracted, again in a controlled process.

5.3.3 Summary: Abstraction Techniques and Conceptual Change

What we have seen in our discussion of the dynamics of conceptual change in science is the potential for acquiring a deeper understanding of the processes through which new scientific representations are constructed and communicated by joining historical analysis with our developing insights into how human beings represent, reason, and solve problems generally. By linking the conceptual and the experiential dimensions of human cognitive processing, mental models theory offers the possibility of capturing and synthesizing theoretical, experimental, and social dimensions of scientific change. Our investigation demonstrated in some detail how cognitive-historical analysis helps us to fathom how the heuristics of analogy, imagistic reasoning, thought experiment, and limiting case analysis, of which we see recurrent use in what has been called "radical" and "revolutionary" conceptual change, could function to create genuinely novel representations by increasing abstraction from existing representations in a problem-solving process.

5.4 Wider Implications

To conclude I would like to underscore the potential fertility of the cognitive-historical method outlined and illustrated above by considering its wider implications for the disciplines it comprises. To do this we need to return to our title query: How do scientists think?

5.4.1 Implications for Philosophy of Science

First, while philosophers would be comfortable with the generality of the question, the detour through language taken by many philosophers of science has prevented its asking. Those who would ask it would prefer it transformed into "How ought scientists to think?" And, quite generally, the creative processes are deemed by philosophers to be too mysterious to be understood. The main point of the investigations above is to show how cognitive-historical analysis opens the possibility of construing the representational and constructive practices of scientists as part of scientific method, and as such within the province of philosophical investigation. The analysis supports and elaborates upon the intuitions of those who have argued that reasoning comprises more than algorithms and for the generative role of such heuristics as analogy. Further, developing criteria for evaluating good and bad uses of heuristics will enable us to show why it is rational to believe inferences resulting from good heuristics are worth testing, holding conditionally if testing is not feasible, etc.

Second, a major problem for historicist philosophers has been how to go from a case study to a more general conclusion. Those who want to use scientific knowledge practices as a basis from which to develop an historicized epistemology recognize the dangers of generalizing from one case, no matter how salient. Placing discovery processes within the framework of human representational and problem solving abilities enables us to extend from case studies without committing the serious injustices of past reconstructive approaches.

Third, as discussed in the body of the chapter, cognitive-historical analysis offers a way of recasting many of the puzzles associated with "incommensurability of meaning." By focusing on the people and practices that create and change representations of a domain, rather than on static linguistic representations that change dramatically from time to time, we open the possibility of understanding how scientists build new and sometimes radically different representations out of existing ones, and thus for explaining the continuous and non-cumulative character of scientific change. And, lastly, we even have a way of making sense of that most paradoxical of all Kuhnian claims: post-revolutionary scientists quite literally understand and experience the world in a manner incommensurable with their pre-revolutionary counterparts (or selves in some cases). If we do negotiate the world by constructing mental models, pro and post-revolutionary scientists would construct different mental models and would, thus, truly have different experiences of the world.

5.4.2 Implications for History of Science

First, historians do not pose the question this way. Those who still do address such issues ask "How did my individual scientist, such as Maxwell, think?" However, every historian–no matter how scrupulously he or she has tried to reconstruct the mosaic of a discovery process in a manner faithful to the historical record must have experienced the nagging doubt "but did they really think this way?" In the end we all face the recorded data and know that every piece is in itself a reconstruction by its author. The diaries and notebooks of a Faraday may be the closest we will ever get to on-line thinking, and even these cannot be taken as involving no reconstruction and as capturing all the shifts and strategies employed. However, if we can show that what the particular scientist claims and/or seems to be doing is in line with what we know about human cognitive functioning generally we can build a stronger case for our interpretation and fill in missing steps in a plausible manner, as I have done in the Maxwell example.

Second, in claiming a generative role for heuristics such as those discussed above one often has the sense of "preaching to the converted" when talking with historians of science. But historians do not always come down on the side of taking apparent uses of problem-solving heuristics at face value. Witness the Maxwell case. It is still controversial as to whether or not he was reasoning through the analogical model he presented.[8] Historians who see such models as off to the side, while some other process is actually generating the representation, have at least tacitly bought the philosopher's assumption that reasoning is only by means of inductive or deductive algorithms.

Cognitive-historical analysis provides support for the idea that such heuristics are not "merely suggestive" (Heimann 1970) or an "unproductive digression" (Chalmers 1986) but are fundamental. i.e.. they constitute the essence of the reasoning process. When they are taken in this way we get a better fit with the data and have less of a need to throw inconvenient pieces, such as Maxwell's "errors," away. Further, insights into how cognitive abilities and limitations contribute to and constrain scientific theorizing, experimentation, assessment, and choice

[8]Berkson (1974), Bromberg (1968), Nersessian (1984, 1986), and Siegel (1986) present arguments in favor of the centrality of the analogical model, while Chalmers (1986), Duhem (1902, 1914), and Heimann (1970) are among those deny its importance.

can enrich the analyses of those who do take such heuristics seriously, irrespective of whether the scientists in question go down dead ends, contribute to winning science, employ different strategies to get to the same point, etc.

Third, controversies have often arisen within the history of science over such questions as "Do we find the concept of inertia in Galileo's physics?" or "Did Faraday have a field concept that guided his research from early on, or did he formulate it only in his last year, or never?" The metatheoretical question that lies at the heart of such seemingly irresolvable disputes—indeed at the core of historical method—has scarcely been noticed by historians. While as historians of science we must not attribute present-day views to past scientists, even though the concepts may look quite familiar, there is no explicit guidance on a theoretical level for how to do this. Intuitive strategies for avoiding the problem are learned with the craft. What is missing is an explicit metatheoretical notion of what constitutes the meaning of a scientific concept.

Now why would an explicit notion yield better results than mere intuitions acquired in the craft? The answer is that underlying many of these controversies is the tacit assumption that a concept is represented by a set of necessary and sufficient conditions. As we have seen in the discussion of kinematics above, this form of representation cannot accommodate a substantial body of historical data. With it we have no criteria other than the modern for determining whether or when Faraday's concept is a field concept; no means for justifying the intuitive sense of family resemblance between what Galileo is discussing and what Newton called "inertia" or for making sense of the fact that we seem able to trace out a distinct line of descent and a pattern of progress over time in a conceptual domain. Seeing these problems as part of the wider representational problem opens a new avenue for their resolution. In an article on Faraday's field concept I have shown in detail how such an analysis can help to resolve standing controversies among historians (Nersessian 1985).

Fourth, many contemporary historians are concerned with issues about the form and rhetoric of presentation of novel ideas. These are usually framed in terms of how scientists adopt certain modes and conventions of writing in order to persuade others of their ideas. What tends to be left out of the analysis is that in order to persuade one has to get one's colleagues to comprehend the new ideas and, again, in order to negotiate, one has to comprehend what is being proposed. Cognitive-historical analysis allows us to take the public communications of scientists presenting new representations as attempts at trying to get others to understand them. That is, we can view such communications as presented in ways that the creators find meaningful for their own construction and understanding. Success at communication does not, of course, entail success at persuasion.

Looked at in terms of the rhetoric of persuasion Maxwell's analogies might seem utter failures. His presentation is quite out of line with the modes and conventions of his contemporaries who are publishing in Philosophical Transactions at that time. And even the person from whom he claims to have poached the technique, William Thomson, did not accept the method of analysis as transformed by Maxwell and therefore Maxwell's results. We can make better sense of what Maxwell is doing in presenting the work in that format if we assume he is trying to get his colleagues to understand his new field representation of forces by leading them through the modeling processes he used to construct the electromagnetic field concept, as well as trying to convince them of its potential.

Finally, we repeatedly find claims in the historical literature about the influence of wider cultural factors on a person's science; notable examples from physics are Faraday's Sandemanian religion on his belief in the unity of forces and a causality in quantum mechanics deriving from Weimar culture. Cognitive-historical analysis can capture the locality that is essential to historical understanding. It offers the potential for determining how it is that representational resources that are part of the scientist's local culture—whether these be construed as within a community of scientists, such as Cambridge mathematical physicists, or as within a wider Weltanschauung, such as obtained in Victorian England—get incorporated into scientific representations. The problem becomes that of how it is that scientists, working individually or collectively combine the cognitive abilities they have in virtue of their biology with the conceptual resources they acquire from the various facets of their lives in a wider community.

5.4.3 Implications for Psychology

First, cognitive psychologists do ask the question, but by themselves lack the means to answer it fully. Revolutionary science is rare and so is the possibility of catching it on line. Cognitive-historical analysis greatly increases the data base for psychological research. A cognitive theory of problem solving, in order to be adequate, needs to take into account the practices of scientists who have created major innovations in its formulation. This has scarcely been done to date. Combining the resources of cognitive psychologists, AI researchers who work on modeling human cognitive processes, and historians and philosophers of science win lead to a more realistic portrayal of the complexities of scientific reasoning than current cognitive models and discovery programs provide.

Second, are the conceptual changes that take place in development and/or learning like those in scientific revolutions? This question is acquiring an important place in the contemporary psychological literature. A growing contingent of cognitive psychologists have been arguing that the processes of cognitive development and conceptual change (or restructuring) in learning are indeed like those of major scientific revolutions (See, e.g., Carey 1985 and Keil 1989). The main support for the psychological hypothesis comes from research that describes the initial states of children and students and compares those states with the desired final state. The kinds of changes necessary to get from one state to the other seem to resemble those that have taken place in scientific revolutions, as they have been construed be Kuhn, whose gestalt switch metaphor of a scientific revolution many psychologists have uncritically adopted. And, as in history and philosophy of science, the nature of the processes through which conceptual change is brought about have not been explored in any depth in psychology. As demonstrated in this chapter, cognitive-historical analysis points the way to a quite different understanding of the kinds of conceptual changes that take place in scientific revolutions and opens an avenue for examining the processes that bring them about.

5.4.4 Implications for Science Education

There is growing interest in how all three disciplines might work together on the problem of how to help students learn science. Cognitive-historical analysis opens a new area of exploration. In fact, it offers a way of fundamentally recasting the old position, proposed by Dewey, Bruner, and Conant among others, that developing an appreciation for the historical roots of scientific ideas will facilitate learning because students will have a context in which to place them.

A cognitive theory of conceptual change views scientific discovery as a process in which scientists actively construct representations by employing problem-solving procedures that are on a continuum with those we employ in ordinary problem-solving. With such a constructionist conception of discovery the cognitive activity of the scientist becomes directly relevant to learning. The historical processes provide a model for the learning activity itself, and, thus, have the potential to assist students in constructing representations of extant scientific theories. The history of science becomes, in this domain, a repository, not of case studies, but rather of strategic knowledge of how to go about constructing, changing, and communicating scientific representations. As I have proposed elsewhere (Nersessian 1989, in press (b)), we should mine historical data—publications, diaries, notebooks, correspondence, etc.—for these strategies and then devise ways of integrating and transforming these more realistic exemplars of scientific problem solving into instructional procedures.

5.5 Return to Galloway

Coming back once more to our opening scene, what would cognitive historical analysis have Maxwell doing that summer day? It would have him searching for a way to make electrostatic phenomena meaningful in terms of mechanical phenomena he believes he understands.

Constructing an analogical model allowed Maxwell to gain access to a systematic body of knowledge: a structure of causal and mathematical relationships with its own constraints. Maxwell generated a continuous-action representation for electromagnetism through a process of fitting the model to the constraints of the new domain. The physical embodiment facilitated his exploration of the kind of mechanical forces that could be capable of producing electromagnetic phenomena at an intermediate level of abstraction: concrete enough to give substance to the relationships he was examining and indicate possible paths to solution, and yet abstract enough to generate a novel representation—one that is dynamical but not mechanical. Once he had understood the dynamical relations through this process he was able to re-derive the mathematical representation without this—or any—specific model, but just with the assumption of a general mapping between electromagnetic and dynamical variables.

The Scene

May 18, 1863, Palace Garden Terrace, Kensington, W. Maxwell is sitting in a parlor sipping tea "Aha!" he thinks, "Now I know how to do it without the model."

The Problem

If we were to take this as our starting point, we could never hope to fathom the nature of conceptual change in science.

Acknowledgments

The research undertaken for this chapter and its preparation was supported by NSF Scholars Award DIR 8821422. The author wishes to thank David Gooding, James Greeno, Mary Hesse, Simon Schaffer, and Robert Woolfolk for valuable discussions of the material in this chapter and Floris Cohen, Richard Grandy, Larry Holmes, Philip Johnson-Laird, Paul Thagard, and Norton Wise for critical and editorial comments on the penultimate version

References

Berkson, W. 1974. *Fields of Force: The Development of a World View from Faraday to Einstein.* New York: John Wiley and Sons.

Bromberg, J. 1968. Maxwell's Displacement Current and His Theory of Light. *Archive for the History of the Exact Sciences* 4: 218–234.

Brown, H. 1986. Sellars, Concepts, and Conceptual Change. *Synthese* 68: 275–307.

Brown, J. R. 1986. Thought Experiments Since the Scientific Revolution. *International Studies in the Philosophy of Science* 1: 1–15.

Campbell, N. R. 1920. *Physics, the Elements.* Cambridge: Cambridge University Press.

Carbonell, J. 1986. Derivational Analogy: A Theory of Reconstructive Problem Solving and Expertise Acquisition. In *Machine Learning: An Artificial Intelligence Approach,* ed. R. Michalski, J. Carbonell, and T. Mitchell, 371–392. Los Altos, Calif.: Morgan Kaufmann.

Carey, S. 1985. *Conceptual Change in Childhood.* Cambridge, Mass.: The MIT Press.

Chalmers, A. F. 1986. The Heuristic Role of Maxwell's Mechanical Model of Electromagnetic Phenomena. *Studies in the History and Philosophy of Science* 17: 415–427.

Clavelin, M. 1968. *The Natural Philosophy of Galileo: Essay on the Origins and Formation of Classical Mechanics* Cambridge, Mass.: The MIT Press.

Clement, J. 1983. A Conceptual Model Discussed by Galileo and Used Intuitively by Physics Students. In *Mental Models,* ed. D. Gentner and A. Stevens, 325–340. Hillsdale, N. J.: Lawrence Erlbaum.

Cohen, H. P. 1990. The Banquet of Truth: An Historiographical Inquiry into the Nature and Causes of the 17th Century Scientific Revolution. Unpublished manuscript.

Drake, S. 1973. Galileo's Experimental Condonation of Horizontal Inertia: Unpublished Manuscripts. *Isis* 64: 291–305.

Duhem, P. 1902. *Les Theories Electriques de J. Clerk Maxwell: Étude Historique et Critique.* Paris: A. Hermann and Cie.

Duhem, P. 1914.*The Aim and Structure of Physical Theory.* New York: Atheneum, 1962.

Einstein, A. 1905. On the Electrodynamics of Moving Bodies. In *The Theory of Relativity,* New York: Dover, 1952.

Einstein, A. 1917. *Relativity: The Special and the General Theory.* London: Methuen, 1977.

Faraday, M. 1839-55. *Experimental Researches in Electricity Reprinted.* New York: Dover, 1965.

Franklin, N. and Tversky, B. 1990. Searching Imagined Environments. *Journal of Experimental Psychology* 119:63–76.

Galilei, G. 1638. *Two New Sciences.* Madison: University of Wisconsin Press, 1974.

Gentnet D. 1989. The Mechanisms of Analogical Learning. In *Similarity and Analogical Reasoning,* ed. S. Vosniadou and A. Ortony, 200–241. Cambridge: Cambridge University Press.

Gentner, D. and Gentner, D. R. 1983. Flowing Waters and Teeming Crowds: Mental Models of Electricity. In *Mental Models,* ed. D. Gentner and A. Stevens, 99–130. Hillsdale, N. J. Lawrence Erlbaum Associates. .

Giere, R. N. 1988. *Explaining Science: A Cognitive Approach.* Chicago: University of Chicago Press.

Goldman, A. I. 1986. *Epistemology and Cognition.* Cambridge, Mass: Harvard University Press.

Gooding, D. 1990. *Experiment and the Making of Meaning: Human Agency in Scientific Observation and Experiment.* Dordrecht: Kluwer Academic Publishers.

Gorman, M. E. and Carlson, W. B. 1989. Interpreting Invention as a Cognitive Process: The Case of Alexander Graham Bell, Thomas Edison, and the Telephone. *Science. Technology and Human Values.*

Heimann, P. M. 1970. Maxwell and the Modes of Consistent Representation. *Archive for the History of the Exact Sciences* 6: 171–213.

Hesse, M. 1966. *Models and Analogies in Science.* Notre Dame: University of Notre Dame Press.

Holmes, F. L. 1985. *Lavoisier and the Chemistry of Life: An Exploration of Scientific Creativity.* Madison: University of Wisconsin Press.

Holyoak, K. and Thagard, P. 1989. Analogical Mapping by Constraint Satisfaction: A Computational Theory. *Cognitive Science* 13: 295–356.

Johnson-Laird, P. N. 1983. *Mental Models.* Cambridge: Harvard University Press.

Keil, F. C. 1989. *Concepts. Kinds. and Conceptual Development.* Cambridge, Mass.: The MIT Press.

Koyré, A. 1939. *Galileo Studies.* Atlantic Highlands, N. J.: Humanities Press, 1979.

Koyré, A. 1968. *Metaphysics and Measurement.* Cambridge, Mass.: Harvard University Press.

Kuhn, T. S. 1964. A Function for Thought Experiments. In *The Essential Tension: Selected Studies in Scientific Tradition and Change.* Chicago: University of Chicago Press, 1977.

Kuhn, T. S. 1965. *The Structure of Scientific Revolutions.* Chicago: University of Chicago Press.

Kuhn, T. S. 1986. Possible Worlds in History of Science: Nobel Symposium—August 1986. Unpublished Manuscript.

Kuhn, T. S. 1987. What are Scientific Revolutions? In *The Probabilistic Revolution.* Volume 1: Ideas in History, ed. L. Kruger, L. J. Daston, and M. Heidelberger, 7–22. Cambridge, Mass.: The MIT Press.

Langley, P., Simon, H. A., Bradshaw, G. L., and Zytkow, I. M. 1987. Scientific Discovery: Computational Explorations of the Creative Processes. Cambridge, Mass.: The MIT Press.

Laudan, L. 1977. *Progress and Its Problems: Towards a Theory of Scientific Growth.* Berkeley: University of California Press.

Larkin, J. H. and Simon, H. A. 1987. Why a Diagram Is (Sometimes) Worth Ten Thousand Words. *Cognitive Science* 11: 65–100.

Mani, K. and Johnson-Laird, P. N. 1982. The Mental Representation of Spatial Descriptions. *Memory and Cognition* 10: 181-187.

Manukian, E. 1987. Galilean Versus Aristotelian Models of Free Fall and Some Modern Concerns in Artificial Intelligence. Unpublished manuscript.

Maxwell, J. C. 1890. *The Scientific Papers of J. C. Maxwell.* ed. W. D. Niven. Cambridge: Cambridge University Press.

McCloskey, M. 1983. Naive Theories of Motion. In *Mental Models,* ed. D. Gentner and A. L. Stevens, 299–324. Hillsdale, N.J.: Lawerence Erlbaum.

McNamara, T. P. and Sternberg, R. J. 1983. Mental Models of Word Meaning. *Journal of Verbal Learning and Verbal Behavior* 22: 449–474.

Morrow, D. G., Bower, G .H., and Greenspan. S. L. 1989. Updating Situation Models during Narrative Comprehension. *Journal of Memory and Language* 28: 292–312.

Murphy, G. L. and Cohen, B. 1984. Models of Concepts. *Cognitive Science* 8: 27–58.

Naylor, R. 1976. Galileo: Real Experiment and Didactic Demonstration. *Isis* 67: 398-419.

Nersessian, N. J. 1984. *Faraday to Einstein: Constructing Meaning in Scientific Theories.* Dordrecht: Martinus Nijhoff.

Nersessian, N. J. 1985. Faraday's Field Concept. In *Faraday Rediscovered,* ed. D. Gooding and F. James, 175–187. London: Macmillan.

Nersessian, N. J. 1986. A Cognitive-Historical Approach to Meaning in Scientific Theories. In *The Process of Science: Contemporary Philosophical Approaches to Understanding Scientific Practice,* ed. N. J. Nersessian, 161–178. Dordrecht: Martinus Nijhoff.

Nersessian, N. J. 1989. Conceptual Change in Science and in Science Education. *Synthese* 80:163–184.

Nersessian, N. J. 1991a. Discussion: The "Method" to Meaning: A Reply to Leplin. *Philosophy of Science.*

Nersessian, N. J. 1991b. Constructing and Instructing: The Role of 'Abstraction Techniques in Developing and Teaching Scientific Theories. In *Philosophy of Science, Cognitive Science, and Educational Theory and Practice,* ed. R. Duschl and R. Hamilton. Albany: SUNY Press.

Nersessian, N. J. and Greeno, J. G. 1990. Multiple Abstracted Representations in Problem Solving and Discovery in Physics. *Proceedings of the Cognitive Science Society* 11: 77-84.

Norton, J. 1986. Thought Experiments in Einstein's Work. Unpublished manuscripts

Qin, P. and Simon, H. A. 1990. Laboratory Replication of Scientific Discovery Processes. *Cognitive Science* 14: 281-308.

Rosch, E. and Mervis, C. 1975. Family Resemblance Studies in the Internal Structure of Categories. *Cognitive Psychology* 7: 573–605.

Roschelle, J. and Greeno, J. G. 1987. Mental Models in Expert Physics Reasoning. Technical Report No. GK-2, University of California, Berkeley.

Sellars, W. 1965. Scientific Realism or Irenic Instrumentalism. In *Boston Studies in the Philosophy of Science 2,* ed. R. Cohen and M. Wartofsky, 171–204. Dordrecht: D. Reidel.

Settle, T. 1961. An Experiment in the History of Science. *Science* 133: 19–23.

Simon. H. A., Langley, P. W., and Bradshaw, G. L. 1981. Scientific Discovery as Problem Solving. *Synthese* 47: 1–27.

Smith, E. and Medin, D. 1981. *Concepts and Categories.* Cambridge, Mass.: Harvard University Press.

Thagard, P. 1988. *Computational Philosophy of Science.* Cambridge, Mass.: The MIT Press.

Tversky, B. 1990. Induced Pictorial Representations. Unpublished manuscript.

Tweney, R. D. 1985. Faraday's Discovery of Induction: A Cognitive Approach. In *Faraday Rediscovered,* ed. D. Gooding and F. A. L. James, 189–210. London: Macmillan.

Tweney, R. D. 1987. What is Scientific Thinking? Unpublished manuscript.

van Fraassen, B. C. 1980. *The Scientific Image.* Oxford: Oxford University Press.

Wise, N. 1979. The Mutual Embrace of Electricity and Magnetism. *Science* 203: 1313–1318.

Wiser, M., and Carey, S. 1983. When Heat and Temperature Were One. In *Mental Models,* ed. D. Gentner and A. L. Stevens, 267–298. Hillsdale, N. J.: Lawrence Erlbaum.

6 Qualitative Spatial Reasoning Framework and Frontiers

Kenneth D. Forbus
Northwestern University

6.1 Introduction

Given the context of this book, we take the importance of spatial reasoning as given. While cognitive science is far from a comprehensive understanding of spatial reasoning, there has been substantial progress in specific subproblems, as the chapters in this book demonstrate. The purpose of this chapter is to look at one of those areas, qualitative spatial reasoning about motion, to show the ideas which worked and to examine how they might be applied more broadly. We begin by outlining the *Metric Diagram/Place Vocabulary* (MD/PV) model of qualitative spatial reasoning (Section 6.2) illustrating it through two examples (FROB and CLOCK). Section 6.3 concludes by discussing three frontiers in spatial reasoning, highlighting how extensions of these ideas might apply, and poses some specific challenge problems to serve as milestones.

6.2 The MD/PV Model

Diagrams and models seem inextricably linked with human spatial reasoning. Why? The wealth of concrete detail in such analog spatial representations at first might seem more than necessary for most spatial questions. Perhaps there are more abstract representations of shape and space which by themselves are sufficient for the tasks an intelligence cares about. If there are, then why don't people use them? Is it due to our highly evolved visual systems, whose computational power makes it cheaper to measure than to infer? Have we simply not discovered them yet? Or is there some deeper reason why humans rely so much on perception for spatial tasks?

We believe there are deep reasons for human reliance on perceptual abilities for spatial reasoning, and that these reasons dominate the structure of theories for spatial reasoning in both people or machines. Our concise statement of this idea is the *Poverty Conjecture* (Forbus, Nielsen, and Faltings 1987, 1991): *There is no problem-independent, purely qualitative representation of space or shape.* By "purely qualitative," we

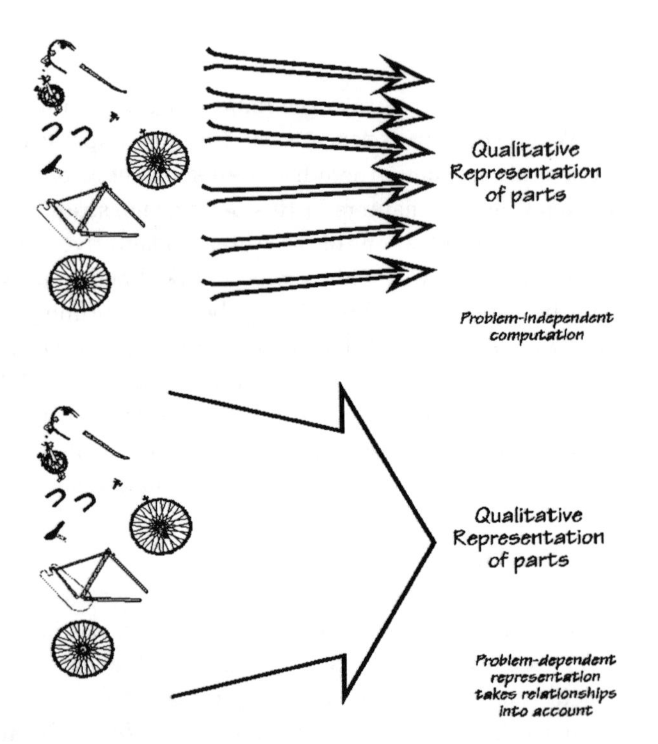

Figure 6.1
Qualitative spatial reasoning appears to require the derivation of task-specific qualitative representations from metric diagrams. A qualitative representation sufficient for figuring out how to assemble a bicycle must support inferences about what parts can fit together, which requires knowing relative sizes. Qualitative abstractions sufficient for this task cannot be computed for each part independently of the others, but good qualitative representations can be computed based on the set of parts. We conjecture that human spatial reasoning involves incrementally calculating such qualitative representations based on metric diagrams.

mean to rule out representations whose parts contain enough detailed information to permit calculation or the operation of perceptual-like processing. (Alas, we do not yet have a more precise definition.) Examples of descriptions that are purely qualitative include describing a two-dimensional shape by a list of signs of curvatures for boundary segments, or stating that two objects are gears which can mesh. Examples of descriptions that are quantitative enough to permit perception-like processes are symbolic descriptions with numerical components, high-resolution arrays, and symbolic algebraic expressions.

By problem-independent, we mean that descriptions in the representation must be able to support, by themselves, a variety of tasks. Suppose we had a collection of physical parts, such as a Lego or Erector set, which can be used to build a variety of physical objects. A good problem-independent representation for such parts would allow us to compute a description for each part independently and then use the parts' descriptions to answer questions about their spatial interactions, without referring back to the original objects. But characterizing the size of, for example, beams *a priori* does not make sense — an important property of beams is the relationship of their size to other elements in the construction kit. For a fixed set of parts, which can be combined only in highly constrained ways, such a qualitative description might be found. But adding even a single new kind of object (e.g., a differential gear box) could require going back to the original parts and computing a new descriptive vocabulary. Figure 6.1 illustrates.

The heavy reliance on metrical information is a general feature of spatial reasoning problems. Consider what a household robot needs to know to navigate. The simplest representation we might consider is a graph whose nodes are pieces of space the robot can be in and whose edges are paths that the robot can fit through from one piece of space to another. Given, say, a bounding diameter of the robot and a floor plan, we can easily design an algorithm that will compute such a graph. But suppose we did not have a detailed floor plan, and instead only knew that doorways and halls were classified as "narrow," "medium," or "wide." If we knew that our robot was "medium" and that medium meant the same thing for robots, doors, and hallways, then we might presume that our robot wouldn't fit in a narrow door, would fit in a wide door, and may or may not fit in a medium door. Dividing widths into arbitrary bins generally doesn't capture the distinctions relevant to the task. Here,

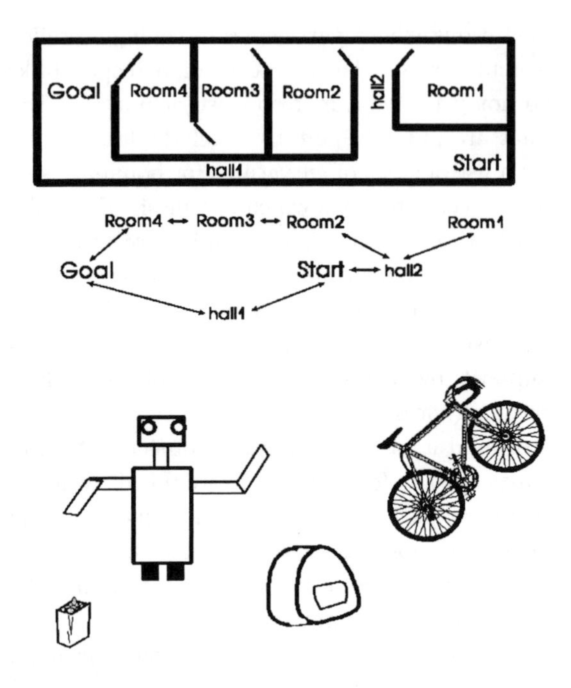

Figure 6.2
Even navigation problems are affected by the poverty conjecture. Figuring out what constitutes a reasonable topological abstraction of a physical space requires information about what objects are passing through the space, in addition to information about the space itself. Thus metric information is required for representations that are independent of specific tasks.

knowing the relative size of the robot and each door is what we really need to know. If we know that the door is wider than the robot then the robot's representation should include an edge between the rooms the door connects, and otherwise not. Knowing metric information (i.e., the robot's width and a floor plan) would certainly allow us to calculate the relevant distinctions, and once we did so, we could simply use this more abstract, topological information to enable the robot to get from one part of the house to another. This graph is an example of a place vocabulary.

This qualitative representation is adequate as long as the robot isn't carrying anything. But what if the robot is carrying (a) your backpack, (b) a sack of groceries, or (c) a bicycle? (Figure 6.2 illustrates.) In a typical house some edges of the original graph of places will not correspond to a legitimate path for the robot and its burden. And the graph of places by itself does not contain the information we would need to compute an improved representation—instead, we have to refer back to whatever source of information allowed us to compute this representation in the first place. This is an example of how purely qualitative representations can fail. Even adding a modicum of quantitative information (e.g., minimum width of each path) can greatly extend the usefulness of the representation. But for very subtle reasoning (e.g., getting a piano up a spiral staircase), a wealth of spatial detail is necessary to determine if a motion is feasible. This does not mean that qualitative representations are useless: far from it! For instance, given the maximum width of a burden we can incrementally compute a problem-specific qualitative representation of space which greatly simplifies path planning. The point is that for spatial reasoning, the interaction between qualitative information and more detailed information needs to be tightly coupled.

What does the poverty conjecture tell us about spatial reasoning? It suggests that spatial representations consist of two parts: a *metric diagram*, which includes quantitative information and thus provides a substrate which can support perceptual-like processing, and a *place vocabulary*, which makes explicit qualitative distinctions in shape and space relevant to the current task. The metric diagram can use floating-point numbers, algebra, or even high-precision arrays—whatever it uses, there must be enough detail to support answering spatial queries by calculation, and it must be capable of supporting the construction of place vocabularies. Place vocabularies consist of *places*, contiguous regions of space where some important property (e.g., in contact with a gear, inside a well) is constant. Computing the place vocabulary according to the needs of the problem ensures that the relevant distinctions are made. Defining the places in terms of elements in the metric diagram makes the diagram a good communication medium for diverse representations. Next we illustrate these ideas through two example systems.

6.2.1 Example: FROB

FROB (Forbus 1980, 1983) reasoned about the motion of balls bouncing around in a two-dimensional diagram. Aside from predicting the specific motion of a given ball, FROB also produced on demand summaries of the eventual fate of a ball and estimates about whether two balls might

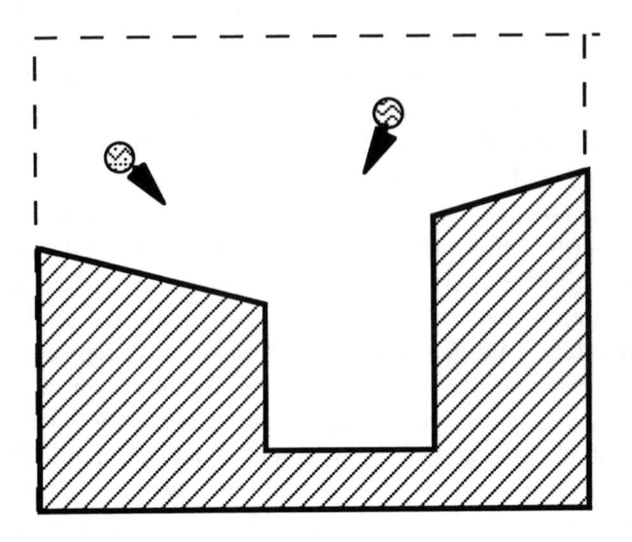

Figure 6.3
A FROB scenario. Can these balls collide? What if the right ball flies over the well and the left ball falls into it? What if both balls fall into the well? Even these simple qualitative stipulations can dramatically affect our judgments concerning their fate.

collide. These problems are an important subset of the spatial reasoning tasks faced by any agent operating in a world of moving objects. For instance, one should be able to quickly figure out that two balls thrown into the same well might collide, while throwing the balls into different wells means they cannot collide, unless one of them escapes.

Figure 6.3 illustrates a typical FROB scenario. The metric diagram is initialized with a set of line segments corresponding to surfaces. Since balls are modeled as point masses, given the surfaces FROB computes a single place vocabulary that is used for all balls. Since gravity acts vertically, free space is divided into places by vertical and horizontal lines emanating from corners. The vertical boundaries distinguish what a ball might hit when dropping downward, and the horizontal boundaries indicate important heights for reasoning about energy. For instance, if a sequence of bounces drops a ball's energy so that the maximum height it can reach is below the top free space segment defining a well, it has become trapped in that well.

FROB's metric diagram consists of a set of symbolic descriptions with numerical attributes. For instance, a line segment includes a pointer to a physical interpretation (e.g., surface) as well as a numerical length and end points, each in turn specified via floating-point coordinates. The numerical information allows spatial queries to be answered by calculation rather than inference, while the physical information guides the selection and interpretation of results. For instance, FROB uses constraint-based simulation (Forbus and de Kleer 1993), rather than traditional incremental-time simulation, to predict motion using numerical data. Constraint-based simulation essentially involves plugging in numerical values for analytic solutions of the original differential equations. This computation uses geometric reasoning in two ways. First, to establish what a ball is doing (flying through the air versus colliding with a surface), we must know where it is. Second, geometric reasoning is required to solve for boundary conditions. Consider a ball flying through the air with a known initial position and velocity. This information suffices to calculate a parabola (or line segment) corresponding to the dynamical constraints on its trajectory, which is then intersected with the surfaces in the scene to figure out what the ball would hit. The new state of the ball after the collision can then be computed, a new trajectory drawn, and so forth.

FROB's place vocabulary allows assimilation of qualitative constraints and supports global reasoning about possible motions. The elements of the place vocabulary and the relationships between them provide the qualitative terms required for qualitative simulation laws for envisioning the possible motions of balls. Certain "obvious" questions about collisions can be answered by comparing envisionments: If two balls are never in the same place, for instance, they can never collide. Furthermore, an envisionment can be pruned to represent the consequences of qualitative constraints on motion (e.g., assuming that a ball doesn't go into a well) or of numerical constraints expressed geometrically (e.g., ruling out motions that would occur if their place is above the maximum height a ball could reach given its energy).

FROB provides a good illustration of the utility of the MD/PV model of spatial reasoning. The metric diagram provides the precision required to calculate boundary conditions for detailed predictions, and provides a substrate for automatic computation of the place vocabulary. The place vocabulary supports sophisticated qualitative reasoning about motion.

But even if the graph of places was provided *a priori*, many interesting questions cannot be answered without grounding the place vocabulary in the metric diagram (e.g., whether a ball is trapped in a well or ruling out collisions between balls). Thus even in FROB's simple domain, both the metric diagram and place vocabulary are required for sophisticated spatial reasoning.

6.2.2 Example: CLOCK

A more complex class of motion problems concerns fixed-axis mechanisms, such as mechanical clocks. The creation of reliable mechanical clocks was a milestone in mechanical engineering; thus the development of systems which can reason about such mechanisms serves as a good milestone for qualitative spatial reasoning. One milestone, the qualitative simulation of a mechanical clock from first principles, was achieved by our group in February 1988 by the CLOCK system (Forbus, Nielsen, and Faltings 1987, 1991) built by Paul Nielsen and Boi Faltings as part of their Ph.D. theses.

CLOCK worked on fixed-axis mechanisms which could be decomposed into two-dimensional interactions. Given a CAD-like description of the parts of a mechanism and their degrees of freedom, CLOCK computed a place vocabulary based on configuration space. Configuration space is the appropriate basis for the place vocabulary because connectivity is central to kinematic state. Faltings developed an elegant characterization of such places and algorithms for computing them (Faltings 1987, 1990). Instead of developing a single, massive high-dimensionality vocabulary, his algorithms created place vocabularies for pairs of parts that could interact, and used elements from these vocabularies to define kinematic states for the whole mechanism. The metric diagram plays a key role in this composition process, since defining consistent combinations of places sometimes requires projecting constraints from one vocabulary to another (and thus introducing new distinct places) when two vocabularies share a part.

CLOCK's metric diagram also played a key role in keeping envisioning tractable. Any diagram has noise, and the well-known sensitivity of kinematics to the details of surface shape means that smoothing the contours of a part in isolation is inappropriate. Nielsen realized that filtering at the level of the place vocabulary allows the interaction of the parts to be taken into account, and developed algorithms for removing "small" places and merging places that were "very close." The resulting simplification of the place vocabulary was dramatic: The number of potential kinematic states dropped from over 10,000 to 58 (Nielsen 1989).

For qualitative reasoning about the dynamics of motion, Nielsen developed a qualitative vector algebra, and showed how shapes should be decomposed qualitatively to define robust notions of mechanical constraint (Nielsen 1990). The requirements of reasoning about mechanical constraint again illustrate the need for interactions between qualitative and quantitative representations: The appropriate qualitative description of an object for figuring out how it can move if pushed depends not just on its shape, but also the qualitative direction to its center of rotation.[1]

6.2.3 Supporting Evidence

The ideas described above are not the only work which supports the claim that the combination of metric diagrams and place vocabularies is necessary for spatial reasoning about motion (c.f. Joskowicz 1987, Joskowicz and Sacks 1991; Narayanan and Chandrasekaran 1991). A more complete examination of the relevant literature and its relation to this model can be found in Forbus, Nielsen, and Faltings (1991). As the household robot example suggests, we believe the MD/PV model is relevant to path-planning problems. Furthermore, the widely reported use of imagery in scientific and engineering reasoning (c.f. Tweney 1990) suggests that similar constraints operate in other forms of spatial reasoning as well. While powerful, self-sufficient, purely qualitative representations for shape and space would in many ways be desirable, none has yet been found and there are good reasons to suspect that they simply do not exist. If this is correct, the necessity of using some form of metric diagram may be the central unifying factor in spatial reasoning.

Many interesting physical systems, including internal combustion engines and pumps, can only be understood by comprehending the interactions of fluids and solid objects through motion. Recently Hyeonkyeong

[1] A simple demonstration: The center of rotation for a book on a table is its center of mass. Pick a side of the book and try pushing it on the corners versus the middle. Notice that the sign of its rotation differs in each case, providing a criteria for decomposing its shape qualitatively. Now drive a nail through the book into the table, somewhere near a corner of the book. The center of rotation will now be different, and hence a different qualitative decomposition of the book's shape is required.

Kim (1993) has developed a set of qualitative representations and reasoning techniques that are sufficient for analyzing such examples. She developed a qualitative account of linkages that can envision up to four-bar linkages, showing that representing relative lengths of links, when combined with a qualitative representation of angle that includes both what quadrant it is in and relative inclination with respect to other links, suffices to solve this problem (Kim 1992a) She developed a qualitative method of computing streamline diagrams for laminar fluid flow, capable of generating explanations about how the Bernoulli effect generates lift over an airplane wing (Kim 1990). Complex processes such as the combustion in a cylinder that drives a piston downward are typically approximated as instantaneous changes, so she developed a qualitative theory of impulses, showing how their effect could be modeled via structural changes in envisionments (Kim 1992b). Finally, figuring out how liquids can move inside containers that contain pistons and valves requires describing fluids in terms of their potential surface contacts. Kim developed such a representation for fluids, exploiting Nielsen's work on representing shapes and surfaces (Kim 1992c). Kim's research is a large step towards a comprehensive qualitative mechanics.

What about the connection of spatial reasoning to perception? As vision researchers begin to grapple with higher-level perception, more attention has been placed on the role of task constraints in visual processing. For example, Ullman has postulated a recognition tasks and is programmable by higher systems (Ullman 1985). An interesting conjecture is that the human metric diagram processor is in fact the same thing as the visual routine processor. Approaching these issues from opposite sides of the cognition/perception borderland has meant that each effort focuses on different tasks, but this conjectured identity raises some interesting avenues for joint empirical inquiry (c.f. Chapman 1991; McDougal and Hammond 1992).

One task for which visual routines are likely to be used is in interpreting line graphs, such as the temperature-entropy diagrams commonly used in thermodynamics to reason about the properties of power plants and refrigerators. Yusuf Pisan (Pisan 1994) has shown how visual processing on metric diagrams can be used to reason with such pictures. His system, SKETCHY, takes as input a diagram, expressed as line segments (curves are approximated by many short line segments). SKETCHY uses the labels associated with the diagram elements to in-

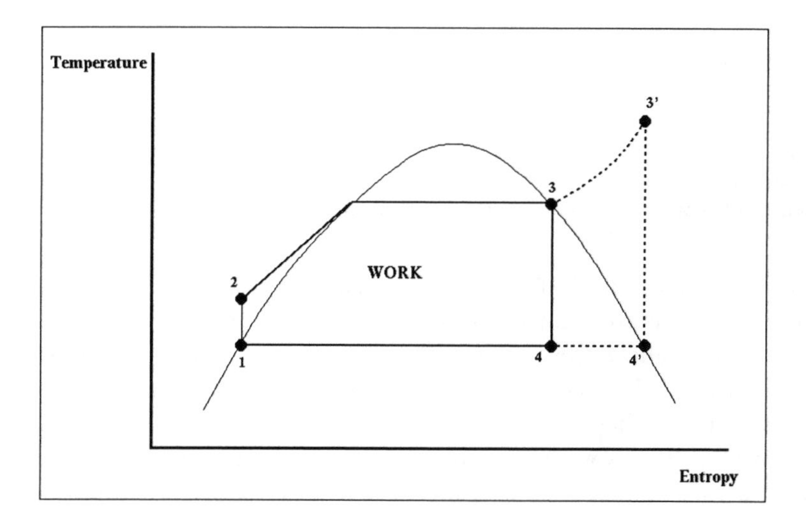

Figure 6.4
An example analyzed by SKETCHY. Comparative analysis can be carried out by visual manipulations on diagrams. Here, the effect of superheating in a steam plant is represented graphically by a change in the position of point 3 in this temperature/entropy diagram. SKETCHY's visual routines enable it to compute that this change increases the area under the curve, and its interpretation of these geometric changes in physical terms allows it to conclude that the efficiency of the system is thus increased.

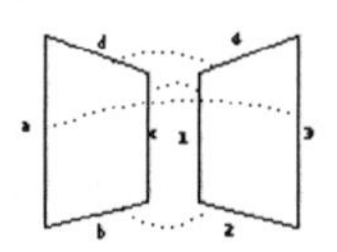

Figure 6.5
MAGI uses SME's ability to produce multiple interpretations to find intuitively plausible symmetries. MAGI produces three mappings for this example. The strongest interpretation is symmetrical, with the axis of symmetry between and parallel to lines c and 1. The other two interpretations correspond to rotations.

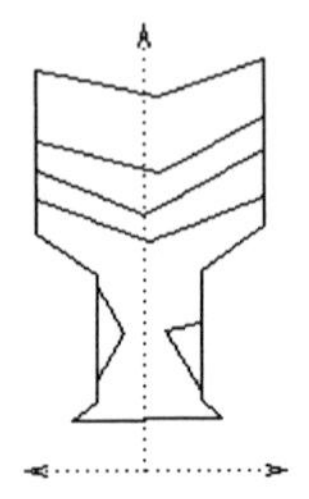

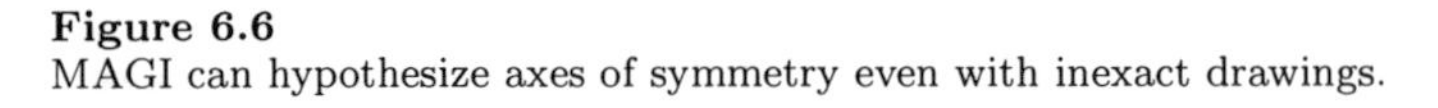

Figure 6.6
MAGI can hypothesize axes of symmetry even with inexact drawings.

fer information about physical properties. For example, SKETCHY uses vision algorithms to estimate curvature, and thus can extract qualitative proportionalities from graphs. An especially interesting and novel aspect of SKETCHY is that it demonstrates Pisan's observation that an important use of diagrams in human reasoning is *comparative analysis* (Weld 1990). Weld's work on comparative analysis argued persuasively that it is an important style of human reasoning about physical systems, but also showed that there were strict limits on how well it could be supported by purely qualitative representations. Pisan argues that the availability of metric information in diagrams makes them a natural representation for comparative analysis. For example, in Figure 6.4 the physical changes caused by superheating the working fluid in a Rankine cycle power plant are depicted in a diagram (from Whalley 1991). SKETCHY uses its visual routines to calculate that this change increases the area under the curve, which it then interprets physically as an increase in the efficiency of the system. To date SKETCHY has analyzed over 60 diagrams from thermodynamics and economics textbooks, supporting these and other inferences.

There is a growing body of psychological evidence that the cognitive processes of similarity are also used in perceptual processing (Markman and Gentner 1993; Medin, Goldstone, and Gentner 1993; Gentner and Markman, in press). Thus we would expect that ideas of symbolic representation and qualitative reasoning would be useful in perceptual computations as well. An example of this is the recent work of Ferguson (1994), who has developed a model of symmetry detection. The key idea of Ferguson's theory is that symmetry is like analogy, specifically, a special kind of mapping involving a scene and itself. His system, MAGI, can detect symmetries in conceptual representations (e.g., an encoding of the O. Henry story "The Gift of the Magi") and perceptual representations. The latter are especially interesting because they show how automatically produced metric diagrams [2] can be used to model human perceptual processing. MAGI uses an incremental version of SME (Forbus, Ferguson, and Gentner 1994), a simulation of Gentner's structure-mapping theory of analogy and similarity (Gentner 1983), to perform the mappings. The ability of SME to produce multiple mappings captures the ability to see several possible symmetries in a figure (c.f. Figure 6.5) The mappings it produces can be used to suggest axes of symmetry (c.f. Figure 6.6). Finally, SME's ability to generate candidate inferences, i.e., plausible inferences suggested by the correspondences, provides an avenue for top-down influences of cognitive processing on perception (c.f. Figure 6.7)

6.3 Frontiers and Challenge Problems

Progress continues in qualitative spatial reasoning about motion, based on the MD/PV model, and this aspect of the problem of spatial reasoning is by no means completely tamed. However, there are many other aspects of spatial reasoning that also deserve attention, and seem ripe for substantial progress as well. Furthermore, the recent improvements in floating point and graphics hardware, along with impressive increases in memory speeds and capacities, means that technological barriers for computational experiments are falling: Spatial reasoning may be one of the few areas in AI where our progress has become more limited by ideas than by technology.

In this spirit, the remainder of this chapter proposes several challenge problems as possible focal points for research on spatial reasoning. Our end goal as Cognitive Scientists remains unchanged, of course: a comprehensive computational account of spatial reasoning, with both an empirically tested explanation for human spatial reasoning capabilities and practical representations and algorithms for mechanical reasoners.

[2] Initial diagrams are drawn with XFIG, a publically available drawing program, and its results are converted into an initial symbolic description with numerical properties, much as in Marr's (1976) Primal Sketch. This initial symbolic description is then further processed via pattern-directed rules to create an initial encoding of spatial relationships.

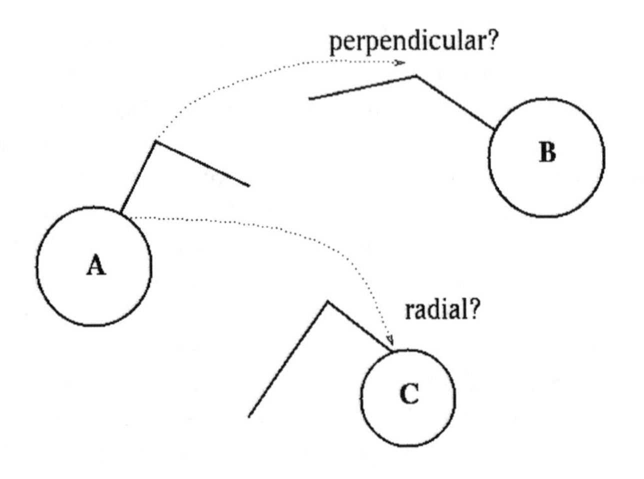

Figure 6.7
MAGI models top-down effects of cognition on perception via candidate inferences. In the subfigure A, one line is normal to the circle at its point of contact (i.e., a radial connection) and the other line forms a right angle. In the mapping that proposes that A corresponds to B, the joint between the corresponding angles is hypothesized to be perpendicular. If the angle was in fact close, rerepresenting it as such might be useful. Similarly, in the mapping that proposes that A corresponds to C, a radial connection between the line and circle are hypothesized. A visual system might use these hypotheses to help guide its exploration of the image, thus constraining visual search.

The problems proposed here are meant to be milestones, in that their solutions would count as substantial progress even though they appear (at least from our current perspective) to be somewhat simpler. In each case we first sketch the general task and why it is important, and then suggest some challenge problems.

6.3.1 Deriving Function from Real Structure

An important engineering skill is interpreting blueprints and schematics, deriving from the description of the structure of the system its intended function. Previous AI work on this problem has focused on analog electronics (e.g., de Kleer 1984), an unfortunate choice from our perspective since that domain is designed to allow geometric considerations to be mostly ignored. The structural descriptions used in more recent qualitative physics research mostly remains quite abstract, ranging from specifying a system in terms of qualitative equations to describing idealized entities such as containers and abstract fluid paths

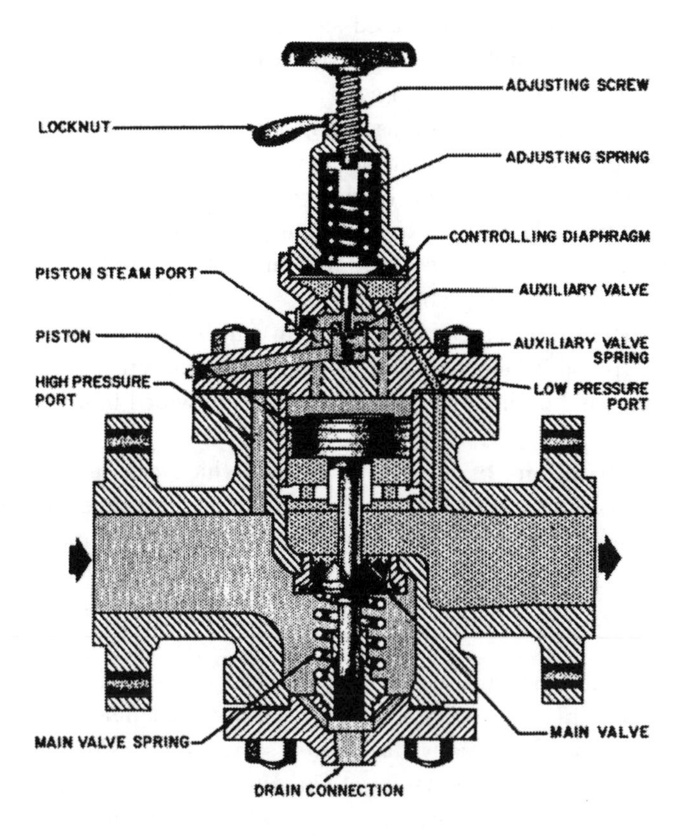

Figure 6.8
A spring-loaded reducing valve. This picture, from a U.S. Navy training manual, is the original source of the abstract reducing valve example widely used as an example in qualitative physics. Many interesting aspects of physical reasoning are involved in translating from this picture into the abstract representations that most qualitative physics work starts with.

(Kim's work, as outlined above, is an exception). Such descriptions may be good candidates for the output of systems which assimilate information from more standard sources, but the problem of deriving abstract structural descriptions from more primitive descriptions itself deserves study. For example, a standard example in qualitative physics is a kind of spring-loaded reducing valve. Figure 6.8 shows the original spring-loaded reducing valve which motivated subsequent work. The process of creating a usable mental model from this geometric description and some supporting text does not seem easy.

Two major issues in such reasoning seem to be (a) how to move from primitive descriptions of shape, material composition, and connectivity to a more abstract interpretation of the parts of the device suitable for other reasoning tasks and (b) how to manage the complexity of the structural descriptions so created (c.f. Liu and Farley 1991). These issues suggest two challenge problems:

Challenge Problem 1: Develop a system which can answer questions about the possible behaviors and uses of pneumatic control components, given the kind of drawings and annotations provided in a typical textbook.

Challenge Problem 2: Develop a system which can, given the blueprints of a complex system such as an automobile engine, derive a decomposition of it into subsystems and provide abstract functional models of the subsystems and overall operation of the system.

6.3.2 Reasoning about Spatially Distributed Systems

Qualitative dynamics has focused on lumped-parameter systems. Many phenomena, including heat transfer, aerodynamics, and fluid dynamics are best modeled as spatially distributed systems. Developing the qualitative version of partial differential equations requires deeper and more flexible integration of spatial reasoning with dynamics. The potential applications are very important: A key problem in today's use of finite element analysis in problems such as computational fluid dynamics is quantizing shapes and space to provide accurate results with the least computational effort. Programs which could automatically produce good meshes would be quite valuable.

One key issue seems to be finding appropriate constraints on place vocabularies. What are the analogs to CLOCK's decomposition of shapes along centers of rotation, or FROB's decomposition of free space along vertical and horizontal axes? The place vocabularies must both support computations with more detailed data and support explanations of overall qualitative features of behavior.

Challenge Problem 3: Develop a system which can automatically set up meshes for finite element analysis programs, given a CAD description of the physical system to be analyzed.

Challenge Problem 4: Develop a system which can, given a sequence of weather maps for a region, provide a consistent qualitative explanation of the atmospheric behavior during that period, or detect if the sequence of maps is inconsistent.

Happily, some progress has been made on each of these problems since this chapter originally appeared in the AAAI Spring Symposium. With regard to generating meshes, Gelsey and his students at Rutgers (Yao and Gelsey 1993) have some interesting results. With regard to reasoning about the weather, Monika Lundell of the Swiss Federal Institute of Technology has developed a promising approach for automatically creating qualitative descriptions of spatially distributed phenomena (Lundell 1994). Each of these is an interesting step towards solving these challenge problems, but much work remains to be done.

6.3.3 Perception in Spatial Reasoning and Learning

In many applications of spatial reasoning the inputs are self-evident (e.g., CAD files or blueprints or weather maps). For cognitive simulation the problem of what the inputs are is a subtle methodological question. Inappropriate assumptions about input can trivialize important problems or divert us into solving non-problems. The psychological aspect of the MD/PV model is the idea that the Metric Diagram is in fact part of our perceptual system, programmed in part according to task and in part bottom-up. Consequently, questions about the nature of high-level perception and the relationship between perception and cognition are crucial to cognitive simulations of spatial reasoning. For instance, in cognitive developmental psychology there is a fascinating set of theories and empirical findings on children's acquisition of ideas concerning motion, objectness, and causality (c.f. Baillargeon and DeVos 1991, Spelke 1991),Furthermore, learning and teaching often involve interaction through mixtures of text, speech, and diagrams (Shrager 1990).

Challenge Problem 5: Simulate the acquisition of commonsense notions of objects, space, or causality, including an artificial vision system as part of the input processing.

Challenge Problem 6: Develop a system which can be taught a qualitative theory of a phenomena, such as aerodynamics or the greenhouse effect, via an interactive, mixed-medium dialog.

Acknowledgments

The research on reported here was supported by the Computer Science Division of the Office of Naval Research. I thank Dedre Gentner, Ron Ferguson, Yusuf Pisan, and David Foster for useful discussions and comments.

References

Baillargeon, R. and DeVos, J. 1991. Object Permanence in Young Infants: Further Evidence. *Child Development* 62: 1227–1246.

Chapman, D. 1991. *Vision, Instruction, and Action.* Cambridge, Mass.: The MIT Press.

de Kleer, J. 1984. How Circuits Work. *Artificial Intelligence* 24.

Faltings, B. 1986. A Theory of Qualitative Kinematics in Mechanisms, Technical Report No. UIUCDCS-R-86-1274, Department of Computer Science, University of Illinois at Urbana-Champaign

Faltings, B. 1990. Qualitative Kinematics in Mechanisms. *Artificial Intelligence* 41(1), June.

Ferguson, R. 1994. MAGI: Analogy-Based Encoding Using Regularity and Symmetry. In Proceedings of the Sixteenth Annual Conference of the Cognitive Science Society.

Forbus, K. 1980. Spatial and Qualitative Aspects of Reasoning about Motion. In Proceedings of the National Conference on Artificial Intelligence. Menlo Park, Calif.: American Association for Artificial Intelligence.

Forbus, K. 1983. Qualitative Reasoning about Space and Motion. In *Mental Models*, ed. D. Gentner, D. and A. Stevens. Hillsdale, N.J.: Erlbaum.

Forbus, K. and de Kleer, J. 1993. *Building Problem Solvers.* Cambridge, Mass.: The MIT Press.

Forbus, K., Ferguson, R. and Gentner, D. 1994. Incremental Structure-Mapping. In Proceedings of the Sixteenth Annual Conference of the Cognitive Science Society.

Forbus, K., Nielsen, P., and Faltings, B. 1987. Qualitative Kinematics: A Framework. In Proceedings of the International Joint Conference on Artificial Intelligence. San Francisco, Calif.: Morgan Kaufmann.

Forbus, K., Nielsen, P. and Faltings, B. 1991. Qualitative Spatial Reasoning: The CLOCK Project. *Artificial Intelligence* 51(1-3), October.

Gentner, D. 1983. Structure-Mapping: A Theoretical Framework for Analogy. *Cognitive Science* 7: 155–170.

Gentner, D. and Markman, A. B. 1995. Similarity Is Like Analogy: Structural Alignment in Comparison. In Proceedings of the Workshop on Similarity at the University of San Marino, ed. C. Cacciari. Milan, Italy: Bompiani.

Joskowicz, L. 1987.Shape and Function in Mechanical Devices. In Proceedings of the Sixth National Conference on Artificial Intelligence. Menlo Park, Calif. American Association for Artificial Intelligence.

Joskowicz, L. and Sacks, E. 1991. Computational Kinematics. *Artificial Intelligence* 51(1-3), October.

Kim, H. 1990. Qualitative Reasoning about the Geometry of Fluid Flow. In Proceedings of the Twelfth Annual Conference of the Cognitive Science Society, Cambridge, Mass., July.

Kim, H. 1992. Qualitative Kinematics of Linkages. In *Recent Advances in Qualitative Physics*, ed. B. Faltings and P. Struss. Cambridge, Mass.: The MIT Press.

Kim, H. 1992. Augmenting Qualitative Simulation with Global Filtering. In Proceedings of the Fourteenth Annual Conference of the Cognitive Science Society.

Kim, H. 1992. Extending the Contained-stuff Ontology with Geometry. In Proceedings of the Sixth International Qualitative Physics Workshop.

Kim, H. 1993. Qualitative Reasoning about Fluids and Mechanics." Technical Report #47, The Institute for the Learning Sciences, Northwestern University, December.

Liu, Z. and Farley, A. 1991. Tasks, Models, Perspectives, Dimensions. In Proceedings of the Fifth International Workshop on Qualitative Reasoning about Physical Systems, Austin, Texas, May.

Lundell, M. 1994. Qualitative Reasoning with Spatially Distributed Parameters. In Proceedings of QR-94, Nara, Japan.

Markman, A. B. and Gentner, D. 1993. Structural Alignment During Similarity Comparisons. *Cognitive Psychology* 25: 431–467.

Marr, D. 1976. Early Processing of Visual Information. *Philosophical Transactions R. Society London Ser. B* 275: 483–524.

McDougal, T. and Hammond, K. 1992.A Recognition Model of Geometry Theorem Proving. In Proceedings of the Fourteenth Annual Conference of the Cognitive Science Society.

Medin, D. L., Goldstone, R. L., and Gentner, D. 1993. Respects for Similarity. *Psychological Review* 100(2): 254–278.

Narayanan, N. H., and Chandrasekaran, B. 1991. Reasoning Visually about Spatial Interactions. In Proceedings of the International Joint Conference on Artificial Intelligence. San Francisco: Morgan Kaufmann.

Nielsen, P. 1990. A Qualitative Approach to Mechanical Constraint. In Proceedings of the National Conference on Artificial Intelligence. Menlo Park, Calif.: American Association for Artificial Intelligence.

Nielsen, P. 1989. The Role of Abstraction in Place Vocabularies. In Proceedings of the Conference of the Cognitive Science Society.

Pisan, Y. 1994. Visual Reasoning about Physical Properties Via Graphs. In Proceedings of QR94, Nara, Japan, June.

Shrager, J. 1990. Commonsense Perception and the Psychology of Theory Formation. In *Computational Models of Scientific Discovery and Theory Formation*, ed. J. Shrager and P. Langley. San Francisco: Morgan-Kaufmann.

Spelke, E. S. 1991. Physical Knowledge in Infancy: Reflections on Piaget's Theory. In *The Epigenesis of Mind*, ed. S. Carey and R. Gellman. Hillsdale, N.J.: Erlbaum.

Tweney, R. D. 1990. Five Questions for Computationalists. In *Computational Models of Scientific Discovery and Theory Formation*, ed. J. Shrager and P. Langley. San Francisco: Morgan-Kaufmann.

Ullman, S. 1985.'Visual Routines. In *Visual Cognition*, ed. S. Pinker. Cambridge, Mass.: The MIT Press.

Weld, D. 1990. *Theories of Comparative Analysis.* Cambridge, Mass.: The MIT Press.

Whalley, P. 1991. *Engineering Thermodynamics.* New York: Oxford University Press.

Yao, K. T. and Gelsey, A. 1993. Spatial Reasoning for Intelligent Control of Numerical Simulators. In Proceedings of QR93, May.

II THEORETICAL FOUNDATIONS

Introduction to Section II
Theoretical Foundations

Patrick Hayes
The University of Illinois

The chapters in this section are all concerned with the idea of reasoning with diagrammatic representations. It seems that reasoning must involve assertions; but what does it mean to assert a diagram? These chapters all give, or assume, rather different answers to this question.

One dimension of contrast involves perception. Stenning, Inder and Neilsen come to this issue from the field of human-computer interaction (HCI), where a diagram is something which people look at or feel. It exists in a physical medium and has a shape and an appearance. Cognitive and perceptual issues are central in their discussion. They are very careful to distinguish differences of medium (spoken versus written language) from differences in modality (text versus pictures). (Their claim that differences in modality have been comparatively neglected is probably less true outside of the HCI community, as the other chapters in this volume may testify.)

At the other extreme, Wang, Lee and Hervat develop a completely algebraic account which removes the notion of diagram completely from perceptual issues. Here, a diagram is thought of not as something existing in a medium, but rather quite abstractly as a complex kind of syntax. Diagrammatic languages are simply a more complex propositional notation than the usual one, a notation whose syntax itself needs a logical description. The result is a system of two multi-sorted first-order theories. The first—called a graphical signature—describes the syntax of possible diagrams, while the second—the graphical theory—describes the inference processes allowed on diagrams. These authors are careful to emphasize that any perceptual aspects of such diagrams are to be ignored: optical illusions, for example, are here required to be illusory. In fact, there is nothing in this account which requires "diagrams" to have a pictorial appearance. Since these signatures are first-order theories, they could be illustrated by any model of these theories without changing the content of the account. In Stenning, Inder and Neilsen's terms, they describe the modality and completely ignore the medium.

Wang, Lee and Hervat raise an issue which bedevils most accounts of diagrammatic reasoning. If we think of a diagram as a picture, it will usually have many properties which are not supposed to convey information, but are mere accidental consequences of the pictorial nature of the diagram. For example, a drawing of two men will indicate their relative height, even if this is not intended to mean anything. How are we to specify which properties of a picture or diagram are meant to be the carriers of information? The graphical signature and theories are intended to make just this selection of the meaningful properties and relations from all those that might be visible in a picture. However, the authors offer little guidance as to how the selection of the right properties might be done, and in some cases it seems a rather subtle problem.

For example, one of the oldest, most beautiful and most convincing proofs of Pythagoras' theorem, described in Dominic Olivastro's *Ancient Puzzles* (New York: Bantam Books 1993), consists simply of the following two pictures together with the single word "Behold!"

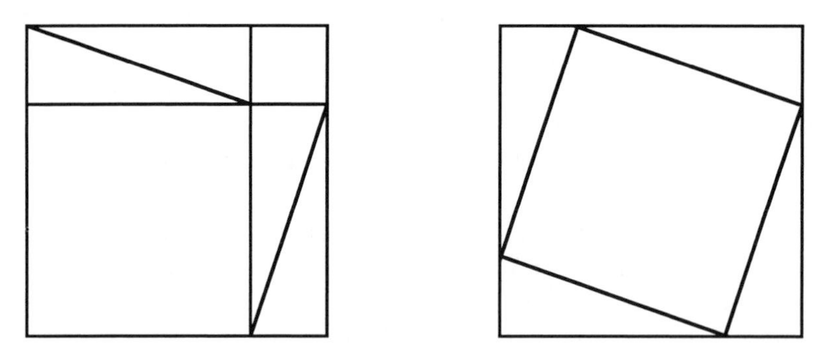

In order to "see" this, one has to see that the large squares are both of side $(a + b)$, that each contains four copies of the same triangle, etc., and to do this it is necessary to see that lines at various places in the figure are the same length as one another. On the other hand, it is also necessary to appreciate that the construction does not depend on these lines being of that particular length. To achieve exactly this amount of precision and generality, the "signature" must be able to express the identity of the relevant line lengths and sufficient geometry to establish all the relevant identities, but must not be able to express any other geometric properties or relations between parts of the diagrams. If this can be done, it is only with considerable care, which amounts to a lot more than the simple injunction which constituted the original text. It seems that something essentially graphic about the old proof has been lost, or perhaps it would be better to say assumed as given, in Wang, Lee, and Hervat's account. They consider a related example, but do not give us details of the relevant signature.

Other authors take still different approaches to what constitutes a diagram.

Barwise and Etchemendy view diagrams and conventional propositional notations as fundamentally different ways of displaying and using information, neither reducible to the other but each describing the same kind of model. This is how the representations are related, in this account: like strange Siamese twins, they are joined only at their denotations. Barwise and Etchemendy share with Stenning, Inder and Neilsen a conviction that diagrams and texts are fundamentally distinct species. However, this perspective arises from mathematics rather than communication, and the differences show. Barwise and Etchemendy are interested in extending the expressive power of diagrams so that they might be able to make assertions which are present beyond them. Like Myers and Konolige, they are driven by a vision of a new kind of reasoning (or perhaps, a modern understanding of a very old kind of reasoning) which has been neglected by contemporary mathematics. In contrast, the central concern of Stenning, Inder and Neilsen is how to transmit and convey information between agents. They are talking about a public language for communication, while Myers and Konolige are talking about a private language of thought. I suspect that Barwise and Etchemendy would reject the distinction.

The justly celebrated Hyperproof system makes clever pedagogic use of the contrast and complement between a diagrammatic representation—which here is a picturelike representation—and a conventional logical description of the same world. Barwise and Etchemendy give a precise semantic account of their pictorial representation. On this account the hyperproof diagram is, like the conventional logical axioms, a description of a possible world. However, the pedagogic utility of this system may arise from the student's regarding the diagram as being a depiction of a model of the axioms, rather than an alternative kind of description. Barwise and Etchemendy point out here that this interpretation is always available. Although it may be somewhat beyond the scope of this collection, this essentially psychological question may be worth some careful study, especially in view of the undoubted success of Hyperproof as a teaching tool.

Myers and Konolige characterize "diagrammatic" at the level of the data structures involved in an implementation of an inference mechanism. This way of describing what "diagram" means, unlike the others, is thus inextricably linked with the computer. Myers and Konolige are careful to insist that the pictures they draw, and the models of these diagrams, are only analytical tools in their metalanguage: all the inference operations are defined on the data structures.

However, it is not entirely clear what this means. For example, Stenning, Inder and Neilsen draw a contrast between tabular and matrix-graphical representations. This makes sense when each of these is presented on a page. But the structure of a datastructure may not be so directly visible. One data structure may be implemented at a lower level by a different data structure with different structural properties. For example, a sparse array may be stored internally as a graph structure, or a collection of ground axioms may be compiled into a compact memory table. The user of the program need not even be made aware of such internal decisions, which are often regarded as matters of optimization. Any characterization of representational mode based on the form of the datastructure seems therefore to be at the mercy of the whim of the implementer of the system.

Myers and Konolige escape this problem by taking a more functional view of what it is to be a datastructure. They treat their representations as encoding assertions, in much the way that sentences do: they have a model-theoretic semantics and the usual notions of consistency and completeness apply to them. While some relations are represented "analogically," the content of the representation can be completely specified by a set of assertions. Indeed, the basic operations on a diagram are to insert a ground assertion into it and extract one from it, so that diagrams are considered to be essentially databases for ground assertions. This perspective has been adopted by other thinkers in AI, notably by Henry Levesque, who introduced the idea of a vivid set of assertions as a way of characterizing the content of diagrammatic representations. This fits naturally with the computer scientist's functionalist perspective towards implemented systems, where what concerns a user of a system is what it does, but how it does it is a private matter between the system and its programmer.

Stenning, Inder and Neilsen also mention Levesque's notion, but they regard it as a "dilemma." To these authors, an account of a representation which blurs the distinction between linguistic and graphic modalities in this way cannot be an adequate account of meaning, and represents a challenge which their semantic theory must overcome. Their response is to extend the ideas of constraints on expressiveness—an essentially functional notion—to talk of how "available" the constraints are to the user. In a graphic modality, they suggest, meaningful constraints of the representation are somehow more directly apparent than they are in a language with a syntax. Clearly they are talking about a situation in which a human being is looking at something.

However, this distinction needs to be made rather more carefully, in my view. In order to appreciate that leftness on a page is transitive (say) requires perception which, while it seems to be effortless, involves substantial mental computation in the mind of the user. It might be argued that detecting grammaticality in sentences is an ability which is just as automatic and immediate for a native speaker as seeing geometric relationships and understanding which aspects of them is considered to be relevant, is to a sighted individual. As the authors say while making their point, the metalogical properties of more complex graphical notations need to be *inferred.* In what representation is this inference performed? Multi-level sentential systems of the kind offered by Wang, Lee and Hervat seem to beckon at this point, but they also lose the essentially graphic essence that Stenning, Inder and Neilsen seek to characterize.

Harel's now classic paper describes and develops a particular diagrammatic notation based on a combination of Euler circles and a generalization of ordinary graphs. These "higraphs" can display in their structure subset relations, cartesian product relations and arbitrary relational assertions, so are amenable to a wide variety of uses. Higraphs are of interest for several reasons. The first is as a kind of challenge to other authors in this area; but they also indicate a rather different approach to the entire subject. Instead of trying to develop a very general descriptive theory of the entire business of representation, Harel's work suggests, it might be constructive to develop new, widely useful notational frameworks, carefully investigate their limitations and properties, and generalize subsequently. Just as in mathematical logic, where much of the subject has progressed by investigating the properties and relationships of particular logical formalisms, this bottom-up approach might at least give us more interesting examples to deal than we can obtain by trying to begin generalizing immediately and directly to a very general-purpose theory from very simple examples.

None of this work seems yet to really give a fully adequate account of such essentially pictorial reasoning as the earlier proof of Pythagoras' theorem. What does seeing this consist of, and why is it so convincing once one has seen it? Can it be connected with the fact that only rigid affine transformations are necessary to convert one figure into the other? Semantic networks, tables, graphs (even hi- and hyper-): none of these are really pictorial in nature, and to follow Levesque in regarding them all simply as compact logical theories is a temptingly coherent path. Stenning, Inder and Neilsen's current response to this strategy takes human perceptual abilities very much for granted. Perhaps, in order to understand how we can often see that things are true, we might need to pay more attention to the the details of how we can see.

7 Heterogeneous Logic

Jon Barwise
Indiana University

John Etchemendy
Stanford University

7.1 Historical Background

A major concern to the founders of modern logic—Frege, Peirce, Russell, and Hilbert—was to give an account of the logical structure of valid reasoning. Taking valid reasoning in mathematics as paradigmatic, these pioneers led the way in developing the accounts of logic which we teach today and that underwrite the work in model theory, proof theory, and definability theory. The resulting notions of proof, model, formal system, soundness, and completeness are things that no one claiming familiarity with logic can fail to understand, and they have also played an enormous role in the revolution known as computer science.

The success of this model of inference led to an explosion of results and applications. But it also led most logicians—and those computer scientists most influenced by the logic tradition—to neglect forms of reasoning that did not fit well within this model. We are thinking, of course, of reasoning that uses devices like diagrams, graphs, charts, frames, nets, maps, and pictures.

The attitude of the traditional logician to these forms of representation is evident in the following quotation, which expresses the standard view of the role of diagrams in geometrical proofs:

> [The diagram] is only an heuristic to prompt certain trains of inference; ... it is dispensable as a proof-theoretic device; indeed, ... it has no proper place in the proof as such. For the proof is a syntactic object consisting only of sentences arranged in a finite and inspectable array. (Neil Tennant, in Tennant 1986)

One aim of our work, as explained in Barwise and Etchemendy 1991b, is to demonstrate that this dogma is misguided. We believe that many of the problems people have putting their knowledge of logic to work, whether in machines or in their own lives, stems from the logocentricity that has pervaded its study for the past hundred years.

Recently, some researchers outside the logic tradition have explored uses of diagrams in knowledge representation and automated reasoning, finding inspiration in the work of Euler, Venn, and especially C. S. Peirce. This volume is a testament to this resurgence of interest in nonlinguistic representations in reasoning.

While we applaud this resurgence, the aim of this chapter is to strike a cautionary note or two. Enchanted by the potential of nonlinguistic representations, it is all too easy to overreact and so to repeat the errors of the past. Just as many in logic and AI once argued (and still argue) that first-order logic is a *universal* representation language, others are now striving toward a universal non-linguistic representation scheme. We want to suggest that the search for *any* universal scheme of representation—linguistic, graphical, or diagrammatic—is a mistake. Efficient reasoning is, we believe, inescapably heterogeneous (or "hybrid") in nature.

7.2 Logic and Information

We approach inference from an informational perspective. Wherever there is structure, there is information. But in order for agents (animals, people, or computers) to traffic in information, the information must in some way or other be presented to or represented by the agent. Typically, a given representation or family of representations will represent certain information explicitly, while other information will be implicit in the information explicitly represented. Inference, as we understand the term, is the task of extracting information implicit in some explicitly presented information.

This informational perspective is part of the modern, semantic approach to logic associated with names like Gödel, Tarski, Robinson, and the like. On this view, a purported rule of inference is valid or not depending on whether it in fact guarantees that the information represented by the conclusion is implicit in the information represented by the premises. But when one takes this informational perspective seriously, the logician's disdain for nonlinguistic representations seems like an oversight, a case of dogma in desperate need of reexamination. The most casual survey of the ways people actually represent information shows an enormous variety of representational devices that go beyond simple text.

In carrying out a reasoning task, part of the solution lies in figuring out how to represent the problem. In problem solving, well begun really is half done. Indeed, this is probably an understatement. Figuring out how to represent the information at hand is often the most important part of the solution. What we need to do, and need to teach students of inference to do, is to use the most appropriate form of representation for the reasoning task at hand. As long as the purported proof really does clearly demonstrate that the information represented by the conclusion is implicit in the information represented by the premises, the purported proof is valid.

Why are logicians so suspicious of diagrams and other forms of nonlinguistic representation? The answer goes back to the tradition in geometry, where diagrams were viewed with suspicion by the founders. Certain mistaken proofs were thought to result from misleading diagrams that accompanied them. So, the tradition went, the diagram should in theory be eliminable from the proof. The textual part of the proof should stand on its own two feet.

This argument is itself a nonsequitur. If we threw out every form of reasoning that could be misapplied by the careless reasoner, we would have little if anything left. Mathematical induction, for example, would certainly have to go. No, the correct response is not to throw out methods of proof that have been misapplied in the past, but rather to give a careful analysis of such methods with the aim of understanding exactly when they are valid and when they are not.

A nice case study along these lines has been carried out by Sun-Joo Shin in Shin 1991a and reported in Shin 1991b. In introductory logic, many people teach the method of Venn diagrams. But often they also tell their students that Venn diagrams are only a heuristic aid to giving proofs. A "real" proof has to be given in first-order logic. Shin shows that this is a mistake. She gives a rigorous analysis of Venn diagrams as a formal system, with its own syntax, semantics, and logical consequence relation. She shows that the usual rules of inference are sound with respect to this consequence relation. Furthermore, she shows that, with some trivial additional rules that had been overlooked, one can give a completeness proof for the deductive system.

An even earlier study is given by John Sowa in Sowa 1984. In the early chapters of that book, Sowa gives a formal treatment of Peirce's existential graphs, including their syntax, semantics, and proof theory. This is a formalism that is expressively equivalent to first-order logic, but it is given in purely diagrammatic terms.

The importance of these results is this. They show that there is no principled distinction between inference formalisms that use text and those that use diagrams. One can have rigorous, logically sound (and complete) formal systems based on diagrams. And while Venn diagrams may seem very simple, they are probably used more frequently in real life than first-order formalisms.

7.3 Homomorphic Representations

By *homomorphic representations* we mean representations that are structurally similar to whatever it is that they represent. (These are what Konolige and Myers (Myers and Konolige 1992) call "analogical" representations. We borrow the term "homomorphic" from modern algebra, though our use of the term is somewhat broader than the technical notion.) Another way to put this is that with homomorphic representations, the mapping ϕ between syntactic structure (that is, the structure of the representation itself) and semantic structure (that is, the structure of the object, situation, or event represented) is highly structure preserving, whereas the corresponding mapping in the case of linguistic representations is anything but structure preserving.

Here are some of the hallmarks of a homomorphic representation system:

1. Objects are typically represented by icon tokens. It is often the case that each object is represented by a unique icon token and distinct tokens represent distinct objects.
2. There is a mapping ϕ from icon types to properties of objects.
3. The mapping ϕ preserves structure. For example, one would expect that:

   (a) If one icon type is a subtype of another (as in the case of shaded squares and squares, for example), then there is a corresponding subproperty relation among the properties they represent.

   (b) If two icon types are incompatible (say squares and circles), then the properties they represent should be incompatible.

   (c) The converses of (a) and (b) frequently hold as well.

4. Certain relations among objects are represented by relations among icon tokens, with the same kinds of conditions as in (3a)–(3c).

5. Higher-order properties of relations among objects (like transitivity, asymmetry, reflexivity, and the like) are reflected by the same properties of relations among icon tokens.

6. Every possibility (involving represented objects, properties, and relations) is representable. That is, there are no possible situations that are represented as impossible.

7. Every representation indicates a genuine possibility.

As these points should make clear, homomorphic representation is not an all-or-nothing affair. A given system may be more or less homomorphic. At one end are representations that are isomorphic to the target domain along certain dimensions. The limiting case of this is reasoning directly with the target domain itself. (If you can't infer which lid fits the jar from the available information, try them on in turn.) At the other extreme are things like Morse code, where the syntactic structure of the representation bears little if any discernible relationship to the structure of whatever the message is about. In between, there can be various degrees of "homomorphicity." For example, the diagrams of *Hyperproof* (see Figure 7.4 for a sample), while highly homomorphic, do not satisfy (3b), since there are incompatible types of icons that represent compatible properties of blocks. Circuit diagrams, by contrast, do satisfy (3b). Venn diagrams are fairly homomorphic, but they do not satisfy condition 7. Linguistic representations occasionally satisfy some of these conditions to a very limited extent, but typically they won't.

7.3.1 Against Universal Schemes of Representation

The literature on diagrammatic representations contains many discussions about why "a picture can be worth 10,000 words." A recurring theme in these discussions is that good diagrammatic representations are homomorphic to what they represent along important dimensions. The homomorphism allows the structure of the representation to carry a great deal of the inferential burden, obviating reasoning that would have to be made explicit in inferences with linguistic representations.

This observation has its up side and its down side. On the positive, we see why good diagrams help make reasoning easier. On the negative, though, they show that a search for a universal representation system in effective reasoning is misguided.

The world is a complex, multi-dimensional affair. Besides the four dimensions of space and time, there are other dimensions as well where other relations most naturally reside. The regularities that we want to exploit reside in and across these dimensions. There just aren't enough regularities in two-space (or three- or four-space) to go around to devise a universal homomorphic representation system.

Let's look at a concrete example from the field of hardware design and verification. (This example comes from Johnson, Allwein, and Barwise 1993. See also Fisler 1994 for a follow-up development.) Think of a computer chip. There are hundreds of different relationships that figure into the design of a new chip or other electronic device. These relationships typically cluster into families, depending on what perspective one takes for the moment. It must be considered from the point of view of control, of logic gates, and of timing, to focus on just three. Each of these has complicated relations that need to be represented in the design of the device. Engineers have solved this representation problem with three separate representational systems: state charts for the representation of control, circuit diagrams for the representation of gate information, and timing diagrams for the representation of timing. Figures 7.1-7.3 show three different representations of a very simple device, a so-called unit pulser.

Diagram 7.1 shows a timing diagram specification for the pulser. It shows that any input pulse should turn into a unit output pulse. Figure 7.2 shows a state diagram for such a device with two internal states. The arcs show transitions between these states. The *I/O* arcs are labeled by pairs of zeros or ones, the first member of the pair representing input and the second output. Finally, Figure 7.3 shows a circuit diagram for such a device. In addition to the usual logic gates, it employs a "storage" device that holds a value for one unit of time before passing it on.

Each of these representational schemes is highly homomorphic to the

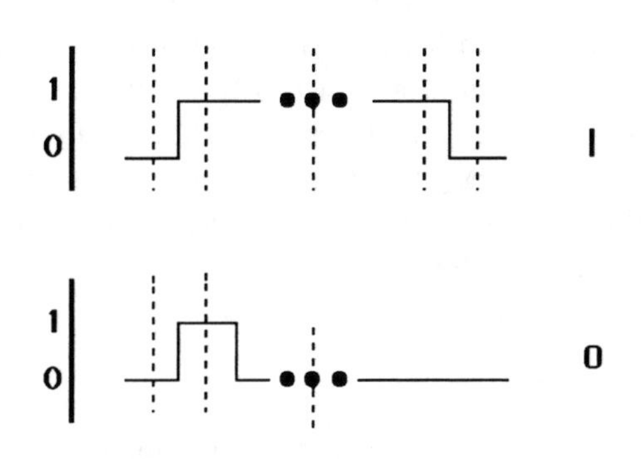

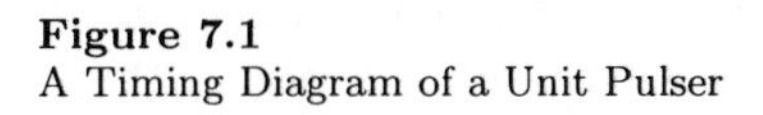

Figure 7.1
A Timing Diagram of a Unit Pulser

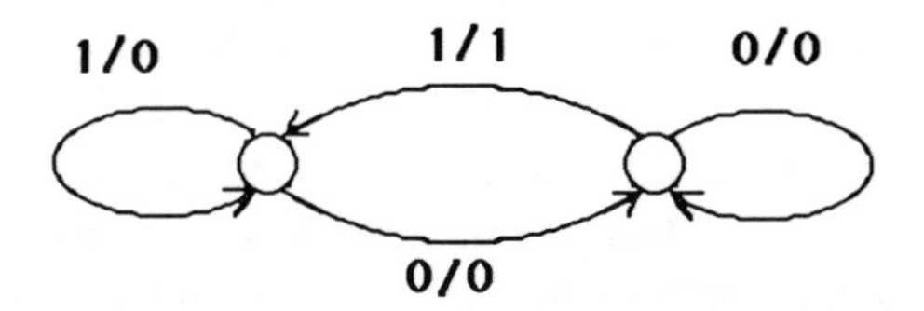

Figure 7.2
A State Diagram of a Unit Pulser

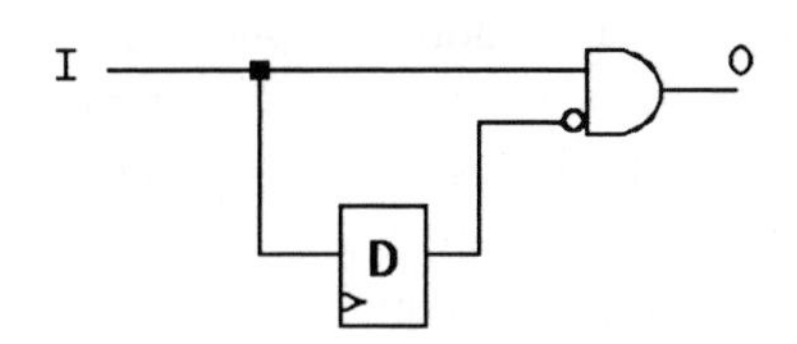

Figure 7.3
A Circuit Diagram of a Unit Pulser

aspect of hardware they represent. Certain spatial relationships among lines and other sorts of tokens represent relationships among various aspects of the operating circuit. But notice that a line in one diagram has quite a different interpretation from that in the others: wiring connections between gates, transitions among states, and the value on a wire through time. When engineers design and reason about hardware, they use all three kinds of diagrams at once. This is a clear example of "heterogeneous" reasoning in real life. They simply use all three sets of conventions, and reason with all of them.

7.3.2 Against an "Interlingua"

People who accept the argument against a universal diagrammatic system, and so accept the idea of a heterogeneous reasoning system, often suppose that in order to have a rigorous heterogeneous system, there must be *some* system of conventions into which all the others can be embedded and compared, some sort of "interlingua" to mediate between the various systems of representations. But this is not correct. Whether it is *useful* to have an interlingua is debatable, but there is certainly no logical necessity to employ one.

The idea that an interlingua is needed to mediate between the various representations misses the crucial fact that these are representations of a single target domain. The semantic mappings that link all of them to a common target domain (circuits in our example) allow for interaction between different forms of representation. Imagine trying to design a hardware system where all three forms of information were represented in a single system. Experience shows that such a system would lose the clarity, crispness, and utility of the systems that have developed in practice. To combine these into one system, the mappings from syntax to semantics would have to be complicated to an extent that they would lose much of their homomorphic character. The more complicated this mapping becomes, the closer we come to having a notational variant of a linguistic scheme of representation, thereby losing the very representational advantages inherent in a homomorphic system.

As a case study in how one can define a useful, truly heterogeneous inference system, one where there is no single form or representation into which all the others are translated, let us consider a working heterogeneous system without an interlingua.

7.4 Hyperproof

Hyperproof is a computer program and textbook that we use in teaching elementary logic courses. The reasoning system it implements is heterogeneous, since it uses both the usual language of first-order logic, plus diagrams. It has all the usual rules of first-order logic, plus a number of rules for dealing with diagrams and the interplay between diagrams and sentences.

In *Hyperproof* every diagram represents partial information about some class of blocks worlds. (We will model these blocks worlds by means of set-theoretic structures below.) A sentence in the first-order language will be true in some of these worlds, false in others. It does not really sound right to say that a diagram is true or false in a world. Rather, a diagram will depict some of these worlds and conflict with others. To adopt a uniform terminology, let us say that a representation r *holds* in a world w if r is a diagram and depicts the world w, or if r is a sentence and is true in w.

When we are given both a diagram and some sentences, the combined information limits us to the worlds in which all the givens hold. Some other sentence or diagram follows from the given sentences and diagram if it holds in all the worlds in which all the given information holds.

Neither of the two forms of representation made available in *Hyperproof* is made redundant by the other. That is, there are things that can be depicted by diagrams that cannot be said in the language, and vice versa. For example, we can depict a block as being on the leftmost, front square, but there is no way to express this in the language, since the language only allows us to speak of relative positions, not absolute positions. Conversely, we can say that there is a large tetrahedron somewhere to the right of block b, but there is no way to depict exactly this with a diagram. Any diagram that depicts a world where there is a large tetrahedron left of b would depict it in some particular place, and so hold in fewer worlds than the sentence. Thus the information content of the sentence and the diagram would be different.

There is an even bigger difference between the forms of representation. If we are given a sentence φ and a diagram d, we can determine whether φ follows from d by inspection. We simply look at d and "see" if the sentence is true in all the worlds it depicts. There is no way to do this the other way around. We cannot "see" the worlds in which a sentence holds in the way we can with a diagram.

What accounts for this asymmetry? We will analyze this in some detail below, but here is a quick gloss of what is going on. A given diagram d can be modeled in two ways. One is as a completed structure in its own right. The other is as a partial structure modeling the pictured facts of the worlds depicted by d. These are distinct structures. For instance, the former will have as objects various pictures of blocks. The latter will have as objects various blocks, not pictures of blocks. There is a mapping from the pictures to the blocks, though, a mapping which preserves a lot of structure. This mapping lets the user easily reinterpret the sentence φ as though it were about the diagram itself. If φ holds of the diagram, under this reinterpretation, then it holds in all the worlds in which the diagram holds. This reinterpretation is possible because of the homomorphic nature of the relationship between diagrams and the worlds they depict. The impossibility of going the other way around stems from a lack of a similar homomorphic relationship between sentences and world.

This asymmetry is also responsible for some of the differences in expressive power between diagrams and sentences mentioned earlier. The homomorphism from diagrams to worlds makes the diagrams better at depicting very particular facts, facts that may not be expressible in the language. Conversely, linguistic devices like quantifiers, negation, and disjunction that allow sentences to represent facts that cannot be represented diagrammatically also block any homomorphism between the sentence and the worlds in which it holds.

7.4.1 Why There Is No Interlingua in *Hyperproof*

It is important to remember that *Hyperproof* maintains two distinct forms of representing information about blocks worlds. There is no sense in which the program has a single underlying representation into which both diagrams and sentences are translated. What holds the two together is not an underlying representation scheme, or interlingua, but simply the fact that they are both about the same worlds. It is this fact that underwrites the rules of inference which govern how we can reason with both at the same time.

This becomes clearer with some examples. Let us examine two of the most important rules of *Hyperproof*, the rules of **Observe** and **Cases Exhausted** (and a special case of the latter, **Apply**).

For any given diagram there are literally an infinite number of sentences that can be observed to hold on the basis of the diagram. The rule **Observe** allows us to extract sentential information from diagrammatic information. (**Apply** allows us to go the other way around.) **Observe** allows the user to infer any sentence which is definitely true in the partial structure that corresponds to the diagram—that is, true according to the truth evaluation schema embodied in the (weak) Kleene three-valued logic. The three values are *true*, *false*, and *unknown*. The implementation of the **Observe** rule in *Hyperproof* is basically just the recursive definition of this Kleene three-valued evaluation scheme.

The most important features of the *Hyperproof* system are the techniques for transferring information from sentences into a range of diagrams. Thus, we are typically given a diagram d and some sentences $\varphi_1, \ldots, \varphi_n$ describing the target world. Based on one of these sentences, say φ, we see that there is a range of possibilities, each of which can be embodied by fleshing out the diagram d in some way. Thus we create some new diagrams $d_1, \ldots, d_k$, each an amplification of d (in that it carries more information than d), and say that these exhaust all the possibilities, given the sentence φ. This step is valid if any way the world could be, consistent with d and φ, is also consistent with at least one of these new diagrams. This is the rule of **Cases Exhaustive**.

A special instance of **Cases Exhaustive** is where $k = 1$, that is, where there is just one new diagram. Using the rule in this case means that the information added to d in the new diagram d_1 is implicit in the sentence φ. We call this special instance **Apply**, since you can think of it as applying the information in φ to add new information to the diagram.

There are many cases where one can infer some sentence from a diagram and other sentences, but where one cannot do this using only the rule of **Observe.** Some version of **Apply** or **Cases Exhausted** is necessary to obtain the inference. Examples of these, together with methods for knowing when they arise, are discussed in the chapter "Logic and Observation" of Barwise and Etchemendy 1994.

To see how we can implement the **Apply** rule without going through an interlingua, let us describe the algorithm. Imagine we are in the following situation. The user has a diagram d and a sentence φ. She wants to apply φ to amplify the diagram to d'.

Ideally, what one would like would be an algorithm that did the fol-

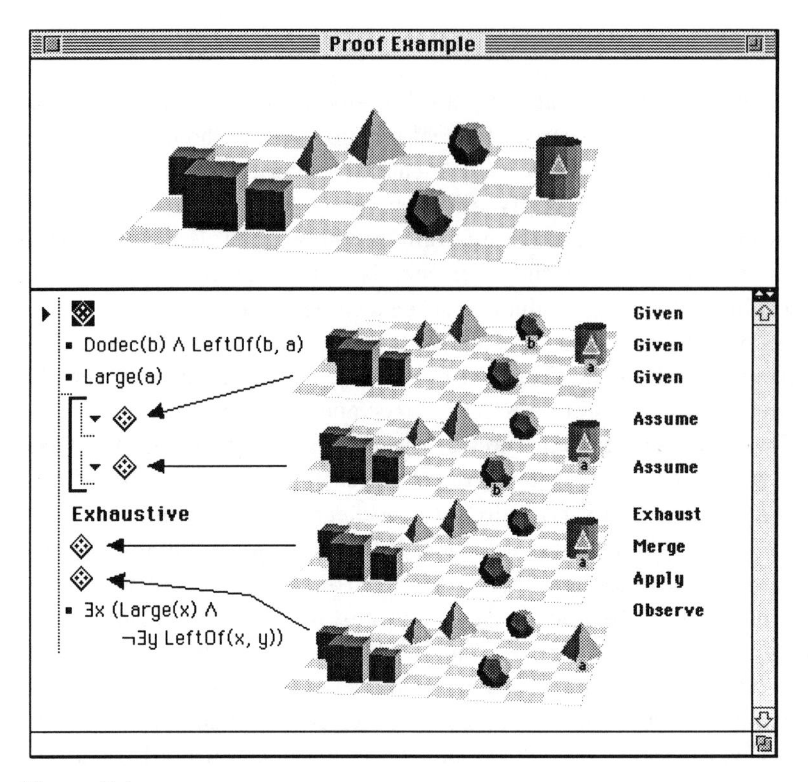

Figure 7.4
A Sample Proof.

lowing: If this **Apply** is legitimate, then say so. That is, look at all diagrams d^* that amplify d in ways that are incompatible with d', and see if any of them make φ true. If not, accept the conclusion d'. Otherwise, reject it and produce a counterexample by displaying an incompatible diagram d^* that amplifies d but in which φ is true.

This is a legitimate form of reasoning (as we will show later in the paper) but it is not in general realizable in a computationally feasible manner. The reason is that it can happen that such a diagram d^* would have to settle too many issues, issues which themselves can be resolved in a variety of ways. Thus one gets lost in a huge search space.

In *Hyperproof* we solve this problem by relying on partial information in two ways. First, we only search for counterexamples among those diagrams that settle just issues raised in d'.[1] If we can find such a

[1]For example, if d' settles the size of a single block b, and that is all, then the only issue we consider is the size of that block. All other amplifications of d are ignored.

diagram in which φ is true, then we will have found a counterexample. But we do not insist that the sentence φ come out as true in d^*, only that it *not* come out as false. If it comes out as neither true nor false in a diagram d^* which is incompatible with d' and which settles all issues raised in d', we call this a possible counterexample, and give it to the user as a possibility that needs to be considered explicitly. In this way, the search space is greatly reduced and the rule is sound, in that it never ratifies an invalid use of **Apply**. The algorithm is not complete, in that it will not be able to recognize some valid uses of **Apply**, but in such cases it returns a possible counterexample for the user to consider.

The point of describing the algorithms that implement the **Observe** and **Apply** rules is to stress the claim made above about there being no need for an interlingua to mediate between the two forms of representation. The rules are sound because of the semantics that relate the two forms of representation, but the semantics itself is not in any sense internal to the program.

7.5 Towards a Mathematical Analysis of *Hyperproof*

In this section we provide a mathematical framework for *Hyperproof* in which to make some of the above claims more rigorous. Our aim here is to carry the development just far enough to put some logical meat on the bones of the informal argument given in the first half of the chapter. In particular, we want to give a rigorous analysis of the *Hyperproof* rules of **Observe** and **Apply**. The logically-minded reader should be able to carry the development further if so inclined.

7.5.1 Syntax

We begin by constructing models of the representations used in *Hyperproof*, namely, the sentences and the diagrams. We start with a standard recursive definition of the sentences.

Definition 1 (Syntax of Sentences)
The *predicates* of our language consist of the following:

- Unary: **Small**, **Medium**, **Large**, **Tet**, **Cube**, **Dodec**
- Binary: =, **Larger**, **LeftOf**, **FrontOf**, **Adjoins**, **SameSize**, **SameShape**, **SameRow**, **SameColumn**

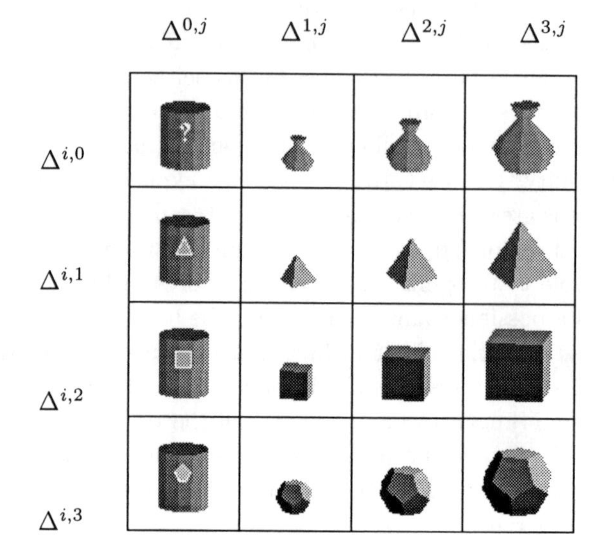

Table 7.1
Icon Types in *Hyperproof.*

- Ternary: **Between**
- The *variables* of our language consist of $\mathbf{v}_1, \mathbf{v}_2, \ldots$

We define the *wffs* as follows:

- The atomic wffs are formed as usual from the variables, names, and predicates.
- The compound wffs are formed recursively as usual from the atomic wffs using $\neg, \wedge, \vee, \rightarrow, \leftrightarrow, \forall, \exists$.

The *sentences* consist of those wffs with no free variables.

By contrast, the syntax of our diagrammatic representations are not presented recursively.

Definition 2 (Syntax of Diagrams)
(Icon types) There are sixteen icon types in our system. For ease of type setting, we refer to these as $\Delta^{i,j}$ for $0 \leq i, j \leq 3$. See Table 7.1 for the form these icons take in *Hyperproof.*

(Icon tokens) We assume that there are an infinite number of icon tokens of each icon type. We indicate an icon token of type $\Delta^{i,j}$ by adding a numerical subscript: $\Delta^{i,j}_n$. We assume that you can always recover the type from any of its tokens, and we refer to the type of token τ as $Type(\tau)$.

(The Grid) We also assume the existence of a *grid* of size $k \times k$. We refer to a grid position by means of a pair $\langle x, y \rangle$ where $1 \leq x, y \leq k$.

(Diagrams) A *diagram* d consists of a triple $\langle Tokens^d, Pos^d, Label^d \rangle$ satisfying the following conditions.

1. $Tokens^d$ is a finite set of icon tokens.
2. Pos^d is a partial, one-to-one function from $Tokens^d$ into grid positions. If $Pos^d(\tau) = \langle x, y \rangle$ we say that the icon token τ has position $\langle x, y \rangle$ on the grid. If $\tau \notin dom(Pos^d)$, then we say that τ is unlocated in d. (In the implementation of *Hyperproof*, unlocated tokens sit off to the right of the grid.)
3. $Label^d$ is a partial function from the set of names into the set $Tokens^d$ of tokens of d. If $Label^d(\mathbf{n})$ is defined, then we say that the name $\mathbf{n}$ *labels* the token $Label^d(\mathbf{n})$ in diagram d.

It should be clear from the definitions of world, sentence, and diagram, that there is a much higher degree of structural similarity between diagrams and worlds than there is between sentences and worlds. We will spell out this similarity in some detail in our discussion of the semantics to follow, since it is this similarity which makes our diagrams a homomorphic representation system.

A proof in the *Hyperproof* system typically involves a sequence of diagrams, not just one. We need to decide how to think about the identity of tokens in different diagrams appearing in the course of a proof. Suppose, for example, that during a proof we have a token τ of type $\Delta^{0,1}$ (representing a tetrahedron of unknown size) with no grid position (representing a lack of information about where the tetrahedron is located) in a diagram d. Suppose further that by means of a valid use of the **Apply** rule, we replace this token by the token τ' of type $\Delta^{1,1}$ (representing a small tetrahedron), and locate it on the grid at some location, obtaining a new diagram d'. Since these tokens are of different types, they are distinct tokens, but they represent the same block. It is only the dynamic aspect of the proof that indicates that the two tokens are being used to represent the same block. To model this history, we follow Shin (Shin 1991a) by introducing the notion of counterpart tokens.

Definition 3 (Counterparts)

- A *counterpart structure* $\mathcal{U} = \langle U, \equiv \rangle$ consists of a universe U of icon tokens and some equivalence relation $\equiv$ on U. Tokens $\tau, \tau' \in U$ are *counterparts* iff $\tau \equiv \tau'$.
- $\mathcal{U}$ *respects* the diagram d if U contains all the icon tokens of d but no two of them are counterparts in $\mathcal{U}$.
- Diagrams d and d' are *counterpart diagrams* (relative to $\mathcal{U}$) if every token in $Tokens^d$ has a counterpart in $Tokens^{d'}$ and vice versa.

In what follows, we work relative to some fixed counterpart structure $\mathcal{U}$. (In order to make the proofs of some of our results go through, we assume that each equivalence class of $\mathcal{U}$ is infinite. This is basically the assumption that given any finite set D of diagrams, we can find a new token which is a counterpart of the tokens which have counterparts in D.) We restrict attention to diagrams respected by this counterpart structure. We will not be discussing proofs explicitly, but if we did, we would insist that all diagrams in any proof be counterparts of one another relative to $\mathcal{U}$. This reflects the fact that the counterpart structure models the process of modifying diagrams in a proof by replacing tokens with more specific tokens. To make this idea more rigorous, we next capture the idea of one token being more specific than another and, using that, the idea that some *Hyperproof* diagrams carry more information than others, not just quantitatively, but qualitatively. This is captured by the notion of one diagram "extending" another.

Definition 4 (Specificity of icons)

- Icon type $\Delta^{i,j}$ is at least as *informative* as $\Delta^{i',j'}$, written $\Delta^{i,j} \geq \Delta^{i',j'}$, iff $i' = 0$ or $i' = i$ and $j' = 0$ or $j' = j$.
- One token is as informative as another if the corresponding relation holds of their types.

Definition 5 (Extension of diagrams)
We say that diagram d is an *extension* of d_0 just in case the following conditions hold:

- d and d_0 are counterpart diagrams.
- Each icon token in d is at least as informative as its counterpart in d_0.
- The function Loc^d extends the function Loc^{d_0}, in the sense that if $Loc^{d_0}(\tau')$ is defined then $Loc^d(\tau) = Loc^{d_0}(\tau')$, where τ and τ' are counterparts.
- The function $Label^d$ extends the function $Label^{d_0}$, in the sense that if $Label^{d_0}(\mathbf{n})$ is defined then $Label^d(\mathbf{n})$ and $Label^{d_0}(\mathbf{n})$ are counterparts.

7.5.2 Semantics

We next turn to modeling the blocks worlds in which both sentences and diagrams hold.

Definition 6 (Worlds)
We assume the existence of an infinite supply of *blocks*, an infinite supply of *names*, and a finite number of possible *locations* arranged in a $k \times k$ array. We refer to a location by means of a pair $\langle x, y\rangle$ where $0 < x, y \leq k$.

A *world* w consists of a tuple $\langle B^w, N^w, Sz^w, Sh^w, Loc^w, Den^w\rangle$ satisfying the following conditions.

1. B^w is a non-empty set of blocks, called the *domain* of w.
2. N^w is a non-empty set of names, called the *names* of w.
3. Sz^w is a function from B^w into the set {Small, Medium, Large} of sizes; $Sz^w(b)$ is called the *size* of the block b.
4. Sh^w is a function from B^w into the set {Tetrahedron, Dodecahedron, Cube} of shapes; $Sh^w(b)$ is called the *shape* of the block b.
5. Loc^w is a one-to-one function from B^w into the set of locations; $Loc^w(b)$ is called the *location* of the block b.
6. Den^w is a function from $U \cup N^w$ into B^w; $Den^w(x)$ is called the *denotation* of x. If x is an icon token (name) then x is said to *depict* (*name*, resp.) the block $Den^w(x)$. Among icon tokens, we require that Den^w respect the counterpart relation; that is, if $\tau \equiv \tau'$, then $Den^w(\tau) = Den^w(\tau')$

Definition 7 (Semantics of sentences)
Let w be a blocks world. A *variable assignment* f is a function from the set of variables into B^w. We extend f to a function on names and

variables by letting $f(\mathbf{n}) = Den^w(\mathbf{n})$ for each name $\mathbf{n}$. We define the notion of f satisfying the wff φ in w, written $w \models \varphi[f]$, by recursion. We give a few examples of the clauses here.

1. (Atomic) $w \models \mathbf{Small(t)}\ [f]$ iff $Sz^w(f(\mathbf{t})) = \text{Small}$.
   $w \models \mathbf{Tet(t)}\ [f]$ iff $Sh^w(f(\mathbf{t})) = \text{Tetrahedron}$.
   $w \models \mathbf{LeftOf(t, t')}\ [f]$ iff $x < x'$ where x is the first coordinate of $Loc^w(f(\mathbf{t}))$ and x' is the first coordinate of $Loc^w(f(\mathbf{t}'))$.
2. (Negation) $w \models \neg\varphi\ [f]$ iff $w \not\models \varphi\ [f]$.
3. (Conjunction) $w \models \varphi \wedge \psi\ [f]$ iff $w \models \varphi\ [f]$ and $w \models \psi\ [f]$.
4. (Universal quantifier) $w \models \forall \mathbf{v}_i \varphi\ [f]$ iff for all assignments f' that agree with f except possibly on $\mathbf{v}_i$, $w \models \varphi\ [f']$.

If φ is a sentence (i.e. a wff with no free variables) we say that φ *holds* in w if φ is satisfied by any assignment f.

Definition 8 (Semantics of diagrams)
Let w be a blocks world and let d be a diagram. We say that d *holds* in w if the following conditions obtain:

1. Every block in w is denoted by some icon token in d.
2. For any icon token $\tau = \Delta_n^{i,j}$ of d:

   if $i = 1$ (2, 3) then the size of the block $Den^w(\tau)$ in w is Small (resp. Medium, Large).
   if $j = 1$ (2, 3) then the shape of the block $Den^w(\tau)$ in w is Tetrahedron (resp. Cube, Dodecahedron).
   if $Pos^d(\tau)$ is defined, say $= \langle x, y \rangle$, then the location of the block $Den^w(\tau)$ in w is $\langle x, y \rangle$.

3. If a name is used to label an icon token τ in d, then the block denoted by τ must have that name in w. That is, if $Label^d(\mathbf{n}) = \tau$, then $Den^w(\tau) = Den^w(\mathbf{n})$.

7.5.3 Logical Notions Defined

Our earlier definitions now allow us to define the main logical notions.

Definition 9 (Logical consequence)

- Let us call any well-formed sentence or diagram a *Hyperproof representation.*

- Let P be a set of representations and q be a single representation. We say that q is a *logical consequence* of P, written $P \models q$, if every blocks world in which every representation in P holds is also one in which q holds.
- We say that a set P of representations is *consistent* if there is a blocks world in which all the representations in P hold.

The following is an easy consequence of our definitions.

PROPOSITION 1 (Autoconsistency) Every diagram is consistent.

We do not present proofs of the results claimed here. None of them are at all difficult, but presenting the details would use up more space than we have at our disposal.

COROLLARY 2 Let d be any diagram and let T be any set of sentences all of which are logical consequences of d. Then $T \cup \{d\}$ is consistent.

A hint that something interesting is going on with the diagrams is given by the following simple, but important, result.

PROPOSITION 3 If d and d' are logical consequences of one another then $d = d'$. Hence, the logical consequence relation, restricted to single diagrams, is a partial ordering.

We write $d \geq d'$ for $d \models d'$ when we want to stress the fact that it is a partial ordering. The following result shows that this relation has a syntactic characterization, modulo the question of which icon tokens are counterparts of one another.

PROPOSITION 4 Given diagrams d and d', the following are equivalent:

1. $d \geq d'$.
2. d is an extension of d'.

This ordering is what rests behind *Hyperproof*'s rule of **Merge**, a rule that lets the user extract all the information common to an exhaustive set of diagrams.

PROPOSITION 5 (Merge) Let D be a finite set of diagrams. The following are equivalent:

1. There is a single diagram d which is the greatest lower bound of the diagrams in D (that is, d is a logical consequence of each diagram in D, and it entails any other diagram d' entailed by every diagram in D).
2. All the diagrams in D are counterparts of one another.

7.5.4 On the Observe and Apply Rules

We conclude our discussion by making precise our earlier claims about the validity of the **Observe** and **Apply** rules. We begin by getting clearer about what we mean when we say we can "see" what is true in a diagram.

We can think of diagrams as first-order structures in their own right. The domain of a diagram d is just the set of icon tokens in the diagram. We can use these structures to give non-standard interpretations of our language. This, in turn, can be used to understand both the cognitive and logical utility of the **Observe** rule of *Hyperproof.*

Definition 10 A *diagrammatic interpretation* I of our language is a function that assigns to each diagram d and each name and predicate of our language an object as follows.

- If $\mathbf{P}$ is an n-ary predicate, then $I(d, \mathbf{P})$ is a pair $\langle T, F\rangle$ of sets of n-tuples of icon tokens in $Tokens^d$ satisfying the conditions that if $\langle \tau_1, \ldots, \tau_n\rangle$ is in T (resp. is in F) then for any model w of d, the n-tuple

  $$\langle Den^w(\tau_1), \ldots, Den^w(\tau_n)\rangle$$

  satisfies (resp. does not satisfy) the predicate $\mathbf{P}$ in w. The set T (resp. F) is called the extension (resp. anti-extension) of $\mathbf{P}$ under the interpretation I.
- If $\mathbf{n}$ is a name and $I(d, \mathbf{n})$ is defined then its value is an icon token τ labeled by $\mathbf{n}$. (Equivalently, τ denotes the same thing as $\mathbf{n}$ in any world which in which d is true.)

The function I is required to be monotone in the following sense.

1. If d' extends d and $\langle \tau_1, \ldots, \tau_n \rangle$ is in the extension (resp. anti-extension) of **P** in d under I then $\langle \tau'_1, \ldots, \tau'_n \rangle$ is in the extension (resp. anti-extension) of **P** in d' under I, where τ'_i is the d'-counterpart of τ_i.
2. Similarly, if **n** is a name with an interpretation in d under I, then it also has an interpretation in d' under I (in which case both interpretations will have to be icon tokens labeled by **n**).

Let's give an example. It is natural to reinterpret **Tet** in d by taking its extension to be the set of icon tokens of type $\Delta^{i,1}$ for any i, and its anti-extension to be the set of icon tokens of type $\Delta^{i,j}$ for any i and any $j > 1$. A less natural reinterpretation, but a reinterpretation none-the-less, would be to take the extension of **Tet** in d to be the set of icon tokens of type $\Delta^{1,1}$, and the anti-extension to be those of type $\Delta^{3,3}$.

A diagrammatic interpretation I gives us a way to associate a partial model of our language with any diagram d. Let us write $d \approx\!\!\!\!|\ _I \varphi$ if φ evaluates as true using the weak Kleene evaluation scheme, when the predicates of φ are reinterpreted according to I.

PROPOSITION 6 (Depiction Lemma) Suppose we have a blocks world w and a diagram d that is true in w. For any sentence φ, if $d \approx\!\!\!\!|\ _I \varphi$ then $w \models \varphi$.

COROLLARY 7 (Observe) If $d \approx\!\!\!\!|\ _I \varphi$ then $d \models \varphi$.

Definition 11 A reinterpretation I *captures* **P** if whenever d is a maximal diagram, $I(d, \mathbf{P})$ is total. That is, the extension and anti-extension of **P** are complements of one another. Similarly, I *captures* **n** if whenever d is a maximal diagram, then $I(d, \mathbf{n})$ is defined.

PROPOSITION 8 Suppose $w \models d$. There is an extension d' of d such that $d' \approx\!\!\!\!|\ _I \varphi$ for every sentence φ all of whose names and predicates are fully captured by I.

COROLLARY 9 Suppose we have a sentence φ such that all the names and predicates in φ are captured by I. If d is consistent with φ then there is an extension d' of d such that $d' \approx\!\!\!\!|\ _I \varphi$.

This result shows that any sentence which is consistent with a diagram and a set of sentences can be shown to be consistent within the

Hyperproof system. This is one of the features we hoped for earlier in a homomorphic system of representation. It likewise shows that non-consequence results can be proven within the system. This is in marked contrast to linguistic systems.

Following the standard terminology in partial orders, we say that two diagrams are *incompatible* if they have no common extension. While this definition makes it look as though it would be computationally difficult to check whether two diagrams were incompatible, the following observation shows that for the *Hyperproof* system, this property is easily checked by reference to the two diagrams in question, without any search over other diagrams. Types $\Delta^{i,j}$ and $\Delta^{i',j'}$ are *incompatible* if i and i' are distinct and non-zero (representing incompatible information about size) or if j and j' are distinct and non-zero (representing incompatible information about shape).

PROPOSITION 10 (Incompatibility check) Diagrams d and d' are incompatible iff there are counterpart tokens in the diagrams which are of incompatible types or located at different positions on the grid, or if there is a name that labels tokens that are not counterparts.

This result, while simple, is quite important in making the notion of proof decidable, and even tractable. Using it, we can now state the result which justifies the rule **Apply**.

PROPOSITION 11 (Apply Lemma) Given a sentence φ and two diagrams d and $d' \geq d$, exactly one of the following holds:

1. d' is a logical consequence of d and φ.
2. There is a diagram d^* which extends d but is incompatible with d' such that $d^* \not\approx_I \varphi$.

In particular, if there is no diagram d^* as in (2), then (1).

As we mentioned earlier, the implementation of this rule in *Hyperproof* is weaker than this for the sake of tractability. Let us conclude by justifying the *Hyperproof* version of **Apply**.

COROLLARY 12 (Tractable Apply Lemma) Given a sentence φ and two diagrams d and $d' \geq d$, at least one of the following holds:

1. d' is a logical consequence of d and φ.

2. There is a diagram d^* which extends d but is incompatible with d' such that not $d^* \models_{I} \neg\varphi$.

In particular, if there is no diagram d^* as in (2), then (1).

We hope it is clear from this discussion that we could give a similar justification for *Hyperproof*'s most important rule, that of **Cases Exhausted.**

Eberle (Eberle 1994) has developed an alternative analysis of the syntax and semantics of *Hyperproof*, and used it to formalize *Hyperproof's* notion of proof. Using this, she has shown the soundness of the *Hyperproof* system, and explored the senses in which the *Hyperproof* system is complete.

7.6 Conclusion

In this chapter we have argued against the idea of a universal diagrammatic system, and against the idea that a system with multiple forms of representation needs some underlying "interlingua" to tie the representations together. On a more positive note, we have argued that *Hyperproof* shows that one can have a effective heterogeneous reasoning system without an interlingua, and we have developed enough of an analysis of the system to show why this is the case. In particular, we have shown how to give rigorous justifications for some of the rules of *Hyperproof* involving both sentences and diagrams without any such interlingua.

References

Barwise, Jon; and Etchemendy, John, 1994. *Hyperproof*, CSLI Lecture Notes. New York: Cambridge Univ. Press.

Barwise, Jon, and Etchemendy, John, 1991a. *Tarski's World.* CSLI Lecture Notes. New York: Cambridge Univ. Press.

Barwise, Jon, and Etchemendy, John, 1991b. Visual Information and Valid Reasoning. In *Visualization in Mathematics,* ed. Walter Zimmerman and Steve Cunningham, 9–24. Washington: Mathematical Association of America.

Barwise, Jon, and Perry, John, 1993. *Situations and Attitudes.* Cambridge, Mass: The MIT Press.

Eberle, Ruth, 1994. Diagrams in Natural Deduction. Ph.D. diss. Visual Inference Laboratory and Department of Philosophy, Indiana University.

Fisler, Kathi. 1994 A Logical Formalization of Hardware Design Diagrams. Technical Report TR416, September, Indiana University.

Johnson, Steven; Allwein, Gerard, and Barwise, Jon, 1993. Toward the Rigorous Use of Diagrams in Hardware Synthesis and Verification. In *Logic and Diagrams: Working Papers*, Visual Inference Lab, Indiana University.

Myers, Karen, and Konolige, Kurt, 1992. Integrating Sentential Reasoning for Perception. Presented at the AAAI Spring Symposium on Reasoning with Diagrammatic Representations, Stanford University, 25-27 March 1992.

Shin, Sun-Joo, 1991a. *Valid Reasoning and Visual Representation.* Ph.D. diss., Department of Philosophy, Stanford University.

Shin, Sun-Joo, 1991b. An Information-Theoretic Analysis of Valid Reasoning with Venn Diagrams. In *Situation Theory and Its Applications, Part 2,* ed. Jon Barwise et al. CSLI Lecture Notes. New York: Cambridge University Press.

Sowa, John, 1984. *Conceptual Structures: Information Processing in Mind and Machine.* Reading, Mass.: Addison-Wesley.

Tennant, Neil, 1986. The Withering Away of Formal Semantics. *Mind and Language* 1: 302–318.

8 On Visual Formalisms

David Harel
The Weizmann Institute of Science

Visualizing information, especially information of complex and intricate nature, has for many years been the subject of considerable work by many people. The information that interests us here is nonquantitative, but rather, of a structural, set-theoretical, and relational nature. This should be contrasted with the kinds of quantitative information discussed at length in Schmid (1983) and Tufte (1983). Consequently, we shall be interested in diagrammatic paradigms that are essentially topological in nature, not geometric, terming them *topovisual* in the sequel.

Two of the best known topo-visual formalisms have their roots in the work of the famous Swiss mathematician Leonhard Euler (1707–1783). The first, of course, is the formalism of graphs, and the second is the notion of *Euler circles,* which later evolved into *Venn diagrams.* Graphs are implicit in Euler's celebrated 1736 paper, in which he solved the problem of the bridges of Königsberg (Euler 1736). (An English translation appears in Biggs, Lloyd, and Wilson [1976.]) Euler circles first appear in letters written by Euler in the early 1760s (Euler 1772), and were modified to improve their ability to represent logical propositions by John Venn in 1880. (See Gardner [1982], chap. 2, for more information.)[1]

A graph, in its most basic form, is simply a set of points, or nodes, connected by edges or arcs. Its role is to represent a (single) set of elements S and some binary relation R on them. The precise meaning of the relation R is part of the application and has little to do with the mathematical properties of the graph itself. Certain restrictions on the relation R yield special classes of graphs that are of particular interest, such as ones that are connected, directed, acyclic, planar, or bipartite. There is no need to elaborate on the use of graphs in computer science—they are used extensively in virtually all branches of the field. The elements represented by the nodes in these applications range from the most concrete (e.g., physical gates in a circuit diagram) to the

[1]Interestingly, both these topo-visual achievements of Euler were carried out during the period in which he could see with one eye only. (Euler lost sight in his right eye in 1735, and in the left around 1766.) It is tempting to attribute this in part to the fact that the lack of stereoscopic vision reduces one's ability to estimate size and distance possibly causing a sharper awareness of topological features.

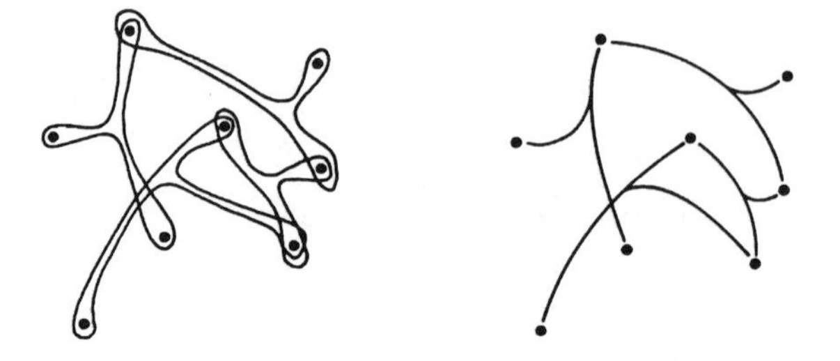

Figure 8.1
Graphical Representation of Hypergraphs.

most abstract (e.g., complexity classes in a classification schema), and the edges have been used to represent almost any conceivable kind of relation, including ones of temporal, causal, functional, or epistemological nature. Obviously, graphs can be modified to support a number of different kinds of nodes and edges, representing different kinds of elements and relationships.

A somewhat less widely used extension of graphs is the formalism of *hypergraphs* (see, e.g., Berge [1973]), though these are also finding applications in computer science, mainly in database theory (see Fagin [1983], Fagin, Mendeizon, and Ullman [1982], and Maier and Ullman [1982]). A hypergraph is a graph in which the relation being specified is not necessarily binary; in fact, it need not even be of fixed arity. Formally, an edge no longer connects a pair of nodes, but rather a subset thereof. This makes hypergraphs somewhat less amenable to visual representation, but various ways of overcoming this difficulty can be conceived (see Figure 8.1). In analogy with graphs, several special kinds of hypergraphs are of particular interest, such as directed or acyclic ones.

It is important to emphasize that the information conveyed by a graph or a hypergraph is nonmetric and captured by the purely topological notion of connectedness (a term taken from Fitter and Green 1979); shapes, locations, distances, and sizes, for example, have no significance.

Although not quite as widely used as graphs, Euler circles, or Venn diagrams, are often used to represent logical propositions, color charts, etc. (see Figure 8.2). The basic idea is to appeal to the two-dimensional case of the Jordan curve theorem (e.g., Dugundji [1966], Lefschetz [1949]), which establishes that simple closed curves partition the plane into disjoint inside and outside regions. A set is then represented by the inside of such a curve[2] giving the topological notions of *enclosure, exclusion,* and *intersection* of the curves their obvious set-theoretic meanings: being a subset of, being disjoint from, and having a nonempty intersection with, respectively.[3]

The bottom line is that, whereas graphs and hypergraphs are a nice way of representing a set of elements together with some special relation(s) on them, Euler/ Venn diagrams are a nice way of representing a *collection* of sets, together with some *structural* (i.e., set theoretical) relationships between them. The difference between the two types of relationships is obvious. The structural ones are uniformly interpreted in the obvious set-theoretic fashion, in much the same way as the = symbol in logical formalisms is uniformly interpreted as the equality predicate, whereas the edge relations of graphs and hypergraphs attain different meanings in different applications.

The main observation motivating the present work is that in numerous computer-related applications the complexity of the objects, systems, or situations under consideration is due in large part to the fact that both capabilities are needed. We have a (usually large) number of sets that are interrelated in nontrivial set theoretic ways, but they are also related via one or more additional relationships of special nature, depending on the application at hand. Furthermore, among the structural, set-theoretic relationships it is often desirable to identify the Cartesian product of some of the sets—an action that can be crucial in preventing certain kinds of representations from growing exponentially in size. In line with these observations, which will be supported by examples in the sequel, the purpose of this article is to extend and combine Euler's two topo-visual formalisms into a tool suitable for dealing with such cases.

In the next section, we introduce *higraphs,*[4] first modifying Euler/ Venn diagrams somewhat, then extending them to represent the Cartesian product, and finally connecting the resulting curves by edges or hyperedges. (Section 8.6 contains the formal syntax and semantics of simple higraphs.) We will then illustrate the power of the formalism

[2]Venn himself was not always consistent in this respect: see Venn (1971) p. 177 or Gardner (1982) p. 43 for a description of his five-set diagram.

[3]The topological paradigm used here is termed *insideness* in Fitter and Green (1979).

[4]This is not a particularly successful choice of term but was chosen nevertheless to be reminiscent of *high graphs* or *hierarchical graphs,* though our diagrams are not limited to being stratified in the way the word hierarchical might imply.

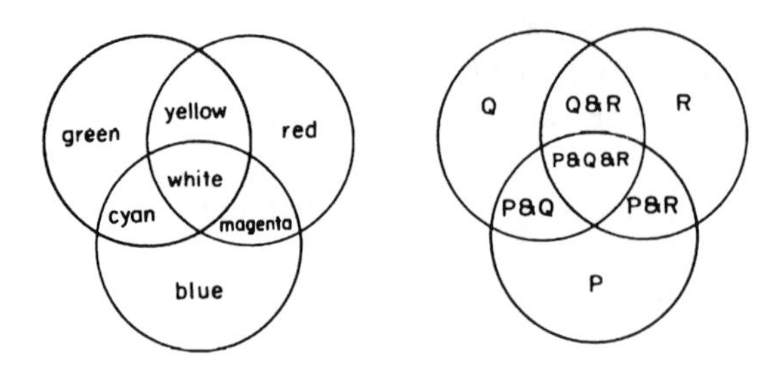

Figure 8.2
Applications of Euler Circles, or Venn Diagrams.

by briefly discussing higraph-based versions of such graphical languages as entity relationship diagrams, semantic and associative networks, and dataflow diagrams. Later we will detail a less obvious application called *statecharts* (Harel 1987), which are essentially a higraph-based version of finite-state machines and their transition diagrams.

8.1 Higraphs

Let us start with a simple example of Euler circles (Figure 8.3). As can be seen, we prefer to use rounded rectangles, or rounded rectilinear shapes *(rountangles?),* rather than circles or unrestricted curves, and shall call the areas, or zones, they enclose *blobs* in the sequel. Second, as the formal definition supplied in Section 8.6 shows, we regard each blob as denoting a certain kind of set, and the nesting of curves denotes set inclusion, not set membership. Thus, Figure 8.3 can be seen to contain several cases of inclusion, disjointness, and intersection of sets.

For our first real departure from Euler and Venn's treatment, we now require that every set of interest be represented by a unique blob, complete with its own full contour. One of the reasons for this is the desire to provide every set with its own area (e.g., for naming or labeling purposes). For example, does the A in Figure 8.3 represent the difference between the sets represented by the two large blobs, or the entire set on the upper left? The answer, following Venn's notational conventions, would appear to be the former; but then how do we label the upper set itself?

Our solution is illustrated in Figure 8.4, where the two large intersecting blobs are clearly labeled A and D, the intersection $A \cap D$ is labeled C, and the difference $A - D$ is called B. In fact, had we left out B and its contour we could not refer to $A - D$ at all. More precisely, with this "unique-contour" convention, the only real, identifiable sets are the *atomic* sets, that is, those represented by blobs residing on the bottom levels of the diagram, containing no wholly enclosed blobs within. Any other blob merely denotes the compound set consisting of the union of all sets represented by blobs that are totally enclosed within it. The atomic blobs of Figure 8.4 are thus $B, C, E, G, H, I, K, L, M, N, O, Q, S$, and, significantly, also T. The fact that T, as a Jordan curve, intersects R in Figure 8.4 does not necessarily mean that the sets represented by[5] T and R really intersect or that $T - R$ is nonempty. In fact, in our formalism, the intersection of two curves does not, in itself, mean anything since unless internal blobs appear in the appropriate places neither the difference nor the intersection of the sets they represent is itself identifiable. Thus, as far as the information present in Figure 8.4, T could just as well have been drawn completely disjoint from R, since R is defined by the figure to be the union of Q and S, whether T's curve intersects it or not. Of course, if T had been entirely enclosed within R, things would have been quite different, with R then being the union of Q, S, and T. All this might sound a little strange, but it is not really restrictive, since one can always let T and R intersect and simply add extra blobs representing $T \cap R$ and $T - R$, as is done in Figure 8.5.

Thus, one might say that empty space in our diagrams always represents nothing at all, except if it is the area of an atomic blob, which is one that contains no enclosed blobs. An atomic blob always represents some identifiable set, though clearly such a set might just happen to be an empty one.

We now add the ability to represent the *Cartesian product.* Figure 8.5 shows the notation used—a *partitioning* by dashed lines. In it J, for example, is no longer the union of K, N, I, L, and M, but, rather, the product of the union of the first two with the union of the last three. Symbolically, $J = W \times X = (K \cup N) \times (I \cup L \cup M)$. We shall call the operands of the product, W and X in this case, the *orthogonal components* of blob J. Actually, the Cartesian product is unordered,

[5]In the sequel, we shall often blur the distinction between a curve. its associated blob, and the set it depicts.

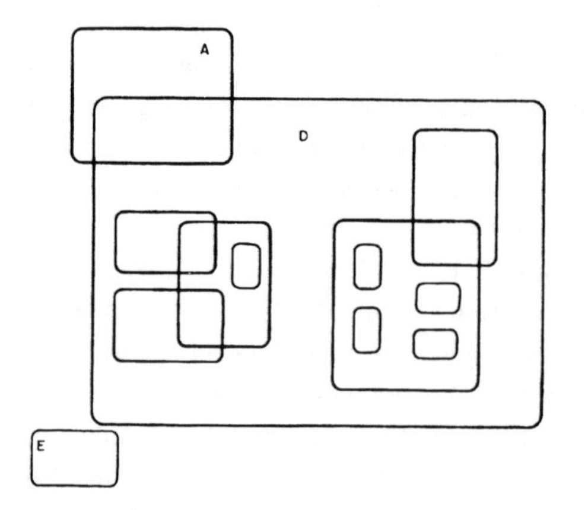

Figure 8.3
Simple Blobs.

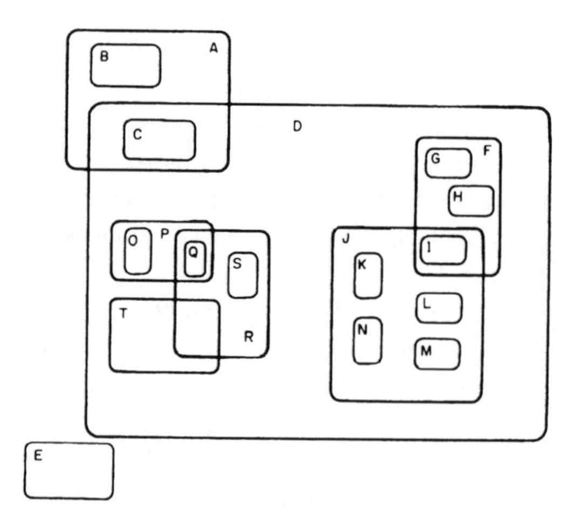

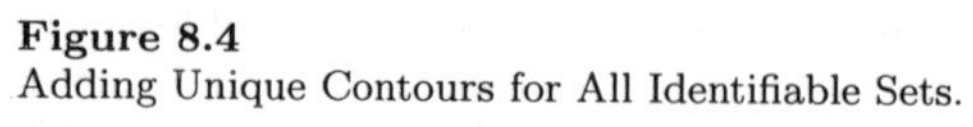

Figure 8.4
Adding Unique Contours for All Identifiable Sets.

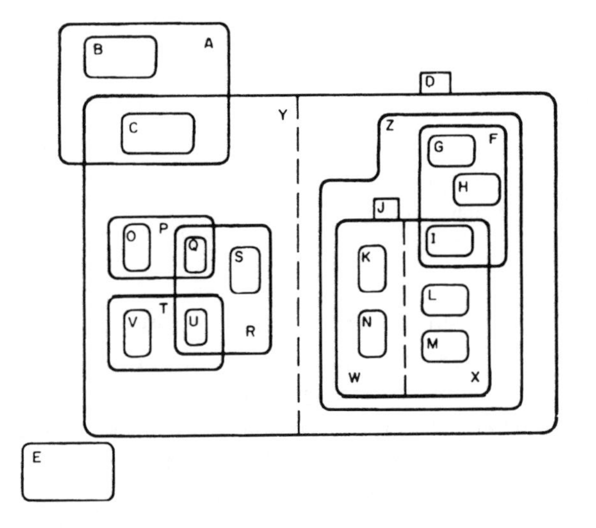

Figure 8.5
Adding Cartesian Product.

in the sense that $A \times B$ is always the same as $B \times A$, so that J is really a set of unordered pairs of elements. Thus, our $\times$ operator is symmetric, and in fact, in Section 8.6 we use the symbol $\otimes$, instead of $\times$, to denote it. Another consequence of this, and of our previous convention regarding set inclusion versus set membership, is that the product is also associative. In this way, if $c \in C, k \in K$, and $m \in M$, then the unordered triple $\{c, k, m\}$ would be a legal element of the set D of Figure 8.5, without the need to distinguish it from $\{c, \{k, m\}\}$. To make this idea work, it helps to assume that all atomic sets are pairwise disjoint (i.e., no element appears in any two of these sets).

Decomposing a blob into its orthogonal components by topologically partitioning the inner area of a Jordan curve yields a unique unambiguous area for each such component. Thus, the labels Y, W, and X in Figure 8.5 label the appropriate components unambiguously. On the other hand, as we shall see, there is another reason for wanting sets to have their own blob contours, and if so desired an orthogonal component can be enclosed in one of its own, as is Z in Figure 8.5. Notice the somewhat awkward location for the labels D and J. There are a couple of other possibilities for locating the label of a product blob, among which is the one illustrated in Figure 8.6, but we shall remain with that

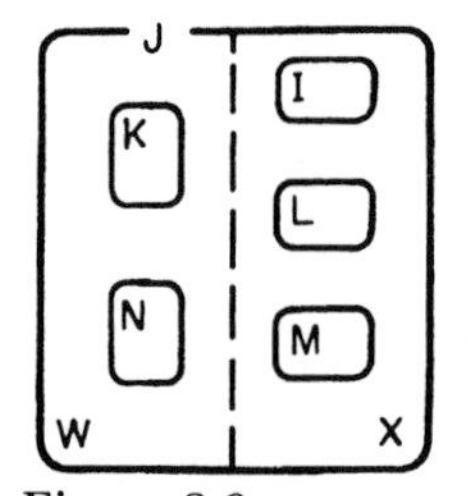

Figure 8.6
An Alternative for Labeling Partitioned Blobs.

of Figure 8.5.

Now that we have a formalism for representing the sets we are interested in and their structural, set-theoretic relationships, it is time to add edges. A *higraph* is obtained by simply allowing edges, or more generally, hyperedges, to be attached to the contour of any blobs. As in graphs, edges can be directed or undirected, labeled or unlabeled, of one type or of several, etc. In Figure 8.7 we have allowed for a single kind of unlabeled directed hyperedge of arity between 2 and 3. Most of the arrows in the figure are simple binary edges, such as the very high-level one connecting E to A, the very low-level one connecting N to K, and the interlevel one connecting U to E. Others are directed three-way hyperedges, such as the one connecting E to both J and T, and the one connecting both R and M to D. Clearly, there is nothing to prohibit self-directed or partially self-directed edges, such as the one connecting A to its subblob B. The formal meaning of such edges (see Section 8.6) in the graph-theoretic spirit simply associates the target blobs with the source blobs via the particular relationship the edges represent. Here, then, is the other reason for wanting each set of interest to have its own contour: to enable it to be connected to others via the edges.

In the sequel the term *higraph* will be used in a very liberal sense, making no real distinction between the various possibilities, for example, the edge-based or hyperedge-based cases.

8.2 Some Immediate Applications

The first thing to notice when attempting to apply higraphs is that edges connect sets to sets, not elements to elements as in graphs. The most common way of interpreting a higraph edge is as a collection of regular edges, connecting each element in one set with each element in the other. In this way, for example, it is possible to represent a 5-clique,

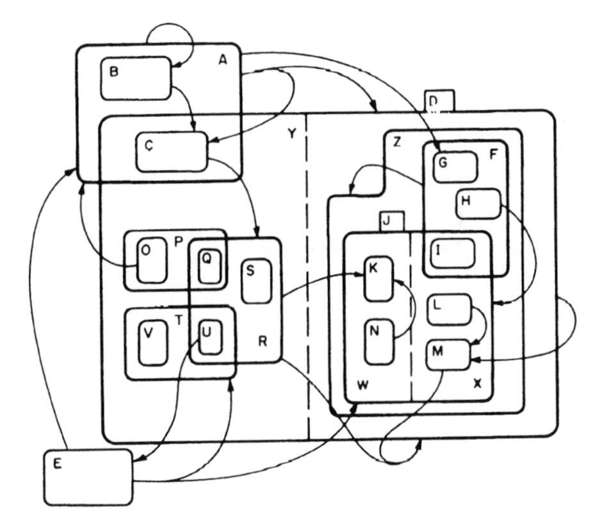

Figure 8.7
Adding Edges, Resulting in a Higraph.

as in Figure 8.8. This all to-all semantics is not mandatory, however, since the bare meaning of a higraph edge is that the relationship it represents holds between the sets it connects. Hence, we are free to attach any meaning at all to the relationship itself and to the way (if any) that it extends downwards to the elements of those sets. Thus, if we take the relationship R represented by ordinary arrows in a higraph to mean "each element in the source set is related to *some* element in the target set by relationship T," then the information conveyed by Figure 8.9, for example, cannot really by captured by an ordinary graph with T-edges, since one would be forced to decide which element in the target set is meant, thus causing an overspecification.

The computer science literature is full of uses of graphs, and it appears that many of these can benefit from the extensions offered by higraphs. Consider the entity-relationship *(E-R)* diagrams used in the conceptual specification of databases (Chen 1976). These are really hypergraphs with a single type of node that is depicted by a rectangle and denotes an entity in the described pool of data. The hyperedges, whose labels are written in small diamond-shaped boxes (that should not be regarded as nodes), capture the intended relationships between entities. Figure

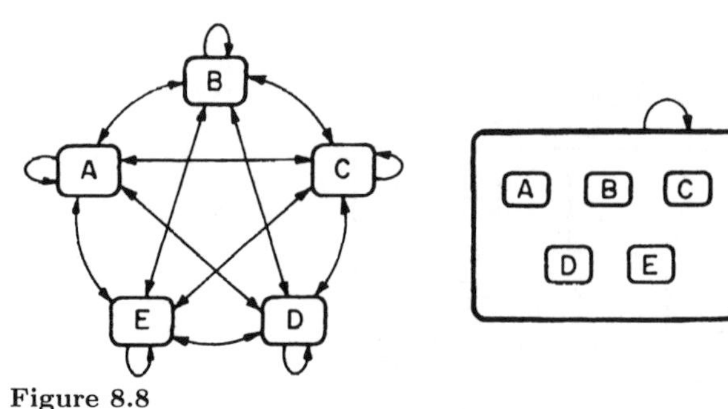

Figure 8.8
Two Representations of the 5-Clique.

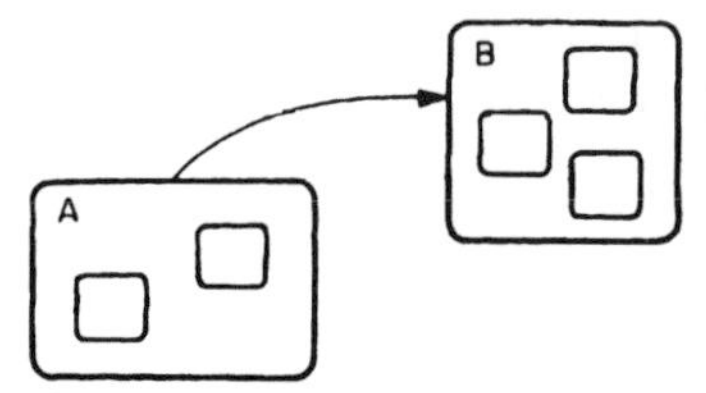

Figure 8.9
A Simple Higraph.

8.10 shows a simple example of such a diagram, representing a small part of the data used by an airline company.[6] Its information content is clear: `pilots` can fly `aircraft`, `secretaries` work for `employees`, and `employees` are paid `salaries` on certain `dates` (the latter being a three-way relationship). Notice, however, the `is-a` edges, informing us that `pilots` and `secretaries` are really `employees` too. These are conveying information of a totally different kind. Indeed, they capture precisely the kind of structural, set-theoretic relations discussed earlier. Using the very same "flat" diagrammatic representation for both kinds of relationships can cause a lot of confusion, especially in large and intricate cases, as a glance at some of the examples in the literature shows.

Figure 8.11 shows the way such information can be represented in a higraph-based extension of E-R diagrams. The set of `employees` is divided into the subsets of interest, `secretaries` and `pilots` (with

[6] Actually, Figure 8.10 does some injustice to the E-R formalism as it is sometimes called, by ignoring the additional features that the formalism supports, such as attributes for both entities. and relationships and the classification of relationships as one-one, many one, etc. Throughout. we shall have to be satisfied with describing only those features of a formalism that are directly relevant to our discussion.

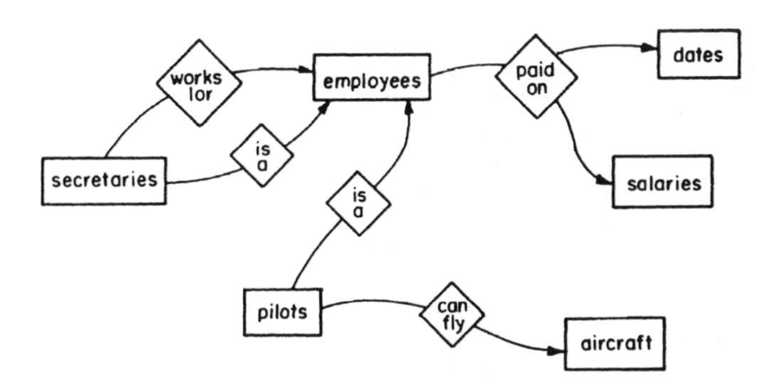

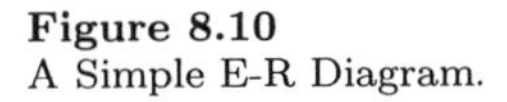
Figure 8.10
A Simple E-R Diagram.

an additional blob for all `others`, if so desired). The `paid-on` edge emanates from the `employees` blob, while the `can-fly` edge emanates from the `pilots` blob—only exactly what one would expect. The `work for` edge rightly connects the `secretaries` blob with its parent blob—`employees`. The new information has been quite easily added: `aircraft` are now just part of the overall `equipment`, which is related to `years` by the relationship `received on`, while the `dates` on which `salaries` are received have been specified as consisting of pairs from the orthogonal components `month` and `year`. Moreover, independent divisions can be represented by overlapping blobs, as illustrated in Figure 8.12, which shows how a new breakup of the `employees` by sex can be added to the previous figure with a couple of additional details. In it we might have reason to relate the `female pilots` or the `male secretaries` to other entities. In practice, overlaps should probably be used somewhat sparingly, as overly overlapping blobs might detract from the clarity of the total diagram, an observation that is in line with the often-made claim that a hierarchy is by far the way humans prefer to structure things (see Touretzky [1986], chapter 1). This opinion is not universally accepted, however, so the human-factors aspects of formalisms like higraphs would appear to require careful experimental research, such as those carried out in Fitter and Green (1979) and Green (1982).

Occasionally, authors have used other labels to capture `is-a` relationships, typically ones that try to describe the special nature of the breakup into subsets. As an example consider Figure 8.13, which is Fig-

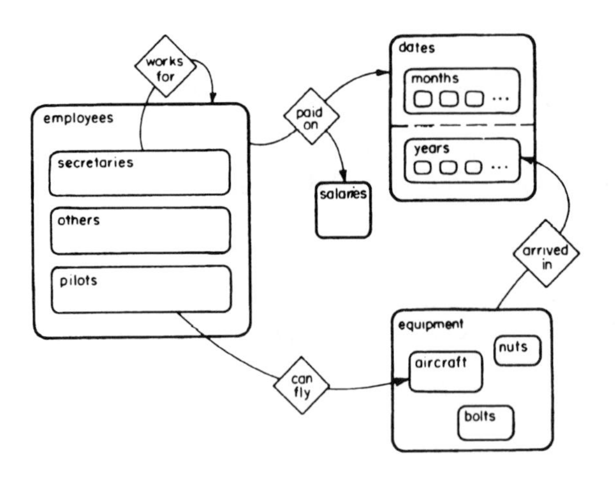

Figure 8.11
A Higraph-Based Version (and Extension) of Figure 8.10.

ure 8.9 of Schiffner and Schuermann (1979) almost verbatim, and our higraph-based Figure 8.14, which contains the same information.

A formalism that is very similar to that of E-R diagrams, and actually predated it by a number of years (see Quillian 1968), is that of *semantic,* or *associative, networks.* These graph-based structures are used widely in artificial intelligence for natural language processing and knowledge representation, and are discussed in numerous books and papers. (A good survey and history appears in Brachman [1979], and more examples can be found in Charniak and McDermott [1985], Nilsson [1980], Shapiro [1971], and Woods [1975] and in the collection of papers in Findler [1979].) Semantic networks can actually be thought of as *concept-relationship diagrams,* with much of the research in the area concerned with the association of rich semantic meaning with the various types of nodes and edges. Here, too, `is-a` edges are used in abundance resulting in large, and at times incomprehensible, diagrams. Often, semantic networks contain more than one distinct type of `is-a` edges, corresponding to set inclusion, set membership, a physical "being-part-of" relationship, etc.[7] The way higraphs can be used here is exactly

[7] A variety of names have been attached to these, such as `isa` and `inst` in Charniak and McDermott (1985), SS and EL in Nilsson (1980) (standing for *is a, instance, subset,* and *element,* respectively), and many others elsewhere. such as `a-kind-of`, `group-of`, `is-part-of`, etc.

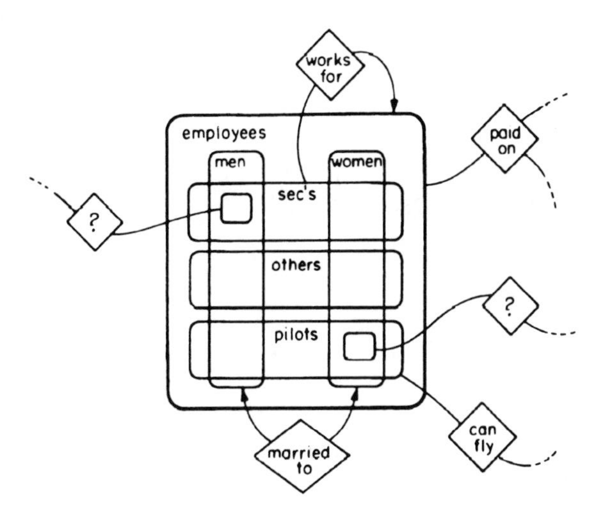

Figure 8.12
Two Breakups of Employees.

as in E-R diagrams, and the advantages become all the more significant if such different shades of structural `is-a` relationships can be made visually distinct (see Section 8.4). Clearly, it would be naive to claim that the profound problematics of knowledge representation can be overcome by diagrammatic considerations alone. Nevertheless, every little improvement helps.

In both E-R diagrams and semantic networks, people have observed that often the relationships, not only the entities and concepts, have to be stratified by levels of detail. This is typically done by considering the diamond-shaped relationship labels to be nodes of a second kind, and involving them also in structural `is-a` relationships with others. Although some people are opposed to this visual blurring of the distinction between entities and relationships, there is nothing to prevent those who are not from transferring this idea to the higraph framework. This would yield a blob structure also for the relationships, with the edges now serving to connect the entities and concepts to their relevant real, nonstructural relationships.

It is noteworthy that the area of the blobs in a higraph can be further exploited in these applications. Full E-R diagrams and semantic networks are typically laden with attributes, or properties, that are attached

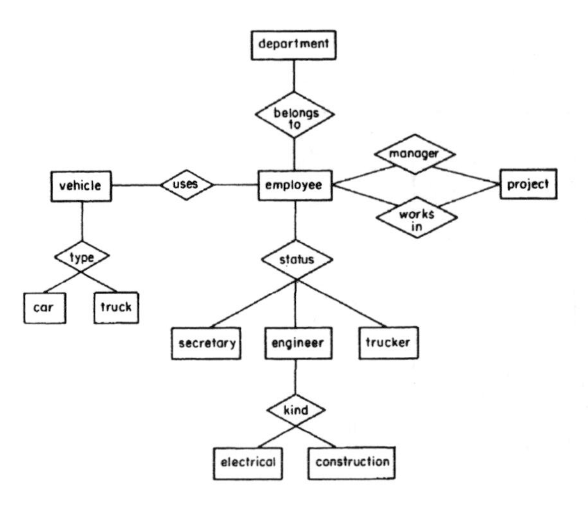

Figure 8.13
Another E-R Diagram (Taken from Schiffner and Schuermann [1986]).

as additional "stump" nodes to the various entities. These attributes are often of the kind that are "inherited down" the `is-a` hierarchy, as the phrase goes. (In fact, there are many interesting issues associated with the very notion of inheritance; see Cardelli [1984], Touretzky [1986].) In a higraph-based representation, the area inside a blob would appear to be an ideal place to list, attach, or otherwise identify any properties, attributes, or explanations that are relevant to that blob and anything enclosed therein. Thus, simple inheritance is made possible quite naturally by the insideness approach to representing the subset relationship.

We should remark that some papers on semantic networks and the ER model have indeed suggested the use of insideness and interblob edges to represent high-level entities and relationships, though the ideas do not seem to have been pursued to their full potential (see dos Santos, Neuhold, and Furtado [1980], al-Fedaghi [1983], Hendrix [1975], McSkimin and Minker [1979], and Nakano [1983]). Also, the idea of basing the decomposition of sets on Cartesian products and OR's is consistent with much of the literature on types. (For example, see Cardelli [1984] where these two features are captured by the notions of a *record* and a *variant*, respectively.)

Among the other graph-based formalisms for which higraphs appear to be useful are data-flow diagrams. A higraph-based version of such

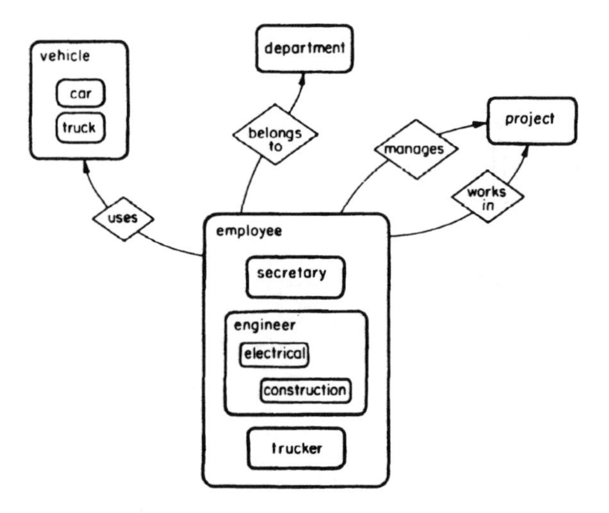

Figure 8.14
A Higraph-Based Version of Figure 8.13.

diagrams, called *activity-charts,* is one of the graphical languages supported by the STATEMATE system of i-Logix and is described in Harel, et al. (1988), and Harel and Politi (1988). In activity-charts the blobs denote functions, or activities, with the subset relation representing the subfunction relationship. The edges denote the possible flow of data. (Cartesian product is not used.) Consider the activity-chart of Figure 8.15, which is a simple part of the functional decomposition of an automatic teller machine. One of the edges therein means that the customer's `account-number` might possibly flow (following, perhaps, a read or write instruction) from the `identify` activity to the `update` account activity, or to anywhere in the `serve-customer` activity, that is, to either (or all) of the `deposit`, `withdraw`, or `balance-query` subactivities. Another of the edges in Figure 8.15 means that the new `amount` with which the customer's balance should be adjusted might flow from any one of the `deposit` or `withdraw` activities to the `update-account` activity.

Higraphs also form the basis of a recent paper (Tygar and Wing 1987), in which a visual language for specifying security constraints in operating systems is presented. The formalism represents access rights and exceptions thereof as distinct kinds of edges in a higraph, the blobs of which represent groups of users, files, and other entities. Cartesian product

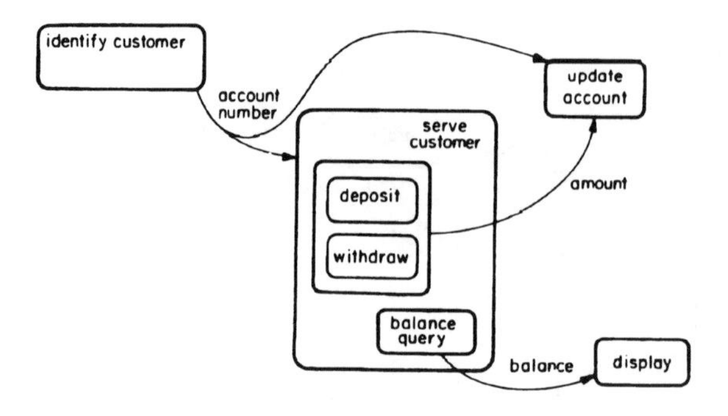

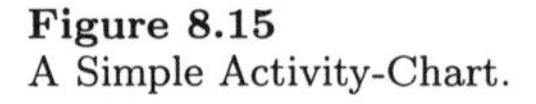
Figure 8.15
A Simple Activity-Chart.

is used to represent the breakup of files into their components. Tygar and Wing (1987) also contains a number of interesting special-purpose extensions to the basic higraph formalism. Another use of higraphlike ideas appears in Manna and Pnueli (1987) and Owicki and Lamport (1982) in the form of proof diagrams for verifying concurrent programs, and there is a simple way of using higraphs as the basis of a hypertext system rather than conventional graph. In part, many issues that arise in the context of hypertext systems, such as multiple hierarchies, superconcepts, and composite nodes are treated naturally in the higraph formalism (Conklin 1987). One can also conceive of additional applications in visualizing interrupt-driven flowcharts and certain kinds of model-collapsing constructions in model theory.

8.3 Statecharts: A Less Obvious Application

The previous section notwithstanding, it would appear that the most beneficial application of higraphs lies in extending state-transition diagrams to obtain the *statecharts* of Harel (1987). It was actually in the process of trying to formulate the underlying graphical concepts embodied in (the earlier) statecharts that higraphs emerged. This section contains a brief description of the statechart formalism; the reader is referred to Harel (1987) for further details.

To motivate the discussion, there appears to be agreement in the literature on software and systems engineering as to the existence of a major problem in the specification and design of large and complex *reactive systems.* A reactive system (see Harel and Pnueli [1985] and Pnueli [1986]), in contrast with a *transformational system,* is characterized by being event driven, continuously having to react to external and internal stimuli. Examples include telephones, communication networks, computer operating systems, avionics systems, VLSI circuits, and the man-machine interface of many kinds of ordinary software. The problem is rooted in the difficulty of describing reactive behavior in ways that are clear and realistic, and at the same time formal and rigorous, in order to be amenable to precise computerized analysis. The behavior of a reactive system is really the set of allowed sequences of input and output events, conditions, and actions, perhaps with some additional information such as timing constraints.

Most notable among the solutions proposed for this problem are Petri nets (see, for example, Reisig [1985]), communicating sequential processing (CSP) (Hoare 1978), the calculus of communicating systems (CCS) (Milner 1980), the sequence diagrams of Zave (1985), ESTEREL (Berry and Cosserat 1985), and temporal logic (Pnueli 1986). Statecharts constitute yet another attempt at solving this problem, but one that is aimed at reviving the classical formalism of finite-state machines (FSMs) and their visual counterpart, state-transition diagrams, trying to make them suitable for use in large and complex applications. Indeed, people working on the design of really complex systems have all but given up on the use of conventional FSMs and their state diagrams for several reasons:

1. State diagrams are "flat." They provide no natural notion of depth, hierarchy, or modularity, and therefore do not support stepwise, top-down, or bottom-up development.
2. State diagrams are uneconomical when it comes to transitions. An event that causes the very same transition from a large number of states, such as a high-level interrupt, must be attached to each of them separately, resulting in an unnecessary multitude of arrows.
3. State diagrams are extremely uneconomical, indeed quite infeasible, when it comes to states (at least when states are interpreted in the usual way as "snapshots" of the situation at a given point in time). As the system under description grows linearly, the number of states grows exponentially, and the conventional FSM formalism forces one to explicitly represent them all.

4. Finally, state diagrams are inherently sequential in nature and do not cater for concurrency in a natural way.[8]

There have been attempts to remove some of these drawbacks, mostly by using various kinds of hierarchical or communicating state machines. Typically, however, these hierarchies provide little help in reducing the size of the resulting description, as they do not condense any information. Moreover, the communication between FSMs is usually one-to-one, being channel or processor based, and allows for only a single set of communicating machines on the highest level of the description. Furthermore, for the most part such extensions are not particularly diagrammatic in spirit, and hence one loses the advantages a visual medium might offer.

Statecharts are a higraph-based extension of standard state transition diagrams, where the blobs represent states and arrows represent transitions. (For additional statechart features, the reader is again referred to Harel 1987.)[9] As to the basics, we might say that

statecharts = state diagrams + depth + orthogonality + broadcast communication.

Depth is represented by the insideness of blobs, as illustrated in Figure 8.16, where 8.16b may replace 8.16a. The symbols e, f, g, and h stand for events that trigger the transitions, and the bracketed c is a condition. Thus, $g[c]$ triggers the transition from A to C if and when g occurs, but only if c is true at that time. The fact that A and C do not overlap and are completely inside D means that the latter is the exclusive-or (XOR) of the former, so that being in D is tantamount to being in either A or C, but not in both. The main point here is that the f-arrow, which leaves the contour of D, applies to both A and C, as in Figure 8.16a. This simple higraph-based principle, when applied to large collections of states with many levels, helps overcome points (1) and (2) above (flatness and multilevel events). The idea of exploiting this kind of insideness in describing levels in a state-transition diagram appears also in Green (1982). It should be noted that the small default arrows depend on their encompassing blobs.

[8]Here modeling a highly concurrent system by its global states only is considered unnatural.

[9]Some encouraging experimental evidence as to the appropriateness of statecharts for system description is discussed in Harel 1987, sect. 9.

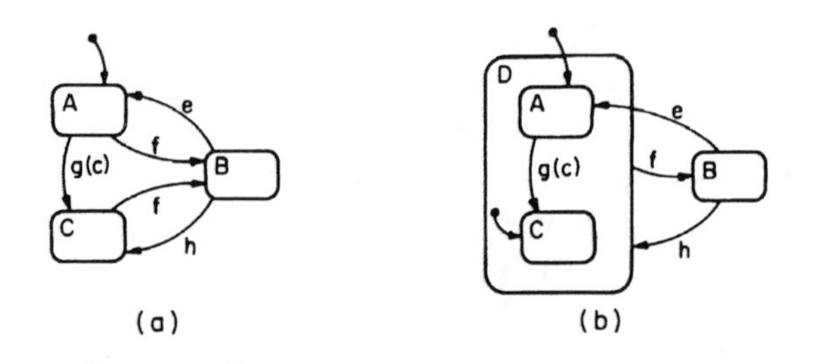

Figure 8.16
Depth in Statecharts.

In Figure 8.16a state A is singled out as being the default, or start state, of the three, a fact represented in 8.16b by the top default arrow. The bottom one, however, states that C is default among A and C if we are already in D and hence alleviates the need for continuing the h-arrow beyond D's boundary.

Orthogonality is the dual of the XOR decomposition of states, in essence an AND decomposition, and is captured by the partitioning feature of higraphs, that is, by the unordered Cartesian product. In Figure 8.17b state Y consists of two orthogonal components, A and D, related by AND: To be in Y is tantamount to being in both A and D, and hence the two default arrows. The intended semantics of Figure 8.17b is given by its equivalent "flat" version 8.17a, which represents a sort of automata product. Notice the simultaneity of transitions that takes place when event e occurs in state configuration (B, F), and the merging and splitting transitions that lead to and from Y. Note also the special condition [$\mathtt{in}(G)$] attached to the f-transition from C, and the way it is reflected in Figure 8.17a. Figure 8.17 illustrates the heart of the exponential blowup problem, the number of states in the explicit version of Y being the product of the numbers of states in the orthogonal components of its higraph version. If orthogonality is used often and on many levels, the state explosion and sequentiality difficulties (points [3] and [4]) are also overcome in a reasonable way. This can be further observed by studying the examples and references in Harel (1987).

Figures 8.16 and 8.17 do not contain any outputs, and hence, orthogonal components can synchronize so far only through common events (like e in Figure 8.17) and can affect each other only through [$\mathtt{in}(\mathit{state})$] conditions. A certain amount of subtlety is added to the way statecharts model concurrency by allowing output events. Here, statecharts can be viewed as an extension of Mealy machines (see Hopcroft and Ullman 1979), since output events, which are called *actions,* can be attached optionally to the triggering event along a transition. In contrast with conventional Mealy machines, however, an action appearing along a transition in a statechart is not merely sent to the "outside world" as an output. Rather, it can affect the behavior of the statechart itself in orthogonal components. This is achieved by a simple broadcast mechanism: Just as the occurrence of an external event causes transitions in all components to which it is relevant (see Figure 8.17), if event e occurs and a transition labeled e/f is taken, the action f is immediately activated, and is regarded as a new event, possibly causing further transitions in other components.

Figure 8.18 shows a simple example of this. If we are in (B, F, J) and along comes the external event m, the next configuration will be (C, G, I), by virtue of e being generated in H and triggering the two transitions in components A and D. This is a *chain reaction* of length 2. If no external event n occurs, the new configuration will be (B, E, J), by virtue of a similar chain reaction of length 3.

This concludes our brief account of the basic features of statecharts, and we now illustrate the formalism with a rather simplified version of the digital watch described in Harel (1987). The watch has four external control buttons, as well as a main display that can be used to show the `time` (hour, minutes, and seconds) or the `date` (weekday, day of month, and month). It has a `chime` that can be enabled or disabled, beeping on the hour if enabled. It has an `alarm` that can also be enabled or disabled, and beeps for 2 minutes when the time in the alarm setting is reached unless any one of the buttons is pressed earlier. It has a `stopwatch` with two display modes (`regular` and `lap`), a `light` for illumination, and a `weak-battery` blinking indication.

Some of the external events relevant to the watch are a, b, c, and d, which signify the pressing of the four buttons, respectively, and `bu-p`, for example, which signifies the release of button b. Another event we shall be using, 2-*min,* signifies that 2 minutes have elapsed since the last time a button was pressed. (We choose not to get involved here in a syntax for the event expressions themselves. In a language of compound events that includes a time-out construct, such as that of Harel, et al. (1988) and Harel and Politi (1988), this last event can be expressed easily.)

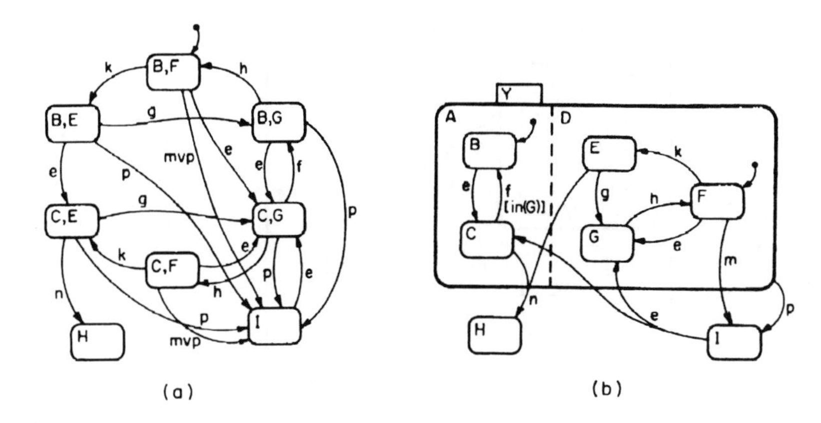

Figure 8.17
Orthogonality in Statecharts.

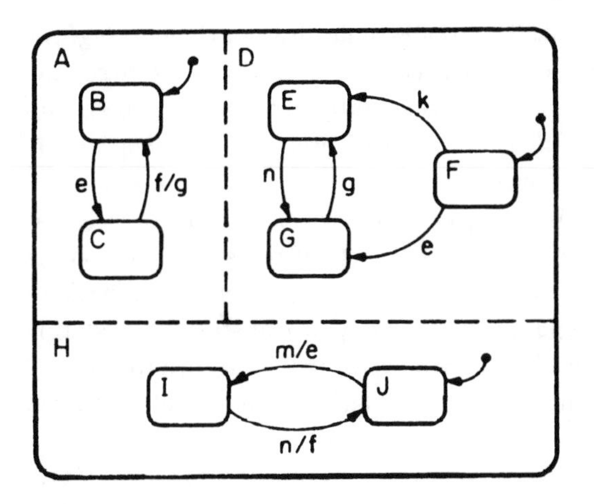

Figure 8.18
Broadcasting in Statecharts.

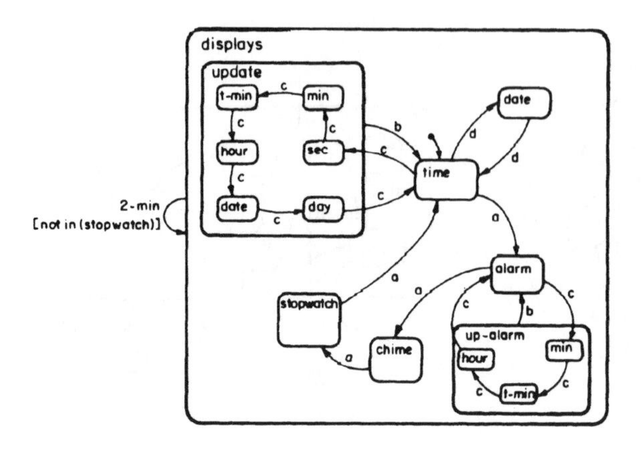

Figure 8.19
Part of the Displays State in a Digital Watch.

Statecharts can be used to describe the behavior of the watch in terms of its human interface; namely, how the user's operations, such as pressing buttons, influence things. It should be noted, however, that the descriptions that follow do not specify the activities carried out internally by the watch, only their control. Thus, nothing is said here about the time elapsing activity itself, or the technicalities of the beeping, the blinking, or the displays. These aspects of a system can be described using other means, and should be incorporated into the overall specification together with the statecharts. (See Harel, et al. [1988] for one approach to this incorporation.)

Figure 8.19 shows the basic `displays` state of the watch. Notice that `time` is the default state, and there is a cycle of pressings of *a* leading from `time` through the `alarm`, `chime`, and `stopwatch` states back to `time`. There is a general `update` state, and a special state for updating the alarm's internal setting. The `2-min` event signifies return to time if 2 minutes have elapsed in any state other than `stopwatch` and no button has been pressed.

The specification of the watch contains examples of orthogonal states on various levels. We should first consider the `stopwatch` state, detailed in Figure 8.20. It has two substates, `zero` and {`disp, run`}, the first being the default. Pressing *b* takes the stopwatch from the former to the latter causing it to start running with a regular display. Repeatedly pressing *b* causes it to stop and start alternately. Pressing *d* can be seen

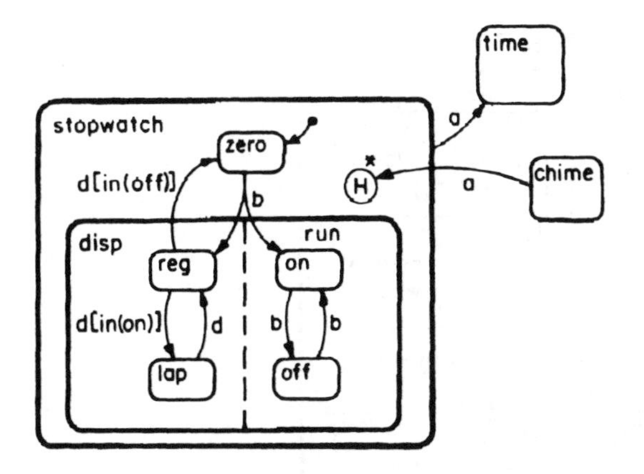

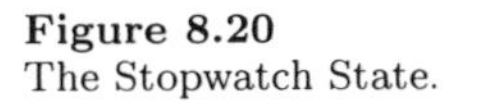
Figure 8.20
The Stopwatch State.

to cause the display to switch to `lap` and back to `reg`, or to leave the orthogonal state and return to `zero` depending, as illustrated, on the present state configuration. The encircled and starred H is one of the additional notations described in Harel (1987), and prescribes that, upon entering `stopwatch` from `chime` by pressing a, the state actually entered will be the one in which the system was in most recently. Thus, we are entering the stopwatch state by "history" hence, the H. The default will be used if this is the first time `stopwatch` is entered, or if the history has been cleared.

The description of the high levels of the watch also uses orthogonality. In Figure 8.21 the watch is specified as being either `dead` or `alive`, with the latter consisting of five orthogonal components. (Notice where the `displays` state fits in.) In this figure the events `bt-in`, `bt-rm`, `bt-dy` and `bt-wk` signify, respectively, the insertion, removal, expiration, and weakening (below a certain level) of the battery. We use `t-hits-tm` to signify that the internal time of the watch has reached the internal time setting of the alarm, and `t-hits-hr` to signify that it has reached a whole hour. Also, `beep-rt` occurs when either any button is pressed or 2 minutes have elapsed since entering `beep`, and `beep-st` occurs 2 seconds after entering `c-beep`. (As mentioned, these events should also be written formally as compound event expressions in a language involving

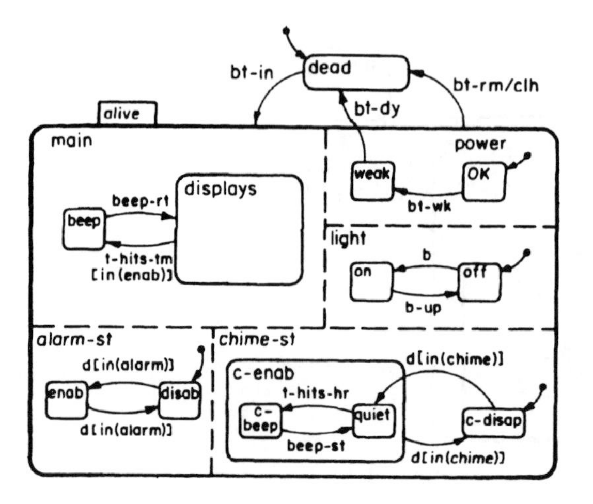

Figure 8.21
A High-Level Description of the Watch.

time-outs, disjunctions, and so on; see Harel and Politi [1987].)

The first of the five components in Figure 8.21, `main`, specifies the transitions between displaying and beeping, where `displays` is simply the state described earlier (see Figure 8.19). (In actuality, the displaying activities themselves do not shut off when the watch is beeping, but cannot be changed until control returns to the displays state.) The `alarm-st` component describes the status of the alarm, specifying that it can be changed using *d* when control is in the `alarm` display state. The `chime-st` state is similar, with the additional provision for beeping on the hour given within. The `power` state is self-explanatory, where the activity that would take place in the `weak` state would involve the displays blinking frantically.

In considering the innocent-looking `light` state, the default is `off`, and depressing and releasing *b* cause the light to switch alternately between `on` and `off`. What is interesting is the effect these actions might have elsewhere. If the entire statechart for the parts of the watch described so far is contemplated (see Figure 8.22), one realizes that pressing *b* for illumination has significant side effects: It will cause a return from an update state if we happen to be in one, the stopping of the alarm if it happens to be beeping, and a change in the stopwatch's behavior if

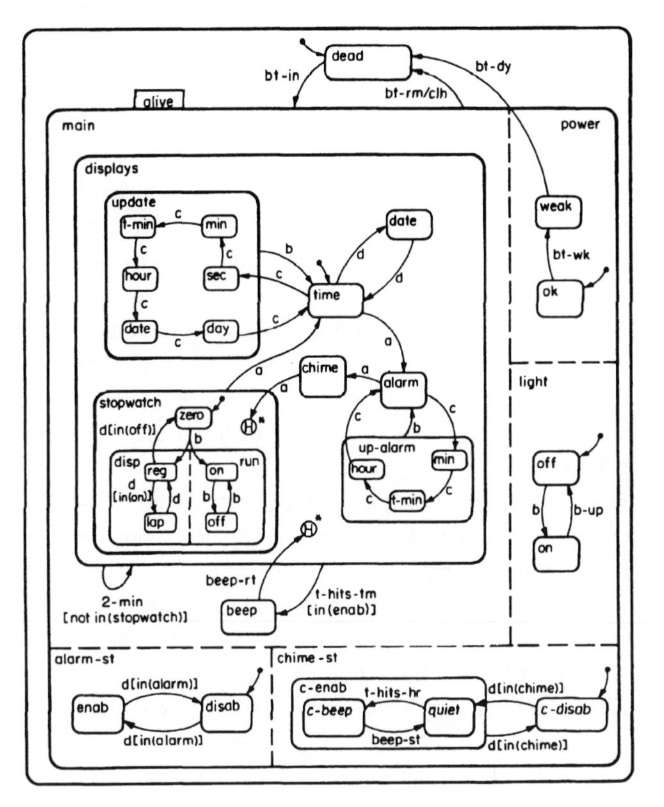

Figure 8.22
A Statechart for the Digital Watch.

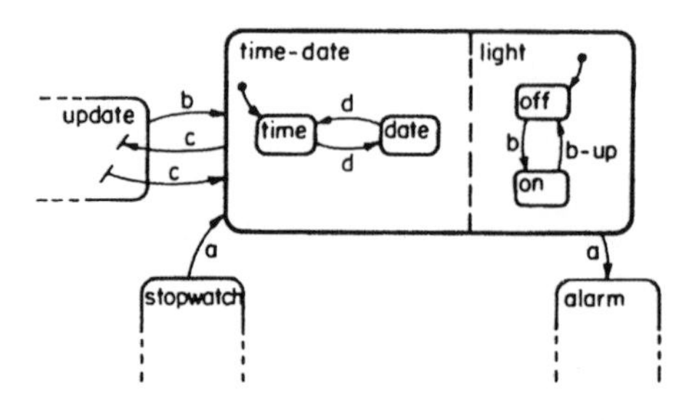

Figure 8.23
A Smaller Scope for the Light.

we happen to be working with it. Conversely, if we use b in `displays` for any one of these things the light will go on, whether we like it or not. These seeming anomalies are all a result of the fact that the `light` component is orthogonal to the `main` component, meaning that its scope is very broad. One can imagine a far more humble `light` component, applicable only in the `time` and `date` states, which would not cause any of these problems. Its specification could be carried out by attaching it orthogonally, not to `main`, but to a new state surrounding `time` and `date`, as in Figure 8.23.

As mentioned earlier, this section has only described the "no-frills" version of the language of statecharts. A more complete treatment appears in Harel (1987), and a formal syntax and semantics appear in Harel, Pnueli, Schmidt, and Sherman (1987). The semantics as implemented in STATECHART appear in Harel and Naamad (1989). The reader may have noticed that we have not used intersecting states in the statecharts. While intersecting blobs in higraphs do not cause any serious semantic problems (see Section 8.6), intersecting states in state charts do. In fact, since not all syntactically legal higraphs make sense as statecharts, it is not even clear how to define an appropriate syntax for statecharts with intersecting states (see Harel 1987, sect. 6.2]). These problems have been dealt with in Harel and Kahana (1992).

8.4 Possible Variations on the Theme

The higraph formalism can be enriched and extended in various ways. We shall point to a few of these possibilities briefly and informally.

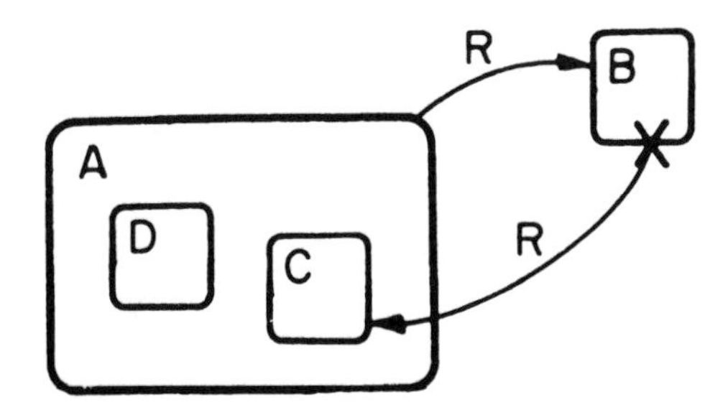

Figure 8.24
Negative Arrows.

At times it becomes useful to base a formalism on a three-valued, rather than a two-valued, underlying model. For example, in certain uses of graphs in databases and artificial intelligence there arises a need to state not only that a certain relationship R holds or does not hold between two objects, but also to capture the situation whereby we do not know which of these is the case. One possibility is to reinterpret the absence of an R arrow as denoting the don't-known situation, and have a new kind of arrow representing the *negative information* that R definitely does *not* hold. This simple idea can be adopted in higraphs too, as in Figure 8.24, which is suppose to indicate that R holds between A and B and does not hold between B and C, and that all other possibilities (including whether or not R holds between C and B)[10] are left open.

Often a don't-know option is needed not only for arrows, but for blobs as well. That is, we might want to represent uncertainty as to the presence or absence of identifiable sets, rather than relationships. Accordingly, we can use a new blob notation (e.g., one with a dashed contour) to denote a set that we are not sure actually exists (here one assumes that all regular blobs stand for nonempty sets). Figure 8.25 asserts our uncertainty as to whether $A - B$ is empty or not, and also states that if it is not empty then the difference is called E and is related to F via relationship R.

When higraphs are used in practice (see Harel [1987], Harel, et al. [1988], Harel and Politi [1988], and Tygar and Wing [1987]), it is use-

[10]This is not determined by the arrow from A to B, since as discussed earlier. the fact that R holds between A and B says nothing about what the case is for A's subsets.

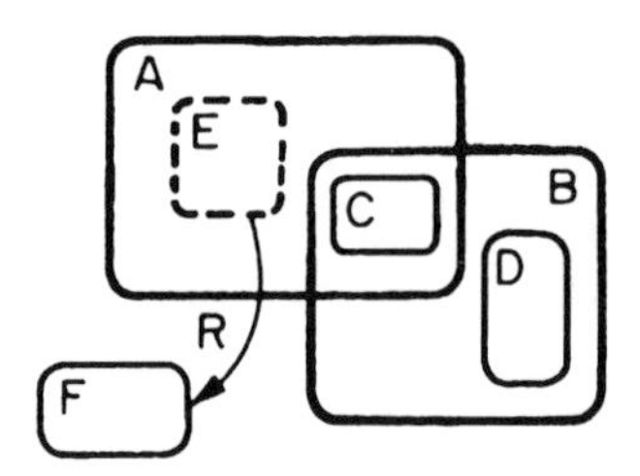

Figure 8.25
"Not-Quite-Sure" Blobs.

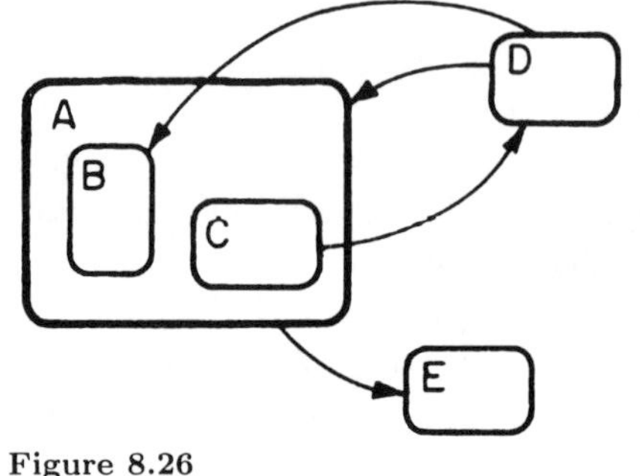

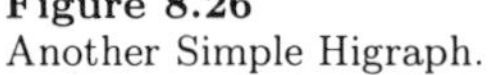

Figure 8.26
Another Simple Higraph.

ful to be able to "zoom out" of a particular view, suppressing low-level details. A good example would be going from Figure 8.22, the detailed state-chart description of the watch, to the less detailed Figure 8.21. In such cases there arises a problem with edges connected to subblobs that are omitted from the new, less detailed view. If we decide to zoom out of the likes of Figure 8.26 by suppressing blobs B and C, it might be a mistake to consider Figure 8.27a as the correct new version, since the two are clearly inconsistent. Figure 8.27b is better, with its stubs that represent relationships to unspecified subblobs. For example, since a statechart arrow whose target is a high-level state A prescribes entrance to none other than the default substate of A, Figure 8.21 is somewhat inconsistent with Figure 8.22. In the present context, a better version would have shown the `beep-rt` arrow crossing the contour of the `displays` state and ending with a stub indicating entrance to a substate (as of now unspecified) that is possibly different from the default substate, `time`.

One weakness of the higraph formalism is its inability to specify both

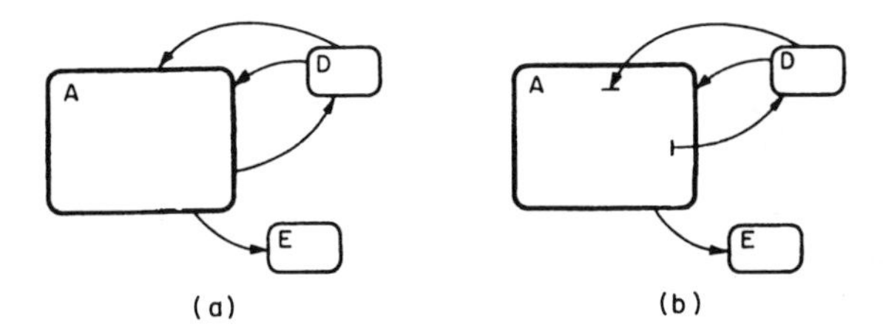

Figure 8.27
Two Possible Zoom Outs for Figure 8.26.

set inclusion and set membership. We have chosen to adopt the former as the meaning of blob enclosure, although we could probably have chosen the latter too without causing too many problems. This weakness is all the more apparent when higraphs are contrasted with their graph-based equivalents, in which set inclusion is depicted by `is-a` edges (see Figure 8.10). In the latter, one need only use an additional type of edge, labeled `elmnt-of`, for instance, to be able to represent set membership. We would like to claim that this is not much more than a notational problem that requires a topovisual way of distinguishing between two different kinds of insideness. Most of the solutions to this notational problem that come to mind are somewhat unsatisfactory, with the exception of the one that calls for a three-dimensional basis for higraphs, in which the third dimension is responsible for such distinctions (e.g., by having set inclusion take place in the same plane and set membership be reflected by different levels of planes).[11]

An additional possible extension to higraphs is to make arrows mean more than a simple connection between source and target. (We are assuming ordinary directed binary edges here, not, say, hyperedges.) Since higraph arrows in general cut across blob contours, we might want to say something more about the sequence of crossovers that the edge takes on its way from the source to the target. This can be achieved trivially by drawing the arrow through the appropriate contours in the desired order (assuming this order is indeed possible, given the basic topology of the blobs). The interesting case occurs when we want to

[11]Visual formalisms that are predominately two-dimensional in nature but make some use of a third dimension are far from being out of the question, even if we are not willing to wait for quality holographic workstations to show up. If all we need as in this case is the ability to tell when two nested blobs are on the same plane or not, then a simple graphical simulation of a dynamic left-right shift in point of view would do the job.

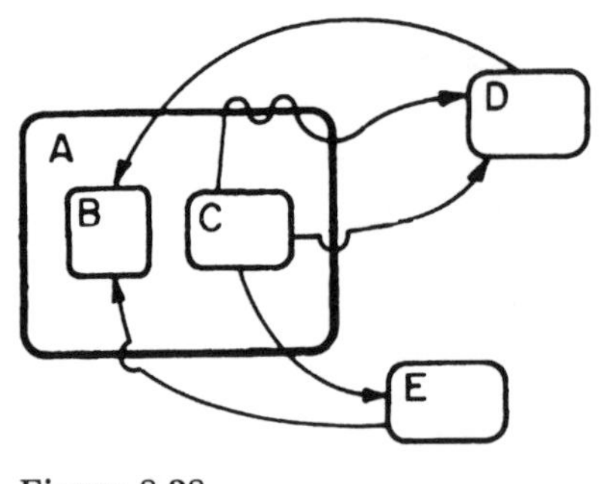

Figure 8.28
Skipping and Multiple Crossovers.

omit from such a sequence one or more of the contours that, topologically speaking, must be crossed by any line from the source to the target. We would like the D–to–B arrow in Figure 8.26, for example, to enter B. but not to enter A in the process. Statecharts with intersections give rise to one interesting motivation for such cases, whereby one wants the system to enter only one of two intersecting states; again, the reader is referred to Harel (1987), section 6.2 for details. This richer notion of an edge can be represented visually by simply allowing arrows to skip edges as in Figure 8.28. Multiple crossovers, if desired, can also be represented as illustrated in the figure. Clearly, the formal semantics would be more elaborate, since a finite sequence of blobs, rather than an ordered pair, is the interpretation of a directed edge, and a finite set thereof, rather than an unordered pair, is the interpretation of an undirected edge.

8.5 Conclusion and Future Work

Higraphs seem to give rise to several interesting mathematical notions adapted to a large extent from graphs and hypergraphs. For example, one can provide reasonable definitions of connectivity, transitive closure, planarity, and acyclicity in higraphs, as well as a couple of different notions of "hitrees." For each of these. we may ask for upper and lower bounds on the computational complexity of the corresponding algorithmic problems. In some cases algorithms and bounds can be carried over from the work on graphs and hypergraphs, but one gets the feeling that in other cases these bounds can be improved by utilizing the special structure of higraphs. Some of these algorithmic problems have indeed arisen during the implementation of the STATEMATE system (Harel, et al. [1988], and Harel and Politi [1988]), which supports three higraph-based formalisms. It would appear that the algorithmics of higraphs forms a fruitful avenue for further research.[12]

The main thesis underlying this chapter is that the intricate nature of a variety of computer-related systems and situations can, and in our opinion should, be represented by *visual formalisms:* visual, because they are to be generated, comprehended, and communicated by humans; and formal, because they are to be manipulated, maintained, and analyzed by computers. (This thesis is consistent with the study in Davis and Anderson (1979), which argues for a more visual, nonverbal approach toward mathematics.)

Part of our motivation in stressing this point, despite the fact that it might appear to be so obvious, is the rather different approach that one occasionally finds elsewhere. For example, Martin and McClure (1985) is a compendium of many computer-related diagrammatic methods (virtually all of which are based on graphs). In our opinion, Martin and McClure (1985) is quite inadequate, since it accepts the *visual,* but apparently rejects the *formal.* For the most part, the methods and languages appearing in Martin and McClure (1985) are described in a manner that is devoid of semantics, and can therefore be used at best as informal aids when working with some other, hopefully more rigorous, nonvisual medium.

One of the implicit points we have tried to make in this article is that a considerable amount of mileage can be gotten out of basing such formalisms on a small number of simple diagrammatic notions, first and foremost among which are those that are topological in nature, not geometric. A lot can be gained by using topo-visual formalisms based on insideness, connectedness, and partitioning, with the semantics as given here, before one attempts to attach special significance to, for example, shapes, colors, and sizes.

We are entirely convinced the future is "visual." We believe that in the next few years many more of our daily technical and scientific chores will be carried out visually, and graphical facilities will be far better and

[12] Since the original version of this paper appeared, work on this has been carried out by O. Grossman and the author. A paper is in preparation.

cheaper than today's. The languages and approaches we shall be using in doing so will not be merely iconic in nature (e.g., using the picture of a trash can to denote garbage collection), but inherently diagrammatic in a conceptual way, perhaps also three-dimensional and/or animated. They will be designed to encourage visual modes of thinking when tackling systems of ever-increasing complexity, and will exploit and extend the use of our own wonderful biological visual system in many of our intellectual activities.

8.6 Supplement: Formal Definition of Higraphs

In what follows we present a formal (nongraphical) syntax and semantics for higraphs with simple binary directed edges. The reader should have no difficulty in extending the edge set E to represent say, hyperedges.

A *higraph* is a quadruple

$$H = (B, \sigma, \pi, E),$$

where B is a finite set of elements, called *blobs,* and E, the set of *edges,* is a binary relation on B :

$$E \subseteq B \times B.$$

The *subblob* function σ is defined as

$$\sigma : B \rightarrow 2^B.$$

It assigns to each blob $x \in B$ its set $\sigma(x)$ of subblobs and is restricted to being cycle free. Thus, if we define

$$\sigma^0(x) = \{x\}, \qquad \sigma^{i+1}(x) = \bigcup_{y \in \sigma^i(x)} \sigma(y),$$

$$\text{and} \quad \sigma^+(x) = \bigcup_{i=1}^{\infty} \sigma^i(x),$$

then σ is restricted so that $x \notin \sigma^+(x)$.

The *partitioning* function π is defined as

$$\pi : B \rightarrow 2^{B \times B},$$

associating with each blob $x \in B$ some equivalence relation $\pi(x)$ on the set of subblobs, $\sigma(x)$. This is really just a rigorous way of specifying the breakup of x into its orthogonal components, which are now defined simply to be the equivalence classes induced by the relation $\pi(x)$. Indeed, for $x \in B$ let us denote these classes by $\pi_1(x), \ldots \pi_{k_x}(x)$. For the orthogonal division into components to be representable graphically (and in order to make the semantics cleaner), we shall require that blobs in different orthogonal components of x are disjoint. Formally, for each x we require that no two elements y and z of $\sigma(x)$ can intersect—that is, can satisfy $\sigma^+(y) \cap \sigma^+(z) \neq \emptyset$—unless they are in the same orthogonal component; that is, unless the relation $\pi(x)$ renders them equivalent. Clearly, $k_x = 1$ means x is not partitioned into components at all.

This concludes the syntax of higraphs; now for the semantics. Two notations are useful. Given a higraph H, define the set of *atomic blobs* to be

$$A = \{x \in B | \sigma(x) = \emptyset\}.$$

(Obviously, the finiteness of B and the cycle-freeness restriction on σ imply A is nonempty.) The *unordered Cartesian product* of two sets S and T is defined as

$$S \otimes T = \{\{s, t\} | s \in S, t \in T\}.$$

Given a higraph H, a *model* for H is a pair $M = (D, \mu)$, where D is a set of unstructured elements[13] called the *domain* of the model M, and μ assigns disjoint subsets of D to the atomic blobs of H. Thus,

$$\mu : A \rightarrow 2^D,$$

where if $x \neq y$ then $\mu(x) \cap \mu(y) = \emptyset$. We now have to show how to extend the association of atomic blobs with sets over D to an association of all blobs with more complex objects over D. Accordingly, extend μ by defining, inductively, for each $x \in B$.

$$\mu(x) = \bigotimes_{i+1}^{k_x} \left(\bigcup_{y \in \pi_i(x)} \mu(y) \right),$$

[13]We want to avoid situations in which, say, x and $\{x\}$ are both elements of D.

the intuition being that to calculate the semantics of a blob x we form the unordered Cartesian product of the meanings of its orthogonal components, each of which, in turn, is simply the union of the meanings of its constituent blobs. In particular, of course, if $k_x = 1$, no product is taken, and we really have

$$\mu(x) = \bigcup_{y \in \sigma(x)} = \mu(y), \text{as expected.}$$

To complete the semantics, note that the edge set E induces a semantic relation E_M on the $\mu(x)s$, defined by

$$(\mu(x), \mu(y)) \in E_M \text{ iff } (x, y) \in E.$$

Acknowledgments

Thanks are due to Ton Kalker, Doug Tygar, and Jeanette Wing for comments on Section 8.6, and to an anonymous referee for a very detailed and thoughtful report. Part of this work was carried out while the author was at the Computer Science Department of Carnegie-Mellon University. Pittsburgh, Pennsylvania.

References

Berge, C. 1973. *Graphs and Hypergraphs.* Amsterdam: North-Holland.

Berry, G., and Cosserat, I. 1985. The ESTEREL Synchronous Programming Language and Its Mathematical Semantics. In *Seminar on Concurrency,* 389–448, ed. S. Brookes and G. Winskel. New York: Springer-Verlag.

Biggs, N. L., Lloyd, E. K., and Wilson, R. J. 1976. *Graph Theory: 1736-1936.* Oxford: Clarendon Press.

Brachman, R. J. 1979. On the Epistemological Status of Semantic Networks. In *Associative Networks: Representation and Use of Knowledge by Computer,* ed. N. V. Findler, 3–50. New York: Academic Press.

Cardelli, L. A. 1984. Semantics of Multiple Inheritance in Semantics of Data Types. In *Lecture Notes in Computer Science,* Vol. 173, 51–67. Berlin: Springer-Verlag.

Charniak, E., and McDermott, D. 1985. *Introduction to Artificial Intelligence.* Reading, Mass.: Addison-Wesley.

Chen. P. P. S. 1976. The Entity-Relationship Model Toward a Unified View of Data. *ACM Trans. Database Syst.* 1(1) (March): 9–36.

Conklin, J. 1987. Hypertext: An Introduction and Survey. *IEEE Computer* 20(9) (September): 17–41.

Davis, P. J., Anderson, J. A. 1979. Nonanalytic Aspects on Mathematics and Their Implication on Research and Education. *SIAM Review* 21(1) (January): 112–127.

dos Santos, C. S., Neuhold, E. J., and Furtado, A. L. 1980. A Data Type Approach to the Entity-Relationship Model. In *Entity-Relationship Approach to Systems Analysis and Design,* ed. P. P. Chen, 103–119. Amsterdam: North Holland.

Dugundji, J. 1966. *Topology.* Boston: Allyn and Bacon.

Euler, L. 1736. Solutio Problematis ad Geometriam Situs Pertinentis. *Comm. Acad. Science Imp. Petropol.* 8: 128–140.

Euler, L. 1772. *Lettres à Une Princesse d'Allemagne.* Vol. 2., Letters No.102–108.

Fagin, R. 1983. Degrees of Acyclicity for Hypergraphs and Relational Database Schemes. *Journal of ACM* 30(3) (July): 514–550.

Fagin, R., Mendeizon, A., and Ullman, J. 1982. A Simplified Universal Relation Assumption and Its Properties. *ACM Transactions Database Syst.* 7(3) (September): 343–360.

al-Fedaghi, S. S. 1983. An Entity-Relationship Approach to Modeling Petroleum Engineering Database. In *Entity-Relationship Approach to Software Engineering,* 761–779, ed. C. G. Davis et al. Amsterdam: Elsevier.

Findler, N. V., Ed. 1979. *Associative Networks: Representation and Use of Knowledge by Computer.* New York: Academic Press.

Fitter, M., and Green, T. R. G. 1979. When Do Diagrams Make Good Computer Languages? *International Journal of Man-Machine Studies* 11(2) (March): 235–261 .

Gardner, M. 1982. *Logic Machines and Diagrams.* Chicago: University of Chicago Press.

Green, T. R. 1982. Pictures of Programs and Other Processes, Or How to Do Things with Lines. *Behavioral Information Technology* 1(1): 3–36.

Harel, D. 1987. Statecharts: A Visual Formalism for Complex Systems. *Sci. Comput. Program* 8(3) (June): 231–274.

Harel, D., and Pnueli, A. 1985. On the Development of Reactive Systems. In *Logics and Models of Concurrent Systems,* NATO, ASI Series, Vol. 13, 477–498. Berlin: Springer-Verlag.

Harel, D., Pnueli, A., Schmidt, J. P., and Sherman, R. 1987. On the Formal Semantics of Statecharts. In Proceedings of the Second IEEE Symposium on

Logic in Computer Science (Ithaca, N. Y., June 22-24), 54–64. New York: IEEE Press.

Harel, D., and Kahana, H.-A. 1992. On Statecharts with Overlapping. *ACM Transactions of Software Engineering Methodology* 1(4): 399–421.

Harel, D., Lachover, H., Naamad, A., Pnueli, A., Politi, M., Sherman. R., and Shtul-Trauring, A. 1988. STATEMENT: A Working Environment for the Development of Complex Reactive Systems. In *Proceedings of the Tenth IEEE International Conference on Software Engineering* (Singapore, April 13-15). New York: IEEE Press. Final version appeared in *IEEE Trans. Soft. Eng.* 16 (1990), 403–414.

Harel, D., and Naamad, A. 1989. The Semantics of Statechart. Tech. Rep., i-Logix, Burlington, Mass.

Harel, D., and Politi, M. 1988. *The Languages of STATEMATE.* Tech. Rep., i-Logix, Burlington, Mass.

Hendrix, G. G. 1975. Expanding the Utility of Semantic Networks Through Partitioning. In Proceedings of the Fourth International Conference on Artificial Intelligence, 115–121. San Francisco: Morgan Kaufmann.

Hoare, C. A. R. 1978. Communicating Sequential Processes. *Communications of the ACM* 21(8) (August): 666–677.

Hopcroft, J. E., and Ullman, J. D. 1979. *Introduction to Automata Theory, Languages, and Computation.* Reading, Mass.: Addison-Wesley.

Lefschetz, S. 1949. *Introduction to Topology.* Princeton, N.J.: Princeton University Press.

Maier, D., and Ullman. J. D. 1982. Connections in Acyclic Hypergraphs. In Proceedings of the ACM Symposium on Database Systems, (Los Angeles, Calif., March 29-31), 34–39. New York: ACM.

Manna, Z., and Pnueli, A. 1987. Specification and Verification of Concurrent Programs by ∀-Automata. In Proceedings of the Fourteenth ACM Symposium on Principles of Programming Languages, 1–12. New York: ACM.

Martin, J., and McClure, C. 1985. *Diagramming Techniques for Analysts and Programmers.* Englewood Cliffs, N.J.: Prentice-Hall.

McSkimin. J. R., and Minker J. 1979. A Predicate Calculus Based Semantic Network for Deductive Searching. In *Associative Networks: Representation and Use of Knowledge by Computer,* ed. N. V. Findler, 205–238. New York: Academic Press.

Milner, R. A. 1980. *Calculus of Communicating Systems.* Lecture Notes in Computer Science, Vol. 92. Berlin: Springer-Verlag.

Nakano, R. 1983. Integrity Checking in a Logic-Oriented ER Model. In *Entity-Relationship Approach to Software Engineering,* ed. C. G. Davis et al., 551–564. Amsterdam: Elsevier.

Nilsson, N. J. 1980. *Principles of Artificial Intelligence.* Palo Alto, Calif.: Tioga.

Owicki, S., and Lamport. L. 1982. Proving Liveness Properties of Concurrent Programs *ACM Transactions Programming Language Systems* 4(3) (July): 455–495.

Pnueli, A. 1986. Applications of Temporal Logic to the Specification and Verification of Reactive Systems: A Survey of Current Trends. In *Current Trends in Concurrency,* ed. J. W. de Bakker et al., 510–584. New York: Springer-Verlag.

Quillian, M. R. 1968. Semantic Memory. In *Semantic Information Processing,* ed. M. Minsky, 227–270. Cambridge. Mass.: The MIT Press.

Reisig, W. 1985. *Petri Nets: An Introduction.* Berlin: Springer-Verlag.

Schiffner, G., and Schuermann, P. 1979. Multiple Views and Abstractions with an Extended-Entity-Relationship Model. *Computer Languages* 4(3–4): 139–154

Schmid, C. F. 1983. *Statistical Graphics: Design Principles and Practices.* New York: Wiley.

Shapiro, S. C. 1971. A Net Structure for Semantic Information Storage, Deduction, and Retrieval. In Proceedings of the Second International Joint Conference on Artificial Intelligence, 512–523. San Francisco: Morgan Kaufmann.

Touretzky, D. S. 1986. *The Mathematics of Inheritance Systems.* London: Pitman.

Tufte, E. R. 1983. *The Visual Display of Quantitative Information.* Cheshire, Conn.: Graphics Press.

Tygar, J. D. and Wing, I. M. 1987. Visual Specification of Security Constraints. In *The IEEE Workshop on Visual Languages* (Linkoping, Sweden, August 19-21). New York: IEEE Press.

Venn, J. 1880. On the Diagrammatic and Mechanical Representation of Propositions and Reasonings. *Phil. Mag.* 123.

Venn, J. 1894. *Symbolic Logic.* New York: Chelsea, 1971.

Woods, W. A. 1975. What's in a Link? Foundations for Semantic Networks. In *Representation and Understanding,* ed. D. G. Bobrow and A. M. Collins, 35–82. New York: Academic Press.

Zave, P. 1985. A Distributed Alternative to Finite-State-Machine Specifications. *ACM Trans. Program. Lang. Syst.* 7(1) (January): 10–36.

9 Reasoning with Analogical Representations

Karen Myers & Kurt Konolige
SRI International

9.1 Introduction

Analogical representations have long been of interest to the knowledge representation community (Gelernter 1963, Hayes 1974, Sloman 1971, Sloman 1975). The attraction of analogical representations lies with their ability to store certain types of information that humans can readily process but are problematic for sentential reasoning systems. Although the power of analogical representations has been acknowledged for many years, little progress has been made in understanding how to exploit the computational advantages that these representations can provide.

Analogical representations encompass both explicit diagrams (as in Furnas 1990, Gardin and Meltzer 1989) and representation structures that are *diagram-like.* Although this latter class is not easily defined, diagram-like representations share with real diagrams the property of certain structural correspondences with the domain being modeled. It is precisely such correspondences that make analogical representations useful. For example, a two-dimensional street map could be represented by graph-theoretic structures in which nodes correspond to intersections and arcs corresponds to road segments. Such a representation is analogical with the world being mapped in two ways. First, paths between nodes in the graph corresponds to road connections in the world being modeled. Second, there is a correspondence between the existence of objects in the world and objects in the representation. For example, all roads are represented in the graph; thus, the closure of the set of roads is implicit. In contrast, expressing such closure information sententially would require an explicit statement that the given roads constitute all roads.

The work described in this chapter applies equally well to both diagrams and diagram-like structures. For this reason, we will not distinguish further between the two types. The terms *diagram* and *analogical representation* will be used interchangeably throughout the chapter.

While analogical representations have received much attention in recent years from the psychology community (Johnson-Laird 1980, Kosslyn 1980, Larkin and Simon 1987), there have been few advances in understanding the computational aspects of analogical reasoning. Until recently, most computationally-oriented work has focused on properties of particular classes of diagrams (*e.g.*, Venn diagrams [Shin 1991b, Shin 1991a], Euler circles [Stenning & Oberlander 1992], qualitative reasoning [Funt 1980, Gardin and Meltzer 1989, Novak and Bulko 1990], geometry [Gelernter 1963]), ignoring more general aspects of reasoning diagrammatically. This document addresses the broader question of domain-independent inference techniques for reasoning involving analogical representations. The work encompasses both reasoning *about* and *with* diagrams. The former involves extraction of information from a diagram and amounts to a passive use of diagrams; the latter further supports modifications to diagrams as a result of the reasoning process, thus constituting an active use of diagrams.

Reasoning with and about diagrams should not be accomplished by simply translating the diagram contents into a sentential language, nor *vice versa*. While analogical structures provide compact representations of information that is cumbersome to express sententially, they generally lack the expressive power of sentential languages. Since sentential theories are a more general representational technology, it is tempting to translate analogical structures into first-order sentences *en masse*. But this strategy would compromise the efficiency of the representation system since the specialized inference mechanisms for the analogical structures are replaced by general-purpose deductive methods; this point is borne out by the experimental results of Myers (1994, 1991a). Here, we adopt a hybrid approach in which separate analogical and sentential subsystems co-exist and inference rules for translating information between the two are defined.

Our hybrid framework is based on a set of generic operations for manipulating analogical structures along with corresponding inference rules that invoke the operations. The operations and rules were chosen for their capacity to increase overall reasoning competency through the appropriate use of analogical information. The framework supports both the incorporation of diagrammatic information into the sentential reasoner and the modification of diagrams to reflect information deduced by sentential reasoning; in other words, both reasoning about and with diagrams.

The incorporation of information back into a diagram distinguishes our work from the closely-related methods of theory resolution (Stickel 1985) and semantic attachment (Myers 1991b, Myers 1994, Weyhrauch 1980). In those methods, procedures are used to compute the truth-value of some predicates or combinations of predicates in a theory. The procedures can be made much more efficient than deductive methods, and so provide an efficient means for incorporating specialized knowledge of subdomains into a theory. Diagrams similarly represent information about a particular subdomain in an efficient way, and we employ procedures for extracting information from diagrams that are equivalent to these other methods. Additionally, however, our work supports the ability to put information acquired from the reasoning process back into the diagram, where it can be used for subsequent reasoning steps.

Adding information to diagrams is a natural inference mode in many domains. One example of a domain for which the ability to add information to diagrams is important is the learning of maps by a mobile robot. We are currently using an implementation of our framework in the construction of a hybrid map-learning architecture for the SRI mobile robot (Myers and Konolige 1992). For concreteness, we focus on examples from this application. The work, however, applies more generally to all types of analogical structures.

9.2 The Hybrid Framework

In this section, we describe the analogical and sentential subsystems along with criteria for their integration. Specific integration rules are presented in Sections 9.3–9.4.

9.2.1 Analogical Subsystem

The details of the analogical component will vary for different applications. Our formal framework isolates the integration methods from the specifics of any particular application through the use of an abstract characterization of the information stored in the analogical system. Since we are interested in reasoning with maps, we employ examples from that domain here.

A typical hallway map used by a mobile robot might contain the kind of information displayed in the following diagram:

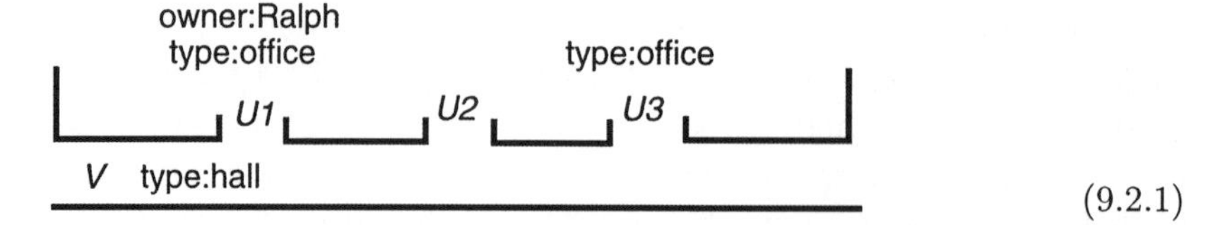

(9.2.1)

The constants V and U_i are symbolic names assigned to the hallway and the three openings on it in the given scene. These objects and the relationships among them are identified by the robot's perceptual interpretation mechanism, which detects relevant geometric properties and segments sensory input into meaningful units (*e.g.*, groups line segments and intersegment spaces into objects such as corridors and significant openings). We use the term *diagram element* for such objects. Prior knowledge about the scene was used to determine the remainder of the information in this diagram, namely that certain U_i are offices and that the leftmost office belongs to Ralph.

Formally, an analogical structure S is a data structure of arbitrary type. Typically we use labeled graphs or trees: to represent the hallway, for example, a labeled linear list is sufficient. Other representations are also possible, although they may be more difficult to manipulate, e.g., a bit-map containing 1's for the walls, and 0's for freespace. What is important is that the structure S be *interpretable* in terms of a set of first-order diagram models M_S. That is, there is a decision procedure $\mathcal{D}(S, M)$ to tell if any particular model M satisfies the structure S.

What do the diagram models look like? For any particular class of applications, there will be a fixed ontology of individuals and a fixed set of properties of interest. We consider two classes of properties: symbolic labels for diagram elements and analogical relations among diagram elements. Thus, diagram models consist of a set of analogical relations A and a set of label relations L over a universe U. Each member of A is a binary relation $E_s \times E_s$, with $E_s \subset U$ the set of diagram elements; each member of L is a relation $E_s \times E_l$, with $E_l \subset U$ the set of labels. Using the "displayed" format of Chang and Keisler (1977), section 1.3, we write these models as $\langle U, A, L, E_s, E_l \rangle$.

As we have said, a diagram model constitutes a possible completion of the partial information provided by a diagram. For example, the type of U_2 and the owners of U_2 and U_3 are unspecified in the above diagram; a diagram model would fully specify those relations. For the scene described by (9.2.1), the diagram elements are $\{V, U_1, U_2, U_3\}$.

We choose the label relations *TYPE*(u, l) and *OWNS*(u, l), and the analogical relations *BES*(u, v) (the opening u is next to the opening v) and *INHALL*(u, v) (opening u is in hall v). The label set contains {*Closet*, *Office*, *Ralph*, *Paul*, *Cyril*} and possibly other values. The choice of relations and elements is important in determining what information in the analogic structure is abstracted in the hybrid system; here, for example, whether an opening is to the right or left of another opening is apparent from the structure, but not in the models.

A key feature of analogical representations is their capacity to implicitly embody constraints that other representations must make explicit. For example, the map structures embed the following constraints:

- Each opening has at most 2 adjacent openings.
- Objects can have exactly 1 type.
- Individuals can own offices but not closets.
- At most one person can own a given office.

These *diagram constraints* can be built into the representation structures directly or into the operations that manipulate the structures, depending on the given implementation. For example, a bit-map representation of (9.2.1) would embed the first constraint directly through its spatial composition; the third constraint would most likely be enforced by operations that manipulate the structure. Either way, diagram constraints are necessarily reflected in diagram models. For instance, all diagram models for (9.2.1) can have only one type relation for a given diagram element, due to the second constraint above.

In diagram (9.2.1), all objects of relevance (the openings and the hall itself) have been noted and the analogical relations *BES* and *INHALL* are fully determined. Although there is type and ownership information missing, the *structure* of the diagram is complete. Not all diagrams share this completeness. When generating maps from perceptual input, noise or faulty sensors may both cause objects of interest to go undetected and leave analogical relations only partially determined. In such circumstances, we say that the diagram contains *structural uncertainty.* We formalize this notion as follows.

Definition 1 *Determined Relation:* A set of models M defined over a class of relations $R = \{r_1, \ldots r_m\}$ *determines* a relation $r_i \in R$ iff every model in M agrees on the extension of r_i.

Definition 2 *Structural Uncertainty:* A diagram S with models M_S is *structurally uncertain* iff some analogical relation of the models is undetermined.

The following diagram constitutes a variation on the scene described by (9.2.1) in which there is structural uncertainty between U_1 and U_3. Here, both the *BES* and *INHALL* relations are undetermined. Dashed lines indicate regions of structural uncertainty:

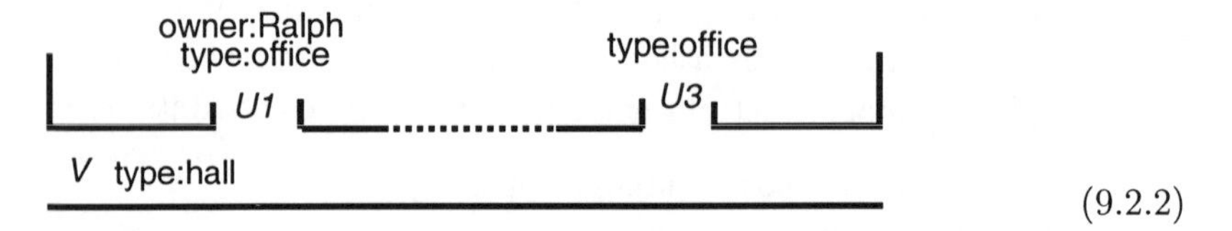

(9.2.2)

As will be seen, our framework provides the means to apply sentential information about a diagram in order to both ascertain the composition of areas of structural uncertainty and flesh out the partial characterizations given by the diagram models for the relations in $L \cup A$.

It is important to note that diagram models are only an analytic tool for characterizing the semantics of information in a hybrid system. The diagrams themselves are data structures that implicitly represent the diagram models. For example, a diagram for the hallway could consist of two linked lists, one for the left-hand side and one for the right-hand side of the hallway. Elements on the lists would represent the rooms on that side, in the order in which they occurred. All inference operations (defined in Sections 9.3 and 9.4) are functions that operate on the data structures.

9.2.2 Sentential Subsystem

The sentential subsystem employs a first-order language

$$\mathcal{L} = \langle \mathcal{P}_A, \mathcal{P}_L, E_s, E_l, \cdots \rangle$$

and a corresponding proof theory. For simplicity, we use the diagram elements E_s and labels E_l as standard names for themselves in $\mathcal{L}$. The predicates $\mathcal{P}_A$ are interpreted by the analogical relations of the diagram models, and $\mathcal{P}_L$ by the label relations. In addition, there may be other predicates and constants that have an indirect relation to the diagram – for example, the predicate $NBR(x, y)$ representing the office-neighbor relationship between two people. This predicate would be related to the diagram predicates $\mathcal{P}_A \cup \mathcal{P}_L$ by an axiom such as

$$\begin{aligned}\forall x, y.\ \mathit{NBR}(x,y) \equiv \exists u, v.\ &\mathit{TYPE}(u, \mathit{Office}) \wedge \mathit{TYPE}(v, \mathit{Office}) \\ &\wedge \mathit{OWNS}(u,x) \wedge \mathit{OWNS}(v,y) \wedge \mathit{BES}(u,v)\ .\end{aligned} \tag{9.2.3}$$

Similarly, the predicate $\mathit{RESIDES}(x,h)$ representing the relationship of an individual x having an office in hallway h would be defined as

$$\begin{aligned}&\forall x, h.\ \mathit{RESIDES}(x,h) \equiv \\ &\quad \exists u.\ \mathit{INHALL}(u,h) \wedge \mathit{TYPE}(u, \mathit{Office})\ \wedge\ \mathit{OWNS}(u,x)\ .\end{aligned} \tag{9.2.4}$$

We refer to axioms of this sort as *grounding* axioms.

As an example of the expression and use of sentential information relative to diagrams, consider the following statements:

Paul and Cyril have offices in hall V.
Ralph and Paul are not neighbors.

Given the grounding axioms (9.2.3, 9.2.4), these statements can be translated into the following formulas of $\mathcal{L}$:

$$\begin{aligned}&\mathit{RESIDES}(\mathit{Cyril}, V)\ \wedge\ \mathit{RESIDES}(\mathit{Paul}, V) \\ &\qquad \neg \mathit{NBR}(\mathit{Ralph}, \mathit{Paul})\ .\end{aligned} \tag{9.2.5}$$

With respect to diagram (9.2.1), the first statement implies that U_2 and U_3 are offices, one each owned by Cyril and Paul. This conclusion follows since $\{U_1, U_2, U_3\}$ constitutes the set of all offices in V and *Ralph* is known to own U_1. Deduction of this result requires information that is implicit in the diagram's structure, namely that each office can be owned by only one individual. With the second statement, the only possible configuration of the scene is:

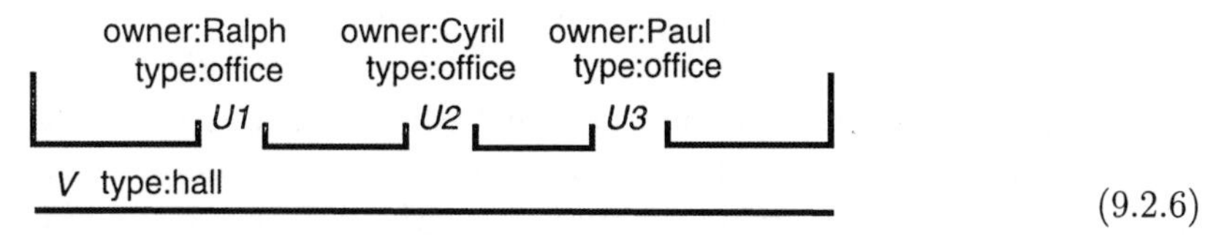

(9.2.6)

Sentential information can also be used to reduce structural uncertainty in diagrams: given the sentences *Ralph and Cyril are neighbors* and *Cyril is Paul's only neighbor*, the diagram (9.2.6) follows from (9.2.2).

9.2.3 Integration Criteria

In order to determine whether a given integration method behaves in an appropriate fashion, it is necessary to provide a semantic account of the over-all hybrid system.

From a model-theoretic perspective, the merging of a diagram S with a set of sentences T that describe the diagram amounts to restricting the models of S to those that are *compatible* with T. Compatibility here means that the diagram model can be expanded to a model for T by providing interpretations for the predicate, function, and constant symbols of $\mathcal{L}$ that do not overlap the diagram model.

Definition 3 *Restricted Models:* Let T be a collection of sentences in $\mathcal{L}$ describing properties of a diagram S and let M_S be the models of S defined for the sublanguage $\langle \mathcal{P}_A, \mathcal{P}_L, E_s, E_l \rangle$ of $\mathcal{L}$. The *restriction of* M_S *relative to* T, written as $M_S(T)$, is the set of models $\langle U, A, L, E_s, E_l \rangle \in M_S$ for which some expansion $\langle U, A, L, E_s, E_l, \cdots \rangle$ is a model of T. The *restriction of* M_T *relative to* S, written as $M_T(S)$, is the set of models of T which are expansions of some model in M_S.

The models in $M_T(S)$ characterize the total information content in the hybrid system while the models in $M_S(T)$ characterize the domain information captured by the analogical structures. The challenge is to provide both *derivation rules* for determining formulas of $\mathcal{L}$ that are logically entailed by $M_T(S)$ and *update rules* for modifying S to eliminate diagram models not contained in $M_S(T)$.

In general, the analogical structures may have weaker representational capabilities than is required to capture the information content of $M_S(T)$. Consider the diagram (9.2.1) and the sentential theory

$$T_0 = \{\mathit{RESIDES}(\mathit{Cyril}, V), \mathit{RESIDES}(\mathit{Paul}, V)\} \ .$$

These two sources of information jointly imply that U_2 and U_3 are offices, one each owned by *Paul* and *Cyril*; however, it is undetermined as to who owns which one. Every model in $M_S(T_0)$ either has both $\langle U_2, \mathit{Cyril} \rangle$ and $\langle U_3, \mathit{Paul} \rangle$ or both $\langle U_2, \mathit{Paul} \rangle$ and $\langle U_3, \mathit{Cyril} \rangle$ in its *OWNS* relation. However, this information cannot be displayed in the diagram since it is not definite about who owns which office and the diagram does not admit disjunctive information about ownership.

Rather than seeking an analogical structure with the models $M_S(T)$, the best that can be attained is a structure that *adequately represents* $M_S(T)$:

Definition 4 *Representational Adequacy:* An analogical structure Q *adequately represents* a set of diagram models M iff $M \subseteq M_Q$ and there is no other diagram R such that $M \subseteq M_R$ and $M_R \subset M_Q$.

For example, when S is the diagram (9.2.1) and T_0 is as defined above, the following diagram adequately represents $M_S(T_0)$:

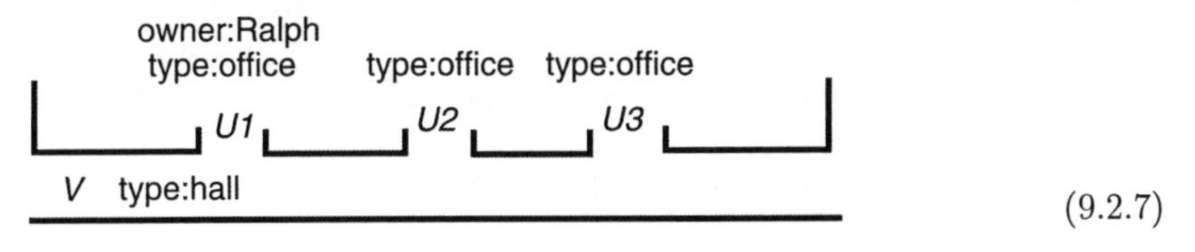

(9.2.7)

This diagram extends (9.2.1) to include the information that U_2 is an office but does not include any new information about ownership.

Soundness and completeness for inference in our hybrid system can be defined using the concepts of restricted models and representational adequacy.

Definition 5 *Soundness:* A diagram update rule is *sound* iff for diagram S and theory T it generates only diagrams whose model set contains $M_S(T)$. A derivation rule is *sound* iff it generates a new theory whose model set contains $M_T(S)$.

We will say that a collection of both diagram update and derivation rules is sound precisely when each of its members is sound.

Definition 6 *Completeness:* A set of derivation and update rules is *derivationally complete* for S and T iff any valid sentence of $M_T(S)$ can be derived by the sentential subsystem. The set is *diagrammatically complete* iff it can generate a diagram that adequately represent $M_S(T)$.

9.3 The Inferential Calculus

The inferential calculus underlying our hybrid framework is defined relative to a class of domain-independent diagram operations. In this section, we describe both the inference rules and operations. We focus exclusively on diagrams without structural uncertainty here; diagrams with structural uncertainty are considered in Section 9.4.

9.3.1 Diagram Operations

Two classes of diagram operations are required for our inference rules: *reflection* and *extraction* procedures.

Reflection procedures provide a means of inserting information into an analogical structure. For each label predicate $P(u, v)$ we require a reflection procedure $\mathsf{INSERT.P}(u, v)$ such that for $e_1, e_2 \in E_s \cup E_l$, the predicate $P(e_1, e_2)$ holds in all models of the diagram obtained by executing $\mathsf{INSERT.P}(e_1, e_2)$. That is, when applied to a diagram S with model set M_S, $\mathsf{INSERT.P}(e_1, e_2)$ yields a diagram S' with model set

$$M_{S'} = \{m \in M_S \mid m \models P(e_1, e_2)\} .$$

For diagrams without structural uncertainty (the focus of this section), insertion procedures for $\mathcal{P}_A$ are unnecessary.

Extraction procedures provide access to the contents of the analogical structure for use by the sentential subsystem. As noted above, whole-scale translation of the analogical structures into first-order sentences is infeasible. Instead, we wish to provide access to the information in the analogical structures on an *as needed* basis, whereby information is accessed as required for individual deduction steps rather than all at once. The two key types of information stored within diagrams are (1) analogical and label relationships for diagram elements, and (2) closure information about those relationships.

For each diagram predicate $P(u, v)$, we require an extraction procedure $\mathsf{EVAL.P}(u, v)$ for evaluating ground instances relative to the diagram S. These *evaluation* procedures provide the sentential reasoner with information about primitive relationships in the analogical structures. The procedure behaves as follows for $e_1, e_2 \in E_s \cup E_l$:

$$\mathsf{EVAL.P}(e_1, e_2) = \begin{cases} \textit{true} & \text{if } M_S \models P(e_1, e_2) \\ \textit{false} & \text{if } M_S \models \neg P(e_1, e_2) \\ \textit{unknown} & \text{otherwise} \end{cases}$$

Closure information for a diagram S is generated by two classes of procedures. Let $P[x]$ represent an instance of a predicate in $\mathcal{P}_L \cup \mathcal{P}_A$ that contains the single variable x, such as $BES(x, U_1)$. (For simplicity, we restrict attention here to predicates containing only one variable.) With respect to the diagram S, the procedure $\mathsf{CLOSURE}^+.P[x]$ generates the set of diagram elements that possibly satisfy $P[x]$ (called the *minimal superclosure*) while the procedure $\mathsf{CLOSURE}^-.P[x]$ generates the set of elements that definitely satisfy $P[x]$ (the *maximal subclosure*).

Definition 7 *Closures:* Let $P[x]$ be a nonground instance of a predicate in $\mathcal{P}_L \cup \mathcal{P}_A$. The *minimal superclosure* of $P[x]$, denoted by $\mathsf{CLOSURE}^+ .P[x]$, and the *maximal subclosure* of $P[x]$, denoted by $\mathsf{CLOSURE}^-.P[x]$, are defined with respect to a diagram S as follows:

$$\mathsf{CLOSURE}^+.P[x] \;=\; \{e \in E_l \cup E_s \;\mid\; m \models P[e] \textit{ for some } m \in M_S\}$$

$$\mathsf{CLOSURE}^-.P[x] \;=\; \{e \in E_l \cup E_s \;\mid\; M_S \models P[e]\}$$

The procedures $\mathsf{CLOSURE}^+.P[x]$ and $\mathsf{CLOSURE}^-.P[x]$ give minimal upper and maximal lower bounds, respectively, for the precise set of values that satisfy $P[x]$. This set is fixed for a given diagram only when the relation $P[x]$ is *determined* by the models of S (in the sense of Definition 1). In terms of the sentential language $\mathcal{L}$, determination of $P[x]$ is equivalent to the condition that for $m_1, m_2 \in M_S$:

$$\forall e \in E_s \cup E_l.\ m_1 \models P[e] \;\equiv\; m_2 \models P[e]\ . \qquad (9.3.8)$$

When a predicate $P[x]$ is determined by a diagram, the maximal sub- and minimal superclosures are equal. We use the term *exact closure* to refer to the set of values in that case.

Note that since we are considering only diagrams without structural uncertainty in this section, all analogical predicates are necessarily determined. More generally though, exact closures are not always available. As will be made apparent in Section 9.3.2, sub- and super-closures are useful sources of diagram information when exact closures cannot be determined.

9.3.2 Inference Rules

The inferential component of the integration framework consists of rules of *evaluation*, *domain enumeration* and *reflection*. Evaluation and domain enumeration utilize information from the diagram as provided by the extraction procedures to derive new sentences describing properties of the diagram. The reflection rule permits the insertion of sentential consequences derived from T into the diagrams using the reflection procedures.

In the definition of the inference rules, we use the notation α_b^c to represent the expression α with all occurrences of the expression b replaced by c.

Reflection The reflection rule sanctions the transfer of information from the sentential to the analogical subsystem. Let $T \vdash \phi$ represent the deducibility of a sentence ϕ from a set of sentences T using the proof theory of the sentential subsystem.

Definition 8 *Reflection Rule:* Let T be a sentential theory and S an analogical structure. If $T \vdash R(t_1, \ldots, t_k)$ for $t_1, \ldots, t_k \in E_s \cup E_l$ and $R \in \mathcal{P}_A \cup \mathcal{P}_L$ then $R(t_1, \ldots, t_k)$ can be *reflected into* S by executing $\mathsf{INSERT.R}(t_1, \ldots, t_k)$.

Evaluation The evaluation rule sanctions replacement of ground instances of a predicate $R \in \mathcal{P}_A \cup \mathcal{P}_L$ by either *true* or *false*, in accordance with the contents of the analogical structure. In the case where the relationship denoted by R is undetermined, the evaluation process has no effect.

Definition 9 *Evaluation Rule:* Let ϕ be a formula that contains an instance $R(t_1, \ldots, t_k)$ of a predicate $R \in \mathcal{P}_A \cup \mathcal{P}_L$. If $\mathsf{EVAL.R}(t_1, \ldots, t_k) = \theta$ where $\theta \in \{\mathit{true}, \mathit{false}\}$ then *evaluation of* $R(t_1, \ldots, t_k)$ *in* ϕ yields $\phi^{\theta}_{R(t_1,\ldots,t_k)}$.

Domain Enumeration The domain enumeration rules allow the elimination of quantifiers in certain cases through the introduction of an appropriate domain of values that covers the relevant instantiations of the quantified variable.

Consider the assertion

$$\exists u.\ \mathit{BES}(u, U_2) \wedge \mathit{OWNS}(u, \mathit{Paul}) \qquad (9.3.9)$$

relative to diagram (9.2.1). The interpretation of this formula is that the diagram element owned by Paul is located beside U_2. The conjunct $\mathit{BES}(u, U_2)$ limits the possibilities for this diagram element: according to (9.2.1), the element must be either U_1 or U_3. As such, the formula $\mathit{OWNS}(U_1, \mathit{Paul}) \vee \mathit{OWNS}(U_3, \mathit{Paul})$ follows from (9.3.9). Similarly, the universally quantified formula

$$\forall u.\ \mathit{INHALL}(u, V) \supset \mathit{TYPE}(u, \mathit{Office}) \tag{9.3.10}$$

can be viewed as a statement about the predicate $\mathit{TYPE}(u, \mathit{Office})$, with $\mathit{INHALL}(u, V)$ serving as a filter on the set of relevant instantiations of the quantified variable. According to the diagram (9.2.1), the only values that satisfy $\mathit{INHALL}(u, V)$ are $\{U_1, U_2, U_3\}$ (*i.e.*, the exact closure of $\mathit{INHALL}(u, V)$ is $\{U_1, U_2, U_3\}$). Thus, the conjunction

$$\bigwedge_{d \in \{U_1, U_2, U_3\}} \mathit{TYPE}(d, \mathit{Office})$$

is equivalent to (9.3.10) with respect to models for diagram (9.2.1).

We refer to the technique used above for applying closure information to eliminate quantifiers as *domain enumeration.* Domain enumeration does not apply to all predicate instances containing a quantified variable. The formula $\exists u.\ \neg \mathit{BES}(u, U_1) \wedge \mathit{TYPE}(u, \mathit{Closet})$ illustrates this point. In this case, the exact closure for $\mathit{BES}(u, U_1)$ is not an appropriate restriction of the terms of $\mathcal{L}$; elimination of the existential quantifier using the exact closure would lead to unsound conclusions.

For existential quantifiers, the domain used in domain enumeration must include all bindings for which the embedded formula (*e.g.*, $\mathit{BES}(x, U_2) \wedge \mathit{OWNS}(x, \mathit{Paul})$ in (9.3.9)) may have truth value *true*; this guarantees that all relevant instantiations of the quantified variable are covered. For universal quantifiers, the domain should exclude values for which the embedded formula is already determined to have truth value *true.* We call a predicate instance whose exact closure satisfies these conditions *focus expressions* for the given quantified formula. In essence, a focus expression prunes from consideration those bindings of a given quantified variable that do not provide useful information.

To formalize the concept of focus expressions, we introduce definitions for the *polarity* and *definiteness* of predicate instances in a formula.

Definition 10 *Polarity:* An instance of a predicate in a formula ϕ is called *positive* if the instance maps to an unnegated literal in the conjunctive normal form of ϕ. The instance is called *negative* otherwise.

Definition 11 *Definiteness:* An instance of a predicate in a formula ϕ is called *definite* if the instance maps to a literal in a clause of length one in the conjunctive normal form of ϕ. The instance is called *indefinite* otherwise.

We will combine the notions of polarity and definiteness, referring to individual instances as *negative indefinite* or *positive definite* as appropriate. The expression $INHALL(u, V)$ has a negative indefinite instance in (9.3.10) and a positive definite instance in

$$\exists u.\ INHALL(u, V) \wedge TYPE(u, Closet)\ .$$

In the definitions below, we employ the notation $\phi[z]$ to denote a formula that contains one or more instances of variable z. For instance, $\phi[z]$ could represent a formula such as $P(x, z) \wedge Q(3, z)$.

Definition 12 (Focus Expression) If ψ is a quantified formula (either $\forall z.\ \alpha$ or $\exists z.\ \alpha$) containing a predicate instance $P[z]$ then $P[z]$ is a *focus expression* for ψ iff either

- ψ has the form $\forall z.\ \alpha$ and the occurrence of $P[z]$ is negative indefinite, *OR*
- ψ has the form $\exists z.\ \alpha$ and the occurrence of $P[z]$ is positive definite.

The domain enumeration rule is formally defined as follows.

Definition 13 *Domain Enumeration Rule:* If ψ is a quantified expression, either $\exists z.\ \alpha$ or $\forall z.\ \alpha$, containing a focus expression $\Phi[z]$ with maximal subclosure D^- and minimal superclosure D^+ then *domain enumeration* for ψ and $\Phi[z]$ yields:

$$\bigvee_{d \in D^+} (\alpha_z^d) \qquad \text{if } \psi \text{ is } \exists z.\ \alpha$$

$$\bigwedge_{d \in D^-} (\alpha_z^d)_{\Phi[d]}^{true} \qquad \text{if } \psi \text{ is } \forall z.\ \alpha\ .$$

Note that when applying domain enumeration to a universally quantified formula $\forall z.\ \alpha[z]$, the embedded formula $\alpha[z]$ need not be fully retained. Instead, the simplification of $\alpha[z]$ in which the focus expression is replaced by *true* suffices, since the focus expression has truth value *true* for all terms in its maximal subclosure. For example, $INHALL(u, V) \supset TYPE(u, Office)$ can be reduced to the expression $TYPE(u, Office)$. In contrast, focus expressions must be retained for existentially quantified formulas: by definition the maximal superclosure may contain terms that are not in the exact closure (and hence do not satisfy the focus expression).

Domain enumeration could be extended to make use of nonatomic focus expressions. For example, the conjunction $BES(x, U_5) \wedge TYPE(x, Office)$ could serve as a focus expression in the formula

$$\forall x.\ BES(x, U_5) \wedge TYPE(x, Office) \quad \supset \quad OWNS(x, Eva)\ .$$

The intersection of the maximal subclosures for the individual conjuncts would serve as a more restricted (and hence more useful) domain for the universally quantified variable x. Similarly, the disjunction $BES(x, U_4) \vee BES(x, U_6)$ could be employed as a focus expression in

$$\exists x.\ (BES(x, U_4) \vee BES(x, U_6)) \ \wedge \ OWNS(x, Ann)\ .$$

The appropriate domain in this case would be the union of the minimal superclosures for each disjunct. Straightforward extensions of Definitions 12–13 support this generalization; we forego their technical statement in this chapter.

9.3.3 Example

We illustrate the workings of our integration rules by applying them to the scenario presented in Section 9.2.2, namely diagram (9.2.1) with sentential theory

$$T_0 = \{\neg NBR(Ralph, Paul),\ RESIDES(Cyril, V), RESIDES(Paul, V)\}\ .$$

A derivation schematic, including both diagrams and sentences, is provided in Figures 9.1–9.2.

Consider first the given formula $RESIDES(Paul, V)$. Rewriting using definition (9.2.4) yields formula S2 in Figure 9.1. The predicate $INHALL(u, V)$ is a focus expression in S2 and its exact closure in diagram (a) is $\{U_1, U_2, U_3\}$. Domain enumeration using this focus expression yields formula S3. Diagram (a) contains the information that U_1 and U_3 are offices, thus $TYPE(U_1, Office)$ and $TYPE(U_3, Office)$ in S3 can be replaced by *true* using the evaluation rule. In addition, since the diagram indicates that *Ralph* owns U_1, evaluation can be used to rewrite $OWNS(Paul, U_1)$ to *false*. This evaluation step exploits the diagram constraint that ownership is unique. The evaluations combined with tautological simplification produce formula S4.

Expansion of the given fact $\neg$*NBR*(*Ralph*, *Paul*) using definition (9.2.3) gives formula S6 in Figure 9.1. This formula contains the focus expression *OWNS*(*Ralph*, x) whose exact closure in diagram (a) is $\{U_1\}$; domain enumeration is applied to produce formula S7. Evaluation of the expression *TYPE*(U_1, *Office*) with respect to diagram (a) leads to formula S8, which contains the focus expression *BES*(U_1, y) whose exact closure is $\{U_2\}$. Domain enumeration for *BES*(U_1, y) yields formula S9, which along with S4 entails *OWNS*(*Paul*, U_3). Application of the reflection rule to this atom yields the diagram (b) in Figure 9.2.

The formula S12 is obtained from the given formula *RESIDES*(*Cyril*, V) by applying the same steps used from S1 to S4 above. The ownership of U_3 was undetermined in the original diagram; however, *OWNS*(*Cyril*, U_3) is necessarily *false* since the new diagram (b) indicates that the owner of U_3 is *Paul*. Evaluation can be applied to the formula S12 using diagram (b) to derive S13. Note that this last deduction could not be made from S12 and the sentence *OWNS*(*Paul*, U_3) alone; again we need the diagram constraint that ownership is unique. Finally, the contents of this last formula can be reflected to produce the diagram (c), which adequately represents $M_S(T_0)$.

9.4 Structural Uncertainty

Consider the diagram

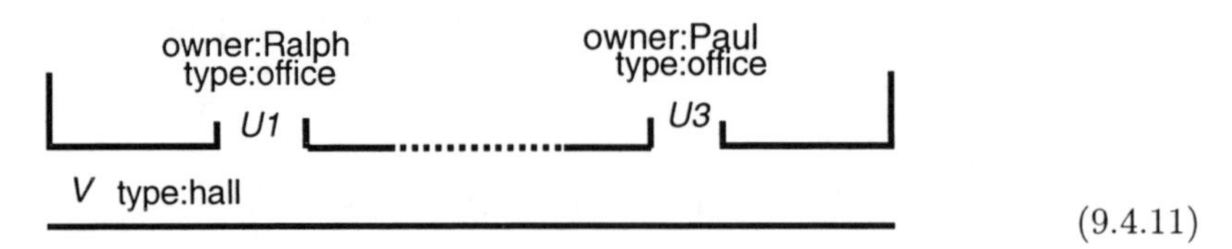

(9.4.11)

containing a region of structural uncertainty between elements U_1 and U_3. This diagram has models in which there are zero, one, two, *etc*, diagram elements in the uncertain area. Without further information, there is no way to determine which of these models corresponds to the actual situation that the diagram is intended to represent.

The presence of structural uncertainty necessitates a slight generalization of the inferential calculus presented in Section 9.3. First of all, reflection operators must be provided for the analogical predicates $\mathcal{P}_A$ so that diagrams can be modified to incorporate new analogical relations

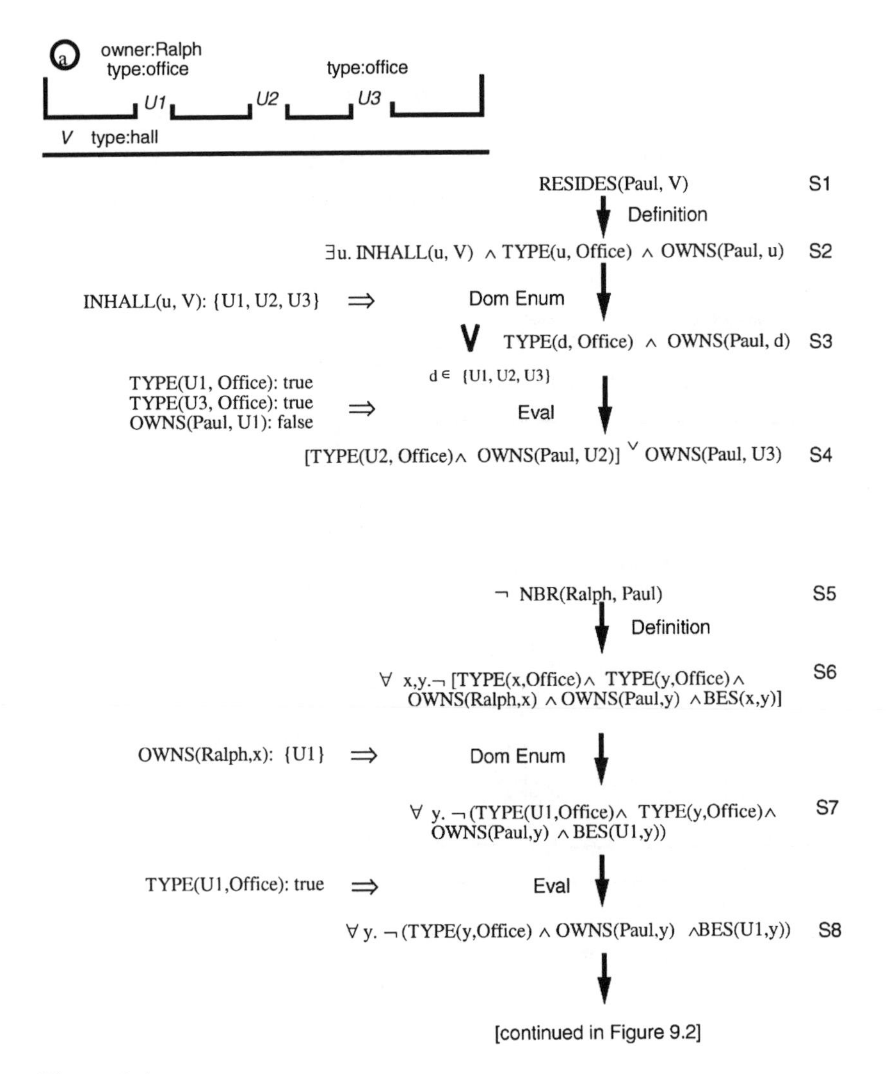

Figure 9.1
An Example Derivation (Part 1)

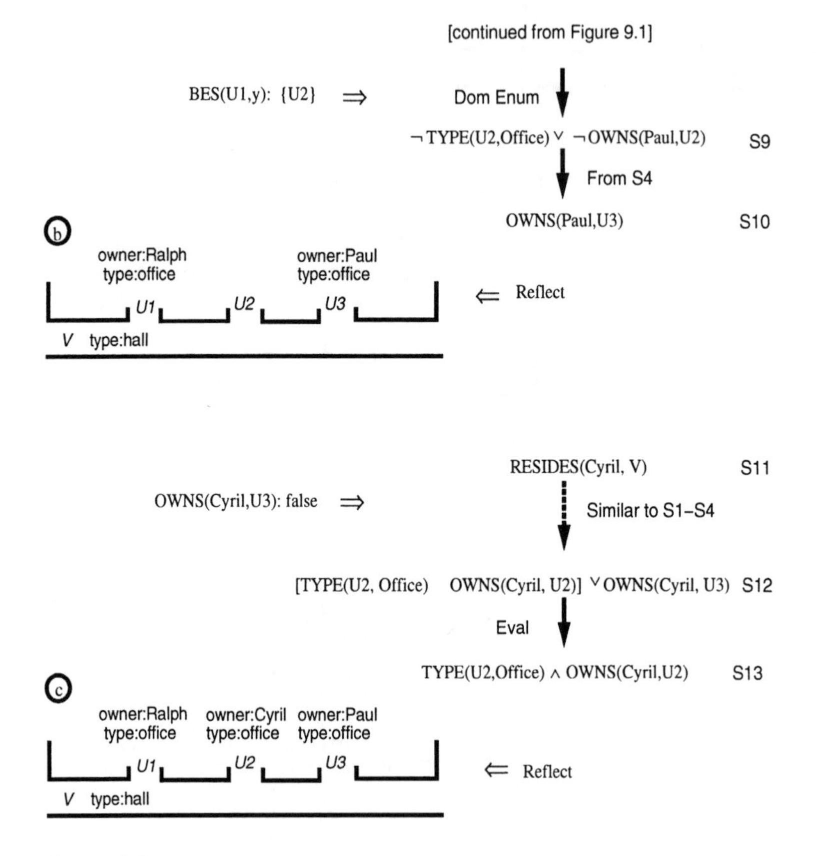

Figure 9.2
An Example Derivation (Part 2).

determined by the sentential subsystem. The definitions of the remaining diagram operations and the various inference rules remain unaltered but the definition of minimal superclosure requires elaboration. Because the minimal superclosure of a predicate must include all possible values for which the predicate holds, it is necessary to consider whether elements inserted in structurally indeterminate regions could satisfy the given predicate. In contrast, the definition of maximal subclosure is not affected by structural uncertainty since diagram elements that do not appear in all models are not included in the maximal subclosure.

9.4.1 Minimal Superclosures with Introduced Names

To account for structural uncertainty in diagrams, we exploit a technique of the natural deduction calculus for dealing with existential elimination. Within this calculus, the existential quantifier of a formula $\exists x.\phi[x]$ can be eliminated by introducing a *new* individual constant c for x, yielding $\phi[c]$. The justification for the introduction is that, since c does not appear elsewhere in the proof, it can refer to an arbitrary individual.

We employ the same principle in formulating minimal superclosures for diagrams containing structural uncertainty. Consider diagram (9.4.11) relative to the sentence $\exists x.\ BES(U_1, x)$. It could be that U_3 is next to U_1, or that there is an intervening element I_1 situated to the right of U_1. The minimal superclosure must take both of these cases into account, yielding the set $\{U_3, I_1\}$.

Employing names for hypothesized individuals introduces a complication to the diagrams, since we have heretofore assumed that all elements were "standardized apart," receiving different names if and only if they were distinct. This is not the case with hypothesized individuals; for example, if we were later to perform domain enumeration on the sentence $\exists y.\ BES(U_3, y)$, introducing the name I_2, it could be the case that both I_1 and I_2 refer to the same individual. To account for naming and identity, we assume that the diagram keeps track of introduced names and their possible referents.[1]

When the exact closure of an analogical predicate $P[x]$ is *determined* by the diagram models (*i.e.*, condition (9.3.8) is satisfied), the minimal superclosure reduces to the exact closure. Otherwise, the minimal su-

[1] In other words, diagram operations must track equalities and inequalities for introduced names.

perclosure consists of those diagram elements that satisfy the predicate in any diagram model, along with an introduced name for a hypothesized element. Even though multiple elements can appear in regions of uncertainty and there may be more than one such region in a diagram, only one introduced element is required for the minimal superclosure. Restriction to one such element is possible because the purpose of domain enumeration is to identify a solitary element satisfying the matrix of the existentially quantified formula.

Definition 14 *Minimal Superclosure for $\mathcal{P}_A$:* Let $P[x]$ represent an instance of a predicate in $\mathcal{P}_A$ that contains the single variable x. The *minimal superclosure* of $P[x]$, denoted by $\mathsf{CLOSURE}^+.P[x]$, is defined for a diagram S as

$$\{e \in E_l \cup E_s \mid M_S \models P[e]\}$$

when $P[x]$ is determined by M_S, otherwise

$$\{e \in E_l \cup E_s \mid m \models P[e] \textit{ for some } m \in M_S\} \cup \{I_k\}$$

where I_k is an introduced name.

For example, the minimal superclosure for $BES(U_1, x)$ relative to diagram (9.4.11) is $\{U_3, I_1\}$, where I_1 is an introduced name.

The new definition of minimal superclosure is used as before in domain enumeration except that when an element name I_k is introduced for a minimal superclosure, the diagram is modified to include inequalities between I_k and all current diagram elements. The referent of an introduced I_k may be determined by future sentential reasoning steps, possibly leading to the insertion of a new diagram element *via* the reflection rule. Such a situation arises in the example presented below.

9.4.2 Example: Structural Uncertainty

Consider diagram (9.4.11) and the theory

$$T_1 = \{NBR(Ralph, Cyril),\ NBR(Paul, Cyril)\}\ .$$

Every model in $M_S(T_1)$ has exactly one element between U_1 and U_3, with this element being labeled as the office of *Cyril*. We show how a new diagram that reflects this information can be generated using the integration calculus.

Applying the same steps used to derive S8 from $\neg NBR(Ralph, Paul)$ in Figure 9.1, we generate the following pair of formulas from T_1:

$$\exists x.\ BES(U_1, x) \wedge TYPE(x, Office) \wedge OWNS(Cyril, x) \tag{9.4.12}$$

$$\exists x.\ BES(U_3, x) \wedge TYPE(x, Office) \wedge OWNS(Cyril, x)\ . \tag{9.4.13}$$

As noted above, the minimal superclosure for $BES(U_1, x)$ relative to diagram (9.4.11) is $\{U_3, I_1\}$. Domain enumeration for the focus expression $BES(U_1, x)$ in (9.4.12) yields

$$\begin{array}{c} BES(U_1, U_3) \wedge TYPE(U_3, Office) \wedge OWNS(Cyril, U_3) \\ \vee \\ BES(U_1, I_1) \wedge TYPE(I_1, Office) \wedge OWNS(Cyril, I_1) \end{array} \tag{9.4.14}$$

along with the naming constraints $U_3 \neq I_1$ and $U_1 \neq I_1$. Evaluation of $OWNS(Cyril, U_3)$ with respect to the diagram returns *false* (since ownership is unique), thus (9.4.14) simplifies to

$$BES(U_1, I_1) \wedge TYPE(I_1, Office) \wedge OWNS(Cyril, I_1)\ . \tag{9.4.15}$$

The conjuncts in this formula can be reflected to produce the new diagram

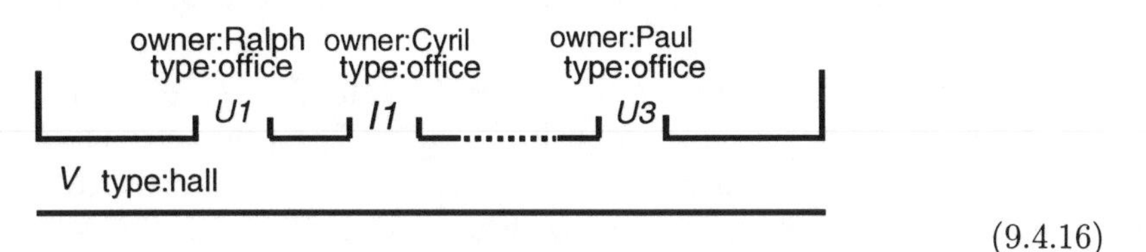

(9.4.16)

Here, a new diagram element has been created to serve as the referent of the introduced name I_1.

In diagram (9.4.16), the expression $BES(x, U_3)$ has minimal superclosure $\{I_1, I_2\}$, for some introduced name I_2. Domain enumeration for $BES(x, U_3)$ in (9.4.13) gives

$$\begin{array}{c} BES(U_3, I_1) \wedge TYPE(I_1, Office) \wedge OWNS(Cyril, I_1) \\ \vee \\ BES(U_3, I_2) \wedge TYPE(I_2, Office) \wedge OWNS(Cyril, I_2) \end{array} \tag{9.4.17}$$

along with the inequalities $I_2 \neq U_1$, $I_2 \neq U_3$, and $I_2 \neq I_1$.

Since the current diagram indicates that *Cyril* owns I_1 (and cannot own I_2 since $I_2 \neq I_1$), the evaluation rule can be applied to eliminate the second disjunct of (9.4.17). Further evaluations lead to the formula $BES(U_3, I_1)$, thus establishing that the introduced name I_2 does not refer to a realizable diagram element. Reflection of this last atom yields the diagram (9.2.6), which adequately represents $M_S(T_1)$.

9.4.3 A Troublesome Example

The new definition of minimal superclosure does not always lead to an adequate representation of the restricted class of diagram models. Suppose that we relate sentences (9.4.12, 9.4.13) to the following diagram D:

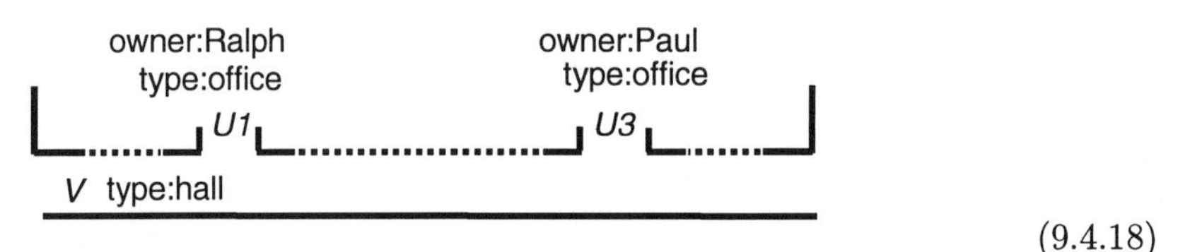

(9.4.18)

The models $M_D(T_1)$ are adequately represented by a diagram similar to (9.2.6) but with regions of uncertainty to the left of U_1 and to the right of U_3. As we will show, our integration calculus cannot produce this diagram.

The minimal superclosure for $BES(U_1, x)$ is again $\{U_3, I_1\}$ as was the case in the previous example (provided we reuse I_1 as the introduced name) and we can similarly derive the formula (9.4.15) from (9.4.12). However, since I_1 could be located on either side of U_1 we cannot insert a new element into the diagram as the referent of I_1. This inability to situate I_1 leads to a different minimal superclosure for $BES(U_3, x)$, namely $\{U_1, I_2\}$ (again we reuse the same introduced name from the previous example). Domain enumeration for $BES(x, U_3)$ in (9.4.13) now gives

$$BES(U_3, U_1) \wedge TYPE(U_1, Office) \wedge OWNS(Cyril, U_1)$$
$$\vee$$
$$BES(U_3, I_2) \wedge TYPE(I_2, Office) \wedge OWNS(Cyril, I_2)$$

with the inequalities $I_2 \neq U_1$ and $I_2 \neq U_3$. Note that in this case, the inequality $I_2 \neq I_1$ is not added since I_1 does not refer to a current diagram element. At this point, no modifications to the diagram are possible, and no further derivations by the sentential subsystem lead to any reflections back to the diagram. While the atoms $BES(U_1, I_1)$, $BES(U_3, I_2)$, $OWNS(Cyril, I_1)$ and $OWNS(Cyril,\ I_2)$ are all derivable, they have no effect on the diagram individually. In combination though, they constrain $I_1 = I_2$ to be the unique office situated between U_1 and U_2. Generating a diagram that adequately represents $M_D(T_1)$ requires reasoning by cases about the possible locations of introduced elements and is beyond the scope of the integration calculus presented in this chapter.

9.5 Properties of the Framework

The three integration rules, *reflection*, *evaluation* and *domain enumeration*, each satisfy the soundness criteria introduced in Section 9.2.3.

PROPOSITION 15 *Soundness of Reflection:* The Reflection rule is sound.

Proof. Let S be a diagram and T a sentential theory such that $T \models R(t_1, \ldots, t_k)$. The reflection rule applies the operation INSERT.R $(t_1, \ldots, t_k)$ to S to produce a new diagram S'. Soundness requires that $M_{S'}(T) \subseteq M_S(T)$. Now $M_{S'} = M_S - \overline{M}$ where $\overline{M} = \{m \in M_S \mid m \not\models R(t_1, \ldots, t_k)\}$; but $\overline{M} \subseteq M_S(T) - M_S$ since $T \models R(t_1, \ldots, t_k)$. The soundness result follows directly.

PROPOSITION 16 *Soundness of Evaluation:* The Evaluation rule is sound.

Proof. Consider a sentential theory T and a diagram S such that $M_S \models \theta \equiv R(t_1, \ldots, t_k)$ for some analogical or label predicate $R(t_1, \ldots, t_k)$. Application of the evaluation rule for $R(t_1, \ldots, t_k)$ in a formula ϕ of T results in the formula $\alpha^{\theta}_{R(t_1,\ldots,t_k)}$. Soundness requires that $M_{T'}(S) \subseteq M_T(S)$ where $T' = T \cup \alpha^{\theta}_{R(t_1,\ldots,t_k)}$. This result directly follows from the facts (1) $R(t_1, \ldots, t_k) \equiv \theta$ is valid in all diagram models of S, and (2) the substitutivity of logically equivalent predicates.

Proposition 17 (Soundness of Domain Enumeration) The Domain Enumeration rule is sound.

Proof. Domain enumeration for a universal quantifier is certainly sound, as it corresponds to multiple instantiations of the sound rule of universal quantifier instantiation.

Consider domain enumeration for the formula $\exists z.\alpha[z]$ in some theory T, relative to a diagram S. Suppose that $\exists z.\alpha[z]$ contains a positive definite instance of a predicate $P[z]$ with minimal superclosure D^+ in S. Soundness requires that $M_{T'}(S) \subseteq M_T(S)$ where $T' = \bigvee_{d \in D^+} \alpha[d]$.

Because $\alpha[z]$ contains a positive definite instance of $P[z]$, we can rewrite $\exists z.\alpha[z]$ in the form $\exists z.P[z] \wedge \alpha'[z]$ for some formula $\alpha'[z]$. Now consider any model $m \in M_T(S)$; necessarily, $m \models \exists z.P[z] \wedge \alpha'[z]$. Thus, there is some term a such that $m \models P[a] \wedge \alpha'[a]$. Since D^+ is the minimal superclosure of $P[z]$, necessarily, $a \in D^+$. Thus, $m \models \bigvee_{d \in D^+} \alpha[d]$ and so $m \in M_{T'}(S)$. Soundness directly follows.

The integration rules are neither derivationally nor diagrammatically complete. The central problem is that the rules focus on properties of individuals and their relationships with other individuals, failing to account for embedded diagram constraints. Thus, although it is implicit in the hallway maps that an office can have at most two offices beside it, the inference rules do not allow the sentential reasoner access to this information. Diagram constraints are certainly made use of at times. In going from S3 to S4 in Figure 9.1, the unique ownership constraint made it possible to conclude that *OWNS*(*Paul*, U_1) had truth-value *false*, given that *OWNS*(*Ralph*, U_1) held in diagram (a). However, it is impossible to directly reason with the diagram constraints.

In the remainder of this section we briefly consider the issue of completeness for propositional sentential theories. We note that the discussion is also of relevance to those first-order theories that can be reduced to propositional theories through appropriate use of the domain enumeration rule.

Derivational completeness demands the derivability in the sentential subsystem of any sentence valid in $M_S(T)$. Suppose we pick a propositionally-complete refutation strategy for the sentential subsystem. Is the resulting system complete? The answer is "no." Consider the following set of statements:

$$\begin{array}{rcl} OWNS(Paul, U_1) & \vee & OWNS(Paul, U_2) \\ OWNS(Ralph, U_1) & \vee & OWNS(Ralph, U_2) \\ OWNS(Cyril, U_1) & \vee & OWNS(Cyril, U_2) \end{array}$$

Given the embedded property of unique ownership, these sentences are inconsistent with respect to *any* diagram in our class of maps. Even so, it is not alway possible to derive the empty clause. In particular, no refutation is possible given a variation of diagram (9.2.1) in which all ownership information has been removed. Because the uniqueness constraint on ownership is embedded in the representations and operations of the analogical structures, the integration rules provide no means of relating this constraint to the sentences above.

Derivational completeness can be attained by extending the evaluation rule to sets of literals. Define:

$$\mathsf{EVAL}^*(l_1, \cdots l_n) = \begin{cases} \textit{inconsis} & \text{if } M_S \models \neg(l_1 \wedge \cdots \wedge l_n) \\ \textit{unknown} & \text{otherwise} \end{cases}$$

Using this evaluation procedure, we can apply total narrow theory resolution (Stickel 1985) as a refutation-complete derivational procedure. This procedure is a variant of hyperresolution in which a set of literals, one from each clause of the resolution, are tested for consistency against the diagram; if they are inconsistent, the result of the resolution is a clause consisting of a disjunction of the remainders of each resolved clause.[2]

Diagram completeness is generally harder to achieve than derivational completeness because it requires the sentential subsystem to be complete for atomic consequence-finding. Consider the theory:

$$T = \{OWNS(Paul, U_3) \vee OWNS(Cyril, U_3)\}$$

relative to diagram (9.2.1). Given the embedded diagram constraint that ownership applies only to offices, it is possible to derive $TYPE(U_3, Office)$

[2]Although we can achieve derivational completeness using theory resolution in a refutation system, in practice we might not want to use theory resolution directly, since it is a multiple-clause inference rule. It would be more efficient to consider a variation on the Davis-Putnam method in which branches are closed when they contain a set of atoms that are inconsistent according to the diagram.

by refutation. But $TYPE(U_3, Office)$ cannot be derived as a consequence of the diagram and T. Arriving at this conclusion requires a form of reasoning by cases that our framework does not currently support. As noted above, reasoning by cases is also required to overcome the form of diagram incompleteness that arose in Section 9.4.3. This capability presents an interesting avenue for further research.

9.6 Summary

We have described a domain-independent formal framework for integrating sentential and analogical representations. We illustrated the workings of the framework for the application of reasoning sententially to extend the information content of maps, both with and without structural uncertainty. The integration rules of the framework are sound as well as derivationally complete in the propositional case.

The integration framework has been implemented on top of the KLAUS automated deduction system (Stickel 1988) using the method of *universal attachment* (Myers 1991b, Myers 1994) to formulate the integration rules. The system has been successfully applied to problems involving reasoning with maps, including the examples presented in this chapter. Much work remains to be done on control issues for the implementation. In particular, the ordering of domain enumerations can greatly impact the efficiency of reasoning.

There has been a resurgence of interest in computational models for diagrammatic/visual reasoning during the past few years. Most similar in nature to our research is the work on Hyperproof (Barwise and Etchemendy 1990). The Hyperproof system combines sentential reasoning with diagrammatic representations of a chessboard containing blocks. In Hyperproof, much of the complexity underlying the integration of diagrammatic and sentential information is implicit in the system; in contrast, our research has sought to provide a domain-independent inferential framework in which all aspects of integration are made explicit. A second difference relates to control: the inference rules presented here automatically combine sentential and diagrammatic reasoning, while Hyperproof requires user interaction to guide the reasoning process.

The work of Narayanan and Chandrasekaran (1991) presents a computational model for reasoning with diagrammatic representations but emphasizes the emulation of human reasoning about visualization. *Computational imagery* (Papadias and Glasgow 1991) defines a representational framework for reasoning with both visual and spatial information but does not address the connection to deductive inference.

Our work also overlaps to a certain extent with research in the hybrid reasoning community (Frisch and Scherl 1991, Frisch 1991). Other than our specialization of hybrid reasoning to analogical representations, the main difference between the material presented there and the hybrid framework presented here is the latter's emphasis on reflecting derived information back into analogical structures.

The work reported here focuses exclusively on the use of a single diagram at any point in time. This simplifying assumption precludes solutions to problems that require explicit reasoning by diagram cases, as noted in Section 9.4.3. We are currently extending this research to include inference rules that reason hypothetically by creating sets of possible diagrams. The use of multiple diagrams in this manner enables indirect reasoning about implicit properties of analogical structures, although it also introduces many control problems that must be addressed in order to provide efficient implementations.

Acknowledgments

This research was supported by the Office of Naval Research under Contract N00014–89–C–0095.

References

Barwise, J. and Etchemendy, J. 1990. Visual Information and Valid Reasoning. In *Visualization in Mathematics,* ed. W. Zimmerman. Washington: Mathematical Association of America.

Chang, C. and Keisler, H. J. 1977. *Model Theory.* New York: Elsevier.

Frisch, A. M., ed. 1991. Principles of Hybrid Reasoning: Papers from the AAAI 1991 Fall Symposium. Technical Report FSS-91-01, American Association for Artificial Intelligence.

Frisch, A. M. and Scherl, R. B. 1991. A Bibliography on Hybrid Reasoning. *AI Magazine* 11(5).

Funt, B. V. 1980. Problem-Solving with Diagrammatic Representations. *Artificial Intelligence* 13.

Furnas, G. W. 1990. Formal Models for Imaginal Deduction. In Proceedings of the Twelfth Annual Conference of the Cognitive Science Society, 662–669. New York: Lawrence Erlbaum.

Gardin, F., and Meltzer, B. 1989. Analogical Representations of Naive Physics. *Artificial Intelligence* 38:139–159.

Gelernter, H. 1963. Realization of a Geometry-Theorem Proving Machine. In *Computers and Thought* ed. E. A. Feigenbaum and J. Feldman. New York: McGraw-Hill.

Hayes, P. J. 1974. Some Problems and Non-Problems in Representation Theory. In *Proceedings of the AISB Summer Conference*, pp. 63–79. University of Sussex.

Johnson-Laird, P. N. 1980. Mental Models in Cognitive Science. *Cognitive Science* 4:71–115.

Kosslyn, S. M. 1980. *Image and Mind.* Cambridge, Mass.: Harvard University Press.

Larkin, J. H. and Simon, H. A. 1987. Why a Diagram Is (Sometimes) Worth Ten Thousand Words. *Cognitive Science* 11:65–99.

Myers, K. L. 1991a. Universal Attachment: An Integration Method for Logic Hybrids. Ph.D diss., Dept. of Computer Science, Stanford University.

Myers, K. L. 1991b. Universal Attachment: An Integration Method for Logic Hybrids. In *Principles of Knowledge Representation and Reasoning: Proceedings of the Second International Conference,* ed. J. A. Allen, R. Fikes, and E. Sandewall. San Francisco: Morgan Kaufmann.

Myers, K. L. and Konolige, K. 1992. Integrating Analogical and Sentential Reasoning for Perception. Presented at the 1992 AAAI Spring Symposium on Reasoning with Diagrammatic Representations, Stanford, California.

Myers, K. L. 1994. Hybrid Reasoning Using Universal Attachment. *Artificial Intelligence* 67:329–375.

Narayanan, N., and Chandrasekaran, B. 1991. Reasoning Visually about Spatial Interactions. In *Proceedings of the Twelfth International Joint Conference on Artificial Intelligence.* San Francisco: Morgan Kaufmann.

Novak, E. P. Jr. and Bulko, W. C. 1990. Understanding Natural Language with Diagrams. In Proceedings of the Eighth National Conference on Artificial Intelligence, 465–470. Menlo Park, Calif.: AAAI Press.

Papadias, D., and Glasgow, J. I. 1991. A Knowledge Representation Scheme for Computational Imagery. In *Proceedings of the Thirteenth Annual Conference of the Cognitive Science Society.* New York: Lawrence Erlbaum Associates.

Shin, S.-J. 1991a. An Information-Theoretic Analysis of Valid Reasoning with Venn Diagrams. In *Situation Theory and its Applications*, ed. J. Barwise, J. M. Gawron, G. Plotkin, and S. Tutiya.

Shin, S.-J. 1991b. Valid Reasoning and Visual Representation. Ph.D. diss., Dept. of Philosophy, Stanford University.

Sloman, A. 1971. Interactions Between Philosophy and AI. *Artificial Intelligence* 2.

Sloman, A. 1975. Afterthoughts on Analogical Representation. In *Proceedings of Theoretical Issues in Natural Language Processing.*

Stenning, K., and Oberlander, J. 1992. Spatial Containment and Set Membership. In *Analogical Connections,* ed. J. Barnden and K. Holyoak.

Stickel, M. E. 1985. Automated Deduction by Theory Resolution. *Journal of Automated Reasoning* 1(4).

Stickel, M. E. 1988. The KLAUS Automated Deduction System. In *Proceedings of the Ninth International Conference on Automated Deduction.*

Weyhrauch, R. W. 1980. Prolegomena to a Theory of Mechanized Formal Reasoning. *Artificial Intelligence* 13.

10 Applying Semantic Concepts to Analyzing Media and Modalities

Keith Stenning & Robert Inder
University of Edinburgh

10.1 Introduction

Interest in multi-media and multi-modal communication systems is currently being driven by the advent of new technologies for human computer interaction. New ways are being developed for us to communicate with machines, and with each other. These innovations present both problems and opportunities for the design of information technology, since they allow designers to use poorer, as well as better, combinations of media in their systems. Designers trying to navigate among the peaks and troughs of this new terrain need principled grounds for evaluating different combinations of media and modalities for expressing the same information. We seek to understand human communication in terms that will provide those grounds, and thus form a basis for rational IT design. But solutions to this practical problem are also a central part of the theoretical enterprise of cognitive science. The ability to construct and interpret new representations for new domains is a distinctively human achievement. Even mundane human reasoning consists largely of selecting appropriate representations which make reasoning tractable for each task that presents itself. This work on the cognitive consequences of allocating the same information to different media and modalities develops work such as Larkin and Simon (1987) and Palmer (1978) in a more semantically oriented direction (Stenning and Oberlander 1994).

Our work is based on the application of techniques developed for the analysis of languages to the analysis of multi-media communication. In turn, we believe that the study of multi-media communication will produce insights into the fundamentals of linguistic communication and give rise to a richer theoretical framework encompassing both sets of phenomena.

A semantic approach to understanding multi-media communication relies on the logical concept of a *representation system*—an explicit definition of the forms that representations within a system can take, coupled with an *interpretation function* which maps elements of a representation onto the entities and relationships they represent. This idea leads us to give very specific meanings to the terms "medium" and "modality": *media* are categories of representing entities and *modalities* are categories of interpretation function. These interpretations conflict with some of the many (and sometimes inconsistent) uses of these terms in the HCI and multi-media communications literature. One of our first goals, therefore, is to clarify these conflicts and explain our chosen interpretation of the terms.

Our analysis is based on an account of the semantics of graphical representations—of the way their parts combine to convey meaning—and we seek to base empirical predictions of the usability of representations on this analysis of their expressive power, as defined in logical/computational theory. Our comparison of the expressive power of graphical and linguistic representations (Stenning and Oberlander 1992) suggests that graphical representations cannot express arbitrary abstractions. A form of graphic that cannot express an abstraction necessary for some task will prove pathological, and will be better replaced by a more expressive language. But where a graphic can express the necessary abstractions, we predict that its weak expressiveness will make it a more efficient representation for performing the necessary inferences. This is so just because weakly expressive systems are computationally more tractable.

Suggesting that forms of representation should be compared on the basis of their logical expressiveness raises an immediate question for a theory of modality allocation. If a certain sentential system is found to have the same logical expressive power as a particular graphical system, such a theory appears to suggest that they should have the same cognitive properties. So why should graphical systems be preferable to weak sentential ones? The answer lies in the *cognitive availability* of the limits of the expressive power. Availability determines whether the weakness of the representation can be exploited. We will offer examples of how graphical notations 'wear their weakness on their sleeves': the nature of these notations makes their weakness available for exploitation. Weak sentential systems, in contrast, lack this property—nothing in the arrangement of symbols on a page constrains the expressive power of the systems. Their weakness cannot be exploited without considerable learning, although where such learning does occur, we would predict it would greatly reduce the discrepancy between equivalent sentential and graphical systems.

Although we discuss only the expressive power of information presentations, we acknowledge that many other factors combine to determine their cognitive characteristics, including, for example, low-level perceptual properties and aesthetic appeal. We do not claim that the expressive properties of representations are the whole of the story, but merely that they must form the core of an account of a cognitive theory, and that they have been given less explicit attention than they deserve.

The next section of the chapter sets out our theoretical perspective in detail. Our proposed interpretation of "medium" and "modality" and their relation to representation systems is elaborated and related to previous work on the effects of assigning information to different media/modalities. The need for conceptual clarification of the terms "medium" and "modality" and their relations to knowledge representation systems is illustrated by reference to inconsistencies and conflicting influences on the usage of these terms in the literature. Particular attention is paid to differences between the system design and cognitive perspectives on these concepts.

Section 10.3 analyses the basis for the contrast between two exemplary modalities, graphics and language. We survey several properties of graphical interpretations which define an ordering on the expressiveness of systems. We focus especially on the enforcement of information presentation by some styles of interpretation. Information enforcement emerges as a critical characteristic of graphical modalities, whereas the nature of linguistic interpretation means that linguistic modalities always can avoid information enforcement. Information enforcement can be related to weak expressiveness and inferential tractability.

In order to link expressiveness to usability it is essential to consider what constraints on expression are *available* to which users with what background information. The observation that the constraints on expression of graphical representations are generally more available to the relatively naive user can be explained in terms of our characterization of graphical modalities. Thus the account explains why graphical representations are often easier to interpret for novices than sentential equivalents, but without resorting to the naive theory that graphical semantics is transparent, or 'realistic'.

Our analysis of graphical semantics ranges examples along a dimension of expressiveness ranging from primitive graphics to powerful languages. In Section 10.4, we illustrate our conceptualization by presenting analyses of representations which are drawn from widely different parts of the dimension: matrix graphics, elementary logic diagrams, and semantic networks. In each case we illustrate how these systems can be analyzed in terms of their constraints to reveal their expressiveness, as defined in logical/computational terms. Some existing empirical evidence on the usability of these different types of representation is discussed, and gaps in current empirical investigation pointed out.

Our concept of modality divides up the space of representations somewhat differently from pre-theoretical intuition. In particular, the more logically expressive interpretations of some kinds of abstract graphics such as semantic networks have the characteristics of linguistic modalities. We believe that this divergence from pre-theoretical intuition may have a role in explaining the mixed results in observation of the usability of these notations. This is an example of the sort of regimentation of psychological data that one might expect to issue from this theoretical approach.

10.2 Semantic Analysis, Media and Modalities

Because HCI research and computer system design brings together workers from several disciplines, the terms "medium" and "modality" are used in several different ways that each appear reasonable against their own background. Clarification of the way we use these terms is essential, but we offer it in the belief that no definition of these terms can be faithful to all usages in this multi-disciplinary field. For example, the psychological terminology of "sensory modalities" is close to the computer scientists use of "media." Having set out our use of these terms, we relate it to some of the other ways they are used in the literature.

10.2.1 Media and Modalities Meet in Representation Systems

We start by presenting some intuitions as landmarks against which we believe definitions of "medium" and "modality" should encompass. For each term we present two intuitions, one which underlies distinctions between cases, and one which underlies abstraction over cases.

1. The very same physical representation can constitute more than one medium when perceived by different sensory systems. Thus embossed diagrams can be 'read' by eye or by finger, and constitute

different media in the two cases. [basis of distinguishing media]

2. At some useful level of abstraction, different representations that are visually perceived in two dimensions can be regarded as the same medium. [basis of abstraction for media]
3. Diagrams and texts are different modalities even though they may be represented in overlapping ranges of media. [basis of distinguishing modalities]
4. Some presentations of language in acoustic and in printed form are examples of information in the *same* modality presented in *different* media. [basis of abstraction for modalities]

The first intuition identifies the perceptual basis of our concept of medium, which involves the physical form of a representation, and the way it is perceived. The second indicates that abstraction is involved—we can regard computer screens, paper, vapor trails in the sky, and other physical expressions of "writing/drawing" as a single abstract medium, because they share a perceptual basis. Media can of course be more finely divided, and our emphasis on the abstraction inherent in our conceptualization does not deny the cognitive significance of finer divisions within these general categories.

Our third intuition, which underlies distinctions between modalities, is that there are clearly different ways of expressing information in a medium, and these differences do not depend on the medium itself. For example, both diagrams and sentences can be presented in visual and tactile media, though their perceptual basis is then quite different. But the *difference* between diagrams and language in each medium is invariant, and it is the basis of this invariant contrast which constitutes modality. Finally, our fourth intuition provides an example of what the basis of this invariance across media might be—language is a modality of information presentation which is invariant across the different visual and acoustic media.

As we shall see below, language is a modality peculiarly free to find expression in different media. Most other modalities are more circumscribed in their media appearances, and an account of the styles of semantics which constitute each modality must explain why this is so. Figure 10.1 summarizes by example the distinctions between a representation's "medium," which is based on how it is perceived, and its "modality," which is based on how it is interpreted.

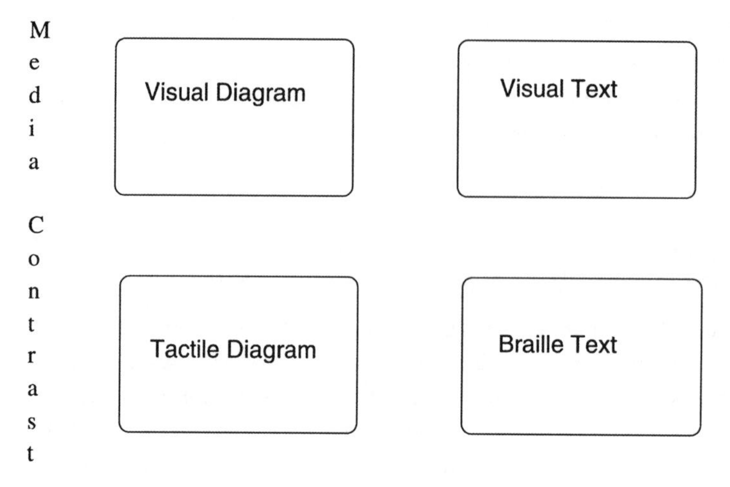

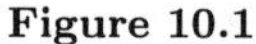

Figure 10.1
The Concepts of *Medium* and *Modality* Applied to Tactile and Visual Diagrams and Texts.

Cognitive theories of information presentation must explain differences between information displays in both *media-variance* and *modality-variance.* Our focus on the expressive power of representations emphasizes the latter, which has been relatively neglected. By defining modalities as categories of interpretation, we can conceptualize cognitive differences between representations which are distinguished from perceptual properties of media.

10.2.2 Interpretation Functions

A representation system consists of a set of physically or perceptually defined representations mapped on to a set of meanings by an interpretation function. In the best understood (and most regimented) examples of representation systems—logics and computer languages—a finite alphabet is used to define a vocabulary which is concatenated into a set of sentences according to syntactic rules. The interpretation function for such a language gives the vocabulary items meaning by mapping them onto (sets of) members of a specified domain. Finally, the statements are given meaning by semantic rules that parallel the syntactic rules for forming them. Thus the physical/perceptual and the interpretational aspects of representation are brought together in interpretation functions.

But languages are a special type of representation system because they are almost independent of their physical form. The only constraint on an alphabet is that the *functional* distinctions and relationships between members are preserved. Thus the shapes of the letters or the acoustic properties of the sounds do not matter, provided one can tell which letter is which, and which follows which. This insight, from de Saussure (1916), explains why a language is a modality which is independent of any medium of expression. This independence of physical medium is not universal. Graphical representation systems are typically interpreted by direct, uniform mappings between relations in the representation and relations in the represented domain. This style of interpretation limits the scope for substituting one physical form of representation for another, because the new form has to provide relations which, within the capabilities of the human perceptual system, precisely mirror those in the old form. This is, for example, why there are visual and tactile diagrams but there is no acoustic equivalent.

Modalities are to be defined in terms of kinds of interpretation functions whereas media are to be understood as physical/perceptual implementations of the representations of those systems. It is the concept of representational system that defines relations between media and modalities. Although choice of media may constrain choice of modality, there is still wide choice of kind of interpretation with a medium, and this choice plays a powerful role in determining usability.

10.2.3 Influences on Current Usage of Terms in HCI, or, Multi-Media Is What We Have—Multi-Modality Is What We Want

Our use of the terms "medium" and "modality" conflicts with common usages in HCI. The practice of describing systems which can handle information in a variety of forms—typically combining text with video and audio—as "multi-media" is close to our usage. But few of these systems can relate information in different media: there is no *fusion* of data. Thus "multi-modality" has become the banner of designers who want to create systems which can inter-relate information received though different media on the basis of meaning (e.g. Coutaz 1992). But this means that any multi-modal system must, by this definition, be multi-media.

We believe that modality and medium are best defined independently. While the above HCI definition would class a system that can integrate speech and text as multi-modal, we would not. We see them as examples of a single modality—language—expressed in different media. On the other hand, since we regard text and diagrams as different modalities, we would ascribe multi-modality to a system which could inter-relate facts in a text with information extracted from a diagram, even though that system might involve only a single medium. This is conspicuously something that current systems generally cannot do: the issue of machine access to meaning is just as difficult within a single medium as between media.

There are obvious reasons for those engaged in constructing software systems to treat speech and written language as separate. Speech is very hard to process by machine, and the procedures for translating between speech and text are necessarily complex, and possibly incomplete. This is because it is, in general, impossible to establish mappings between the two at the level of 'alphabetic' correspondences. Properly interpreting either requires taking account of features of extended portions of the representation, such as intonation and stress in speech, and punctuation and layout in text. For this reason, lexically equivalent samples of speech and text may not be equivalent in meaning. Nevertheless, we contend that when speech and writing samples are deemed equivalent they then differ in medium, not modality.

The computer science approach in which media are *physically* defined tends to underplay the abstraction that is involved in the concept of medium. A screen and a sheet of paper are very different physically but we need to abstract over these differences to capture what is in common between 2-D visual displays. Exactly what abstraction is appropriate will depend on what range of possibilities are actually being exploited in using the displays. In one context, the fact that the computer screen is capable of dynamic and unobtrusive change, whereas the paper is a static display, may be of vital importance. In another context, where the dynamic characteristics of the screen are only used for 'scrolling' through a document, the difference may be unimportant. We should not generalize from the legitimate interests of system builders and assume that "medium" is a simple physical concept that does not have an ineluctably perceptual and therefore cognitive component.

The psychological approach to conceptualizing media and modalities also runs counter to our usage. *Sensory modalities* provide the physical or perceptual access of user to representation. Psychology does not have a systematic use of the term media, nor a systematic term for what we have called modalities of information presentation. Near reversal of terminology relative to computer science appears to result from the difference between the experimental analytic, as opposed to engineering synthetic, methodologies in the two disciplines. The result in psychology has been neglect of systematic study of the nature of styles of interpretation of different representation systems.

Tensions between ways the terms "medium" and "modality" are used make it unlikely that any definitions of medium, multi-media, modality and multi-modality will gain universal acceptance in our multi disciplinary field. For our present purposes, what is critical is to relate both medium and modality to the concepts of *representational system* and *interpretation function.* When we do this (below) it emerges that the concepts we need for our theory lead to unexpected classifications for many currently available systems. Given the pragmatic influences on the current uses of the terms, this seems to be a price worth paying for a perspicuous theory.

10.3 Graphical and Linguistic Modalities

Modalities are kinds of interpretation function that relate representing things to represented things. That different kinds of interpretation function have different consequences for the tractability of computations based on them is a commonplace of computer science. In this section, our aim is to develop a theory for predicting the cognitive characteristics of representation systems based on the nature of their interpretation functions, and on users' access to them.

The contrast between graphics and language is our touchstone modality distinction. It has received much attention from philosophers throughout the history of semantics. We here assume that at least the outlines of an adequate account of this contrast will transfer to treatments of other modalities.

We take the basic structure of the interpretation functions for sentential languages, sketched briefly in the previous section, to be relatively well understood. We therefore focus initially on accounts of the semantics of graphical representations and then return to compare what we find with the situation with sentential languages.

The traditional view of graphical representations is that they represent by virtue of their resemblance to what they represent. As Goodman (1968) says "Vestiges of this view, with assorted refinements, persist in most writings on representation" (page 3). As Goodman elegantly illustrates, this view suffers from basic problems as an account of even any subspecies of representation. Closeness of resemblance is neither necessary nor sufficient for establishing *denotation,* the core of representation. Resemblance is a reflexive relation whereas representation is not. Things are most closely resembled by themselves but are rarely represented by themselves. Tokens of types may resemble each other as closely as we wish but rarely represent each other—each of the identical cars rolling off a production line resembles all the others but does not, in general, represent them.

Global properties such as resemblance are unsatisfactory for theory. They prove hard to apply in detail to actual cases because they fail to distinguish between:

1. 'lexical' and 'propositional' semantics (roughly between unstructured and structured semantic relations);
2. properties of *systems* of representation and *token* representations;
3. what various different classes of user may or may not know about interpretations;
4. different grades of correspondence between representation and represented; and
5. different interpreting relations operating on different aspects of the same complex representation system.

We take each of these issues in turn:

1) The contrast between icons and words is one of the points at which modality differences arise in HCI discussions most frequently. Paradoxically, the semantics of most computer icons is essentially lexical semantics. The relevant issues are about how a visual pattern denotes a class of objects, rather than about how a configuration of parts of a pattern expresses a relation between elements in a domain. There are differences

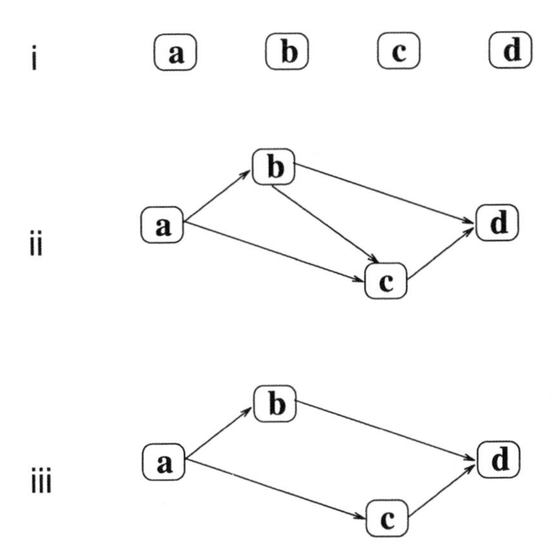

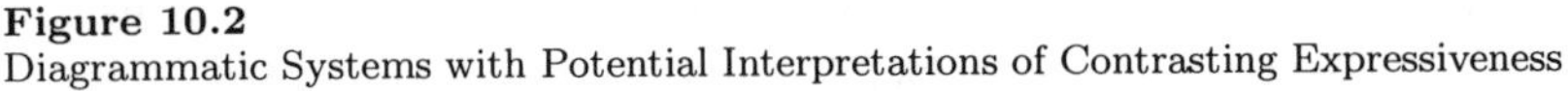
Figure 10.2
Diagrammatic Systems with Potential Interpretations of Contrasting Expressiveness

between how icons do this and how words do this, differences that have an impact on memorability, but semantically there is little difference because the lexical relation of denotation has relatively little structure. In what follows we will mainly be concerned with propositional semantics.

2) The contrast between the level of representation *system* and the level of *individual* representations can be illustrated by Figure 10.2. Figure 10.2 i is intended to be interpreted as a token representation from a system of representations in which placement of square icons in a field represents the size of the elements they denote—say, larger to the left. Other individual representations from this system would have different numbers of icons with different labels in different arrangements. There is an isomorphism between every individual representation of the system, and the sizes of any set of truthfully represented objects. For such an inexpressive system, there is also a system-level isomorphism between the left-of representing relation and the bigger-than represented relation.

However, for the system of representation from which Figure 10.2 ii and iii are drawn, the system-level and the token-level relations diverge. The intended interpretation of these diagrams is that the representing relation (arrow-from-x-to-y) represents that the thing denoted by **x** is bigger than the thing denoted by **y**[1]. For the individual representation in Figure 10.2 ii and any of its models, there is still a complete correspondence between the arrow relation and the bigger than relation—if there is an arrow from **a** to **b** then a is bigger than b, *and visa versa.* But this correspondence breaks down at the system-level as witnessed in iii where the diagram does not represent whether b is bigger than, equal to, or smaller than c. Individual representations *may* correspond completely to their models, but other representations of the same system do not.

3) This distinction between token-level and system-level properties is critical for applications of semantic theory to the cognitive properties of representations. Users often have to infer the scope of systems of representation and the properties of their interpretation from examples. In doing so they can extrapolate from their experience in different ways. If we knew only of Figure 10.2 ii, we might suppose that it was drawn from a representation system in which all individual representations had sets of icons which were completely and consistently connected, thus excluding iii, and restoring a system-level correspondence between 'arrow' and 'greater than'. Since knowledge of the system will prove a critical determinant of cognitive properties of modalities, we require a treatment which clearly distinguishes system- and token-level correspondences.

Approaching graphical modalities in terms of the *enforcement of information* by representation systems has just this effect of distinguishing system and token levels of analysis. Enforcement only makes sense at a system level. As far as token representations go, if it is possible to represent a relation between some elements, it is *possible* to represent it between all elements. The issue is whether representation is *avoidable.* Are there other tokens of the same system which fail to exhibit the expression of the information?

4) Distinguishing token and system levels of analysis reveals the need to distinguish different grades of correspondence between representations and what they represent. How does the enforcement of information arise in systems of representation like that in Figure 10.2 i but not in the system from which ii and iii are drawn? Why can the second system express abstractions (assert only partial orderings of elements) while

[1]More precisely a correspondence between 'x is connected to y by a directed arrow-path, and 'x is greater than y.

the first must determine relative size relations between every pair of elements represented? The answers reveal that far from there being a single type of 'resemblance' between a graphic and what it represents, there is a hierarchy of relations.

Consider the case in which we take the representation system of Figure 10.2 ii and iii and not only interpret the arrow relation as meaning 'greater than', but also interpret its failure to hold as meaning 'not greater than'. Under this interpretation, Figure 10.2 iii *does* determine size relations between all pairs of represented elements, specifically that $b = c$.

What determines whether information about size relations is enforced is the *exhaustiveness* of the interpretation of the representing relations. We define the interpretation of a representing relation to be *exhaustive* if the negation of the representing relation is interpreted as indicating the negation of the relation's interpretation. Under our original interpretation for Figure 10.2 iii, the absence of an arrow from **b** to **c** was not interpreted as meaning that the negation of the interpreting relation held. When this stronger condition is imposed, information enforcement appears.

Although this new interpretation restores the system-level information enforcement noted in Figure 10.2 i, the new system retains a property of its old interpretation which contrasts with i. Whereas the interpretation of i guarantees consistency for all representations drawn from the system, this is not true of either the old or the new interpretation of ii and iii. A diagram such as Figure 10.3 has no model under this exhaustive interpretation, because the lack of an arrow implies equivalence, which means that c is equivalent to both a and b, which the arrow shows are non-equivalent. Figure 10.3 could only be consistent if there were an arrow between **c** and one of the other nodes.

Information enforcement is a feature of interpretations which are exhaustive in the sense defined above. This condition is less restrictive than the full isomorphism of 10.2 i which results from a match between the logical properties of representing and represented relations. The representing relation 'left of' is anti-symmetrical, anti-reflexive and transitive, just as is the represented relation 'greater than'. The result is that the system of Figure 10.2 i, under the interpretation described, cannot represent inconsistent sets of propositions. This property of the isomorphic style of interpretation we call *self-consistency* (Barwise 1993).

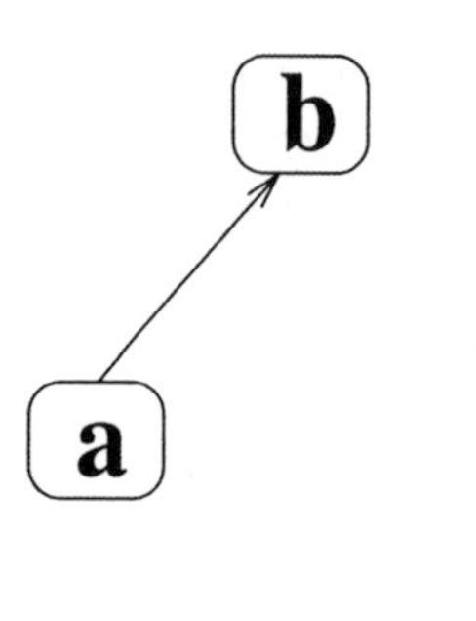

Figure 10.3
A Diagram that Is Inconsistent Under an Exhaustive Interpretation of Arrows.

Mere exhaustive interpretation does not yield this property. For example, the representing relation of "having an arrow from x to y" is non-symmetrical, non-reflexive and non-transitive. When this representing relation is exhaustively interpreted, far from being self-consistent, most of the system's diagrams have no model.

In emphasizing the importance of distinguishing different types of correspondence, we have distinguished three grades of mapping between representing and represented relations. In the least expressive, there is a correspondence between the logical properties of the representing and represented relations which results in a self-consistency property of these systems; a more expressive system results from relaxing the correspondence of logical properties but maintaining exhaustive interpretation in which the negation of a representing relation is interpreted as the negation of the represented relation; the most expressive system relaxes even this constraint. Below, when we consider linguistic semantics, we will make a further sub-division of the last category. So far we have only considered systems in which there is a single representing relation, relating a single category of elements. When links become typed (or equivalently nodes become typed), then even more expressive systems result.

5) Finally, our fifth difficulty in analyzing graphical semantics through such global properties as similarity, is the problem that in complex real representation systems, these different types of correspondence coexist in the same system. This can be illustrated by further development of our current examples. We have so far tacitly supposed that the letters in the icons in the figures are logical constants interpreted according to a single-names axiom (things only have a unique name) i.e. we have

supposed that $a \neq b \neq c \neq d$. This tendency to interpret labels in this way in all the diagrams amounts to interpreting the sameness-of-position relation as isomorphic with the identity relation. Note that this is just as true of Figure 10.2 iii when the arrow relation is *not* exhaustively interpreted, as it is of Figure 10.2 i when it is. This interpretation of position as identity is a particularly pervasive characteristic of graphics which we return to below under the heading of *token referential* systems when we contrast linguistic and graphical semantics.

For the present, we note that representation systems sometimes interpret one relation in a way which enforces information, and another relation in a way that does not. We will see this illustrated in real graphical systems in the next section, and for languages later in this one. This is yet one further reason for understanding graphical semantics in terms of relations less global than resemblance or similarity.

10.3.1 Availability of Constraints

Both information enforcement resulting from the exhaustive interpretation of representing relations, and the even stronger property of self-consistency resulting from correspondence between representing and represented relations, can be directly related to inferential tractability, through such concepts as "vividness" (Levesque 1988) and "limited abstraction representation systems" (LARS) (Stenning & Oberlander 1992).

As we noted in the introduction, establishing the weak expressiveness and inferential tractability of graphical representations is only half way to relating graphics to its cognitive characteristics. The very demonstration that the logical expressiveness of graphical systems is weak is achieved by showing a correspondence to a weak *sentential* system (see for example Levesque's definitions of vivid fragments of FOL). If weakly expressive graphical systems can be simulated in weakly expressive sentential systems having therefore the same resulting tractability, then the appeal to computational complexity has destroyed any account of *differences* between linguistic and graphical modalities. If computational tractability is the underlying explanation of why graphical systems are easily usable, then these weak sentential systems should also be easily usable, and the differentiation of graphical and sentential systems is lost.

An insightful response to this dilemma requires supplementing an account of computational complexity with an account of what we will call the *availability* of constraints on expressiveness. We must ask what information a user requires to identify and to exploit the constraints in a representation system? In a sentential system with abstract syntax, such weaknesses of expression that exist do not arise from the way that representations map onto their semantics. A considerable amount of exploration and learning may be required to be able to tailor a theorem prover to exploit the weak expressiveness of the system. In graphical systems, the situation is more complicated, but at least sometimes, the weaknesses of expression of the system can be 'inspected' because they are consequences of a few relatively central properties of the graphical representations and their interpretations. In our example in Figure 10.2 i, just knowing that 'greater than' was represented by 'left of' is sufficient to know that only full orderings can be represented, because 'left of' shares logical properties with 'greater than'. As we shall see in more complicated examples described below (matrix graphics, Euler's Circles), quite intricate meta-logical properties of the graphics can be inferred from a few basic facts about the diagrams' geometry/topology and its interpretation.

What users with different background knowledge and learning opportunities can understand about the constraints on expressiveness of diagrams is potentially determined by several sources of knowledge about interpretations. We have distinguished several interpretations of figures 10.2 ii and iii which cannot be inferred from anything in the diagrams. Even when the graphical relation in these diagrams is interpreted exhaustively, imposing an expressive weakness, exploiting this fact relies on being aware of it. Computational tractability can only predict usability when supplemented by an account of the availability of constraints to users with different contextual knowledge. The discussion of example systems below will illustrate this point.

Providing we can substantiate the claim that there are differences between languages and some graphical systems in the availability of their constraints, the claim can offer a possible explanation of an often noted psychological fact about modality differences. Graphics are frequently used in the introductory teaching of abstract subjects but abandoned by students as they gain proficiency, often in favor of some algebraic generalization of the topic. If the cognitive advantage of diagrams is that they make constraints of expression available to someone with little background knowledge of a new topic, then one might expect graphics to lose their advantage over sentential systems as the user learns to exploit the hidden weaknesses in sentential systems.

10.3.2 Linguistic Expressiveness

Having described a hierarchy of expressiveness amongst interpretations of graphics, we now turn to a comparison with the semantics of sentential languages. This comparison will make clear why constraints on the expressiveness of sentential representations are less available. We use the term *language* here to refer only to sentential representation systems even though it is often used more broadly. Our discussion of languages will assume the printed medium as most relevant to the present comparison with graphics. Though we believe the essence of our account will transfer to spoken languages, there are certainly many interesting issues which arise but which will not divert us here.

Pure texts consist of sequences of tokens of alphabetical characters (including characters such as parentheses) drawn from a set of types of character. Sequences of characters combine to make 'words' which in turn combine to form sentences. Artificial languages may be characterized in terms of different constitutents, but for current purposes the issues are the same. The only property of a *tokens* which is relevant to its interpretation is the *type* of which it is an instance. The only properties of texts relevant to their interpretation are the sequences of token words classified into types.[2]

The essential property of pure linguistic modalities that sets them off from graphical ones is that the only inter-word relation which is interpreted is concatenation. Because concatenation is the only interpreted spatial relation its interpretation has to be differentiated by the types of elements which are concatenated. For there to be more than a single uniform semantic interpretation of concatenation there must therefore be an abstract syntax which provides a diversity of abstract relations to be interpreted. It is the paucity of interpreted temporal/spatial relations in language which requires an abstract syntax to express many semantic relations. Conversely, it is the abstract syntax which means that the representation of semantic relations is not direct.

With this account of the semantic bases of graphics and language, we can now see how it explains some intuitively gross differences be-

[2]This is, of course, a simplification: actual texts are more than sequences of characters, since they assign significance to such features as spatial layout and font. But at this level of analysis, it is a useful simplifications.

tween graphical and sentential representations. One key is the style of representation of identity relations which are distinguished as type- and token-referential systems. In *token* referential systems, multiple tokens of icons of the same type refer to *distinct* entities (generally with shared properties denoted by the features of the type). In *type* referential systems (such as sentential languages), names refer in virtue of their type—multiple token occurrences of the *same* name-type refer to the same entity. Different attributions are made to them by attaching different predicates to separate occurrences.

Token referential systems enforce the representation of identity—it is not possible to represent two elements (say the evening star and the morning star) without representing whether they are one and the same, or distinct. Tokens of icons are typically identified by their positions at some suitable level of granularity, and all identity relations are determined between the referents of all icons in all token representations. 'Having the same position as' is a relation which is interpreted isomorphically with identity in these systems.

Type referential systems generally do not enforce representation of identity relations because name-type identity is not generally interpreted exhaustively. Different names do not necessarily denote different things. In sub-languages with 'unique names' restrictions, the relation between name-type and reference is restored. But information enforcement only results if names are the *only* referring expressions. Only in that case is isomorphism established and every reference determines the identity relations of its referent to all other references. These successive conditions on languages bring them closer to the highly restricted systems Goodman (1968) defines as *notations,* for which the main condition is that there be a unique representation for each state of affairs represented.

If a representation system is token referential, it can only use a 'name' (or icon) once within an individual representation, since any recurrence of the name signals a distinct reference and simultaneously asserts non-identity of its denotation with the denotation of its previous occurrence. This limitation to a single occurrence of each referring element in token referential systems also limits the number of properties of entities represented, because unless nodes for abstract properties are used to introduce abstraction, each property must be represented by a feature of a single icon, and the number of dimensions on which icons can vary is limited. As has often been observed, graphics runs out of carrier dimensions (e.g.

Barwise 1993; Hovy and Arens 1990). While token-referential systems exhibit these limitations, they thereby purchase considerable facility of processing. For example, problems such as anaphor resolution can only occur in a type-referential system where multiple occurrences of an icon which may share reference are possible.

Cartoon strips are an interesting hybrid of token and type referentiality which get around some of the limitations of token-referential systems by introducing a form of 'type identity' across frames. Multiple-frame graphics are a clear reminder that we have so far been addressing issues of interpretation of homogeneous graphical spaces. One symptom of the breakdown of graphical homogeneity is the inability to interpret spatial relations across frames. That a character appears in one frame to the left of another character in another frame is not interpretable as meaning they bear this relation in the domain. The terms of between-frame semantics are not the same as those of within-frame semantics (the subdiagrams of Figure 10.2 are another example of this phenomenon).

We can now summarize our account of the contrast between linguistic and graphical modalities. In graphical representations, a hierarchy of interpretations imposes increasing constraints on the interpretation of spatial representing relations. In linguistic modalities, concatenation is the only graphical relation which is directly and uniformly interpreted, and it is generally interpreted as yielding an abstract syntax. Semantic interpretation then applies to relations within this abstract syntax. There is therefore no semantically uniform interpretation of concatenation, and therefore no constraint on expression arises from the nature of the interpretation of spatial relations.

This theory of the graphical/linguistic modality contrast departs from intuitive classifications of representation systems both for extremely weakly expressive languages (which it shows to share the critical property of information enforcement with graphical systems) and for highly expressive graphics (which it shows to share with languages the possession of abstract syntax—see Section 10.4 below where expressive semantic networks are considered). This conflict with pre-theoretical intuition is just what one expects to follow on the development of theory. We believe that the application of the approach to practical examples below fully justifies this departure from intuition by demonstrating unintuitive correspondences of usability with its analyses.

Having developed this framework for comparing modalities, the remainder of the paper considers three classes of common representation, ranging from the most weakly to the most strongly expressive, applying the analysis and reviewing its predictions against some of what is known empirically about the usability of each type of representation.

10.4 Three Example Families of Representation Systems

In order to test the usefulness of the conceptualization we have proposed, we now apply it to three widely occurring families of representation. In each case we first apply the theoretical framework. We then review some of what is known about the cognitive properties of the example and ask whether the observations are in accordance with the framework's predictions.

An important principle in selecting examples to analyze is that they should be representation systems for which there is a reasonable presumption of usefulness. Constructing hypothetical examples would be much easier, but a much less secure foundation for theory. Not much empirical evidence is available from careful experimental investigation of the usefulness of informationally equivalent representations, but at least analyzing frequently used systems encourages the presumption that the examples are useful for something. We here take matrix graphics, logic diagrams, and semantic networks as our three example families of representations. We begin with the most constrained and progress to the more expressive.

10.4.1 Matrix Graphics

We use *matrix graphics* as a convenient term for graphical representations of populations of data cases which are usually multi-dimensional and in which all cases are specified on all dimensions. 'Business' graphics —graphs, pie-charts, histograms, Gant charts etc.—are common examples. The meaning of these graphics is determined by isomorphisms between representation and data.

Since Bertin (1974), presentational issues associated with this type of graphic have been extensively researched in the HCI literature. Most of this work has, however, concentrated either on the ergonomic aspects of the display of a particular type of graphic (e.g. Salvendy 1987, Kolski and Millot 1991) or on the fine detail of alternative presentations of

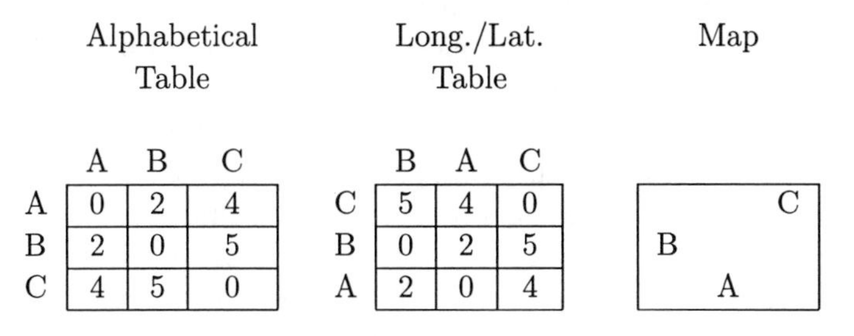

Alphabetical Table

	A	B	C
A	0	2	4
B	2	0	5
C	4	5	0

Long./Lat. Table

	B	A	C
C	5	4	0
B	0	2	5
A	2	0	4

Figure 10.4
A Table of Intercity Distances Equivalent to a Map

closely related graphical forms (Tufte 1983). The latter type of work has been extended to automatic control of data presentation (Cleveland 1985, Mackinlay 1983, Mackinlay 1986).

Tables are one point at which textual and matrix graphical systems meet[3]. Simple algorithms can turn tables into running text by combining row and column headings with cell contents. From that perspective, tables are two-dimensionally laid out language. Tables therefore represent a mixed modality in which some spatial relations are directly semantically interpreted in a way which intertwines them with the interpretation of their linguistic components. In the other direction, towards the more graphical, lies the transformation of tables to maps illustrated in Figure 10.4.

Both tables and matrix graphics are weakly expressive, in that they cannot represent data cases which are not specified on all axis dimensions. Both can omit cases entirely but neither can include partially specified cases. There are some fine-grained differences of expressiveness within matrix graphics. For example, graphs are more weakly expressive than tables or histograms because graphs require an ordering on the categories ranged along axes, which then allows direct semantic interpretation of another spatial relation.

So, corresponding examples of tables, histograms and the tabular texts generated from tables, are different expressions of the same information, and as such each sub-family of the modality is equally expressive. The

[3]It is perhaps no accident that archeological evidence suggests that in every known case of the invention of writing systems, the initial use was to express tabulations of data, generally in the service of account keeping.

equivalences to be found between tabular language and graphical presentations is an example which underlines the dependence of analysis on the *system* level of description. The equivalence presumes that we understand tabular texts as ones generated from complete tables. As soon as texts are permitted which omit some but not all of the information about cells, the textual system becomes more expressive. The example also illustrates how the availability to users of constraints on expression will determine cognitive properties. A user faced with a text generated by translation from a whole table can make no use of this constraint unless it is known to hold. If the same text is presented *as a table,* the spatial properties of the layout may be sufficient to allow immediate exploitation of the constraints in reasoning.

Our theory predicts that matrix graphics as a family of representation systems should have broadly similar cognitive properties. This view is supported by the empirical literature which mostly focuses on fine-grained interactions between specific tasks and different types of matrix-graphic presentation. Access mechanisms will differ in their facility according to the exact tasks at hand—judging whether a difference is positive or negative will be done more easily on the graph because it can be done by using only perceptual mechanisms. Retrieving an exact figure, or a figure for a difference should be easier from the table than the histogram. In terms of the classification scheme described in Stenning and Oberlander (in press), matrix graphics and tables are Minimal Abstraction Representation Systems: one graphic represents just one model.

10.4.2 Logic Diagrams

While matrix graphics align categories along axes, diagrams exploit a wide range of spatial relations in representing their domains.

Work on the teaching of abstract subjects such as geometry and mechanics has demonstrated the advantages for students of using diagrams and has presented theories of why graphics have the effect they have. Larkin and Simon (1987) draw a distinction between *informational* and *computational* equivalence of representation. They see the advantages of graphics in terms of their computational tractability, citing searchability by parallel mechanisms and other properties of graphics as computational advantages of what they take to be informationally equivalent representations. Our approach can be seen as both a generalization and a refinement of theirs. We agree that the central cognitive advantages of graphics come from their computational tractability. But we trace this tractability to their weak expressiveness, which in turn rests on the fact that at the representation *system* level, graphics are not informationally equivalent to languages. On this account, the computational advantages of graphics are more fundamental than architecture dependent features like parallel searchability (though these may well be the *result* of the possibility of implementing weakly expressive representations). To see where the accounts diverge, consider the case of processing a weakly expressive sentential language equivalent to a graphical system. It will be possible to construct a processor which makes this sentential language equally tractable (and therefore computationally equivalent). The difference between the graphical and sentential systems lies in the discoverability of the limitations on expression and the necessary methods of exploiting them in inference.

We illustrate our theory in a domain where we can precisely assess the match between the expressive power of the representation and the expressive demands of the task: logic diagrams based on using areas to represent sets. There are several such approaches, including Venn Diagrams and Euler's Circles. They are good examples because they combine complete abstraction in some aspects (the relation between the circles and the sets represented is entirely arbitrary) with, in some cases, complete isomorphism of interpretation of topological relations to set relations. The domain also has the added attraction that a great deal is known about human reasoning ability in this domain and theories of mental process have been based both on graphical and non-graphical methods. Euler's circles have been the subject of well documented misinterpretation in the literature, and this misinterpretation is of some interest to our cognitive theory (e.g. Erickson 1975, Johnson-Laird 1983), discussed in Stenning and Oberlander (1995).

Venn Diagrams Some circle-diagram systems provide a link with the preceding section's discussion of tables since they start out as nothing more than tables organized according to a specialized method of spatial layout which facilitates search. Venn's system, for example, uses a single diagram of three circles intersecting as a 'table' of the eight possible 'types' of element defined by three properties. Figure 10.5 illustrates this correspondence between diagram and table.

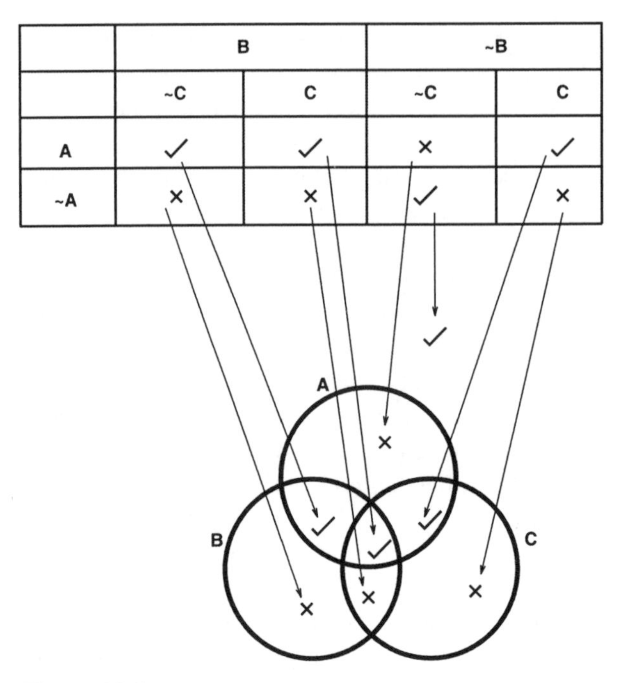

Figure 10.5
Venn Diagram as a Variant of a Table: Table Cells Map to Diagram Sub-Regions. Empty ones have crosses, non-empty ones ticks.

The system annotates regions in this table to reflect presence or absence of types of individual in the model. There are different systems of annotation with different expressiveness. Shin (1991) shows how the system can be extended through a node-and-link notation for relations between cells to express much of monadic predicate logic.

The mapping of the several representing relations on to the relations they represent illustrates the different kinds of mapping distinguished in Section 10.3. The fundamental idea of using spatial inclusion to represent set membership is fully isomorphic. A transitive, anti-symmetrical and anti-reflexive representing relation is mapped onto a represented relation with the same logical properties. In fact, the interpretation is such that spatial inclusion of points in a closed curve is actually an *example* of inclusion of members in a set.

This notation can be augmented to allow an arc between two marked sub-regions to be used to indicate a disjunction—that one *or other* (or

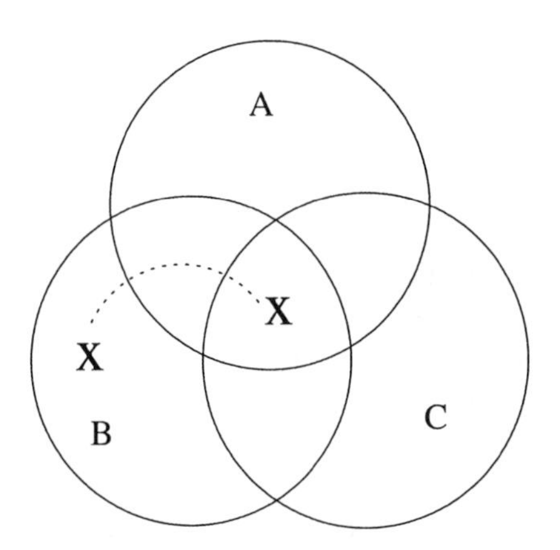

Figure 10.6
Interpretation of the Link Notation in Venn Diagrams. The arc connecting the Xs asserts that *either* ABCs *or* $\tilde{A}B\tilde{C}$ exist. Absence of a link between regions is not interpreted as the negation of equivalent disjunctions.

more than one) of the individuals linked by the arc definitely exists (see Figure 10.6)

But when augmented in this way, the representation scheme loses its isomorphism. The links cannot be interpreted exhaustively—absence of a link between two areas does not designate the negation of a disjunction between the linked regions. Adding the links notation is what takes the system beyond matrix graphics in expressiveness, but this addition intuitively makes the system much harder to understand. Anecdotal evidence from teaching with the system bears this out though we know of no systematic experimental test.

Euler's Circles Venn Diagrams are only one system of diagrammatic reasoning based on the same fundamental representing relation. Euler's circles (Euler 1772) exploit graphical constraints more fully than Venn diagrams, using many different arrangements of circle and incorporating a dynamic element into their use—reasoning can be modeled by mechanical constraints on movement of circles. Euler's Circles provide an interesting example of the complexities of analyzing even apparently simple graphical systems and predicting their usability.

Euler's Circles is a system of logic diagrams for doing syllogistic reasoning (Euler 1772). Elsewhere we have developed a detailed reconstruction of Euler's algorithm and shown that when the system is correctly interpreted, it is a Limited Abstraction Representation System (LARS), rather than a Minimal Abstraction Representation System (MARS) (Stenning and Oberlander 1995, Stenning and Oberlander 1994). The reader is referred to that discussion for the detailed application of the current theory.

Briefly, a simple application of the analogy of spatial inclusion for set membership leads to a MARS interpretation and an explosion in the number of diagrams necessary to perform the abstract reasoning required. For example, the premise *Some A are B* is satisfied by four of the five possible 2-circle diagrams representing the sets A and B.[4] This means that to discover that the syllogism *Some A are B, Some B are C* does not have any valid conclusions using this concrete interpretation of the diagrams requires consideration of 16 pairs of diagrams. In each case it is necessary to show that there is no conclusion involving A and C which holds in all possible 'unifications' of these diagram pairs. This typically requires consideration of several arrangements of the three circles, each consistent with the premises, and leads to a total of about sixty diagrams to consider.

But no logic teacher, least of all Euler, ever proposed such exhaustive methods to a pupil. By strategically selecting what can be seen as 'weakest' cases it is possible to prune the search space. Using Euler's system the reasoner can solve any syllogism by algorithmic construction of a single diagram. A simple notational device, along with a subtle but far reaching reinterpretation of the ontology of the diagrams, provides a mechanically defined algorithm which allows this dramatic difference in effectiveness. Marks distinguish the sub-regions which designate *minimal* models of the premise from regions designating types merely consistent with the premise. A strategy of choosing unifications of diagrams with the most possible sub-regions ensures exhaustive search of the logical space. By adding a simple topological rule for 'canceling marks' under some conditions after unification, the system is transformed from one which requires concrete examination of every single possible logical model, to an elegant one-pass algorithm which constructs a single diagram, and bases complete and valid reasoning on it.

Figure 10.7 provides an example syllogism solution using Euler's method.

[4]The four diagrams differ in what they say about whether there are A that are not B, or Bs that are not A, or both, or neither. The fifth diagram represents the case where A and B are disjoint

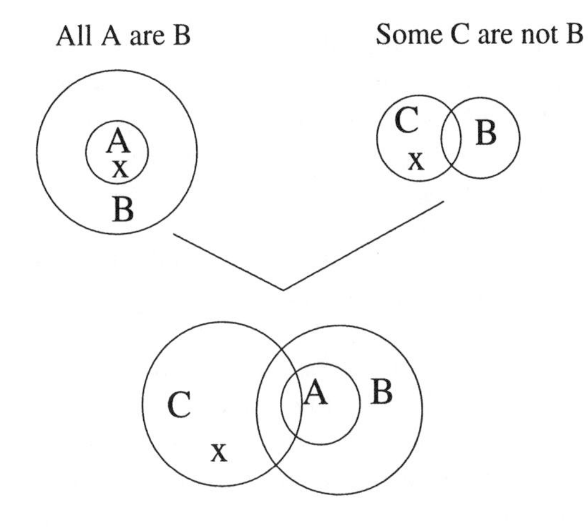

Figure 10.7
An Example Graphical Syllogism Solution. 'x' indicates a region corresponding to a minimal model. In unifying premise diagrams, 'x'-marked regions bisected by the third circle become unmarked. Final 'x'-marked regions license valid conclusions.

Unlike Shin's extension of Venn, this elucidation of Euler stays within a strongly graphical interpretation of its diagrams. Although it captures the whole of the syllogism, it is considerably logically less expressive than Shin's system.

What do we know of the cognitive impact of this diagrammatic system? Although there are few systematic studies using this graphical reasoning technique its very longevity as a didactic technique speaks for its cognitive efficacy. Psychologists have mainly been attracted by using the system as the basis for a psychological model of 'mental' reasoning rather than an external teaching/reasoning aid. One teaching study (Grossen and Carnine 1990) which compares Euler's Circles with sentential teaching does show quite radical facilitation of learning by graphics, bringing 'learning impaired' subjects up to superior performance levels, but only in a condition in which subjects actively manipulated the diagrams. The importance of manipulation may be due to temporal information enforcements.

When the diagrams are 'animated' by movements of the circles, the resulting operations have certain computationally attractive properties of continuity. The movements transform models from one to another with minimal additions or subtractions of sub-regions denoting single types of individual. The 'relevant' models to consider in verifying a conclusion are always 'adjacent' in this space of models.

Analysis If Euler's system, correctly used, is a cognitively efficient representation for learning and performing a rather difficult fragment of reasoning, what does that say about the general theoretical framework? This diagrammatic system clearly takes us beyond matrix graphics in its expressive power. Syllogistic reasoning is inherently abstract, and a matrix graphic system requires exhaustive inspection of up to 60 diagrams to demonstrate the lack of any conclusion from some pairs of premises. Shin's Venn-based system augments the power of the basic matrix-graphic core by notations which are not graphically constrained, capturing a larger fragment of logic but, we suspect, losing some cognitive efficacy. The Euler system shows that diagrams can be extended in expressive power to be just adequate to capture the abstractions required for this fragment of reasoning *without giving up logically interpretable graphical constraints.*

Although there is clearly a need for empirical investigation, the framework encompasses some important observations. If the graphics are interpreted as only primitively expressive (MARS), they really are useless for this abstract task—viz the arguments that Euler's Circles cannot be the basis of mental syllogistic reasoning (Johnson-Laird 1983). It was Euler's genius to see that suitable strategies of selection and combination could remain within a graphically constrained interpretation and yield a tractable system for this limited domain of reasoning. Even minimal extensions of the logic to say, disjunctive syllogisms are beyond the expressive power of Euler's graphical formalism.

This graphical system provides a good example of the differential availability of constraints in graphical and sentential representations described in Section 10.3. Once a diagram user understands the core of the interpretation of the diagrams, their weakness of expression immediately follows from their basic geometrical properties. Any point in a plane corresponds to a maximally specified individual. Spatial containment, like set inclusion, is a transitive, non-symmetric, reflexive relation like the monadic universal quantifier. Intersection models existential quantification; exclusion models ground negation. The five possible topological relations between two circles exhaust the possibilities and are each interpreted as the corresponding set relations. This exhaustiveness is particularly compelling because all the primitive topological relations are included. In contrast, deriving these properties from the sentential formulation of the syllogism takes a sophisticated grasp of model theory and considerable inference and enumeration of cases.

These important properties of Euler's Circles are available by inspection to a user with prior knowledge of only the core semantic concept behind the spatial-containment-as-set-inclusion interpretation. But there is still a big difference in ease of use between the primitively interpreted system with its explosion of diagrams to be checked, and the abstractive version presented here, even though both share the same core concept. Isomorphism is of little use if it blocks the expression of abstractions which are required for a tractable performance of the task at hand. We would still expect the usefulness of the system for reasoning by naive users to be determined by the pedagogical details of how the system is introduced.

In summary, Euler's Circles maximally exploit graphical constraints in capturing the domain of syllogistic reasoning. They are more constrained than Venn's system and the theory therefore predicts that for syllogistic reasoning they should be more effective. Our intuition and what observation is available supports this view but it stands in need of experimental test. Euler's system illustrates how constrained graphical representations make properties of reasoning systems available to users with only core knowledge of their semantic basis, but also reveals the need for a complete analysis of strategies of use and details of interpretation to fully predict usability. The usability of the system is determined by the combinatorics, and these are dependent on the subtleties.

10.4.3 Semantic Networks

In Section 10.3, we adopted node-and-link examples to illustrate interpretations of different expressiveness because this single formalism can bear interpretations of such a wide range of expressiveness. Semantic networks, one category of these formalisms, are therefore an important case for developing a theory based on constraints on expressiveness. Semantic networks are an insightful case for our purposes because much is known of their formal properties, and something of their usability. Networks are an important class of applied notation which has evolved in close association with computational technology. Much of their practical use is dependent on that technology. They have an intimate relation to linguistic representations in programming languages. The origins of semantic networks go back at least to Peirce (Roberts 1973), who developed graphical notations for predicate calculus contemporaneous with Frege's development of sentential versions (see Sowa 1993), but did not achieve widespread use until the advent of computers.

A further interesting feature of semantic networks is that an important motivation for their development has been cognitive theorizing about human mental representation. Semantic networks have been used as the basis of models of human semantic memory and lexical representation (Collins and Quillian 1969); in simulation models of human text comprehension (Anderson and Bower 1972, Anderson 1983); and as a notation for human memory representations in discourse (Kintsch and van Dijk 1978). Even early formulations of mental models employed a variety of semantic network notation (Johnson-Laird and Steedman 1978).

We first review commonly occurring examples of these formalisms of various expressive powers, and then review some evidence of their usability. We begin with the most expressive examples.

Semantic networks can be interpreted as logically highly expressive languages (Schubert 1976, Hendrix 1979, Sowa 1979). Schubert shows how simple nets can be extended in expressive power to equivalence with the lambda-calculus by progressively adding devices for capturing connectives, quantifiers, and abstraction operators. Schubert's point is to understand the semantics of networks by assimilating them to logical languages whose semantics is already understood.

These expressive interpretations of semantic networks are possible because an abstract syntax is imposed on the networks. Nodes appear which have syntactic categories connected to their syntactic arguments by links. Sometimes the 'abstract' nodes are eliminated in favor of labelings on links. Either way the semantic interpretation is defined not directly on the representing relation (the links) but on a syntactical categorization of the links based on configuration. Node-and-link formalisms can thus be seen as introducing multi-dimensional concatenation to the design of languages. Whereas sentential languages use one dimensional concatenation, networks, by allowing indefinitely many arcs leading to and from any node, expand the dimensionality of concatenation available. As such our theory classifies these networks as essentially of a linguistic modality that exploits no graphical constraints.

The next less expressive grade of interpretation we distinguished in Section 10.3 was representations in which there was uniform interpretation of a representing relation (no abstract nodes), but this relation was not exhaustively interpreted (the initial interpretation of Figure 10.2 ii and iii). We saw that such diagrams were capable of expressing partial orderings. When these partial orderings are interpreted as expressing partial knowledge of a completely ordered world, the resulting representation system retains the discursiveness of a language—representation is selective.

Tree diagrams of taxonomies are an example of interpretation which applies the further constraint of exhaustive interpretation. Trees are probably the commonest representation of taxonomies. In a common interpretation, the transitive closure of their link relations are interpreted as ISA relations. Any two nodes which are not connected by a path of arrows are interpreted as being related by the negation of this relation. Whether the links are explicitly asymmetrical arrows, or whether this asymmetry is implicit in the vertical or horizontal layout, the interpretation is certainly asymmetrical. Because the logical properties of the representing arrows (non-symmetric, transitive) do not match those of the represented relation ISA (anti-symmetric, transitive), trees do not have the guaranteed consistency property (for example, all cyclic graphs interpreted in this fashion represent inconsistent taxonomies).

Finally, an example of the most constrained interpretations of networks, in which the semantic interpretation of the representing links does share all their logical properties, is the circuit diagram. Here links are interpreted as physical connections, and their absence as the absence of physical connections. Nodes are interpreted token-identically as components, labeled according to their type. The result is a graphical MARS in which each graphic has a single model.

How does the empirical evidence of the usefulness of semantic networks map onto this classification of examples? The most systematic empirical studies of the cognitive properties of expressive semantic networks as compared to equivalent sentential counterparts come from the assessment of 'graphical' programming languages (e.g. Meyers 1990). Results of studies of usability are mixed as our theory would predict, with some studies showing advantage but more showing roughly equal usability. But this review does not address expressiveness explicitly. At the most expressive end of the dimension, there is little indication that semantic networks are a useful formalism for lambda calculus (Schubert's intention was, of course, always analytical). Some have claimed that these formalisms are useful for teaching predicate calculus. We know of no controlled studies, and our general intuition is that when sentential and network systems are carefully equated for expressiveness, they have roughly the same pedagogical efficacy. This empirical issue is worthy of investigation.

As we descend the expressivenes dimension, the first semantic networks for which we find solid evidence of wide employment are ones which stop short of employing variables. Systems like ACT*, which contain a semantic network representation as their declarative memory, certainly have typed arcs (or abstract syntactic nodes), but they signally restrict their entity nodes to logical constants, and are token-referential. Here there is real evidence of usefulness of the network formalism (relative to sentential equivalents) at least in theorizing about human memory. Intuitively, much of the benefit probably stems from the ease of search which results from the token referential nature of the systems. Interestingly, the property of complete connectedness (having no unconnected 'islands' of nodes in a network representation) has been used to predict comprehensibility and memorability of texts the networks represent.

Our example of networks which impose exhaustive interpretations on their link relations was trees interpreted as representing taxonomies. The widespread use of this representation is sufficient testimony to its usefulness. The question arises as to how the limitations on their expression are understood since, as we have seen, they do not arise from any graphical constraint. So widely are these formalisms used that it is quite hard to answer questions about the origins of the knowledge required to interpret them. Just what does generate the inference that two classes of entity on different descending branches are mutually exclusive? What generates the related assumption that a class labeled "a" at one node is a different class than one on another branch labeled "b"? Is it the token referentiality of the system? Or the exhaustiveness of interpretation of the link relation? Or the 'formal' perception that cyclic graphs are not well formed members of the system? Or knowledge that what is presented is a taxonomy? Or ...? Whatever the right answer is for any particular example, predictions of usability from expressiveness will have to be relative to availability of contextual knowledge. At this level of expressiveness there is clear evidence of the usefulness of these graphical formalisms. When we take the final step to circuit diagrams usefulness can hardly be challenged. Sentential equivalents to these systems only arose in the process of computerization of circuit design, and are rarely used in non-automated systems.

This brief journey along the dimension of expressiveness suggests that a thorough study of the interpretations of the many node-and-link formalisms used in computer science and elsewhere would be a valuable preliminary to a deeper study of the cognitive properties of these graphical representations. Although we can point to few systematic experimental comparisons of network and sentential systems, even the samples discussed here support the view that there is good evidence for usefulness at the inexpressive end of the continuum, but decreasing evidence as the formalisms' interpretations grow more expressive. Token referentiality appears to be an important watershed—there is little evidence that node-and-link formalisms that are so expressive that they have jettisoned this feature have any advantage over sentential systems. By and large, the complexity of the existing empirical literature on the usability of network representations bears out the theoretical framework developed here.

10.5 Conclusion

We believe that our proposals for the terminology of media and modalities, however terminologically distinct, capture concepts widely but implicitly held in the community concerned with the usability of representations. We believe they are the basis for a firmer foundation for research into cognitive properties of representations based on semantic analysis. Using semantic concepts to predict cognitive properties of representations turns theoretical analyses from logic and computer science back onto human information processing. Expressiveness of representation was first studied in connection with understanding processing by machine, but at a fundamental level the theory applies to the humans who devised it. This discussion of the family of graphical modalities is suggestive of the richness of classification this conceptualization offers and of ways semantic analysis can contribute to the study of usability.

Elsewhere (Stenning and Oberlander 1992) we have proposed a hierarchy of expressivness based on the ability of representing systems to express partitionings of the space of all their possible models. This characterizes representation systems as Minimal Abstraction, Limited Abstraction or Unlimited Abstraction representation systems (MARS, LARS and UARS respectively). Our present description of grades of interpretation function, drawn in terms of constraints on the mapping between represented and representing relations, is the beginnings of a 'syntactically' or formally motivated taxonomy. It is clear that the two classifications are not independent. Our hope is that in the future it may be possible to give an exact characterization of their relations.

Our semantic conceptualization of modalities focuses attention on the availability of information about interpretations to different classes of user. Degrees of expressiveness (and therefore tractability) of systems cannot predict usability unless combined with accounts of the availability to the user of constraints on expressive power. We have given some examples which illustrate how some graphical systems wear their weakness on their sleeves. As almost a side effect, we have emphasized what we all knew all along, that human cognition is as much about *selecting* representation systems to perform a task as about computation *within* a given representational scheme.

The current vogue for 'visualization' which is witnessed in fields as disparate as programming methodology, the analysis of large data sets, human-computer interaction, mathematical proof, and education, is a powerful force for liberalizing practice in many fields. But if we are to separate the value from the hype, it will take a more sophisticated distinction between modalities of presentation than the apparently simple one between graphics and language.

Acknowledgments

The support of the Economic and Social Research Council UK (ESRC) is gratefully acknowledged. The work was partly supported by the ESRC funded Human Communication Research Centre. We also wish to acknowledge partial support from Grants # 9018050 from the JCI in Cognitive Science and HCI and # GR/J586129 from SERC/DTI

References

Anderson, J. R. and Bower, G. H. 1972. Configurational Properties in Sentence Memory. *Journal of Verbal Learning and Verbal Behavior* 11:594–605.

Anderson, John. R. 1983. *The Architecture of Cognition.* Cambridge, Mass.: Harvard University Press.

Barwise, Jon 1993. Heterogeneous Reasoning. Working Papers IULG-93-24, Indiana University, Bloomington.

Bertin, J. 1974. *Graphische Semiologie.* Berlin: Diagramme Netze Karten. Trans. from *Semiologie Graphique,* 1967.

Cleveland, W. S. 1985. *The Elements of Graphing Data.* Monterey, Calif.: Wadsworth.

Collins, A. M and Quillian, M. R. 1969. Retrieval Time from Semantic Memory. *Journal of Verbal Learning and Verbal Behavior* 8:240–247.

Coutaz, Joëlle 1992. A Taxonomy for Multimedia and Multimodal User Interfaces. In *EWCHCI,* 229–240, Moscow.

de Saussure, Ferdinand 1916. *Cours de Linguistique Generale.* Paris: Payot.

Erickson, J. R. 1975. A Set Analysis Theory of Behaviour in Formal. In *Information Processing and Cognition,* ed. Robert L. Solso. Hillsdale, N.J.: Lawrence Erlbaum Associates.

Euler, L. 1772. *Lettres a une Princesse d'Allemagne,* volume 2, 102–108.

Goodman, Nelson 1968. *Languages of Art.* Indianapolis, Indiana: Bobbs-Merrill.

Grossen, G. and Carnine, D. 1990. Diagramming a Logic Strategy: Effects on Difficult Problem Types. *Learning Disability Quarterly* 13:168–182.

Hendrix, Gary 1979. Encoding Knowledge in Partitioned Networks. In *Associative Networks,* ed. Nicholas V Findler, 51–92. New York: Academic Press.

Hovy, Eduard and Arens, Yigal 1990. When Is a Picture Worth a Thousand Words?—Allocation of. Presented at the 1990 AAAI Symposium on HCI, Stanford, Calif.

Johnson-Laird, Philip N. 1983. *Mental Models.* Cambridge: Cambridge University Press.

Johnson-Laird, Philip N., and Steedman, Mark J. 1978. The Psychology of Syllogisms. *Cognitive Psychology* 10:64–99.

Kintsch, W. and van Dijk, T. A 1978. Towards a Model of Text Comprehension and Reproduction. *Psychological Review,* 85:363–394.

Kolski, Christophe and Millot, Patrick 1991. Evaluation of a Rule-based Approach to the Ergonomic "Static." *International Journal of Man-Machine Studies* 35:657–674.

Larkin, J. H. and Simon, H. A. 1987. Why a Diagram Is (Sometimes) Worth Ten Thousand Words. *Cognitive Science* 11:65–99.

Levesque, Hector 1988. Logic and the Complexity of Reasoning. *Journal of Philosophical Logic,* 17:355–389.

Mackinlay, Jock 1983. Intelligent Presentation: The Generation Problem for User Interfaces. Technical Report No. HPP-83-34, Heuristic Programming Project, Stanford University.

Mackinlay. Jock 1986. Automating the Design of Graphical Presentations of Relational Information. *ACM Transactions on Graphics* 5(2):110–1416.

Meyers, B. A. 1990. Taxonomies of Visual Programming and Program Visualization. *Journal of Visual Languages and Computing* 1(1):97–125.

Palmer, Stephen E. 1978. Fundamental Aspects of Cognitive Representation. In *Cognition and Categorization,* ed. Eleanor Rosch and Barbara B. Lloyd, 259–303. Hillsdale, N.J.: Lawrence Erlbaum Associates.

Roberts, Don D. 1973. *The Existential Graphs of Charles S. Peirce.* The Hague: Mouton.

Salvendy, Gavriel 1987. *Handbook of Human Factors.* New York: John Wiley and Sons.

Schubert, Lenhart 1976. Extending the Expressive Power of Semantic Networks. *Artificial Intelligence* 7(2):163–198.

Shin, Sun-Joo 1991. A Situation-theoretic Account of Valid Reasoning with Venn. In *Situation Theory and its Applications,* ed. Jon Barwise, Jean Mark Gawron, Gordon Plotkin, and Syun Tutiya, 581–605. Stanford, Calif.: Center for the Study of Language and Information.

Sowa, John F. 1979. Semantics of Conceptual Graphs. In Proceedings of the 17th Annual Meeting of the Association for Computational Linguistics, 39–44, La Jolla, Calif.

Sowa, John F. 1993. Relating Diagrams to Logic. In *Conceptual Graphs for Knowledge Representation* ed. G. Mineau, B. Moulin, and J. F. Sowa. Berlin: Springer.

Stenning, Keith, and Oberlander, Jon 1992. Implementing Logics in Diagrams. Presented at the AAAI Spring Symposium on Reasoning, Stanford, California.

Stenning, Keith, and Oberlander, Jon 1994. Spatial Containment and Set Membership: A Case Study of Analogy at Work. In *Analogical Connections,* ed. J. Barnden and K. Holyoak, 446–486. Hillsdale, N.J.: Lawrence Erlbaum Associates.

Stenning, Keith, and Oberlander, Jon 1995. A Cognitive Theory of Graphical and Linguistic Reasoning: Logic and Implementation. *Cognitive Science.*

Tufte, E. R. 1983 *The Visual Display of Quantitative Information.* Cheshire, Connecticut: Graphics Press.

11 Reasoning with Diagrammatic Representations

Dejuan Wang & John Lee
University of Edinburgh

Henk Zeevat
University of Amsterdam

11.1 Introduction

Diagrams can be used for reasoning about certain problems. A well-known example is syllogistic reasoning using Euler circles. In Figure 11.1, two diagrams represent the premises and another the conclusion. If we use the +-symbol and the arrow as indicated for connecting a set of premises to a conclusion, we can make distinctions here between valid and invalid reasoning and develop a logic of diagrams for the particular application of syllogistic logic.

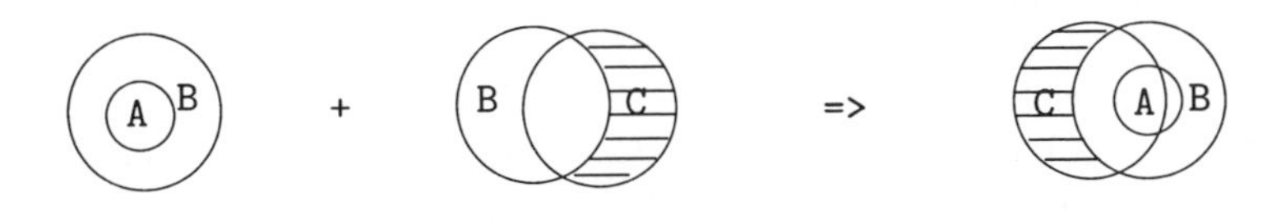

Figure 11.1
All A Are B + Some C Are Not $B \Rightarrow$ Some C Are Not A.

That diagrams can be used for this purpose should come as no surprise, once one accepts that diagrams contain information. In this respect, diagrams are like the formulas of a logical system or the sentences of natural languages. It is then reasonable that we can combine the information expressed in several diagrams to obtain a diagram that incorporates all or some of the information present in the premises. This conclusion diagram then expresses only information contained in the premises. Expressed in this way, there seems to be no particular problem about graphical reasoning and this chapter could be short. There are however a series of difficulties that considerably complicate the situation.

The most important is the characterization of what information a diagram contains. This problem first of all necessitates the assignment of a structure to diagrams and an interpretation of that structure as making a statement about some application domain. In contrast to logical languages, where within categories the assignment of meaning can be arbitrary, the interpretation of graphical constants cannot be arbitrary in the same way. This has to do with the problem of emergent objects and emergent facts in the construction of a diagram. Generally, if we have entered some facts (true about the application domain) in a diagram, other facts emerge. Whether these new facts are true about the application domain depends on the chosen interpretation. For example, the fact that circle A is included in circle B means that John (B) is the father of Bill (A). That circle B is included in circle C means that Charles is John's father. But we would be wrong to infer that Charles is Bill's father, even though this is what we should read from the picture if inclusion means fatherhood.

The second major departure from the usual symbolic logic comes as a consequence of a distinction in the structure of diagrams and formulas. In the latter, it is always possible to distinguish a main operator, a circumstance that considerably alleviates the characterization of the formal relationship between premises and conclusion. In diagrams, we end up with a non-trivial relation, that cannot in general be decomposed into minimal reasoning steps[1].

A third departure arises through the specificity properties inherent in graphical representation.[2] Graphical conclusions may be forced to overrepresent the information in the premises: there is more information in the conclusion than in the combined premises. In case this can happen in only one way and our interpretation is sound, we are dealing with the power of graphical reasoning: a new atomic fact has been inferred. But often, there is not a unique combination; there are various ways in which the specificity can be reached. In general therefore, we are dealing with inference relations, where a set of diagrammatic conclusions (interpreted disjunctively) is inferred from a (conjunctively interpreted) set of premises.

We can see an example of such a disjunction in Figure 11.1, where the shading is supposed to indicate that a certain area is known to be non-empty. We know that in the first premise it would be appropriate

[1]See however Sun-Joo (1991) for an account of how this may be achieved in the particular case of Venn-diagrams.

[2]See Stenning (1993) for a defence of the view that specificity is the main property dividing the graphical from the symbolic mode.

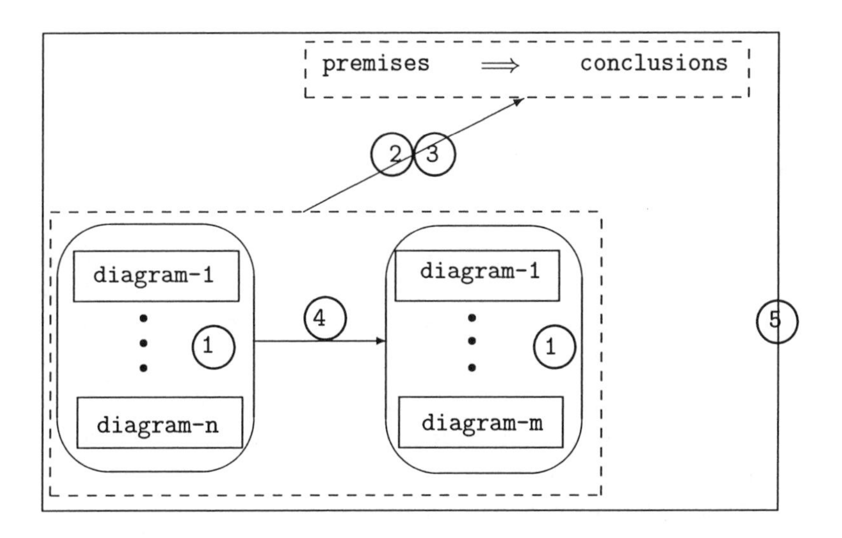

Figure 11.2
A Model of Reasoning with Diagrammatic Representations.

to shade the A circle—but what about in the conclusion? The A circle is cut by the C circle, and either or both parts of it could in fact be shaded, to give three distinct ways of modeling the combination of the premises, each of which however leads to the same conclusion. Later, in Section 11.6, we discuss the implications of this situation in more detail.

In this chapter, we attempt to give a formal framework for diagrammatic logic, and in particular a framework which can provide a basis for a computational treatment.

A model of diagrammatic reasoning must have the following three components: (a) a theory of the diagrams representing the premise and the conclusions, (b) a characterization of the inference, and (c) an interpretation which associates the diagrams to inferences about the application problem (see in Figure 11.2).

The chapter consists of the following parts, that can be derived from the model.

1. *Geometrical description of diagrams.* First, we need a formal description of the diagrams. This description should correctly reflect what one sees in a diagram when it is used in visual reasoning.
2. *Interpretations.* On the basis of the geometrical description of

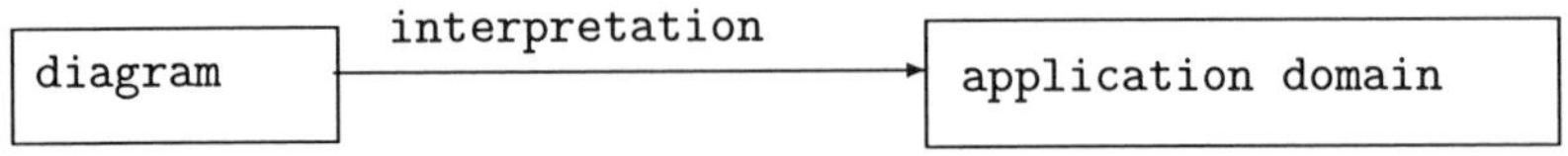

Figure 11.3
A Model of Simple Visual Reasoning.

diagrams, a notion of interpretation is developed relating diagrams to the domain objects. For example, if one interprets *circles* as *sets* and the *in* relation between circles as the $\subseteq$-relation between sets, then the diagram on the left in Figure 11.1 represents $A \subseteq B$.

3. *Correctly using diagrams.* Before studying reasoning with diagrammatic representations, we study a simpler form of visual reasoning which contains only *one* diagram, an interpretation and an application domain (see in Figure 11.3).

   First, we give a logical characterization of the conclusions one can draw from a single picture. We then discuss under which circumstances diagrams can be used successfully in visual reasoning. This comes down to answering the question: which properties must an interpretation have for it to represent correctly the subject matter of the application domain.

4. *Mapping rules between diagrams.* On this basis, we can investigate reasoning with diagrammatic representations. We start with introducing some mapping rules which can produce the possible conclusion diagrams from the premise diagrams. For example, a rule, which unifies the same labeled objects in two diagrams, forms the third diagram from the first two in Figure 11.1 (here the circles labeled with B are unified).

5. *A logical characterization of the reasoning.* This gives a formal semantics for reasoning with diagrammatic representations, which includes the meaning of a conclusion diagram and, if there is more than one conclusion diagram, the relationship between each of them and the real domain.

The above topics will occupy Section 11.2 to Section 11.6. Section 11.7 contains a discussion of some examples of reasoning with diagrammatic representations and Section 11.8 discusses related work and further research.

11.2 Geometrical Description of Diagrams

In this Section, we study the geometrical description of diagrams. Consider the following diagram:

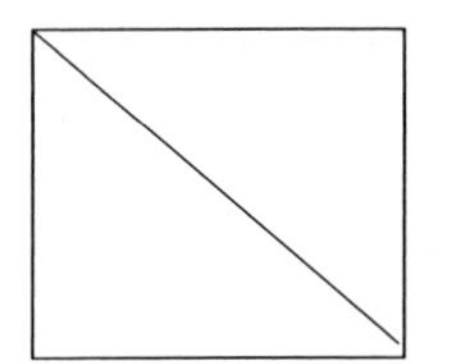

This diagram may be described as: *two triangles sharing one side*; *a square with a diagonal line* or *five lines* and so on. There are some problems that arise in such descriptions. First, although each of the descriptions seems to be acceptable, there is no reason to choose one instead of the others. Second, none of the descriptions seems to be complete in the sense that no more details can be added to the description. For instance, the first one can be enriched by describing the triangles as *right angled* triangles, by describing the shared side as *hypotenuse*, by describing the length of each side, its orientations, its positions in the plane. Thinking in this way, we may find it hard to have a description in which one can say that every detail in the diagram has been included. However, when we use diagrams to communicate with each other we are never troubled by such problems. In specific circumstances, we know how to describe a diagram and we also know to what extent we need to describe it. For instance, if we use *squares* to represent *sets* and *diagonal lines* to represent the fact that *the sets are empty*, we will describe the diagram as *a square with a diagonal line*. Though it is clear that the diagonal line divides the square into two triangles, this does not interest us. If we use *triangles* to represent *sets* and *two triangles sharing one side* to represent *two sets having the same size*, the above diagram will be described as *two triangles sharing one side*. Furthermore, if the *right angled* property is also used, e.g. to represent *integer sets*, the description will be *two right angled triangles sharing one side*.

We can conclude from this example that a diagram can be described in many different ways and that our choice of a description is guided by the intended *use* of the diagram. Choosing the proper description of a diagram in virtue of some interpretation seems a natural ability of human beings. It also seems one of the reasons why visual communication is so popular.

We now present a formal method for describing diagrams, in which the formal process is analogous to the retrieval by human beings of geometrical information from diagrams in visual communication.

In order to give diagrams a geometrical characterization, a graphical descriptive language is needed. As the above example tells us, a single diagram can be read in different ways depending on the intended use of the diagram. This suggests that we are concerned with the abstract structure of graphical descriptive languages and not with any particular language. The structure is abstract in the sense that for a particular application, suitable graphical entities can be entered into the structure to obtain a particular graphical language for the special purpose. The notion of graphical descriptive language consists of a graphical signature and a graphical theory. The expressions of a language are generated by a graphical signature and the geometrical meanings of the language expressions are characterized by a graphical theory over the graphical signature. The graphical signature we will use is an order-sorted signature (Goguen & Meseguer 1989) which can express classes of graphical objects as well as individual ones. In the order among its sorts, it reflects the inheritance relationship between classes of diagrams and gives a natural way of describing possible relations and operations on graphical entities. The graphical signature embodies a well-ordered structure which, on one hand, reflects the internal relationships between graphical objects and on the other provides a natural way to associate diagrams with applications via interpretations. Having a graphical theory as part of a graphical language allows a logical characterization of graphical inference. By *graphical inference* we mean in this chapter the algorithmic computation which deduces the spatial properties of graphical objects. It is one of our assumptions that one can model, by the algorithms for graphical inference, the ability of people to see the properties of graphical objects in a diagram.

The descriptions of particular diagrams should correctly reflect all that one sees in the diagram. We achieve this by a set of principles through which a diagram is described as a set of graphical objects and a set of formulae representing properties of and relations between the graphical objects. The set of principles consists of the following aspects: (1) a *partial graphical signature* reflecting the fact that in a particular diagram there are only some graphical objects; (2) *basic facts* (a basic fact is either an atomic formula or its negation) reflecting the fact that one can only see basic facts in a diagram; (3) *consistency* which guarantees that the basic facts included in the description of the diagram are only those contained in the diagram and (4) *maximality* which guarantees that the basic facts included in the description of the diagram exhaust what the diagram tells us.

11.2.1 Graphical Languages

In this section, an abstract notion of graphical (descriptive) language is presented.

Using diagrams in visual communication, one can see in a diagram not only a set of basic graphical objects (e.g. circles) and their properties (e.g. one circle is in the other) but also emergent graphical objects (e.g. a closed curve emerges from two overlapping circles) and their properties. Therefore, a graphical language should be able to express not only basic but also emergent graphical objects and their possible properties. Furthermore, one often uses a class of graphical objects (e.g. Venn diagrams) to represent a class of objects (e.g. sets) in the application domain. It is therefore natural to use a typed graphical language. Finally, between many classes of graphical objects there are inheritance relationships in the sense that one class (e.g. that of circles) is a subclass of another (e.g. the class of closed curves). A graphical language reflecting such natural relationships is suitable for supporting natural choices of graphical representations and their implementation.

Based on the above considerations, we will use order-sorted logical languages[3] (cf. Goguen & Meseguer 1989) as our graphical descriptive languages. The syntax of an order-sorted language is presented by an *order-sorted signature*, from which the expressions of the language are generated.

---

[3]For generality, except for the order-sorted syntactical structure, we do not fix a logical system here. See, for example, Goguen and R. Burstall (1984 & 1992) and Meseguer (1989) for discussions of "general logics." However, order-sorted first-order logic is assumed in examples.

Graphical Signature Informally, an order-sorted signature of a graphical language consists of

- a set of *sorts* standing for (the names of) classes of diagrams,
- a set of *function symbols*, standing for operations over graphical objects to represent graphical objects by means of terms, where constants (i.e. nullary functional symbols) express basic graphical objects and complex expressions express emergent graphical objects,
- a set of *predicate symbols*,standing for basic properties of and relations between graphical objects, and
- a partial-order between sorts expressing the subclass relationship between classes of graphical objects.

The *atomic formulas* of the language are formed by the predicate symbols and formulas are generated by logical connectives and quantifiers from the atomic formulas. Formulas which do not have free variables are called *sentences*.

The following gives a precise definition of graphical signature.

Definition 11.2.1
Order-Sorted & Graphical Signature
An *order-sorted signature* Σ is a quadruple $\Sigma = (\mathcal{S}, \leq, \mathcal{F}, \mathcal{P})$, where

- $(\mathcal{S}, \leq)$ is a partially ordered set of *sorts*, with a largest sort and a smallest sort.
- $\mathcal{F}$ is a set of *function symbols* (including constants), each of which is associated with a principal type of the form $s_1 \times \ldots \times s_n \rightarrow s$, where $n \geq 0$ and $s_i, s \in \mathcal{S}$. In $\mathcal{F}$, there is a constant $\perp$ with the smallest sort as its principal type.
- $\mathcal{P}$ is a set of *predicate symbols*, each of which is associated with a principal domain of the form $s_1 \times s_2 \times ... \times s_n$, where $n \geq 0$ and $s_i \in \mathcal{S}$.

A *graphical signature* is just an order-sorted signature, whose sorts, function symbols and predicate symbols are called *graphical sorts* (with the largest *Graph* and the smallest *Null*), *graphical operations* and *graphical predicates*, respectively.

Figure 11.4
An Example Graphical Signature Σ_0.

$\mathcal{S}$	*Point*, *Circle*, *Closed_curve*, *Graph*, *Null*
$\leq$	$Null \leq s \leq Graph$, for all $s \in \mathcal{S}$ $s \leq s$ for all $s \in \mathcal{S}$ $Circle \leq Closed\_curve$
$\mathcal{F}$	a, b, c, d : *Point*; A, B, C, D : *Circle*; E, F : *Closed_curve*; $\perp$: *Null*; *overlap* : *Circle* $\times$ *Circle* $\rightarrow$ *Closed_curve*; *merge* : *Closed_curve* $\times$ *Closed_curve* $\rightarrow$ *Graph*; ... ...
$\mathcal{P}$	in_1, *outside* : *Point* $\times$ *Circle*; in_2, *overlapping* : *Circle* $\times$ *Circle*; ... ...

We give some further explanations, using the graphical signature given in Figure 11.4.

The graphical sorts represent classes of graphical objects (e.g. Circle for the class of circles). The partial order over the graphical sorts describes a subclass relationship between the classes of graphical objects. For instance, "$Circle \leq Closed\_curve$" expresses that every circle is a closed curve. A function symbol with principal type $s_1 \times ... \times s_n \rightarrow s$ also has $s'_1 \times ... \times s'_n \rightarrow s'$ as its type, if $s_i \geq s'_i$ and $s \leq s'$. Similarly, a predicate symbol with principal domain $s_1 \times ... \times s_n$ also has $s'_1 \times ... \times s'_n$ as its domain, if $s_i \geq s'_i$. For instance, for the signature in Figure 11.4, *merge* also has *Circle* $\times$ *Circle* $\rightarrow$ *Graph* as its type.

Every graphical signature has a largest sort *Graph*, a smallest sort *Null* and a constant $\perp$ of type *Null*. $\perp$ represents a *null* object and *Graph* stands for the class of arbitrary graphical objects. Note that every graphical sort has $\perp$ as an object and hence is non-empty. The sorts *Graph* and *Null* play an important role in avoiding partial function problems. For example, applying *overlap* to two non-overlapping circles forms a null object, and merging two arbitrary closed curves together may not form an object of any graphical sort except *Graph* (see the operation *merge* in Figure 11.4). By introducing a largest sort, a graphical language becomes complete in the sense that any diagram can be described by the language. For instance, if there is no largest sort in a graphical signature then no matter how many sorts the signature has, there is a diagram which includes a graphical object which does not belong to any of the sorts. So the graphical language fails to describe this diagram. However, if a graphical signature has a largest sort, even if it has only few sorts it will be able to describe any kind of diagram since all graphical objects at least have the largest sort *Graph* as their sorts.

The graphical function symbols are the possible operations over graphical objects, which are used to generate the language *terms*. The terms in a graphical signature denote expressible graphical objects. Examples of terms in the graphical signature in Figure 11.4 are: a, A, $\perp$, $overlap(A, B)$, $overlap(\perp, A)$, $merge(overlap(A, B), A)$, $merge(A, E)$. There are two kinds of graphical objects, basic graphical objects and emergent graphical objects. All the constants in the set of function symbols (e.g. points a, b, circles A, B) represent basic graphical objects and applying a function symbol (e.g. *overlap*) to terms (e.g. A, B) forms emergent graphical objects (e.g. $overlap(A, B)$ representing an emergent closed curve if A and B are overlapping or a null object otherwise).

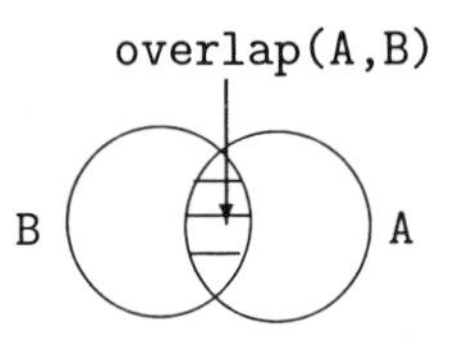

The predicates (more precisely, the atomic formulae generated from them) describe the basic properties of and relationships between graphical objects. For example, in the signature in Figure 11.4, the atomic formulae, $in_1(a, A)$ and $overlapping(\perp, A)$, can be generated, which describe properties of graphical objects like a *point is inside a circle*. Formulae like $\forall x, y, z : Circle.\ in_2(x, y) \wedge in_2(y, z) \Rightarrow in_2(x, z)$ can also be generated to represent the transitivity of the "inside" relation between circles.

Definition 11.2.1 only gives the structure of a graphical signature. Following this structure one may build any kind of graphical signature. Though the notion of graphical signature is purely syntactic, the choice of certain graphical sorts, function symbols and predicate symbols in one's graphical signature must be based on semantic considerations. In practice, a graphical signature is built as consisting of all of the possible sorts, function symbols and predicates which one may wish to use for a certain application. Therefore, once a graphical signature is selected, the graphical objects and those of their properties which are of interest are the ones expressible in the signature. For instance, if one chooses the graphical signature in Figure 11.4, one would not be interested in talking about triangles, although they may be regarded as arbitrary graphs of type *Graph*. If one builds a graphical language for solving syllogisms, circles and various operations and predicates over circles (e.g. overlapping, merge) will be included in the graphical signature. However, if the application is about diagram chasing (Arbib and Manes 1975) (see the system GROVER [Plummer and Bailin 1992]) all the functions and predicates related to circles do not need to be included in the graphical signature.

Notation Let Σ be a signature. We shall use $T(\Sigma)$, $F(\Sigma)$ and $At(\Sigma)$ to denote the sets of terms, formulae and atomic formulae over Σ, respectively.

Graphical Inference: An Axiomatic Characterization A graphical signature presents the syntax of the graphical language. In the above explanation of the graphical language, we pretended that there was a "common-sense" understanding of the graphical sorts, operations and predicates. In fact, the real meaning of the symbols and expressions in the language is determined by the associated mechanism of graphical inference.

Graphical inference is the computation of the graphical objects formed by graphical operations such as *overlap* and to infer the properties of graphical objects in a diagram such as whether a triangle is inside a circle. In practice, graphical inference is realized by geometrical algorithms. In other words, graphical operations and predicates are implemented by programs which give an (operational) semantics to graphical expressions in the language. A theoretical characterization of graphical inference can be given in an axiomatic way, that is to characterize by a logical theory the general properties of all diagrams.

More specifically, we assume that graphical inference is axiomatizable by a logical theory over the graphical signature, called *the graphical theory* of the graphical language. Let Σ be the graphical signature of a graphical language. Then the graphical theory $\mathcal{T}$ is a set of logical formulas over Σ which is consistent and closed under the consequence relation of the underlying logical system and characterizes the graphical inference.

Figure 11.5
Example Formulas in a Graphical Theory.

$\mathcal{T}$	$in_1(x,y) \Rightarrow \neg(outside(x,y))$ $in_2(x,y) \Rightarrow overlapping(x,y)$ $overlapping(x,y) \Rightarrow overlapping(y,x)$ $in_1(x,y) \wedge in_2(y,z) \Rightarrow in_1(x,z)$ ......

Formally, a graphical theory is just a consistent logical theory. However, the intention here is that the graphical theory $\mathcal{T}$ gives an adequate axiomatic characterization of the general properties of diagrams and graphical inference (the behavior of graphical algorithms in particular). Being closed under logical inference, a graphical theory is necessarily infinite, but it usually (and always in practice) has a finite presentation.[4] It should also be emphasized that the graphical theory contains *only* the general properties that all diagrams (intended models) share, but *not* the specific properties of particular diagrams. For example, the presentation of the graphical theory over the graphical signature in Figure 11.4 would contain (among others) the formulae listed in Figure 11.5, where it is assumed that the variables are universally quantified (over appropriate sorts). But, the theory does not contain any of the atomic facts such as $in_1(a, A)$.

It is useful to emphasize that we think of the graphical theory as fixed once and for all. For a given graphical language, we can restrict the graphical theory to the signature of the language. Also, it is possible to allow for preferred modes of geometrical expression (e.g. take *in* between circles as *reflexive* or not). The graphical theory intuitively expresses the geometrical truth about the graphical screen.

Therefore, a graphical language $\mathcal{L}$ is completely presented by a graphical signature together with the graphical theory that characterizes graphical inference. From now on, we shall use the following notation.

Notation Let $\mathcal{L}$ be a graphical language. Then, $\Sigma(\mathcal{L})$ and $\mathcal{T}(\mathcal{L})$ will be used to denote the graphical signature and the graphical theory of $\mathcal{L}$,

[4]It is an interesting topic to study what kind of presentation of graphical theory is suitable for implementation of a system of visual communication. Some related research develops suitable graphical theories for specific applications, e.g. the study of Venn Diagrams (Sun-Joo 1991) and the discussion of Euler circles and syllogisms (Stenning 1993).

respectively; that is, $\mathcal{L} = (\Sigma(\mathcal{L}), \mathcal{T}(\mathcal{L}))$.

11.2.2 A Geometrical Characterization of Diagrams

Pictures are expressed by terms in our graphical language and can be viewed as models of the graphical theory of the language. In order to describe diagrams, we shall introduce a notion of *situation* [5] based on which we give the geometrical characterization of diagrams to express *what one can see in a diagram.*

There are two aspects that must be characterized to describe the information that a diagram carries: (a) the graphical objects that occur in the diagram and (b) the properties those graphical objects have. For the first, one has to delimit those graphical objects that occur in the diagram and exclude those that do not appear in it. To meet this demand, we introduce the notion of a *subsignature.*

Definition 11.2.2
Subsignature
A signature $\Sigma = (\mathcal{S}, \leq, \mathcal{F}, \mathcal{P})$ is a *subsignature* of another, $\Sigma' = (\mathcal{S}', \leq', \mathcal{F}', \mathcal{P}')$, if and only if:

1. $\mathcal{S}$ is a subset of $\mathcal{S}'$ and contains the largest and smallest sorts *Graph* and *Null*;
2. $\leq$ is the restriction of $\leq'$ over $\mathcal{S}$;
3. $\mathcal{F}$ and $\mathcal{P}$ are subsets of $\mathcal{F}'$ and $\mathcal{P}'$, respectively.

We shall write $\Sigma \sqsubseteq \Sigma'$ when Σ is a subsignature of Σ'.

The graphical objects that occur in a diagram can be presented by the terms generated from a subsignature of the graphical signature. For example, consider the diagram shown in Figure 11.6 (1). The graphical objects in it correspond to the subsignature Σ_0 (see in Figure 11.6[2]) of the graphical signature in Figure 11.4.

The properties of the graphical objects in a diagram are to be characterized axiomatically. We introduce a notion of "situation" to characterize several important ideas which give the geometrical semantics of diagrams. A situation is a maximal set of formulas expressing basic properties over a subsignature consistent with respect to the graphical

[5] We use *situation* here in a way that is unrelated to the notion of situation as developed by Barwise and Perry (1983),

theory (graphical inference). The notions of basic fact and of situation are given in the following definitions, followed by explanations why the latter gives an adequate characterization of pictorial properties.

Definition 11.2.3
Basic Facts
Let Σ be an order-sorted signature. A *basic fact* over Σ is either an atomic sentence over Σ or the negation of an atomic sentence over Σ. The set of basic facts over Σ is denoted by $\mathcal{B}(\Sigma)$.

Definition 11.2.4
Situation
Let $\mathcal{L}$ be a graphical language and $\Sigma \sqsubseteq \Sigma(\mathcal{L})$ be a subsignature of the graphical signature of $\mathcal{L}$. A *situation* S over Σ is a maximal set of basic facts over Σ consistent with respect to the graphical theory $\mathcal{T}(\mathcal{L})$, that is, S is a set of formulae over Σ such that

1. $S \subseteq \mathcal{B}(\Sigma)$;
2. S is consistent with respect to $\mathcal{T}(\mathcal{L})$, i.e. $\mathcal{T}(\mathcal{L}) \cup S \nvdash \mathit{false}$; and
3. S is maximal, i.e. for any set $M \subseteq \mathcal{B}(\Sigma)$ of basic facts over Σ, $M = S$ if $S \subseteq M$ and M is consistent with respect to $\mathcal{T}(\mathcal{L})$.

A situation over a subsignature contains the properties of a diagram whose graphical objects are characterized by the subsignature. For instance, the situation in Figure 11.6 (3) contains the properties that the diagram shown in Figure 11.6 (1) has.

The notion of situation captures three important aspects of the properties of those graphical objects occurring in a diagram: basic facts, consistency and maximality.

Basic Facts The first condition, basic facts, captures an important observation:

- The properties that can be seen in a diagram are the basic ones (expressed by the basic facts).

A diagram is only a concrete model of the graphical theory;in a particular diagram, one can only see the basic properties of the graphical objects, but *not* those general properties or general laws about the graphical inference which are characterized by the graphical theory. For example, consider the following diagram.

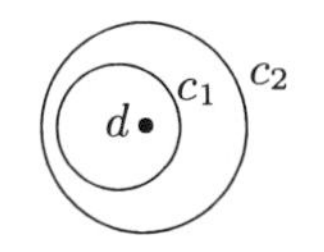

One can see that the dot is inside both of the circles and the smaller circle is inside the larger one. However, one can *not* see in the above diagram the general properties such as "for any dot x and any circles y and z, x is inside z if x is inside y and y is inside z," which is expressed by the following logical formula (cf. , Figure 11.5):

$$\forall x : Dot\ \forall y, z : Circle.\ in_1(x,y) \wedge in_2(y,z) \Rightarrow in_1(x,z).$$

Some people may argue that they can see such general properties in a diagram. In our view, however, such general properties are *not* what they *see* in a diagram, but rather what they *realize* by associating them with the basic facts they see in the diagram, which are particular instances of the general properties. Such a possibility of associating the basic facts seen in a particular diagram with certain general properties by generalization is one of the interesting and important aspects of visual communication, which allows people to *illustrate* (but not to prove) some general principles such as general algebraic laws on set operations using particular diagrams such as Venn diagrams.

A remark here is necessary. We have only included the basic facts into the geometrical semantics of a diagram, but excluded those properties of the graphical objects in a diagram expressed by other composite sentences such as $in_1(d, c_1) \wedge in_2(c_1, c_2) \Rightarrow in_1(d, c_2)$. It is debatable whether the logical consequences of the basic facts can be seen in a diagram. It may be reasonable to say that the conjunction of depictable basic facts can be seen in a diagram. We think that this is already covered by the set of depictable basic properties. However, it would be more questionable whether one can see a disjunctive fact (and similarly, an implication). So we believe that we do not lose any generality by our characterization via the basic facts.

Consistency The *consistency* condition for a situation reflects the fact that diagrams cannot convey contradictory graphical information. In other words, for a basic property represented by an atomic sentence P

about some objects in a diagram (say, a point is inside a circle), it is impossible to see both P and $\neg P$ in the diagram. E.g. it would be absurd to see a point both as inside and as outside a circle.

Some may hold that there are diagrams which convey contradictory information. For instance, a reasonable graphical theory should reflect the fact that in a 3D space, for any plane there is at most only one of its sides which can be seen. However, if we consider the following diagram

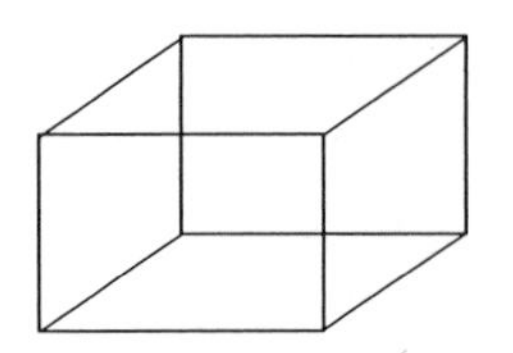

we may be confused by sometimes seeing the top sides of the horizontal planes and other time seeing their reverse sides. Does this mean that diagrams may convey contradictory information? In our view, such a contradiction does not directly come from the basic facts conveyed by a diagram but is formed by another process. For the above diagram, the inconsistent observation results from moving the apparent horizon above the cube at one time and below it at another time. That means that the cube has been viewed twice and each time in a different reference system which should be represented by different graphical theories. It is clear that in one reference system we can only see either the top or its reverse side.

One distinction between inconsistency and optical illusion can be mentioned here. A diagram may cause an optical illusion but will never convey inconsistent information. Optical illusions can be described as: a property P in a diagram is not recognized as such but rather as its negation. But this does not mean that both P and $\neg P$ exist in the diagram. For example, consider the following diagram.

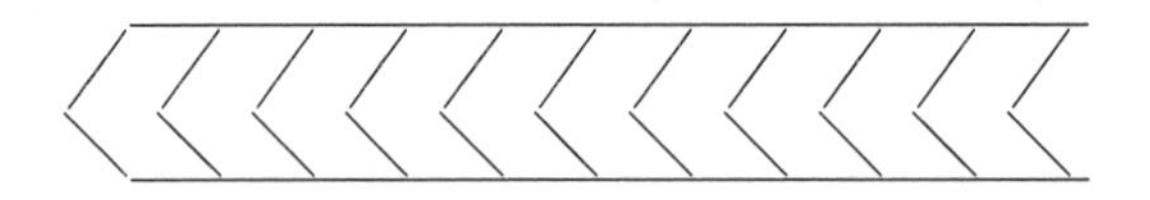

The optical illusion in this diagram results from the set of arrows which causes us to see a pair of non-parallel lines which are in fact parallel according to the geometrical definition. However, this only means that the diagram shows one property which *we* read as its negation rather than as both the property and its negation.

Maximality Finally, diagrams do give us *maximal* information about the properties of the graphical objects, as characterized in the third condition in the definition of situation. In other words, for a basic property represented by an atomic sentence P about some objects in a diagram, either P or $\neg P$ can be seen in the diagram. This consideration leads to the maximality condition for situations.

The distinction between maximality and the perceptual Gestalt that a diagram may have can be mentioned here. Consider the following diagram.

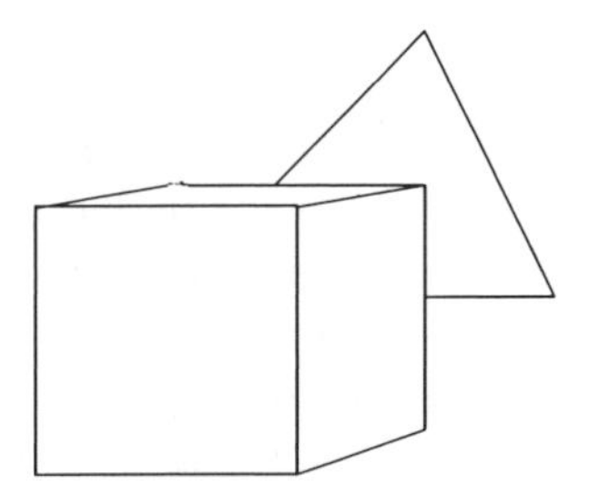

Usually, people view the shape connected with the cube as a triangle behind the cube, though it is just a partial triangle. Some may be confused by our claim of maximality with respect to such a perceptual Gestalt, saying that diagrams do not always give us maximal information, as in this example the shape seen by us is a triangle while in the diagram it is only a partial triangle. However, in our view, the complete triangle is *not* what we *see* in the diagram, but what we *guess*. What we see in the diagram is indeed a partial triangle. The above perceptual Gestalt could be described by introducing a special graphical language whose signature included sorts for various classes of incomplete triangles, which would be seen as triangles by Gestalt. Then we could describe triangles in a diagram by looking not only for complete triangles but also for the Gestalt triangles. However, we do not discuss the Gestalt issue in this chapter but only point out the difference between perceptual Gestalt and the maximality condition for situations.

Maximality, together with the consistency condition, implies the completeness of basic facts of a situation. To emphasize this aspect, *Maximality is a key notion to capture the information that a diagram provides.* Also note that a situation S over Σ is necessarily closed with respect to the graphical theory $\mathcal{T}(\mathcal{L})$ of the graphical language in the sense that $\{P \in \mathcal{B}(\Sigma) \mid \mathcal{T}(\mathcal{L}) \cup S \vdash P\} \subseteq S$, that is, *every basic property of the graphical objects in a diagram is included in a situation provided that it is a logical consequence of the graphical theory $\mathcal{T}(\mathcal{L})$ and the basic facts in the situation.*[6]

Invisible Properties The above notion of situation has essentially captured the geometrical semantics of diagrams, except for the following minor point concerning the "null" graphical objects represented by the constant $\perp$. A diagram may correspond to more than one situation because, for any invisible property involving null objects such as $in_1(\perp, A)$, there are (at least) two different situations corresponding to the same diagram, one containing $in_1(\perp, A)$ and the other its negation $\neg in_1(\perp, A)$. Since the properties of any null graphical object (say, $in_1(\perp, A)$) can not be seen in a diagram, one is not interested in these properties. To deal with this, we can define an observational equivalence between the situations over the same subsignature Σ by taking the sort *Null* as a non-observable sort (cf., the study of observational equivalence in program specification; see, for example, Sannella and Tarlecki [1987]). Then, a diagram $\mathcal{G}$ corresponds to an equivalence class $[S_{\mathcal{G}}]$ of the situations corresponding to the diagram $\mathcal{G}$.

Taking account of the above consideration, the geometrical characterization of a diagram $\mathcal{G}$, whose graphical objects are characterized by subsignature $\Sigma_{\mathcal{G}}$, is given by the following set of basic facts:

$$\mathcal{A}_{\mathcal{G}} = \bigcap [S_{\mathcal{G}}]$$

where the invisible properties of null graphical objects are excluded by taking the intersection of the equivalent situations subject to observational equivalence (taking $Null$ as a non-observable sort).

---

[6]This can be simply proved as follows. Any $P \in \mathcal{B}(\Sigma)$ being a logical consequence of $\mathcal{T}(\mathcal{L}) \cup S$, $\mathcal{T}(\mathcal{L}) \cup S \cup \{P\}$ is logically consistent, by the consistency of the underlying logical system. Therefore, $S \cup \{P\}$ is consistent with respect to $\mathcal{T}(\mathcal{L})$, and hence $P \in S$ by the maximality of the situation S.

When we build a graphical language, the "null" graphical object ($\perp$) should be treated in a careful way. Besides some obvious way in which the "null" graphical object is made (e.g. overlap of two separated circles), overlapping a filled area and an object may also make the "null" object. The characterization of such overlapping in the graphical theory should be treated carefully so that the geometrical characterization of diagrams meets the requirements of the visual communication. It is our opinion that the graphical objects used in visual communication should always be seen by the users. It does not make sense from a visual point of view to think that there is a square inside the filled circle in the following diagram (1), unless it can be seen as in the diagram (2) or it can be partially seen and can be recognized as a square according to the perceptual Gestalt (3).

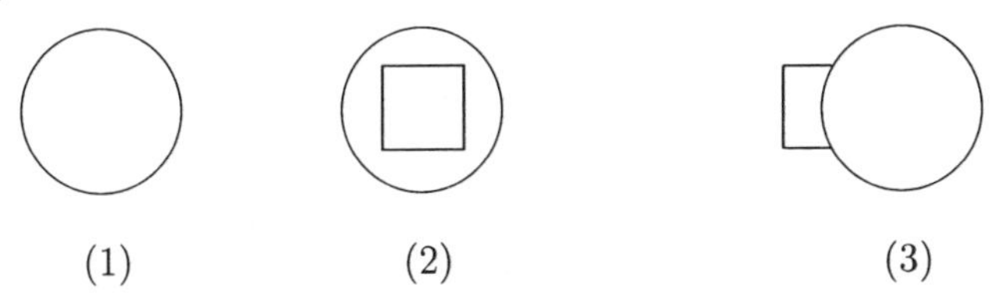

(1) (2) (3)

Therefore, we suggest that the drawing system makes every drawing visible (see the above diagram (2) as an example) in a visual communication supporting environment, otherwise, the graphical theory should give correct axioms so that the geometrical characterization of a diagram correctly reflects what one can see in the diagram.

A Geometrical Characterization of Diagrams To summarize, a diagram is given a formal geometrical characterization by capturing its graphical objects by means of a subsignature and characterizing its properties axiomatically as above.

Definition 11.2.5
The Geometrical Characterization of Diagrams
Let $\mathcal{L}$ be a graphical language and $\mathcal{G}$ a diagram. The geometrical characterization of $\mathcal{G}$ in $\mathcal{L}$ is given as a pair:

$$[\![\mathcal{G}]\!] = (\Sigma_{\mathcal{G}}, \mathcal{A}_{\mathcal{G}})$$

where $\Sigma_{\mathcal{G}}$ is the subsignature of $\Sigma(\mathcal{L})$ characterizing the graphical objects of $\mathcal{G}$, and $\mathcal{A}_{\mathcal{G}}$ is the set of basic facts as defined above.

Figure 11.6
An Example Diagram and Its Geometrical Semantics.

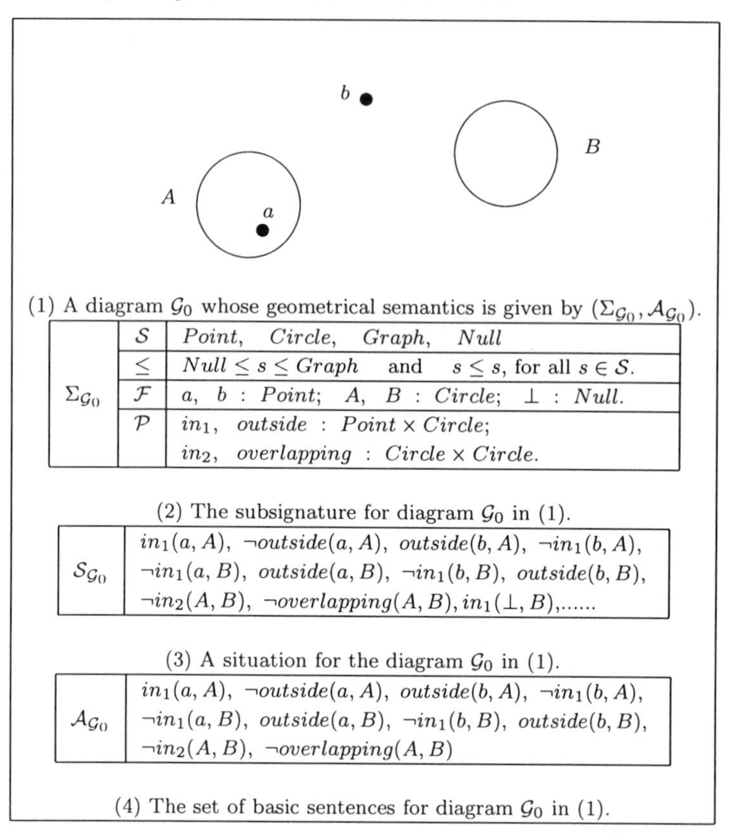

(1) A diagram $\mathcal{G}_0$ whose geometrical semantics is given by $(\Sigma_{\mathcal{G}_0}, \mathcal{A}_{\mathcal{G}_0})$.

$\Sigma_{\mathcal{G}_0}$	$\mathcal{S}$	*Point, Circle, Graph, Null*
	$\leq$	$Null \leq s \leq Graph$ and $s \leq s$, for all $s \in \mathcal{S}$.
	$\mathcal{F}$	$a,\ b$: *Point*; $A,\ B$: *Circle*; $\perp$: *Null*.
	$\mathcal{P}$	in_1, *outside* : *Point* × *Circle*; in_2, *overlapping* : *Circle* × *Circle*.

(2) The subsignature for diagram $\mathcal{G}_0$ in (1).

$\mathcal{S}_{\mathcal{G}_0}$	$in_1(a, A)$, $\neg outside(a, A)$, $outside(b, A)$, $\neg in_1(b, A)$, $\neg in_1(a, B)$, $outside(a, B)$, $\neg in_1(b, B)$, $outside(b, B)$, $\neg in_2(A, B)$, $\neg overlapping(A, B)$, $in_1(\perp, B)$,......

(3) A situation for the diagram $\mathcal{G}_0$ in (1).

$\mathcal{A}_{\mathcal{G}_0}$	$in_1(a, A)$, $\neg outside(a, A)$, $outside(b, A)$, $\neg in_1(b, A)$, $\neg in_1(a, B)$, $outside(a, B)$, $\neg in_1(b, B)$, $outside(b, B)$, $\neg in_2(A, B)$, $\neg overlapping(A, B)$

(4) The set of basic sentences for diagram $\mathcal{G}_0$ in (1).

For example, the geometrical characterization of the diagram in Figure 11.6 (1) is given by the subsignature $\Sigma_{\mathcal{G}_0}$ in Figure 11.6 (2) and the set of depictable basic properties $\mathcal{A}_{\mathcal{G}_0}$ in Figure 11.6 (4).

11.3 Interpretation

It is often said that a picture is worth a thousand words, but it seems hard to say which picture is worth which thousand words. In fact, if this could be figured out, a universal visual communication language could have been defined and we would study very different questions in the research of visual communication. However, according to our experience of using pictures in communication, a picture can be worth many different thousands of words. It depends on how we assign meanings to pictures, i.e. it depends on the interpretations. This interpretation makes the picture worth this thousand words and that interpretation makes it worth that thousand. Furthermore, on an improper interpretation, the picture may not be worth anything at all.

In other words, there is a variety of meanings in the use of pictures in communication. This *variety* of meanings in use seems to be essential in understanding the general structure of visual communication. The variety of meanings does *not* just refer to the fact that the graphical entities in a diagram may be assigned (or understood) to have many different meanings, although that is an important aspect of the use of diagrams in communication. Another aspect of this variety is that, in the use of diagrams in communication based on one's *intended* interpretation of the graphical entities, one often sees that the information carried by a diagram is subject to a certain kind of *abstraction*. In other words, one often emphasizes some of the properties of the graphical objects, but at the same time intentionally ignores (or abstracts away from) the other properties. For instance, using Venn diagrams to illustrate the algebraic laws about sets, one ignores irrelevant properties of the diagrams such as the size of the circles. Also, one does not (and should not) think that the fact that two circles are overlapping implies by itself that the represented sets have common elements. What this says is that, when using diagrams in communication, one does not and should not regard all of the information one can see in the diagrams as being relevant to the subject matter. This shows that the intended interpretation should concern only the relevant information and ignore the irrelevant. It is this possibility of abstraction by interpretations that enables diagrams to be useful in visual communication.

Meaning variety is a key notion for understanding the use of diagrams in visual communication. Our study of graphical interpretation will be guided by this observation to provide a general and flexible formal framework for interpretations.

In visual communication, usually, it is not just a diagram as a whole that is assigned a meaning; more importantly, the component graphical entities such as subpictures and emergent graphical objects, and their possible properties must be regarded as having meanings so that they contribute information in communication. For example, using a Venn diagram to illustrate the distributive law of the set-theoretic operations $\cup$ and $\cap$, the emergent graphical object formed by the overlapping of two circles represents $B \cap C$, and what is obtained by merging this emergent graphical object with another circle represents $A \cup (B \cap C)$. Therefore, the meaning interpretation framework should reflect this aspect as well.

Summarizing the above, the notion of interpretation should reflect the following three aspects.

- The same class of graphical objects and properties may be interpreted and hence used to represent different objects and properties in different applications.
- The notion of interpretation should be flexible to reflect the uses of diagrams where the communication concerns and concentrates on only a part of the properties of the graphical objects in a diagram and ignores the rest.
- What can be interpreted (used) in communication includes not only the simple graphical components of a diagram and their properties, but also the more complicated components such as emergent graphical objects and their properties.

11.3.1 Interpretations

Intuitively, an interpretation maps graphical entities to entities in an application domain in a coherent way so that it respects the necessary relationships between objects. The simplest way to formalize such a notion of interpretation in our formal framework is to consider the notion of signature morphisms (renaming maps),[7] which map sorts to sorts, function symbols to function symbols and predicate symbols to predicate symbols. However, in practice, we find that it is sometimes helpful to use a single graphical function/predicate symbol to represent a composed function (term) or predicate (propositional function). For example, we may need this generality to allow a binary graphical operation with principal type $s \times s \rightarrow s$ to be used to represent a composed operation $\lambda xy.(\overline{\overline{x} \cap \overline{y}})$ in set theory. This can be done by allowing the

[7] It may be the case that reasoning in an application domain is based on a logical system which is different from the logical system for graphical inference. If that is the case, to interpret graphical inference into the application domain, one has to consider a map from the logic for graphical inference to that in the application domain. See, for example, Meseguer's discussion in Meseguer (1989) on general logics and interpretations between them. Here, for simplicity, we consider the case where the same logical system is used and this is enough to explain our ideas.

interpretation of a function symbol (predicate symbol) into a "generalized term (formula)."[8] A generalized term may have an "arrow sort" (e.g. $\lambda xy.\overline{\overline{x} \cap \overline{y}} \ : \ set \times set \rightarrow set$) and a generalized formula may be a propositional function over some domain.

Notation Let Σ be a signature. Then, $GT(\Sigma)$ and $GF(\Sigma)$ denote the sets of generalized terms and generalized formulas, respectively.

Definition 11.3.1
Interpretation
Let $\mathcal{L}$ be a graphical language and $\Sigma = (\mathcal{S}, \leq, \mathcal{F}, \mathcal{P})$ an order-sorted signature (of the application language). An *interpretation* $\mathcal{I}$ from the graphical language to Σ $\mathcal{I}$: $\Sigma(\mathcal{L}) \rightharpoonup \Sigma$ is a quadruple $(\Sigma_{\mathcal{I}}, \mathcal{I}_{\mathcal{S}}, \mathcal{I}_{\mathcal{F}}, \mathcal{I}_{\mathcal{P}})$, where

- $\Sigma_{\mathcal{I}} = (\mathcal{S}_{\mathcal{I}}, \leq_{\mathcal{I}}, \mathcal{F}_{\mathcal{I}}, \mathcal{P}_{\mathcal{I}})$ is a subsignature of the graphical signature $\Sigma(\mathcal{L})$, called the *signature of* $\mathcal{I}$;
- $\mathcal{I}_{\mathcal{S}} \ : \ \mathcal{S}_{\mathcal{I}} \rightarrow \mathcal{S}$ is a function which preserves the partial order between sorts and the largest and smallest sorts;
- $\mathcal{I}_{\mathcal{F}} \ : \ \mathcal{F}_{\mathcal{I}} \rightarrow GT(\Sigma)$ is a type-preserving function; and
- $\mathcal{I}_{\mathcal{P}} \ : \ \mathcal{P}_{\mathcal{I}} \rightarrow GF(\Sigma)$ is a domain-preserving function.

Figure 11.7 describes an example subsignature $\Sigma_{\mathcal{I}}$ of the graphical signature Σ_0 in Figure 11.4, a signature Σ for the domain of sets and an interpretation $\mathcal{I}: \Sigma_0 \rightharpoonup \Sigma$ whose signature is $\Sigma_{\mathcal{I}}$.

Partial Mapping ($\Sigma_{\mathcal{I}}$) The above notion of interpretation from a graphical language to an application domain reflects the requirements we have described in last section. In particular, an interpretation is a *partial* map over the graphical signature in the sense that it is defined only over a part of the graphical signature (the signature of the interpretation). This reflects the second aspect of use of pictures and allows the user to specify an interpretation that allows her to concentrate on certain kinds of graphical objects and properties but ignores the others. In other words, choosing an interpretation over a certain subsignature can provide the necessary control over how pictures are used in

[8] Roughly speaking, a generalized term (formula) is a term where λ-notation is used to represent complex functions.

Figure 11.7
An Interpretation.

$\Sigma_{\mathcal{I}}$	$\mathcal{S}_{\mathcal{I}}$	*Point, Circle, Graph, Null*
	$\leq_{\mathcal{I}}$	$Null \leq s \leq Graph$ and $s \leq s$, for all $s \in \mathcal{S}$.
	$\mathcal{F}_{\mathcal{I}}$	a, b : *Point*; A, B : *Circle*; $\perp$: *Null*.
	$\mathcal{P}_{\mathcal{I}}$	in_1 : *Point* $\times$ *Circle*;
Σ	$\mathcal{S}$	*Elem, Set,* ... ...
	$\leq$	... ...
	$\mathcal{F}$	a, b, c, d : *Elem*; A, B, C, D : *Set*; ... ...
	$\mathcal{P}$	$\in$: *Elem* $\times$ *Set*; $\subseteq$: *Set* $\times$ *Set*; ... ...
$\mathcal{I}$	$\mathcal{I}_{\mathcal{S}}$	*Point* $\mapsto$ *Elem*, *Circle* $\mapsto$ *Set*, ...
	$\mathcal{I}_{\mathcal{F}}$	$A \mapsto A$, $B \mapsto B$, $a \mapsto a$, $b \mapsto b$,
	$\mathcal{I}_{\mathcal{P}}$	$in_1 \mapsto \in$.

communication. This also sheds some light on the implementation of a supporting system, where the implemented graphical language is rather rich for wide applications and, for a particular application, only a part of the graphical language is under consideration.

Sorts ($\mathcal{I}_{\mathcal{S}}$) Mapping graphical sorts to the sorts in an application domain naturally reflects the fact that in visual communication, we always use a class of graphical objects to represent a class of objects in an application domain [9]. It only creates confusion if one maps one class of graphical objects to two different kinds of things in the application. For example, by mapping some circles into sets, other circles into elements and *inside* into the *subset* relation for sets or the *membership* relation for elements, the following picture confuses us because it is unclear whether B is an element of A or a subset of A.

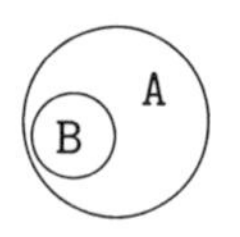

[9]Here, we assume that the underlying graphical signature $\Sigma(\mathcal{L})$ is rich enough to support any choice of picture classes. However, in practice, it may be the case that there is not a suitable class of graphical objects in the graphical language which can be used to represent the class of objects in the application domain. This can be solved by introducing a picture specification mechanism (Wang & Lee 1993) which supports users in creating new classes of graphical objects (i.e. adding new sorts into the graphical signature) according to the requirements of the problem solving.

An interpretation must also respect the subtyping relation (i.e. partial order preserving) which guarantees the accuracy of the use of classes of pictures in representing classes of objects in an application domain. For example, mapping circles to men and closed curves to persons is only valid if the type of men is a subtype of type of persons in the application domain. It might be argued by some that the fact that they use circles to represent men and closed curves to represent cats does not mean that all men are cats. This claim can only be maintained if the closed curves are specified to be closed curves excluding circles.

During visual communication, people use conventions according to their needs, whether they are aware of these or not. And in our formal framework, such conventions determine graphical languages and interpretations.

Objects and Properties ($\mathcal{I_F}$ and $\mathcal{I_P}$) Graphical objects (and their spatial properties) are allowed to be used in visual communication by means of the mapping of graphical function symbols (and graphical predicate symbols) to application objects, functions and predicates. $\mathcal{I_F}$ ($\mathcal{I_P}$) must be type (domain) preserving so that the mapping between functions (predicates) is consistent with the mapping between sorts. For example, if *Circle* is interpreted to *Set* then all the null-ary function symbols (i.e. the representations of graphical objects) with sort *Circle* must be mapped into the objects of sort *Set*. Furthermore, emergent graphical objects can be used by the mapping of n-ary (n $\geq$ 1) function symbols such as mapping $overlap : Closed\_curve \times Closed\_curve \rightarrow Closed\_curve$ into $\cap : Set \times Set \rightarrow Set$. A function (predicate) symbol can be mapped to a generalized term (formula). For example, if $\mathcal{I_S}(s) = set$ and $union : s \times s \rightarrow s$, we may have $\mathcal{I_F}(union) = \lambda xy.(\overline{\overline{x} \cap \overline{y}})$.

An interpretation as defined above is naturally extended to the terms and formulas over the signature of $\mathcal{I}$ (cf. Goguen and R. Burstall 1992). For example, $\mathcal{I}(merge(A, overlap(B,C)))=\mathcal{I}(merge)(\mathcal{I}(A), \mathcal{I}\,(overlap)$ $(\mathcal{I}(B), \mathcal{I}(C)))$. We shall use the following notation.

Notation Let $\mathcal{I}$ be an interpretation. For any set M of terms or formulas over $\Sigma_{\mathcal{I}}$, $\mathcal{I}(M) =_{\text{df}} \{\mathcal{I}(m) \mid m \in M\}$.

11.4 Correct Uses of Diagrams in Visual Reasoning

In this section, we study the use of interpreted diagrams in visual reasoning. By visual reasoning we mean a reasoning system which consists of a diagram, an interpretation and an application domain theory. The study addresses among others the questions: (1) which conclusions are deduced in this reasoning system? and (2) what kind of interpretation makes the conclusions in this reasoning system correct with respect to the facts in the application domain? This study is the basis for subsequent investigation of reasoning with diagrammatic representations.

11.4.1 A Logical Characterization of Visual Reasoning

A visual reasoning system consists of diagrams, an application domain theory $\mathcal{T}$ and an interpretation $\mathcal{I}$. To characterize visual reasoning is to answer the question: Given a diagram $\mathcal{G}$, what can be concluded from this diagram in this reasoning system? According to Section 11.2, the diagram $\mathcal{G}$ can be geometrically characterized as $[\![\mathcal{G}]\!] = (\Sigma_{\mathcal{G}}, \mathcal{A}_{\mathcal{G}})$, where $\mathcal{A}_{\mathcal{G}}$ is a set of basic facts deduced from $\mathcal{G}$, which characterize what one sees in the diagram. However, in visual reasoning, not all the facts in $\mathcal{A}_{\mathcal{G}}$ interest us, but only those parts representing the subject matter of the application domain. Therefore, we only take into account that part of $\mathcal{A}_{\mathcal{G}}$ which covers the interpretation signature, i.e. $\mathcal{A}_{\mathcal{G}} \cap F(\Sigma_{\mathcal{I}})$. Interpreting that part, i.e. $AF = \mathcal{I}(\mathcal{A}_{\mathcal{G}} \cap F(\Sigma_{\mathcal{I}}))$, we get a set of facts AF in the application domain. Each fact in AF is a conclusion of the diagram $\mathcal{G}$ in this reasoning system. Furthermore, taking AF and the domain theory $\mathcal{T}$ as defining the premises, all the conclusions in the domain reasoning system can also be viewed as the conclusions of the diagram $\mathcal{G}$ in this visual reasoning system.

We characterize this more precisely by defining a consequence relation which incorporates graphical inference as well as domain reasoning in such a way that the properties deduced from diagrams are incorporated in reasoning about application domains.

Definition 11.4.1
Logical Characterization of Visual Reasoning
Let $\mathcal{L}$ be a graphical language, $\mathcal{T}$ the logical theory over a signature Σ of the application language. Then,

1. A *state of visual reasoning* (in $\mathcal{T}$) is a pair $\sigma = (\mathcal{I}, \mathcal{G})$ consisting

of an interpretation $\mathcal{I}$ from $\mathcal{L}$ to Σ whose signature is $\Sigma_\mathcal{I}$ and a diagram $\mathcal{G}$ whose geometrical characterization is $[\![\mathcal{G}]\!] = (\Sigma_\mathcal{G}, \mathcal{A}_\mathcal{G})$.

2. The *consequence relation for visual reasoning* $\vdash^\sigma$, determined by a state of visual reasoning σ, is defined as follows: for any sentence A over Σ, $\vdash^\sigma A$ iff $\mathcal{T} \cup \mathcal{I}(\mathcal{A}_\mathcal{G} \cap F(\Sigma_\mathcal{I})) \vdash A$.

Consider the diagram and its geometrical characterization in Figure 11.6 (which reappear, for convenience, in Figure 11.8) and the interpretation in Figure 11.7. Figure 11.8 lists:

- $F(\Sigma_\mathcal{I})$: the set of formulae over the interpretation signature;
- $\mathcal{A}_{\mathcal{G}_O} \cap F(\Sigma_\mathcal{I})$: the intersection between $F(\Sigma_\mathcal{I})$ and the geometrical characterization of the diagram, and
- $\mathcal{I}(\mathcal{A}_{\mathcal{G}_O} \cap F(\Sigma_\mathcal{I}))$: the facts in the application domain deduced from the diagram.

According to the above logical characterization of visual reasoning, the properties of graphical objects in a diagram that are carried over by an interpretation to an application domain are those basic facts in the geometrical characterization of the diagram which are interpreted by the interpretation. Put another way, those and only those *interpreted* depictable properties of the *interpreted* graphical objects of the diagram are used in reasoning about the application domain. Those graphical objects and properties which are either uninterpreted or cannot be seen in the diagram have no effect in domain reasoning. For instance, the fact $\neg overlapping(A, B)$ in the diagram in Figure 11.8 plays no role in the reasoning because *overlapping* is not interpreted; so it is ignored, even though it can be seen in the diagram. Properties like $in_1(\bot, A)$, which although they are interpreted cannot be seen in the diagram, do not effect the reasoning either. It may also be worth remarking that we do not assume the subsignature corresponding to the diagram ($\Sigma_\mathcal{G}$) to be a subsignature of the signature of the interpretation (Σ_I); this allows a diagram used in visual reasoning to contain graphical objects that are not interpreted and hence not used in the reasoning. This results in a certain robustness and is useful in practice.

11.4.2 The Syntactic Correctness of Interpretation

Interpretations are used in visual reasoning to capture the different uses of graphical entities with possible different meanings. A correct use of

Figure 11.8
An Example of Sentences Under the Consequence Relation for Visual Reasoning.

$\mathcal{G}_O$	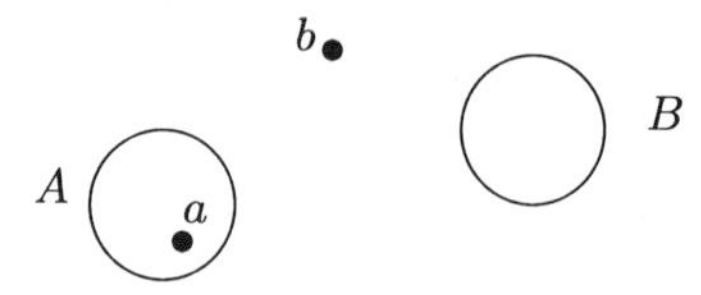
$\mathcal{A}_{\mathcal{G}_O}$	$in_1(a,A)$, $\neg outside(a,A)$, $outside(b,A)$, $\neg in_1(b,A)$, $\neg in_1(a,B)$, $outside(a,B)$, $\neg in_1(b,B)$, $outside(b,B)$, $\neg in_2(A,B)$, $\neg overlapping(A,B)$
$F(\Sigma_\mathcal{I})$	$in_1(a,A)$, $\neg in_1(a,A)$, $in_1(a,B)$, $\neg in_1(a,B)$, $in_1(b,A)$, $\neg in_1(b,A)$, $in_1(b,B)$, $\neg in_1(b,B)$, $in_1(\bot,A)$, $\neg in_1(\bot,A)$, $in_1(\bot,B)$, $\neg in_1(\bot,B)$, ...
$\mathcal{A}_{\mathcal{G}_O} \cap F(\Sigma_\mathcal{I})$	$in_1(a,A)$, $\neg in_1(a,B)$, $\neg in_1(b,A)$, $\neg in_1(b,B)$
$\mathcal{I}(\mathcal{A}_{\mathcal{G}_O} \cap F(\Sigma_\mathcal{I}))$	$a \in A$, $a \notin B$, $b \notin A$, $b \notin B$

diagrams in reasoning is reflected in the suitable choice of graphical entities to represent entities in the application domain. The correctness of use is mainly reflected in the choice of interpretations. Correctness of interpretation can be considered to have two aspects: syntactic correctness and semantic correctness.

By syntactic correctness we mean that the interpretation has to satisfy the definition of interpretation (Definition 11.3.1). For instance, a system for supporting visual reasoning (such as GAR [Wang & Lee 1993]), may require the user to specify interpretations according to the formal structure of interpretations described in its definition. Whether a given specification is syntactically correct can be checked automatically by the supporting system, which prevents the user from making mistakes. These may be trivial but happen quite frequently in specifying interpretations.

An example will indicate how syntax-checking for interpretations can be helpful. Consider the graphical operation *overlap* (in Figure 11.4), whose principal type is $Circle \times Circle \rightarrow Closed\_curve$. With the partial order specified in Figure 11.4, *overlap* also has types such as $Circle \times Null \rightarrow Closed\_curve$ and $Circle \times Circle \rightarrow Graph$, and so on, as long as the domain sorts are less than or equal to *Circle* and the range sort is greater than or equal to *Closed_curve*. Any mapping supposed to be an interpretation which does not satisfy this will be considered as syntactically incorrect. The guarantee of such syntactic correctness of meaning specification is helpful to avoid certain misuses of diagrams in reasoning. For instance, in using Venn diagrams, a beginner might have thought that circles represent sets. Such mistakes can be prevented by syntax-checking. To explain, if one interpreted *Circle* as *Set*, there would be no sensible graphical operation that could be used to represent set operations such as intersection ($\cap$). The graphical operation *overlap* could not be used to represent $\cap$ since in general overlapping two circles makes a closed curve, rather than a circle. A correct interpretation would be to represent sets by closed curves, which include circles since *Circle* is a subsort of *Closed_curve*. Then the interpretation mapping *overlap* to $\cap$ is syntactically correct.

11.4.3 Semantic Properties of Interpretations

The absence of syntactically incorrect interpretations can exclude some mistakes which happen quite often in visual reasoning. However, even when it is syntactically correct, an interpretation may be semantically incorrect in that it still does not conform with one's intentions. Intuitively, a semantically correct interpretation guarantees that the properties of graphical objects which are depictable in a diagram are, under the translation along the interpretation, among the properties of the depicted objects in the application domain. The semantic correctness of the interpretation is the basis of the correctness of the use of diagrams in reasoning. It is obvious that semantical correctness can only be achieved by the user with the help of the supporting system through a good understanding of the application domain problem as well as the graphical language.

The logical characterization of visual reasoning contributes to the understanding of the correct use of diagrams. On this basis, we discuss several semantical properties of interpretations to explain how diagrams can be used correctly in visual reasoning to reflect the user's intentions and hence to obtain adequate (and intended) results. In particular, we are interested in the following three properties of interpretations.

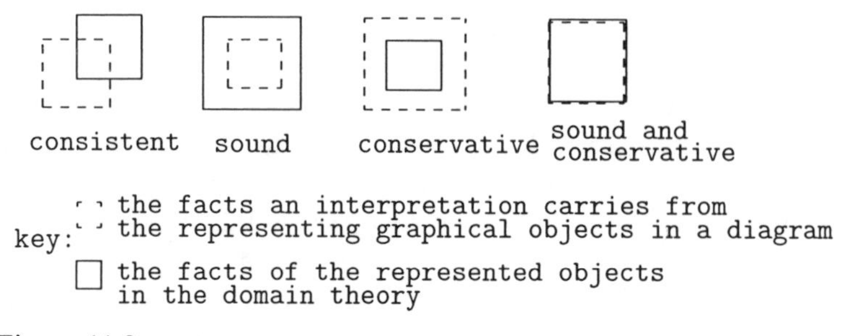

Figure 11.9
An Illustration of the Three Properties

Definition 11.4.2
Consistency, Soundness, and convervativity
Let $\mathcal{L}$ be a graphical language, $\mathcal{T}$ a domain theory over signature Σ of the application language, $\mathcal{I}$ an interpretation from $\mathcal{L}$ to Σ whose signature is $\Sigma_{\mathcal{I}}$, and $\mathcal{G}$ a diagram with geometrical semantics $[\![\mathcal{G}]\!] = (\Sigma_{\mathcal{G}}, \mathcal{A}_{\mathcal{G}})$. Then,

1. $\mathcal{I}$ is *consistent* with respect to $\mathcal{G}$ and $\mathcal{T}$ if and only if $\mathcal{T} \cup \mathcal{I}(\mathcal{A}_{\mathcal{G}} \cap F(\Sigma_{\mathcal{I}}))$ *is consistent if* $\mathcal{T}$ *is consistent.*
2. $\mathcal{I}$ is *sound* with respect to $\mathcal{G}$ and $\mathcal{T}$ if and only if $\mathcal{I}(\mathcal{A}_{\mathcal{G}} \cap F(\Sigma_{\mathcal{I}})) \subseteq \mathcal{T}$.
3. $\mathcal{I}$ is *conservative* with respect to $\mathcal{G}$ and $\mathcal{T}$, if and only if $\{ A \in At(\Sigma_{\mathcal{I}}) \cap At(\Sigma_{\mathcal{G}}) \mid \mathcal{I}(A) \in \mathcal{T} \} \subseteq \mathcal{A}_{\mathcal{G}}$, where $At(\Sigma_{\mathcal{I}})$ and $At(\Sigma_{\mathcal{G}})$ are the sets of atomic formulae over $\Sigma_{\mathcal{I}}$ and $\Sigma_{\mathcal{G}}$, respectively.

Intuitively, the above three properties of interpretations reflect the relationship between the properties that a diagram presents and those in the logical theory of the application domain. *Consistency* of an interpretation means that the information transformed by the interpretation from the diagram does not introduce contradiction into the domain theory; however, a consistent interpretation may introduce new facts into the domain theory which were not previously derivable and, on the other hand, the information it carries may not cover all of the properties of the corresponding objects in the domain theory. *Soundness* means that all of the properties that an interpretation carries from a diagram are already derivable from the domain theory. *Conservativity* means that the properties carried by an interpretation include all of the properties of the corresponding objects in the domain theory. Without explanation, it might not be clear why we use the word *conservativity* instead of *completeness* here. Usually, completeness is used to discuss the relation between a logic system and its models and conservativity is used to compare systems, i.e. the relation between a system and its subsystems. In visual reasoning, we do not treat diagrams as models of application domain theories (though in some applications they may behave like models). Instead we treat them as graphical representations of application domain theories. The properties of interpretations are investigated by comparing two systems, where one corresponds to the interpretation related part of the application domain and the other is the system obtained by interpreting the set of formulae deduced from a diagram. If an interpretation is conservative (and also consistent) the system which results from the diagram can be viewed as a conservative expansion of the application domain system. If an interpretation is both sound and conservative, the facts that an interpretation carries coincide with the properties of the corresponding objects in the domain theory. Figure 11.9 gives an illustration of these three properties, where a solid box represents the facts of the represented objects in the domain theory and a dash box represents the facts an interpretation carries from the representing graphical objects in a diagram.

Now, we give examples to explain the above properties of interpretations. Let $\mathcal{T}(\mathcal{L})$ be the graphical theory over $\Sigma(\mathcal{L})$ and $\mathcal{T}$ be the domain theory over Σ as described in Figure 11.10. We consider three interpretations $\mathcal{I}_i: \Sigma(\mathcal{L}) \rightharpoonup \Sigma$ and their properties.

1. $\mathcal{I}_1$ interprets the graphical sort *Circle* as *Set* and *line_connect* (X, Y) as $\mathcal{I}(X) \subseteq \mathcal{I}(Y)$, for X, Y : *Circle*, see Figure 11.11. $\mathcal{I}_1$ is inconsistent with respect to the diagram in Figure 11.11 and $\mathcal{T}$. Giving the diagram in Figure 11.11 a geometrical characterization based on the graphical language in Figure 11.10, we get the following set of formulae: $line\_connect(C_1, C_2)$, $line\_connect(C_2, C_1)$, $line\_connect(C_2, C_3)$, $line\_connect(C_3, C_2)$. After interpreting the formulae, we arrive at the following set of formulae in the application domain: $a \subseteq b$, $b \subseteq a$, $b \subseteq c$, $c \subseteq b$, $b \subseteq a$ and $c \subseteq b$ are

Figure 11.10
A Graphical Language $\mathcal{L} = (\Sigma(\mathcal{L}), \mathcal{T}(\mathcal{L}))$ and a Domain Signature and Theory.

<table>
<tr><td rowspan="4">$\Sigma(\mathcal{L})$</td><td>$\mathcal{S}$</td><td>$Circle,\ Line,\ ...\ ...$</td></tr>
<tr><td>$\leq$</td><td>$...\ ...$</td></tr>
<tr><td>$\mathcal{F}$</td><td>$C_1, C_2, C_3, ...\ :\ Circle,\ L_1,\ L_2,\ L_3,\ ...\ :\ Line,\ ...$</td></tr>
<tr><td>$\mathcal{P}$</td><td>$line\_connect\ :\ Circle \times Circle,$
$in\ :\ Circle \times Circle,$
$t\_joint\ :\ Line \times\ Line$</td></tr>
<tr><td>$\mathcal{T}(\mathcal{L})$</td><td colspan="2">$line\_connect(x, y) \Leftrightarrow line\_connect(y, x)$
$in(x, y)\ \wedge\ in(y, z) \Rightarrow in(x, z)$
$...\ ...$</td></tr>
<tr><td rowspan="4">Σ</td><td>$\mathcal{S}'$</td><td>$Set,\ ...\ ...$</td></tr>
<tr><td>$\leq'$</td><td>$...\ ...$</td></tr>
<tr><td>$\mathcal{F}'$</td><td>$a, b, c\ :\ Set,\ ...\ ...$</td></tr>
<tr><td>$\mathcal{P}'$</td><td>$\subseteq :\ Set \times Set,\ ...\ ...$</td></tr>
<tr><td>$\mathcal{T}$</td><td colspan="2">$\subseteq$ is the partial order generated by
$a \subseteq b \subseteq c$.</td></tr>
</table>

in contradiction with the formulae $\neg b \subseteq a$ and $\neg c \subseteq b$ in the domain theory $\mathcal{T}$ in Figure 11.10. The reason why $\mathcal{I}_1$ is inconsistent results from the fact that the binary predicate *line_connect* in the graphical theory is symmetric, and $\subseteq$ is an asymmetric predicate.

2. $\mathcal{I}_2$ interprets the graphical sort *Line* as *Set* and *t_joint* as $\subseteq$, see in Figure 11.12. Then, $\mathcal{I}_2$ is sound (and hence consistent) with respect to the diagram in Figure 11.12 and $\mathcal{T}$. But it is not conservative, for there are some facts in the application domain (e.g. $a \subseteq a$, $a \subseteq c$ etc.) which have no corresponding representation in the diagram in Figure 11.12. The reason for this is the fact that *t_joint* is neither transitive nor reflexive in the graphical theory.

3. $\mathcal{I}_3$ interprets *Circle* as *Set* and *in* as $\subseteq$, see in Figure 11.13. $\mathcal{I}_3$ is sound and conservative with respect to the diagram in Figure 11.13 and $\mathcal{T}$.

The above examples illustrate what we mean by the three properties of interpretations. However, the examples may give the false impression that the semantic correctness of an interpretation is determined by the coincidence of the properties of the graphical entities with those in the application domain. In our examples, when the properties of the graphical predicate and the $\subseteq$ relation are conflicting (as *line_connect* is

Figure 11.11
I_1 Is Inconsistent with $\mathcal{T}$ and the Diagram.

$\Sigma_{\mathcal{I}}$	$\mathcal{S}_{\mathcal{I}}$	*Circle, ...*
	$\leq_{\mathcal{I}}$	
	$\mathcal{F}_{\mathcal{I}}$	$C_1,\ C_2,\ C_3 : \ Circle;$
	$\mathcal{P}_{\mathcal{I}}$	$line\_connectCircle \times Circle;$
$\mathcal{I}_1$	$\mathcal{I}_{\mathcal{S}}$	$Circle \mapsto Set,$
	$\mathcal{I}_{\mathcal{F}}$	$C_1 \mapsto a, \quad C_2 \mapsto b, \quad C_3 \mapsto c$
	$\mathcal{I}_{\mathcal{P}}$	$line\_connect \mapsto \subseteq.$

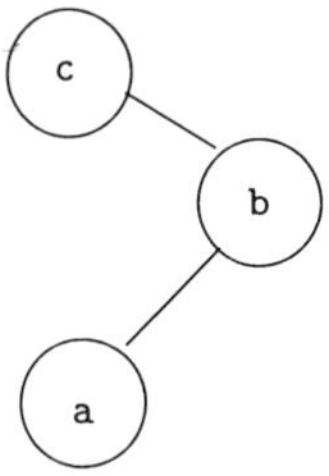

symmetric but $\subseteq$ is asymmetric), the interpretation ($\mathcal{I}_1$) is inconsistent; when the set of properties of the graphical predicate is a proper subset of the properties of $\subseteq$ (as *t_joint* is asymmetric), the interpretation ($\mathcal{I}_2$) is sound but not conservative; only when both properties are the same (as *in* is reflective, asymmetric and transitive, and $\subseteq$ also has exactly these three properties), the interpretation ($\mathcal{I}_3$) is both sound and conservative. So it seems easy to believe that the relations between the two sets of properties determine the properties of an interpretation. Unfortunately, this is not in general correct. We know the relation *father* is not transitive, and the graphical predicate *in* in the graphical language in Figure 11.10 is transitive. Nevertheless, if $\mathcal{I}$ interprets *in* into *father*, $\mathcal{I}$ is sound and conservative with respect to $\mathcal{T}$ and the diagram in Figure 11.14.

Once again, we emphasize that we can only see *basic* facts in a diagram, as we concluded in section 11.2.2, and in visual reasoning only those *basic* facts in the diagram are interpreted in the application domain as we defined in section 11.4.1.

The above analysis provides a formal understanding of the semantic correctness of interpretations. Semantic correctness cannot be automatically checked; technically, it is undecidable, and in practice, the

Figure 11.12
I_2 Is Sound with $\mathcal{T}$ and the Diagram.

$\Sigma_{\mathcal{I}}$	$\mathcal{S}_{\mathcal{I}}$	*Line*, ...
	$\leq_{\mathcal{I}}$	
	$\mathcal{F}_{\mathcal{I}}$	$L_1,\ L_2,\ L_3 :\ Line;$
	$\mathcal{P}_{\mathcal{I}}$	$t\_joint\ :\ Line \times Line;$
$\mathcal{I}_2$	$\mathcal{I}_S$	$Line \mapsto Set,$
	$\mathcal{I}_{\mathcal{F}}$	$L_1 \mapsto a,\quad L_2 \mapsto b,\quad L_3 \mapsto c$
	$\mathcal{I}_{\mathcal{P}}$	$t\_joint \mapsto \subseteq.$

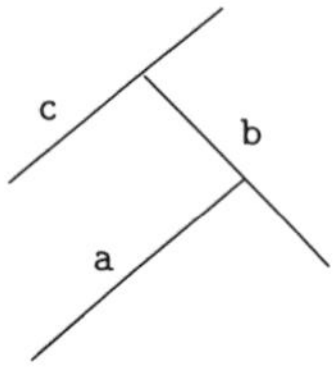

supporting system has no way to get a complete grasp of the semantics of the application domain. However, it is our opinion that such an understanding is important for providing useful guidance to help users, both conceptually and by machine, to choose correct interpretations to reflect their intentions. For instance, a supporting system may give the user useful information about the graphical entities chosen, such as the symmetry property of *line_connect* in the interpretation $\mathcal{I}_1$ and in this case the user will realize that something explicitly directional, such as *arrow_connection*, should be used in a partial order representation.

11.4.4 Pythagoras' Theorem: An Example of Abstract Reasoning

Having discussed the correct use of diagrams in visual reasoning in rather abstract terms and using artificial examples, we discuss, in this section, how the notion of interpretation is critically used in a well-known but more subtle example of visual reasoning— the use of graphical objects to represent arbitrary objects and properties in a proof of Pythagoras' Theorem.

One may distinguish two different kinds of reasoning about an application domain. The first may be called *concrete reasoning*, where properties of particular objects are concerned; for example, when one

Figure 11.13
I_3 is Sound and Conservative with $\mathcal{T}$ and the Diagram.

$\Sigma_{\mathcal{I}}$	$\mathcal{S}_{\mathcal{I}}$	*Circle*, ...
	$\leq_{\mathcal{I}}$	
	$\mathcal{F}_{\mathcal{I}}$	$C_4,\ C_5,\ C_6$: *Circle*;
	$\mathcal{P}_{\mathcal{I}}$	*in* : *Circle* × *Circle*;
$\mathcal{I}_3$	$\mathcal{I}_{\mathcal{S}}$	*Circle* ↦ *Set*,
	$\mathcal{I}_{\mathcal{F}}$	$C_4 \mapsto a,\ \ C_5 \mapsto b,\ \ C_6 \mapsto c$
	$\mathcal{I}_{\mathcal{P}}$	$in \mapsto \subseteq$.

Figure 11.14
In is Transitive and *Father* is Anti-Transitive, But the Interpretation of *in* to *Father* is Sound and Conservative with $\mathcal{T}$ and the Diagram.

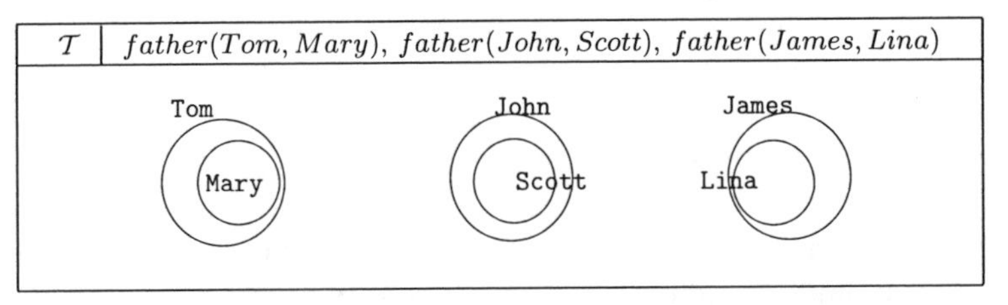

wants to show that a particular set is a subset of another. The second kind of reasoning, which we may call *abstract reasoning*, is to prove some (e.g. universal) properties that an arbitrary object of a certain kind has; for example, to prove Pythagoras' theorem which gives the relationship between the lengths of sides of an *arbitrary* right triangle.

Using diagrams to help concrete reasoning, one uses particular graphical objects in a diagram to represent the particular objects in a domain, and graphical inference under an interpretation provides a direct answer to the questions one may ask about the represented objects. For example, we may use particular Venn diagrams to illustrate (not to prove!) the distributive laws about the set operations of union and intersection by showing that the particular cases satisfy the laws.

However, since diagrams are particular models of the graphical theory, it is natural to ask whether and how one can use diagrams to help in

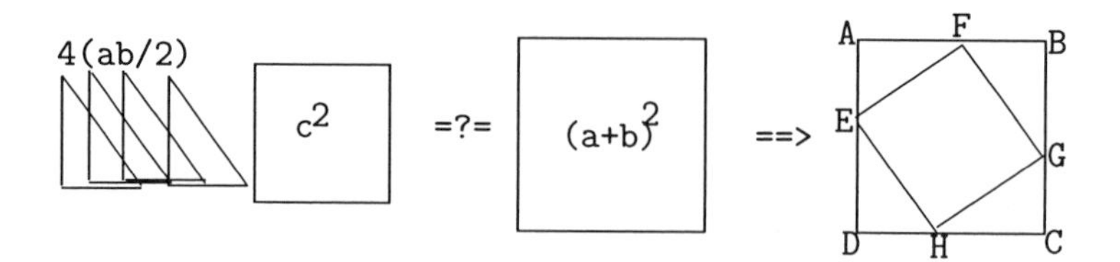

Figure 11.15
Pythagoras' Theorem.

proving universal properties in abstract reasoning. For example, can we use diagrams to help in proving Pythagoras' theorem? If so, how can one regard an arbitrarily chosen (but particular) right triangle in a diagram as an arbitrary right triangle? It is obvious that, if we are not careful, it is easy to deduce incorrect conclusions from such a use of diagrams in reasoning; for example, if the particular right triangle representing the arbitrary right triangle happens to be an isosceles triangle, one might get the absurd conclusion that every right triangle is an isosceles triangle.

In the following, we consider the example of proving Pythagoras' Theorem in our setting of visual reasoning. We shall give a brief analysis and explain how diagrams may be used to help abstract reasoning. In particular, through the discussion, we emphasize that interpretations are the key tool in understanding and controlling how diagrams (and which parts of them and what properties of them) are used in reasoning about the application domain.

Pythagoras' Theorem is a well-known theorem in geometry, which asserts that, in a right triangle, the square of the hypotenuse is equal to the sum of the squares of the other two sides. Thus, if the hypotenuse has length c and the other two sides have lengths a and b, then $a^2 + b^2 = c^2$.

An elegant proof is obtained by forming two squares using four identical right triangles (see Figure 11.15) and equating areas; that is, one shows that the diagram contains two squares and then the fact that the area of the smaller square is equal to that of the outer minus four times the area of the right triangle gives the proof of the theorem.

It is obvious that, in this argument, the diagram plays an essential role, without which one could not proceed with the argument (or even find it). However, on the other hand, it is not completely clear how the diagram helps in the proof and what information provided by it is used

Figure 11.16
The Graphical Signature, Domain Signature and Theory, and the Interpretation for Proving Pythagoras' Theorem.

$\Sigma_{\mathcal{I}}$	$\mathcal{S}$	*Angle*, *Edge*, ...
	$\leq$	...
	$\mathcal{F}$	$EAF,\ FBG,\ GCH,\ HDE : Angle,\quad EF,\ FG,\ GH,\ HE : Edge$ $AFE,\ BGF,\ CHG,\ DEH : Angle,\quad AE,\ BF,\ CG,\ DH : Edge$ $AEF,\ BFG,\ CGH,\ DHE : Angle,\quad AF,\ BG,\ CH,\ DE : Edge$ $EFG,\ FGH,\ GHE,\ HEF : Angle$
	$\mathcal{P}$	...
Σ'	$\mathcal{S}'$	*R'Triangle*, *S'quare*, *A'ngle*, *E'dge*, ...
	$\leq'$	...
	$\mathcal{F}'$	$R : R'Triangle,\quad C : S'quare$ $RA,\ RB,\ RC,\ C_1,\ C_2,\ C_3,\ C_4 : Angle$ $Ra,\ Rb,\ Rc : Edge$
	$\mathcal{P}'$	...
$\mathcal{T}$	$RA + RB = RC = C_1 = C_2 = C_3 = C_4 = \pi/2$ (1) axioms about triangles and squares	
$\mathcal{I}$	$\mathcal{I}_{\mathcal{S}}$	$Angle \mapsto A'ngle,\quad Edge \mapsto E'dge$, ...
	$\mathcal{I}_{\mathcal{F}}$	$EAF,\ FBG,\ GCH,\ HDE \mapsto RC,\quad EF,\ FG,\ GH,\ HE \mapsto Rc$ $EFG \mapsto C_1,\ FGH \mapsto C_2,\ GHE \mapsto C_3,\ HEF \mapsto C_4$ $AFE,\ BGF,\ CHG,\ DEH \mapsto RA,\quad AE,\ BF,\ CG,\ DH \mapsto Ra$ $AEF,\ BFG,\ CGH,\ DHE \mapsto RB,\quad AF,\ BG,\ CH,\ DE \mapsto Rb$

in the proof. For example, the particular fact that one of the sides in a triangle is longer than another, is not (and should not be) used in the proof.

Using such a diagram to prove Pythagoras' theorem, we must understand that the triangles in the diagram represent an arbitrary right triangle in the domain. Therefore, particular properties such as that one of the edges is longer than another should not be used in domain reasoning[10]. This can be controlled by means of interpretation, since, according to the logical characterization of reasoning, only the interpreted pictorial components (and their interpreted properties) can be used. In other words, giving a correct and intended interpretation is a most important step in using diagrams in reasoning.

In the interpretation (see Figure 11.16) for proving Pythagoras' theo-

[10] Such a possible fallacy in a proof of the Pythagoras theory has also been discussed by Barwise and Etchemendy (1990). Here, we analyze this phenomenon and clarify it in our framework.

rem, numerical attributes like *length* of edges are not interpreted (that is, they are not included in the signature of the interpretation), since an arbitrary triangle represented by the triangles in the diagram does not necessarily have the particular (numerical) properties that these pictorial objects may have. This prevents us from deducing incorrect conclusions in the graphical inference. Having given such an interpretation, one can use the diagram in Figure 11.15 to guide and help to find the proof as sketched above. For instance, in order to prove that (the area represented by) $ABCD$ is a square, it is necessary to prove that (the lines represented by) AF and FB are collinear. To do this, one may point at the diagram to prove that the sum of degrees of (the angles represented by) AFE, BFG and EFG is equal to π. Note that, by pointing at the diagram and using "$ABCD$," "AF," "AFE" etc., the developer of the proof is really referring to the corresponding objects in the domain theory which are represented by these graphical objects! For example, by pointing at the angles AFE, BFG and EFG the reasoner should be seen to intend the angles RA, RB and C_1 in the application domain according to the interpretation; applying the axiom (1) in the domain theory $\mathcal{T}$ results in the conclusion that the sum of the three angles is equal to π, so AF and FB are collinear. In other words, by pointing to graphical objects one is referring to the referents of these graphical objects under the interpretation. Through this, the diagram plays an essential role in guiding the development or explanation of the proof.

Note that, on the basis of the interpretation in Figure 11.16, there is no way the user can, for example, use the size of an angle in the diagram (say AFE) to refer to the size of the represented angle in the domain theory, since the attribute *angle size* (except for the *right angle*) is not interpreted. Similarly, the attribute *length* is not interpreted either. Otherwise, if *degree* and *length* were interpreted, one would be able to prove the Pythagoras theorem simply by computing the values of the graphical attributes (say, the lengths of the edges of a right triangle which may be 3, 4 and 5 respectively) and calculate that $c^2 = a^2 + b^2$ ($5^2 = 3^2 + 4^2$); this certainly does not prove the theorem in general. In our terminology, such an interpretation is only *consistent*, but *not sound*; it carries unintended information (like the numerical attributes) over to the domain and makes the represented triangle become a particular triangle, and no longer arbitrary.

In conclusion, diagrams are useful in both concrete and abstract reasoning. In fact, interpretations may also provide ways to deal with both abstract and concrete reasoning in a flexibly mixed situation. When abstract reasoning is considered, interpretations should be given more carefully, especially with respect to the geometrical attributes of graphical objects.

11.5 G-Mappings

In this section, we address in detail the issues of reasoning with diagrammatic representations. We first study the relations between premise and conclusion diagrams. We call this relation a *G-mapping* (Graphical mapping). The G-mapping relation can be thought of as a transformation which allows the premise diagrams to be combined in certain ways, and then take a number of different forms corresponding to different consistent representations of the information contained in the premises. It is obvious that there must be a geometrical description and an interpretation for each of the diagrams, and we will use these to characterize how the information contained in the individual premise diagrams can be combined to obtain the conclusion diagrams. We have studied geometrical description and interpretation in terms of the simpler form of visual reasoning, where only one diagram is involved in a reasoning state; but now there are two groups of diagrams involved in the reasoning. The geometrical descriptions (and the interpretations) of each of them should be consistent with each other. To ensure this, we introduce some conventions on the descriptions and on the interpretations of the diagrams.

11.5.1 Descriptions of Diagrams

When a G-mapping transforms a set of diagrams into another, it maps each graphical object in the premise diagrams into another object in the conclusion diagram. A direct representation of such a mapping is a set of pairs like (O_i, O_j) which represents the graphical object O_i being mapped to O_j. However, if we consider the use of G-mappings in real world reasoning, a real world object is usually represented by several different graphical objects (in different diagrams). For instance, in Figure 11.1, the set B is represented by three different circles whose sizes may be the same but whose relative spatial positions are different from each other. Though they are different graphical objects, they are recognized to be (representations of) the same object in that application because the label B is attached to each of them. When we look at a G-mapping (e.g. the transformation between diagrams in Figure 11.1) we usually view a label and the graphical objects attached to it as a whole (e.g. B and the circles labeled B in Figure 11.1)[11].

Therefore, we define the following conventions for the description of the diagrams in a G-mapping.

Convention:

1. There is a *label* attached to each graphical object in a diagram. More precisely, we use (g, l) : to represent a graphical object, where g is the name of the graphical object (i.e. a term in the graphical language) and l is a label attached to the graphical object. For instance, consider the diagram in Figure 11.17. If we relate the graphical objects p_1, p_2, C_1, C_2 and $overlap(C_1, C_2)$ with labels a, b, A, B and C respectively, then the objects are re-represented as (p_1, a), (p_2, b), (C_1, A), (C_2, B) and $(overlap(C_1, C_2), C)$. For any diagram $\mathcal{D}$, we use $B\mathcal{L}_\mathcal{D}$ (*basic* label set) to represent the set of the labels attached to the original graphical objects and $E\mathcal{L}_\mathcal{D}$ (*emergent* labels set) to represent the labels attached to the emergent graphical objects in the diagram, e.g. $B\mathcal{L}_\mathcal{D} = \{a, b, A, B\}$ is the basic label set and $E\mathcal{L}_\mathcal{D} = \{C\}$ the emergent label set of the above diagram.

2. For any diagram $\mathcal{D}$ and label l, l appears in $\mathcal{D}$ at most once. Usually labels are the names of the represented objects in an application domain. This convention means we always use one graphical object to represent a domain object. One may wonder whether it should be allowed to have several graphical objects represent a single domain object; to have, for instance, both a square and a triangle represent a house. In our view, it is more natural to treat the square and the triangle as one (complex) graphical object instead

[11] In the foregoing sections, a label informally attached to a graphical object is sometimes the name of the graphical object and at other times the name of the represented object in the application domain. When only one diagram is used in a visual communication state it is not important to distinguish the name of a graphical object and the name of the represented object, because in most cases we can use the same name for both. But the distinction becomes important in the study of G-mappings, because several different graphical objects (or one graphical object) may represent one object (or several different objects) in an application domain.

of two graphical objects. If we must have several graphical objects to represent a single domain object in one diagram, we can still start with different labels for each of the graphical objects and then map all of the labels to the represented object. Hence the graphical objects in a diagram can be represented unambiguously by just their labels. In the following, if there is no ambiguity, constants (i.e. the representation of original graphical objects) in a graphical signature will also be represented by just their labels. The labels for emergent objects can be formed from the labels of their components. For example, if (C_1, a) and (C_2, b) are two overlapping circles, $(overlap((C_1, a), (C_2, b)), overlap(a, b))$ may be used to represent the emergent closed curve, and $overlap(a, b)$ is the new label attached to it.

3. There are no labels attached to empty graphical objects. A graphical object may be transformed away into nothing, in which case its associated label disappears. This happens when premise pictures are inconsistent with each other, as we will discuss in the definition of G-mapping.

4. As we indicated before, giving a diagram a geometrical characterization must be based on an underlying graphical signature and a graphical theory in the signature. The geometrical characterization of each diagram in a G-mapping must be based on a single graphical signature and theory.

Notation Let $\mathcal{L}$ be a graphical language. $P(\mathcal{L})$ denotes a set of diagrams such that: for each diagram $p \in P(\mathcal{L})$ whose geometrical characterization is $[\![p]\!] = (\Sigma_p, \mathcal{A}_p)$, $\Sigma_p \sqsubseteq \Sigma(\mathcal{L})$ and $\mathcal{A}_p$ is the intersection of the equivalent situations which are consistent and maximal with respect to $\mathcal{T}(\mathcal{L})$.

11.5.2 Interpretations

For each diagram in a G-mapping, there is an interpretation which relates the diagram to an application domain. It seems reasonable to assume that all the diagrams in a G-mapping should be interpreted by means of a common interpretation. But this might not always be apparent; e.g. in Figure 11.1 the circle labeled B in the second premise diagram has exactly the same geometrical shape and relative spatial position as the one labeled C in the conclusion diagram, but this graphical

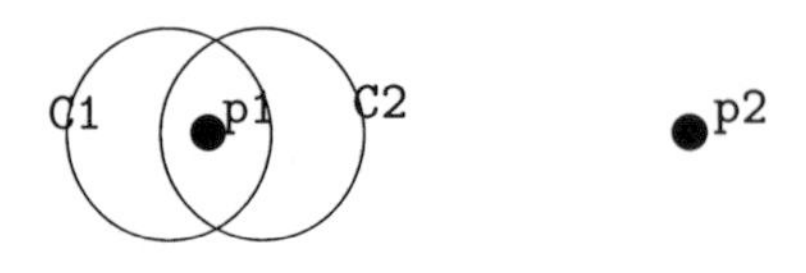

Figure 11.17
C1, C2, p1 and p2 are Names (*not Labels*) of the Graphical Objects.

object has been interpreted as a different set in each of the diagrams. Fortunately, we introduced a label for each graphical object, and hence what appears to be an identical graphical object can be viewed as a different one by having a different label. This avoids conflicting interpretations which might arise in applications. In our discussion, consistency of interpretation for the diagrams will be defined in terms of the labels instead of the graphical objects. This leads to the following convention.

Convention
Let $\mathcal{L}$ be a graphical language, Σ an application domain signature, and $\mathcal{I}$ an interpretation from $\mathcal{L}$ to Σ whose signature is $\Sigma_{\mathcal{I}}$. $P(\mathcal{L}_{\mathcal{I}})$ denotes a set of diagrams such that:

1. $P(\mathcal{L}_{\mathcal{I}})$ is $P(\mathcal{L})$;
2. for any two terms, $t_i = (O_i, l_i)$ and $t_j = (O_j, l_j)$, generated from $\Sigma_{\mathcal{I}}$, if the labels $l_i = l_j$ then $\mathcal{I}(t_i) = \mathcal{I}(t_j)$ (i.e. those graphical objects whose labels are the same must be interpreted as the same object in the application domain);
3. for each diagram $p \in P(\mathcal{L}_{\mathcal{I}})$, whose geometrical characterization is $[\![p]\!] = (\Sigma_p, \mathcal{A}_p)$, $\mathcal{A}_p^{\mathcal{I}}$ denotes $\mathcal{A}_p \cap F(\Sigma_{\mathcal{I}})$.

11.5.3 G-Mapping

Definition 11.5.1
G-Mapping
Let $\mathcal{L}$ be a graphical language, Σ an application domain signature and $\mathcal{I}$ an interpretation from $\mathcal{L}$ to Σ, whose signature is $\Sigma_{\mathcal{I}}$. A G-mapping G in $\mathcal{T}$ with $\mathcal{I}$ is a pair $(P_1(\mathcal{L}_{\mathcal{I}}), P_2(\mathcal{L}_{\mathcal{I}}))$ (where $P_1(\mathcal{L}_{\mathcal{I}})$ is the set of premise diagrams and $P_2(\mathcal{L}_{\mathcal{I}})$ the set of conclusion diagrams) which satisfies the following conditions:

- *Identity*: For any $P_2 \in P_2(\mathcal{L}_\mathcal{I})$, the basic labels that occur in P_2 must occur among the basic labels of a premise diagram, i.e.

  $$B\mathcal{L}_{P_2} \subseteq \bigcup_{P_1 \in P_1(\mathcal{L}_\mathcal{I})} B\mathcal{L}_{P_1}.$$

  New labels are never introduced, unless they come from new emergent objects.
- *Consistency*: For any $P_1 \in P_1(\mathcal{L}_\mathcal{I})$ and $P_2 \in P_2(\mathcal{L}_\mathcal{I})$ the basic facts in P_1 and P_2 must be consistent with each other, i.e.

  $$\mathcal{A}^\mathcal{I}_{P_1} \cup \mathcal{A}^\mathcal{I}_{P_2} \textit{ is consistent.}$$

- *Maximality*: Any basic fact in a premise diagram which is consistent with a conclusion diagram (and also with all the other premise diagrams) must occur in that conclusion diagram. Namely, $\forall P_2 \in P_2(\mathcal{L}_\mathcal{I}), \forall P_1 \in P_1(\mathcal{L}_\mathcal{I})\ \forall A \in \mathcal{A}^\mathcal{I}_{P_1}, \{A\} \cup \mathcal{A}^\mathcal{I}_{P_2}$ *is consistent* and $\forall P_1' \in P_1(\mathcal{L}_\mathcal{I}), \{A\} \cup \mathcal{A}^\mathcal{I}_{P_2} \cup \mathcal{A}^\mathcal{I}_{P_1'}$ *is consistent* $\Rightarrow A \in \mathcal{A}^\mathcal{I}_{P_2}$.

The *Identity* condition is justified, because in practice the label of a graphical object will be used to indicate the (semantic) relationship between that object and some object in the real world. A G-mapping can change the graphical representation of an object in the real world but should not be seen to change the link (i.e. the label) between the world-object and its graphical representation. New labels for basic objects would introduce unjustified new objects in the application domain. On the other hand, new emergent graphical objects can be introduced in conclusion diagrams, which play an important role in many applications (see the examples in Section 11.7). Besides this, a label can also be transformed by a G-mapping into an empty object (i.e. it disappears). This happens because a G-mapping satisfying the *consistency* condition, may not be able to put all the information in the premise diagrams into a conclusion diagram. For example, suppose there are two premise diagrams, P_1 and P_2, where in P_1 two circles labeled as A and B overlap but in P_2 two circles which have the same labels do not overlap and that *overlapping* is interpreted. Then the conclusion diagrams are single object diagrams in which only one of A or B appears (see Figure 11.18), since the consistency condition is not satisfied for diagrams depicting both A and B.

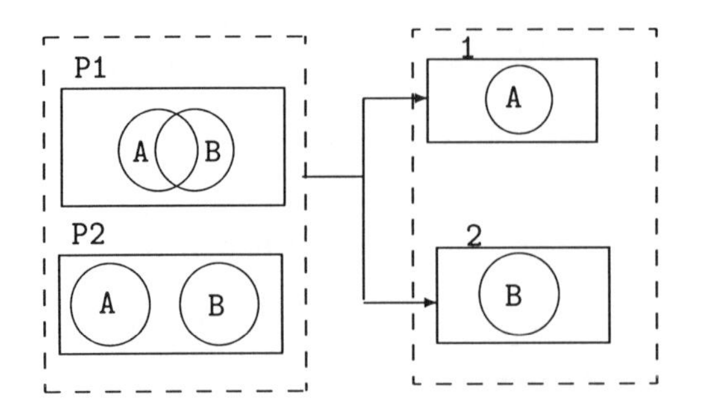

Figure 11.18
Premise Diagrams P_1 and P_2 are contradictory with each other if the predicate *overlapping* is included in the Graphical Language and the Interpretation. In order to satisfy the consistency condition, either A (2) or B (1) must not exist in each of the conclusion diagrams.

Consistency tells us that the conclusion diagram should not contain any facts contradict its premises. This is the most basic condition which should hold for a reasoning system.

The above two conditions only tell us what kinds of objects and properties should not be included in a conclusion diagram. A trivial way to satisfy these two conditions is to define a G-mapping which maps any diagram to an empty diagram. It is obvious that we also need some condition which limits a G-mapping to preserve all the proper objects and their properties. This leads us to consider maximality.

Maximality guarantees that objects and their spatial properties in the premise diagrams should be mapped to the conclusion diagram as much as possible.

Figure 11.19 gives an example of a G-mapping which maps two premise diagrams, P_1 and P_2, to four conclusion diagrams. Figure 11.20 gives another example where the map is not a G-mapping with respect to the same graphical theory.

The above definition allows G-mappings from an inconsistent premise set. The conclusion set in that case contains just the maximal consistent pictures that take facts from the premises. Alternative notions are possible, where inconsistent premises do not allow G-mappings. To obtain such a notion, a G-mapping must obey the following demand instead of the maximality demand.

Figure 11.19
An Example G-Mapping.

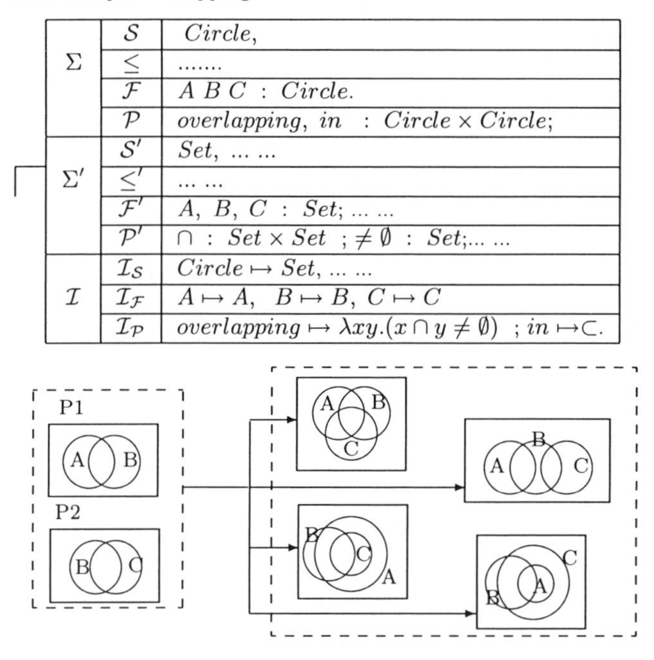

Σ	$\mathcal{S}$	*Circle,*
	$\leq$	....
	$\mathcal{F}$	$A\ B\ C\ :\ Circle.$
	$\mathcal{P}$	$overlapping,\ in\ \ :\ Circle \times Circle;$
Σ'	$\mathcal{S}'$	*Set,* ... ...
	$\leq'$	... ...
	$\mathcal{F}'$	$A,\ B,\ C\ :\ Set;$ ... ...
	$\mathcal{P}'$	$\cap\ :\ Set \times Set\ \ ; \neq \emptyset\ :\ Set;$... ...
$\mathcal{I}$	$\mathcal{I}_\mathcal{S}$	$Circle \mapsto Set,$ ... ...
	$\mathcal{I}_\mathcal{F}$	$A \mapsto A,\ \ B \mapsto B,\ C \mapsto C$
	$\mathcal{I}_\mathcal{P}$	$overlapping \mapsto \lambda xy.(x \cap y \neq \emptyset)\ \ ; in \mapsto \subset.$

- *Consistent premises*: For any conclusion diagram P_2

$$\bigcup_{P_1 \in P_1(\mathcal{L}_\mathcal{I})} \mathcal{A}^\mathcal{I}_{P_1} \subseteq \mathcal{A}^\mathcal{I}_{P_2}.$$

11.6 Reasoning with Diagrammatic Representations

In the last section, we discussed the relations between premise and conclusion diagrams mainly from a graphical point of view. Though interpretation was mentioned in the definition of G-mapping, it served only as a filter to exclude those parts of a diagram in which a user may not be interested. In this section, we study what the conclusion diagrams really mean in an application domain, i.e. the formal semantics of reasoning with diagrammatic representations.

Considered as a consequence relation for reasoning with diagrammatic

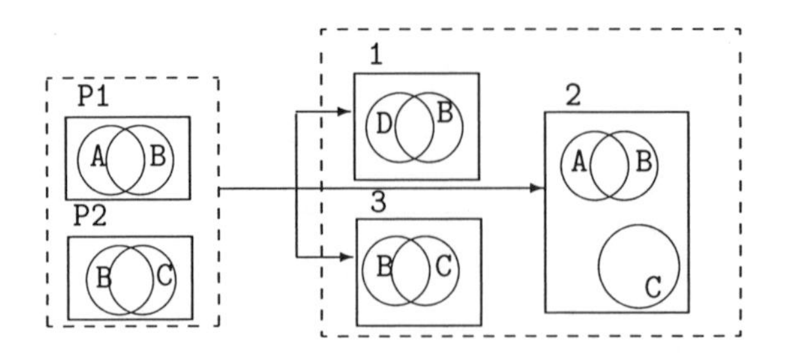

Figure 11.20
These Are Not G-mappings With Respect to the Graphical Theory and the Interpretation In Figure 15.19 because: (1) does not satisfy the identity condition; (2) is not consistent and (3) is not maximal.

representations, the meaning of reasoning with diagrammatic representations can be characterized as follows.

Definition 11.6.1
Reasoning with Diagrammatic Representations
Let $\mathcal{L}$ be a graphical language, $\mathcal{T}$ the logical theory over a signature Σ of the application language, $\mathcal{I}$ an interpretation from $\mathcal{L}$ to Σ, $G = (P(\mathcal{L}_\mathcal{I}), P'(\mathcal{L}_\mathcal{I}))$ a G-mapping. The *consequence relation* $\vdash^G$ *determined by* G is defined as follows: for any sentence A over Σ

$$\vdash^G A \quad \text{iff} \quad \bigvee\{\bigwedge \mathcal{I}(\mathcal{A}_P^\mathcal{I}) \mid P \in P'(\mathcal{L}_\mathcal{I})\} \;\vdash\; A$$

A is a theorem iff it consists of the disjunction of expressions giving the interpretation for each conclusion diagram (these expressions each being formed by conjoining the interpretations of the diagram's basic facts).

From this, we see that conclusion diagrams must be inconsistent with each other and the conclusion of reasoning with diagram representations is an exclusive disjunction rather than the conjunction of all the facts in each conclusion diagram. The meaning of the reasoning in Figure 11.19 is:

$\vdash^G$

$$(A \cap C \neq \emptyset \;\wedge A \cap B \neq \emptyset \;\wedge B \cap C \neq \emptyset) \vee (A \cap C = \emptyset \;\wedge A \cap B \neq \emptyset \;\wedge B \cap C \neq \emptyset)$$

$$\vee\ (A \subset C \;\wedge A \cap B \neq \emptyset \;\wedge B \cap C \neq \emptyset) \vee (C \subset A \wedge A \cap B \neq \emptyset \;\wedge B \cap C \neq \emptyset).$$

Note that this neglects certain areas which appear salient in the diagram, e.g. $A \cap B \cap C$. This is a consequence of the definition of the original graphical signature and theory in Figure 11.19, where it can be seen that *overlapping* is defined only between pairs of circles; there is no predicate relating the relations between three circles or circles with other closed-curves. This emphasizes the need for choosing a particular graphical language for a particular purpose, as we discussed in Section 11.2.

Besides carefully selecting the graphical signature and the theory, to use G-mappings in real world reasoning correctly we also need reasonable interpretations. A correct interpretation should guarantee that the basic facts in each conclusion diagram under the interpretation are consistent with the application domain theory.

The conclusion of each reasoning with diagrammatic representations is an exclusive disjunction. This means (1) any one of the conclusion diagrams can be true, but (2) in a specific model, only one of them can be true. So the set of conclusion diagrams can match a set of *specific* models, or all of them together can be seen to satisfy a model which, in the sense defined by Stenning and Oberlander (1992), has *limited abstraction*.

In order to make the meanings represented by the set of conclusion diagrams more easily accessible to the user, we can also exploit Stenning and Oberlander's notion of a *minimal case of animation*, by dynamically transforming one conclusion diagram into another in a cyclical fashion. This is defined here as the following sequence of diagram transformations:

Definition 11.6.2
Conclusion Displaying Cycle
Let $G = (P, P')$ G-mapping, where, $P' = \{P'_0, P'_1, ..., P'_{m-1}\}$. A conclusion displaying cycle of G is a diagram transformation sequence, from P'_i to $P'_{mod(i+1,m)}$, $i = \{0, 2, ..., m-1\}$.

11.7 Examples

In this section, some examples are presented to provide further clarification of the above formal description of diagrammatic reasoning, and to show how it might be used in solving real problems.

11.7.1 Using Euler Circles to Solve Syllogisms

Using Euler circles to solve syllogisms is a well known example of reasoning with diagrammatic representations. Here, we elucidate the formal process of G-mapping by going through a syllogism example, based on the formal considerations presented in this chapter.

Consider the syllogism in which *All A are B* and *Some C are not B* are premises and one of the valid conclusions is *Some C are not A*. This is actually the syllogism mentioned at the beginning of the chapter and presented using Euler circles in Figure 11.1. A more complete depiction of the relation between the premises and the conclusion can be seen in Figure 11.21 (2). We are now in a position to understand the difference between these figures, and its implications.

Suppose the underlying graphical signature is as in Figure 11.21 (1) and we assume that the graphical theory over this signature (which we omit) gives the common-sense meanings to the graphical symbols. An interpretation is given in Figure 11.21 (2): the premises *All A are B* and *Some C are not B* are represented respectively by diagrams P_1 and P_2 in Figure 11.21 (2). By applying a G-mapping to these two premise diagrams, the set of conclusion diagrams is produced (see P_1', P_2' and P_3' in Figure 11.21 (2)).

Let $S = \{in(A,B), overlapping(B,C), overlapping(C,B)\}$; then the geometrical semantics of each conclusion diagram is as follows:
$\mathcal{A}_{P_1'} = \{in(A,C), out(C,A)\} \cup S$
$\mathcal{A}_{P_2'} = \{overlap(A,C), overlap(C,A)\} \cup S$
$\mathcal{A}_{P_3'} = \{separate(A,C), separate(C,A)\} \cup S$
According to definition 3.1, the following conclusion in the application domain is obtained under the interpretation in Figure 11.21 (1): $(all\_are(A,C) \wedge some\_are\_not(C,A)) \vee (some\_are\_not(A,C) \wedge some\_are\_not(C,A)) \vee (all\_are\_not(A,C) \wedge all\_are\_not(C,A))$ and, since *all_are_not* implies *some_are_not* (a rule in the application domain), this implies that $some\_are\_not(C,A) \wedge (all\_are(A,C) \vee some\_are\_not(A,C) \vee all\_are\_not(A,C))$ which tells us that *Some C are not A* is always true (see the animation diagram in Figure 11.21 (2)), and this is also the conclusion obtained by the traditional algorithm that uses Euler circles.

It will be noticed that there is no shading in the diagrams presented in this section, and this relates to an interesting aspect of the interpreta-

Figure 11.21
An Example of Using G-Mapping to Solve Syllogisms.

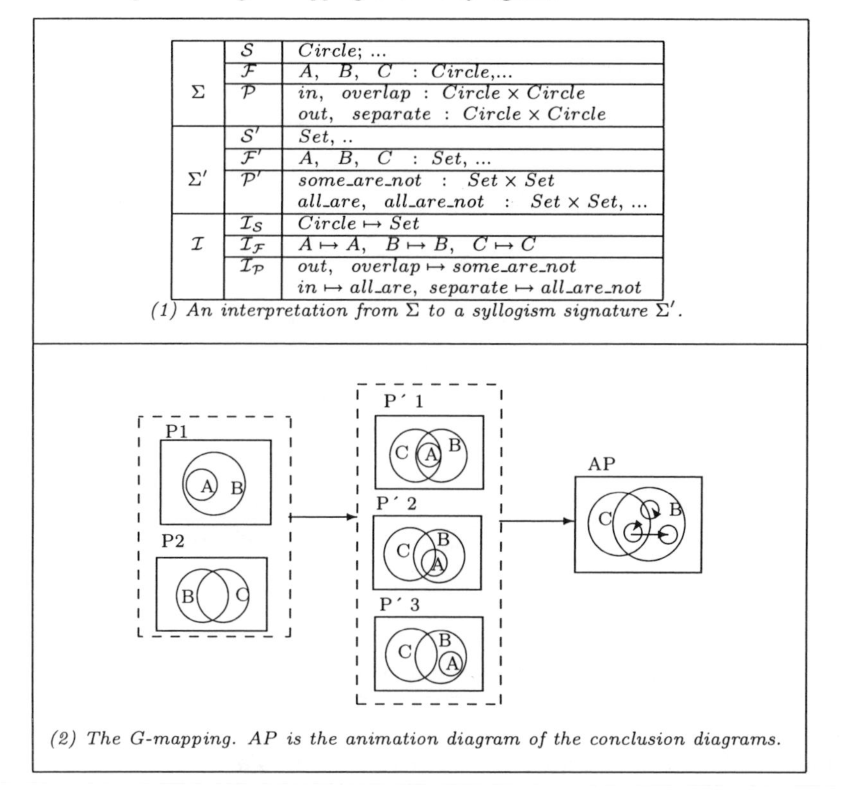

Σ	$\mathcal{S}$	*Circle*; ...
	$\mathcal{F}$	*A*, *B*, *C* : *Circle*,...
	$\mathcal{P}$	*in*, *overlap* : *Circle* × *Circle* *out*, *separate* : *Circle* × *Circle*
Σ'	$\mathcal{S}'$	*Set*, ..
	$\mathcal{F}'$	*A*, *B*, *C* : *Set*, ...
	$\mathcal{P}'$	*some_are_not* : *Set* × *Set* *all_are*, *all_are_not* : *Set* × *Set*, ...
$\mathcal{I}$	$\mathcal{I}_{\mathcal{S}}$	*Circle* ↦ *Set*
	$\mathcal{I}_{\mathcal{F}}$	*A* ↦ *A*, *B* ↦ *B*, *C* ↦ *C*
	$\mathcal{I}_{\mathcal{P}}$	*out*, *overlap* ↦ *some_are_not* *in* ↦ *all_are*, *separate* ↦ *all_are_not*

(1) An interpretation from Σ to a syllogism signature Σ′.

(2) The G-mapping. AP is the animation diagram of the conclusion diagrams.

tion scheme. The relation *overlap* is interpreted as *some_are_not*—this is an approach that works for the given syllogism, but could cause problems if we needed also to deal with the relation *some_are*. The shading in Figure 11.1 would allow the distinction to be made, in effect by using an implicitly different interpretational scheme where closed curves directly represent sets, and *overlap* represents set intersection, the syllogistic implications then having to be derived by a more complex chain of reasoning. This difference emphasizes the importance of being very clear about the precise nature of the semantics defined in any particular case of diagrammatic reasoning.

Figure 11.22
An Example of Using Diagrams to Solve Resultant Forces Applied on Objects, Where Emergent Graphical Objects Are Used in the Problem Solving.

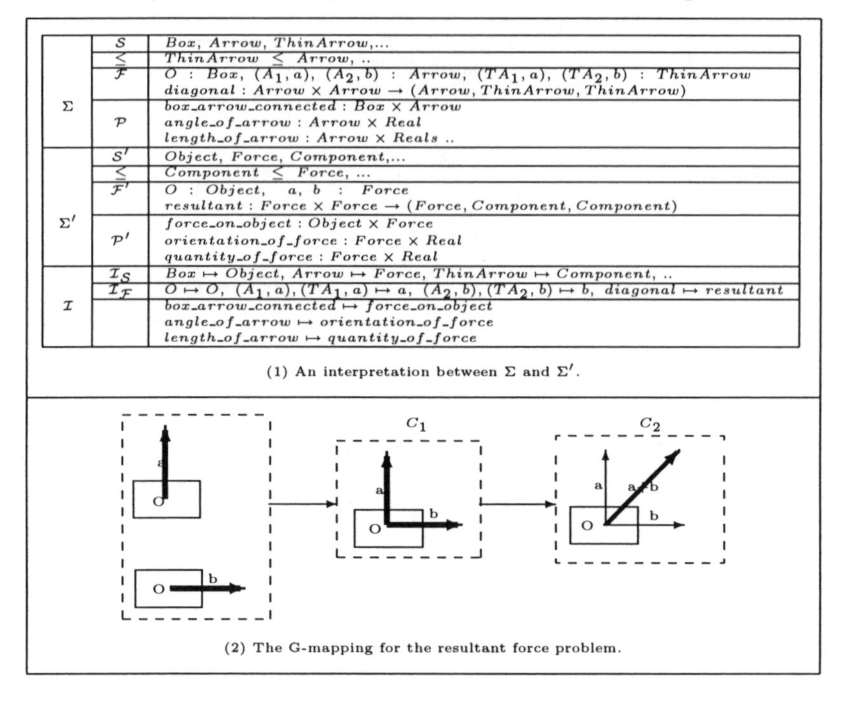

Σ	$\mathcal{S}$	Box, Arrow, ThinArrow,...
	$\leq$	ThinArrow $\leq$ Arrow, ..
	$\mathcal{F}$	O : Box, (A_1, a), (A_2, b) : Arrow, (TA_1, a), (TA_2, b) : ThinArrow diagonal : Arrow $\times$ Arrow $\rightarrow$ (Arrow, ThinArrow, ThinArrow)
	$\mathcal{P}$	box_arrow_connected : Box $\times$ Arrow angle_of_arrow : Arrow $\times$ Real length_of_arrow : Arrow $\times$ Reals ..
Σ'	$\mathcal{S}'$	Object, Force, Component,...
	$\leq$	Component $\leq$ Force, ...
	$\mathcal{F}'$	O : Object, a, b : Force resultant : Force $\times$ Force $\rightarrow$ (Force, Component, Component)
	$\mathcal{P}'$	force_on_object : Object $\times$ Force orientation_of_force : Force $\times$ Real quantity_of_force : Force $\times$ Real
$\mathcal{I}$	$\mathcal{I}_{\mathcal{S}}$	Box $\mapsto$ Object, Arrow $\mapsto$ Force, ThinArrow $\mapsto$ Component, ..
	$\mathcal{I}_{\mathcal{F}}$	$O \mapsto O$, $(A_1, a), (TA_1, a) \mapsto a$, $(A_2, b), (TA_2, b) \mapsto b$, diagonal $\mapsto$ resultant
		box_arrow_connected $\mapsto$ force_on_object angle_of_arrow $\mapsto$ orientation_of_force length_of_arrow $\mapsto$ quantity_of_force

(1) An interpretation between Σ and Σ'.

(2) The G-mapping for the resultant force problem.

11.7.2 Using Diagrams to Solve Resultant Force

In this section, we give another example, where emergent objects are used in reasoning.

Suppose two forces a (5kg and 90°) and b (5kg and 0°) are applied to an object O, and we ask what is the resultant force on O.

Solving this problem by means of G-mapping, we first assume a graphical signature (the graphical theory over this signature being omitted here), the application domain signature and an interpretation as shown in Figure 11.22–(1). The premises, forces a and b on object O, are represented as two premise diagrams in Figure 11.22–(2). Applying G-mapping to these two premise diagrams, a conclusion diagram is obtained (see in Figure 11.22–(2)).

The graphical object labeled as $a + b$ in the conclusion diagram is an emergent graphical object, which represents the resultant force applied on the object O. This emergent object is an inevitable outcome of the operation of our theoretical framework. Using G-mappings, the conclusion diagram may only consist of the two arrows a and b (see C_1 in Figure 11.22–(2)). However, when we give the diagram a geometrical characterization (as described in Section 11.2) the graphical subsignature reflects all the possible graphical objects in the diagram. For this case, the subsignature for the conclusion diagram contains not only arrows a and b but also the emergent object formed by applying the graphical function, *diagonal*, to a and b. By drawing it explicitly, an expected conclusion diagram is obtained (see C_2 in Figure 11.22–(2)).

In this graphical signature, there is a special kind of arrow, *ThinArrow* which is a subsort of *Arrow*, corresponding to *Component* force which is a subsort of *Force* in the application domain. The graphical function *diagonal* produces a diagonal line, and meanwhile changes the pair of arrows in its domain into thin arrows. This prevents the conclusion diagram from producing an infinity of arrows by applying the function *diagonal* to each new arrow and the existing arrows.

In the graphical signature in Figure 11.22–(1), labels a and b relate to both arrows and thin arrows. The representations of the graphical objects are (A_1, a), (A_2, b), (TA_1, a) and (TA_2, b), and (A_1, a) and (TA_1, a) are interpreted as force a and (A_2, b) and (TA_2, b) as b. This example shows that it is not necessary to preserve the sorts of the graphical objects in a G-mapping. It suffices to preserve the labels of the graphical objects (e.g. an arrow (A_1, a) is mapped to a thin arrow (TA_1, a)). However, in this case, if the mapping changes the size or orientation of the arrow it won't be a G-mapping any more, since that change does not satisfy the consistency condition.

11.8 Related Work and Further Research

11.8.1 Related Work

The work presented in this chapter consists of three parts: diagram description, interpretation and reasoning with diagrammatic representations. We consider these in turn.

Diagram Description Diagram description consists of two parts: an abstract notion of a graphical descriptive language, and the geometrical characterization of particular pictures. The notion of a graphical descriptive language is related to various lines of work on picture description. The main distinction between our work and most of these results stem from the different purposes for which diagrams are described. Much work in this field aims at picture recognition and generation (Fu 1974, Duce & Fielding 1986, Mallgren 1983, Onodera & Kawai 1986), and constraint based picture specification (Borning 1981, Helm & Marriott 1991, Wang & Lee 1993). Such work is mainly concerned with describing pictures on the basis of current computer graphics techniques to serve a particular kind of visualization or, in other kinds of application domain, with the recognition of objects from photographs etc.

However, what we are interested in are those respects in which diagrams are used as a communication medium by or among people. Therefore, techniques for computer graphics and visualization are not immediately applicable here, but, instead, we are mainly concerned with features which pictures have in their uses as visual languages for communication and reasoning.

Our approach to diagram description is an algebraic approach. Such an algebraic approach to picture description was introduced by Pineda in his system *GRAFLOG* (Pineda 1990), which has been a source of inspiration. There are, however, some divergences. The graphical descriptive language used in *GRAFLOG* is based on a many-sorted algebra (Goguen, Thatcher & Wagner 1978), whereas ours is based on order sorted algebras (Goguen & Meseguer 1989). We believe this to be a technically more suitable approach, avoiding the various problems resulting e.g. from partial functions in many-sorted algebras. Another difference lies in the treatment of semantics: in *GRAFLOG* the meanings of the graphical entities in the language are given by geometrical algorithms, while ours are given by a set of logical formulae (in a graphical theory) which describe the behavior of geometrical algorithms. This makes it possible to give diagrams an accurate geometrical characterization based on the graphical descriptive language, without the need of considering the merits of different algorithms.

Interpretations and Visual Reasoning There has been a good deal of recent research on the semantic characterization of pictures. Most of the work in this field is the study of semantics in situations where a recognized interpretation for a class of graphical representations already exists, as for example in the use of Euler's circles (Stenning 1993) or Venn diagrams (Sun-Joo 1991), and various lines of work in the field of visual languages (as regularly reported e.g. in the *Journal of Visual Languages and Computing*), in all of which cases the graphical representation of the application domain is well established (e.g. Venn diagrams and set theory, Euler's circles and syllogisms, various charts and binary relations, flow charts and programs, and so on). Our objective, however, is to examine the way in which pictures are assigned meanings by explicit interpretations. For us, the study of interpretations is a crucial first step towards providing the computational environment for supporting general visual communication where pictures do not have a fixed meaning. Much of Sections 11.2 to 11.4 of this chapter are an elaboration of some of our earlier work (Wang & Lee 1993), where a visual reasoning system *GAR* was also introduced. *GAR* allows users to give interpretations to graphical entities and answers users' queries by demonstrating graphical inferences. For example, a user interprets *Closed-curve* as *Set*, and the graphical operations *overlap*, *union* and *difference* between closed curves as $\cap$, $\cup$ and $-$ between sets. *GAR* can then answer various queries about these set operations (e.g. $A \cup (B \cap C) = (A \cup B) \cap (A \cup C)$?) by not only giving an answer as *Yes* or *No* but by also showing the corresponding graphical representations step by step as we do when we use Venn diagrams. This paper develops that formal framework, through the concept of G-mapping and its evident relation to rules of inference, in the direction of a fully-fledged proof system.

11.8.2 Further Research

The current definition of the G-mapping has various limitations. The example of *counting the tangled forest*, demonstrated by the system BIT-PICT (Furnas 1992), can be viewed as a reasoning with diagrammatic representations. In this example, a picture of a tangled forest (consisting of many intertwined but not intersecting curved lines) is mapped to another picture by mapping a curve to a dot; then dots are mapped to Roman numerals which give the number of the trees in the tangled forest. Though we can describe this mapping in our framework by choosing a suitable graphical language and interpretation, we cannot get each of the conclusion diagrams by just seeking things which meet our definition of the G-mapping. In order to solve problems like this, a framework is needed for putting mapping rules into a G-mapping in a flexible and easily-revisable way, according to the application. It would be nice to develop such a framework on the basis of the work presented here.

Acknowledgments

This chapter is a revision and extension of Wang and Lee (1993). Parts of the work have been supported by the UK Joint Research Councils' Initiative in Cognitive Science and HCI, and by the Economic and Social Research Council (UK) *via* the Human Communication Research Centre.

References

Arbib, M. A. and Manes, E. G. 1975. *Arrows, Structure and Functors—The Categorical Imperative.* New York: Academic Press.

Barwise, J. and Perry, J. 1983. *Situations and Attitudes.* Cambridge, Mass.: The MIT Press.

Barwise, Jon and Etchemendy, John 1990. Visual Information and Valid Reasoning. Tech. Report, CSLI, Stanford University.

Borning, A. 1981. The Programming Language Aspects of Thinglab, A Constraint-Oriented Simulation Laboratory. *ACM Trans. Program. Lang. Syst.* 3.

Duce, D. A. and Fielding, E. V. C. 1986. Towards a Formal Specification of the GKS Output Primitive. In Proceedings of Eurographics 86. Amsterdam: North-Holland.

Fu, K. S. 1974. *Syntactic Methods in Pattern Recognition.* New York: Academic Press.

Furnas, George W. 1992. Reasoning with Diagrams Only. In Reasoning with Diagrammatic Representations: Papers from the 1992 AAAI Spring Symposium. Tech. Report SS-92-02, American Association for Artificial Intelligence, Menlo Park, Calif.

Goguen, J. and Burstall, R. 1984.Introducing Institutions. *LNCS* 164.

Goguen, J. and Burstall, R. 1992. Institutions: Abstract Model Theory for Specification and Programming.*Joural of the Association for Computing Machinery* 39(1) (January): 95–146.

Goguen, J. and Meseguer, J. 1989. Order-Sorted Algebra 1: Equational Deduction for Multiple Inheritance, Polymorphism, Overloading and Partial Operations. Technical Report SRI-CSL-89-10, SRI International.

Goguen, J., Thatcher, J. and Wagner, E. 1978. An Initial Algebra Approach to the Specification, Correctness and Implementation of Abstract Data Types. In

Current Trends in Programming Methodology, ed. R. Yeh. Englewood Cliffs, N.J.: Prentice-Hall.

Helm, Richard and Marriott, Kim 1991. A Declarative Specification and Semantics for Visual Languages. *Journal of Visual Languages and Computing* 2: 311–331.

Mallgren, W. R. 1983. *Formal Specification of Interactive Graphics Programming Language.* Cambridge, Massachusetts: The MIT Press.

Meseguer, J. 1989. General Logics. In *Logic Colloquium,* ed. H.-D. Ebbinghaus. Amsterdam: North-Holland.

Onodera, T. and Kawai, S. 1986. A Formalization of the Specification and Systematic Generation of Computer Graphics Systems. *Visual Computer.*

Pineda, L. A. 1990. GRAFLOG: a Theory of Semantics for Graphics with Applications to Human-Computer Interaction and CAD Systems. PhD diss., University of Edinburgh.

Plummer, D. B. and Bailin, S. C. 1992. Proofs and Pictures Proving the Diamond Lemma with the Grover Theorem Proving. In Reasoning with Diagrammatic Representations: Papers from the 1992 AAAI Spring Symposium. Tech. Report SS-92-02, American Association for Artificial Intelligence, Menlo Park, Calif.

Sannella, D. and Tarlecki, A. 1987. On Observational Equivalence and Algebraic Specification. *Computer and System Science* 34.

Stenning, Keith 1993. *Logic as a Foundation for a Cognitive Theory of Modality Allocation.* Edinburgh: Human Communication Research Center, Edinburgh University.

Stenning, Keith and Oberlander, Jon 1992. Implementing Logics in Diagrams. In Reasoning with Diagrammatic Representations: Papers from the 1992 AAAI Spring Symposium. Tech. Report SS-92-02, American Association for Artificial Intelligence, Menlo Park, Calif.

Sun-Joo, Shin 1991. A Situation-Theoretic Account of Valid Reasoning with Venn Diagrams. *Situation Theory and Its Applications* 2. Stanford, Calif.: CSLI.

Wang, Dejuan, and Lee, John R. 1993. Pictorial Concepts and a Concept-Supporting Graphical System. *Journal of Visual Languages and Computing* 4:177–199.

Wang, Dejuan, and Lee, John R. 1993. Visual Reasoning: Its Formal Semantics and Applications. *Journal of Visual Languages and Computing* 4:327–356.

III COGNITIVE AND COMPUTATIONAL MODELS

Introduction to Section III
Cognitive and Computational Models

David L. Waltz
NEC Research Institute and Brandeis University

Diagrammatic reasoning is an area of immense importance, both practical and theoretical, especially given the rush toward multimedia systems and services, and the scientific objective of understanding perception, at the same time the richest and one of the least-well understood aspects of cognition. I first became interested in this area when I was working on my thesis, a constraint propagation system for understanding scenes of simple polyhedral objects (Waltz 1975). The late Max Clowes, whose work on scene labeling had profoundly influenced me, argued in a talk at the MIT AI Lab that vision is "controlled hallucination," illustrating his point by showing perfectly intelligible scenes that featured for example edges hidden in shadows and subjective contours. This, together with the difficulty I and others encountered in obtaining "perfect line drawings" of scenes, even when we had full control lighting and used specially prepared objects, caused me to realize that vision was not going to be solved by a pure bottom-up strategy, then and now the most common approach.

Later, having worked in the interim on natural language processing, I thought hard about what was wrong with Schank's Conceptual Dependency (Schank 1975) as a basis for language understanding, and concluded that it was fundamentally incapable of differentiating such concepts as "eating" from "devouring," "wolfing," and "nibbling at," and that what was needed was a visually enriched representation (Waltz 1982). This led me, with my student Lois Boggess (Waltz & Boggess 1979), to an investigation of analogical constructs for representing the meaning of natural language prepositions (e.g. on, in, near, etc.), a topic also investigated at about the same time by Annette Herskovitz (Herskovitz 1985), and closely related to Johnson-Laird's work on mental models (Johnson-Laird 1983). At about the same time I also wrote two papers outlining the requirements for a system that could understand natural language scene descriptions (Waltz 1981a, 1981b), as well as other pieces that investigated the relationships of images, objects, and words. In retrospect, these papers had little impact, due no doubt in part to the quality of the work and my own lack of follow-through, but in addition, I believe, because the time was not yet ripe for such work. Logical representations were generally viewed as theoretically universal and the sufficient basis for all manner of expert systems. It was widely believed that logic could successfully model images and scenes, even though the baroque improbability of that effort should have long been clear to everyone who read Pat Hayes' Naive Physics Manifesto (Hayes 1969).

Well, the time is now ripe. These chapters represent some, though by no means all, of the best work from a rapidly expanding field. The chapters in this section are concerned with models of diagrammatic reasoning. They utilize a wide spectrum of methodologies, and draw their inspiration from a wide range of different problem areas. Yet there are common themes; I'll return to this below, after saying a bit about the goals, methodology, and results of the work reported in the chapters comprising this section.

In their fascinating chapter, Y. Qin and H. Simon report on their exploration of the role of diagrams in understanding scientific concepts. In their research, Qin and Simon tested subjects on their understanding of sections of Einstein's original paper on special relativity—which was published with no diagrams—and found close links between the quality and accuracy of diagrams that subjects drew and their understanding of the concepts in the paper.

Janice Glasgow and Dimitri Papadias' chapter, reprinted from *Cognitive Science* (Glasgow & Papadias 1992), presents a family of multi-perspective, hierarchical models for mental images, and explores the use of these models for representing and reasoning about images of scenes, maps, and objects. The chapter is partially motivated by human mental imagery and its use in representation and problem solving, but most of Glasgow and Papadias' emphasis is on computational efficiency and the appropriateness of representations for supporting different types of reasoning.

In contrast, Erika Rogers presents a model of human visual problem-solving, concentrating on the interactions between bottom-up, visually driven processing and top-down, expectation-driven processing. Rogers' goal is ultimately the design of better interfaces and support systems for human problem-solving, but the bulk of her chapter here is on a model of human performance, which she argues must be understood in order to enable appropriate interface design. Rogers shows how her model can be used to represent protocols of radiologists reading chest x-rays, illuminating interactions between top-down and bottom-up strategies.

The chapters in this volume by Narayanan, Suwa and Motoda, and by Mary Hegarty both are concerned with inferring the behavior of mechanical systems from diagrams. Like Rogers, Narayanan *et al* are concerned with the interactions between bottom-up and top-down processes and problem-solving methods that direct attention and draw inferences from diagrams. They present a computer model that is inspired by verbal protocols, and that features image representations in many ways similar to those of Glasgow and Papdias. The algorithm for their model combines both rule-based and diagram-based reasoning.

While her goals are closely related to those of Naryanan *et al*, Hegarty takes reaction-time and eye-fixation data as her starting point for investigating how people infer the kinematics of mechanical systems through "mental animation" in her chapter reprinted from *JEP: Learning, Memory & Cognition* (Hegarty 1992). Using qualitative motion analysis of pulley systems for her testing, Hegarty finds that eye movements and reaction times suggest that subjects solve these types of problems by piecemeal operations, that the sequencing of these operations is isomorphic to the causal sequencing of events in the pulley systems, and that errors increase as the causal chains lengthen.

Kenneth Koedinger and John Anderson use verbal protocols as their basis for formulating a model of human skill in the domain of geometry proof problems, in another chapter reprinted from *Cognitive Science* (Koedinger & Anderson 1990). They report that, unlike previous models of geometric problem solving, experts tend to focus on key portions of the diagrams, that they tend to skip steps – even in the initial planning phase of a proof – and moreover that experts tend to skip the same steps. Their model parses geometry problems into perceptual chunks that cue relevant schemas, some of which are multi-step macro-operators, dramatically cutting down the proof search space.

Habel, Pribbenow and Simmons take a quite different direction from the rest of the chapters in this section. They concentrate on the representation of objects, especially part-whole relationships, and on the use of vision or mental images for verification in planning or reasoning.

Much of the chapter is concerned with the segmentation of objects – especially complex or articulated objects – into parts, and the representation of objects in hybrid partonomy and taxonomy structures for support of more traditional logical reasoning.

The work reported here only scratches the surface, considering a tiny set of domains. I came away from reading the chapters in this section with a greater appreciation for the difficulties of understanding human image-based reasoning even to the degree that we understand human verbal reasoning, and of building systems that deal fluently with images and diagrams, even if such systems are restricted to narrow domains. Still, some common themes are already evident: hybrid representation structures that shade from image analogs to hierarchies; and heterogeneous processing modules and control structures that support bottom-up and top-down interactions, cuing higher level schemas from low-level features, and using expectations to drive attentional mechanisms.

References

Glasgow, J. and Papadias, D. 1992. Computational Imagery. *Cognitive Science* 16(3): 355–394.

Hayes, P. J., 1969. The Naive Physics Manifesto. In *Expert Systems in the Electronic Age,* ed. D. Michie. Edinburgh: Edinburgh University Press.

Hegarty, M. 1992. Mental Animation: Inferring Motion from Static Displays of Mechanical Systems. *JEP: Learning, Memory & Cognition* 18(5): 1084–1102.

Herskovits, A. 1985. Semantics and Pragmatics of Locative Expressions. *Cognitive Science* 9(3): 314–378.

Johnson-Laird, P. 1983. *Mental Models,* Cambridge, Mass.: Harvard University Press.

Koedinger, K. and Anderson, J. 1990. Abstract Planning and Perceptual Chunks: Elements of Expertise in Geometry. *Cognitive Science* 14(4): 511–550.

Schank, R. C. 1975. *Conceptual Information Processing,* Hillsdale, N.J.: Erlbaum.

Waltz, D. L. 1975. Understanding Scenes with Shadows. In *The Psychology of Computer Vision*, ed. Winston. New York: McGraw-Hill.

Waltz, D. L. and Boggess, L. 1979. Visual Analog Representations for Natural Language Understanding. In Proceedings of the International Joint Conference on Artificial Intelligence., 926–934. San Francisco, Calif.: Morgan Kaufmann.

Waltz, D.L. 1981a. Toward a Detailed Model of Processing for Language Describing the Physical World. In Proceedings of the International Joint Conference on Artificial Intelligence., 1–6. San Francisco, Calif.: Morgan Kaufmann.

Waltz, D. L. 1981b. Generating and Understanding Scene Descriptions. In *Elements of Discourse Understanding*, ed. Joshi, Sag, and Webber. Cambridge: Cambridge University Press.

Waltz, D. L. 1982. Event Shape Diagrams. In Proceedings of the National Conference on Artificial Intelligence, 84–87. Menlo Park, Calif.: AAAI Press.

12 Imagery and Mental Models

Yulin Qin & Herbert Simon
Carnegie Mellon University

For some decades, imagery has been an active research area in cognitive science (c.f., Paivio 1971; Shepard and Metzler 1971; Simon 1972; Pylyshyn 1973; Kosslyn 1980, 1983; Shepard and Cooper 1982; Pinker 1985; Finke 1989). Research is also going on regarding imagery's neuropsychological base (Farah 1985; Kosslyn 1987; Kosslyn, Sokolov and Chen 1989; etc.). And the role of imagery in education has been developed (e.g., Martel 1991). However, there are only a few publications of experimental work concerned mainly with imagery in problem solving (e.g., Simon and Barenfeld 1969; Hayes 1973; and some aspects in Larkin and Simon 1987; Novak 1976; Tabachneck and Simon 1995).

Understanding how users interact with pictorial and diagrammatic displays on computer screens is crucial to the design of interfaces for expert systems and other sophisticated applications of computers. To be effective, computer displays must be compatible with human capabilities for creating mental and external diagrams and for drawing inferences from them In this paper we illustrate how experimental methods can be used to discover how subjects use mental images and drawings created from them to comprehend a difficult text. We will draw some general conclusions from the experiment about the nature of mental imagery and its relation to diagrams drawn on paper.

Our project, in which subjects were asked to read and try to understand the first part of Einstein's 1905 paper on special relativity, focuses on imagery in understanding and problem solving, in mental modeling (c.f. Gentner and Stevens 1983; Johnson-Laird 1983; Norman 1988) and in qualitative reasoning (c.f. Iwasaki 1989; Weld and de Kleer 1990) . In Qin and Simon (1990, 1992), we discussed some results of our project relating to problem solving success. We summarize briefly here the major findings about imagery that will be developed in our paper:

1. All of our subjects can form mental images to derive or justify the essential equations of special relativity, including those subjects who, when meeting difficulties in reasoning, usually claimed not to be able to do so;

2. Subjects can follow the processes in an evolving mental image as they would track processes in the real world. In tracking processes, subjects note key events and construct before-and-after images and (when permitted to do so) corresponding external diagrams that relate successive key events and enable inferences to be drawn from static relations between the events By following the processes in this way, subjects can draw qualitative conclusions, and then infer quantitative relations, i.e., the equation to be derived. Without images or with incorrect images, subjects find the task very difficult. They are not able to derive the equations or even derive wrong results;

   One of the differences between observing a mental image and observing a real-world object is that the components of the image are better understood, because they are formed by the observers themselves, who know what they should include;

3. In the process of going from a qualitative result to a quantitative equation, some subjects, with the help of their images, can create new concepts, quantities, and form semi-quantitative equations;

4. The basic pieces of information for forming a mental image are the components of the situation, their organization and structure, the kinematic relations among them, and the process (if the image is used to represent a process). There are two basic ways of forming images: that used while reading for comprehension and that used for problem solving, such as deriving an equation. The difference between them is that the first is based on attention to the reading matter, and the second is guided by the goal of problem solving. There is active interaction between the processes of problem solving and of forming mental images. The images used in problem solving are usually as simple as possible. Irrelevant components are lost very soon. Subjects frequently switch between reasoning and forming and watching images. They carry a heavy load in short-term memory (STM);

5. To form mental images, subjects draw upon information in their mental models, stored in long-term memory (LTM). By mental model we mean the structure of the subjects' knowledge about the world. This is a different usage from Johnson-Laird's (1983), which

employs "mental model" for what we prefer, in accord with earlier usage (Newell and Simon, 1972) to call a problem representation.

A mental model, in our use of the term, is deeper and more stable, systematic and general than the images formed in (STM) for a specific task, and provides a source of information for such imaging. As shown by Novak 1976, the mental model influences the process of getting information from the reading material, and determines what kind of image will be formed. Bugs in the mental model may cause subjects to form an image that does not correspond to the real situation, or to form the right picture but with wrong values of the quantities of the components (e.g., in our text on relativity, the velocity of light measured in the stationary system);

6. Understanding reading material often involves changing the reader's mental model. It is not easy to change one's mental model totally. Furthermore, a mental model is not very complete and may be inconsistent. So, when reading a paper that fundamentally changes their world model, as our reading material does, subjects may for some time have a confused mental model. They are learning non-Galilean transformations, but still hold the concept of Galilean transformations in their minds. They can give the superficial meaning of an equation, but find it difficult to accept a deep one (e.g.,that the synchronism of two events is relative). Encountering and resolving this kind of conflict while reading may be a way to change the mental models.

12.1 Experiment

First, we describe our experiment, including the reading material used. We also discuss briefly the processes we use for inferring mental images from verbal protocols and external diagrams, and the prior empirical evidence that supports these kinds of inferences.

12.1.1 Reading Material

Except for a few modifications, such as equations and some explanatory material to help readers derive formula , the reading material used in this experiment is simply a copy of the first three sections of the first part, the kinematical part, of Einstein's 1905 paper: "On the Electrodynamics of Moving Bodies" (Einstein, 1905). As shown in the following outline of the reading material, Einstein employed a "divide then integrate" strategy and motivated each of his initial equations by inviting the reader to form a mental picture that exemplifies it. The equations can, so to speak, be read directly from these mental pictures, so that the reader who has found the picture understands the corresponding equation. interestingly enough, the published paper contains no diagrams to guide or assist this process. For the convenience of the discussion later, in square brackets [ ] we give the numbers of the paragraphs cited in the reading material.

Definition of Simultaneity In this section, some basic concepts are introduced:

1. Stationary and moving systems;
2. Simultaneous events and time;
3. Definition of synchronous clocks:

   [10] "Let a ray of light start at the 'A time' t_A from A towards B, let it at the 'B time' t_B be reflected at B in the direction of A, and arrive again at A at the 'A time' t'_A. In accordance with definition the two clocks synchronize if

   $$t_B - t_A = t'_A - t_B.\text{"} \qquad (12.1.1)$$

4. Velocity of light:

   [16] "In agreement with experience we further assume the quantity

   $$2AB/(t'_A - t_A) = c \qquad (12.1.2)$$

   to be a universal constant—the velocity of light in empty space."

On the Relativity of Lengths and Times

1. Two principles:

   - The principle of relativity.

     [19] "The laws by which the states of a physical system undergo change are not affected, whether these changes of state be referred to the one or the other of two systems of coordinates in uniform translatory motion."

- The principle of the constancy of the velocity of light.

  [20] "Any ray of light moves in the 'stationary' system of co-ordinates with the determined velocity c, whether the ray be emitted by a stationary or by a moving body. Hence

  $$velocity = lightpath/timeinterval \tag{12.1.3}$$

  where time interval is to be taken in the sense of the definition in 12.1.1."

2. The relativity of lengths.

   [21] "Let there be given a stationary rigid rod; and let its length be l as measured by a measuring-rod which is also stationary. We now imagine the axis of the rod lying along the axis of x of the stationary system of co-ordinates, and that a uniform motion of parallel translation with velocity v along the axis of x in the direction of increasing x is then imparted to the rod."

   [22] "We now inquire as to the length of the moving rod, and imagine its length to be ascertained by following two operations:"

   (a) Measured in the moving system: according to the principle of relativity, the length of the rod must be equal to l.

   (b) Measured in the stationary system: "we shall find that it differs from l." [Einstein did not give the value of the length at this time.]

   [27] "Current kinematics tacitly assumes that the lengths determined by these two operations are precisely equal, ..."

The Relativity of Times. [28] "We imagine further that at the two ends A and B of the rod, clocks are placed which synchronize with the clocks of the stationary system, that is to say that their indications correspond at any instant to the 'time of the stationary system' at the place where they happen to be. These clocks are therefore 'synchronous in the stationary system.'"

[29] "We imagine further ... Let a ray of light depart from A at the time t_A, let it be reflected at B at the time t_B, and reach A again at the time t'_A."

[30] "Taking into consideration the principle of the constancy of the velocity of light we find that

$$t_B - t_A = r_{AB}/(c - v) \tag{12.1.4}$$

and

$$t'_A - t_B = r_{AB}/(c + v) \tag{12.1.5}$$

where r_{AB} denotes the length of the moving rod—measured in the stationary system."

[31] "Observers moving with the moving rod would thus find that the two clocks were not synchronous, while observers in the stationary system would declare the clocks to be synchronous."

[32] "So we see that we cannot attach any absolute signification to the concept of simultaneity, ..."

Theory of the transformation of co-ordinates and times from a stationary system to another system in uniform motion of translation relative to the former. .

[33] "Let us in 'stationary' space take two systems of coordinates,..."

[34] "Now to the origin of one of the two systems (k) let a constant velocity v be imparted in the direction of the increasing x of the other stationary system (K), ..."

[36] "To any system of values x, y, z, t, which completely defines the place and time of an event in the stationary system, there belongs a system of values ξ, η, ζ, τ determining that event relatively to the system k, and our task is now to find the system of equations connecting these quantities."

[38] "If we place $x' = x - vt$, it is clear that a point at rest in the system k must have a system of values x', y, z, independent of time. We first define τ as a function of x', y, z, and t ..."

1. Along the X-axis

   [39] "From the origin of system k let a ray be emitted at the time τ_0 along the X-axis to x', and at the time τ_1 be reflected thence to the origin of the co-ordinates, arriving there at the time τ_2;"

   [40] "we then must have

$$\frac{1}{2}(\tau_0 + \tau_2) = \tau_1 \tag{12.1.6}$$

[41] "or, by inserting the arguments of the function τ and applying the principle of the constancy of the velocity of light in the stationary system:

$$\frac{1}{2}[\tau(0,0,0,t)+\tau(0,0,0,t+\frac{x'}{c-v}+\frac{x'}{c+v})] = \tau(x',0,0,t+\frac{x'}{c-v}) \quad (12.1.7)$$

[42] "To simplify the mathematical operations, losing no generality, let $t=0$ and $\tau_0=0$. We get:

$$\frac{1}{2}[\tau(0,0,0,0)+\tau(0,0,0,\frac{x'}{c-v}+\frac{x'}{c+v})] = \tau(x',0,0,\frac{x'}{c-v})\text{''} \quad (12.1.8)$$

2. Along the Y-axis

   [51] "Imagine an analogous consideration—applied to the axes of Y and Z—it being borne in mind that light is always propagated along these axes, when viewed from the stationary system, with the velocity

$$\sqrt{c^2-v^2}. \quad (12.1.9)$$

   Then we can have:

$$\frac{1}{2}[\tau(0,0,0,0,)+\tau(0,0,0,\frac{2y}{\sqrt{c^2-v^2}})] = \tau(0,y,0,\frac{y}{\sqrt{c^2-v^2}} \quad (12.1.10)$$

3. The Lorentz transformation equations

   Based on the above key equations, by algebraic reasoning, we can get the Lorentz transformation equations:

$$\begin{aligned} \tau &= \beta(t-vx/c^2) \\ \xi &= \beta(x-vt) \\ \eta &= y \\ \zeta &= z \end{aligned}$$

   where

$$\beta = \frac{1}{\sqrt{1-\frac{v^2}{c^2}}}$$

12.1.2 Method and Subjects

To understand Einstein's paper, subjects need to read it with comprehension, to modify or build concepts (e.g., time, simultaneous events, synchronous clocks), and to understand and/or derive the equations. The latter involves building images, and doing qualitative and quantitative reasoning. In this chapter, we will focus on the images and the reasoning required to derive the equations in Section 12.2 and in Section 12.3 (as shown above) before the Lorentz transformation equations are derived.

The experiment consists of a pretest, reading and exercises, and posttest. The tests and exercises do not have "right answers." They are used for testing the degree of understanding of the subjects.

We obtain information about the images from the diagrams drawn by the subjects, the subjects' gestures (recorded by the experimenter), and their tape-recorded protocols. That is, we postulate a consistency between these observable data and their mental images. The hypothesis that there is a close relation between the kinds of diagrams people draw on paper and their mental images, generally known as the Mind's Eye Hypothesis, is supported by a substantial body of empirical evidence. The evidence has been summarized recently by Tabachneck and Simon (in press):

1. On the behavioral side, Kosslyn (1980) concludes that "generally speaking . . . people judge similarities in the same way when stimuli are evoked from memory or when they are physically present (p. 274)." He observes that such results make perfect sense if images evoked by perception and memory produce the same configuration in the mental visualization locus and use the same procedures.

   Finke and Shepard (1986) review research that relates mental imagery to visual perception to determine whether "the observed performances in perceptual and imagery tasks are in fact mediated by similar or overlapping internal processes (pp. 37-38).' They conclude that "the [hypothesis of] functional equivalence [between external and internal images] provides the single best overall explanation for the results (p. 37)."

2. Kosslyn and Koenig (1992) review research on imagery and perception in both neurophysiology and cognitive science, as well as

research on brain-damaged people, all supporting the hypothesis that processes and locus are shared by perception and memory.

3. The third kind of evidence comes from computational research, which establishes the sufficiency of the Mind's Eye claim. Kosslyn (1980) shows how existing models of long-term memory representations could produce imagery: he defines an image locus as well as the types of processes this locus allows. Many different data from experiments on imagery are accounted for with this model. Computational evidence for the sufficiency of a Mind's Eye is also given by Baylor (1971), who models performance in Guilford's Block Visualization Task with the aid of simulated mental imagery.

The Mind's Eye hypothesis does not require that "pictures in the head" be exactly the same as pictures on a piece of paper. Tabachneck and Simon observe that the two representations may contain different amounts of detail, that the percepts stored in memory may be mingled with previous percepts of the same type, and that certain operations may be more difficult with mental imagery than with perception of external diagrams.

Figures 12.2 and 12.3 show the diagrams drawn by the subjects while they were studying Section 12.2. Most of them focused on three (or at first two) special events, i.e., light starting to go from A to B, light arriving at B, and light going back and arriving at A again, while the rod was moving. In Figure 12.1 we use a time-space coordinate system to show the subject's dynamic image which represents the process of the rod and light traveling. Focusing on the special events of the emission, reflection and return of the light ray, and projecting the process to the X-axis, one can get a diagram similar to S_g, S_m (three events) or S_b, S_j (c) (first two events) in Figures 12.2 and 12.3. A good deal of work must be done on the relation between internal and external representations to check this postulate and the conditions under which it holds. For the present, we can use the data from diagrams, gestures and protocols to see what processes are used to form an image from the reading material and how the image is used to understand the material. In general, we will not find it necessary for our purposes to distinguish between the internal images and the information contained in the diagrams the subjects drew.

Most of our subjects were undergraduate or graduate students in electrical engineering or computer science at Carnegie Mellon University

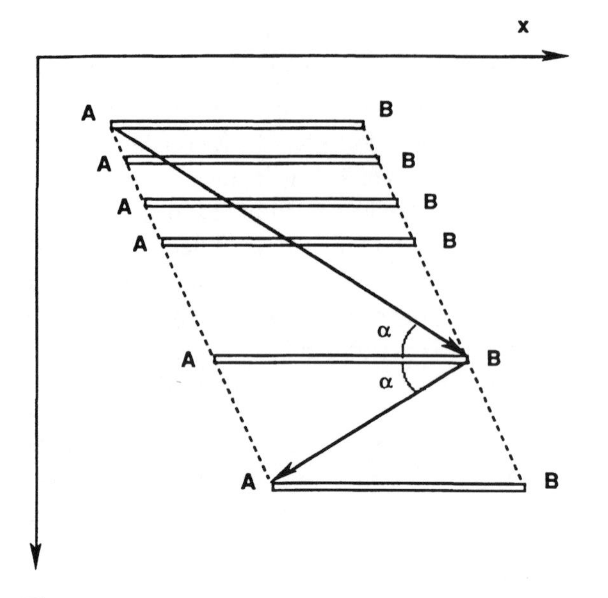

Figure 12.1

with little prior knowledge of the theory of special relativity. All, except S_m, had learned in physics courses that in a moving system time is slowed and lengths are shortened; but none had read Einstein (1905), and none were familiar with derivations of the Lorentz equations or could derive them. They did not know how the alterations of times and lengths were derived from considerations of simultaneity of clocks, invariance of physical laws, and constancy of the speed of light. None of them were aware that the reading material was from Einstein (1905), until, they were told at the end of the experiment.

Of the six subjects, two, S_m and S_r, were allowed to draw diagrams and to use them while performing the tasks we set them; two, S_s and S_g, were allowed to draw diagrams, but these were taken away from them while they performed the tasks; two, S_j and Sb, were not allowed to draw diagrams unless requested to do so by the experimenter (S_j was guilty of two minor violations). Their diagrams were drawn after they had answered the questions. As these differences in condition were not related in any important way to the subjects' uses of imagery, or their ability to perform the tasks, we will not distinguish among the subjects

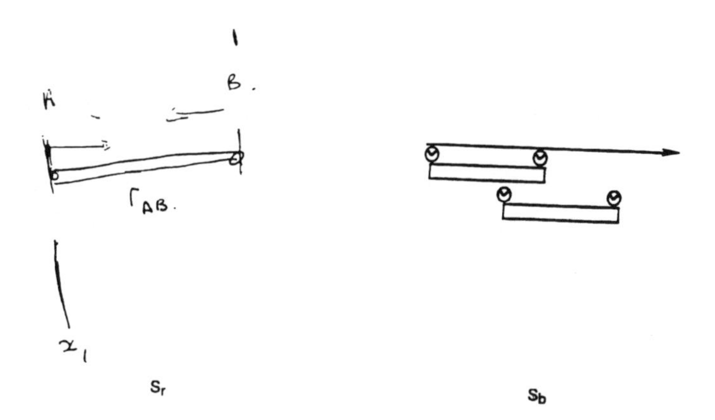

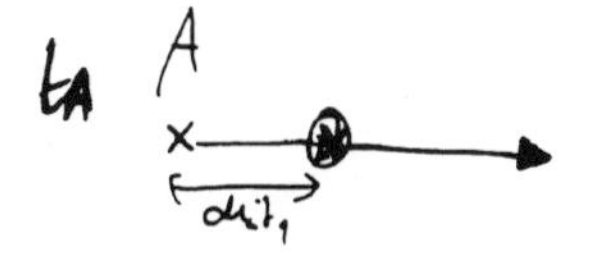

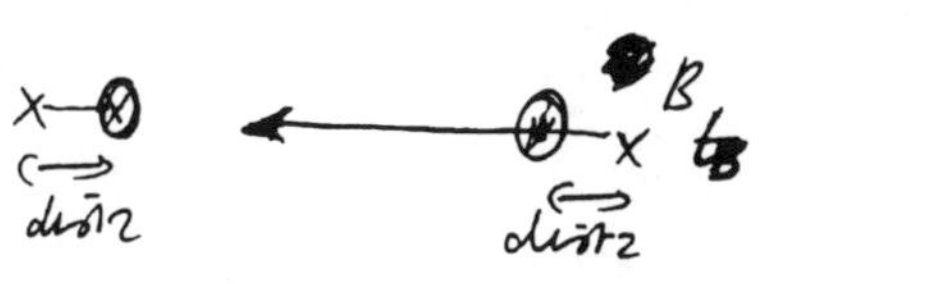

S_m

Figure 12.2

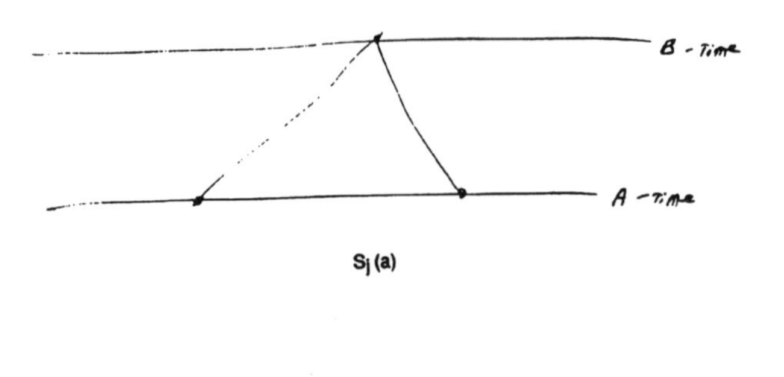

Sj (a)

Sj (b)

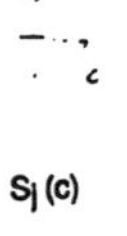

Sj (c)

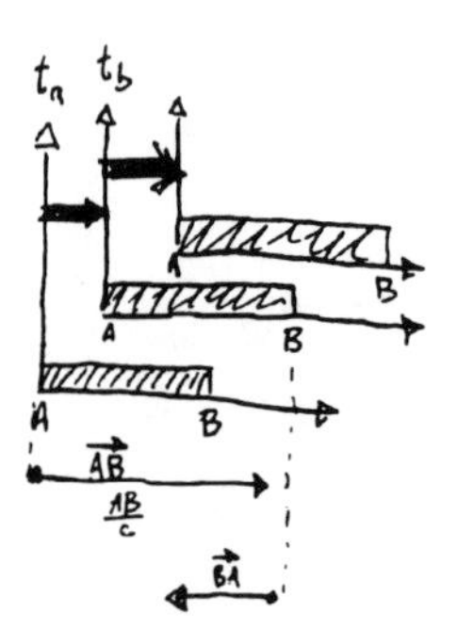

Sg

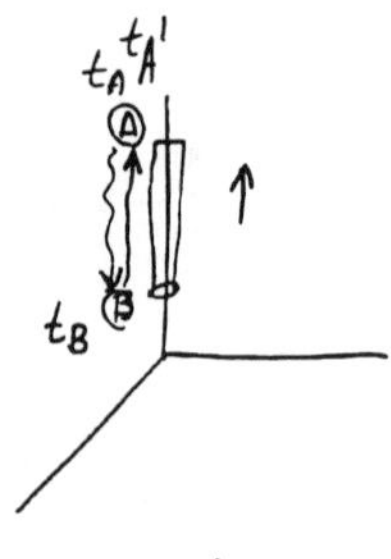

initial - light opposite rod
final - light moving with rod

Ss

Figure 12.3

Table 12.1
Times Required by Subjects to Derive Equations and to Understand the Explanations (Subjects S_j and S_s derived the equations twice: S_j by two methods, S_s after an error. The numbers in parentheses show times for first derivation, the larger numbers, total times).

Subject	Time for equations	Time for paragraphs
	[minutes]	[minutes]
S_m	90	100
S_r	6	6
S_j	119 (21)	96
S_b	9	5
S_s	500 (57)	149
S_g	24	14

in this respect, only noting that S_g, the subject whose data we analyse here in most detail, drew diagrams but did not have them available while answering questions.

Individual sessions extended for about 1.5 to 2 hours. Subjects who had not completed the material at the end of a session returned for one or more additional sessions. Their total times for the entire task ranged from a little more than four hours to about twenty hours.

12.2 The Relativity of Time: Section Two of Einstein's Paper.

The time each subject used to derive equations 12.1.4 and 12.1.5, and the time used to understand paragraphs [31] and [32], which interpret the meanings of the these equations, are shown in Table 12.1.

Subjects reach an understanding of the equations in two ways. The first method is to equate the distance the light travels with the sum of the length of the rod and the distance the rod travels while the light is in route (length method). The second method is to use the formula $Time = lightpath/velocity$ and measure the velocity of light relative to the moving rod in the stationary system (velocity method). That is, they set this velocity equal to $(c - v)$, then to $(c + v)$. Some subjects began with the velocity method, but found that they could attain a clearer understanding of the equations by switching to the length method. S_j derived the equations by the velocity method in 21 minutes. He created

Table 12.2
Comparison of Subjects' Reasoning, Imaging and Alternative Reasoning Methods.
V: Velocity method; L: Length method; I: Imaging; R: Reasoning

	S_m	S_r	S_j	S_b	S_s	S_g
Number of Diagrams Drawn	12	3	2	0	9	3
Number of Gestures	2	0	3	1	1	1
Number of Words	224	203	8	12	203	108
First reasoning method:	V-L	L	V	V	V	L
Number of Switches			7			
between Reasoning Methods	0	0	0	1	1	2
First Step to Derive the Equations:	R	R	R	I	R	I
Number of Times Forming or Watching Images	10	1	6	3	6	6
Number of Times Switching between Imaging and Reasoning	10	2	7	5	8	11

a new concept "apparent velocity" to interpret $c-v$ and $c+v$. Because the experimenter asked him try to state his reasons more clearly, he changed his method. After spending 98 more minutes, he derived the equations again, but by the length method.

By observing their images, subjects obtain a qualitative understanding, and then find the values of relative quantities to derive the quantitative equations. They found it difficult to keep the whole image and the reasoning path in STM simultaneously and switched frequently between forming, changing, and observing images and reasoning. Almost all of the subjects in this experiment used gestures to help reasoning, watching their own gestures as they made them.

Some subjects, such as S_s and S_g, wrote many details on paper. It appears that diagrams offer external storage for images. These subjects used words to keep some information, lowering the load of information transport between STM and LTM.

The number of diagrams drawn by the subjects after reading paragraph [28], the number of their gestures, the number of times they switched between reasoning methods, and the number of times they switched between imaging and reasoning after reading the equations are shown in Table 12.2. In the table, mathematical symbols and operators count as words.

Subjects sometimes formed different images while reading the situation statements and while deriving the equations. In these cases we see different diagrams drawn by the same subject. Figures 12.2 and 12.3 give the final diagrams drawn by each subject. S_b's diagram is his mental image as inferred from his protocol. S_j's (a) was drawn when the experimenter asked him to show his "triangle" image before he derived the equations. S_j's (b) and (c) were drawn so fast that the experimenter could not keep up with him. His images changed from "triangle" to images similar to those drawn by other subjects while deriving the equations. Before deriving the equations, some subjects' images depicted observers and clocks etc, but then they focused on the process of light traveling, without other details.

Although these diagrams may not be exactly the same as the images used by subjects in deriving the equations,, the diagrams show the similarities and differences of images among the subjects. For example, most of the subjects drew the X-axis horizontally and put A at the left end of the rod. This is what Einstein intended, but he did not say it explicitly (c.f. paragraph [21], [28]). S_s' diagram is very interesting. He used the vertical axis as X, and, as he is a left-handed person, put A above B. Keeping this kind of image in mind, he could not draw the correct diagram. He derived equations consistent with his image, but inconsistent with the reading material. He never questioned his image, and tried in a lot of ways to correct his reasoning for about 7.5 hours. It seems that an image has considerable stability. If there were diagrams in the reading material, subjects would not face this kind of difficulty.

In Qin and Simon (1990) we discussed, using S_g's protocol as an example, how subjects used images to derive the equations. Figures 12.4, 12.5 and 12.6 shows the diagrams drawn by another subject, S_m, during this period. Diagrams (1) to (6) were drawn the first day; Diagrams (7) to (12), the second day. To show the relation between her images and her reasoning, we give her reasoning as she constructed the equations that she wrote down in (13) and (14) (Figures 12.4, 12.5, and 12.6). Her images are as simple as possible. For example, when reading paragraph [28] she represented the rod, AB, by two points, as in (1). She separated the process of light traveling from the motion of the rod. The diagrams were too simple to allow her to derive the equations (See (1) (2) and (8) (9)). By interaction between imaging and reasoning, the later more complete images not only helped her follow the whole process to get the qualitative result (the distance the light travelled was longer than the length of the rod), but also helped her to derive the quantitative equation from her qualitative result. She divided the distance the light travelled into two parts. One part, with the help of (12), and supposing the rod was not moving, is equal to the length of the rod. She could not find the value of the other part immediately and introduced a new quantity, named dis1 (See (13)). Then she tried to find the value of the new quantity and succeeded. The last step of her reasoning was checking the quantitative equation against the qualitative relations among the quantities in the equations (See (14)).

Why did some subjects chose the velocity method first, and then shift to the length method? Probably, from the form of the equation, they could recall: *time* = *distance/velocity*. Finding they could not reach a clear conclusion, they changed to the length method, which, as its components are spatial lengths and distances, corresponded to an image easier to see clearly. Table 12.3 (lower half) shows, for special relativity, the values of the velocity of light, the length of the rod, the distance of light traveling, and $t_B - t_A$, measured in the stationary system but relative to two different systems, the stationary system and the moving system, in the situation of equation 12.1.4. For comparison (Table 12.3, upper half), we give the values based on classical mechanics (Galilean transformations).

The velocity of light $c - v$, measured in the stationary system but relative to the moving system based on special relativity, was a new concept to the subjects, not mentioned explicitly by Einstein till then, and was not very easily stated by all of the subjects.

It is also interesting that subjects usually required a rather long time to understand paragraphs [31], [32]. The time ranges from 6 to 149 minutes. The ratio of this to the time for deriving the equation ranges from 29 percent to 110 percent. Subjects can derive the equation, once they know the surface meaning of the equation, as S_m checked qualitatively. Why did they meet difficulty here? The likely reason is that the claim in these paragraphs involves knowing new concepts, such as synchronous clocks, offered in this reading material. It was not easy for them to acquire these new concepts.

To model this phenomenon, and the interaction between the image and problem solving process, and also the switching of the reasoning methods, we postulate two different levels of mental representation. One is the general knowledge structure the subject holds of the real world. This structure is relatively stable, systematic, and general. It includes

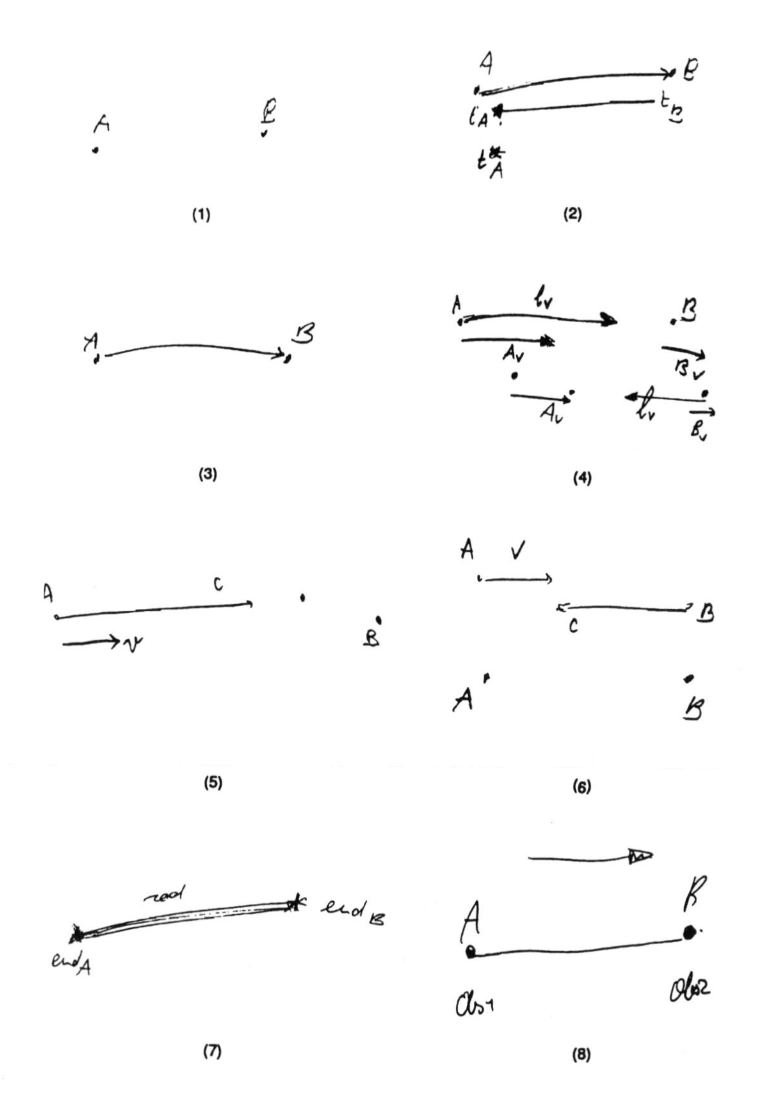

Figure 12.4

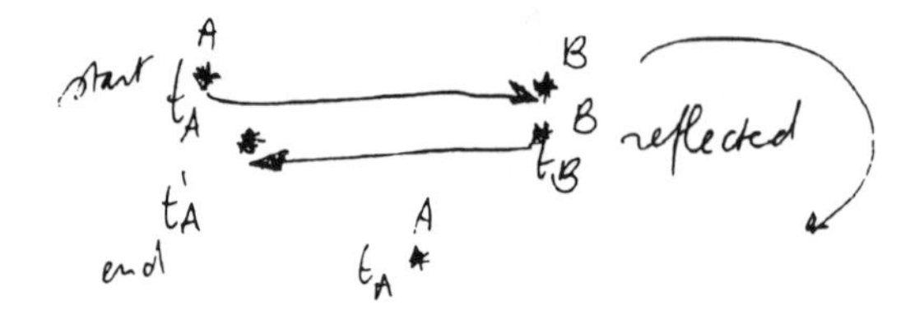

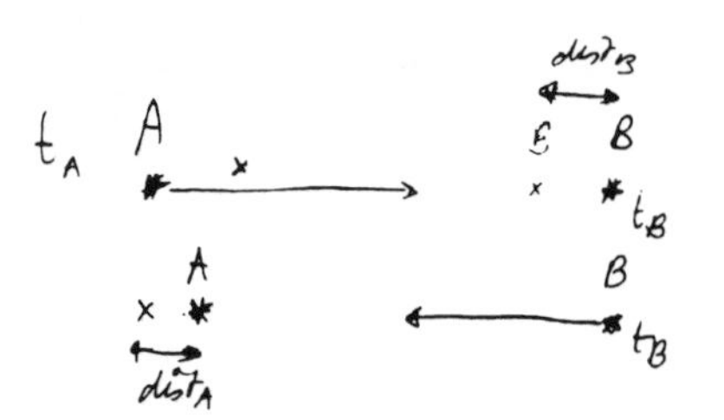

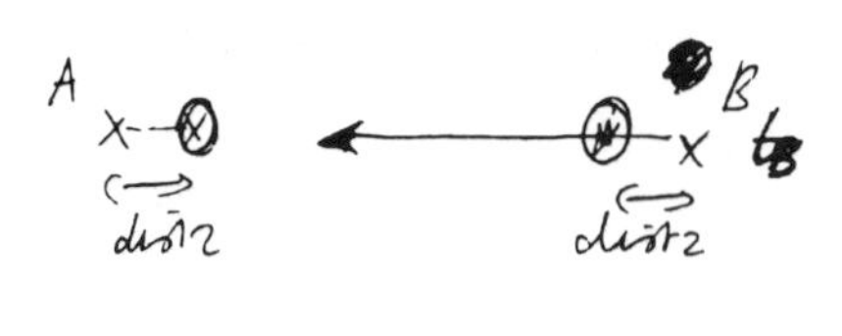

(11)

Figure 12.5

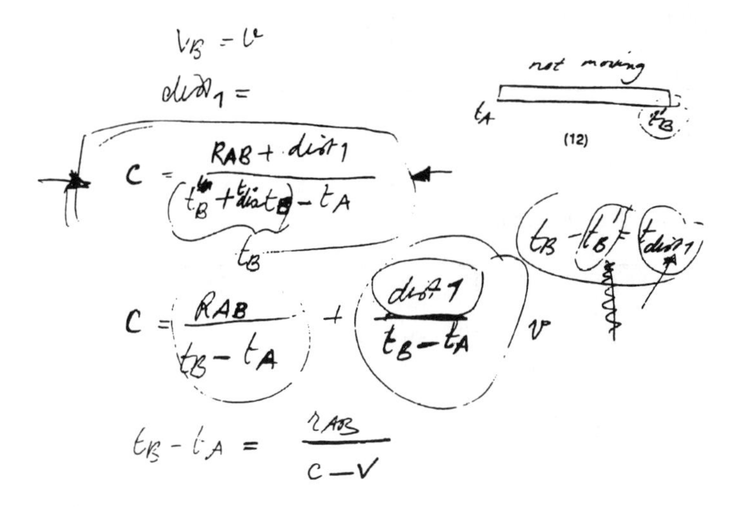

(13)

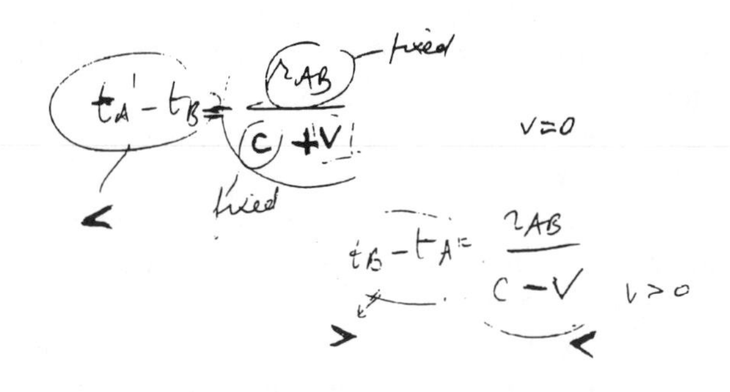

(14)

Figure 12.6

Table 12.3

		Measured in the	stationary system
		Relative to the	Relative to the
	stationary system	moving system	
	The velocity of light	$c + v$	c
Classical mechanics	The length of the rod	l	l
	The distance of light traveling	$l + v(t_B - t_A)$	l
	$t_B - t_A$	l/c	l/c
	The velocity of light	c	$c - v$
Special relativity	The length of the rod	r_{AB}	r_{AB}
	The distance of light traveling	$r_{AB} + v(t_B - t_A)$	r_{AB}
	$t_B - t_A$	$r_{AB}/(c - v)$	$r_{AB}/(c - v)$

relevant general knowledge, science concepts, and common sense that guides the subjects' reading, shapes and limits what they can "see," their problem solving and the ways in which they generate and use images and get information from them. As previously indicated, we called this knowledge structure the subjects' mental model.

The mental image is a representation of the specific situation on which attention is currently focused. It can be manipulated, controlled and "run" on the basis of the reading material and the task requirements to simulate the system's dynamic process—in the case of the text on relativity, the process whereby the beam of light moves from one end of the rod and is then reflected to the point of origin. Most of the information in the image is temporary, but part of it may be stored and reused later. The relations among the mental model, the mental image, the reading material and the problem solving activity are depicted in Figure 12.7.

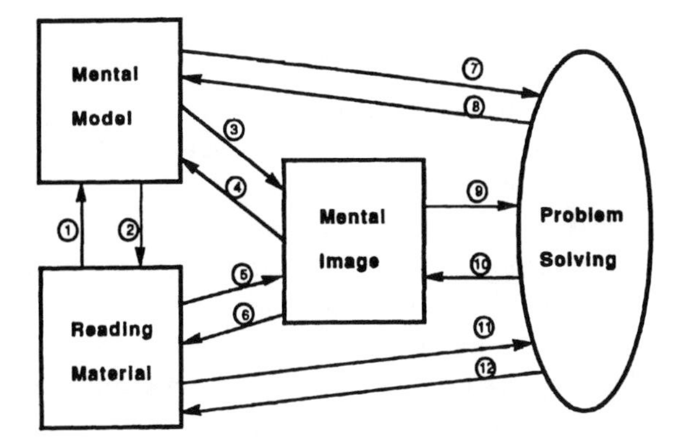

Figure 12.7
Relationships. 2): The mental model guides the attention in reading, and influences the process of getting information from the reading material. 3, 5, 10): Mental model, reading material, and the feedback from problem solving are the information sources for image. 7), 9), 11): Mental model, reading material, and image offer information in problem solving. 1), 4), 8): Reading, image, and problem solving offer information for changing mental model. 6), 12): Image and problem solving also influence reading.

12.3 Theory of the Transformation of Co-ordinates and Times from a Stationary System to Another System in Uniform Motion of Translation Relative to the Former

In [36], Einstein states that the "task is now to find the system of equations connecting these quantities": the system of values x, y, z, t, which completely defines the place and time of an event in the stationary system and the system of values ξ, η, ζ, τ determining that event relative to the system k, i.e., the Lorentz transformation equations. We will discuss how our subjects learned the key equations.

12.4 Along the X-axis

The basic problem in deriving these equations is that one cannot form a single image to show the system of values of an event measured in both stationary and moving systems. However, Einstein has prepared most of the necessary material from previous sections. After carefully specifying the two systems (See [33] to [39]), he needs only to put them together: according to 12.1.1 to get 12.1.6, and insert the arguments of the function t, according to 12.1.4 and 12.1.5, in 12.1.6 to get 12.1.7, the first key equation. If the equations describing the two component systems have been understood from the previous imaging and reasoning, they can be assembled algebraically without imaging the events in two distinct reference systems simultaneously.

Only one subject, S_s, tried to form and watch images again to derive equation 12.1.6 and the arguments in 12.1.7. Others, with some help from separate images to find the clues and by interpreting the physical meaning of the equations and their arguments (for 12.1.7), tried to identify what previously analyzed processes the equations and the arguments (for 12.1.7) described, and then derived the equations.

The key points in understanding equation 12.1.6 are that time t is measured in the moving system and the clocks are synchronous in the moving system. After studying this section, four subjects could point out these facts. Two others could interpret the physical meaning of equation 12.1.6. For example, S_r said "Time taken for light to travel from origin to x' is $\frac{1}{2}$ of time taken to go from origin to x' and back to origin." They did not mention the points noted above explicitly.

At first, S_m was confused about the two different processes described by equation 12.1.6 and by the arguments in equation 12.1.7. She tried to derive both equations 12.1.6 and 12.1.7 simultaneously, but failed. Only after she became aware that "You have to look at it (them) separately", could she derive the equations.

Immediately after reading paragraph [39], the situation statement before equation 12.1.6, three of six subjects, S_g, S_b and S_j, tried to predict the equation which described the process, but all of their predictions were wrong. They mis-identified the process as the one discussed in Section 12.2, which they had just dealt with, instead of the correct one discussed in the earlier section, Section 12.1.

On reading the situation statement, S_g formed an image that was unrealizable. The time is τ, measured in the moving system, but the light travels as if he had seen it in the stationary system. One can not see this situation when watching a real world event. Having the wrong image led him to make the wrong prediction and impeded him from deriving the equation. Only when he used means-ends analysis was he able to rewrite the equation, find the meaning of τ, and then derive equation 12.1.6 by the definition of synchronous clocks (1.0).

Because of his mistaken prediction, S_b experienced surprise (Kulkarni and Simon 1988), in finding that equation 12.1.6 was not as he expected. He said "Why would that be?" and then, by checking the condition of the equation "Are these clocks synchronized?" he correctly identified the process of the equation described. Comparing the situation statements in Section 12.2 and Section 12.3, i.e., [29] and [39], we can find their similarity. The only difference is that in Section 12.2 the measuring system is the stationary system, and in section 3 it is the moving one. We can infer that after learning Section 12.2, S_b formed a production system. His mistake is based on partially matching the productions, i.e., he did not check what the measuring system was .(the condition part of his production was not perfect). This interpretation implies that the mental structure can be a production system, and the reading process is a process of modifying the mental model. Modifying the mental model is not an easy process. We will now see another example of difficulty in changing it.

12.5 What Is X'?

In [38], Einstein introduced a quantity $x' = x - vt$. There are three levels of interpretation of the meaning of x':

1. General quantitative equation $x' = x - vt$;
2. According to [38], for any point at rest in the moving system, k, the system of values (x', y, z) is a transform of (x, y, z), the coordinates of the point in the stationary system, K.

   One of the benefits of introducing x' is that x', unlike x, is independent of time. On this basis, Einstein could introduce the function $\tau(x', y, z, t)$ with all of the arguments independent of each other. Note that x' is not equal to ξ. In the previous paragraphs of this section, it was given that system k is moving in the direction of increasing x of system K with constant velocity v. And it was also given [36]:

   > To any system of values x, y, z, t, which completely defines the place and time of an event in the stationary system, there belongs a system of values ξ, η, ζ, τ, determining that event relatively to the system k, and our

> task is now to find the system of equations connecting these quantities.

To a point at rest in system k, (ξ, η, ζ) are its coordinates in the moving system (and measured in the moving system) and (x, y, z) are its coordinates in the stationary system (and measured in the stationary system). At any time t, the X coordinate of the origin of the moving system is vt. So $x - vt$, the distance on axis x between the origin of the moving system and that point (measured in the stationary system), will not change with time. In a Galilean transformation system, $\xi = x' = x - vt$. But this relation does not hold here. We can only say that x' is the x coordinate of a point at rest in the moving system, but measured in the stationary system.

3. According to [39], x' is the coordinate of the reflector of the moving light.

Einstein used all of these three meanings in equation 12.1.7.

When reading [38], all of our subjects felt x' to be strange. They read the definition of x' several times before they dealt with the equations. Two subjects even thought that, according to the definition $x' = x - vt$, x' would decrease with the increase in time t and eventually would become negative. If x were fixed, this inference would be true. Also they thought x' was independent of time τ but dependent on t, even though in [38] it is clearly said: "... x', y, z, independent of time." It seems that they did not understand the second meaning of x' well. After reading [39], all of the subjects caught the "operative meaning" of x', the coordinate of the reflector of the moving light, although one subject initially thought the moving system was moving in the negative direction of the X-axis in the stationary system.

In Section 12.2 (See operation (b) after paragraph [22]), Einstein said that the length of a moving rod measured in the moving system was different from that measured in the stationary system. Some subjects were surprised by that statement. As we mentioned above, Einstein did not point out explicitly the difference between ξ and x'. None of our subjects could say clearly that x' was not the same as ξ, instead, most of them thought the two were identical.

When studying a paper about non-Galilean transformations, subjects still had the Galilean transformation system in mind. When subjects read a paper that fundamentally changes their world model, as our reading material did, subjects may for a time hold a mental model that contains elements from both systems.

12.5.1 Along the Y-axis

In our reading material we added the following sentences after formula (3.3) to decrease the difficulty of deriving it:

> Suppose an observer in the moving system sees a light ray go a distance $c\tau$ along the Y-axis perpendicular to X. Then, since the axis will have moved a distance, $v\tau$, in the same time, in the direction of the X-axis but parallel to itself, an observer in the stationary system will see the same light ray take a diagonal path of length ct from the initial origin of the perpendicular axis to the point of reflection, and a diagonal path back to the new location of the origin. By the Pythagorean Theorem, this implies that, viewed from the stationary system, the Y-component of the velocity of the ray will be $\sqrt{(c^2 - v^2)}$.

As in section 12.2, subjects formed and observed their mental images to derive that "the Y-component of the velocity of the ray will be $\sqrt{(c^2 - v^2)}$" And then, by comparing with equation 12.1.8, they analogized the reasoning process and justified equation 12.1.10. Every subject's protocol was much shorter than before. S_b only uttered two sentences while deriving 12.1.9. These processes are, in general, consistent with what we have discussed. It seems that there was some positive learning transfer here. For example, S_j reported his image after reading formula (3.3) but before reading our added paragraph:

> So from the stationary system, it looks like a triangle. It takes. It doesn't go straight out and straight back because it is moving, so it goes out and by the time it hits it it has moved way over here. So it is a triangle out and then by the time it gets back it has moved even farther out. So it takes a triangular path and not a straight path. Whereas if you are moving with it, it just goes out and back.

Also, based on their images, the subjects used velocity or length methods to derive (3.3) as we discussed in section 2. One new thing about

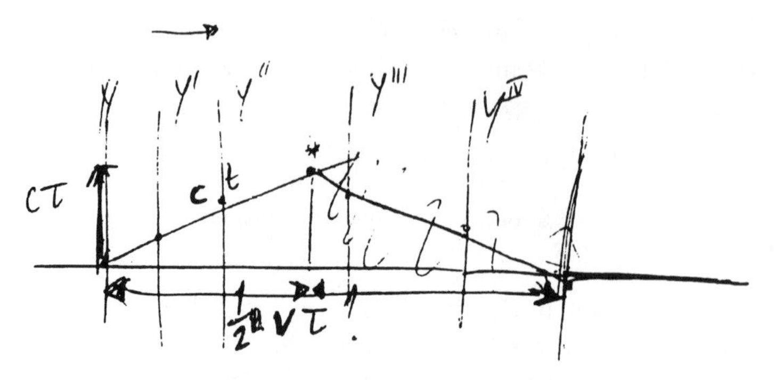

Figure 12.8

the process of forming the image appears in S'_ms protocol. Her image was based on watching the path of light step by step. By imagining the axis moving to the right a small distance and at the same time light traveling up a small distance, she fixed a point of the path of the moving light. Continuing the process, she found the path of the light. Figure 12.8 is her diagram drawn to show her image. Notice that, like the other subjects, she staticized her image; but in her case, she depicted a whole sequence of near-neighbor events instead of just a few critical events.

However, most of the subjects did encounter troubles in deriving (3.3). Their pictures of the images were good but they could not at first assign the right value to the y component of the light velocity or to the length of its path in the y direction. Four subjects automatically assigned c as the y component of the light velocity, or assigned ct as the length of the light's path in the y direction. Then the velocity along the diagonal path was the square root of $(c^2 + v^2)$. This is different from the reading material. S_j was confused about these values and claimed several times "I can't visualize things."

With the help of our new sentences, sooner or later the subjects were aware that the value of the y component of the light velocity was unknown and needed to be found, but the length of the diagonal path was known and equal to ct, and they then solved the problem. After solving the problem, S_j said "It is so simple and I just didn't see it right away."

Based on Galilean transformation formulas, it is true that light travels in the Y direction with velocity c and that the velocity in the diagonal path is the square root of $(c^2 + v^2)$. The subjects automatically used

Galilean transformation formulae because they did not comprehend the principle of the constancy of the velocity of light very well. This required a change of mental model.

We have seen three instances of the gap between Einstein's relativity model and the readers' mental models, which commonly exist in our subjects: the relativity of simultaneity in Section 12.2, the relativity of the length in the x' problem, and the constancy of the velocity of light discussed above. The first and the third problems became foci of explicit conflict, the second one had not yet been noticed by the subjects when deriving equations 12.1.6 and 3.1. Encountering and resolving these kinds of conflicts may be like experiencing and reacting to surprises in scientific discovery (Kulkarni and Simon 1988). Readers may change their mental models in this way. When deriving one of the Lorentz transformation equations,$\xi = \beta(x - vt)$, some subjects were aware that this meant ξ was equal to $\beta x'$ instead of x' as they had believed. Discussing this reaction to surprise in detail, however, is beyond the scope of this chapter.

12.6 Discussion and Conclusion

In this chapter, we have discussed the processes used by subjects in forming and watching dynamic mental images, drawing qualitative conclusions and then deriving the quantitative equations. We saw that the reading and understanding processes required subjects to change their mental models. Mental models provide the substrate for the more transient mental images that subjects form. They consist of the relevant knowledge already held in subjects' memories that shapes their attempts to form the new representations needed in problem solving.

Kosslyn et al (1990) discussing the uses of imagery in everyday life, found that "relatively few images were reported to be used in the service of what we took to be the primary purpose of imagery, that is, recall and mental simulation." "Most of the images the subjects reported had no recognizable purpose; most images occurred in isolation, not as part of a sequence..." It seems that when imagery is used in problem solving, the behavior is different than when it is used in everyday life. While deriving the equations, imagery was used with obvious purpose: to represent the process of light traveling. The data show that subjects can use images in two ways:

1. To simulate the process (by discrete steps) and derive the equations that describe it;

   For example, to derive the equations $t_B - t_A = r_{AB}/(c - v)$ and $t'A - tB = r_{AB}/(c + v)$, the process looks like this:

   - Guided by the goal (why is the equation right?), they formed their images of the successive stages of the situation;
   - By watching the images, and comparing the related quantities, they could derive the qualitative relations. For example, the distance of light traveling was longer than the length of the moving rod;
   - By assigning the known values to the given quantities and deriving the values of the unknown quantities, they inferred the quantitative relations among the quantities, i.e., the equations.

   Using the terms in Kosslyn et al (1990), forming and watching the image to get the qualitative conclusion is the process of navigation and tracking objects moving relative to each other, while the process of assigning and deriving the values of quantities is the process of recognition (and reasoning).

   If there are some bugs in their mental models, subjects may make mistakes in assigning the values, even though they have the right picture, as we have seen in their deriving the Y-component of the velocity of the ray: $\sqrt{(c^2 - v^2)}$.

2. To simulate the process and identify its type. In the process of inserting the arguments of function τ in equation 12.1.6

   $$\frac{1}{2}(\tau_0 + \tau_2) = \tau_1 \qquad (12.6.11)$$

   to get equation 12.1.7

   $$\frac{1}{2}[\tau(0,0,0,t) + \tau(0,0,0,t + \frac{x'}{c-v} + \frac{x'}{c+v})] = \tau(0,0,0,t + \frac{x'}{c-v}), \qquad (12.6.12)$$

some subjects reported their images. But, except for S_s, they did not really use their images to derive the values of these arguments. Instead, by observing the image, they identified the process as identical with that discussed in the previous section and then simply used the results derived there to insert the co-ordinate values in this new equation. This process combines the simulation and recognition processes.

When used in problem solving, subjects' images are as simple as possible. In this situation, there are two ways of forming the images: construction and generation. When the moving situation is relatively simple, e.g., in the images used to derive the equation $t_B - t_A = r_{AB}/(c-v)$, subjects formed the components of the image, such as the rod and light (a line, maybe, with arrow), and then simply moved the whole rod and extended the light line to form a before-and-after dynamic image. we call this *construction.* However, when the movement of objects is relative complex, some subjects found it difficult to see the trace of the movement. For example, in the process of deriving the formula, $\sqrt{(c^2 - v^2)}$ light moved in the Y direction while the rod was moving in the X direction. To see the trace of light traveling, one subject moved the rod step by step and watched the corresponding positions of light. We call this *generation.*

It seems that there was a heavy STM load while subjects were keeping the image and reasoning simultaneously. Subjects shifted frequently between forming and watching images and reasoning. There was active interaction between the process of forming images and of problem solving. On the one hand, the way subjects derived the equations was closely related to their images. On the other hand, subjects might totally change their images when they met trouble in using their original images to solve problems, or they might modify their images, shifting their attention in the process of problem solving.

Understanding relativity required some basic changes in the subjects' mental models before they could construct and build mental images to help them draw the necessary inferences about the situation and derive the equations describing it. Our notion of mental model appears to be close to what Norman (1988) had in mind in speaking of "the models people have of themselves, others, the environment, and the things with which they interact."

Mental models, even when appropriately modified, are not enough for understanding the concepts of relativity. Our subjects also had to construct mental images that could be manipulated to reveal the relations among the successive events that Einstein introduces to describe the transmission of light in the world of special relativity. When they were successful in constructing appropriate images, they could derive from them both the qualitative properties of the situation and the equations that described it quantitatively, and in this way, were able to change their mental models. However, deriving an equation does not mean understanding the equation. We have seen three cases where, without explicitly encountering and solving the conflicts, some part of a subjectsU old mental model may not be affected and changed.

Acknowledgements

This research was supported by the Personnel and Training Programs, Psychological Sciences Division, Office of Naval Research, under Contract No. N00014-86-k-0678; and by the Defense Advanced Research Projects Agency, Department of Defense, ARPA Order 3597, monitored by the Air Force Avionics Laboratory under contract F33615-81-k-1539. Reproduction in whole or in part is permitted for any purpose of the United States Government. Approved for public release; distribution unlimited.

References

Baylor, G. W. 1971. A Treatise on the Mind's Eye. Ph.D. diss., Carnegie Mellon University, Pittsburgh, Penn.

Einstein, A. 1905. On the Electrodynamics of Moving Bodies. In *The Principle of Relativity,* ed. A. Einsten et. al. New York: Dover.

Einstein, et al. 1923. *The Principle of Relativity.* New York: Dover Publications.

Farah, M. J. 1985. The Neurological Basis of Mental Imagery: A Componential Analysis. In *Visual Cognition,* ed. S. Pinker. Cambridge Mass.: The MIT Press.

Finke, R. A. 1989. *Principles of Mental Imagery.* Cambridge Mass.: The MIT Press.

Finke, R. A. and Shepard, R. N. 1986. Visual Functions of Mental Imagery. In *Handbook of Perception and Human Performance,* ed. K. T. Boff, L. Kaufman, and J P. Thomas. New York: Wiley-Interscience.

Gentner, D. and Stevens, A. L. (Eds.). 1983. *Mental Models.* Hillsdale, N.J.: Lawrence Erlbaum Associates.

Hayes, J. R. 1973. On the Function of Visual Imagery in Elementary Mathematics. *Visual Information Processing,* ed. W. G. Chase. New York: Academic Press.

Iwasaki, Y. 1989. Qualitative Physics. In *Handbook of Artificial Intelligence,* ed. A. Barr, P. R. Cohen, and E. A. Feigenbaum. Los Altos, Calif.: William Kaufmann, Inc.

Feigenbaum E. A. (ed.). *The Handbook of Artificial Intelligence.* Vol., 4. Reading, Mass.: Addison-Wesley.

Johnson-Laird, P. N. 1983. *Mental Models.* Cambridge, Mass.: Harvard University Press.

Kosslyn, S. M. 1980. *Image and Mind.* Cambridge, Mass.: Harvard University Press.

Kosslyn, S. M. 1983. *Ghosts in the Mind's Machine—Creating and Using Images in the Brain.* New York: W. W. Norton and Company.

Kosslyn, S. M. 1987. Seeing and Imagining in the Cerebral Hemispheres: A Computational Approach. *Psychological Review* 94: 148–175.

Kosslyn, S. M. and Koenig, O. 1992. *Wet Mind: The New Cognitive Neuroscience.* New York: The Free Press.

Kosslyn, S., Seger, C. Pani, J. R., and Hillger, L. A. 1990. When Is Imagery Used in Everyday Life: A Diary Study. *Journal of Mental Imagery* 14(3 –4): 131–152.

Kosslyn, S. M., Sokolov, M. A. and Chen, J. C. 1989. The Lateralization of BRAIN: A Computer Theory and Model of Visual Hemispheric Specialization. In *Complex Information Processing—the Impact of Herbert A. Simon,* ed. D. Klahr and K. Kotovsky. Hillsdale, N.J.: Lawrence Erlbaum Associates.

Kulkarni, D. and Simon, H. A. 1988. The Process of Scientific Discovery: The Strategy of Experimentation. *Cognitive Science* 12: 139–175.

Larkin, J. H. and Simon, H. A. 1987. Why a Diagram Is (Sometimes) Worth Ten Thousand Words. *Cognitive Science* 11(1): 65–100.

Martel, L. D. 1991. The Role of Guided Imagery in Educational reform: The Integrative Learning System. In *Mental Imagery,* ed. R. G. Kunzendorf, New York: Plenum Press.

Norman, D. A. 1988. *The Psychology of Everyday Things.* New York: Basic Books, Inc.

Novak, G. S. 1976. Computer Understanding of Physics Problems Stated in Natural Language. Ph.D. Diss., The University of Texas at Austin.

Paivio, A. 1971. *Imagery and Verbal Processes.* New York: Holt, Rinehart and Winston.

Pinker, S. (Ed.) 1985. *Visual Cognition.* Cambridge Mass.: The MIT Press.

Pylyshyn, Z. W. 1973. What the Mind's Eye Tells the Mind's Brain: A Critique of Mental Imagery. *Psychological Bulletin* 80(1): 1–24.

Qin, Y. and Simon, H. A. 1990. Imagery and Problem Solving. In Proceedings of the Twelfth Annual Conference of the Cognitive Science Society, 646–653. Hillsdale, N.J.: Lawrence Erlbaum Associates.

Qin, Y. and Simon, H. A. 1992. Imagery as Process Representation in Problem Solving. In Proceedings of the Fourteenth Annual Conference of the Cognitive Science Society, 1050–1055. Hillsdale, N.J.: Lawrence Erlbaum Associates.

Shepard, R. N. and Cooper, L. A. 1982. *Mental Images and Their Transformations.* Cambridge Mass.: The MIT Press.

Shepard, R. N. and Metzler, J. 1971. Mental Rotation of Three-Dimensional Objects. *Science* 171: 701–703.

Simon, H. A. 1972. What Is Visual Imagery? An Information Processing Interpretation. In *Cognition in Learning and Memory,* ed. L. W. Gregg. New York: John Wiley and Sons.

Simon, H. A. and Barenfeld, M. 1969. Information Processing Analysis of Perceptual Processes in Problem Solving. *Psychological Review* 76 473– 483.

Tabachneck, H. J. M. and Simon, H. A. 1995. Alternative Representations of Instructional Material. In *Alternative Representations: An Interdisciplinary Theme,* ed. Donald Peterson. London: Interdisciplinary Books.

Weld, D. S. and de Kleer, Johan, 1990. *Readings in Qualitative Reasoning about Physical Systems.* San Mateo, Calif: Morgen Kaufmann.

13 Computational Imagery

J. I. Glasgow & D. Papadias
Queen's University

Numerous psychological studies have been carried out and several, often conflicting, models of mental imagery have been proposed. This chapter does not present another computational model for mental imagery, but instead treats imagery as a problem solving paradigm in artificial intelligence (AI). We propose a concept of computational imagery, which has potential applications to problems whose solutions by humans involve the use of mental imagery. As a basis for computational imagery, we define a knowledge representation scheme that brings to the foreground the most important visual and spatial properties of an image. Although psychological theories are used as a guide to these properties, we do not adhere to a strict cognitive model; whenever possible we attempt to overcome the limitations of the human information processing system. Thus, our primary concerns are efficiency, expressive power and inferential adequacy.

Computational imagery involves tools and techniques for visual-spatial reasoning, where images are generated or recalled from long-term memory and then manipulated, transformed, scanned, associated with similar forms (constructing spatial analogies), pattern matched, increased or reduced in size, distorted, etc. In particular, we are concerned with the reconstruction of image representations to facilitate the retrieval of visual and spatial information that was not explicitly stored in long-term memory. The images generated to retrieve this information may correspond to representations of real physical scenes or of abstract concepts that are manipulated in ways similar to visual forms.

The knowledge representation scheme for computational imagery separates visual from spatial reasoning and defines independent representations for the two modes. Whereas visual thinking is concerned with *what* an image looks like, spatial reasoning depends more on *where* an object is located relative to other objects in a scene (complex image). Each of these representations is constructed, as needed, from a descriptive representation stored in long-term memory. Thus our scheme includes three representations, each appropriate for a different kind of processing:

- An image is stored in long-term memory as an hierarchically organized, descriptive, *deep representation* that contains all the relevant information about the image.
- The *spatial representation* of an image denotes the image components symbolically and preserves relevant spatial properties.
- The *visual representation* depicts the space occupied by an image as an occupancy array. It can be used to retrieve information such as shape, relative distance and relative size.

While the deep representation is used as a permanent store for information, the spatial and visual representations act as working (short-term) memory stores for images.

A formal theory of arrays provides a meta-language for specifying the representations for computational imagery. Array theory is the mathematics of nested, rectangularly-arranged data objects (More 1979). Several primitive functions, which are used to retrieve, construct and transform representations of images, have been specified in the theory and mapped into the functional programming language Nial (Jenkins, Glasgow and McCrosky 1986).

The knowledge representation scheme for computational imagery provides a basis for implementing programs that involve reconstructing and reasoning with image representations. One such system, currently under investigation, is a knowledge-based system for molecular scene analysis. Some of the concepts presented in the chapter will be illustrated with examples from this application area.

Research in computational imagery has three primary goals: a cognitive science goal, an AI goal and an applications goal. The *cognitive science goal* addresses the need for computational models for theories of cognition. We describe a precise, explicit language for specifying, implementing and testing alternative, and possibly conflicting, theories of cognition. The *AI goal* involves the development of a knowledge representation scheme for visual and spatial reasoning with images. Finally, the *applications goal* involves incorporating the knowledge representation scheme for computational imagery into the development of programs for solving real world problems.

The chapter begins with an overview of previous research in mental imagery, which serves as a motivation for the representations and processes for computational imagery. This is followed by a detailed description of the deep, visual and spatial representations for imagery, and the primitive functions that can be applied to them. The chapter concludes with a summary of the major contributions of computational imagery to the fields of cognitive science, AI and knowledge-based systems development, and a discussion of the relationship between our scheme and previous research in the area.

13.1 Mental Imagery

In vision research, an image is typically described as a projection of a visual scene on the back of the retina. However, in theories of mental imagery the term image refers to an internal representation used by the human information processing system to retrieve information from memory.

Although no one seems to deny the existence of the phenomenon called imagery, there has been a continuing debate about the structure and the function of imagery in human cognition. The imagery debate is concerned with whether images are represented as *descriptions* or *depictions*. It has been suggested that descriptive representations contain symbolic, interpreted information, whereas depictive representations contain geometric, uninterpreted information (Finke, Pinker and Farah 1989). Others debate whether or not images play any causal role in the brain's information processing (Block 1981). According to Farah (1988a), in depictive theories the recall of visual objects consists of the top-down activation of perceptual representation, while in descriptive theories visual recall is carried out using representations that are distinct from those in vision, even when it is accompanied by the phenomenology of "seeing with the mind's eye". Further discussions on the imagery debate can be found in various sources (e.g. Anderson 1978; Kosslyn and Pomerantz 1977; Block 1981).

The purpose of this chapter is not to debate the issues involved in mental imagery, but rather to describe effective computational techniques for storing and manipulating image representations. To accomplish this, however, requires an understanding of the broad properties of representations and processes involved in mental imagery.

13.1.1 Research Findings in Mental Imagery

Many psychological and physiological studies have been carried out in an attempt to demystify the nature of mental imagery. Of particular interest to our research are studies that support the existence of multiple image representations and describe the functionality of mental imagery processes. In this section we overview relevant results from such studies and, based on these results, propose some important properties of mental imagery which we use to motivate our representation scheme for computational imagery.

Several experiments provide support for the existence of a visual memory, distinct from verbal memory, in which recognition of verbal material is inferior. Paivio's (1975) dual-code theory suggests that there is a distinction between verbal and imagery processing. This theory leaves the exact nature of mental images unspecified, but postulates two interconnected memory systems, verbal and imaginal, operating in parallel. The two systems can be independently accessed by relevant stimuli but they are interconnected in the sense that nonverbal information can be transformed into verbal and vice versa. Furthermore, it has been indicated that visual memory may be superior in recall (Standing 1973).

The issue of visual memory is an important one for computational imagery. What it implies to us is the need for a separate descriptive and depictive representations. This is reinforced by the experiments carried out by Kosslyn (1980) and his colleagues, who concluded that images preserve the spatial relationships, relative sizes and relative distances of real physical objects. Pinker (1988) suggested that image scanning can be performed in two and three-dimensional space, providing support for Kosslyn's proposal that mental images capture the spatial characteristics of an actual display. Pinker also indicates that images can be accessed using either an object-centered or a world-centered coordinate system.

A series of experiments suggest that mental images are not only visual and spatial in nature, but also structurally organized in patterns; that is, they have an hierarchical organization in which subimages can occur as elements in more complex images (Reed 1974). Some researchers propose that under certain conditions images can be reinterpreted: they can be reconstructed in ways that were not initially anticipated (Finke et al. 1989). Experiments also support the claim that creative synthesis is performed by composing mental images to make discoveries (Shepard

1978; Finke and Slayton 1988).

The relationship between imagery and perception has been considered by Brooks (1968), who demonstrated that spatial visualization can interfere with perception. Farah (1988a) also suggests that mental images are visual representations in the sense that they share similar representations to those used in vision, but notes that this conclusion does not imply that image representations are depictive since both imagery and perception might be descriptive. She argues, from different evidence however, that they are in fact spatial.

Findings, provided by the study of patients with visual impairments, point toward distinct visual and spatial components of mental imagery. Mishkin, Ungerleider and Macko (1983) have shown that there are two distinct cortical visual systems. Their research indicates that the temporal cortex is involved in recognizing *what* objects are, while the parietal cortex determines *where* they are located. Further studies verify that there exists a class of patients who often have trouble localizing an object in the visual field, although their ability to recognize the object is unimpaired (De Renzi 1982). Other patients show the opposite patterns of visual abilities; they cannot recognize visually presented objects, although they can localize them in space (Bauers and Rubens 1985). Such patients are able to recognize objects by touch or by characteristic sounds. It has also been suggested that the preserved and impaired aspects of vision in these patients are similarly preserved or impaired in imagery (Levine, Warach and Farah 1985). In experimental studies, subjects with object identification problems were unable to draw or describe familiar objects despite being able to draw and describe in detail the locations of cities in a map, furniture in a house and landmarks in a city. Patients with localization problems were unable to describe relative locations, such as cities on a map, although they could describe from memory the appearance of a variety of objects. Such findings have been interpreted by some researchers (e.g. Kosslyn 1987) as suggesting two distinct components of mental imagery, the spatial and the visual, where the spatial component preserves information about the relative positions of the meaningful parts of a scene and the visual component preserves information about how (e.g., shape, size) a meaningful part of a scene looks.

Although there are varying strategies for retrieving spatial information and solving problems concerning spatial relations, research has suggested that humans typically use mental imagery for spatial reasoning (Farah 1988b). Experimental results also support an isomorphism between physical and imaged transformations (Shepard and Cooper 1982). A premise of Kritchevsky (1988) is that behavior can be divided into spatial and nonspatial components. For example, determining the color of an object is a nonspatial behavior whereas determining relative positions of objects is a spatial behavior. Kritchevsky assumes that the spatial component of behavior is understood in terms of elementary spatial functions. Furthermore, these functions are independent of any particular sensory modality (Ratcliff 1982).

While individually the results described above do not imply a particular approach to computational imagery, collectively they imply several properties that we wish to capture in our approach. Most importantly, an image may be depicted and reasoned with visually or spatially, where a visual representation encodes what the image looks like and the spatial representation encodes relative location of objects within an image. As well, images are inherently three-dimensional and hierarchically organized. This implies that computational routines must be developed that can decompose, reconstruct and reinterpret image representations. Results from studies comparing imagery and vision imply that the representations and processes of imagery may be related to those of high-level vision. Thus, we should also consider the representations and functionality of object recognition when defining computational imagery. Finally, we must be able to consider an image from either an object-centered or a viewer-centered perspective.

The numerous experiments that have been carried out in mental imagery not only suggest properties for the representation scheme, but also support the premise that mental imagery is used extensively to reason about real world problems. Thus, computational imagery is an important topic to investigate in relation to AI problem solving.

The subjective nature of mental imagery has made it a difficult topic to study experimentally. Qualities like clarity, blurring and vividness of images are not directly observable and may differ from one person to another. Furthermore, it has been argued by some researchers that it is impossible to resolve the imagery debate experimentally, since depictive and descriptive representations do not have distinct properties from which behavioral consequences can be predicted (Anderson 1978). As a result, several alternative accounts have been proposed to explain the findings mentioned above. The most important of these are: tacit knowledge, experimenter bias, eye movements and task induced characteristics (Intons-Peterson 1983). These difficulties involved in experimental studies emphasize the need for computer models for mental imagery. While the knowledge representation scheme for computational imagery is not meant to model a particular theory of imagery, it does provide the tools for specifying, testing and formally analyzing a variety of theories, and thus can contribute to resolving the imagery debate.

13.1.2 Theories and Principles of Mental Imagery

Pylyshyn (1981), a forceful proponent of the descriptive view, argues that mental imagery simply consists of the use of general thought processes to simulate perceptual events, based on tacit knowledge of how these events happened. He disputes the idea that mental images are stored in a raw uninterpreted form resembling mental photographs and argues for an abstract format of representation called propositional code. Kosslyn's (1980) model of mental imagery is based on a depictive theory which claims that images are quasi-pictorial; that is, they resemble pictures in several ways but lack some of their properties. According to Kosslyn's model, mental images are working memory, visual representations generated from long-term memory, deep representations. A set of procedures, which is referred to as the "mind's eye", serves as an interface between the visual representations and the underlying data structures, which may be decidedly non-pictorial in form. Hinton disputes the picture metaphor for imagery and claims that images are more like generated constructions (Hinton 1979). In this approach, as in Marr and Nishihara's (1978) *3D* model, complex images can be represented as an hierarchy of parts.

Finke (1989) takes a different approach to the imagery debate. Instead of proposing a model, he defines five "unifying principles" of mental imagery:

- The principle of *implicit encoding* states that imagery is particularly useful for retrieving information about physical properties of objects and relations among objects whenever this information was not previously, explicitly encoded.
- The principle of *perceptual equivalence* states that similar mechanisms in the visual system are activated when objects or events

are imagined, as when the same objects or events are actually perceived.

- The principle of *spatial equivalence* states that the spatial relations between objects are preserved, although sometimes distorted, in mental images.
- The principle of *structural equivalence* states that the structure of images corresponds to that of perceived objects, in the sense that the structure is coherent, well organized and can be reinterpreted.
- The principle of *transformational equivalence* states that imagined and physical transformations exhibit similar dynamic characteristics and follow the same laws of motion.

These principles provide a basis for evaluating the representations and functions for computational imagery; in the development of our scheme we have attempted to address each of the underlying principles for mental imagery.

13.1.3 Stages of Image Representations

The hypothesis of multiple representations for mental imagery can explain several experimental results that cannot be explained independently by either a propositional, spatial or visual representation. For instance, after a series of experiments Atwood (1971) concludes that memory for high image phrases is disrupted if followed by a task requiring the subject to process a visually presented digit in contrast to abstract phrases. Although other researchers found difficulty in replicating Atwood's experiments, Jannsen (1976) succeeds consistently over several experiments and claims that other failures stem from using an interfering task that is spatial rather than visual. Baddeley and Lieberman (1980) interpret these results as pointing towards distinct visual and spatial components of mental imagery.

When images are retrieved, it is possible to recall information about what objects constitute a scene and their spatial relationships with other objects without remembering what the object looks like. Furthermore, we are able to recognize objects independent of any context. Distinct spatial and visual components for imagery can explain such phenomena, where the spatial component can be considered as an index that connects visual images to create a scene.

Intuitively, we can distinguish between visual and spatial representations by considering the type of information we wish to retrieve. Consider, for example, answering the following questions: *How many windows are there in your home? What city is further north, Seattle or Montreal? What objects are sitting on top of your desk? Who was sitting beside Mary in class?* These questions can typically be answered without constructing an explicit visual image; that is, you could possibly recall that John was sitting beside Mary without knowing what John looked like or what clothes he was wearing. Each of these questions does rely on knowing the relative locations of objects within a recalled image, information that is embodied in a spatial representation. Now consider questions such as: *What is the shape of your dog's ears? What does a particular image look like if you rotate it ninety degrees? What is larger, a rabbit or a racoon? Is Montreal or Toronto closer to Ottawa?* To answer these questions you may need to reconstruct a representation that preserves information such as size, shape or relative distance, information that is embodied in a visual representation.

From the computational point of view, a single representational system cannot always effectively express all the knowledge about a given domain; different representational formalisms are useful for different computational tasks (Sloman 1985). In perceptual systems, for instance, multiple representations have been proposed to derive cognitively useful representations from a visual scene. For computational imagery, we propose three stages of image representation, each appropriate for a different type of information processing. The deep representation stores structured, descriptive information in terms of a semantic network, long-term memory model. The working memory representations (spatial and visual) are consciously experienced and generated as symbolic and occupancy arrays, as needed, using information stored in the deep representation. Details about the computational advantages of each of the image representations involved in the scheme will be presented in the following section.

13.2 Knowledge Representation Scheme

Research in AI has long been concerned with the problem of knowledge representation. AI programs rely on the ability to store descriptions of a particular domain and formally manipulate these descriptions to derive new knowledge. Traditional approaches to knowledge representation include logic representations, which denote the objects and relations in the world in terms of axioms, and structural knowledge representation schemes, which denote concepts and relations in terms of structural hierarchies.

In addition to general schemes, there exist specialized schemes concerned with the representation of the visual representation of images. In discrimination trees, objects are sorted by discriminating on their coordinates, as well as other quantitative and qualitative discriminators (McDermott and Davis 1984). A simple way of describing volume or shape is with occupancy arrays, where cells of the array denote objects filling space. For computer vision applications, an occupancy array is often called a grey level description, since the value of the cells encode the intensity of light on a grey scale from white to black. For our molecular scene analysis application, we use three-dimensional occupancy arrays that correspond to electron density maps resulting from X-ray diffraction experiments. The values of the cells in such maps correspond to the electron density in a unit cell of a crystal.

According to Biederman (1987), the visual representation for objects can be constructed as a spatial organization of simple primitive volumes, called geons. Other researchers have proposed alternative primitive volumes, like generalized cones, spheres etc. A major contribution in representational formalisms for images is the progression of primal sketch, *2-1/2D* sketch and *3D* sketch (Marr and Nishihara 1978). The primal sketch represents intensity changes in a *2D* image. The *2-1/2D* sketch represents orientation and depth of surface from a particular viewer perspective. Finally, the *3D* sketch represents object-centered spatial organization.

The representation schemes discussed above are not suggested as structures for representing human knowledge and do not necessarily commit to addressing questions about mental processes. Although many AI researchers believe that the best way to make true thinking machines is by getting computers to imitate the way the human brain works (Israel 1987), research in knowledge representation often is more concerned with expressiveness and efficiency, rather than explanatory and predictive power. Thus, although our knowledge representation scheme attempts to preserve the most relevant properties of imagery, whenever possible

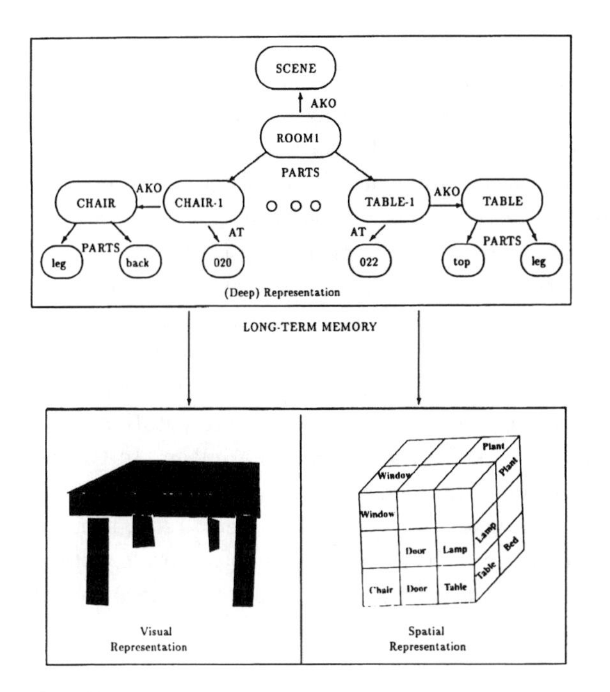

Figure 13.1
Representations for Computational Imagery.

we try to overcome the limitations of the human information processing system. For example, theories of divided attention argue that attention can be concentrated on, at most, a few mental processes at a time. Our proposed scheme has the capability of relatively unrestrictive parallel processing of spatial images. Furthermore, although the resolution of mental images is limited by the capabilities of the human mind, in the knowledge representation scheme the resolution restrictions are imposed by the implementation architecture.

A theory of arrays provides a formalism for the representations and functions involved in computational imagery. Array theory (More 1979) is the mathematics of nested, rectangularly-arranged collections of data objects. Similar to set theory, array theory is concerned with the concepts of nesting, aggregation and membership. Array theory is also concerned with the concept of data objects having a spatial position relative to other objects in a collection. Thus, it provides for a multi-dimensional, hierarchical representation of images, in which spatial relations are made explicit.

We consider computational imagery as the ability to represent, retrieve and reason about information not explicitly stored in long-term memory. In particular, we are concerned with visual and spatial information. Recall that the visual component of imagery specifies how an image looks and is used to retrieve information such as shape, size and volume, while the spatial component of imagery denotes where components of an image are situated relative to one another and is used to retrieve information such as neighborhoods, adjacencies, symmetry and relative locations. As illustrated in Figure 13.1, the long-term memory representation is implemented as a description of the image and the working memory representations correspond to representations that make explicit the visual and spatial properties of an image. In the remainder of this section, we describe each of the representations in detail and discuss the primitive functions that operate on them. First, though, we overview the theory of arrays, which provides the basis for describing and implementing the representations and functions for computational imagery.

13.2.1 Array Theory

Results of empirical studies suggest that images may be organized using both a hierarchical and a spatial structure. Components of an image may be grouped into features and stored based on their their topological relations, such as adjacency or containment, or their spatial relations, such as above, beside, north-of, etc. Because of the relevance of storing and reasoning about such properties of an image, we base the development of the knowledge representation scheme for computational imagery on a theory of arrays. This mathematical theory allows for a multi-dimensional, hierarchical representation of images in which spatial relations are made explicit. Furthermore, functions can be defined in array theory for constructing, manipulating and retrieving information from images represented as arrays. For example, functions that compose, translate, juxtapose and compare images have been defined within the theory.

The development of array theory was motivated by efforts to extend the data structures of APL and has been influenced by the search for total operations that satisfy universal equations (More 1981). In this theory, an array is a collection of zero or more items held at positions

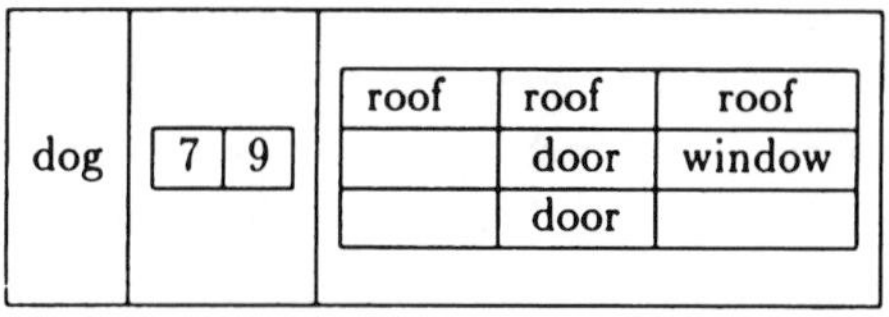

dog
7 9
roof roof roof
door window
door

Figure 13.2
Example of Nested Array Diagram.

in a rectangular arrangement along multiple axes. Rectangular arrangement is the concept of data objects having a position relative to other objects in the collection. The interpretation of this structure can be illustrated using nested, box diagrams. Consider the array diagram in Figure 13.2. In this array the pair formed from 7 and 9 is an array nested within the larger array. Nesting is the concept of having the objects of a collection be collections themselves. This is an important concept in array theory since it is the power of aggregating arbitrary elements in an array that gives the theory much of its expressive power. The third element of the array is a symbolic array, which denotes an image of a house containing three parts. The indexing of the array allows us to make explicit such properties as *above(roof,door)* and *left-of(door,window)* in a notation that is both compact and accessible.

Array theory has provided a formal basis for the development of the *N*ested *I*nteractive *A*rray *L*anguage, *Nial*. This multi-paradigm programming language combines concepts from APL, Lisp and FP with conventional control mechanisms (Jenkins, Glasgow and McCrosky 1986). The primitive functions of array theory have all been implemented in Q'Nial (Jenkins and Jenkins 1985), a commercially available, portable interpreter of Nial developed at Queen's University.

Operations in array theory are functions that map arrays to arrays. A large collection of total, primitive operations are described for the theory. They are chosen to express fundamental properties of arrays. Nial extends array theory by providing several syntactic forms that describe operations, including composition, partial evaluation of a left argument, and a lambda-form. Array theory also contains second-order functions called transformers that map operations to operations.

It has previously been shown that the syntactic constructs of array theory facilitate both sequential and parallel computations (Glasgow, Jenkins, McCrosky and Meijer 1989). This is an important feature when considering computational imagery as a basis for specifying cognitive processes, which themselves may be sequential or parallel. The potential parallelism in array theory comes from three sources: inherent parallelism in the primitive operations, parallelism expressed by syntactic constructs, and parallelism in operation application controlled by primitive transformers. The potential parallelism of the primitive operations results from treating an entire array as a single value; each array takes an array as a single argument and returns an array as its result. Array theory includes transformers that allow expression of the parallel application of an operation to subparts of an array.

The software development associated with AI problem solving in general, and with computational imagery in particular, differs from traditional computer applications. AI problems are solved at the conceptual level, rather than a detailed implementation level. Thus, much of the programming effort is spent on understanding how to represent and manipulate the knowledge associated with a particular problem, or class of problems. This imposes certain features on a programming language, including interactive program development, operations for symbolic computation, dynamically created data structures and easy encoding of search algorithms. While Lisp and Prolog both address capabilities such as these, they provide very different and complementary approaches to problem solving. The language Nial is an attempt at finding an approach to programming that combines the logic and functional paradigms of Prolog and Lisp (Glasgow and Browse 1985, Jenkins et al. 1986). It has been demonstrated that array theory and Nial can provide a foundation for logic programming (Glasgow, Jenkins, Blevis and Feret 1991), as well as other other descriptive knowledge representation techniques (Jenkins, Glasgow, Blevis, Chau, Hache and Lawson, 1988). These techniques have been implemented and tested on a variety of knowledge-based applications.

13.2.2 Deep (Long-Term Memory) Representation

The deep representation for computational imagery is used for the long-term storage of images. Earlier work has suggested that there exists a separate long-term memory model which encodes visual information descriptively (Kosslyn, 1980; Pinker 1984). This encoding can then be used to generate depictive representations in working memory. As pointed out in (Marschark, Richman, Yuille and Hunt 1987), most of the research in vision and imagery has focused on the format of the on-line conscious representations, in exclusion of long-term storage considerations. Our point of view is that the deep representation falls more in the limits of research in long-term memory than imagery and we base its implementation on the hierarchical network model of semantic memory (Collins and Quillian 1969). This model is suitable for storing images since they have a structured organization in which subimages can occur as elements in more complex images.

The deep representation in our scheme is implemented using a frame language (Minsky 1975), in which each frame contains salient information about an image or class of images. This information includes propositional and procedural knowledge. There are two kinds of image hierarchies in the scheme: the AKO (a kind of) and the PARTS. The AKO hierarchy provides property inheritance: images can inherit properties from more generic image frames. The PARTS hierarchy is used to denote the structural decomposition of complex images. The deep representation for imagery can be characterized as non-monotonic, since default information (stored in specific slots, or inherited from more generic frames) is superseded as new information is added to a frame.

A frame corresponding to the image of a map of Europe and part of the semantic network for a map domain is illustrated in Figure 13.3. Each node in the network corresponds to an individual frame and the links describe the relationships among frames. The AKO slot in the frame of the map of Europe denotes that the frame is an instance of the concept "Map-of-Continent". The PARTS slot contains the meaningful parts that compose the map, along with an index value that specifies their relative locations. The POPULATION slot contains a call to a procedure that calculates the population of Europe, given the populations of the countries. As well, the frame could incorporate several other slots, including ones used for the generation of the spatial and visual representations.

For the molecular scene analysis application, the frame hierarchy is more complex than the simple map example. The structure of a protein is described in terms of a crystal, which consists of a regular three-dimensional arrangement of identical building blocks. The structural motif for a protein crystal can be described in terms of aggregate (complex or quaternary) three-dimensional structures. Similarly, tertiary structures can be decomposed into secondary structures, and so on.

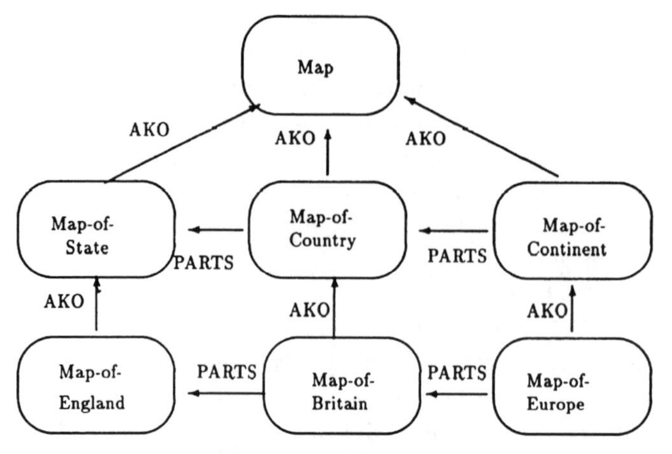

a) Semantic network representation

FRAME	Map-of-Europe
AKO	Map-of-Continent
PARTS	Sweden (0, 5) Britain (1.1)(1.2)(1.3) ...
POPULATION	'find-population'
...	...

Figure 13.3
Example of Deep Representation.

Each level in this decomposition hierarchy corresponds to a conceptual frame denoting a molecular fragment at a meaningful level of abstraction. If we consider a fully determined crystal as a molecular scene, there exist databases containing over 90,000 images of small molecules and over 600 images of protein structures (Allen, Bergerhoff and Sievers 1987). These databases include the three-dimensional geometry of the molecular scenes that forms a basis for our long-term memory model for molecular images.

Semantic networks and frames have previously been suggested as representations for images in vision research. One example of this deals with the interpretation of natural scenes (Levine 1978). In Levine's system, the spatial relations are represented as arcs such as *left-of, above,* or *behind.* A classic example of the use of semantic networks is the work of Winston (1975) on structural descriptions. In this study on scene understanding, common structures, such as arches and pedestals, are represented in terms of their decomposition into parts and a description of the spatial relations among these parts. While this approach may be useful for some applications, we argue later that explicitly representing spatial relations in terms of an indexed array provides increased computational efficiency for spatial reasoning.

Our implementation of the deep representation has several attractive properties. First it provides a natural way to represent knowledge since all the information about an image (or a class of images) can be stored in a single frame and the structure of images is captured by the PARTS hierarchy. It is assumed that a property is stored at the most general level possible (highest level in the conceptual hierarchy) and is shared by more specific levels, thus providing a large saving in space over propositional or database formulations of property relations. The deep representation also incorporates the psychological concept of semantic networks in an implementation that provides features such as procedural attachment. The non-monotonic feature of the frame allows for reasoning with incomplete information; default information can be stored in conceptual frames and inherited and used for depicting or reasoning about subconcepts or instances of images. Despite its attractive properties, however, the deep representation is not the most suitable representation for all of the information processing involved in imagery. Thus, we require alternative representations to facilitate the efficiency of the scheme.

13.2.3 Working-Memory Representations

Mental images are not constantly experienced. When an image is needed, it is generated on the basis of stored information. Thus, unlike the deep representation, which is used for the permanent storage of information, the working-memory representations of an image exist only during the time that the image is active, i.e., when visual or spatial information processing is taking place.

The distinct working memory representations were initially motivated by results of cognitive studies which suggest distinct components in mental imagery (Kosslyn 1987). More importantly, separate visual and spatial representations provide increased efficiency in information retrieval. The visual representation is stored in a format that allows for analysis and retrieval of such information as shape and relative distance. Since the spatial representation makes explicit the important features

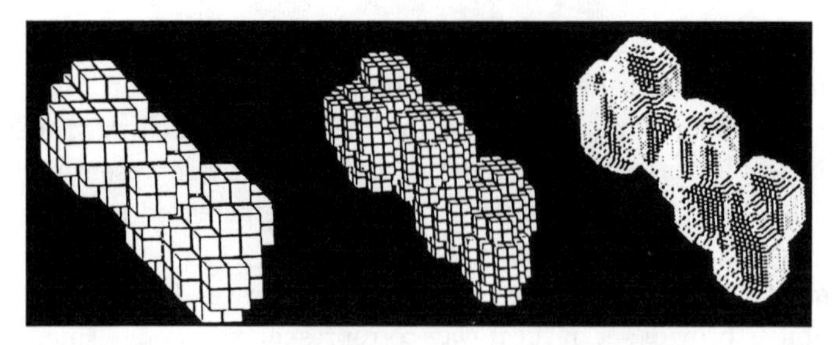

Figure 13.4
Example of Occupancy Arrays for Visual Representations.

and structural relationships in an image, while discarding irrelevant features such as shape and size, it provides a more compact and efficient depiction for accessing spatial and topological properties.

Visual Representation The visual representation corresponds to the visual component of imagery, and it can either be reconstructed from the underlying deep representation or generated from low level perceptual processes. Similar to Kosslyn's (1980) skeletal image, this representation is depictive and incorporates geometric information. Unlike Kosslyn's approach, we assume that the visual representation can be three-dimensional and viewer-independent.

For the current implementation of the visual representation we use *occupancy arrays*. An occupancy array consists of cells, each mapping onto a local region of space and representing information such as volume, lightness, texture and surface orientation about this region. Objects are depicted in the arrays by patterns of filled cells isomorphic in surface area to the objects. Figure 13.4 illustrates depictions of three-dimensional occupancy arrays corresponding to a molecular fragment at varying levels of resolution. These arrays were constructed using geometric coordinates and radii of the atomic components of the molecule.

Representing occupancy arrays explicitly in long-term memory can be a costly approach. As a result other approaches to storing or generating this information (like generalized shapes) have been developed. Such approaches can be incorporated into an application of the scheme for computational imagery.

Spatial Representation A primary characteristic of a good formalism for knowledge representation is that it makes relevant properties explicit. While an occupancy array provides a representation for the visual component of imagery, it is basically uninterpreted. For the spatial component of imagery we are best served by a representation that explicitly denotes the spatial relations between meaningful parts of an image, corresponding to the mental maps created by humans. Thus we use a multidimensional symbolic array to depict the spatial structure of an image, where the symbolic elements of the array denote its meaningful parts (Glasgow 1990). The symbolic array preserves the spatial and topological relationships of the image features, but not necessarily relative sizes or distances. The arrays can be interpreted in different ways depending on the application. If, for example, we use the scheme to reason about geographic maps, interpretations could include predicates such as *north, east, south* and *west*; if the array is used to represent the image of a room, then the interpretation would involve predicates such as *above, behind, left-of, beside,* etc. For molecular scene analysis we are more concerned with properties such as *symmetry* and *adjacency* (bonding), which are made explicit by a symbolic array. The spatial representation can also denote non-spatial dimensions. For example, the symbolic array could be used to index features such as height or speed.

<table>
<tr><td></td><td></td><td></td><td></td><td>Norway</td><td>Sweden</td><td>Finland</td></tr>
<tr><td></td><td rowspan="3">Britain</td><td></td><td></td><td>Denmark</td><td></td><td></td></tr>
<tr><td>Ireland</td><td></td><td>Holland</td><td rowspan="2">Germany</td><td>Poland</td><td></td></tr>
<tr><td></td><td></td><td>Belgium</td><td>Czech Republic</td><td>Slovakia</td></tr>
<tr><td></td><td></td><td colspan="2" rowspan="2">France</td><td>Switzerland</td><td>Austria</td><td>Hungary</td></tr>
<tr><td></td><td></td><td rowspan="2">Italy</td><td colspan="2">? Yugoslavia ?</td></tr>
<tr><td>Portugal</td><td colspan="2">Spain</td><td></td><td></td><td>Greece</td></tr>
</table>

Figure 13.5
Example of Symbolic Array for Spatial Representation.

The symbolic array representation for the spatial component of imagery is generated, as needed, from information stored explicitly in the frame representation of an image. For example, in Figure 13.3 the PARTS slot contains the indices needed to reconstruct the spatial representation for a simplified map of Europe. Figure 13.5 illustrates this symbolic array. Note that some parts occupy more than one element in an array (e.g., Italy, France). This is necessary to capture all the spatial relationships of the parts of an image. We may also wish to denote more complex relations, such as one object being "inside" another. This is illustrated in Figure 13.6, which displays a spatial image of a glass containing water.

glass	water	glass
glass	glass	glass

Figure 13.6
Symbolic Array Depiction of Inside Relation.

According to Pylyshyn (1973), images are not raw uninterpreted mental pictures, but are organized into meaningful parts which are remembered in terms of their spatial relations. Furthermore, we can access the meaningful parts; that is, we are able to focus attention on a specific feature of an image. Nested symbolic arrays capture these properties by representing images at various levels of abstraction as prescribed by the PART hierarchy of the deep representation; each level of embedding in an array corresponds to a level of structural decomposition in the frame hierarchy. For instance, focusing attention on Britain in the array of Figure 13.5 would result in a new array in which the symbol for Britain is replaced by its spatial representation (see Figure 13.7). This subimage is generated using the PARTS slot for the frame of Britain in the deep representation.

It has been suggested that people can reconstruct and reinterpret mental images (Finke 1989). The proposed scheme also provides the capability to combine and reconstruct images, using special functions that operate on the symbolic array representations. For instance we can combine a portion of the array of Figure 13.5 with a portion of the array that corresponds to the map of Africa and create a new array that contains the countries of the Mediterranean Sea.

Recall that Pinker (1988) has pointed out that images are represented and manipulated in three-dimensions. Similar to the visual representation, a symbolic array can be two or three-dimensional, depending on the application. In the domain of molecular scenes, fragments of molecules are represented as three-dimensional symbolic arrays at vary-

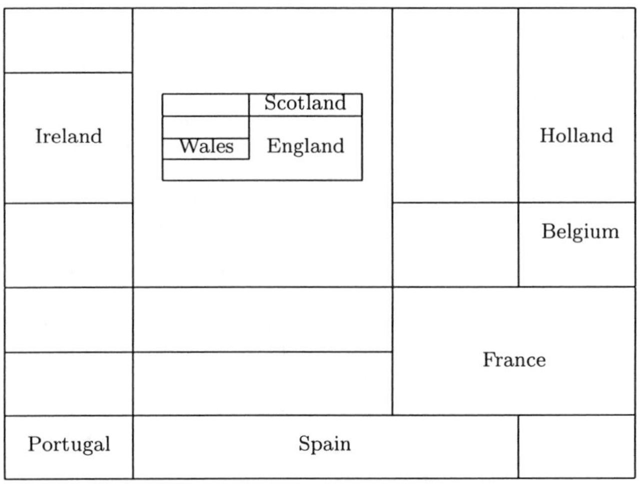

Figure 13.7
Embedded Symbolic Array Representation for Western Europe.

ing levels of abstraction, corresponding to the level of decomposition in the frame hierarchy. For example, a protein can be represented as a three-dimensional array of symbols denoting high-level structures, which can be decomposed into nested arrays of symbols denoting progressively more detailed substructures. Because of the size and complexity of molecular structures, it is essential to be able to reason at multiple levels of abstraction when analyzing a particular molecular scene. Figure 13.8 depicts a three-dimensional image of a fragment of a protein secondary structure, and an embedded amino acid residue substructure containing symbols denoting atoms. Bonding at the residue and atomic level is made explicit through structural adjacency in the representation.

For image recognition and classification, it is necessary to pick out characteristic properties and ignore irrelevant variations. One approach to image classification is on the basis of shape. While the visual representation provides one approach to shape determination, the spatial representation allows for an hierarchical, topological representation for shape. This approach is particularly useful in applications where images are subject to a large number of transformations. For example, a human body can be configured many ways depending on the positions of arms, legs, etc. While it is impossible to store a separate representation for every possible configuration, it is possible to represent a body us-

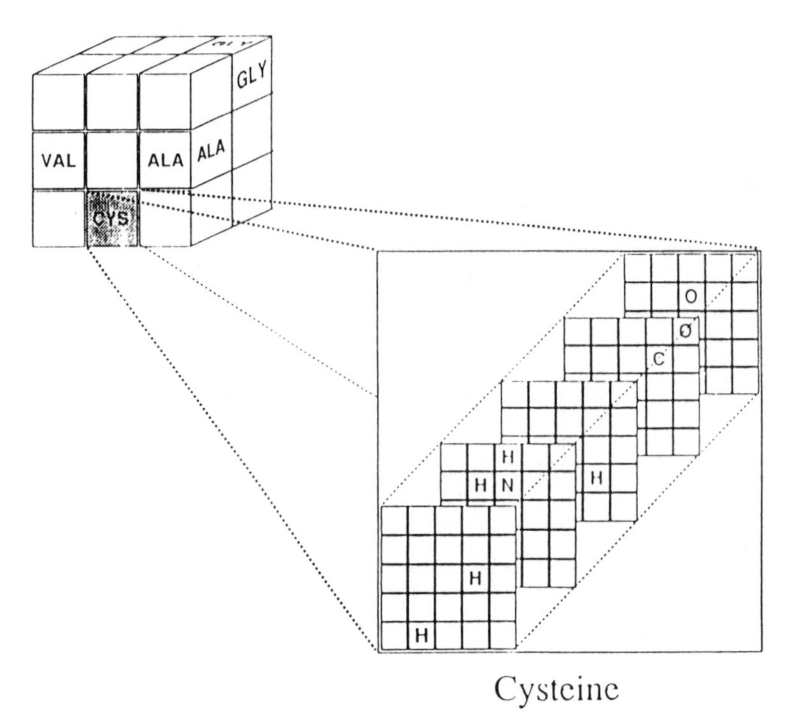

Figure 13.8
Symbolic Array of Molecular Fragment.

ing a symbolic array that makes explicit the parts of the body and the relations between parts that remain constant under allowable transformations. Figure 13.9 illustrates such a spatial representation. Combined with a primitive shape descriptor (such as generalized cylinder), the spatial representation provides for multi-dimensional shape descriptors as proposed by Marr (1982).

The spatial representation can be thought of as descriptive since it can be expressed as a propositional representation, where the predicates are spatial relationships and the arguments are concrete, imaginable, objects. Although information in the spatial representation can be expressed as propositions, the representations are not computationally equivalent; that is, the efficiency of the inference mechanisms is not the same. The spatial structure of images has properties not possessed by deductive propositional representations. As pointed out by Lindsay (1988), these properties help avoid the "combinatorial explosion of correct but trivial inferences that must be explicitly represented in a propositional system". Lindsay also argues that the spatial image repre-

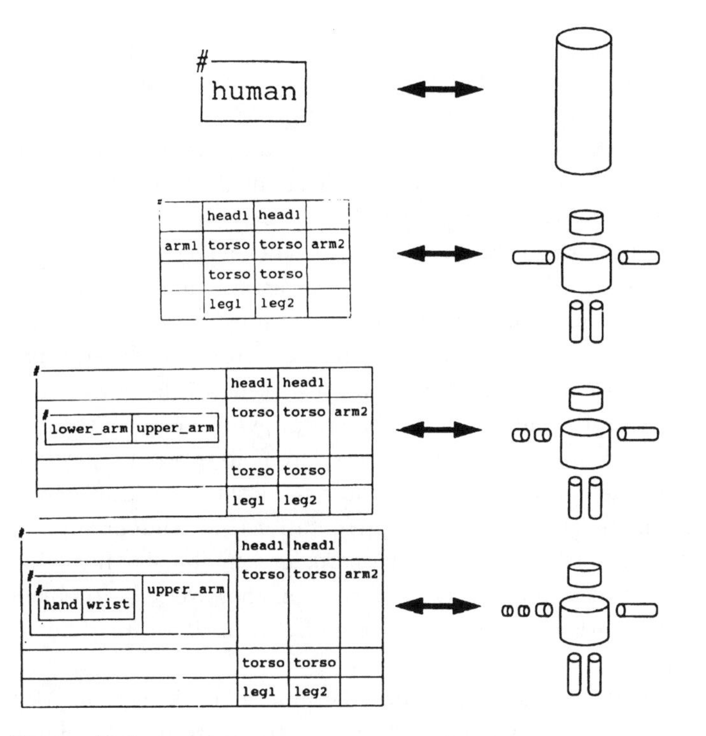

Figure 13.9
Spatial Representation for Topological Shape Description.

sentations (symbolic representations in our case) support non-deductive inference using built-in constraints on the processes that construct and access them. Consider, for example, the spatial representation of the map of Europe. To retrieve the information about what countries are north of Germany, we need only search a small portion of the symbolic array. Alternatively, in a propositional approach the spatial relations would be stored as axioms such as: *north-of(Britain,Portugal)*, *north-of(France,Spain)*, *north-of(Holland,Belgium)*, ... and general rules such as: $north\text{-}of(X,Y) \wedge north\text{-}of(Y,Z) \rightarrow north\text{-}of(X,Z)$.

To determine what countries are north of Germany using this representation involves considering all axioms plus recursive calls to the general rule. Thus, although the information embodied in the spatial representation is derivable from propositional knowledge the indexing of this information using an array data structure can make spatial reasoning more efficient.

Another advantage of symbolic arrays, with respect to propositional representations, concerns temporal reasoning. Any cognitive system, natural or artificial, should be able to deal with a dynamic environment in which a change in a single item of knowledge might have widespread effects. The problem of updating a system's representation of the state of the world to reflect the effects of actions is known as the *frame problem* (Raphael 1971). Representing an image as a symbolic array has advantages when considering this problem. Consider, for example, that we change the position of a country in our map of Europe. In a propositional representation we would have to consider all of the effects that this would have on the current state. Using the symbolic array to store the map, we need only delete the country from its previous position and insert it in the new one. Since spatial relationships are interpreted, not logically inferred, from image representations, we eliminate some of the problems associated with non-monotonicity in domains involving spatial/temporal reasoning. There still remains, however, the problem of dealing with truth maintenance if we desire to preserve relations as changes are made.

The representation scheme provides the ability to extract propositional information from symbolic arrays and to create or manipulate symbolic arrays with respect to propositional information. It should be noted, though, that the spatial representation does not provide the full expressive power of first-order logic; we cannot express quantification or disjunction. For example, it is not possible to represent an image of Europe that denotes the fact that Britain is either north of *or* south of Portugal. But mental images cannot express such information either. The representation scheme can be integrated with a logic representation through Nlog, a logic programming environment based on the theory of nested arrays (Glasgow et al. 1991). In this environment, the spatial information extracted through imagery processes can be used as propositions in logical deductions.

13.2.4 Primitive Functions for Computational Imagery

Approaches to knowledge representation are distinguished by the the operations performed on the representations. Thus, the effectiveness of our scheme can be partially measured by how well it facilitates the implementation of imagery related processes. In this section we review some of the primitive imagery functions that have been defined for the scheme. We also discuss how these functions provide the building blocks for more complex processes.

In his computational model for imagery, Kosslyn (1980) considers three basic categories of image processes: procedures for image generation (mapping deep representations into visual representations), procedures for evaluating a visual image, and procedures for transforming an image. While we attempt to capture much of the functionality of the procedures described by Kosslyn, and in fact can categorize our operations similarly, the nature of our representations lead to differences in the implementations. For example, we define operations for both visual and spatial reasoning of three dimensional images. As well, since our images can be organized hierarchically, we have defined functions that allow us to depict parts of an image at varying levels of abstraction using embedded arrays. When considering spatial functions, we were also influenced by the work of Kritchevsky (1988), who defines (but does not implement) a classification scheme for elementary spatial functions that includes operations for spatial perception, spatial memory, spatial attention, spatial mental operations and spatial construction. As well as attempting to capture much of the functionality derived from cognitive studies of behavior, we have been influenced by our desire to incorporate our tools in reasoning systems for knowledge-based system development. Thus, we have been concerned with issues such as efficiency and reusability of our primitive functions.

The implementation of the imagery functions assumes global variables corresponding to the current states of long-term and working memory. The primitive functions modify these states by retrieving images from memory, transforming the contents of working memory or storing new (or modified) images in long-term memory.

We consider the primitive functions for imagery in three classes corresponding to the three representations: deep, visual and spatial. Functions for deep and visual memory have been considered previously in research areas such as semantic memory, vision, computational geometry and graphics. Thus we provide a brief overview of these classes and concentrate on the more novel aspect of our research, the functions for spatial reasoning. We also discuss the processes involved in transforming one representation into another, a powerful feature of our knowledge representation scheme. Note that the proposed functions have been specified using array theory and implemented in the programming language Nial.

Long-Term Memory Functions The frame concept was initially proposed as a model for analogy-driven reasoning (Minsky 1975). In the context of imagery, this type of reasoning involves the understanding of an image in a new context based on previously stored images. The functions for the deep representation of imagery in our implementation are exactly those of the Nial Frame Language (Hache 1986). In this language, imagery frames contain information describing images or classes of images, where knowledge is organized into slots that represent the attributes of an image.

Like most frame languages, the Nial Frame Language uses a semantic network approach to create configurations of frame taxonomies. The hierarchical network approach supports AKO links for implementing an inheritance mechanism within the frame structure. Frames in the language are implemented and manipulated as nested association lists of slots and values. Creating a generic or instance frame for an image requires assigning values to its slots, which is achieved using the function *fdefine*. Information is modified, added to or deleted from an existing frame using the *fchange, fput* and *fdelete* operators. Knowledge is retrieved (directly or through inheritance) from frames using the *fget* function. These and many other frame functions are implemented as part of the Nial AI Toolkit (Jenkins et al. 1988).

The decomposition of images into their components is an important concept of computational imagery. This is achieved through a PARTS slot that contains the meaningful parts of an image and their relative location. Since the spatial representation of an image is stored relative to a particular axis, an instance frame may also contain an ORIENTATION slot. As described later, the PARTS and ORIENTATION slots allow for reconstruction of the spatial representation of an image.

Functions for Visual Reasoning Functions for visual reasoning have been studied extensively in areas such as machine vision and graphics. Similar to previous work, we consider visual images as surface or occupancy representations that can be constructed, transformed and analyzed.

The occupancy array representation for the visual component of imagery can be constructed in a number of ways, depending on the domain of application. For example, the visual representation can be stored as generalized shape descriptions and regenerated at varying levels of resolution. They may also be reconstructed from geometric information stored in the deep representation.

Imagery functions for manipulating occupancy arrays include *rotate, translate* and *zoom*, which change the orientation, location or size of a visual image. Functions for retrieving *volume* and *shape* are also being implemented. Whereas many of these functions are generic, domain specific functions can also be implemented for a particular application. For example, when considering molecular scenes we are concerned with a class of shape descriptors that correspond to the shape of molecular fragments at varying levels of abstraction (e.g. residues, secondary structure, molecule, etc.).

Functions for Spatial Reasoning Whereas functions for visual and memory-based reasoning have been studied previously, the primitive functions for spatial imagery are more unique to our representation. The importance of spatial reasoning is supported by research in a number of areas, including computer vision, task planning, navigation for mobile robots, spatial databases, symbolic reasoning, etc. (Chen 1990). Within the imagery context we consider spatial reasoning in terms of a knowledge representation framework that is general enough to apply to various problem domains. We also consider the relationship of spatial image representations to visual and deep representations.

As mentioned earlier, the functions for computational imagery are implemented assuming a global environment consisting of the frame knowledge base and the current working memory representation. Generally, the working memory representation consists of a single symbolic array (for spatial reasoning) or an occupancy array (for visual reasoning). One exception to this case is when we are using the spatial array to browse an image by focusing and unfocusing attention on particular subimages. In this case we need to represent working memory as a stack, where we push images onto the stack as we focus and pop images from the stack as we unfocus. Table 13.2.4 presents a summary of some of the functions for spatial imagery. We specify these functions as mappings with parameters corresponding to: deep memory (DM), working memory (WM), image name (N) and relative or absolute location (L).

In order to reason with images, it is necessary to provide functions that

Table 13.1
Primitive Functions for Spatial Reasoning.

Name	Mapping	Description
retrieve	$DM \times N \rightarrow WM$	Reconstruct spatial image
put	$WM \times N \times N \times L \rightarrow WM$	Place one image component relative to another
find	$WM \times N \rightarrow L$	Find location of component
delete	$WM \times N \rightarrow WM$	Delete image component
move	$WM \times N \times L \rightarrow WM$	Move image component to new location
turn	$WM \times Direction \rightarrow WM$	Rotate image 90° in specified direction
focus	$WM \times N \rightarrow WM$	Replace specified subimage with its spatial representation
unfocus	$WM \rightarrow WM$	Return to original image
store	$WM \times DM \times N \rightarrow DM$	Stores current image in long-term memory
adjacent	$WM \times N \rightarrow N^*$	Determine adjacent image components

allow us to interpret the spatial representations in terms of propositions within a given domain. For example, consider the three-term series problem: *John is taller than Mary, Sam is shorter than Mary, who is tallest?* It has been suggested that people represent and solve such a problem using an array where the spatial relationships correspond to the relative heights (Huttenlocker, 1968):

John	Mary	Sam

As discussed earlier, describing and solving such a problem using a propositional approach involves an exhaustive search of all the axioms describing the relation. The symbolic array representation allows direct access to such information using a domain specific array theory function *tallest*, which returns the first element of the array:

tallest is operation A {first A}

If our array is representing a map domain, we could similarly define domain specific functions for *north-of, east-of, bordering-on,* etc.

Cognitive theories for pattern recognition support the need for *attention* in imagery, where attention is defined as the ability to concentrate tasks on a component (or components) of an image. The concept of attention is achieved using the spatial representation by defining a global variable that corresponds to a region of attention (and possibly an orientation) in a spatial representation of an image and implementing functions that implicitly refer to this region. For example, we have defined functions that initialize a region of attention (*attend*), shift attention to a new region (*shift*), retrieve the components in the region of attention (*at-attend*), focus on the region of attention to retrieve detail (*focus-attend*), etc. These functions are particularly useful for applications where we may wish to describe and reason about a scene from an internal, rather than external, perspective. Consider, for example, a motion planning application where the spatial representation reflects the orientation and current location of the moving body.

Complex Functions for Imagery Using the primitive functions for computational imagery we can design processes corresponding to more complex imagery tasks. For example, a function for visual pattern matching can be defined using the *rotation* and *translation* functions to align two visual representations of images, and a primitive *compare* function to measure the similarity between these occupancy arrays.

To retrieve properties of an image, it may be necessary to focus on details of subimages. For example, we may wish to determine all the regions of countries on the border of an arbitrary country X. This can easily be determined by applying the *focus* function to the countries *adjacent* to country X and then determining the *content* of these subimages. This can be expressed as the array theory function definition *border,* where the body of the definition is enclosed by the curly brackets: *border is operation X {content (EACH focus) adjacent X}*

A key feature of our approach to knowledge representation for imagery is the underlying array theory semantics, which allows us to consider all representations as array data structures and implement functions that transform one representation of an image to another. Figure 13.10 illustrates the transformations supported by the scheme. While the implementation of functions used for storage, retrieval and interpretation may be complex and domain specific, the primitive functions for imagery provide a basis for their implementation. For further details of the use of imagery for image interpretation in the domain of molecular scene analysis see (Glasgow, Fortier and Allen, 1991).

13.3 Contributions of Computational Imagery

In the introduction of the chapter we proposed three goals for our research in computational imagery: the cognitive science goal, the AI goal and the applications goal. Combined these goals attempt to address the fundamental question: *What are the underlying processes involved in*

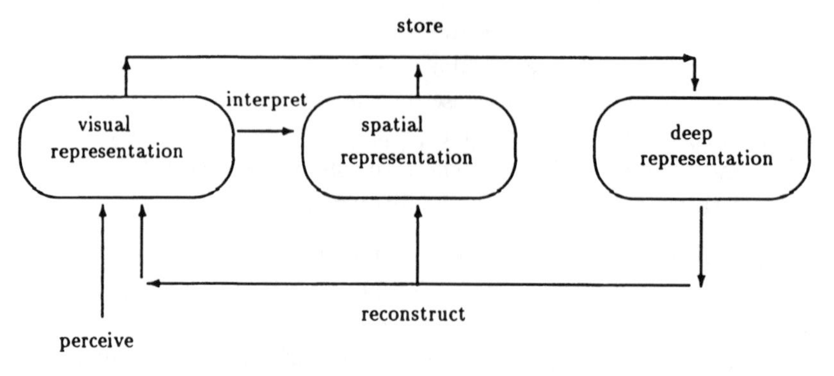

Figure 13.10
Stages of Image Representation.

mental imagery, and how can corresponding computational processes be efficiently implemented and used to solve real world problems?. We do not believe that the three goals can be approached independently. The representations and functionality of computational imagery are motivated by empirical results from cognitive science, as well as the pragmatic needs of applications in AI. Also, the tools that have been developed for computational imagery can be used to implement and test cognitive theories and thus increase our understanding of mental imagery. In this section we discuss the major contributions of computational imagery to each of the prescribed goals.

13.3.1 Cognitive Science Goal

A primary objective of research in cognitive science is to study and explain how the mind works. One aspect of work in this area is the theory of computability. If a model is computable, then it is usually comprehensible, complete and available for analysis; theories that are implemented can be checked for sufficiency and used to simulate new predictive results. In a discussion of the issues of computability of cognitive theories for imagery, Kosslyn (1980) expresses frustration with existing implementation tools:

> There is a major problem with this approach however; the program will not run without numerous "kluges", numerous ad hoc manipulations required by the realities of working with a digital computer and a programming language like

ALGOL or LISP.

Kosslyn goes on to state that:

> "The ideal would be a precise, explicit language in which to specify the theory and how it maps into the program" (p. 138).

Array theory, combined with the primitive functions and representations for computational imagery, provides such a meta-language. Moreover, it allows us to represent an image either visually or spatially, and provides for the implementation and testing of alternative, and possibly conflicting, models for mental imagery imagery.

Consider the problem of mental rotation. Although empirical observations conclude that rotation involves an object representation being moved through intermediate orientations (Shepard and Cooper 1982), a still unresolved issue is the actual content of the representation used. One obvious representation is a visual depiction of the object which preserves detailed three-dimensional shape information. An alternative approach is one in which the object is represented as vectors corresponding to the major axes of the object (Just and Carpenter 1985). This type of representation can be considered as spatial in nature; it preserves connectivity of parts but discards surface information about the image. Furthermore, while some researchers argue that images encode size (e.g. Kosslyn 1980), others claim that mental images preserve information about relative positions but not size (e.g. Kubovy and Podgorny 1981). This conflict, as possibly others, could be attributed to the different representations used by subjects in the different experimental tasks. Using the primitives of computational imagery and array theory, such theories could be simulated and analyzed. While we are not interested in entering into the imagery debate, we suggest that such simulations could contribute to discussions in this area. As another example, consider that Pylyshyn's (1981) main criticism of depictive theories of imagery is that they confuse physical distance in the world with the representation of distance in the head. The visual representation for computational imagery does in fact attach a real distance to the representation, in terms of the number of cells in the array depicting the image. The spatial representation, on the other hand, does not necessarily preserve distance information. Thus, the distinct representations could be used to model conflicting theories of image scanning.

The use of abstract representations for storing and manipulating three-dimensional images has been supported by research in cognition. Attneave (1974) has suggested that humans represent three-dimensional objects using an internal model that at some abstract level is structurally isomorphic to the object. This isomorphism provides a "what-where" connection between the visual perception of an object and its location in space. A similar connection exists between the visual and spatial representations for imagery.

The human brain is often compared to an information processing system where computations can either be serial or parallel. Ullman (1984) has suggested that there may be several forms of parallelism involved in mental imagery. One form is spatial parallelism, which corresponds to the same operations being applied concurrently to different spatial locations in an image. Functional parallelism occurs when different operations are applied simultaneously to the same location. Funt (1983) has also argued that many spatial problems are amenable to parallel processing. In developing a parallel computational model for the rotation problem, he was able to simulate the linear-time behaviour corresponding to the human solution of the problem.

As well as allowing for multiple representations for testing cognitive theories, the array theory underlying computational imagery also provides both sequential and parallel constructs for specifying the processes involved in imagery. For example, the *EACH* transformer of array theory is a primitive second-order function that applies an operation to all of the arguments of an array, i.e. $EACH f[A_1, ..., A_n] = [f(A_1), ..., f(A_n)]$. Thus, we could specify a spatial parallel operation such as *EACH focus*, which would simultaneously reconstruct all of the subimages in a given image. Functional parallelism can be captured using the *atlas* notation of array theory. An atlas is a list of functions that may be applied in parallel to an array. For example, the expression $[f_1, f_2, ..., f_n]A$ specifies simultaneous application of the functions $f_1, ..., f_n$ to the array A. Using the atlas construct and the functions of computational imagery we can specify such spatial parallelism as $[turn, move]$, which expresses the simultaneous updating of working and deep memory to reflect the translation and rotation of an image.

A full study of the relationship between parallel processing in mental imagery and computational parallelism is a topic for future research. It has previously been demonstrated that the constructs of array theory are powerful enough to express a variety of concurrent processing styles (Glasgow et al. 1989). It may then be possible to analyze the limitations of parallel processing in cognitive tasks by analyzing the limitations when specifying these in array theory; if we cannot express a parallel algorithm for a task then perhaps it is inherently sequential, cognitively as well as computationally.

A detailed discussion of the relationship between mind and computer has been presented by Jackendoff (1989), who addresses the issue of studying the mind in terms of computation. More specifically, he suggests that to do so involves a strategy which divides cognitive science into studies of structure and processing. Our functional approach to computational imagery is complimentary to this philosophy; image representations are array data structures, which can be considered distinctly from the array functions that operate on them. Jackendoff also supports the possibility of different levels of visual representation with varying expressive powers.

In summary, the underlying mathematics for computational imagery satisfies Kosslyn's ideal by providing a precise and explicit language for specifying theories of mental imagery. Visual and spatial representations are implemented as arrays and manipulated using the primitive functions of computational imagery, which themselves are expressed as array theory operations. Finally, the primitives of array theory and computational imagery have been directly mapped into Nial programs which run without any "kluges" or "ad hoc manipulations". Note, that the theory can also provide the basis for other implementations of computational imagery, as illustrated by the Lisp implementation of Thagard and Tanner (1991).

13.3.2 AI Goal

AI research is concerned with the discovery of computational tools for solving hard problems that rely on the extensive use of knowledge. While traditional approaches to knowledge representation have been effective for linguistic reasoning, they do not always embody the salient visual and spatial features of an image. Also, they do not allow for an efficient implementation of the operations performed on this information, such as comparing shapes and accessing relevant spatial properties.

Whereas representations and operations for visual reasoning have previously been studied in imagery, as well as other areas such as computer vision and graphics, there has been little attention given to knowledge representations for spatial reasoning. We suggest that the proposed scheme for representing and manipulating spatial images has several advantages over visual or propositional representations. First, the spatial structure imposed by symbolic arrays supports efficient, non-deductive inferencing. Furthermore, the symbolic array representation for images can deal more easily with dynamic environments.

The symbolic array representation for computational imagery has also provided the basis for analogical reasoning in spatial problems (Glasgow 1991; Conklin and Glasgow 1992). A thesis of this work is that the structural aspects of images, in particular the spatial relations among their parts, can be used to guide analogical access for spatial reasoning. Preliminary results in the conceptual clustering of chess game motifs has illustrated that computational imagery can be applied to the area of image classification. Currently we are extending this work to include classification of molecular structures based on spatial analogies.

13.3.3 Applications Goal

Since the time of Aristotle, imagery has been considered by many as a major medium of thought. Einstein stated that his abilities did not lie in mathematical calculations but in (Holton 1971) "visualizing ... effects, consequences, and possibilities". Similarly, the German chemist Kekulé stated that it was spontaneous imagery that led him to the discovery of the structure of benzene (MacKenzie 1965). Mental simulations provide insights that contribute to effective problem solving techniques. Thus, it is only natural to use the representations and functions of computational imagery to develop knowledge-based systems that incorporate the imagery problem solving paradigm. One such system is an application to the problem of molecular scene analysis (Glasgow et al. 1991), which combines tools from the areas of protein crystallography and molecular-database analysis, through a framework of computational imagery.

In determining structures, crystallographers relate the use of visualization or imagery in their interpretation of electron density maps of a molecular scene. These maps contain features that are analyzed in terms of the expected chemical constitution of the crystal. Thus, it is natural for crystallographers to use their own mental recall of known molecular structures, or of fragments thereof, to compare with, interpret and evaluate the electron density features. Since molecular scenes can be represented as three-dimensional visual or spatial images, this mental pattern recognition process can be implemented using the primitive functions of computational imagery.

In molecular scene analysis, we attempt to locate and identify the recognizable molecular fragments within a scene. As in Marr's (1982) definition of computational vision, it is the *"process of discovering what is present in the world, and where it is"*. The integrated methodology for molecular scene analysis is being implemented as a knowledge-based system, through the development of five independent, communicating processes: 1) retrieval and reconstruction of visual representation of anticipated motifs from the long-term memory (deep representation) of molecular images; 2) enhancement and segmentation of the visual representation of the three-dimensional electron density map molecular scene; 3) visual pattern matching of the segmented image features with the retrieved visual motifs; 4) analysis and evaluation of the hypothesized partially interpreted spatial representation of the perceived image; and 5) resolution and reconstruction of the molecular image. These processes are applied iteratively, resulting in progressively higher resolution images, until ultimately a fully interpreted molecular scene is reconstructed.

The organization of the comprehensive information on crystal and molecular structures into a deep representation is crucial to the overall strategy for molecular scene analysis. This representation stores concepts and instances of molecular scene in terms of their structural and conceptual hierarchies. A serious problem in this domain, and in general, is to find appropriate visual and spatial depictions. This involves determining what features (visual or spatial) we wish to preserve in each of the representations. Initial algorithms have been developed to construct visual representations that depict the surface structure of an image and spatial representations that preserve bonding and symmetry information. Whether these are the most appropriate structures for all our reasoning in the domain is still an open question.

A full implementation of the knowledge-based system for molecular scene analysis is an ambitious and on-going research project. To date we have been encouraged by preliminary results in the development of a long-term memory model (deep representation) for molecular scenes and the implementation of some of the essential tasks of molecular imagery. These tasks include transforming geometric information into spatial and visual representations, evaluation of partially interpreted images, classification and retrieval of images, and visual and spatial comparison of molecular scenes.

While molecular scene analysis shares many features with visual scene analysis, it also differs in many ways. Both tasks involve segmentation of perceived images, retrieval and reconstruction of image templates and pattern matching for object classification. The problem of molecular scene analysis is more tractable, however. Molecular images are perceived in three dimensions, thus eliminating the bottleneck of early vision routines. As well, the molecular domain is highly constrained: molecular interactions and symmetry constraints impose hard restrictions on the image representations. Finally, there exists a wealth of knowledge about molecular scenes and molecular interactions in existing crystallographic databases. Using machine learning techniques, we hope to ultimately generalize, correlate and classify this information.

Although molecular scene analysis is only one of many potential applications for computational imagery, we feel that it is important to apply our reasoning paradigm to a complex problem which involves extensive imagery abilities when carried out by humans. Because of the experience embodied in existing crystallographic databases and algorithms, the availability of experts in the field and the natural constraints that exist in the domain, we feel that the important and real problem of molecular image reconstruction is an ideal test case for the concepts and implementations of computational imagery. It also suggests that the multiple representations of the scheme provide the framework for a complete computational model for the complex reasoning tasks involved in scene analysis.

Other potential applications for imagery-based systems include haptic perception and medical imaging. Literature in haptic perception provides evidence for an interdependence between haptic perception and visual imagery (Katz 1989). Of special interest, are applications such as motion planning and game playing which combine spatial and temporal reasoning. As suggested earlier, the spatial representation for computational imagery facilitates nondeductive reasoning, thus precluding many of the nonmonotonicity problems involved in deductive approaches in these areas. Preliminary work in imagery and machine learning has demonstrated that the spatial representation for imagery can be used to depict and reason about structural motifs in a chess game (Conklin and

Glasgow 1992). As well, the representations for computational imagery have been used to describe the role of visual thinking in such complex domains as atomic theory development (Thagard and Hardy 1992).

13.4 Discussion

This chapter introduces the concept of computational imagery, which treats imagery as a problem solving paradigm in AI. By proposing a knowledge representation scheme that attempts to capture the fundamental principles of mental imagery, we provide a foundation for implementing systems that rely on imagery-based reasoning.

Aside from related research in perception and early work in frame representations, the AI community has given little attention to the topic of imagery. Thus, we rely on relevant theories of cognition to provide initial guidance for our research. We are also driven by the need to apply the scheme to real world applications. The representation scheme is not intended to be a model of mental imagery; we do not claim that in human working-memory two "mind's eyes" exist that process visual and spatial representations identical to the ones that we have implemented. What we do suggest is that the internal image representations are informationally equivalent to representations involved in our scheme; that is, information in one representation is inferable from the other (Larkin and Simon 1987).

The knowledge representation scheme for computational imagery includes three image representations, each appropriate for a different kind of information processing. A set of primitive functions, corresponding to the fundamental processes involved in mental imagery, has been designed using the mathematics of array theory and implemented in the functional array language Nial. These functions provide the building blocks for more complex imagery-related processes.

The most relevant previous contribution to imagery is the work of Kosslyn, who proposed a computational theory for mental imagery. In this theory images have two components: a surface representation (a quasi-pictorial representation that occurs in a visual buffer), and a deep representation for information stored in long-term memory. Like Kosslyn, we consider a separate long-term memory model for imagery, which encodes visual information descriptively. Unlike Kosslyn, we consider the long-term memory to be structured according to the decomposition and conceptual hierarchies of an image domain. Thus we use a semantic network model, implemented using frames, to describe the properties of images. The long-term memory model in Kosslyn's theory is structured as sets of lists of propositions, stored in files.

The surface representation in Kosslyn's theory has been likened to spatial displays on a cathode ray tube screen; an image is displayed by selectively filling in cells of a two-dimensional array. Our scheme for representing images in working memory is richer in two important ways. First, we treat images as inherently three-dimensional, although two-dimensional images can be handled as special cases. As pointed out by Pinker (1988), images must be represented and manipulated as patterns in three-dimensions, which can be accessed using either an object-centered or a world-centered coordinate system. Second, we consider two working memory representations, corresponding to the visual and spatial components of mental imagery. Just as the long-term memory stores images hierarchically, the visual and spatial representations use nested arrays to depict varying levels of resolution or abstraction of an image. While the functionality of many of the primitive operations for computational imagery were initially motivated by the processes defined for Kosslyn's theory, their implementation varies greatly because of the nature of the image representations.

Possibly the most important distinction between our approach to computational imagery and Kosslyn's computational theory is the underlying motivations behind the two pieces of work. Kosslyn's model was initially developed to simulate and test a particular theory for mental imagery. While computational imagery can be used to specify and implement cognitive theories, its development was based on the desire to construct computer programs to solve hard problems that require visual and spatial reasoning. Thus, efficiency and expressive power, not predictive and explanatory power, are our main concerns.

As a final illustration of the knowledge representation scheme, consider the island map used by Kosslyn to investigate the processes involved in mental image scanning. Figure 13.11 presents a visual depiction of such a map, as well as a spatial representation that preserves the properties of closeness (expressed as adjacency) and relative location of the important features of the island. It does not attempt to preserve relative distance. Consider answering such questions as: *What is the shape of the island?*

or *Is the beach or the tree closer to the hut?* These properties can be retrieved using the visual representation of the map. For example, we could analyze the surface of the island and compare this with known descriptions in the deep representation to retrieve shape information. Now consider the queries: *What is north of the tree?* and *What is the three-dimensional structure of the hut?* While it may be possible to derive this information from the visual representation, it would be a costly process. Using the symbolic array representation, however, we can easily access and retrieve spatial information using an efficient constrained search procedure. While it may be argued that it is also costly to initially construct the spatial representation, the process of determining the structure of this representation can be carried out once and then the results stored in the deep representation for later use.

More detailed information can be accessed from the spatial representation using the *focus* function to construct and inspect spatial images at lower levels of the structural hierarchy. For this particular example, there is not sufficient information to determine all of the three-dimensional features of the hut from the two-dimensional visual depiction. Using the computational imagery paradigm, which incorporates inheritance in the deep representation, we can construct the three-dimensional symbolic array using information stored in the generic frame for the concept "hut" to fill in missing details.

It is worth noting here that the spatial representation is not just a low resolution version, or approximation, of the visual representation of an image. As well as capturing the structural hierarchy of an image, the symbolic array may discard, not just approximate, irrelevant visual information. For example, in particular molecular applications we are primarily concerned with bonding information, which is made explicit using adjacency in a three-dimensional symbolic array. Visual and spatial properties such as size, distance, relative location (i.e. above, behind, left-of, etc.) may not important for such applications and thus not preserved.

Another approach to visual reasoning was presented by Funt (1980), who represented the state of the world as a diagram, and actions in the world as corresponding actions in the diagram. Similar to Kosslyn, Funt uses two-dimensional arrays to denote his visual images. A more recent model describes how visual information can be represented within the computational framework of discrete symbolic representations in such

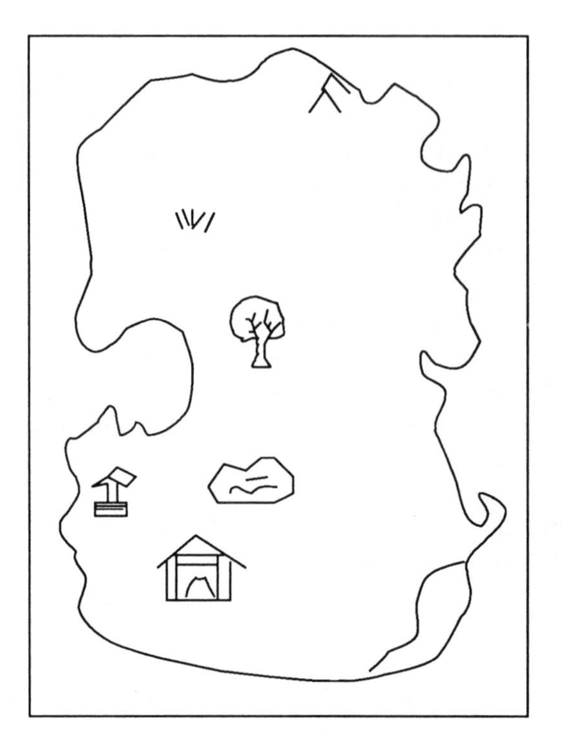

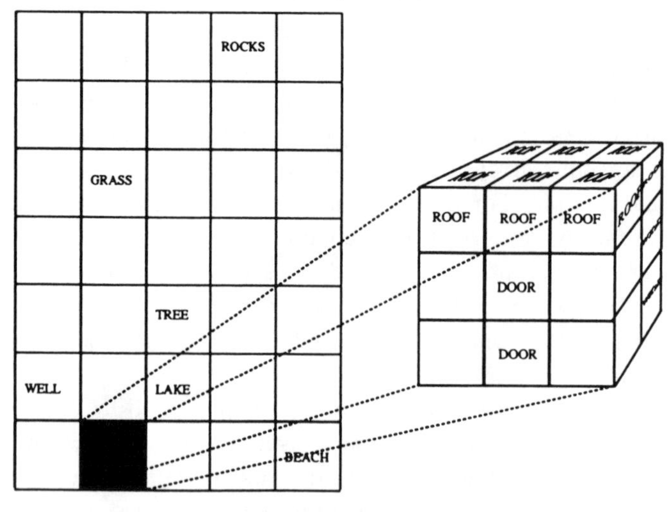

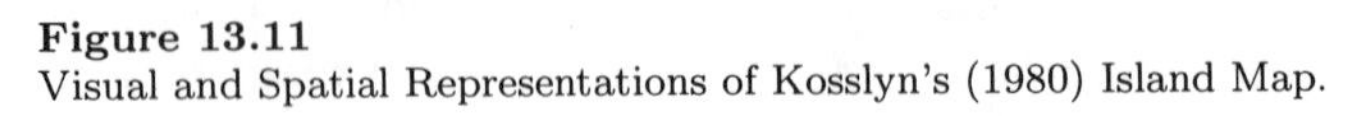

Figure 13.11
Visual and Spatial Representations of Kosslyn's (1980) Island Map.

a way that both mental images and symbolic thought processes can be explained (Chandrasekaran and Narayanan 1990). While this model allows a hierarchy of descriptions, it is not spatially organized.

One way of evaluating our approach to computation imagery is in terms of the fundamental principles of mental imagery, as described in (Finke 1989). In particular, the scheme was designed around the principle of *implicit encoding*, which states that imagery is used to extract information that was not explicitly stored in long-term memory. We retrieve information such as shape and size using the visual representation and information pertaining to the relative locations of objects in an image using the spatial representation for working memory. The principle of *perceptual equivalence* is captured by our assumption that perception and imagery share common representations. In fact the processes involved in transforming a visual representation to a spatial representation are just those of scene analysis - taking a raw uninterpreted image (visual representation) and identifying the subcomponents and their relative positions (spatial representation). The spatial representation captures the principle of *spatial equivalence*, since there is a correspondence between the arrangement of the parts of a symbolic array of an image, and the arrangement of the actual objects in the space. Note though that Finke argues for a continuous space of mental images, while the spatial representation assumes a discrete space. The principle of *structural equivalence* is preserved by the deep and the spatial representations, which capture the hierarchical organization of images. Furthermore, images in our representation scheme can be reorganized and reinterpreted. The scheme captures the functionality required of the principle of *transformational equivalence* by providing primitive array functions that can be used to manipulate both the visual and spatial representations of images.

When questioned on the most urgent unresolved difficulties in AI research, Aaron Sloman (1985) replied:

> I believe that when we know how to represent shapes, spatial structures and spatial relationships, many other areas of AI will benefit, since spatial analogies and spatial modes of reasoning are so pervasive.

Experimental results suggest that people use mental imagery for spatial reasoning. Thus, by facilitating an efficient implementation of the processes involved in mental imagery, computational imagery provides a basis for addressing the difficulties suggested by Sloman and for developing AI systems that rely on representing, retrieving and reasoning about visual and spatial properties of images.

Acknowledgements

The research described in this chapter was supported by grants from the Intelligent Robotics and Information Systems Federal Network Center of Excellence, the Information Technology Research Center of Ontario, and the Natural Science and Engineering Research Council of Canada. The authors would like to acknowledge crystallographers Suzanne Fortier and Frank Allen for their collaboration and contributions in the area of molecular scene analysis.

References

Allen, F. H., Bergerhoff, G., and Sievers, R. (eds.) 1987. *Crystallographic Databases.* Chester, England: IUCr.

Anderson, J. R. 1978. Arguments Concerning Representations For Mental Imagery. *Psychological Review* 85: 249–277.

Attneave, F. 1974. Apparent Movement and the What-Where Connection. *Psychologica* 17: 108–120.

Atwood, G. E. 1971. An Experimental Study of Visual Imagination and Memory. *Cognitive Psychology* 2.

Baddeley, A. D., and Lieberman, K. 1980. Spatial Working Memory. In *Attention and Performance* VIII, ed. R. Nickerson, 521–617. Hillsdale, N.J.: Lawrence Erlbaum, .

Bauer, R. M., and Rubens, A. B. 1985. Agnosia. In *Clinical Neuropsychology,* ed. Heilman and Valenstein. 187–241. New York: Oxford University Press.

Block, N., (ed.) 1981. *Imagery.* Cambridge, Mass.: The MIT Press.

Biederman, I. 1987. Recognition-By-Components: A Theory of Human Image Understanding. *Psychological Review* 94: 115–147.

Brooks, L. R. 1968. Spatial and Verbal Components In the Act of Recall. *Canadian Journal of Psychology* 22: 349–368.

Chandrasekaran, B., and Narayanan, N. H. 1990. Integrating Imagery and Visual Representations. In Proceedings of the 12th Annual Conference of the Cognitive Science Society. Hillsdale, N.J.: Lawrence Erlbaum, 670–677.

Chen, S., (ed.) 1990. *Advances in Spatial Reasoning* (Vols. 1 and 2). New York: Ablex Publishing Corporation.

Collins, A. M., and Quillian, M. P. 1969. Retrieval Time From Semantic Memory. *Journal of Verbal Learning and Verbal Behavior* 8: 240–247.

Conklin, D., and Glasgow, J. I. 1992. Spatial Analogy and Subsumption. In *Machine Learning: Proceedings of the Ninth International Conference on Machine Learning*, 111-116. San Francisco: Morgan Kaufmann.

De Renzi, E. 1982. *Disorders of Space Exploration and Cognition.* New York: John Wiley and Sons.

Farah, M. J. 1988a. Is Visual Imagery Really Visual? Overlooked Evidence from Neuropsychology. *Psychological Review* 95: 307–317.

Farah, M. J. 1988b. The Neuropsychology of Mental Imagery: Converging Evidence From Brain-Damaged and Normal Subjects. In *Spatial Cognition—Brain Bases and Development,* ed. Stiles-Davis, Kritchevsky, and Bellugi, 33–56. Hillsdale, N.J.: Lawrence Erlbaum, 111–140.

Finke, R. A. 1989. *Principles of Mental Imagery.* Cambridge, Mass.: The MIT Press.

Finke, R. A.; Pinker, S.; and Farah, M. J. 1989. Reinterpreting Visual Patterns In Mental Imagery. *Cognitive Science* 13: 51–78.

Finke, R. A., and Slayton, K. 1988. Explorations of Creative Visual Synthesis In Mental Imagery. *Memory and Cognition* 16: 252–257.

Funt, B. V. 1983. A Parallel-Process Model of Mental Rotation. *Cognitive Science* 7: 67–93.

Funt, B. V. 1980. Problem-Solving With Diagrammatic Representations. *Artificial Intelligence* 13: 201–230.

Glasgow, J. I. 1990. Artificial Intelligence and Imagery. In Proceedings of the Second IEEE Conference on Tools for AI.

Glasgow, J. I. 1991. Imagery and Classification. In *Advances in Classification Research and Application,* ed. Humphrey. Medford, N.J.: Learned Information,

Glasgow, J. I., and Browse 1985. Programming Languages For Artificial Intelligence, *Computers and Mathematics with Applications* 11(5): 431–448.

Glasgow, J. I.; Fortier, S.; and Allen, F. H. 1991. Crystal and Molecular Structure Determination Through Imagery, In *Artificial Intelligence and Molecular Biology,* ed. Hunter. Menlo Park, Calif.: AAAI Press.

Glasgow, J. I.; Jenkins, M. A.; Blevis, E.; and Feret, M. 1991. Logic Programming With Arrays. *IEEE Transactions on Knowledge and Data Engineering* 3(3) 307–319.

Glasgow, J. I.; Jenkins, M. A.; McCrosky, C.; and Meijer, H. 1989. Expressing Parallel Algorithms in Nial. *Parallel Computing* 11: 331–347.

Hache, L. 1986. The Nial Frame Language. Masters thesis, Queen's University, Kingston.

Hinton, G. 1979. Some Demonstrations of the Effects of Structural Descriptions in Mental Imagery, *Cognitive Science* 3: 231–250.

Holton, G. 1972. On Trying to Understand Scientific Genius. *American Scholar* 41: 95–119.

Huttenlocker, J. 1968. Constructing Spatial Images: A Strategy in Reasoning. *Psychological Review* 4: 277–299.

Intons-Peterson, M. J. 1983. Imagery Paradigms: how Vulnerable Are They to Experimenters' Expectations? *Journal of Experimental Psychology: Human Perception and Performance* 9: 394–412.

Israel, D. J. 1987. Some Remarks On the Place of Logic in Knowledge Representation. In *The Knowledge Frontier,* ed. Cercone and McCalla, 80–91. Berlin: Springer Verlag.

Jackendoff, R. 1989. *Consciousness and the Computational Mind.* Cambridge, Mass.: The MIT Press.

Jannsen, W. H. 1976. Selective Interference during the Retrieval of Visual Images. *Quarterly Journal of Experimental Psychology* 28.

Jenkins, M. A.; Glasgow, J. I.; Blevis, E.; Chau, R.; Hache, E.; and Lawson, E. 1988. The Nial AI Toolkit. In Proceedings of Avignon '88 Eighth International Workshop on Expert Systems and their Applications.

Jenkins, M. A.; Glasgow, J. I.; and McCrosky, C. 1986. Programming Styles in Nial, *IEEE Software* 86: 46–55.

Jenkins, M. A., and Jenkins, W. H. 1985. *The Q'Nial Reference Manual.* Kingston, Ontario: Nial Systems Ltd.

Just, M. A., and Carpenter, P. A. 1985. Cognitive Coordinate Systems: Accounts of Mental Rotation and Individual Differences in Spatial Ability. *Psychological Review* 92, 137–172.

Katz, D. 1989. *The World of Touch.* Hillsdale, N.J.: Lawrence Erlbaum.

Kosslyn, S. M. 1980. *Image and Mind.* Cambridge, Mass.: Harvard University Press.

Kosslyn, S. M. 1987. Seeing and Imagining in the Cerebral Hemispheres: A Computational Approach. *Psychological Review* 94 148–175.

Kosslyn, S. M., and Pomerantz, J. P. 1977. Imagery, Propositions and the Form of Internal Representations. *Cognitive Science* 9 52–76.

Kritchevsky, M. 1988 The Elementary Spatial Functions of the Brain. In *Spatial Cognition—Brain Bases and Development,* ed. Stiles-Davis, Kritchevsky, and Bellugi. Hillsdale, N.J.: Lawrence Erlbaum.

Kubovy, M., and Podgorny, P. 1981. Does Pattern Matching Require the Normalization of Size and Orientation? *Perception and Psychophysics* 30: 24–28.

Larkin, J., and Simon, H. A. 1987. Why a Diagram Is (Sometimes) Worth Ten Thousand Words. *Cognitive Science* 10.

Levine, D. N.; Warach, J.; and Farah, M. J. 1985. Two Visual Systems in Mental Imagery: Dissociation of "What" and "Where" in Imagery Disorders Due to Bilateral Posterior Cerebral Lesions. *Neurology* 35 1010–1018.

Levine, M. 1978. A Knowledge-Based Computer Vision System. In *Computer Vision Systems,* ed. Hanson and Riseman. New York: Academic Press. Academic Press.

Lindsay, R. K. 1988. Images and Inference. *Cognition* 29: 229–250.

MacKenzie, N. 1965. *Dreams and Dreaming.* London: Aldus Books.

Marr, D. 1982. *Vision: A Computational Investigation in the Human Representation of Visual Information.* San Francisco: W. H. Freeman.

Marr, D., and Nishihara, H. K. 1978. Representation and Recognition of the Spatial Organization of Three Dimensional Shapes. In Proceedings of the Royal Society B200, 269–294.

Marschark, M.; Richman, C. L.; Yuille, J. C.; and Reed, Hunt 1987. The Role of Imagery in Memory: On Shared and Distinctive Information. *Psychological Bulletin* 1987.

McDermott, D. V., and Davis, E. 1984. Planning Routes Through Uncertain Territory. *Artificial Intelligence* 22.

Minsky, M. 1975. A Framework For Representing Knowledge. In *The Psychology of Computer Vision,* ed. Winston, 211–277. New York: McGraw Hill.

Mishkin, M.; Ungerleider, L. G.; and Macko, K. A. 1983. Object Vision and Spatial Vision: Two Cortical Pathways. *Trends in Neuroscience* 6: 414–417.

More, T. 1979. The Nested Rectangular Array as A Model of Data. From Proc. APL79, *APL Quote Quad* 9.

Paivio, A. 1975. Perceptual Comparisons Through the Mind's Eye. *Memory and Cognition* 3: 635–647.

Papadias, D., and Glasgow, J. I. 1991. A Knowledge Representation Scheme for Computational Imagery. In Proceedings of the 13th Annual Conference of the Cognitive Science Society. Hillsdale, N.J.: Lawrence Erlbaum.

Pinker, S. 1984. Visual Cognition: An Introduction. *Cognition* 18: 1–63.

Pinker, S. 1988. A Computational Theory of the Mental Imagery Medium. In *Cognitive and Neuropsychological Approaches to Mental Imagery,* ed. Denis, Engelkamp, and Richardson, 17–36. Dordecht: Martinus Nijhorff Publishers.

Pylyshyn, Z. W. 1973. What the Mind's Eye Tells the Mind's Brain: A Critique of Mental Imagery. *Psychological Bulletin* 80: 1–24.

Pylyshyn, Z. W. 1981. The Imagery Debate: Analogue Media Versus Tacit Knowledge. *Psychological Review* 88: 16–45.

Raphael, B. 1971. The Frame Problem in Problem-Solving Systems. *Artificial Intelligence and Heuristic Programming,* ed. Findler and Meltzer, 159–169. Edinburgh: Edinburgh University Press.

Ratcliff, G. 1982. Disturbances of Spatial Orientation Associated with Cerebral Lesions. In *Spatial Abilities: Development and Physiological Foundations,* ed. Potegal, 301–331. New York: Academic Press.

Reed, S. K. 1974. Structural Descriptions and the Limitations of Visual Images. *Memory and Cognition* 2 329–336.

Shepard, R. N. 1966. Learning and Recall as Organization and Search. *Journal of Verbal Learning and Verbal Behavior* 5: 201–204.

Shepard, R. N., and Cooper, L. A. 1982. *Mental Images and Their Transformations.* Cambridge, Mass.: The MIT Press.

Sloman, A. 1985.*Artificial Intelligence* 25: 386.

Standing, L. 1973. Learning 10000 Pictures. *Quarterly Journal of Experimental Psychology* 25: 207–222.

Thagard, P., and Hardy, S. 1992. Visual Thinking in the Development of Dalton's Atomic Theory. In Proceedings of AI–92, ed. Glasgow and Hadley, 30–37.

Thagard, P., and Tanner, C. 1991. *Lisp Implementation For Computational Imagery* [Computer program]. Princeton, University.

Ullman, S. 1984. Visual Routines. In *Visual Cognition,* ed. Pinker. Cambridge, Mass.: The MIT Press. 97–159.

Winston, P. H. 1975. Learning Structural Descriptions from Examples. In *Psychology of Computer Vision,* ed. P. H. Winston. New York: McGraw-Hill.

14 A Cognitive Theory of Visual Interaction

Erika Rogers
Clark Atlanta University

The research described in this chapter was inspired by an interest in how visual information is used by a human practitioner to solve scientific problems. There are certain applications where understanding and interpretation of visual images are inherent parts of the problem-solving process (e.g., medical imaging, satellite imaging, geographical information systems, etc.). The increasing amount and complexity of these images mean that computers must play an important role in this type of task, in terms of data processing, graphical and image processing, and also knowledge processing. Current research has emphasized the development of improved high-resolution displays, together with sophisticated toolboxes for manipulating those images. However, this puts the burden on the user to not only be an expert in the field, but also to master the interface of the software, and to understand when to use the various tools provided. The emphasis taken in our work is to apply cognitive science and artificial intelligence techniques to the design of computer systems which can cooperate with humans as they integrate the perceptual and problem-solving knowledge needed in such visual reasoning tasks. To accomplish this, however, we need to know about visual perception, about problem-solving, and most importantly, about how perception and problem-solving exchange information. This is termed *visual interaction,* and the modeling of this process is the subject of the remainder of this chapter.

14.1 Related Work

Despite the ill-structured nature of the problem under consideration, the evolution of our model has benefited particularly from the information-processing view of cognition, where human mental activities are expressed as a set of separable components. These include memories and processors, together with principles of operation. However, generally, these components are treated individually, with the details of interaction (particularly between perception and problem-solving) left largely unspecified (e.g., Card et. al 1983, Norman 1985). More recent theories of cognition in artificial systems, exemplified by the work on the Soar architecture (Newell 1990), make a stronger attempt to deal with some of the issues of interaction between perception and cognition, but this work emphasizes machine-based cognitive processes, whereas our interest is primarily in modeling human capabilities.

Perception itself has been described as "the act of sensing something and knowing its meaning and value (Bolles 1991)." Fodor says that perception must represent the world so that it is accessible to thought (Fodor 1983), while Neisser describes it as an ongoing transaction with the external world, where *anticipatory schemata* act as "plans for perceptual action as well as readinesses for particular kinds of optical structure (Neisser 1976)." Explicit integration of the bottom-up approach to low-level vision (e.g., Marr 1982), with top-down effects of contextual knowledge on high-level vision (e.g., Kosslyn et al 1990, Ullman 1988) is important to our research, since the practitioner must be engaged in looking at the visual stimulus throughout the problem-solving task. This also suggests the importance of the role of attention. The work on visual "pop out," and the role of attention in visual search (Treisman 1982, Treisman 1985, Treisman and Gelade 1980), is of particular interest, as well as the control-oriented approach advocated in Allport (1989). Combined with other theories of attention (e.g., Kahneman 1973, Norman and Bobrow 1975, Posner 1980), these studies suggest that there is not only stimulus input to perception from the sensory systems, but also directional input formed from internal intentions or expectations. The latter may control where to look and what to look for or look at. Current theories of perception seem to emphasize one or the other type of input to perception, but do not address the impact of *both* types of input on visual process and representation.

These internal intentions and expectations are products of the problem-solving activity, which is characterized in the information-processing view as a directed or goal-oriented cognitive process (Mayer 1983). Differences between expert and novice performance (e.g., Chi, Glaser, and Farr 1988) have led to the theory of *schema-based problem-solving*, where a triggering process may cause a particular schema to suddenly pop into mind very early in the perception of the problem, and set up expectations about specific subschemas needed for subsequent processing.

In studies specific to diagnostic radiology, the basic steps of recording, perception and interpretation of critical roentgen shadows, have been identified in (Tuddenham 1962). Later work by Blesser and Ozonoff formalized this approach into a three-stage model, including a psychophysical stage, a psychological stage, and a nosological stage (Blesser and Ozonoff 1972). In a more recent study on expert radiological behavior, verbal protocols were collected from radiologists reading chest x-ray films (Lesgold 1981). The process of radiological diagnosis is described as "an interaction between the information content of the specific film and the knowledge base of the radiologist (Lesgold 1983)." The radiologists are characterized as opportunistic planners, who are "very sensitive to new information and know when to seek additional data (Lesgold 1983)."

14.2 Background

Our initial work also consisted of a number of experiments involving radiologists reading chest x-rays. Several different types of abnormalities were included in the study, and the subjects themselves ranged in experience from first-year resident to thirty-year expert. The largest body of data was collected in the form of videotaped think-aloud reports based on the radiologists examining the cases in a computer-displayed format. Extensive data analysis resulted in a number of insights about the task of radiological diagnosis, and a short summary of these results is presented here to set the scene for the discussion of the model development. A more detailed treatment can be found in Rogers (1992).

Several different levels of oversights suggested a possible transition between perception and problem-solving. At the perceptual level, a *detection* oversight occurred when the subject did not notice or see the abnormal object or feature at all. On the other hand, at the identification level, a *labelling* error occurred when the subject saw the abnormality in question, but labelled it incorrectly. Finally, at the problem-solving level, difficulty with *integration* was encountered when the subject saw and labelled the abnormality correctly, but failed to use this information in the generation of diagnostic hypotheses.

Several data-driven and expectation-driven reasoning patterns were discerned, and the specific types of information used in these patterns were also determined. Visual information about abnormal objects or findings in the image was also expressed in three levels of abstraction: a perceptual level, which had some descriptive value but little diagnostic value (e.g., "density"); a more general level, which carried additional connotations regarding features which might be associated with the object, and was labelled in a more diagnostically meaningful way (e.g., "mass"); and, finally, a specialized level, which carried a great deal of diagnostic meaning, and even some expectations about values of associated features (e.g., "malignant tumor"). Support for two kinds of context was also found in the data: declarative context, which consists of the organization of the domain knowledge, and procedural context, which involves plan-like activity associated with the use of the domain knowledge. Immediate visual capture and deliberate landmark search were identified as two types of attentional activity used in the task, and the role of expectation was also examined.

All of these issues are closely coupled in the problem-solving task under consideration. Context sets the scene for a particular collection of declarative and procedural knowledge to be retrieved from memory and brought to bear on the problem. This knowledge creates expectations of what the practitioner is likely to see, and plans to explore these expectations emerge, that then guide the attention process in deliberate search. However, there are often unexpected phenomena in the image, which seem to capture attention immediately, and cause currently active plans to be interrupted or abandoned in favor of new exploratory activity. Descriptive features are used to characterize findings, which, in turn, are labelled at different levels of abstraction.

In the interplay between these different issues, a pattern of interaction between perception and problem-solving begins to emerge. Descriptive features can be said to lie closer to the perceptual side, while context seems to originate with more abstract thought related to problem-solving. Expectations appear to lie between these two poles, originating with problem-solving, but resulting in the activation of perceptual schemas through focus of attention, which direct acts of looking. These schemas allow perceptual information to be delivered back, and the levels of abstraction mentioned above provide a way to transform the information between expectation and perceptual schema, so that it can be used by the process concerned with achieving a solution to the problem.

14.3 Model Development

This work begins with the premise that perception and problem-solving can be considered as distinct processes, which differ in purpose, function and structure, but which are related to each other in some way. It is the establishment and nature of this relationship that forms the core of our modeling effort.

In the field of human endeavor, many problems actually arise from the external environment, and therefore, many of the goals of problem-solving involve new ways of interacting with the environment. Neisser points out that human knowledge must be grounded, and that "[w]hatever we know explicitly depends for its meaning on a more immediate form of knowledge, i.e., on perception (Neisser 1991)." So it can be said that problem-solving needs a link to perception in order to perform its task. On the other hand, if it is true that problems can arise from the environment, then there is also a good argument for perception to need a link to problem-solving. Neisser also claims that "perception, like evolution, is surely a matter of discovering what the environment is really like and adapting to it (Neisser 1976)." Objects in the environment often have the potential for more than one function, and when the environment changes, it may be that a new label (or schema) is needed for the same object. Anderson states that often, "solutions to problems depend on the solver's ability to represent the objects in his or her environment in novel ways (Anderson 1985)." The well-known experiments by Maier (1931) and Duncker (1945) on the phenomenon of *functional fixedness* illustrate this point. In these experiments, subjects are asked to solve problems which require them to perceive novel functions of familiar objects. It can be argued, then, that perception needs some kind of access to problem-solving, in order to establish new representations for objects that are meaningful to the problem-solving task. This idea is also supported by researchers such as Hochberg (1981), who point out that there are certainly cases where "cognitive processes must intervene in perception" and that "perception involves some sort of problem solving."

From the descriptions above, it can be deduced that perception needs to deliver information to the problem-solving process, and, conversely, depending upon the goals of the organism, the problem-solving process has to communicate directions to the perceptual process (e.g., I need *this* type of information rather than *that* type). Based on current models of perception and problem-solving, the mechanisms for such two-way communication are already potentially in place. The internal representation which is the output of the perceptual process as described by Fodor (1983), allows the perceptual process to deliver its information about the current state of relevant knowledge about the world. It is this current state which the problem solver needs to examine in order to determine whether the current state matches the goal state. In this sense, it can be said that the internal representation can be a means by which the perceptual process delivers its information to the problem-solving process. On the other hand, since the methods for solving a problem are frequently formulated as "plans for action" (where some of these actions may be mental, and some physical), and it is also by means of plans for action at a different level that the perceptual process receives its direction, it can be concluded that the problem-solving process may provide direction to the perceptual process via these plans.

An initial, sequential model would simply connect perception to problem-solving in a bottom-up manner through the internal representation, and indicate a top-down relationship from problem-solving to perception through plans. In bottom-up activity, perceptual beliefs, or percepts, arise from interactions with the environment or stimulus (in this case with an image), leading to a modification of the internal representation. This information is then tested by the problem-solving process to decide whether it constitutes a solution. If not, new exploratory activities are initiated which lead to new percepts. A question that arises at this point is the following: Is the internal representation modified in such a way that it can be directly utilized by the decision-making process?

Top-down activity is similar, except that the cycle begins with a goal to solve a problem, so there is high-level direction from the beginning. This means that particular perceptions related to the goal will be sought, and that any other perceptions should be considered in light of their contributions towards the goal. However, problem-solving in a visual reasoning task must not only include the gathering of appropriate perceptual data, but must allow reasoning over the information that forms the current problem-solving state. This may lead to further reasoning, or it may lead to gathering of more evidence, and it may be asked whether these various levels of planning may be accounted for by a simple, sequential model.

Thus, two major questions arise with respect to the sequential approach: 1) Is the information delivered by the perceptual system via the internal representation in such a form that the problem solver can make a decision without further processing? and 2) How do the plans evolve to reflect sufficient detail to direct further perceptual exploration? To answer these questions, the model must address the following issues. First, the internal representation should be able to accommodate knowledge from both sides: visual information delivered by the perceptual process (e.g., percepts that describe findings in the image), and decision-related knowledge based on the current state of the problem-solving process (e.g., which hypotheses are active, what kinds of information do they need for evidence, etc.). Therefore a way is needed to reconcile and combine these different types of information in the internal representation. Furthermore, there should be a way to account for different levels of plans. For example, a plan to pursue hypothesis-directed search versus data-driven search is at a different level of abstraction than the detailed plan for gathering the specific perceptual evidence required by a particular hypothesis. Therefore a mechanism is needed that coordinates these different levels, and ensures that the plans are executed, modified or abandoned according to both current perceptual information, and the current state of the decision-making process.

A more fruitful approach is to take advantage of the cyclic or feedback nature of some of the current theories of perception and problem-solving. Fig. 14.1 demonstrates a non-sequential conceptual interaction between perception and problem-solving. This more complex model maintains the basic components, but introduces additional relationships, that may come closer to answering some of the questions raised above.

An interesting feature of the cyclic model is that it introduces a new relationship, namely, an interaction between the plans component and the internal representation component. From the perceptual cycle, we note that some change in the internal representation (that comes from perceptual input) may impact plans for perceptual action. From the problem-solving cycle, the plans for problem-solving action modify the internal representation in a way that may lead to immediate testing for a solution, rather than to further perceptual activity. Thus there appears to be an "inner loop" which is not directly under the control of either perception or problem-solving. A high-level plan, generated by problem-solving, may result in the reorganization of the information in the internal representation in a way that leads to a solution. On the other

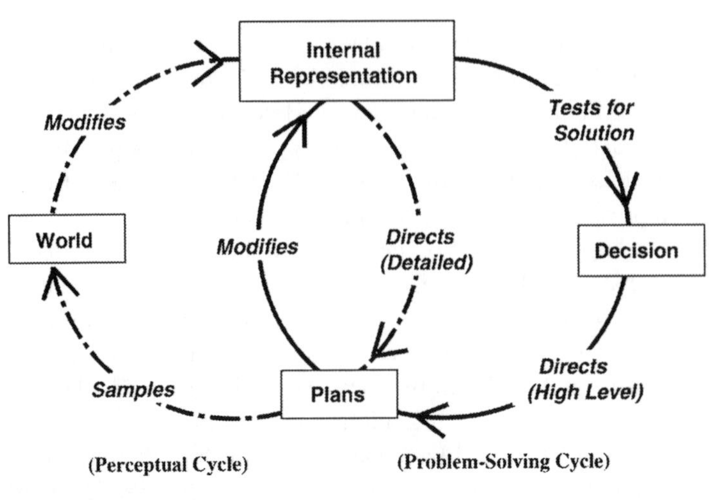

Figure 14.1
Initial Conception of Perception—Problem-Solving Interaction.

hand, this new internal representation may result in a perceptual plan that guides the acquisition of new information from the environment, in this case, the image.

If this interacting cyclic model is recast in terms of the information-processing paradigm, then the inputs and outputs of both the perceptual process and the problem-solving process require a mediating process to account for the transfer of information and instructions. This is designated the *Visual Interaction Process* (VIP), and it is assigned the responsibility for maintaining the internal representation depending on current information from both of the other two processes, and also for managing the transition from high-level reasoning plans to detailed perceptual plans.

In addition to the three processes, this preliminary information-processing model must also include the notion of memory. The typical standard model of cognition includes, amongst other things, two principal memories: a short term or working memory, characterized by rapid access and limited capacity, and a long term memory, characterized by an associative organization and a virtually unlimited capacity (Simon and Kaplan 1989). While the interactions portrayed in our model occur primarily in working memory, long term memory is also included, since neither perception nor problem-solving function in the absence of

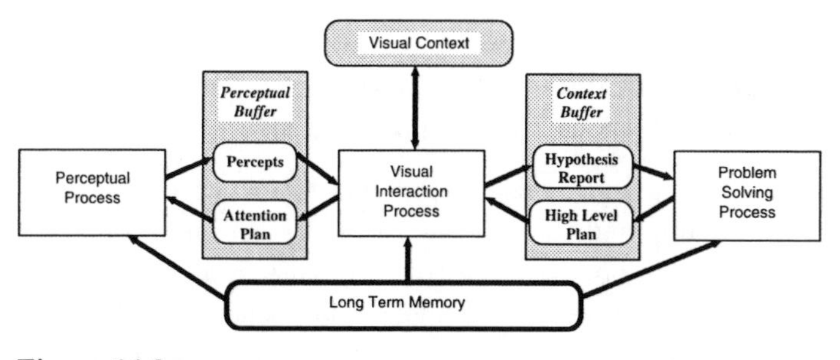

Figure 14.2
Model of Visual Interaction.

experience. Besides general knowledge about the world, the long term memory also contains domain-specific knowledge that is relevant to the problem-solving task, and persists over long periods of time (e.g., the career of an active radiologist). Based on our data, this knowledge includes anatomical landmarks, a variety of abnormalities at different levels of abstraction together with descriptive features, previous theoretical knowledge, diagnostic methods, disease characterizations, and previous experiences. Thus, for the purposes of our model, long term memory is the repository of domain-specific knowledge, which is accessed at various times during the problem-solving task by the three primary processes. (The issue of learning is not addressed at this time). Fig. 14.2 illustrates the complete information-processing model of visual interaction.

14.3.1 Functions of the Visual Interaction Process

It is important to note that the visual interaction process does not usurp any of the functions of either problem-solving or perception. Rather it acts as a *transformer* at those points in the visual reasoning task where the problem-solving process requests perceptual input, and where the perceptual process is delivering such relevant information. Otherwise, the VIP is transparent to the regular functioning of these processes. Following are some concrete examples. Suppose that there are a number of active candidate diagnostic hypotheses, and the problem-solving process has decided to adopt the strategy of trying to rule-out some of these hypotheses. It might then construct a plan that looks like the following:

- Find features to rule out competing hypotheses.
- Check those features in the image.
- Update hypothesis list based on what you see.

An examination of this plan reveals two different types of goals: *reasoning* goals such as the first and third in the list, which act on information in the internal representation, and what could be called a *perceiving* goal, which is a signal that some perceptual information is needed before the plan can be completed. When the VIP sees this plan, it extracts the perceiving type of goal, and expands it with knowledge from the internal representation that indicates what kind of perceptual information is already known about the image. This is coupled with appropriate perceptual schemas that are retrieved from long term memory to form a plan which directs attention that might look like the following:

- LOOK-AT(mass)
- LOOK-FOR(edges=smooth)
- ACTIVATE(perceptual-schema(mass with edge=smooth))

This is then directed to the perceptual process which may activate the perceptual schema. If a purely reasoning plan comes from the problem-solving process, then the VIP just lets it pass through and execute in the regular problem-solving cycle. Thus, the first major function of the VIP can be called *Attention Direction* of both problem-solving and perception.

Now let us consider the perceptual aspect of the VIP. Assume that some abnormality has been noticed in the image (immediate visual capture). The perceptual process does the noticing and the initial labelling of this object, and delivers this percept to the VIP. The VIP then examines the internal representation for relevant information, and retrieves one or more hypotheses that suggest a more specific labelling of this object in terms of the current problem-solving context. For example, if a "round white density" is seen, and it is in the lung, then possible labels for this object include "mass," "consolidation," or "infiltration." These labels are retrieved from associations in long term memory, and the VIP brings up the entire associative chain for this object. In the case of experts, this chain may contain very detailed levels of abstraction, terminating in diagnostic hypotheses, triggered by only a small amount of perceptual evidence[1]. On the other hand, those who are less experienced or confident may only have a limited number of levels of abstraction readily available in associative memory. In these cases, further levels of abstraction are explored by the VIP as new evidence is accumulated. This is consistent with Fodor's view that "the computations that input systems perform typically proceed via the assignment of a number of intermediate analyses of the proximal stimulation (Fodor 1983)." However, he also claims that "the output of the visual processor must be reasonably shallow" (Fodor 1983), and therefore it is claimed that the VIP fulfills the role of evolving the hypotheses of what is seen as far as possible toward the problem-solving level. In this way, the information in the internal representation may be as useful as possible in the iterative attempts to converge upon a solution. Thus the second main function of the VIP consists of *Hypothesis Management*, and this is seen as a supplement to the activities of the problem-solving process.

14.3.2 Components of Working Memory

The above discussion regarding the functionality of the visual interaction process strongly suggests a finer grained partitioning of the working memory than was initially described. What has been referred to until now as the internal representation can be more specifically described as the *Visual Context*. It contains the accumulated knowledge about the current problem under consideration: the visual evidence gathered, current hypotheses, including those regarding what's in the image, as well as diagnostic candidates, and a model of the current patient that includes anatomical, clinical and case history information. This does not necessarily represent *all* of the information used by the radiologist to solve the problem. It is only a part of working memory that is devoted to the aspects of the problem that require integration of visual and abstract problem knowledge.

Our definition of how the visual interaction process communicates with the perceptual and problem-solving processes suggests that there must also be a mechanism to allow asynchronous communication between the processes, as suggested in Newell (1990). Therefore the working memory devoted to the current problem is further partitioned into

[1]This would account for the very fast (almost immediate) generation of diagnostic hypotheses, described by some experts as "seeing the Gestalt."

two buffers, each of which enables flow of both declarative and procedural information. The *Perceptual Buffer*, links the perceptual process and the visual interaction process. From the stream of percepts, produced by the perceptual process, the VIP selects those which are relevant to the current problem. In addition, the VIP sends directions for attention, together with appropriate perceptual schemas or templates to the perceptual process for execution. These are assembled in the attention plan, which is intimately linked with the high-level expectations of the problem solver. On the other hand, the *Context Buffer* allows asynchronous communication between the visual interaction process and the problem-solving process. In particular, it provides a mechanism for the problem-solving process to set or change the current problem-solving context in the form of high level plan(s). This is done in an opportunistic manner, allowing the problem-solver to switch contexts according to the current needs of the diagnostic reasoning process. Since new perceptual information is constantly arriving, the VIP composes this into hypotheses about what has been seen in the current problem-solving context. These are called visual hypotheses, and are delivered by the VIP to the problem-solving process for further evaluation and incorporation via the hypothesis report.

14.4 Model Evaluation

In the previous sections, the evolution of the model of visual interaction has been described, particularly with respect to how empirical and theoretical work have been combined in order to generate a cognitively-consistent theory. However, cognitive consistency also implies that the model can account for some of the results of the data analysis, and perhaps even tell us something new which was unanticipated.

Oversights and Errors

It was noted previously that our experimental results revealed a number of conditions under which subjects could overlook or fail to use relevant image information in the diagnostic process. (These results were also compared to those in Lesgold [1981]). The following descriptions demonstrate how the model may help to account for such oversights, and where it would be possible for an intelligent system to intervene in the diagnostic process to try to preempt such errors. The model suggests that for many problems, there may be both a bottom-up and a top-down explanation, depending on where the user is in the diagnostic process. This implies that for the same problem, different types of assistance must be considered, according to the current needs and problem-solving state of the user.

At the perceptual level, the quality of the image, coupled with the user's perceptual talent will affect the visibility of anatomical landmarks and abnormalities. The dual nature of the selection mechanism of the visual interaction process is illustrated in the following discussion.

The case of bottom-up processing is considered first. This appears to be especially important at the beginning of the examination of a case, where little or no information has yet been obtained. To improve the image quality, either better acquisition techniques must be used, or the image itself may be pre-processed to some extent, in order to make detection easier. It is also possible that the user *perceives* particular areas in the image, but that these percepts pass through the selective mechanism of the visual interaction process, and are not even brought to the labelling level. This type of slip is expected particularly of the less experienced user, who may not yet have a large repertoire of labelled percept associations in long term memory. In this case, the VIP selection mechanism serves a more passive role, and the error occurs because its granularity may be too coarse. This means that percepts which should be examined more closely as possible abnormalities slip through unnoticed. A related type of problem occurs in "over-reading," that is, incorrectly labelling normal percepts as abnormal. This may be an indication that the VIP criteria for selection may be too fine, again, possibly due to inexperience.

If the user is further along in the diagnostic process, there may be several top-down effects that impact whether or not an abnormality or an anatomical landmark is detected. Expectations generated as a result of the current problem-solving context may influence the active selection function of the VIP so that it seeks particular percepts, and is tuned to accept them when they are seen. This could be due to two reasons: the user has a "mental template" or model of what the percept should "look" like, and/or the expectation causes an attention plan to be constructed that directs more careful, deliberate search. A different type of effect occurs when there is negative expectation; that is, the user is expecting *not* to see something that may actually be there.

The identification level is where subjects have detected either a potential abnormality, or perhaps an anatomical object, which must be labelled in a manner that is not only relevant to the current problem-solving context, but which will be conducive to furthering the diagnostic process. Problems with this type of labelling can occur for a number of reasons. If the object is difficult to see, perhaps due to poor image quality, then there may be more than one plausible label that can be associated with it. (For example, a questionable increased density found in one of our cases was variously labelled a lesion, an artifact of image quality, and a nodule.) Furthermore, such labels are likely to be closer to the perceptual level of abstraction than to the problem-solving level. This means that more effort would need to be devoted to sorting out perceptual ambiguity before higher-level diagnostic reasoning could be done efficiently. An incorrect labelling of a percept carries repercussions that can lead the entire diagnostic process astray, as Lesgold also found (Lesgold 1981).

When the top-down point of view is considered, there are two possible effects. If a strong diagnostic hypothesis dominates the current context, then it may influence the mislabelling of a weak percept. On the other hand, data from one of our cases presenting bronchogenic carcinoma (cancer) suggests that the *absence* of a strong diagnostic hypothesis may also influence incorrect labelling of a weak percept. In this case, one of the subjects who had not generated a diagnostic hypothesis, even late in the protocol, saw a secondary abnormality which would have supported a conclusion of cancer, but labelled it as something normal.

The third type of oversight to be considered is at the problem-solving level, and this concerns what could be termed a lack of closure, i.e., when a subject has accumulated some evidence, but then fails to utilize it explicitly in the diagnosis. A specific example of this is seen in the previously-mentioned bronchogenic carcinoma case. This time the subject saw the bony abnormality, and correctly labelled it as a lesion. However, the final dictated diagnosis was not bronchogenic carcinoma, for which such a lesion is strong supporting evidence. The model suggests that this type of problem-solving behavior could be attributed to two kinds of situations. The first is that the information "fades" from working memory (Visual Context) if it is not utilized within some period of time. This means that the finding has not been connected to a diagnostic hypothesis in any meaningful way. Refresh could occur if the subject looked at that area of the image again, but, unless the finding becomes incorporated in a diagnostic context, it may be replaced in working memory by more interesting or relevant information.

A top-down explanation for this type of mistake involves weak diagnostic associations and/or methods. The subject's knowledge may be impoverished due to lack of experience, or forgetting. On the other hand, the knowledge may be there, but the subject only explores a shallow level of what Lesgold would call the problem-solving schema. This means that the subject may concentrate on the investigation of primary evidence for a particular diagnostic hypothesis, without considering secondary findings that are known to support such a hypothesis.

Clearly, all of the above situations could also be affected by a number of user-specific characteristics: paucity of domain knowledge, or difficulty in retrieving domain knowledge, which may be due to inexperience; cognitive overload during the task itself - working memory may be poorly organized, or overloaded so that relevant or important information gets replaced before it can be used for problem-solving; or varied levels of perceptual talent or acuity, i.e., the ability to discern features of the image which can later be incorporated into the problem-solving context. Although this appears to improve with training and experience, there is still great variation across subjects. These types of variables are not surprising, and would have to be considered regardless of the nature of model we were proposing.

14.4.1 Dynamic Mappings

The model can also be used in a dynamic fashion to examine the diagnostic activities suggested by the talking-aloud statements of the subjects' protocols[2]. Fig. 14.3 shows excerpts from one subject's protocol, where the original statements are numbered and presented in order, accompanied by an iconic representation of the model of visual interaction.

In this icon, PP corresponds to the perceptual process, VIP is the visual interaction process, and PSP denotes the problem-solving process of the model. The arrows linking these boxes represent the hypothesized information flow between the processes, and the boldface arrows or boxes

[2]Note: The following results were originally obtained by animating the model using Stasko's Xtango (Stasko 1990) algorithm animation program. A static representation has been adopted for illustrative purposes.

8. I'm looking at the mass, it's...

9. I can see very clearly the aortic shadow.

10. so it's not adjacent to the aorta.

11. That means it's either anterior or posterior to that.

12. There's not much room anterior.

13. I think it's probably a posterior mass,

14. which will mean it's some kind of neurogenic mass,

15. probably, a neurofibroma or neurenteric cysts or a neuroma [...]

16. Although it's got some lobulated edges.

17. You can see these lobulations, and the lesions I just described are usually smooth and round.

18. And this is lobulated, which makes me wonder if this may be a cancer.

19. Immediately, I, you know, went to the ribs,

20. and I see an area of rib that's discontinuous right there.

21. The cortex goes, stops, and then goes again so.

22. There's a litic lesion in one of the left posterior ribs,

23. so cancer is higher up on my list now.

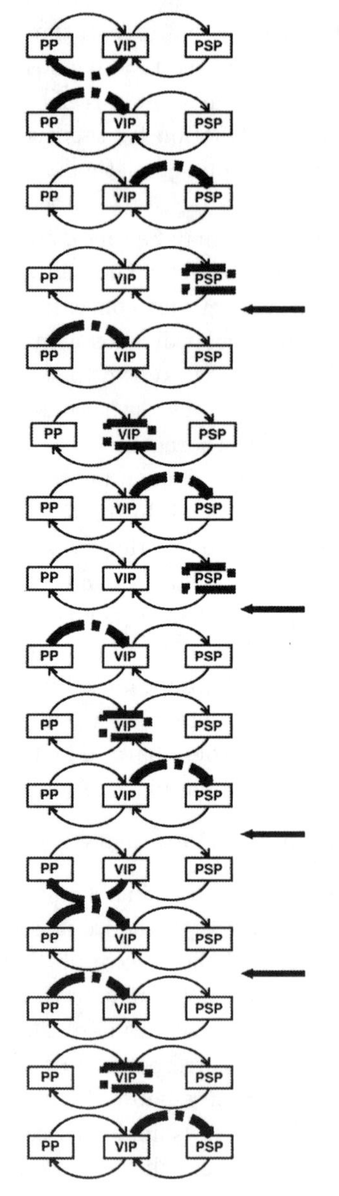

Figure 14.3
Dynamic Mapping Example.

indicate the locus of activity which corresponds to the statement next to it. Since often think-aloud reports do not express all of the mental activities of the subject, it is sometimes necessary to infer an intervening activity, and this is represented by the solid black arrows on the right hand side of the figure.

The statements of this subject demonstrate a traversal of the model that is similar to what might be expected in typical hypothetico-deductive reasoning. The movement from the problem-solving side of the model to the perceptual side and vice versa appears to lead to a fairly efficient convergence upon a correct solution, even though an incorrect diagnosis was hypothesized early in the process.

However, a similar analysis of a second subject examining the same case revealed a completely different pattern of diagnostic activity. This subject gathered a great deal of perceptual information about the primary abnormality, but never generated a diagnostic hypothesis. Although there was also an explicit indication of attention direction toward the abnormal rib, the subject finally concluded that it was normal, and ended with a final finding hypothesis of "pulmonary lesion." The use of model animation has revealed a marked contrast between this subject's dynamic pattern and that of the previous subject, which was not obvious from simple protocol comparison. In the former case both sides of the model were traversed in such a way that a correct diagnostic hypothesis was generated and supported. On the other hand, the pattern of the second subject showed a kind of fixation on the perceptual side of the model, leading to a weak solution hypothesis. Even more interesting than the lack of a diagnostic-level hypothesis is the question of whether it was this very lack that influenced the subject to mislabel the secondary finding of bone lesion? This cannot be judged on the basis of this single case, but further investigation in this direction is certainly warranted.

14.5 Conclusions

The characterization of the mediating visual interaction process in this model leads to more explicit boundaries on the inputs and outputs of perception and problem-solving. Furthermore, the dynamic nature of the model indicates that the form of the internal information flow may vary, depending on the direction of the processing. For example, an initial percept which results from data-driven processing is relatively shallow, with little semantic content beyond a preliminary object label, and some low-level features. However, a percept which is the outcome of expectation-driven processing, where a schema or perceptual template awaits confirmation, is going to be richer in semantic content. This suggests that the percept representation itself may need to be flexible, especially if it is also used to accommodate the different levels of abstraction revealed in the case of findings.

The transformation of percepts into visual hypotheses suitable for use by the problem-solving process is one of the functions of the visual interaction process. This provides a more explicit description of how information obtained by the perceptual process can be used as input to the problem-solving process. On the other hand, one of the intermediate products of the problem-solver is the high level plan, which informs the user of what type of information is needed next, and how to go about getting it. The transformation of this plan into a more detailed plan for attention that impacts the actual direction of glances provides an internal source of input to the perceptual process. What the model demonstrates is that a non-sequential, dynamic interaction seems to occur in the task of visual diagnostic reasoning, and that this suggests complex representations and characterizations of the internal information flow.

The model has been used as the foundation for design of a knowledge-based computer system called VIA (visual interaction assistant). VIA is based on a blackboard-style architecture incorporating the user, the image display and the program modules into a cooperative, problem-solving system. The panels of the blackboard are representative of the components of working memory expressed in the model, while the general control flow is based on the functions of the visual interaction process itself. This design has been instantiated in a prototype system for diagnostic radiology called VIA-RAD, and was tested in a small observational study with radiologist subjects (Rogers 1994). The results of this work show promise for the further development of computer systems which can cooperate with humans in the execution of visual reasoning tasks.

References

Allport, A. 1989. Visual Attention. In *Foundations of Cognitive Science,* ed. M. J. Posner, 631–682. Cambridge, Mass.: MIT Press.

Anderson, J. R. 1985. *Cognitive Psychology and Its Implications.* New York: W. H. Freeman.

Blesser, B., and Ozonoff, D. 1972. A Model for the Radiologic Process. *Radiology* 103: 515–521.

Bolles, E. B. 1991. *A Second Way of Knowing.* New York: Prentice Hall.

Card, S. T., Moran, T. P., and Newell, A. 1983. *The Psychology of Human-Computer Interaction.* Hillsdale, N.J.: Erlbaum.

Chi, M. T. H., Glaser, R., and Farr, M. J. 1988. *The Nature of Expertise.* Hillsdale, N.J.: Erlbaum.

Duncker, K. 1945. On Problem Solving. *Psychological Monographs* 58(270).

Fodor, J. A. 1983. *The Modularity of Mind.* Cambridge, Mass.: MIT Press.

Hochberg, J. 1981. On Cognition in Perception: Perceptual Coupling and Unconscious Inference. *Cognition* 10: 127–134.

Kahneman, D. 1973. *Attention and Effort.* New York: Prentice Hall.

Kosslyn, S. M., Flynn, R. A., Amsterdam, J. B., and Wang, G. 1990. Components of High-Level Vision: A Cognitive Neuroscience Analysis and Accounts of Neurological Syndromes. *Cognition* 34: 203–277.

Lesgold, A. 1983. Acquiring Expertise. Learning Research and Development Center, Technical Report No. PDS-5, Univ. of Pittsburgh.

Lesgold, A., Feltovich, P., Glaser, R., and Wang, Y. 1981. The Acquisition of Perceptual Diagnostic Skill in Radiology. Learning Research and Development Center, Technical Report No. PDS-1, Univ. of Pittsburgh.

Maier, N. R. F. 1931. Reasoning in Humans: II. The Solution of a Problem and Its Appearance In Consciousness. *Journal of Comparative Psychology* 12: 181–194.

Marr, D. 1982. *Vision.* New York: W. H. Freeman.

Mayer, R.E. 1983. *Thinking, Problem Solving, Cognition.* New York: W. H. Freeman.

Neisser, U. 1991. Without Perception, There is No Knowledge: Implications for Artificial Intelligence. Emory Cognition Project Report #18, Dept. of Psychology, Emory University.

Neisser, U. 1976. *Cognition and Reality.* San Francisco: W. H. Freeman.

Newell, A. 1990. *Unified Theories of Cognition.* Cambridge, Mass.: Harvard University Press.

Newell, A., Rosenbloom, P. S., and Laird, J. E. 1989. Symbolic Architectures for Cognition. In *Foundations of Cognitive Science,* ed. M. J. Posner, 93–131. Cambridge, Mass.: The MIT Press.

Norman, D. A. 1985. Twelve Issues for Cognitive Science. In *Issues in Cognitive Modeling,* eds. A. M. Aitkenhead, and J. M. Slack, 309–337. Hillsdale, N.J.: Erlbaum.

Norman, D. A., and Bobrow, D. G. 1975. On Data-Limited and Resource-Limited Processes. *Cognitive Psychology* 7: 44–64.

Posner, M. I. 1980. Orienting of Attention. *Quarterly Journal of Experimental Psychology* 32: 3–25.

Rogers, E. 1994. VIA-RAD: A Blackboard-Based System for Diagnostic Radiology. *Artificial Intelligence in Medicine.*

Rogers, E. 1992. Visual Interaction: A Link Between Perception and Problem-Solving. Ph.D. Diss., Technical Report No. GIT-CC-92/59, Georgia Institute of Technology.

Simon, H. A., and Kaplan, C. A. 1989. Foundations of Cognitive Science. In *Foundations of Cognitive Science,* ed. M. J. Posner, 1–47. Cambridge, Mass.: MIT Press.

Stasko, J. T. 1990. Tango: A Framework and System for Algorithm Animation. *Computer* 23: 27-39.

Treisman, A. 1985. Preattentive Processing in Vision. *Computer Vision, Graphics, and Image Processing* 31: 156–177.

Treisman, A. 1982. Perceptual Grouping and Attention in Visual Search for Features and for Objects. *Journal of Experimental Psychology, Human Perceptual Performance* 8(2): 194–214.

Treisman, A., and Gelade, G. 1980. A Feature Integration Theory of Attention. *Cognitive Psychology* 12: 97–136.

Tuddenham, W. 1962. Visual Search, Image Organization, and Reader Error in Roentgen Diagnosis. *Radiology* 78: 694–704.

Ullman, S. 1988. Visual Routines. In *Readings in Cognitive Science,* ed. A. Collins and E. E. Smith, 548–579. San Mateo, Calif.: Kaufmann.

15 Hypothesizing Behaviors from Device Diagrams

N. Hari Narayanan
Georgia Institute of Technology

Masaki Suwa, & Hiroshi Motoda
Hitachi Advanced Research Laboratory

15.1 Introduction

In this chapter we introduce a problem solving task involving common sense reasoning that humans are adept at, but one which has not received much attention within the area of cognitive modeling until recently. The task is to predict the operation of a simple mechanical device by hypothesizing the behaviors of its components, from a labeled schematic diagram of the device showing the spatial configuration of its components and an initial behavior. We conducted an exploratory study of problem solving in this task. Concurrent think-aloud protocols and gestures of subjects solving a set of device behavior hypothesis problems presented as labeled diagrams were collected. The gestures and marks made by the subjects were examined and used to annotate encoded verbal data, which was then analyzed. We propose a cognitive process model of diagrammatic reasoning in this task, illustrate it using the example of a pressure gauge, and compare it with results of analyzing the protocols. Besides lending support to results of previous experimental studies, this study also revealed some interesting aspects of diagrammatic reasoning that merit further research. We also describe the architecture of a corresponding computer model.

Humans quite often make use of diagrams while solving problems or explaining things to themselves or others. Reading a book like *How Things Work* (1967) and understanding the multi-modal descriptions of machines it contains provides a persuasive illustration of how diagrams aid common sense reasoning. The problem solving task of hypothesizing qualitative behaviors of a device from its diagram is another example. The main roles of the diagram in this task are to situate the problem solving process and to guide it along the direction of causality. Besides, features of the diagram facilitate the recall of prior knowledge relevant to the problem.

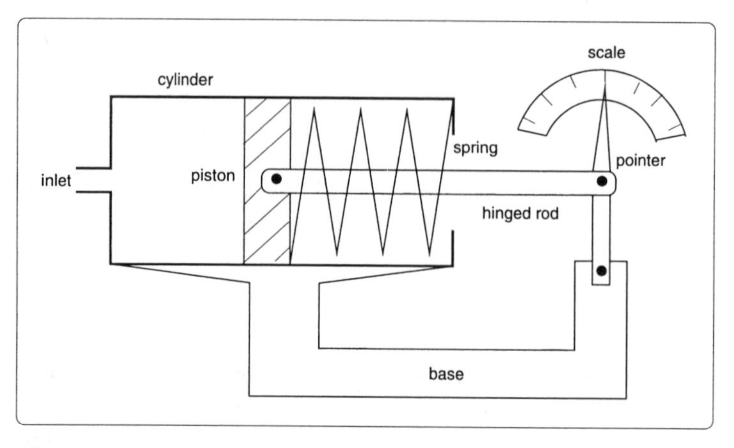

Figure 15.1
Schematic Diagram of a Device.

Consider someone with a basic knowledge of mechanical components examining the schematic diagram of a mechanical device, such as the pressure gauge shown in figure 15.1, and reasoning about its operation. This requires that the person reason about spatial processes occurring inside the device. Information used in this type of reasoning is of two kinds: *visual* and *conceptual.* Visual information is obtained from the diagram, and includes spatial configurations and shapes of the device and its components. Conceptual information comes from the prior domain knowledge of the reasoner, and includes predictive knowledge used for making inferences about the device's operation.

In such reasoning situations diagrams clearly serve as compact representations of spatial information. However, this is only part of the story of the role diagrams play in this task. Diagrams also facilitate the indexing of relevant problem solving knowledge. Furthermore, diagrams support mental visualizations of spatial behaviors of device components during the course of reasoning. Such mental visualizations guide human reasoning along the direction of causality.

The rest of this chapter is organized as follows.[1] The task that we

[1]This chapter describes early results from an ongoing research program on diagrammatic reasoning. It is based on research conducted at the Advanced Research Laboratory of Hitachi Limited, and previously published in Narayanan, Suwa, and Motoda (1993); Narayanan, Suwa, and Motoda (1994a); Narayanan, Suwa and Motoda (1994b).

studied, hypothesizing behaviors from labeled schematic diagrams, is first described. Second, we propose a model of how people might execute this task. Third, the method and results of an experimental study that we conducted, in order to investigate how people actually solve behavior hypothesis problems using diagrams, are presented. Fourth, we provide the outline of a computational model of diagrammatic reasoning in this task. In the final section we discuss interesting aspects of diagrammatic reasoning that the verbal and gestural data revealed and which merit further investigations, limitations of our computational model, and related work.

15.2 A Study of Diagrammatic Reasoning

15.2.1 Research Methodology

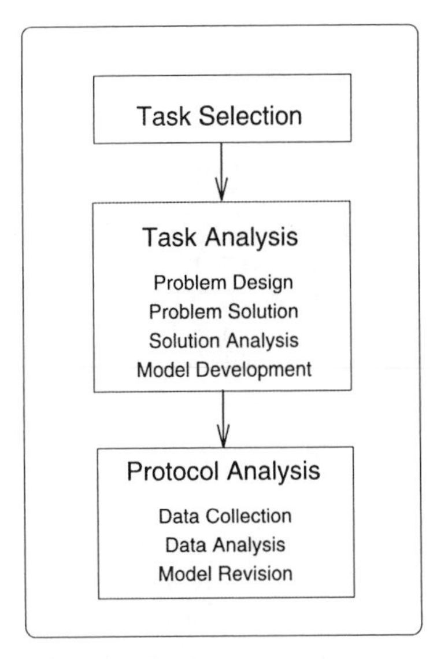

Figure 15.2
Three Stages of the Experimental Study.

The main goal of our research is to characterize how visual information from the diagram and conceptual information (prior knowledge) interact, and influence the direction of reasoning, during problem solving. In general, we have adopted the three-stage approach illustrated in figure 15.2

to study and model diagrammatic reasoning. First, a task in which diagrams are used as a medium to represent, reason with, or communicate information is selected. Second, a set of problems that exemplify the task are designed. We then solve these problems, and in the course of that develop a detailed step-wise enumeration of the solution process. These steps are then carefully analyzed in order to generate hypotheses about how the diagram cued conceptual knowledge, facilitated inferences, and influenced the course of reasoning. The aim here is to develop a descriptive characterization of diagrammatic reasoning in the task. Based on this, a process model of problem solving in the task is developed. Third, protocol analysis experiments of subjects solving these problems are carried out to collect data on actual human performance, to compare with the previously developed descriptive characterization. The raw data is encoded, analyzed, and compared with the process model. This may result in the model being revised.

15.2.2 Hypothesizing Device Behaviors

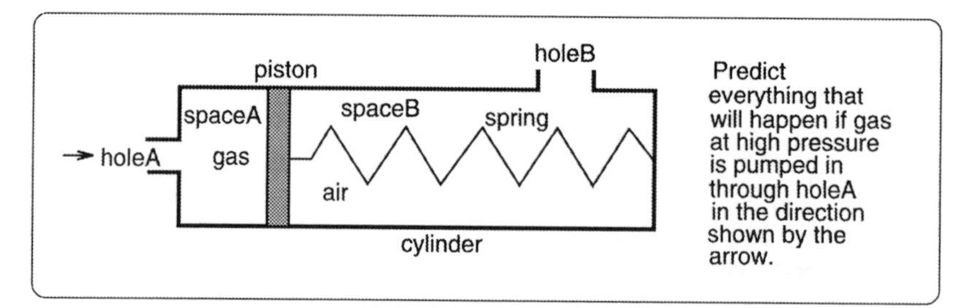

Figure 15.3
A Behavior Hypothesis Problem.

The diagrammatic reasoning task that we selected for this study was *hypothesizing device behaviors from labeled schematic diagrams.* Given the schematic diagram of a mechanical device depicting the spatial configuration of its (labeled) components[2] and an initial behavior, the goal in this task is to hypothesize the ensuing operation of the device in terms of behaviors of its components. Figure 15.3 shows a sample problem.

This study is part of a larger effort to understand how diagrams are used in reasoning. We are interested in how diagrams support problem

[2]We use the term *components* to mean components, individual parts of components, and substances.

solving by directing attention and facilitating visualization, and reduce search during problem solving by indexing appropriate knowledge. The task of hypothesizing how a device might behave, solely from its diagram, is appropriate for this because of its following characteristics.

- A device's diagram depicts the spatial layout and configuration of its components. This depiction contains cues that influence how *focus of attention*[3] is shifted during problem solving.
- Behaviors of physical devices include many spatial behaviors such as sliding, tilting, rotating, filling, and deforming. Therefore such problems are ideal vehicles for studying visualization during problem solving.
- For problems involving physical devices, only part of the information required to solve them can be gleaned from the diagram. Hence such problems are well suited for studying the interaction of conceptual (non-diagrammatic) knowledge and diagrammatic information during problem solving. How diagrammatic information cues conceptual and inferential knowledge is a particularly interesting aspect of this interaction.

15.2.3 Task Analysis

After designing and solving sample problems of the type that figure 15.3 illustrates and upon analyzing the solution steps thus generated, we observed that the problem solving steps required for this task could be classified into seven types.

1. *Diagram Observation*: Observe the diagram to locate and retrieve spatial information.
2. *Conceptual Knowledge Retrieval*: Index and retrieve related conceptual knowledge from long term memory.
3. *Inferential Knowledge Retrieval*: Index and retrieve applicable procedural or problem solving knowledge from long term memory.
4. *Conceptual Inference*: Making an inference based only on conceptual knowledge from short term and long term memories.

[3]We use the term *focus of attention* to mean an element in the diagram (a component, a part of a component, or a substance) or a conceptual aspect of an element in the diagram (such as the mass of a component) that is being heeded at any given moment during problem solving.

5. *Visual Inference*: Making an inference based only on visual information from the diagram.
6. *Hybrid Inference*: Making an inference based on both conceptual knowledge and visual information.
7. *Visualization*: Imagination of spatial behaviors of components in the diagram.

Among these, the hybrid inference is an interesting type of inference. It is typically accomplished by first generating an abstract or relatively incomplete inference based on prior conceptual knowledge, and then completing it (making it concrete) by using visual information from the diagram. For instance, one may initially infer that the input of high pressure gas will force the piston in a piston-cylinder assembly to move, based on prior conceptual knowledge about such mechanisms while solving the problem in figure 15.3. This inference is then completed by observing the diagram and concluding that this motion will be constrained to the rightward direction by the orientation of the cylinder walls. This instantiation of an abstract inference is an example of reasoning that is situated in the diagram.

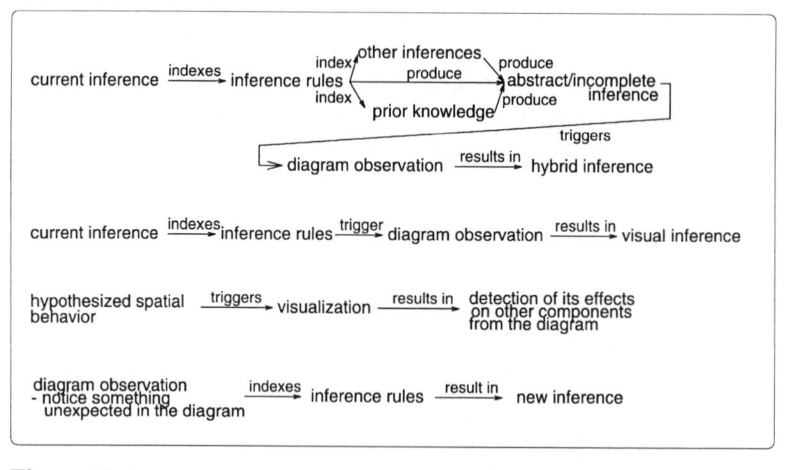

Figure 15.4
Inference Patterns Involving the Diagram.

The enumerated solution steps of sample problems were scanned to detect any regularities that might indicate repeating patterns of inference. We discovered four such interesting inference patterns involving the diagram of the problem, shown in figure 15.4.

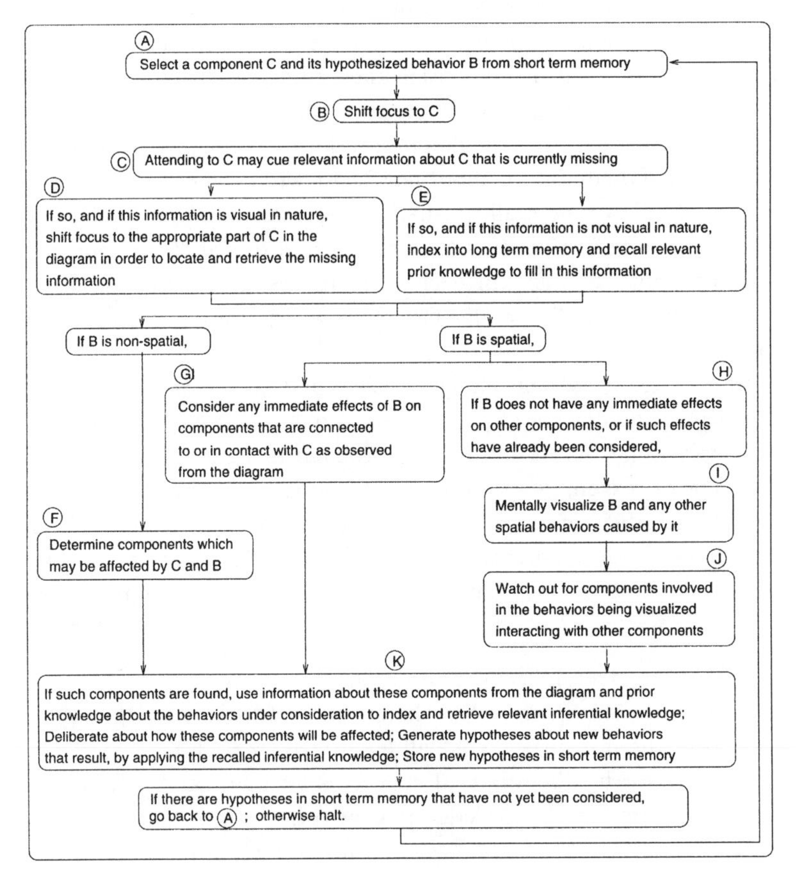

Figure 15.5
A Process Model.

The cognitive process model of problem solving in this task resulting from task analysis is shown in figure 15.5. It explicates a reasoning strategy for solving qualitative behavior hypothesis problems from diagrams. Reasoning starts with a component and its behavior mentioned in the initial condition, and proceeds in cycles. In later cycles, a component and its behavior to focus on will be selected from among the hypotheses in short term memory. The diagram facilitates the indexing and recall of knowledge in two different ways: (i) attending to a component may cue relevant properties of it, information regarding which is either recalled from long term memory or retrieved from the diagram, and (ii) configurational and shape information about components from the diagram together with prior knowledge about components and behaviors allow the indexing and recall of inferential knowledge. New hypotheses are generated in three ways: (i) by deliberating about effects of non-spatial behaviors, (ii) by observing the diagram to locate connected/contacting components and deliberating about how these will be affected by spatial behaviors, or (iii) by mentally visualizing spatial behaviors, detecting interactions among components that result, and deliberating about effects of these interactions. In each of these cases, the application of the recalled inferential knowledge creates new hypotheses in short term memory.

In order to explicate the model further, and to provide a flavor of the step-wise enumeration of problem solutions that were done as part of task analysis, let us reconsider the problem in figure 15.3 and enumerate steps of reasoning according to this model. Following each step the alphabetic labels of corresponding parts of the process model from figure 15.5 are given in parentheses. This enumeration does not contain steps corresponding to every part of the process model in each reasoning cycle.

1. Consider the given initial condition (A).
2. Observe from the diagram that holeA opens to spaceA (D).
3. Infer that the pressurized gas will enter spaceA (G,K).
4. Observe from the diagram that spaceA is a closed cavity (A,D).
5. Recall the inferential knowledge that pressurized gas contained in a closed cavity will exert a force in the normal direction on walls of the cavity (G,K).
6. Observe from the diagram that the cylinder and piston form walls surrounding spaceA (A,D).
7. Infer that a force in the normal direction will be exerted on the piston and cylinder (G,K).
8. Recall the inferential knowledge that force can induce motion in a movable component (K).
9. Recall the conceptual knowledge that the piston is movable in a piston-cylinder assembly (K).
10. Infer that the piston will move (K).

11. Observe the piston in the diagram and conclude that it is free to move left or right (A,D).
12. Infer that the piston will move right (K).
13. Observe from the diagram that the piston is connected to a spring, and is in contact with air in spaceB; consider each in turn (A, D).
14. Recall the inferential knowledge that if a component is connected to another, and the former starts moving in one direction, it will exert a force on the latter in the same direction (G,K).
15. Infer that when the piston starts moving right, it will exert a rightward force on the spring (K).
16. Recall the inferential knowledge that a force applied on a spring will either compress it or expand it depending on the direction of the force (K).
17. Infer that the spring will compress (K).
18. Consider the air inside spaceB (A).
19. Observe from the diagram that spaceB is an open cavity with holeB (D).
20. Recall the inferential knowledge that if gas inside an open cavity is pushed, it will escape through the cavity's openings (G,K).
21. Infer that air in spaceB will exit through holeB (K).
22. All immediate effects of the hypothesized piston motion have now been considered (A,H).
23. Visualize the piston's rightward motion and the spring's compression (I).
24. Notice that the spring gets compressed more and more as the piston moves (J).
25. Recall the inferential knowledge that as a spring gets compressed or expanded, it will exert an increasing force in the opposite direction (K).
26. Infer that the spring will exert a force on the piston which, at some point, will equal the force exerted by the pressurized gas on the piston (K).
27. Observe from the diagram that this may happen before or after the piston reaches holeB; consider each case (A,D).
28. In the former case, infer that the piston will stop somewhere before holeB (K).
29. Infer that the spring compression will cease (K).

Subsequent to analyzing this task, we conducted an experiment to find out how people typically solved such problems. This involved recording, observing and analyzing subjects' verbal and gestural behaviors as they solved behavior hypothesis problems using diagrams. The following sections describe the method and results of this study.

15.2.4 Experimental Method

Subjects. Three adult high school graduates volunteered as subjects.

Materials The subjects were seated at a table and presented with one sheet (per problem) containing a labeled diagram with an initial condition and instructions written below the diagram. A pen was kept on the table. The subjects were told that they could use it to point or draw on the problem sheet.

Procedure. All subjects attended an initial session in which concurrent think-aloud verbal reporting (Ericsson and Simon 1983) was explained and illustrated by the experimenter. Each subject attended two problem solving sessions lasting approximately 45 minutes each, separated by a week. Subjects were asked not to discuss the experiments among themselves during this period. In each session a subject was first given a general instruction sheet that explained what was expected of them in terms of think-aloud reporting. These instructions followed the guidelines presented in Ericsson and Simon (1983). They were then given three training problems followed by the actual problems. The four actual problems we used are shown in figures 15.6 and 15.7. Concurrent verbal and gestural data were collected. Verbal reports in Japanese were tape-recorded and gestures with hands and pen were video-taped.

15.2.5 Protocol Analysis

The verbal reports were transcribed and translated into English. Gestures and drawings that the subjects made were examined using both the video recording and the problem sheets on which subjects drew. These gestures appeared concurrently with verbalizations or during pauses. Gestures were hierarchically categorized as shown in figure 15.8. At the top level there are three categories of gestures: subjects pointed to diagram elements, made gestures indicative of spatial behaviors such as motion and deformation of device components, or sketched on the

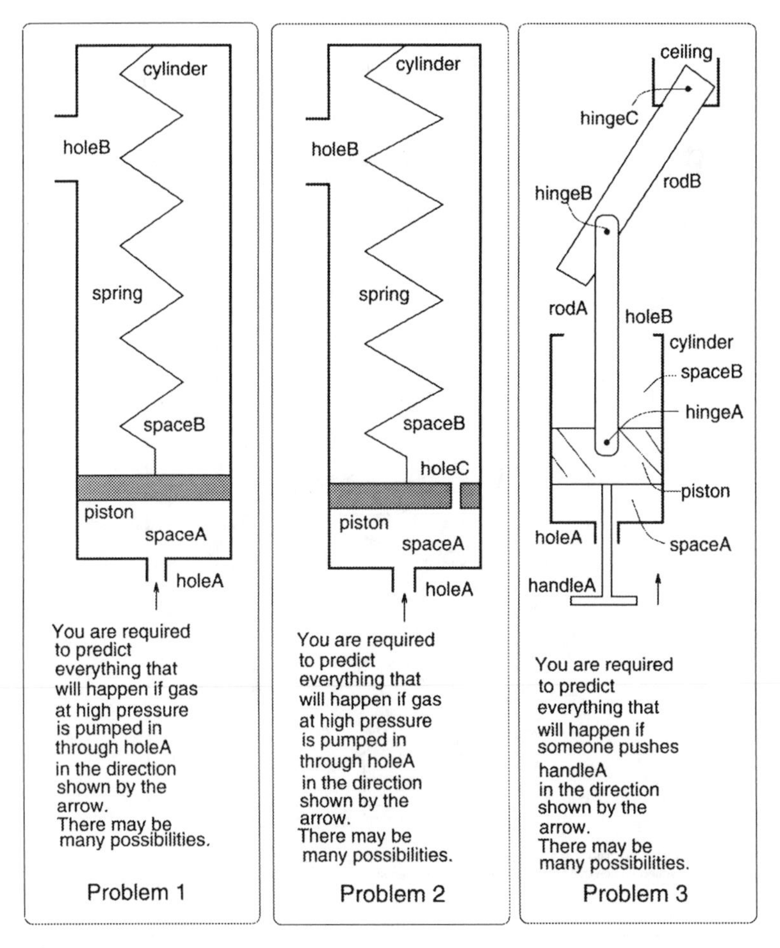

Figure 15.6
First Three Problems Used in the Experiment.

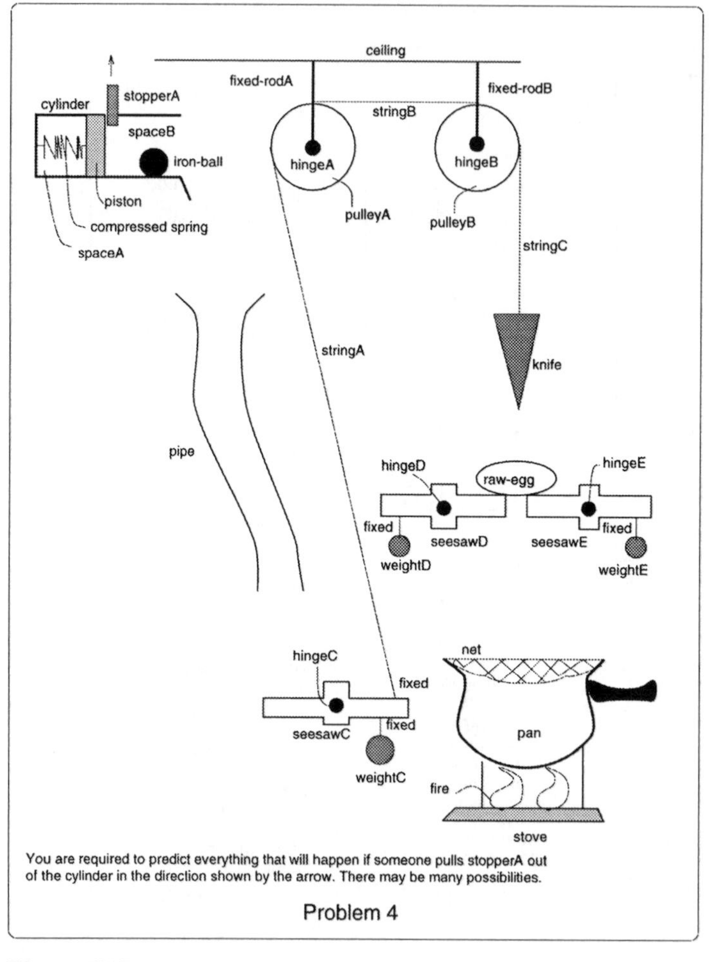

Figure 15.7
The Fourth Problem.

sheet containing the diagram and statement of the problem. Pointing activities either referred to components or areas, or circumscribed the boundary of a component. Spatial behaviors were indicated by gestures such as moving the tip of the pen along their trajectories, or by richly expressive gestures involving fingers, hands, and the pen imitating the spatial behaviors of one or more components. We call the former class of gestures *projection* and the latter class of gestures *simulation*. Subjects illustrated spatial behavior trajectories by moving the tip of the pen from one diagram location to another, from one device component to another, or from one component along a particular direction (e.g., of a motion). Drawing gestures were divided into two classes: drawing the new state (new location and/or orientation) of a moving component or redrawing a component at another location on the problem sheet. The verbal protocols were then annotated with encoded gestures.

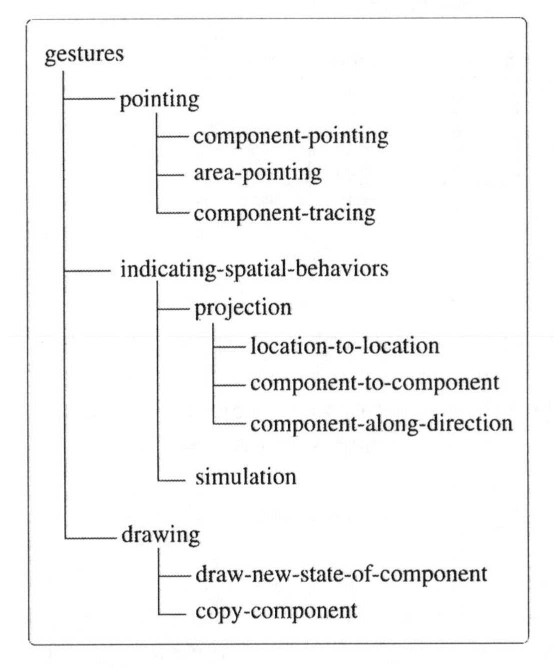

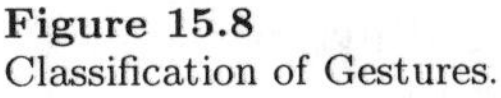
Figure 15.8
Classification of Gestures.

The annotated protocols were segmented. A segment was defined to be a meaningful clause (or clauses) separated from the rest of the transcript by pauses, commas, expressions such as "hmmm," "let me see," etc., question marks or connectives, or a gesture occurring during a pause. Figure 15.9 contains the number of segments obtained per protocol. Based on its verbal and gestural content, each segment was tagged with one or more of the following labels: diagram observation (DO), visualization (V), recall of known/given information (R), and inference (I). The segments were encoded using the following four types of expressions.

Focus(components) lists components that constitute the focus of reasoning in a segment. We assumed that a subject was focusing on a component if it was explicitly mentioned in a segment and/or gestures involving that component (pointing, tracing the boundary, drawing, simulating its motion with the pen, etc.) were made within that segment. We assumed that a subject was focusing on some conceptual aspect of a component if an explicit mention of it appeared in a segment.

	problem1	problem2	problem3	problem4	total
subject1	26	25	28	36	115
subject2	31	40	46	69	186
subject3	43	27	66	86	222
total	100	92	140	191	523

Figure 15.9
Number of Segments

Behavior(component; behavior; type) describes any given or hypothesized component behaviors mentioned in the segment.

Knowledge(statements) contains a restatement of any facts, assumptions, conditions or descriptions of component states that the segment contains.

Comment(statements) consists of any elaborations or inferences by the encoder.

The encoding vocabulary for the first two types of expressions consists of all component labels, two words for characterizing the type of a behavior—*known* or *hypothesis*—and terms for component behaviors (e.g., move-up, rotate-clockwise, etc.) derived from analyzing the problems and examining the verbal protocols. Figure 15.10 shows an excerpt from annotated protocols combining verbal and gestural data and its encoding. Gestures and verbalizations were encoded by one person each.

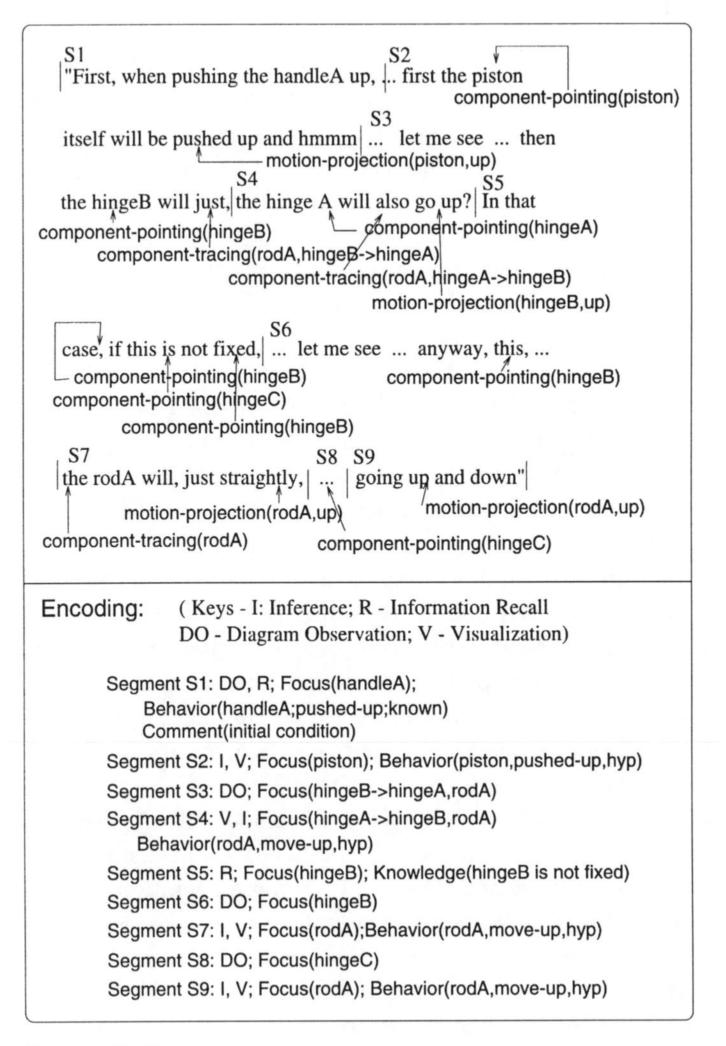

Figure 15.10
An Excerpt from Annotated Protocols for Problem 3 and Its Encoding.

So a measure of the reliability of the encoding, such as inter-coder agreement, was not computed.

15.2.6 Results

Figure 15.11 shows three samples of hypothesis sequences that subjects generated. We concentrated our analysis on two issues: the order in which subjects shifted their focus of attention during problem solving and the recall of prior knowledge cued by spatial information from the diagram.

The process model of figure 15.5 predicts that reasoning will start with the given initial condition, and will proceed with attention focussed on one or more components. The verbal reports show that reasoning began with the initial condition in all cases.

When attention is focussed on multiple components, the model predicts that these will either be connected/contacting components or components related by the propagation of causality. We counted the number of distinct components indicated by each individual verbalization[4] and accompanying gestures. This number ranged from 0 to 9. In 95% of the verbalizations with more than one component, the components could be classified as connected/contacting components or components causally related by their spatial behaviors. This finding supports the hypothesis in Hegarty (1992) that subjects decompose the representation of a device into smaller units corresponding to the machine components during diagrammatic reasoning. Our study suggests that such units may contain more than one component and that this decomposition may be guided by spatial adjacency, causality, or both.

The model predicts that in each cycle the component and behavior selected from short term memory and the hypotheses subsequently generated will be causally related. For a device whose operation can be described in terms of a linear sequence of causally connected events, this means that each pair of successive hypotheses will have a cause-effect relationship. However, for a device whose operation involves branching component behaviors (such as one whose operation can be described by a tree of causally connected events), the model's implication is only that each hypothesis in a sequence generated according to this model can be

[4] A sentence, a question, or a set of clauses separated from the rest of the protocol by pauses at both ends. Such verbalizations were split into multiple segments during the encoding process.

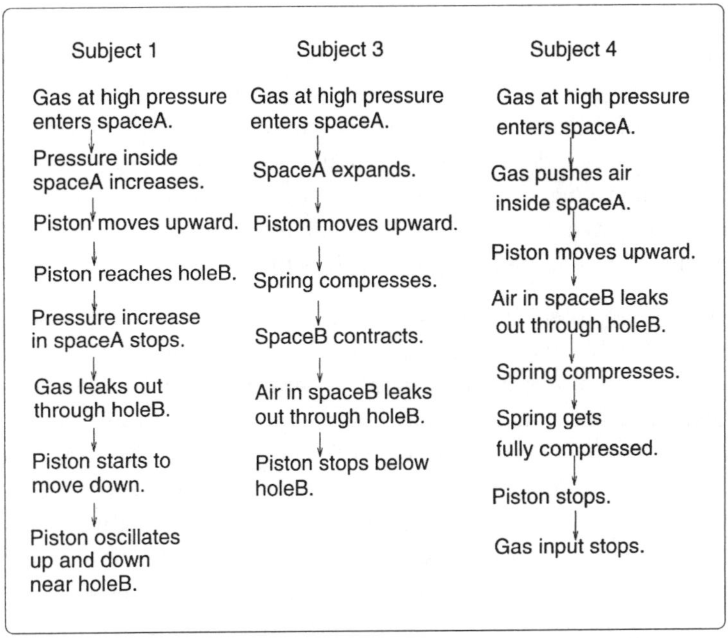

Subject 1

Gas at high pressure enters spaceA.
↓
Pressure inside spaceA increases.
↓
Piston moves upward.
↓
Piston reaches holeB.
↓
Pressure increase in spaceA stops.
↓
Gas leaks out through holeB.
↓
Piston starts to move down.
↓
Piston oscillates up and down near holeB.

Subject 3

Gas at high pressure enters spaceA.
↓
SpaceA expands.
↓
Piston moves upward.
↓
Spring compresses.
↓
SpaceB contracts.
↓
Air in spaceB leaks out through holeB.
↓
Piston stops below holeB.

Subject 4

Gas at high pressure enters spaceA.
↓
Gas pushes air inside spaceA.
↓
Piston moves upward.
↓
Air in spaceB leaks out through holeB.
↓
Spring compresses.
↓
Spring gets fully compressed.
↓
Piston stops.
↓
Gas input stops.

Figure 15.11
Sample Sequences of Hypotheses for Problem 1.

identified as the effect of some preceding hypothesis in the sequence. The structure and instructions of our problems encouraged subjects to consider many different, possibly branching, behaviors. However, their hypotheses appeared in the verbal reports as linear sequences. This means that even if subjects were following the direction of causality in their reasoning, successive hypotheses may not always be related causally. Therefore, we computed the percentage of times a hypothesis about a correct event in the operation of the device, which has another event as its cause and which is appearing in the sequence of hypotheses for the first time, was in fact preceded in the sequence by its cause[5]. This averaged to 88% over all 12 protocols. This also supports the conclusion that diagrammatic reasoning about mechanical devices typically proceeds along the direction of causality (Hegarty 1992).

[5]The formula used was "(X/X+Y) times 100" where X = the number of correct hypotheses appearing for the first time and whose causes appeared earlier in the sequence and Y = the number of correct first-time hypotheses whose causes did not appear earlier in the sequence.

The model predicts that focus shifts are mediated by three factors—search for information, connectivity/contacts, and visualization. Component connectivity and contacts, detection of spatial interactions among components during visualization of hypothesized behaviors, and search for information were indeed found to be factors, in decreasing order of importance, influencing focus shifts during problem solving. However, these three accounted for only 62% of all focus shifts, indicating that there must be additional factors guiding the shifts of focus.

Focus Shifts Focus shifts were induced from the protocol data based on contents of verbalizations and specific gestures. Therefore, it is a coarser measure than eye fixation data. It was found that connectivity/contacts, visualization, and search for information explain about three-fifths of the observed focus shifts. Figure 15.12 summarizes results from analyzing the number and types of focus shifts found in the segments[6], and the different types of focus shifts are explained below.

Connectivity/contacts: A focus shift based on connectivity or contact occurs when a subject, after deliberating about a component and its behavior, starts to heed another component that is connected to or in contact with the former one. Such shifts typically occur when the behavior under consideration affects the shape, position, or orientation of the component. Such shifts of focus guide reasoning along the direction of causality. This appears to be a very common type of focus shift since 39% of all focus shifts in the 12 protocols could be classified into this category.

Visualization: A focus shift based on visualization occurs when a subject, during deliberations about a component and its behavior accompanied by verbalizations or gestures indicating mental visualization, starts to heed another component that, while not connected to or in contact with the original one, has the potential to interact with the original component as a result of its behavior. Such shifts typically occur when subjects are deliberating about spatial behaviors such as deformation or motion, after considering immediate effects due to connectivity/contact. A shift of focus from the iron ball to the pipe in problem 4 is a typical

[6] The following abbreviations are used in this figure: C - the number of focus shifts explained by component connectivity or contacts; V - the number of focus shifts explained by detection of spatial interactions between components during visualization; I - the number of focus shifts explained by search for information; and O - the number of focus shifts that could not be classified as C, V or I.

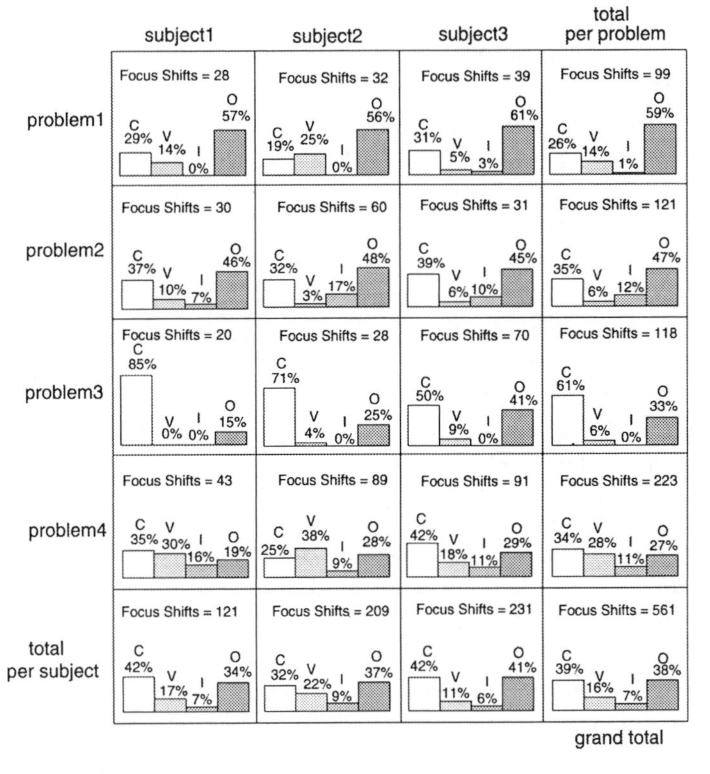

Figure 15.12
Focus Shift Data

example. These shifts also guide reasoning along the direction of causality. Among all focus shifts in the 12 protocols, 16% could be classified into this category.

Search for information: Attending to a component may cue prototypical knowledge that a subject has about that component. The indexing and recall of such knowledge (about the component's typical parts or function) may reveal that information about some aspects—visual aspects such as whether a typical part of the component is present in the diagram and conceptual aspects such as the mass of a component—of this particular component is currently lacking. This will cause a shift of the subject's focus of attention to the corresponding element/location in the diagram (in the case of a visual aspect) or to the corresponding conceptual aspect. Unlike the previous two types of focus shifts, the occurrence of these focus shifts depends on the type of component being considered rather than its behavior. An example is the shift of focus from the left end of seesawC to weightC in problem 4. In this case, considering the left end of a horizontal seesaw might have created an expectation regarding the presence/absence of a balancing weight at the other end, resulting in the focus shift. Since parts of a complex component are typically connected together, it can be difficult to separate this type of focus shifts from those due to connectivity. However, when a shift occurs to a conceptual aspect, or when it bypasses intermediate parts or selects one part when there are other parts that could have been selected based on connectivity alone, we feel that classifying such shifts into this category is appropriate. Only 7% of all focus shifts could be so classified. This may be due to the fact that most of the device components in the four problems were quite simple.

Knowledge Indexing Many instances of the recall of relevant conceptual knowledge triggered by diagram elements (e.g., *mass* of the ball and *purpose* of the knife in problem 4) appeared in the protocols. One problem in which diagrammatic information—in this case the presence and size of a hole—directly cued relevant inferential knowledge was problem 2, although the recalled knowledge and resulting inferences differed among the subjects. All subjects inferred leakage of gas after noticing holeC in the piston. One subject explicitly considered three possibilities—holeC being very small, normal, or very large—and made hypotheses regarding the piston's motion in each case. The other two subjects, perceiving holeC to be very small, ignored its effect and hypothesized the same behavior of the piston (upward motion) as in problem 1.

15.3 An Architecture for Diagrammatic Reasoning

In this section we propose elements of a computational architecture for implementing diagrammatic reasoning and problem solving, and describe its elements. This proposal is based on the results of analysis and modeling efforts described in the previous section. There are five main elements: a user interface, a knowledge base, a rule base, a working memory, and an inference engine (see figure 15.13). The user interface allows the user to specify both descriptive and diagrammatic aspects of a problem, and to watch manipulations of the input diagram that the system carries out during the course of reasoning. The knowledge base contains two kinds of representations: descriptive and visual. The rule base contains domain-specific inference rules. The inference engine generates new inferences by accessing and manipulating information from both kinds of representations in the knowledge base in accordance with rules selected from the rule base. The generated inferences are stored in the working memory.

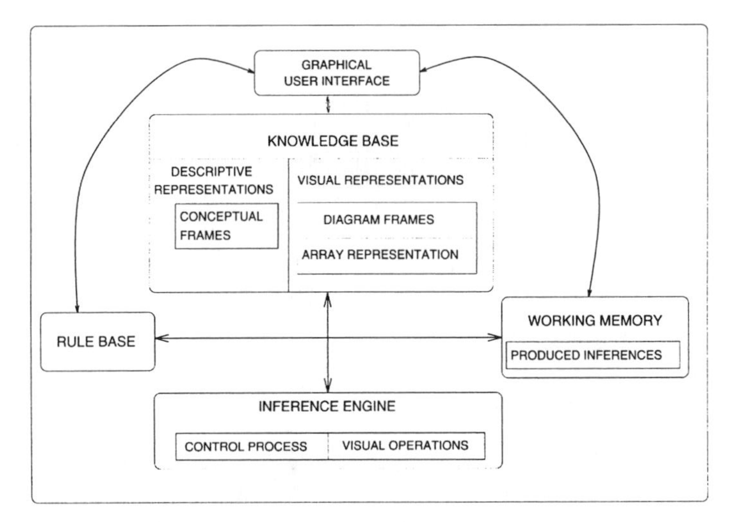

Figure 15.13
Elements of a Diagrammatic Reasoning System.

Descriptive representations store domain-specific conceptual information. For the behavior hypothesis task, this includes both general knowledge about component types in the domain and particular knowledge about components of the device in the input problem. We use a frame-based representation that organizes knowledge around component types, but other types of descriptive representations may also be used. Visual representations contain diagrammatic information and have two parts. One part (called diagram frames) contains information about diagram elements like segments, boundaries and areas, which stand for components or parts of components of the device. The other is an array representation (Glasgow and Papadias 1992) in which the diagram is literally depicted by filling appropriate array elements with symbolic labels of components and substances that "occupy" the corresponding locations. This captures shape, geometry and configuration information.

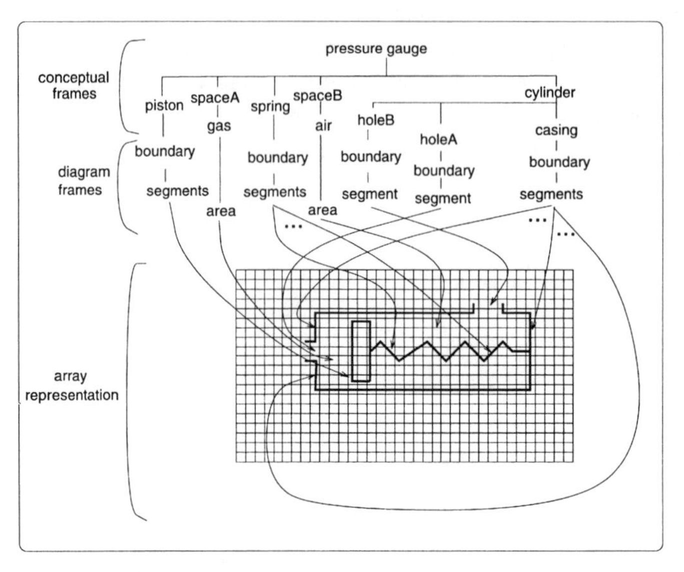

Figure 15.14
Descriptive and Visual Representations.

A behavior hypothesis problem can be provided to the system by specifying, via the user interface, conceptual information about components of a device (component types, labels, etc.), the device diagram, the pairings between components and diagram elements, and an initial condition. The user interface program takes this specification and (i) stores information about the device's components in the descriptive part of the knowledge base, (ii) uses given information about component types to link this knowledge with general knowledge about various types of components that already exists in the knowledge base, (iii) represents the 2-D device diagram using both diagram frames and array representation, and (iv) stores the initial condition in the working memory in a last-in-first-out queue (LIFO-Q). Thus, the user interface generates internal representations of the form shown[7] in figure 15.14. This representation is hierarchical, with conceptual frames linked to diagram frames and diagram frames at the lowest level containing pointers to

[7]Note that filled adjacent array elements imply contact. Therefore, contrary to appearance, the piston is not free to tilt and separates spaceA from spaceB.

the array. Symbolic labels stored in array elements provide connections in the reverse direction. This organization allows reasoning procedures to move between conceptual and diagrammatic information easily—an important characteristic of human reasoning with diagrams.

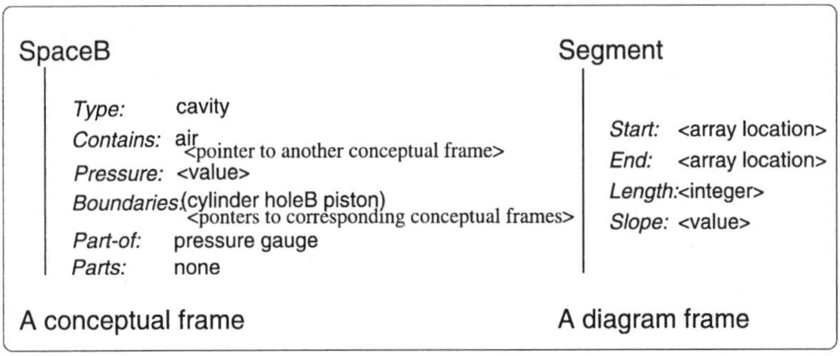

SpaceB

Type: cavity
Contains: air
<pointer to another conceptual frame>
Pressure: <value>
Boundaries: (cylinder holeB piston)
<ponters to corresponding conceptual frames>
Part-of: pressure gauge
Parts: none

A conceptual frame

Segment

Start: <array location>
End: <array location>
Length: <integer>
Slope: <value>

A diagram frame

Figure 15.15
Descriptive Frames of Representation.

Conceptual frames *descriptively* encode conceptual knowledge about the device and its components, whereas diagram frames *descriptively* encode geometric attributes of diagram elements. Figure 15.15 shows an example of each. The array representation, on the other hand, *depictively* encodes diagram elements. It may be thought of as a "bitmap" except that each element (bit) contains symbolic labels of parts or substances instead of an intensity value. Conceptual and diagram frames are created at problem specification time by instantiating templates of the various types of frames that already exist in the knowledge base. Indices of array elements corresponding to each diagram frame are then computed and filled with labels of the corresponding part or substance. The user specifies the basic elements constituting the diagram (at present these are line segments and individual locations) and how they are to be grouped together to form open and closed boundaries or define areas.

Each inference rule in the rule base has three parts: an antecedent that refers to descriptive and/or diagrammatic information, a consequent containing new inferences that the system will assert in the working memory if conditions in the antecedent are verified, and side-effects, which are procedures that manipulate both descriptive and visual representations in the knowledge base and which get activated when the corresponding rule is fired. Figure 15.16 shows a sample inference rule.

The working memory is the computer equivalent of short term memory, except that it is not subject to capacity limitations of human short term memory. The LIFO-Q of inferences is maintained in the working memory. It also contains all new information generated during the course of problem solving.

The reasoning steps carried out by the inference engine fall into the following seven classes (which correspond to the classification in Section 15.2.3).

1. *Diagram Observation*: Accessing the diagram frames and/or the array representation to retrieve spatial information.
2. *Conceptual Knowledge Retrieval*: Retrieving information from descriptive representations.
3. *Inference Rule Retrieval*: Matching and retrieving rules from the rule base.
4. *Conceptual Inference*: Generating an inference using only conceptual information from descriptive representations.
5. *Visual Inference*: Generating an inference using only spatial information from visual representations.
6. *Hybrid Inference*: generating an inference using both conceptual and spatial information.
7. *Visualization*: Simulating spatial behaviors by incrementally modifying the visual representations.

In order to facilitate accessing and manipulating the visual representations, a set of "visual operations" are made available to the inference engine. These are procedures for accessing and manipulating both types (diagram frames and the array representation) of visual representations. There are four kinds of visual operations: basic operations, indexing operations, scanning operations and visualization operations.

Basic Operations. These are operations on individual array elements. *Read* (x, y) returns labels l of the array element at location (x, y). *Write* (x, y, l) marks the array element at location (x, y) using labels l. Other basic operations are *erase*, *test*, *add-label*, and *remove-label*.

Indexing Operations. Indexing operations generate indices or addresses of array elements. At least four such operations are required.

If a gas enters a cavity which is closed except for the opening through which it is entering, it will fill the cavity.

```
(and
("descriptive" (substance-move ?1<gas> ?2<part> ?3<opening> ?4<cavity>))
("diagrammatic" (closed ?4<cavity> ?3<opening>)))
                ↓
(assert (fill ?1<gas> ?4<cavity>))
```

Side effects:

Update "contains" and "pressure" slots of the conceptual frame of the cavity bound to ?4<cavity> with values of ?1<gas> and "pressure" slot of ?1<gas> respectively; Update the array by adding the symbolic label of gas bound to ?1<gas> to array elements representing ?4<cavity>.

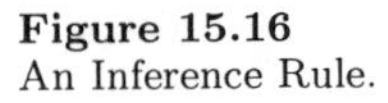

Figure 15.16
An Inference Rule.

Directional indexing: Given an index (x, y) and a direction[8], generate the sequence of indices of cells which fall in that direction from (x, y).
Boundary indexing: Given an index (x, y) and a symbol s, generate a sequence of indices of cells, each of which is adjacent to the previous one and contains s as a label.
Neighborhood indexing: Given an index (x, y), generate the sequence of indices of its neighboring cells.
Fill indexing: Given an index (x, y), generate a sequence of indices of cells such that these gradually cover the area surrounding (x, y) until a boundary is reached.[9]

Scanning Operations. Scanning operations use indexing operations to generate sequences of array elements and basic operations to test those elements for various conditions. At least three different kinds of scanning operations are required.
Directional Scanning: Given a starting point in the array, a direction, and one or more conditions, test all array elements from the starting point that fall along a line in the given direction for the given conditions.
Boundary Following: Given a starting point on a boundary and one or

[8] At present sixteen discrete directions are defined on the array, with each differing from the next by 22.5 degrees; this is an arbitrary choice.

[9] This is meant for areas enclosed by a boundary or bounded by the array itself. The system represents holes in boundaries with "imaginary" segments, so that fill indexing will terminate.

more conditions, follow the boundary from the starting point and test the boundary elements or their neighborhoods for the given conditions. *Sweeping*: Like directional scanning, except that an area is scanned.

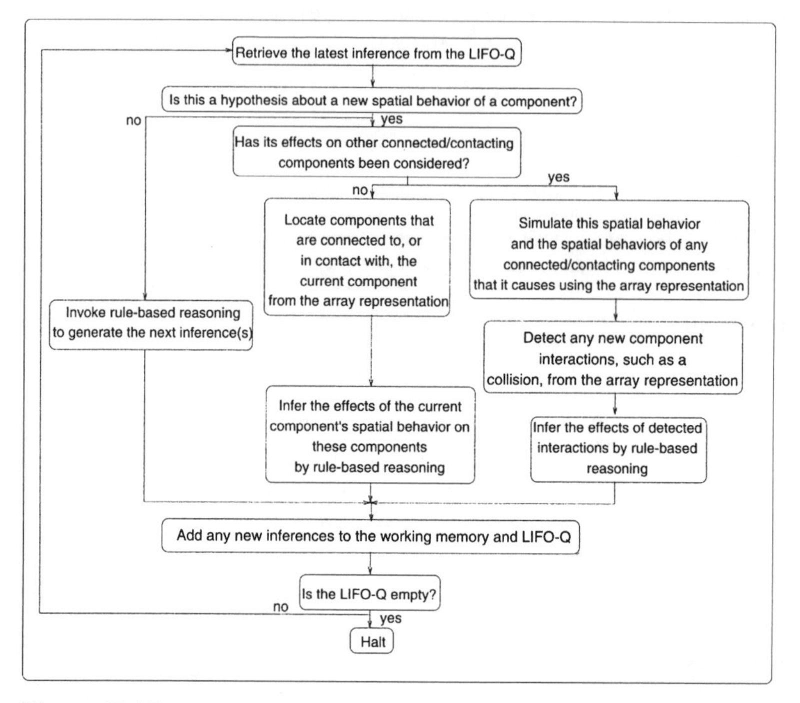

Figure 15.17
Control Flow Chart.

Visualization Operations. Visualization operations transform the represented diagram by manipulating diagram elements that represent individual components. Both general operations like *move*, *rotate*, *copy*, and *delete*, and component-specific ones such as *compress-spring* have been defined.

The inference engine's operation is governed by the control flow chart of figure 15.17. This is based on the process model of figure 15.5, with knowledge representations and operations on those representations substituted for corresponding mental representations and mental operations. For example, the storage and selection of an inference at the beginning of each cycle from short term memory is implemented using the LIFO-Q data structure in working memory. The inferential knowledge recalled from long term memory during deliberation is represented by inference rules. The computational process corresponding to mental visualization is the simulation of spatial behaviors that visualization operations carry out on the array representation, combined with scanning for component interactions in the cells of the array.

The inference engine combines rule-based reasoning with diagram-based reasoning. Each reasoning cycle begins by extracting an element from the LIFO-Q. Reasoning changes to a diagram-based mode when either this inference is a hypothesis about a spatial behavior of a component and its immediate effects on connected/contacting components need to be determined, or it is a hypothesis about a spatial behavior whose immediate effects have already been determined. In the former case scanning the array representation will detect other connected/contacting components. Then rule-based reasoning can be applied to infer effects of the current component's spatial behavior on these components. These inferences are then stored in the LIFO-Q and the working memory. In the latter case, we have a behavior whose immediate effects (which may be spatial behaviors of connected/contacting components) have already been determined. So the next action will be to simulate this behavior and its effects by incrementally changing the array representation. This simulation will proceed until new interactions between components are detected (or it becomes clear that no interactions will occur within the diagram boundaries). Once interactions are detected, their effects are determined by rule-based reasoning and stored in the LIFO-Q and the working memory.

For illustrative purposes, figure 15.18 shows the trace of a simple example requiring about twenty rules. Reasoning begins with the given initial condition, *(enter gas holeA source)*. The next inference is derived from the application of an inference rule that checks the diagram to ensure that holeA is not blocked. The inference *(fill gas spaceA)* requires both knowledge about gases at high pressure filling spaces and a diagram observation to ensure that spaceA is closed except for holeA. At this point rule-based reasoning generates two inferences, one of which leads to a dead end. The other leads to the hypothesis *(move piston right)*. Since this is a hypothesis concerning a spatial behavior, the array representation is scanned to detect components connected to or in contact with the piston. Rule-based reasoning is invoked to infer effects of the piston's motion on any such component. This results in four new

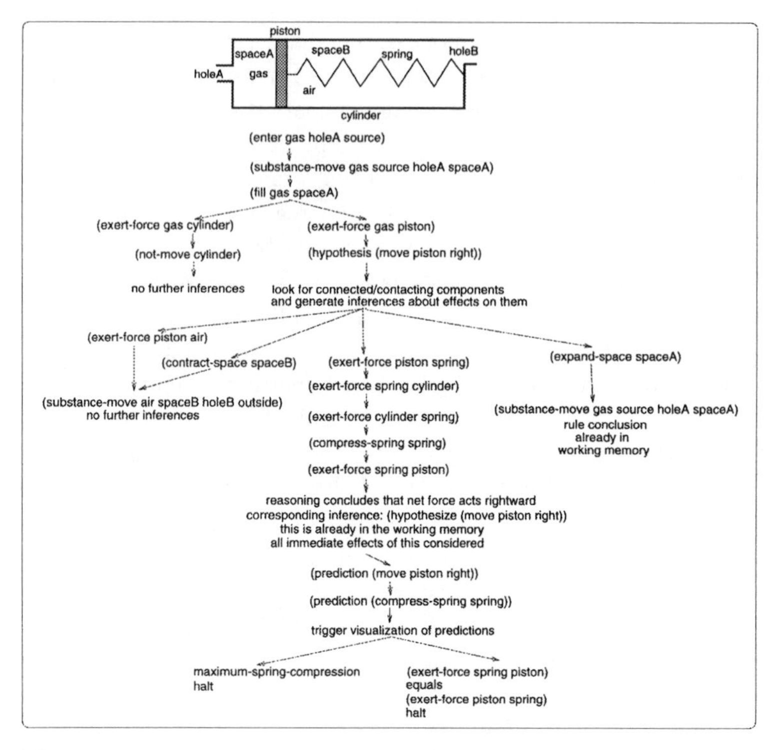

Figure 15.18
An Example and Corresponding Inferences.

inferences. The first two lead to the same inference *(substance-move air spaceB holeB outside)* for which no further rules are found to be applicable. The fourth inference generates another which already exists in the working memory. So the only path further followed by the inference engine is that leading from the third, *(exert-force piston spring).* This eventually leads to the inference *(exert-force spring piston).* At this point two forces on the same object have been hypothesized. Knowledge about springs leads the system to conclude that the initial force exerted by the spring is small. The resulting hypothesis, that of a rightward move of piston, is already in the working memory. At this point all immediate effects of this hypothesized motion have been considered and therefore two spatial behaviors—motion of the piston and compression of the spring—can be predicted. This triggers a simulation of these. This simulation will detect the fact that as the piston moves, the spring will get progressively more compressed. Based on knowledge about behaviors of springs and using rules for reasoning about inequalities, the system will then discover two possibilities: either the spring will get maximally compressed or the piston will reach a point at which the two forces are in equilibrium. At this point there are no more entries in the LIFO-Q and the inference process will come to a stop. These inferences amount to a series of hypotheses about the given device's operation, generated along the direction of causality.

15.4 Concluding Discussion

Diagrammatic reasoning may be defined as the act of reasoning, and solving problems, using diagrams as external representations. Though diagrams are static external representations, reasoning with them involves mental simulations of behaviors that change the configurations depicted in them, which therefore may be supported by underlying cognitive processes that are imagistic in nature. Whereas mental imagery has a colorful history of research in cognitive science, research on diagrammatic reasoning is of more recent vintage (Hegarty 1992; Hegarty and Sims 1994; Larkin and Simon 1987; Lindsay 1988). In this chapter we explored diagrammatic reasoning in the context of a particular task. Analyzing this task and examining hypotheses generated by human subjects allowed us to formulate a cognitive process model of problem solving in this task, and using this model as a basis, to describe elements of a diagrammatic reasoning system. In this concluding section we discuss interesting aspects of diagrammatic reasoning that the verbal and gestural data revealed and which deserve further research, limitations of our computational model, and related work. We close on a speculative note about the potential benefits of studying, and computationally modeling, cognitive processes involved in reasoning with diagrams.

15.4.1 Interesting Aspects of Diagrammatic Reasoning

The analyses we carried out—both of the task and the experimental data—indicated that the diagram plays two important roles during problem solving.

- The diagram facilitates the indexing and recall of both conceptual knowledge regarding components and inferential knowledge using which the reasoner generates new hypotheses.

- The diagram supports a visualization of hypothesized spatial behaviors of components, which in turn enables the reasoner to detect effects of these behaviors.

Additionally, our study revealed the following as interesting aspects of diagrammatic reasoning that deserve to be researched further.

Focus Shifts As Figure 15.12 shows, connectivity/contacts, visualization, and search for information explain only 62% of the total number of focus shifts observed over all 12 protocols. What other factors might explain focus shifts? Some may be explainable in terms of subjects' goals. One particular pattern appeared many times: after shifting focus to a new component and predicting its behavior, focus shifted back and forth between it and the component perceived to be causing this new behavior. An internal goal to confirm the newly made hypothesis may be the cause of this iterative shifting. Uncovering other determinants of focus shifts and using eye fixation data to track focus shifts more finely are issues deserving further research.

Knowledge Indexing We believe that as in the domain of geometry (Koedinger and Anderson 1990), diagrams facilitate the indexing of inferential knowledge, thereby reducing search, during problem solving in the domain of mechanical devices as well. This role of diagrams in problem solving needs to be experimentally investigated further, using problems that are specifically designed to elicit the indexing and recall of inferential knowledge.

Visualization. Video-taped gestural data—showing gestures that simulate motions with pen, fingers and hands, and drawings of intermediate and final states of components undergoing motion or deformation—makes a persuasive case for the mental visualization of spatial behaviors. Cognitive processes underlying such visualizations ought to be investigated further.

Reasoning by Visual Analogy In the case of problem 2, *all* subjects recalled their solution to problem 1. Subjects solved these two problems in different sessions separated by a week. Nevertheless, they recalled and tried to adapt and fit the earlier solution to the current problem instead of starting from the beginning. Clearly, the diagram cued the recall of the solution from a previously experienced problem solving episode in this case. Such visual analogies (Thagard, Gochfeld, and Hardy 1992) and their computational modeling (Narayanan 1992a, McDougal 1993) are fertile topics for further research.

15.4.2 Limitations

The computational model we proposed is fairly limited in scope, in that it does not by any means capture the full generality of human diagrammatic reasoning. The indexing of "relevant" knowledge is a case in point. In the present computer model, slots of conceptual frames constitute the relevant facts, and rules retrieved from the rule base constitute the relevant inferential knowledge. Humans, on the other hand, employ much more sophisticated relevance criteria in deciding what to retrieve from long term memory and which inferences to entertain. For instance, theoretically feasible but practically unlikely scenarios were almost never reported by subjects in our experiments. Therefore, a computer system also requires a more sophisticated and operational notion of relevance to filter facts and rules in order to efficiently deal with large amounts of conceptual information and a large rule base.

Support for visualization and support for indexing and recall of conceptual and inferential knowledge were mentioned earlier as the two major roles that diagrams seem to play in problem solving. Operation of the inference engine as currently defined, with its forward chaining strategy, implements only the former. In order to implement the latter (for instance, noticing something unexpected in the diagram may cue conceptual knowledge or inferential knowledge that leads to a new prediction), additional strategies (e.g., an opportunistic scanning strategy that, upon noticing some interesting, unusual or unexpected feature, uses that for indexing into the rule base and descriptive representations) ought to be designed and implemented. Another aspect requiring more work is the development of visual indexing schemes for conceptual knowledge and inference rules. Our current work is addressing these issues, so that the model can be scaled up to more complex problems.

The array representation is designed to support 2-D visualizations of spatial behaviors such as translations, rotations, and deformations. This can in principle be extended to 3-D by using a three dimensional array representation. But these visualizations do not capture temporal aspects of spatial behaviors. Granularity of the array representation is another aspect requiring further work. It is not critical for relatively abstract schematic diagrams that do not depict shape in great detail. At present, the user must decide on the resolution and select an appropriate array size. Automatically selecting an appropriate grain size to ensure that component interactions are not missed during visualizations and compensating for information loss that occurs when continuous shapes are represented by discrete arrays are issues that need to be addressed. For example, positional errors introduced by the discreteness of the representation could accumulate over a number of simulation steps and affect the accuracy of component interaction detection.

15.4.3 Related Work

The coupling between perception and reasoning is bidirectional. On one hand, high level knowledge, goals and reasoning can significantly influence aspects of perception such as directing the focus of attention and disambiguating image interpretations (Brand, Birnbaum, and Cooper 1993). On the other hand, visually perceived spatial properties and the mental manipulation of visual representations can considerably aid reasoning and problem solving. More work needs to be done on studying this latter phenomenon in various problem solving tasks. Despite previous pioneering work (Sloman 1971; Funt 1980; Forbus, Nielsen, and Faltings 1987), only recently has the cognitive capability for common sense reasoning using diagrams and imagery begun to receive renewed attention in artificial intelligence (Narayanan 1992b). The computer modeling of visual reasoning has been shown to be of benefit in a variety of domains and applications, e.g., automating expert reasoning using phase diagrams (Yip 1991), geometry theorem proving (McDougal and Hammond 1993), and analysis of load-bearing structures (Iwasaki, Tessler, and Law 1995).

Principles and models of problem solving derived from studies of visual and diagrammatic reasoning in real world domains (for example, see Rogers 1993) can form the basis of intelligent visualization and instruction systems that, instead of merely presenting pretty displays, can understand and intelligently manipulate these in order to assist and reduce the cognitive load of their human users. Studies of the role of visual reasoning in scientific thought (Nersessian 1991), of differences in visualization skills between individuals (Hegarty and Sims 1994) and between experts and novices, and of common mistakes that novices are prone to, can lead to intelligent tutoring systems that facilitate the development of visualization skills in problem solving among students of science (Dreyfus 1991) and engineering. Current research on cognitive and computational aspects of diagrammatic and visual reasoning is still exploratory in nature. However, its maturity promises many applications in intelligent multi-modal interfaces, knowledge-based graphics, and instructional systems. This motivates our research on diagrammatic reasoning.

References

Brand, M., Birnbaum, L., and Cooper, P. 1993. Sensible Scenes: Visual Understanding of Complex Structures Through Causal Analysis. In Proceedings of the Eleventh National Conference on Artificial Intelligence, 588–593. Menlo Park, Calif.: AAAI Press.

Dreyfus, T. 1991. On the Status of Visual Reasoning in Mathematics and Mathematics Education. In Proceedings of the Fifteenth International Conference on the Psychology of Mathematics Education, 33–48, ed. F. Furinghetti.

Ericsson, K. A. and Simon, H. A. 1983. *Protocol Analysis: Verbal Reports as Data.* Cambridge, Mass.: The MIT Press.

Forbus, K. D., Nielsen, P., and Faltings, B. 1987. Qualitative Kinematics: a Framework. In Proceedings of the Tenth International Joint Conference on Artificial Intelligence, 430–436. San Francisco: Morgan Kaufmann.

Funt, B. V. 1980. Problem-Solving with Diagrammatic Representations. *Artificial Intelligence* 13: 201–230.

Glasgow, J. and Papadias, D. 1992. Computational Imagery. *Cognitive Science* 16(3): 355–394.

Hegarty, M. 1992. Mental Animation: Inferring Motion from Static Displays of Mechanical Systems. *Journal of Experimental Psychology: Learning, Memory, and Cognition* 18(5): 1084–1102.

Hegarty, M. and Sims, V. K. 1994. Individual Differences in Mental Animation During Mechanical Reasoning. *Memory and Cognition* 22: 411–430.

How Things Work: The Universal Encyclopedia of Machines. London: George Allen and Unwin Ltd, 1967.

Iwasaki, Y., Tessler, S. and Law, K. H. 1995. Qualitative Structural Analysis Through Mixed Diagrammatic and Symbolic Reasoning. In this volume. Menlo Park, Calif.: AAAI Press.

Koedinger, K. R. and Anderson, J. R. 1990. Abstract Planning and Perceptual Chunks: Elements of Expertise in Geometry. *Cognitive Science* 14: 511–550.

Larkin, J. H. and Simon, H. A. 1987. Why a Diagram Is (Sometimes) Worth Ten Thousand Words. *Cognitive Science* 11: 65–100.

Lindsay, R. K. 1988. Images and inference. *Cognition* 29: 229–250.

McDougal, T. F. 1993. Using Case-Based Reasoning and Situated Activity to Write Geometry Proofs. In Proceedings of the Sixteenth Annual Conference of the Cognitive Science Society. Hillsdale, N.J.: Lawrence Erlbaum Associates.

McDougal, T. F. and Hammond, K. J. 1993. Representing and Using Procedural Knowledge to Build Geometry Proofs. In Proceedings of the Eleventh National Conference on Artificial Intelligence, Menlo Park, Calif.: AAAI Press.

Narayanan, N. H. 1992a. Imagery, Diagrams and Reasoning. Ph.D. diss., Department of Computer and Information Science, Ohio State University, Columbus, Ohio.

Narayanan, N. H., (ed.). 1992b. Reasoning with Diagrammatic Representations: Papers from the 1992 AAAI Spring Symposium. AAAI Tech. Report SS-92-02. Menlo Park, Calif.: AAAI.

Narayanan, N. H., Suwa, M., and Motoda, H. 1993. Behavior Hypothesis from Schematic Diagrams: a Hybrid Approach. In Proceedings of the IJCAI-93 Hybrid Representation and Reasoning Workshop, 50–61.

Narayanan, N. H., Suwa, M., and Motoda, H. (1994a). How Things Appear to Work: Predicting Behaviors from Device Diagrams. In Proceedings of the Twelfth National Conference on Artificial Intelligence, 1161–1167, Menlo Park, Calif.: AAAI Press.

Narayanan, N. H., Suwa, M., and Motoda, H. 1994b. A Study of Diagrammatic Reasoning from Verbal and Gestural Data. In Proceedings of the Sixteenth Annual Conference of the Cognitive Science Society, 652–657, Hillsdale, N.J.: Lawrence Erlbaum Associates.

Nersessian, N. J. 1991. How do Scientists Think? Capturing the Dynamics of Conceptual Change in Science. *Minnesota Studies in the Philosophy of Science 15,* ed. R. Giere. Minneapolis, Minn.: University of Minnesota Press.

Rogers, E. 1993. Visual Interaction : A Link Between Perception and Problem Solving. Ph.D. diss., College of Computing, Georgia Institute of Technology, Atlanta, Georgia.

Sloman, A. 1971. Interactions Between Philosophy and AI: The Role of Intuition and Non-Logical Reasoning in Intelligence. *Artificial Intelligence* (2): 209–225.

Thagard, P., Gochfeld, D., and Hardy, S. 1992. Visual Analogical Mapping. In Proceedings of the Fourteenth Annual Conference of the Cognitive Science Society, 522–527, Hillsdale, N.J.: Lawrence Erlbaum Associates.

Yip, K. M. 1991. Understanding Complex Dynamics by Visual and Symbolic Reasoning. *Artificial Intelligence* 51: 179–221.

16 Mental Animation

Mary Hegarty
University of California, Santa Barbara

Understanding the operation of deterministic systems, such as mechanical or electronic devices, includes the ability to infer the state of one component of the system given information about the states of the other system components, and the relations between the components. This type of understanding is central to how people design, troubleshoot, and operate devices. This chapter describes how people infer the motion of components of a simple mechanical system (a pulley system) from knowledge of the configuration of the system and the movement of one of the system components. It provides an account of the process of inferring motion, the type of knowledge that allows people to infer motion, and the characteristics of human information processing that constrain the inference process. I will refer to this process as *mental animation.*

16.1 Mental Animation

16.1.1 Mechanical Reasoning

Mechanical reasoning has previously been characterized as a process of running a mental model of a machine (DeKleer and Brown 1984; Forbus 1984; Gentner and Stevens 1983; Reiger and Grinberg 1977; Williams, Hollan, and Stevens 1983). These accounts suggest that the inferential processes involved in mechanical reasoning involve mentally simulating the operation of the system. The usefulness of mental models as a theoretical construct has been questioned, because of terminological inconsistencies, lack of precision, and limitations on the testability of the theoretical proposals (Rips 1986; Rouse and Morris 1986). Rather than arguing for or against the construct of a mental model, the approach taken in this chapter is to investigate in what senses and to what extent the mental processes involved in reasoning about a mechanical system are isomorphic to the physical processes in the operation of the system.

The mental animation task investigated in this study involves imagining the related motions of components in a mechanical system. In other tasks in which people have to imagine a series of spatial manipulations, such as paper-folding or surface-development tasks used in tests of spatial abilities (French, Ekstrom, and Price 1963), solution time is proportional to the number of spatial manipulations that need to be performed, suggesting an isomorphism between the physical processes and their mental analogs (Shepard and Feng 1972). Since all components of a mechanical system move at once, if the mental process is physically isomorphic to the motion in the machine, all components of the machine should be mentally animated at once. An alternative possibility, explored in this chapter, is that the components of the machine are animated piecemeal.

16.1.2 Possible Accounts of Mental Animation.

As a specific example of mental animation, consider the pulley system depicted in Figure 16.1. What are the mental processes involved in inferring how each component of the pulley system will move when the rope is pulled? In this section possible accounts of the mental animation of this type of system are outlined.

One possible account is that the mental animation process simulates the physical behavior of the device. When the rope of the pulley system is pulled, all of the components move simultaneously. Since people's representations of mechanical phenomena are probably based on perception of mechanical systems in operation (McCloskey 1983; Kaiser, Proffit, and McCloskey 1985), it is possible that these representations reflect the actual behavior of the system. Thus, a person might determine the motion of a component in a pulley system, by mentally animating the whole system at once, and then determining how the component in question is moving in his or her animated representation of the system. Anecdotal accounts of the reasoning of prominent scientists and engineers suggest that the ability to animate a system all at once may be characteristic of expert reasoning (Ferguson, 1977; Shepard 1978). However, given the limited capacity of working memory (Miller 1956; Baddeley and Hitch 1974), it is unlikely that novices can mentally animate all the components of a machine at once, unless the machine is very simple.

An alternative account is that the mental animation process simulates the kinematics of the system piecemeal. It has been proposed that mental models of specific machines or devices, consist of rules al-

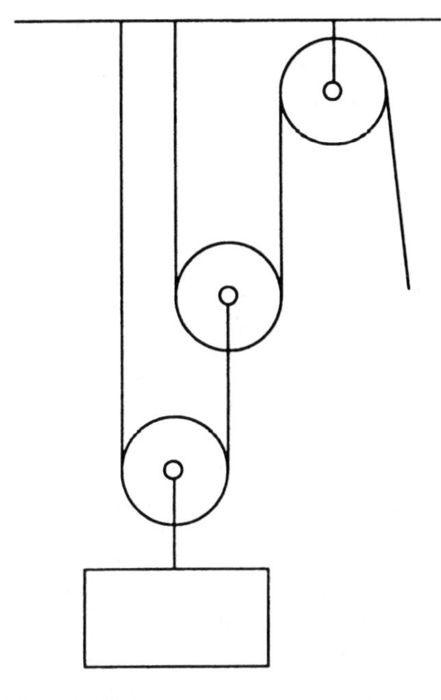

Figure 16.1
Pully System 1.

lowing the reasoner to infer the states of individual components of the machine from the states of other adjacent components (De Kleer and Brown 1984; Forbus 1984; Reiger and Grinberg 1977; Williams, Hollan, and Stevens 1983). Note that there are two differences between the proposed accounts; (1) whether the components are animated all at once or piecemeal and (2) whether the animation process involves spatial-visualization processes or more abstract rules of inference. Only the first of these differences is directly investigated in this chapter. According to the piecemeal hypothesis, mentally animating a system consists of a series of cognitive processes, in which the individual components are animated one by one rather than a single process of animating the whole system. For example, in the case of the pulley system in Figure 16.1, the kinematics of the system components might be inferred by making a chain of inferences beginning with the knowledge that the free end of the rope is being pulled. From this knowledge, the reasoner might first infer the motion of the upper pulley and then infer the motion of each successive component, ending with the inference that the weight is being lifted. I will refer to this as inferring the causal chain of events in the system, reflecting the fact that the immediate cause of the motion of each component is the motion of the adjacent component that precedes it in this chain of events.

If subjects mentally animate a system piecemeal, they may not necessarily infer the motion of components in order of the causal chain of events. For example, to infer the motion of a component later in the causal chain of events (e.g., the lower pulley in Figure 16.1), they might first infer that when the rope is being pulled, the weight is being lifted (which presumably is included in people's general knowledge of pulley systems). They might then infer the motion of the lower pulley from the motion of the weight. In this case the direction of inference would be in the opposite direction to the causal chain of events (from a later component to an earlier one). The experiments reported in this chapter examine the order in which people infer the motion of components of a pulley system, or whether people determine the motion of all components at once. The existing empirical evidence does not differentiate between the above accounts of mental animation. Providing subjects with causal models of machines improves their ability to operate and solve problems about machines (Kieras and Bovair, 1984; Mayer 1989), but it is not clear how causal models are used in subjects' reasoning. The time to determine the state of a component in a system is related to the complexity of the system (Spoehr and Horvath 1989), however this could indicate that subjects are making a chain of inferences or that they determine the states of all components at once within a capacity limited system, so the more components in the system, the more time it takes to animate the system.

16.1.3 A Theoretical Framework

In order to formalize the above accounts of mental animation and to test their specific predictions, the accounts will be described within the framework of a production system. This ensures continuity with previous theoretical accounts of reasoning about physical systems in particular (Fallside 1989; Hegarty, Just, and Morrison 1988; Kieras 1984; 1990; Larkin and Simon 1987) and higher level cognitive skills in general (Newell and Simon 1972; Anderson 1983). The proposed production system model is a theory of how the mental animation process is decomposed, but not of the algorithm that performs the mental animation process. As stated above, the evidence presented in this chapter does not differentiate between a process of matching production rules against a propositional representation of a mechanical system or a more analog process of transforming a mental image of a mechanical system. The model consists of a declarative representation of a static pulley system and a set of inference rules for deriving the kinematic representation of the pulley system from the static representation.

Representation of a Static Pulley System A static pulley system can be represented as a structural description, consisting of objects and spatial relations between these objects (Hegarty, Just and Morrison 1988; Larkin and Simon 1987). For the purposes of this chapter I defined the basic objects in the pulley system to be units whose motion can be described by a single transformation. This necessitated the representation of ropes as subdivided into rope strands. For example, the lower rope in Figure 16.1, was subdivided into three strands, the left side of the rope, which shortens when the pull rope is pulled, the section lying under the lower pulley which moves to the right under the pulley, and the right side of the rope which moves up. This specific decomposition of the system is largely intuitive. However the notion of subdivision of the pulley-system representation is central to the piecemeal hypothesis.

The basic objects in the representation are pulleys, rope strands, weights being lifted by the pulley system and stationary objects in the environment to which the pulleys and ropes can be fixed, the ceiling or floor. Table 16.1 lists the objects in the static representation of the pulley system depicted in Figure 16.1 and Table 16.2 lists the spatial relations between these objects. An object is defined as fixed if it is connected to an environmental object (the ceiling or floor) and as attached if it is connected to an object that is free to move (e.g. a free pulley). In addition to these connections, rope strands can lie over or lie under a pulley. Finally if an object is not connected to another object it is free.

Representation of a Pulley System in Motion The kinematic representation of a pulley system describes the movements of the components that result when the free end of the rope is pulled. Pulleys, rope strands and the weight can move up or move down. Pulleys can rotate clockwise or rotate counterclockwise. Rope strands can move to the right or left over or under a pulley. Finally rope strands can lengthen or

Table 16.1
Static and Kinematic Representations of the Pulley System Depicted in Figure 16.1. The Static Representation: Objects

Pulleys:	upper pulley, middle pulley, lower pulley
Ropes:	upper rope, lower rope
Rope Strands:	upper rope strands 1-5, lower rope strands 1-3
Weight:	weight
Environmental Objects:	ceiling

Table 16.2
Static and Kinematic Representations of the Pulley System Depicted in Figure 16.1. The Static Representation: Spatial Relations Between Objects

1.	The upper pulley is fixed to the ceiling 2. The middle pulley is free
3.	The lower pulley is attached to the weight
4.	Upper rope strand 1 is free at the lower end and is attached to upper rope strand 2 at the upper end.
5.	Upper rope strand 2 lies over the upper pulley.
6.	Upper rope strand 3 to Upper rope strand 2 at the upper end and to upper rope strand 4 at the lower end.
7.	Upper rope strand 4 lies under the middle pulley.
8.	Upper rope strand 5 is attached to upper rope strand 4 at the lower end and is fixed to the ceiling at the upper end.
9.	Lower rope strand 1 is attached to the middle pulley at the upper end and to lower rope strand 2 at the lower end.
10.	Lower rope strand 2 lies under the lower pulley.
11.	Lower rope strand 3 is attached to lower rope strand 2 at the lower end and is fixed to the ceiling at the upper end.
12.	The weight is attached to the lower pulley.

shorten. Table 16.3 lists the movements of the components of the pulley system in Figure 16.1. In this table, the statements are presented in the order of the causal chain of events from the input of the pulley system (the rope being pulled) to its output (the weight being lifted). In this ordering, it is assumed that the movement of a rope strand over a pulley causes the pulley to rotate and that the shortening of a rope strand that lies under a pulley causes the pulley to rise.

Inferring the Kinematic Representation from the Static Representation The process of inferring the kinematic representation from the static representation can be accomplished by a set of production rules in which the conditions are the spatial relations between pulley system components and the motion of one of these components and the action is the inference of the motions of the other components. For example, the following production would infer the motion of the rope strand hanging over the upper pulley (motion B in Table 16.3) from the

Table 16.3
Static and Kinematic Representations of the Pulley System Depicted in Figure 16.1. The Kinematic Model: Motions of the Pulley System Components When the Rope Is Pulled

1.	Upper rope strand 1 moves down.
2.	Upper rope strand 2 moves to the right over the upper pulley.
3.	The upper pulley turns clockwise.
4.	Upper rope strand 3 moves up.
5.	Upper rope strand 4 moves to the right under the middle pulley.
6.	The middle pulley turns counterclockwise.
7.	Upper rope strand 5 shortens.
8.	The middle pulley moves up.
9.	Lower rope strand moves up.
10.	Lower rope strand 2 moves to the right under the lower pulley.
11.	The lower pulley turns counterclockwise.
12.	Lower rope strand 3 shortens.
13.	The lower pulley moves up.
14.	The weight moves up.

knowledge that the free end of the rope is moving down.

IF a rope strand (RS1) lies over a pulley and it is attached to another rope strand (RS2) on the right and RS2 is moving down

THEN infer that RS1 is moving to the right over the pulley. Again, the actual inference process carried out under these conditions might be a process of imaging the movement of the pull rope and pulley.

The basic question addressed in this study asks how people infer the kinematics of a pulley system from a static description of the system. If people propagate through the causal chain of events in the system to mentally animate the pulley system, then their knowledge is best described by a set of production rules relating the motion of each pulley system component to the components that it affects directly. If subjects can infer the motion of components from non-adjacent components (e.g., the pull rope and the weight), then productions linking the motion of these components should be included in the model. Finally, if people determine the motion of all components at once, then their knowledge is best described by more complex production rules in which the conditions include the configuration of a whole pulley system and the actions include inferring the motions of all the components of the pulley system, Thus, further specification of the model was based on the empirical data and will be described below.

16.2 Experiment 1

The mental animation process was investigated using a sentence-picture verification task. Subjects were shown a diagram of a pulley system and a sentence describing either a static property or a kinematic property of one or more components of the system, and were required to verify whether the sentence correctly described the pulley system depicted in the diagram. When the sentence described a static property of the system (the spatial relation between two components) the task was a standard sentence-picture verification task, which involves constructing representations of the text and the diagram and comparing these representations (Clark and Chase 1972; Carpenter and Just 1975). When the sentence described a kinematic property of the system (the movement of one or more components) the task involved the process of mental animation in addition to these encoding and comparison processes. Subjects were asked to determine the motion of system components at the beginning, middle, and end of the causal chain. If people determine the motion of a component by making a chain of inferences from the input of the system, the time to verify the motion of a particular component should be an increasing function of its distance from the beginning of the causal chain. If subjects can infer the motion of components from either the beginning or the end of the kinematic chain, statements about components in the middle of the causal chain should take longest to verify. If subjects infer the motion of all components at once, the animation time should be equal for all components. Experiment 1 contrasted the verification of sentences describing static and kinematic properties of pulley systems, examining how the position of a component in a pulley system affects a subject's accuracy, response latency, and eye fixations. Eye fixation data have provided important insights into a number of other cognitive tasks that involve operating on a spatial display, for example reading (Just and Carpenter 1987; Rayner and Pollatsek, 1989), processing subtitles (D'Ydewalle, Muylle and Van Rensbergen 1985; D'Ydewalle, Van Rensbergen, and Pollet 1987) scene perception (Loftus 1972; Loftus and Mackworth 1978) mental rotation (Just and Carpenter 1976, 1985), sentence picture verification (Just and Carpenter 1976), visual analogies (Carpenter, Just, and Shell 1990), and construction of mental models from text and diagrams (Hegarty, in press; Hegarty and Just 1991). These studies assume that when a person is using a visual display to

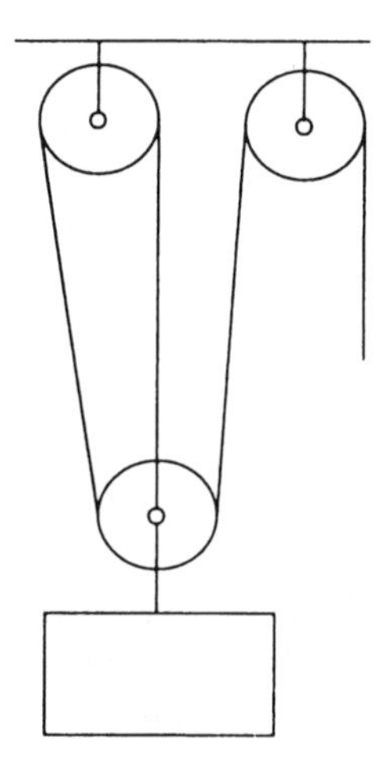

Figure 16.2
Pully System 2. *Static Statement:* The upper left pulley is attached to the ceiling. *Kinematic Statement:* The upper left pulley turns counterclockwise.

perform a cognitive task, the part of the display that he or she is fixating at any point in time corresponds to the symbol that he or she is currently processing in working memory (Just and Carpenter 1976). For example, if a person determines the motion of a given component of a mechanical system by mentally animating the system components from the beginning of the chain to this component, then they should fixate components of the system that precede the given component in the causal chain of events.

16.2.1 Method

Subjects Eleven undergraduate students from the University of California, Santa Barbara participated in the experiment for course credit.

Stimuli and Apparatus Each stimulus was composed of a sentence on the left of the screen and a diagram of a pulley system on the right (see the examples in Figure 16.2). The subjects' task was to state whether the sentence was true or false of the depicted pulley system.

The sentences described either static relations between component of the pulley system or kinematic events that occur when the free end of the pull rope is pulled. The referents of these sentences were components in three different locations in the pulley system, components involved in interactions towards the beginning of the causal chain of events in the system, components in the middle of the causal chain, and components towards the end of the causal chain. The legend of Figure 16.2 gives examples of a static and a kinematic relation between objects at the end of the kinematic chain. An example of a statement about a kinematic event at the beginning of the causal chain would be "the rope moves to the right over the upper right pulley." An example of a kinematic event in the middle of the causal chain would be "the lower pulley turns counterclockwise." Subjects were presented with the pulley system diagrams presented in Figures 16.1 and 16.2, and the mirror images of these diagrams (producing left and right isomers of the two systems). From now on, the system in Figure 16.1 will be referred to as pulley system 1 and the system in Figure 16.2 as pulley system 2. Half of the sentences were true and half were false. For each combination of the other factors there were two sentence-diagram pairs, yielding a total of 96 unique sentences. These were presented in two blocks of 48 stimuli each and the subjects saw each block twice, for a total of four blocks and 192 trials. Half the subjects saw block 1 first and half saw block 2 first. Stimuli were presented in a random order within a block.

The false trials were included in order to make the verification task realistic, but no effort was made to standardize their difficulty. Thus, only the true trials (96 trials) were analyzed.

The stimuli were presented on a DEC VR 260 Monochrome Video Monitor, situated approximately 3 meters from the subject. The subjects' eye fixations were monitored using an Iscan corneal-reflectance and pupil-center eye tracker (Model RK-426), that has a resolution of less than 1 degree of visual angle. The tracker sampled the position of the subjects' gaze every 16 milliseconds, and output the x and y coordinates to a DEC Vaxstation 3200. Further processing of the data is described below.

Procedure First, the experimenter presented written and verbal instructions, which introduced the subjects to pulley systems and to the labels used to refer to the pulley system components in the stimuli. Following these instructions, a headrest was fitted comfortably to the subject's head and the subject was asked to move as little as possible during the experiment. After the eye-tracking equipment had been calibrated, the subject was asked to fixate an asterisk that appeared in the top-left corner of the screen and to push a button in order to begin and end each trial. As soon as the button was pressed, a sentence and diagram appeared on the screen. The subject viewed the sentence and diagram, and responded either "true" or "false" verbally and by pressing one of two buttons, marked "true" and "false." These two responses were later checked for consistency, and if they were inconsistent, the verbal response was taken as the subjects' response.

16.2.2 Results and Discussion

Errors The overall error rate was low (6.5 %). As Figure 16.3 shows, subjects made more errors verifying kinematic relations than static relations between components ($F(1,10) = 12.54, MS_e = .01, p < .01$). Subjects also made more errors verifying statements about components at the end of the causal chain of events than at the beginning and middle ($F(2,20) = 8.49, MS_e = .005, p < .01$) and there was a significant interaction between type of statement (static or kinematic) and position of the referent in the pulley system ($F(2,20) = 8.49, MS_e = .005p < .01$), such that position had a greater effect on errors in verifying kinematic relations ($F(2,20) = 7.63, MS_e = .01, p < .01$) than static relations ($F(2,20) = 3.13, MS_e = .001, p = .07$). Although there was a trend for subjects to make fewer errors on the second repetition of the stimuli ($.05, SD = .11$) than the first ($.08, SD = .15$), this was not statistically significant ($F = 1.21$). None of the other factors had significant effects on errors.

Reaction Time The mean reaction times for different trial types are indicated by the height of the bars in Figure 16.4. These data are based on correct trials only, but the results do not change appreciably if error trials are also included in the analysis. There was a practice effect such that subjects had faster reaction times on the second repetition of the stimuli (Mean $= 5.45 seconds, SD = 1.96$) than on the first repetition (Mean $= 6.67 seconds, SD = 2.19, F(1,10) = 74.75, MS_e = 1.3, p < .001$). Since practice did not interact with any other factor, reaction times were collapsed over repetitions. The reaction times for the two pulley systems were analyzed separately, because of configural differences between the two pulley systems.

As Figure 16.4 shows, subjects spent more time verifying kinematic statements than static statements about both pulley systems ($F(1,10) =$

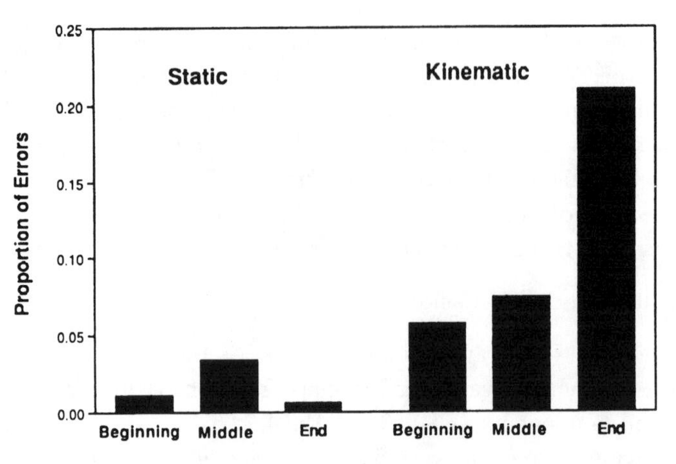

Figure 16.3
Statement to be Verified. Mean proportions of errors made by subjects in verifying static and kinematic statements describing components at different positions in the causal chain of events in the pulley systems.

$35.35, MS_e = 2.19, p < .001$ for pulley system 1; $F(1, 10) = 83.84, MS_e = 1.17, p < .001$ for pulley system 2). This is consistent with the proposal that verifying kinematic relations involves the process of mental animation in addition to the processes of encoding and comparing the representation of the text and diagram.

For statements about both pulley systems, there was a significant effect of location of the referent on reaction time ($F(2, 20) = 9.29, MS_e = 1.21, p < .01$ for pulley system 1; $F(2, 20) = 17.21, MS_e = 1.02, p < .01$ for pulley system 2), and a significant interaction of location with type of statement (static or kinematic) ($F(2, 20) = 17.63, MS_e = 1.32, p < .001$ for pulley system 1; $F(2, 20) = 25.81, MS_e = 0.49, p < .001$ for pulley system 2).

As Figure 16.4 shows, the reaction times for kinematic trials increased from the beginning to the end of the causal chain and simple effects analyses revealed a significant effect of location on verification times for statements about kinematic events in both pulley systems ($F(2, 20) = 14.97, MS_e = 2.11, p < .001$ for pulley system 1; $F(2, 20) = 25.69, MS_e = 1.16, p < .001$ for pulley system 2). This is consistent with the proposal that subjects mentally animate pulley system components by imagining a causal chain of events from the input of the system so that they spend more time verifying sentences describing kinematic events later in this

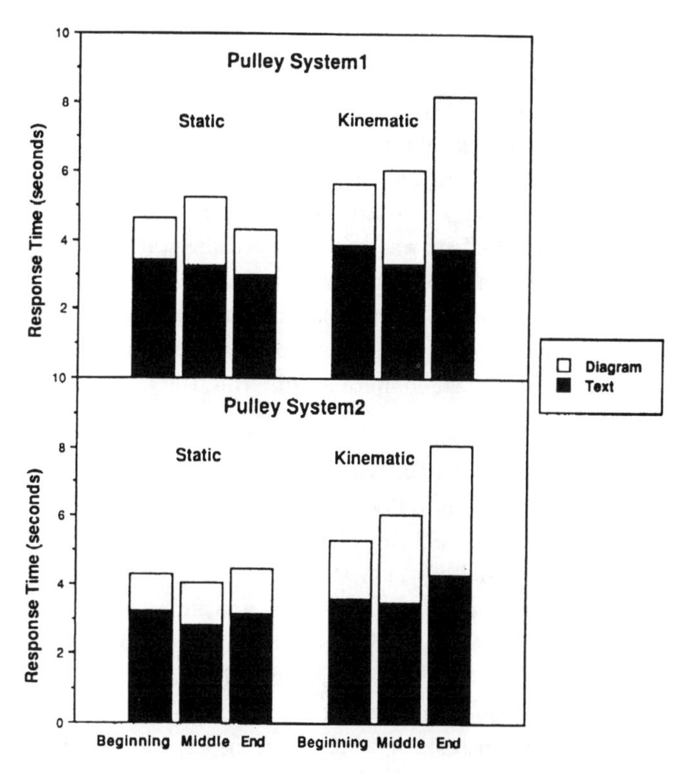

Figure 16.4
Statement to be Verified. Mean response times to verify sentences describing static and kinematic relations between system components at the beginning, middle and end of the causal chain of events in the pulley systems, broken down into time spent inspecting the text and time spent inspecting the diagram.

causal chain.

In contrast, these trends were not observed in the verification times for statements about static relations. Thus, they were not due to differences in subjects' ability to locate and encode information about components at different positions in the pulley system. For static statements about pulley system 1, the effect of location on the verification of static relations ($F(2, 20) = 7.01, MS_e = 0.42, p < .01$), was due to longer verification times for statements about the middle pulley. The spatial relations of the middle pulley to other system components are particularly complex, since the upper rope lies under this pulley, while the lower rope is attached to it. For static statements about pulley system 2, there was no effect of location of the components ($F < 1$).

In conclusion, errors and reaction times increased with the distance of the referent from the beginning of the causal chain. This effect is not consistent with an account of mental animation in which all components of a pulley system are animated at once nor an account in which components at the end of the causal chain are inferred from the motion of the weight. Furthermore, the effect was not observed for static stimuli, indicating that it is not due to differences in subjects' ability to locate or encode information about components at different positions in the pulley system. The results suggest that people animate pulley systems in increments, by inferring a causal chain of events from the input of the system.

Development and Evaluation of a Model of Mental Animation The reaction-time and eye-fixation data were matched to a production system model that infers the kinematics of a pulley system in such an incremental manner. This model begins with a representation of a static pulley system and the movement of the pull rope, and infers the movement of each successive component in the causal chain, stopping when the motion of the component in question is determined. Thus, the model simulates the mental animation stage but not the encoding and comparison stages of the experimental task. The productions express relations between spatially adjacent components so that the movement of a component can only be inferred from knowledge of the motion of another component that touches it (i.e., is fixed, attached, lies over, or lies under the component) and is earlier in the causal sequence of events in the system.

Thus, the model predicts the number of inferences required to determine the motion of any component in a pulley system. Table 16.4 lists the model's predictions of the number of inferences required to verify the true sentences describing kinematics for both pulley systems. The chain of events listed in Table 16.3 corresponds to the order in which the component motions in pulley system 1 are inferred within the model, with the exception that the direction of rotation of a pulley is determined only if this rotation is the referent of the sentence to be verified.

The model was evaluated in terms of its ability to predict the location of subjects' eye fixations. The first hypothesis tested is that the time to verify a sentence describing the movement of a pulley system component

Table 16.4
Predictions of the Number of Inferences Required to Verify Statements about the Kinematics of the Pulley Systems and Statistics Describing the Time Subjects Spent Inspecting the Diagram to Verify Each Statement.

Pulley System 1

Statement	Number. of Inferences	*M*	*S*
The upper rope moves to the right over the upper pulley.	1	1.88	1.2
The upper pulley turns clockwise.	2	1.96	1.0
The upper rope moves to the right under the middle pulley.	3	2.60	1.0
The middle pulley turns counterclockwise.	4	2.85	0.9
The lower rope moves to the right under the lower pulley.	7	3.88	1.7
The lower pulley turns clockwise.	8	4.82	2.3

Pulley System 2

Statement	Number of Inferences	*M*	*S*
The rope moves to the right over the right upper pulley.	1	1.52	0.7
The right upper pulley turns clockwise.	2	1.85	0.9
The rope moves to the right under the lower pulley.	3	2.47	0.9
The lower pulley turns counterclockwise.	4	2.72	1.1
The rope moves to the left over the left upper pulley.	5	3.51	1.6
The left upper pulley turns counterclockwise.	6	4.14	2.0

is proportional to the number of inferences required to determine that component's motion. The second hypothesis tested is that in order to verify the motion of a component, subjects inspect that component and components whose motions occur earlier in the causal chain of events in the pulley system.

Time Spent Inspecting the Diagram. As Figure 16.4 shows, a breakdown of reaction time into time spent reading the text and time spent inspecting the diagram indicated that reaction time differences are largely due to differences in diagram inspection time.[1] Time spent inspecting the diagram was highly related to the number of inferences required to verify a kinematic statement (see Table 16.4). A regression analysis in which this was the single independent variable accounted for 90% of

[1] Differences in time spent reading the text in Experiment 1 are difficult to interpret, because the length of the text varied across conditions.

the variance in diagram time ($F(1,22) = 201.53, MS_e = .11, p < .001$). The slope of the regression equation indicated that the estimated time to infer the movement of a component in these pulley systems is .44 seconds. The intercept (1.10 seconds) was close to the average time to verify static statements (1.34 seconds), which is consistent with the fact that both are measures of the time to encode and compare the information in a sentence and a diagram without the additional mental animation process. Furthermore, the intuitive assumption that the movement of a rope strand over a pulley causes the pulley to rotate was supported by the data. At all pulley system locations, it took longer to infer the motion of the pulley than that of the rope strand lying over or under the pulley ($F = 5.01, MS_e, = .703, p < .05$ for pulley system 1, $F(1,10) = 3.83, MS_e = .69, p = .08$ for pulley system 2).

Location of Eye Fixations. To further evaluate the model's predictions, eye fixations were aggregated to gazes, consisting of a single fixation or group of sequential eye fixations on a particular sector of the display. The display sectors were rectangles enclosing the pulleys, rope strands, the weight, and sections of the ceiling which were defined so that each section contained a single connection to a rope or pulley. The sectors corresponded to the objects in the static representation of the pulley system listed in Table 16.1, with the exception that the rope strands lying above or below a pulley were included in the same sector as the pulley.

Time spent inspecting the diagram was classified further as (1) time spent fixating the component(s) described in the sentence read (the referents of the sentence), (2) time spent fixating pulley system components whose motions occur before the referents in the kinematic chain of events (3) time spent fixating pulley system components whose motions occur after the referents in the kinematic chain and (4) time spent fixating all other parts of the display. The order of events presented in Table 16.3 defined the components whose motions were before or after a given motion in the causal chain of events. This breakdown of reaction time is presented in Figure 16.5.

Most of the time spent inspecting the diagram on kinematics trials ($.91, SD = .08$ for pulley system 1 and $.88, SD = .09$ for pulley system 2) was spent fixating the referents of the sentence and components whose motions precede these in the causal chain of events in the system. To verify statements about the motion of components

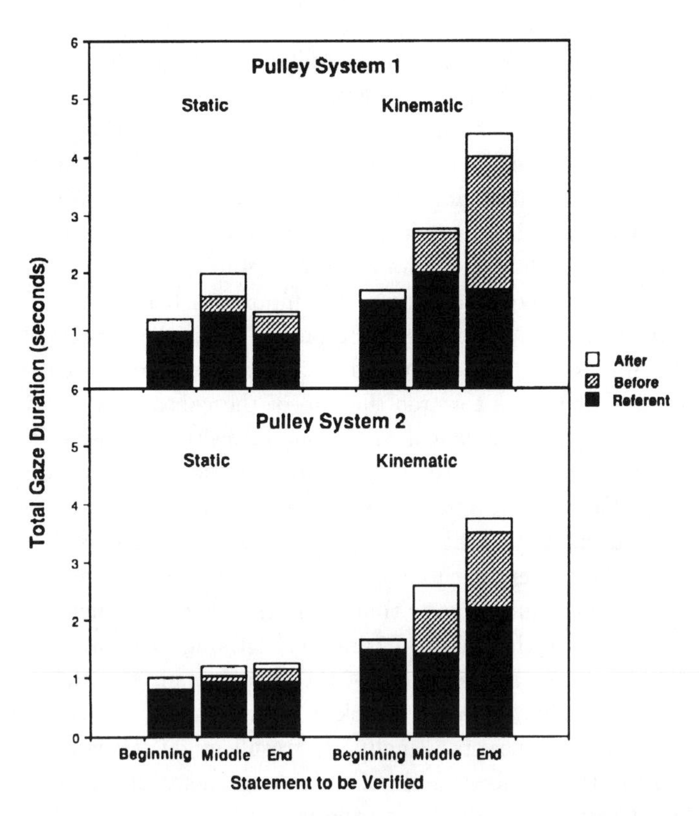

Figure 16.5
Statement to be Verified. A breakdown of total gaze duration on the diagram into time spent inspecting the referent(s) of the sentence, time spent inspecting components before the referent in the causal chain of events, and time spent inspecting components after the referent in the causal chain. The total gaze duration is the sum of the durations of all gazes on that section of the diagram.

at the beginning of the kinematic chain, subjects primarily inspected the referents of the statement (.84 of time on the diagram, $SD = .09$ for pulley system 1, $.86, SD = .12$ for pulley system 2). There was a linear increase in gaze duration on components before the referent in the chain of events from the beginning to the end of the causal chain (indicated by the crosshatched portions of the bars in Figure 16.5; $F(1, 10) = 33.35, MS_e = .86, p < .001$ for pulley system 1; $F(1, 10) = 23.81, MS_e = .38, p < .001$ for pulley system 2).

On kinematics trials, subjects should spend more time inspecting components earlier than the referent in the causal chain than components later in this chain. The most appropriate test of this prediction is to examine trials in which the referent was in the middle of the causal chain, since when the referent is towards the beginning of the causal chain, there are very unequal numbers of components before and after the referent (relatively few earlier components when the referent is towards the beginning of the causal chain and relatively few later components when the referent is towards the end of the causal chain). In this middle condition, subjects spent more time inspecting components earlier in the causal chain ($F(1, 10) = 22.04, p < .001$ for pulley system 1; $F(1, 10) = 5.97, MS_e = .08, p < .05$ for pulley system 2).

It must be noted, however, that subjects did spend some time fixating components after the referent in the causal chain, especially in the case of pulley system 2. This result suggests that subjects may have sometimes made inferences against the chain of causality, although the strategy of inferring motion from the beginning of the causal chain was clearly dominant. Subjects might also have looked to the end of the causal chain as a check on their answers. Finally, this result might reflect some calibration error in the eye-fixation data, since components classified as after the referent were often adjacent to the referent.

When verifying sentences describing static relations, the majority of the time spent inspecting the diagram, was spent fixating the referents of the sentence ($.73, SD = .12$ of diagram time for pulley system 1, .79 of diagram time, $SD = .12$ in the case of pulley system 2). Furthermore, when the referent was in the middle of the causal chain, there was no difference in the amount of time spent inspecting components earlier and later than the referent.

In summary, assuming that subjects' eye fixations are indicative of their mental processes (Just and Carpenter 1976), the eye-fixation location data provide support for a model of this mental animation task stating that the components of a pulley system are animated piecemeal, in order of the causal sequence of events in the system.

Strategies Subjects typically read the sentence before inspecting the diagram, (on 98.5% of trials, $SD = 1.7$) suggesting that their overall strategy was to first construct a representation of the text and then verify this representation against the diagram. To provide further information about subjects' mental animation strategies, the sequence of eye fixations on the diagram was examined for a subset of the mental animation trials. Since subjects typically inspected only the referent when the sentence described an event at the beginning of the causal chain (see Figure 16.5), the most interesting sequence data occurred on trials describing events at the middle or end of the causal chain. The eye-fixation sequences of the 11 subjects were examined for the 8 trials describing kinematic events at the middle and end of the causal chain in the second block of trials (with the exception of one subjects' data on one trial in which calibration was lost). Examples of typical sequences of fixations on the text and diagram are presented in Figures 16.6 and 16.7.

If we assume that subjects fixate the part of the visual display that they are mentally processing at any given time, then the theory suggests that when animating a pulley system, people should inspect the components of the pulley system in a sequence corresponding to their positions in the causal chain. This pattern can be observed in gazes 2 to 5 and 7 to 9 of the protocol in Figure 16.7 and is approximated by gazes 5 to 12 of the protocol in Figure 16.6. In 6 of the 8 trials examined ($SD = 1.55$) subjects scanned from the beginning of the causal chain to the referent at least once, suggesting that this pattern was typical.

It was also quite common for a subject to first inspect the referent before scanning back to the beginning of the causal chain, as in the example in Figure 16.6. On 4.2 of the 8 trials examined, subjects began by fixating the referent ($SD = 1.8$). This result suggests that the most common strategy was to locate the referent of the sentence in the diagram before mentally animating the pulley system. It may also reflect a process of inferring motion against the direction of causality (i.e., from the referent to an earlier component). This step was not always necessary. In a further 2.2 of trials ($SD = 1.5$) the subject began by fixating

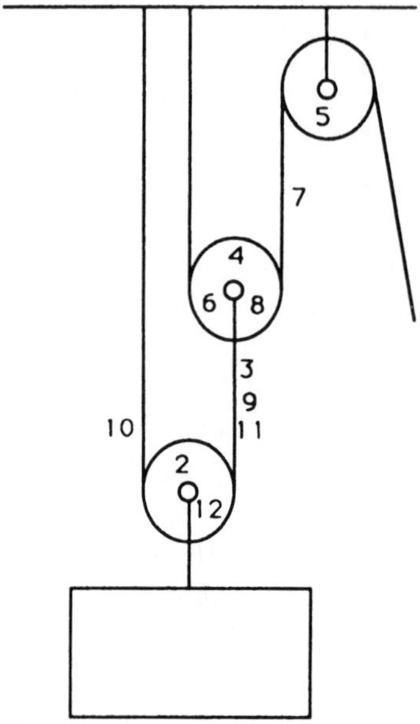

Gaze	Object Fixated	Gaze Duration
1	text	901 milliseconds
2	pull rope	417
3	right lower rope	266
4	middle pulley	918
5	upper pulley	885
6	middle pulley	433
7	right upper rope	167
8	middle pulley	1852
9	right lower rope	733
10	left lower rope	250
11	right lower rope	234
12	lower pulley	500
13	text	200

Figure 16.6
Example of an Eye-Fixation Protocol. 1,13. The lower pulley turns counterclockwise. The numbers on the diagram indicate the sequence of the subjects gazes on the text and on components of the diagram.

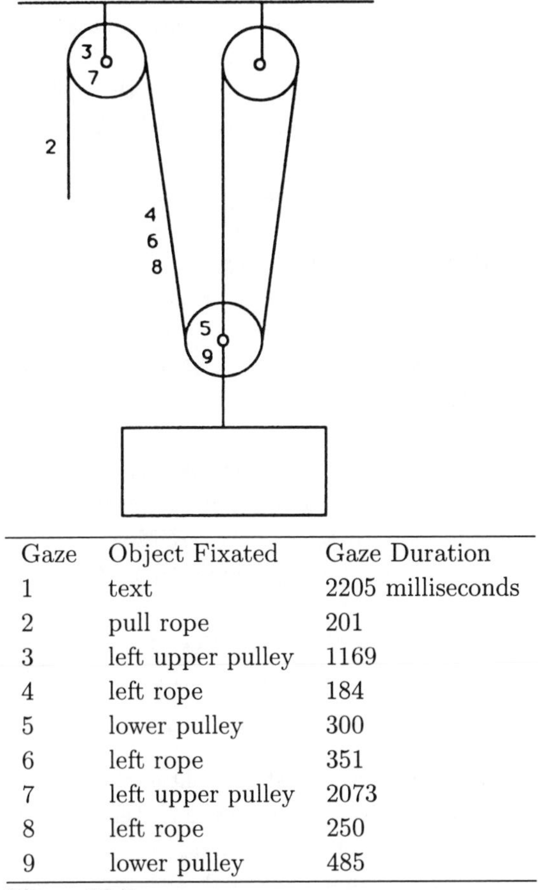

Gaze	Object Fixated	Gaze Duration
1	text	2205 milliseconds
2	pull rope	201
3	left upper pulley	1169
4	left rope	184
5	lower pulley	300
6	left rope	351
7	left upper pulley	2073
8	left rope	250
9	lower pulley	485

Figure 16.7
Example of an Eye-Fixation Protocol. The rope moves to the left under the lower pulley. The numbers on the diagram indicate the sequence of the subjects gazes on the text and on components of the diagram.

a component at the beginning of the causal chain in the pulley system, as in the example in Figure 16.7.

Subjects often scanned between the referent and other components in the pulley system, more than once in a trial. For example in Figure 16.7 the subject scanned from the pull rope to the referent (gazes 2 to 5), then back to the first pulley in the kinematic chain (gazes 6 and 7) and then forward to the referent again (gazes 8 and 9). Subjects inspected the referent on average 2.7 times per trial ($S.D = 1.00$). Thus, the mental animation may not always have been successfully completed during the first attempt.

Subjects sometimes reread the text during a trial. They read sentences describing events at the end of the causal chain (2.39 times, $S.D = .58$) more often than sentences describing events at the beginning (1.98 times, $SD = .52$) or middle (1.97 times, $SD = .58$) of the causal chain. On these trials the demands of inferring the motion of more components and storing the intermediate results of these computations may have overloaded working memory so that the sentence representation decayed and had to be reactivated by rereading.

Finally, to assess whether any of the above characteristics of the protocols were related to success on the mental animation task, the strategies of subjects who made fewer than 10 errors ($N = 7$, Mean $= 4.6$, $SD = 3.21$) were compared with those who made more than 10 errors ($N = 4$, Mean $= 27.25, SD = 8.96$). None of the above measures of subjects' strategies significantly differentiated the high- and low-error groups.

16.2.3 Conclusion

In conclusion, the results of Experiment 1 suggest that subjects are able to determine the motion of a component of a pulley system given a static diagram of the system and knowledge of the input motion to the system. The reaction-time and eye-fixation data suggest that the dominant strategy is to determine the motion of a pulley system component by first encoding the configuration of the pulley system and then tracing the causal chain of events from the input of the system to the component in question. Inspection of the static diagram seems to be central to this mental animation process.

16.3 Experiment 2

In Experiment 1, subjects were asked to verify the motion of a pulley system component, given that the free end of the rope in the pulley system was being pulled. Thus, they were given the motion of one component, the pull rope, which is the input to the system, and were required to determine the motion of a component that is later in the causal chain of events. The results suggested that subjects determined the motion of any component by making a chain of inferences from the input of the system to this component. If this characterization of mental animation is correct, then people should be able to determine the motion of a component from that of any other component that is earlier in the causal chain of events. In Experiment 2 this was tested by asking subjects to verify the motion of components of a pulley system given the motion of another component, which was earlier in the kinematic chain, but not the input to the system.

Assuming that subjects determine the motion of a component of a pulley system by making a chain of inferences, if the motion that they are given is earlier in the chain of events, then the required inference chain is in the direction of causality. In Experiment 1, rules of inference expressing causal relations between adjacent components accounted for most of the data. However, there was also some suggestion that subjects made inferences against the direction of causality.

In Experiment 2, subjects were required to make inferences either from an earlier component in the causal chain of events in the system or from a later component. Presuming that they can make inferences against the causal chain, there are two possible explanations of this process. First, it is possible that subjects' rules of inference express co-occurrences between component motions that are not necessarily in the direction of causality, for example "when the rope is moving to the right over the upper pulley, the rope is being pulled." In this case, there should be no differences in errors or reaction times between inferences from an earlier component in the causal chain and inferences from a later component.

Second, it is possible that subjects rules only express causal relations. In this case, they should have more difficulty making inferences from a later event in the causal chain than from an earlier event. When given a later event, one possible strategy is backward chaining, i.e., making a chain of inferences in which an earlier component is located and the subject infers which motion of this earlier component causes the motion of the later component. Another possible strategy is to infer both the given and the motion in question from the input of the system, i.e., in the direction of causality.

16.3.1 Method

Subjects Ten undergraduate students at the University of California, Santa Barbara participated in the experiment for course credit.

Stimuli and Apparatus As in Experiment 1, each stimulus was composed of a sentence on the left of the screen and a diagram of a pulley system on the right. The subjects' task was to state whether the sentence was true or false of the depicted pulley system.

The sentences described the motion of one component of the system, given the motion of another component. For example, on one trial, the diagram in Figure 16.1 was accompanied by the sentence "when the rope is moving to the right over the upper pulley, the middle pulley is turning counterclockwise." In this sentence, the motion of the rope over the upper pulley is the given motion and the motion of the middle pulley is the motion in question. The given motion was an event at either the beginning or the end of the causal chain of events in the pulley system (in the case of pulley system 1, the movement of the rope over the upper pulley and the movement of the rope under the lower pulley respectively). The motion to be determined was either a motion at the beginning, the middle or the end of the kinematic chain (in the case of pulley system 1, the movement of the upper, middle and lower pulleys respectively).

The diagrams depicted left and right isomers of the two pulley system configurations used in Experiment 1. Half of the sentences were true and half were false. A false sentence was composed to correspond to each true sentence so that the given motion was the same in both sentences and the motion to be determined was opposite. There were a total of 48 sentence-diagram pairs which were presented in a random order to subjects in one block of trials.

The procedure and apparatus were the same as in Experiment 1.

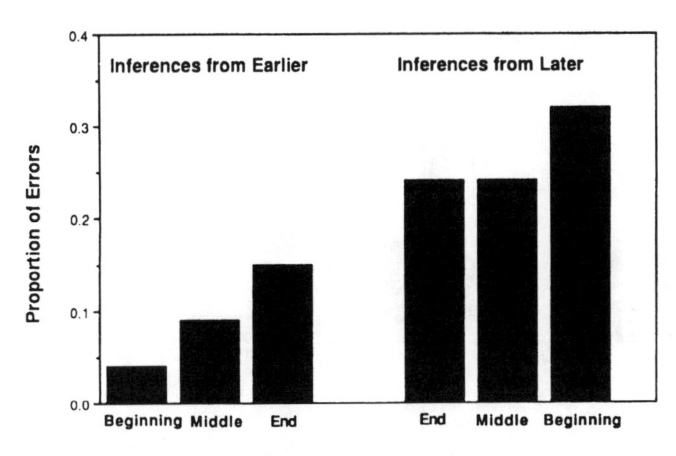

Figure 16.8
Position of the Motion in Question in the Causal Chain. Mean proportion of errors made by subjects in inferring the motion of pulley system components at different positions in the causal chain of events when the given motion was at the beginning of the causal chain (inference from earlier in the causal chain) and when it is at the end (inference from later in the causal chain).

16.3.2 Results and Discussion

Errors The error data replicate the distance effects observed in Experiment 1 and suggest that inferences from the end of the causal chain of events are more difficult than inferences from the beginning of the causal chain. The overall error rate in this experiment was 18.0%. As Figure 16.8 shows, subjects made more errors when the inference process involved tracing more links in the causal chain of events in the pulley system ($F(2,18) = 8.86, MS_e = .03, p < .01$). There was also a marginally significant trend for subjects to make more errors when the given motion was at the end of the causal chain of events than when it was at the beginning ($F(1,9) = 4.06, MS_e = .02, p = .07$).

Reaction Time The overall reaction times for correct trials are represented by the height of the bars in Figure 16.9. Inferences from events later in the causal sequence took longer than inferences from events earlier in this sequence ($F(1,9) = 5.33, MS_e = 21.4, p < .05$ for pulley system 1; $F(1,9) = 17.49, MS_e = 10.8, p < .01$ for pulley system 2). Thus, the inference process is more effortful when the chain of inferences to be made is inconsistent with the direction of causality, suggesting that

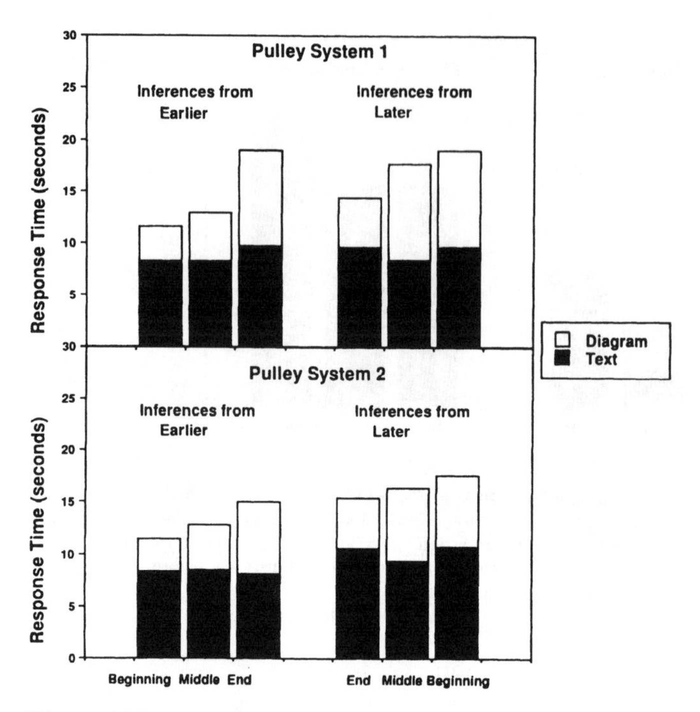

Figure 16.9
Position of Motion in Question in the Causal Chain. Mean response times to infer the motion of components in a pulley system from events earlier and later in the causal chain, broken down into time spent inspecting the text and time spent inspecting the diagram.

the inference rules are directional.

Reaction times for inferences from earlier in the causal chain replicated the results of Experiment 1. Figure 16.9 shows that for these trials, the time to verify a statement increased with the distance of the motion in question from the given motion ($F(2,18) = 15.16, MS_e = 12.11, p < .001$ for pulley system 1; $F(2,18) = 4.75, MS_e = 7.8, p < .05$ for pulley system 2).

In the case of inferences from the end of the causal chain, verification times also increased with distance of the motion in question from the given motion, i.e. they were longest when the motion in question was an event at the beginning of the causal chain and shortest when it was an event at the end of the causal chain (see Figure 16.9). However the increase in reaction time with distance reached statistical significance only in the case of pulley system 1 ($F(2,18) = 3.86, MS_e = 17.2, p < .05$).

Reaction times for inferences from earlier and later in the causal sequence were compared to a model of mental animation assuming that people can infer the motion of a component from that of an adjacent component and that the inference takes the same amount of time, regardless of whether this component is earlier or later in the causal chain of events. A multiple regression analysis indicated the relation of the mean time to verify the 48 sentences to two independent measures, the number of inferences predicted by this model ($r = .61$), and whether the given motion was earlier or later in the causal chain ($r = .58$). Both variables had significant contributions to the regression equation ($t(1,45) = 3.50, p < .01$ for number of inferences; $t(1,45) = 3.01, p < .01$ for location of given motion), and together they accounted for 47.9% of the variance in reaction times ($F(2,45) = 20.68, MS_e = 7.54, p < .001$).

This model was a better predictor of time to make inferences from earlier in the causal chain ($r = .77$) than time to make inferences from later in the causal chain ($r = .55$). The difference may be due to variability in subjects' strategies for inferring motion from later events in the causal chain, which will be outlined below.

A comparison of the reaction times with those observed in of Experiment 1 indicates that the times in Experiment 2 were considerably longer. This was partially due to reading time because the sentences used in this study were longer. However, subjects also spent more time inspecting the diagram in this study, and the regression analyses indicated that the increment in reaction time with each additional inference was greater in Experiment 2 (.73 seconds) than in Experiment 1 (.44 seconds).

A possible explanation of this result suggests that there were additional storage demands on working memory in Experiment 2 and that these interfered with the speed of the mental animation process. In Experiment 1 the given motion was the same on all trials. It was also the input motion to the system (the rope being pulled). This motion is probably particularly salient for subjects, since they presumably subjects know that pulley systems are operated by pulling the pull rope. For these reasons, subjects might not have had to represent the given motion explicitly while performing the mental animation task. In Experiment 2 on the other hand, the given motion varied from trial to trial and was probably not as salient since it was the motion of one of the internal components of the system, In this task it is more likely that the given motion was represented explicitly during the mental animation process. This additional storage demand may have interfered with the speed of the mental animation processes (cf., Baddeley and Hitch 1974; Baddeley and Lieberman 1978).

Inferences from Earlier in the Causal Chain The locations and sequence of eye fixations on the display provided information about the strategies that subjects employed to infer motion from an earlier component in the causal chain.

Location of Eye Fixations. As the height of the bars in Figure 16.10 shows, gaze duration on the diagram increased with distance of the motion to be determined from the given motion ($F(2,18) = 17.20, MS_e = 5.56, p < .001$ for pulley system 1; $F(2,18) = 10.08, MS_e = 3.68, p < .01$ for pulley system 2) and this was due to an increase in gaze duration on components earlier in the chain of events (shown by the crosshatched sections of the bars in Figure 16.10, $F(2,18) = 39.57, MS_e = 2.41, p < .001$ for pulley system 1; $F(2,18) = 29.78, MS_e = 1.12, p < .001$ for pulley system 2). In the middle condition, in which there were approximately equal numbers of components before and after the referent in the causal chain of events, more time was spent inspecting the components before the referent ($F(1,9) = 57.37, MS_e = .25, p < .001$ for pulley system 1; $F(1,9) = 22.09, MS_e = 1.53, p = .001$ for pulley system 2. Gaze duration on the text, on the component whose motion was in question, and on components later in the kinematic chain did not vary significantly with distance.

Sequence of Eye Fixations. To gain further insight into subjects' strategies, the sequence of eye fixations on the display was examined for the true kinematics trials describing pulley system 1. As in Experiment 1, the most interesting sequence data occurred on trials in which the motion to be determined was at the middle (2 trials) or end (2 trials) of the causal chain, since when both the given motion and the motion to be determined were at the beginning of the causal chain, subjects typically inspected only components at the beginning of the chain (see Figure 16.10).

As in Experiment 1, subjects switched between processing the text and diagram more often when the motion in question was at the end of the

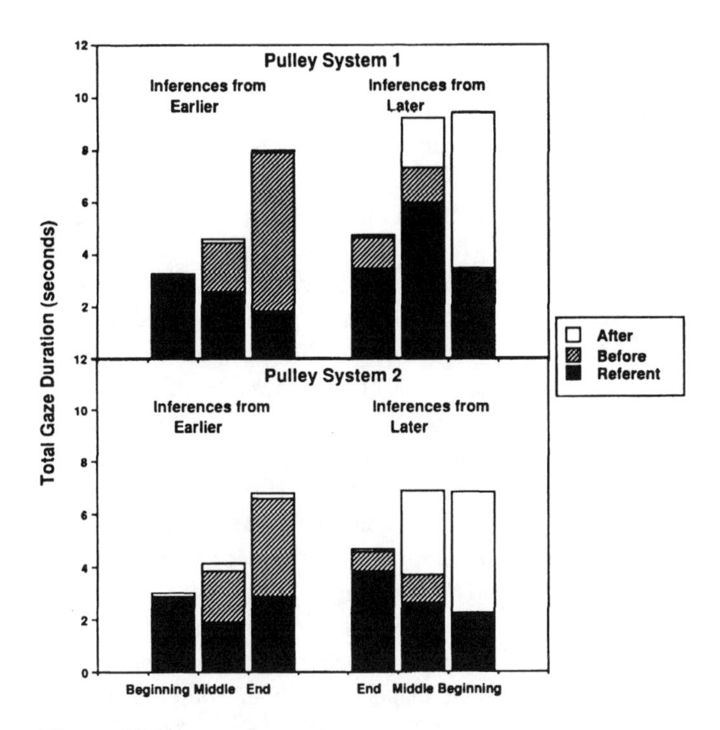

Figure 16.10
Position of Motion in Question in the Causal Chain. Breakdown of gaze duration on the diagram into time spent inspecting the component in question, time spent inspecting components before this component in the causal chain of events, and time spent inspecting components after this component in the causal chain.

causal chain (4.05 times, $SD = .64$) than when it was at the middle of the causal chain (2.55 times, $SD = 1.14, t(10) = 4.03, p < .01$). Within a trial, subjects first inspections were typically on components at the beginning of the causal chain only, suggesting that they first constructed a representation of the given motion (2.4 trials, $SD = 1.35$) and inferred the motion of the component in question on later inspections.

The pattern of scanning from the beginning of the causal chain to the referent was observed in 2.9 of the 4 trials examined ($SD = 1.4$) and in almost all of these trials (Mean $= 3.8, SD = .42$), subjects inspected the beginning of the causal chain before their final inspection of the referent. These patterns suggest the process of inferring the motion in question from the given motion. Subjects' final inspections were often focussed on the referent alone, suggesting a final check on the motion in question (in 1.6 trials, SD = 1.35).

Inferences from Later in the Causal Chain *Location of Eye Fixations.* In the case of inferences from the end of the causal chain, time spent inspecting the diagram was again affected by the distance of the motion to be determined from the given motion ($F(2,18) = 6.08, MS_e = 11.62, p < .01$ for pulley system 1; $F(2,18) = 2.67, MS_e = 5.91, p < .10$ for pulley system 2; see Figure 16.10). This was largely due to an increase in gaze duration on components after the component in question ($F(2,18) = 13.24, MS_e = 6.83, p < .001$ for pulley system 1; $F(2,18) = 15.27, MS_e = 3.43, p < .001 for pulley system 2$), shown by the white sections of the bars in Figure 16.10. This result is consistent with a model of mental animation in which people can infer an earlier event in the causal chain from a later event. However subjects also spent a greater amount of time fixating components earlier in the causal chain when the component in question was at the middle or end of the causal chain ($F(2,18) = 6.26, MS_e = .76, p < .01$ for pulley system 1, $F(2,18) = 6.63, MS_e = .43, p < .01$ for pulley system 2). Furthermore, in the middle condition, the time spent inspecting later components significantly exceeded the time spent inspecting earlier components only in the case of pulley system 2 ($F(1,9) = 66.99, MS_e = .34, p < .001$). These results would not be predicted by a model in which inferences from later in the causal chain are made purely by backward chaining.

Sequence of Eye Fixations. The location of subjects' eye-fixations on the display provided further insight into the inference process, suggesting that when the given motion is an event at the end of the causal chain, subjects animate the component in question either by backward chaining, by inferring its motion from the beginning of the causal chain, or a combination of these strategies.

The eye-fixation protocols were examined for all 10 subjects for trials in which the given motion was at the end (2 trials) or the middle (2 trials) of the causal chain. If subjects use the backward chaining strategy they should begin by inspecting components at the end of the causal chain, and then scan from these components to the middle of the pulley system. In fact, subjects were as likely to begin by inspecting components at the beginning of the causal chain (1.4 trials, $SD = 1.4$) than at the end (1.2 trials, $SD = .1.3$) on these 4 trials (on the remaining trials they began by inspecting the referent). Furthermore, although the pattern of scanning between the end of the causal chain and the referent occurred during the majority of these 4 protocols (3.4, $SD = .69$), the protocols typically also included inspections on components at the beginning of the causal chain (2.4 trials, $SD = 1.07$). These data suggest that subjects attempted to infer the motion in question both from the end and from the beginning of the causal chain. Although there were individual differences in how often subjects inspected the beginning of the causal chain, all subjects did so on at least 1 of the 4 trials examined.

This combination of strategies is illustrated by the eye-fixation protocol in Figure 16.11, in which the motion in question is in the middle of the causal chain. On this trial, the subject's first two diagram inspections (fixations 2 and 4) are on the upper pulley, a component at the beginning of the causal chain. Her subsequent diagram inspections include scans both between the referent and the end of the causal chain (fixations 6 to 8 and 13 to 15) and between the upper pulley and the referent (fixations 10 to 13).

These data support the view that subjects' rules of inference are in the direction of causality. They suggest that subjects' default preference is to infer the motion of a component from the beginning of the causal chain of events in the machine. When the text requires subjects to infer its motion from the end of the causal chain, this strategy is not completely overcome by the alternative strategy of backward chaining.

16.3.3 Conclusion

In conclusion, the results of Experiment 2 supported to the theory that people determine the motion of pulley system components by making a chain of inferences to determine the motion of successive components. These results add to the account of mental animation by showing that people can make inferences against the direction of causality. This process is effortful, and appears to compete with the default strategy of inferring the motion of the system from the beginning of the causal chain, suggesting that subjects rules of inference are directional and that inferences against the causal chain of events are more effortful. Finally, assuming that the given motion is represented more explicitly in this experiment, and that this additional storage demand interferes with the rate of mental animation, the results of Experiment 2 suggest further evidence of capacity limitations in the mental animation process.

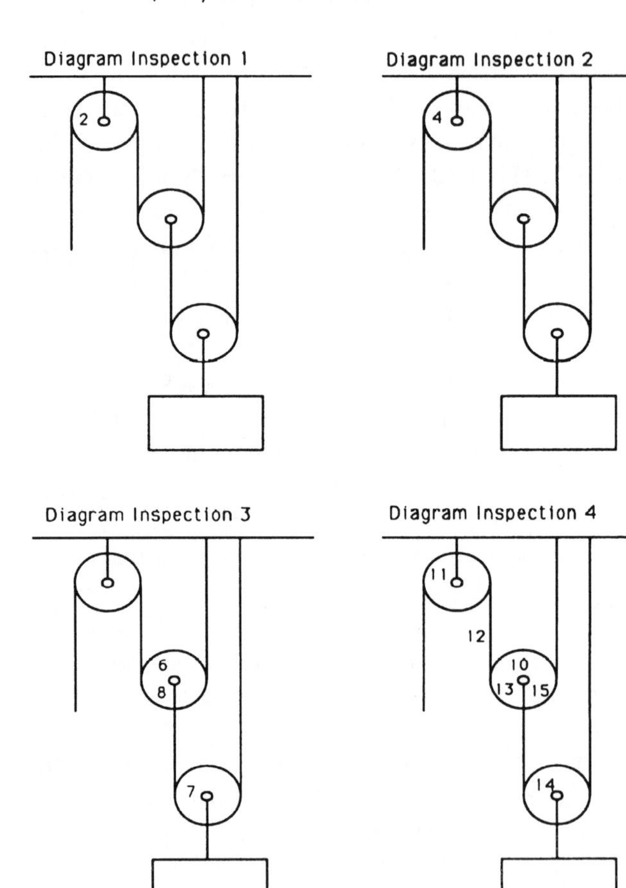

Figure 16.11
Eye-Fixation Protocol. Examples of an eye-fixation protocols for a trial where the subject was required to infer the motion of a component from the end of the causal chain. The subject read the text and inspected the diagram four times. The numbers on the diagram indicate the sequence of the subjects gazes on the text and on components of the diagram.

16.4 General Discussion

Mental animation is the process of inferring the kinematics of a mechanical system from information about the static configuration of the system. The research presented in this chapter suggests that when people mentally animate a pulley system, they decompose their representation of the machine into smaller units corresponding to the machine components, and animate these components in a sequence corresponding to the causal sequence of events in the machine's operation. Although people can make inferences against the chain of causality in the machine, these inferences are more difficult and people have a preference for making inferences in the direction of causality. Thus, for the task studied in this research, the mental animation process is more isomorphic to the causal sequence of events in the machine's operation than to the physical movement of the machine, in which all components move at once.

These results provide empirical support for the view that running a mental model of a mechanical system involves applying a set of causal rules to determine the states of successive components of the system. Although this theory of mechanical reasoning has been well developed in the artificial intelligence literature (de Kleer and Brown 1984; Forbus 1984; Reiger and Grinberg 1977), there have been few attempts to study it empirically (e.g., Spoehr and Horvath 1989). This study provides a precise specification of this theory for one specific mechanical reasoning task and shows that this can account for on-line measures of cognitive processing, such as reaction times and eye fixations.

16.4.1 Limitations of the Mental Animation Process

A major conclusion of this study is that the mental animation process is limited. People cannot mentally animate a mechanical system all at once at the level of detail required in this task, but do so in increments. There are two possible reasons why this task decomposition is necessary. One possibility is that it is due to capacity limitations, i.e., that the process of animating a whole pulley system at once overloads working memory. Another possibility is that it is due to knowledge limitations, i.e., that people only have knowledge of the kinematic relations between spatially contiguous components in a mechanical system.

Several of the results in this chapter can be interpreted as effects of working memory limitations. First, the account of mental animation proposed in this chapter is an example of the general strategy of decomposing a complex problem into subproblems that are manageable within the constraints of working memory (Carpenter, Just and Shell 1990). Second, subjects were more likely to reread the text on trials that involved animating more components, suggesting that the animation task interfered with the storage of the text representation. Third, the difference in the rate of mental animation observed in Experiments 1 and 2 can be interpreted by assuming that the given motion is represented more explicitly in the task in Experiment 2 and that this additional representation decreases the rate. The second and third points reflect the tradeoff between storage and processing in working memory (Baddeley and Hitch 1974; Baddeley and Lieberman, 1978; Carpenter and Just 1989). Clearly, these interpretations are highly speculative given the data collected to date on the mental animation task. They could be tested more directly in future experiments by observing subjects' ability to mentally animate systems of different complexity or by observing the mental animation process under memory-load conditions.

The data also suggest that knowledge is limited in that people are not able to infer the motion of a component of a pulley system from any other component, but only from adjacent components. Furthermore, if the effects reported in this chapter were due to capacity limitations alone, there would not have been a difference between the processes of inferring motion from the beginning and end of the causal chain, as was observed in Experiment 2.

In the model proposed in this chapter the limitations are expressed as knowledge limitations. The production rules in the model only express relations between spatially contiguous components. This type of knowledge base is an efficient method of storing mechanical knowledge, since it ensures that people have the ability to infer the kinematics of any novel mechanical system, provided that they have knowledge of the local interactions between components of the system. If mechanical systems were animated all at once, it would be necessary to have a separate and complete knowledge structure for inferring the kinematics of every individual mechanical system with which one is familiar and in this case, mechanical knowledge would be highly redundant.

The theory of mechanical knowledge presented here does not exclude the possibility that people develop more complex knowledge structures corresponding to a complete mental model of mechanical systems with which they are highly familiar. In fact, it is likely that with familiarity, the groups of related components of a mechanical system are "chunked" (cf. Chase and Simon 1973; Egan and Schwarz 1979) so that instead of analyzing a mechanical system into individual components, the system is analyzed into groups of components that directly affect each others' motions. By the mechanism of production composition (Anderson, 1983), the production rules proposed here could be combined to form more complex productions, which allow the motions of such a group of components to be inferred all at once. Thus, the intuitions of gifted scientists and engineers that they can imagine the operation of a familiar mechanical system all at once (Ferguson, 1977; Shepard 1978) are not implausible. However the amount of practice that subjects received in this experiment was not sufficient to produce significant chunking effects. Although a practice effect was observed in Experiment 1, practice did not affect the slope of the reaction time curve, which would be the case if chunking had occurred.

16.4.2 Visual-Spatial Processes in Mental Animation

The eye-fixation data suggest that inspection of the relevant part of the visual display is related to the mental animation process. There are several possible interpretations of this relation between diagram inspection and internal inference processes. First, it is possible that eye-fixations on the visual display might relieve the subject of the need to store a static representation of the system, so that more mental capacity can be devoted to the animation processes. Second, as Larkin and Simon (1987) have proposed, the visual display might serve to index the information that must be related in solving a problem, so that subjects' fixations on the display might allow them to focus on a particular subgoal of the problem or to keep track of their progress in solving a problem. Third, subjects' eye movements might mediate their determination of the movement of the system components. That is, the process of imagining an external object moving might be accompanied by the movement of parts of one's own body, including eye movements. The precise roles of the visual display in a task such as mental animation need to be investigated in future research. One possible future approach would be to monitor how mental animation is affected when the static display is not present for the duration of the task.

A related question concerns the extent to which the inference of motion involves spatial visualization processes. Although the current model is expressed as a production system, the current understanding of this task does not differentiate between a rule-based inference process and one based on spatial visualization. The role of spatial visualization in mental animation could be investigated in experiments, modelled after Brooks (1968), in which students are given either a spatial or a non-spatial interference task to perform while mentally animating a diagram.

16.4.3 Development of the Model

The production system model described in this chapter is quite successful in accounting for the reaction time data and the location of subjects' eye fixations. The central proposals of this model, that the mental animation process is piecemeal and that it is isomorphic to the causal sequence of events in the model are well supported by the data. However the model also includes some more specific proposals that are less central to the theory, e.g. that the movement of the rope over a pulley and the rotation of the pulley are separate events. Although some of these specific proposals were supported by the data, they are largely intuitive at present and need to be tested further in future research.

The current model has some other limitations. It accounts for aggregate performance across subjects, rather than the performance of individual subjects. The small number of subjects in this study did not allow for more than a cursory examination of individual differences. However, there was large variation among subjects in both reaction times and eye fixation patterns and an account of these individual differences should contribute to the theory of mental animation. Second, an important addition to the model would be to impose working memory limitations on the mental animation process. Third, the model of mental animation should eventually be embedded in a more complete model of the sentence-picture verification task, including the encoding and comparison processes in this task and the process of selecting a mental animation strategy.

16.4.4 Generality of the Results

In order to develop a precise specification of the mental animation process, it was necessary to confine the task analysis and empirical investigation in this chapter to a specific mental animation task, the inference of the motions of individual components of a pulley system. Pulley systems are typical machines in that they are composed of elementary components which constrain each others' motions and work together to achieve the function of the machine. Thus, a model of the type described here might also account for mental animation of many other types of machines that fit this description, although the basic components of these machines and the relations between their motions would be different. In fact, the model described here is similar to a more general production system model developed by Kieras (1984, 1990) to simulate mental models of a variety of electronic devices in that in both cases the inference of system behavior is based on a declarative description of the configuration of the system, also known as the device topology.

There are also some aspects of the model that we would not expect to generalize to other mechanical systems. For example, many systems such as pumps and electrical circuits do not have a distinct input and output, but are more cyclical in their operation. People might be more flexible in being able to mentally animate these systems given the state of any component in the system. Furthermore, many complex machines have multiple potential causal chains so that mental animation of these machines might first involve identifying a causal chain to use in inferring kinematics.

Finally, answering different questions about the same mechanical system may involve different processes. For example, it does not appear to involve a chain of inferences to determine that when the rope of a pulley system is pulled the weight moves up, possibly because this motion directly related to the function of a pulley system. Furthermore, answering quantitative questions, e.g., how high the weight will rise when the rope is pulled by a given amount, or questions about pulley system dynamics have been found to be more difficult than the questions asked in this study and to involve processes such as counting the ropes in the system (Hegarty, Just, and Morrison 1988). The mental animation process studied in this research is probably just one of a number of strategies that people have at their disposal when they are required to infer the behavior of deterministic systems. Future research will identify the conditions under which this process is used and how it varies for different systems and for the inference of different types of information.

Acknowledgements

This research was supported by a grant from the Academic Senate of the University of California, Santa Barbara.

I wish to thank Andy Beall, Ted Bicknell, Erika Ferguson, Peter Hegarty, Valerie Sims and Tom Fikes for assistance with data collection and analysis. I am also grateful to Marcel Just, Cathy Reed, Jeff Shrager and three anonymous reviewers for comments on earlier drafts of this manuscript.

References

Anderson, J. R. 1983. *The Architecture of Cognition.* Cambridge Mass.: Harvard University Press.

Baddeley, A. D. and Hitch, G. 1974. Working Memory. In *The Psychology of Learning And Motivation,* ed. G. H. Bower, 47–89. New York: Academic Press.

Baddeley, A. D. and Lieberman, 1978. Spatial Working Memory. In *Attention and Performance,* ed. R. Nickerson, 521–539). London: Academic Press.

Brooks, L. R. 1968. Spatial and Verbal Components of the Act of Recall. *Canadian Journal of Psychology* 22: 349–368.

Carpenter, P. A. and Just, M. A. 1975. Sentence Comprehension: A Psycholinguistic Processing Model of Verification, *Psychological Review* 82(1): 45–73.

Carpenter, P. A. and Just, M. A. 1989. The Role of Working Memory In Language Comprehension. In *Complex Information Processing: The Impact of Herbert A. Simon,* ed. D. Klahr and K. Kotovsky. Hillsdale, N.J.: Lawrence Erlbaum Associates.

Carpenter, P. A., Just, M. A. and Shell, P. 1990. What One Intelligence Test Measures: A Theoretical Account of The Processing in the Raven Progressive Matrices Text. *Psychological Review* 97(3): 404–431.

Chase, W. G., and Simon, H. A. 1973. Perception in Chess. *Cognitive Psychology* 4: 55–81.

Clarke, H. H. and Chase, W. G. 1972. On the Process of Comparing Sentences Against Pictures. *Cognitive Psychology* 3: 472–517.

de Kleer, J., and Brown, J. S. 1984. A Qualitative Physics Based on Confluences. *Artificial Intelligence* 24: 7–83.

D'Ydewalle, G., Muylle, P., and Van Rensbergen, J. 1985. Attention Shifts in Partially Redundant Information Situations. In *Eye Movements And Hu-*

man Information Processing, ed. R. Groner, G. W. McConkie, and C. Menz. Amsterdam: North Holland.

D'Ydewalle, G., Van Rensbergen, J., and Pollet, J. 1987. Reading A Message When the Same Message Is Available Auditorily in Another Language: The Case Of Subtitling. In *Eye Movements: From Physiology To Cognition,* ed. J. K. O'Regan and A. Levy-Schoen. Amsterdam: North Holland.

Egan, D. E., and Schwartz, B. J. 1979. Chunking In Recall of Symbolic Drawings. *Memory and Cognition* 7(2): 149–158.

Fallside, D. C. 1988. Understanding Machines In Motion. P.hD. diss., Carnegie Mellon University.

Ferguson, E. S. 1977. The Mind's Eye: Non-Verbal Thought in Technology. *Science* 197: 827–836.

Forbus, K. D. 1984. Qualitative Process Theory. *Artificial Intelligence* 24: 85–168.

French, J. W., Ekstrom, R. B., and Price, L. A. 1963. *Manual for a Kit of Reference Tests for Cognitive Factors.* Princeton N.J.; Educational Testing Service.

Gentner, D., and Stevens, A. L. 1983. *Mental Models.* Hillsdale, N.J.: Lawrence Erlbaum Associates.

Hegarty, M. (Forthcoming). The Mechanics of Comprehension and Comprehension of Mechanics. In *Eye Movements and Visual Cognition: Scene Perception and Reading* , ed. K. Rayner. New York: Springer Verlag.

Hegarty, M. and Just, M. A. 1991. Constructing Mental Models of Machines from Text and Diagrams. Unpublished.

Hegarty, M., Just, M. A. and Morrison, I. M. 1988. Mental Models of Mechanical Systems: Individual Differences in Qualitative and Quantitative Reasoning. *Cognitive Psychology* 20: 191–236.

Just, M. A., and Carpenter, P. A. 1976. Eye Fixations and Cognitive Processes. *Cognitive Psychology* 8: 441–480.

Just, M. A., and Carpenter, P. A. 1985. Cognitive Coordinate Systems: Accounts of Mental Rotation and Individual Differences in Spatial Ability. *Psychological Review* 92: 137–172.

Just, M. A., and Carpenter, P. A. 1987. *The Psychology of Reading and Language Comprehension.* Newton, Mass.: Allyn and Bacon.

Kaiser, M. K., Proffitt, D. R., and McCloskey, M. 1985. The Development of Beliefs about Falling Objects. *Perception and Psychophysics* 38 (6): 533–539.

Kieras, D. E. and Bovair, S. 1984. The Role of a Mental Model in Learning to Operate a Device. *Cognitive Science* 8: 255–273.

Kieras, D. E. 1984. A Simulation Model for Procedural Inference from a Mental Model for a Simple Device. Technical Report No. 15, UARZ/DP/TR–84/ONR–15, Department of Psychology, University of Arizona.

Kieras, D. E. 1990. The Role of Cognitive Simulation Models in The Development of Advanced Training and Testing Systems. In *Diagnostic Monitoring of Skill and Knowledge Acquisition,* ed. N. Frederiksen, R. Glaser, A. Lesgold, and M. G. Shafto, 51–73. Hillsdale, N.J.: Lawrence Erlbaum Associates.

Kosslyn, S. M. 1980. *Image and Mind.* Cambridge, Mass.: Harvard University Press.

Larkin, J. H., and Simon, H. A. 1987. Why a Diagram Is (Sometimes) Worth Ten Thousand Words. *Cognitive Science* 11: 65–99.

Loftus, G. R. 1972. Eye Fixations and Recognition Memory for Pictures. *Cognitive Psychology* 3: 525–551.

Loftus, G. R. and Mackworth, N. H. 1978. Cognitive Determinants of Fixation Location During Picture Viewing. *Journal of Experimental Psychology: Human Perception and Performance* 4: 565–572.

McCloskey, M. 1983. Intuitive Physics. *Scientific American* 248(4): 122–130.

Mayer, R. E. 1989. Models for Understanding. *Review of Educational Research* 59: 43–64.

Miller, G. A. 1956. The Magical Number Seven, Plus Or Minus Two: Some Limits On Our Capacity for Processing Information. *Psychological Review* 63: 81–97.

Newell, A., and Simon, H. 1972. *Human Problem Solving.* Englewood Cliffs, N.J.: Prentice-Hall.

Rayner, K. and Pollatsek, A. 1989. *The Psychology of Reading.* Englewood Cliffs, N.J.: Prentice-Hall.

Reiger, C. and Grinberg, M. 1977. The Declarative Representation and Procedural Simulation of Causality in Physical Mechanisms. In Proceedings of the Fifth International Joint Conference on Artificial Intelligence. San Francisco: Morgan Kaufmann.

Rips, L. J. 1986. Mental muddles. In *Problems in the Representation of Knowledge and Belief,* ed. M. Brand and R. M. Harnish. Tucson Ariz.: University of Arizona Press.

Rouse, W. B. and Morris, N. M. 1986. On Looking Into the Black Box: Prospects and Limits in the Search for Mental Models. *Psychological Bulletin* 100(3): 349–363.

Shepard, R. N., 1978. Externalization of Mental Images and the Act of Creation. In *Visual Learning, Thinking and Communication,* ed. B. S. Randhava and W. E. Coffman, 33–189. New York: Academic Press.

Shepard, R. N. and Cooper, L A. 1982. *Mental Images and Their Transformations.* Cambridge, Mass.: The MIT Press.

Shepard, R. N. and Feng, C. 1972. A Chronometric Study of Mental Paper Folding. *Cognitive Psychology* 3: 228–243.

Spoehr, K. T. and Horvath, J. A. 1989. Running a Mental Model: Evidence from Reaction Time Studies. Presented at the Conference of the Psychonomic Society, Atlanta, Georgia.

Williams, M. D., Hollan, J. D., and Stevens, A. L. 1983. Human Reasoning About a Simple Physical System. In *Mental Models,* ed. D. Gentner and A. L. Stevens. Hillsdale N.J.: Lawrence Erlbaum Associates.

17 Abstract Planning and Perceptual Chunks

Kenneth R. Koedinger & John R. Anderson
Carnegie Mellon University

17.1 Introduction

In this chapter, we present a new model of skilled performance in geometry proof problem solving called the Diagram Configuration model (DC). While previous models plan proofs in a step-by-step fashion, we observed that experts plan at a more abstract level—they focus on the key steps and skip the less important ones. DC models this abstract planning behavior by parsing geometry problem diagrams into perceptual chunks, called diagram configurations, which cue relevant schematic knowledge. We provide verbal protocol evidence that DC's schemas correspond with the step-skipping inferences experts make in their initial planning. We compare DC with other models of geometry expertise and then, in the final section, we discuss more general implications of our research. DC's reasoning has important similarities with Larkin's display-based reasoning approach and Johnson-Laird's mental model approach. DC's perceptually-based schemas are a step towards a unified explanation of 1) experts' superior problem solving effectiveness, 2) experts' superior problem-state memory, and 3) experts' ability, in certain domains, to solve relatively simple problems by pure forward inferencing. We also argue that the particular and efficient knowledge organization of DC challenges current theories of skill acquisition as it presents an end-state of learning that is difficult to explain within such theories. Finally, we discuss the implications of DC for geometry instruction.

Detailed study of successful performance in difficult task domains can provide a strong basis for understanding the processes of problem solving and the nature of thought in general. To become an expert in a difficult field calls upon the full adaptive and flexible nature of human intelligence. Characterizing the adaptive processes that bring about the acquisition of expertise is an important goal of cognitive science and much progress has been made in creating general mechanisms of skill acquisition and learning (Anderson 1983; Newell 1990; Holland, et. al. 1986). However, progress in these areas is limited by the depth and accuracy of theories of expertise. Some of our efforts towards developing a general mechanism that models human learning may be wasted if we do not have an accurate and detailed understanding of the end-state such mechanisms are designed to reach.

Newell and Simon (1972) pioneered the use of verbal protocol analysis and computer simulation as complementary tools for the study of successful performance in difficult task domains and the identification of the mechanisms behind such performance. The analysis of verbal reports given by subjects as they solve problems can provide both initial ideas for proposing a workable mechanism and empirical evidence to support one. In a complementary way, computer simulation provides a test of both the coherence and sufficiency of a proposed mechanism.

In this chapter we present verbal report data and a computer simulation of geometry proof problem solving. This domain is a difficult one for human problem solvers and has been studied by a number of cognitive science researchers (Gelernter 1963; Nevins, 1975; Greeno 1978; Anderson, et. al. 1981). We were motivated to take another look at this domain by the observation that skilled problem solvers are able to focus on key problem solving steps and skip minor ones in the process of generating a solution plan. We found a surprising regularity in the kinds of steps expert subjects skipped and built a computer model, called DC, to account for this regularity.

17.2 The Execution Space of Geometry

Geometry proof problem solving is hard. For a typical geometry proof, the search space of possible geometry rule applications (i.e., theorems, definitions, and postulates) is quite large. Problem 7 in Figure 17.1 is a typical high school geometry proof problem. At the point in the high school curriculum where this problem is introduced there are 45 possible inferences that can be made from the givens of this problem, from these inferences another 563 inference can be made, from these greater than 100,000 can be made.

While it is true, as Newell and Simon (1972) pointed out, that there are multiple possible problem spaces for any problem, there is one problem space for geometry which is perhaps the most natural extension of the way geometry is typically taught. This problem space is the one analyzed above and has the definitions, postulates, and theorems of ge-

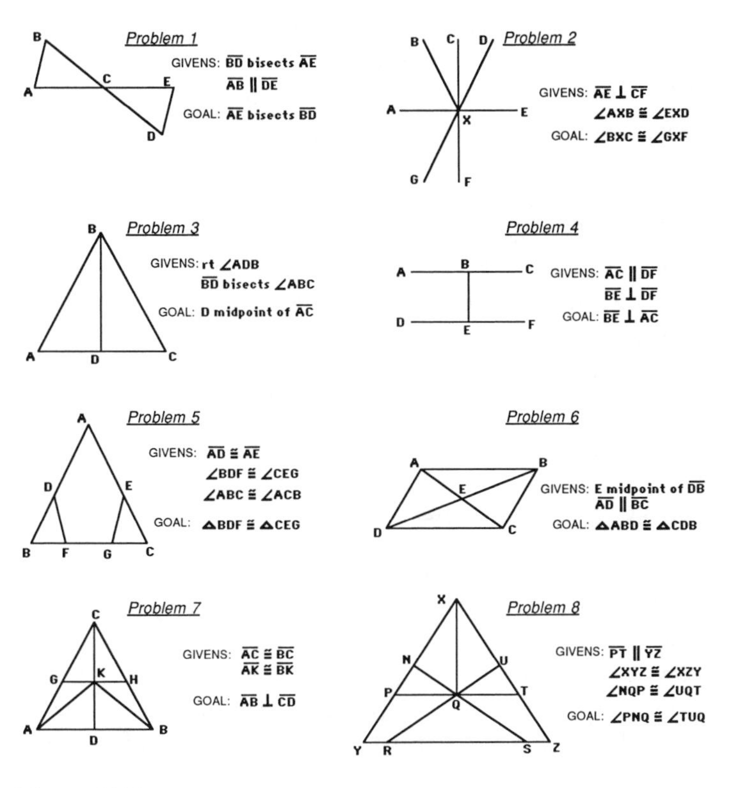

Figure 17.1
Geometry Problems Given to Subjects and Solved by DC.

ometry as operators. We call it the *execution space* of geometry because the operators correspond with the steps that a problem solver writes down in the solution of a problem.

As illustrated above, the geometry execution space is enormous. In the DC model described below, we achieve search control by initially planning a solution sketch in a problem space that is more abstract, i.e., more compact, than the execution space. In contrast, the traditional approach has been to look for better search strategies and heuristics to use within the execution space. Gelernter's (1963) geometry theorem proving machine used a backward search strategy in the execution space and used the diagram as a pruning heuristic. More recently, the second author and colleagues (Anderson, Boyle and Yost, 1985) built a geometry expert system as a cognitive model of students and a component of an intelligent tutoring system. The Geometry Tutor expert (GTE) used an opportunistic or best-first bidirectional search strategy in the execution space and used various contextual features as heuristics for predicting the relevance of an operator. (We review these systems and a couple others in Section 17.6.) While GTE provided a reasonably good model of students, as evidenced by the success of the Geometry Tutor (Anderson, Boyle, Corbett and Lewis 1990), we found that the mode of attack of human experts was distinctly different from that of GTE. It seemed important to be able to characterize this expertise both as a goal in and of itself and for pedagogical purposes.

17.3 Expert Human Problem Solving

17.3.1 Step Skipping and Abstract Planning

One feature that distinguishes geometry experts is that they do not make all the steps of inference that students do while developing a solution plan. Consider the protocol in Table 17.1 of an expert (subject R) solving problem 3 shown in Figure 17.1. The top of the table contains the protocol and bottom indicates our coding of the subject's actions.

This expert had a reliable solution sketch for this problem in 13 seconds at the point where he said "we're done" (emphasis ours). He plans this solution sketch without looking at the goal statement (more on this curious behavior in Section 17.5.3) and in the remainder of the protocol he elaborates the solution sketch, reads the goal statement, and explains how it is proven. His words "we're done" indicate his realization that the two triangles ABD and CBD are congruent and that therefore he knows everything about the whole problem—as he explains later: "we can determine anything from there in terms of corresponding parts".

Figure 17.2 shows the solution to the problem in a proof tree notation. Apart from the givens and goal, the statements which the expert mentioned while solving this problem are numbered in Figure 17.2 while the skipped steps are circled. Assuming this expert's verbalizations accurately reflect his working memory states (Ericsson and Simon 1984), we conclude that the expert only makes certain key inferences in his search for a solution while skipping other, apparently minor inferences.

Table 17.1
A Verbal Protocol for a Subject Solving Problem 3.

B1:	We're given a right angle–this is a right angle
B2:	perpendicular on both sides [makes perpendicular]
B3:	BD bisects angle ABC [marks angles ABD and CBD]
B4:	and *we're done*
B5:	We know that this is a reflexive [marks line BD],
B6:	we know that we have congruent triangles; we can determine anything from there in terms of corresponding parts
B7:	and that's what this [looking at the goal statement for the first time] is going to mean ... that these are congruent [marks segments AD and DC as equal on the diagram].
	Planning Phase
B1:	Reading given: $rt\angle ADB$
B2:	Inference step 1: $AC \perp BD$
B3:	Reading given: BD *bisects* $\angle ABC$
B4:	Inference step 2:$\triangle ABD \cong \triangle CBD$
	Execution Phase
B5-7:	In this phase, the subject refines and explains his solution to the experimenter.

Abstraction. In the terminology of the problem solving literature, it seemed clear that experts were initially planning their proof in an *abstract problem solving space* (Newell and Simon 1972; Sacerdoti 1974; Unruh, et. al. 1987). They were ignoring certain distinctions such as the distinction between congruence and equality and they were skipping over certain kinds of inferences, particularly the algebraic inferences. It turns out that ignoring the algebraic inferences considerably reduces the size of the search space. We establish this fact in the analysis of the model below by comparing the size of the execution space for problem 7 with and without the algebraic inferences (see section 17.5.1).

We distinguish two types of abstract planning, risky and safe. *Risky abstraction* is a type of abstraction where details can be ignored that are sometimes critical to arriving at a correct solution. Newell and Simon (1972) showed that during planning, subjects solving logic problems

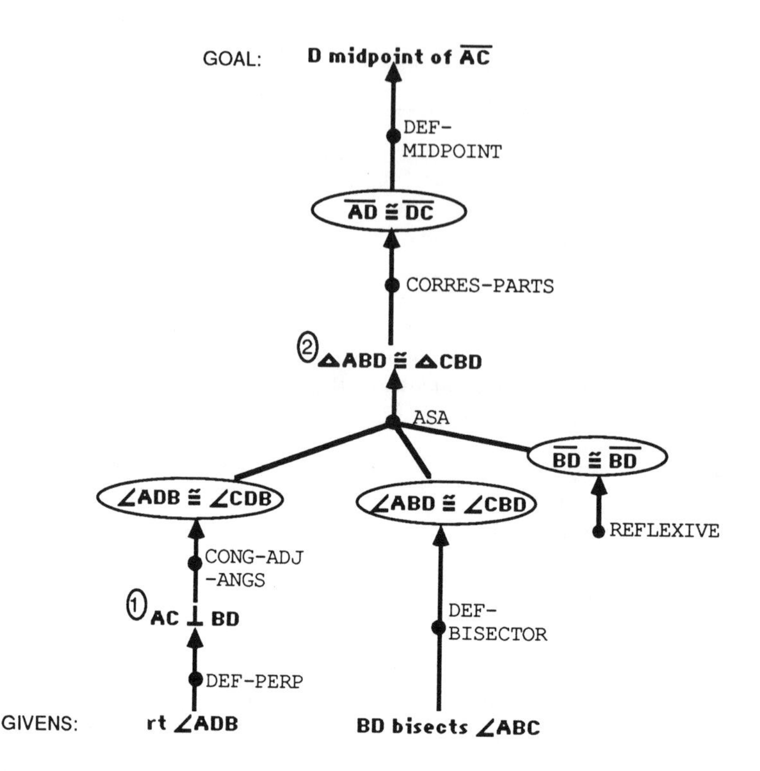

Figure 17.2
The Final Solution for Problem 3. The givens of the problem are at the bottom and the goal is at the top. The lines represent inferences with the conclusion at the arrow head, the premises at the tails, and the justifying geometry rule at the dot in between. The statements subject R mentioned during planning (see Table 17.1) are numbered while the ones he skipped are circled.

would often ignore certain aspects of the expressions they were working with. This abstraction was often very effective in guiding their problem solving search. However, sometimes subjects failed to successfully refine an abstract plan because one of the details ignored in the abstraction process turned out to be critical.

A *safe abstraction* only ignores irrelevant details, i.e., details which only discriminate between objects that are functionally equivalent with respect to the problem solving task. For example, in ignoring the details that distinguish between congruence statements, e.g., AB $\cong$ CD, and measure equality statements, e.g., mAB = mCD, geometry problem solvers are performing a safe abstraction since these statements are equivalent with respect to making proof inferences. Any inference that can be made from one can be made from the other.

Macro-Operators. In addition to performing useful abstractions, expert problem solvers have been characterized by the fact that they often collapse multiple problem solving steps into a single step (Anderson 1983; Larkin, et. al. 1980b). In the field of problem solving this is known as the formation of macro-operators (Nilsson 1972; Korf 1985). Macro-operators are the chunking together of a sequence of operators which are often used consecutively to achieve a particular goal. Although geometry experts appear to have certain macro-operators, these operators are not just arbitrary compositions of geometry rules which can be used in sequence. Rather, there is a regularity in the kinds of macro-operators experts have. Not only does the same expert skip the same kinds of steps on different occasions, but different experts appear to skip the same kinds of steps in similar situations.

In summary, we found that experts were not planning solutions in the execution space as previous models have. In addition, it appeared that expert's planning space could not be accounted for by a straightforward application of standard learning mechanisms to the execution space. Typical abstraction methods lead to risky abstractions, while experts' abstractions were safe. Typical macro-operator learning methods do not predict the kind of regularity in step-skipping that we found of the experts. Thus, we were led to search for a new problem space for geometry theorem proving—one that was a safe abstraction of the execution space and that left out the same kind of steps as the experts did.

17.3.2 Use of the Diagram

Besides not working in the execution space, experts' inference making was largely tied to the diagram. We found that the regularity in experts' step-skipping can be captured by knowledge structures that are cued by images in the problem diagram. In contrast, execution space inferences are cued off the known and desired statements in the problem. Larkin and Simon (1987) suggest two reasons why diagrammatic representations might be critical to problem solving in domains like geometry. First, one can use *locality* of objects in the diagram to direct inference and second, perceptual inferences can be made more easily than symbolic inferences.

Let us consider their point about locality first. A familiar strategy of high school geometry students is to record proof steps by marking the problem diagram as an alternative to writing them down in statement notation. Such an annotated diagram aids students in holding together information that they need to make further inferences. (This is even true if they do not explicitly mark the diagram as long as they think in terms of it.) In contrast, information within a list of written statements may be visually separated and require search to identify. For instance, to use the side-angle-side rule for inferring triangle congruence a problem solver must locate three congruence relationships—two between corresponding sides of the triangles and one between corresponding angles. In searching a list of statements for these three relationships, one might need to consider numerous possible combinations of three statements that exist in the list. However, if these relationships are marked on a diagram, one can quickly identify them since the side-angle-side configuration comes together in each triangle at a single vertex. In other words, related information is often easier to find in a diagram because it is typically in the same locality whereas the same information may be separated in a list of statements. This is the *locality feature* of diagrams.

The example above illustrates the role of the diagram in aiding knowledge search—i.e., the search for applicable knowledge. The geometry diagram can also be used to aid problem search—i.e., the search for a problem solution.[1] The idea is that images in the diagram can be used to cue chunks of knowledge which serve as operators in an abstract planning space. The notion that external representations can play a major role in guiding problem solving is the central notion of Larkin's display-based reasoning approach (Larkin 1988). Our approach elaborates on this one by showing how the organization of an external representation can be used to cue abstract planning operators. These abstract operators reduce problem search by packing many execution steps into a single inference.

Larkin and Simon's second point, that diagrams allow easy perceptual inferences to replace hard symbolic ones, is based on an assumption that perceptual inferences are generally easier than symbolic inferences.

[1]See chapter 2 in Newell (1990) for more discussion on the distinction between knowledge search and problem search.

While we agree with this assumption, we feel it is unlikely that perceptual inferences are somehow inherently easier (except in terms of the locality feature noted above). Rather, it is possible that perceptual inferences appear easier because, in general, they have been much more highly practiced than symbolic inferences. Nevertheless, since it is likely that students of geometry have had more prior experience with geometric images than with formal notations and since diagrams typically have the locality feature, students are likely to find perceptual inferences in this domain easier.

17.4 The Diagram Configuration Model

Based on our observations of experts, we tried to design a system for geometry theorem proving that would be both more powerful and more like human experts than previous systems. The model we came up with, the Diagram Configuration model (DC), has one major knowledge structure, diagram configuration schemas, and three major processes: diagram parsing, statement encoding, and schema search. Section 17.4.1 describes DC's diagram configuration schemas, while section 17.4.2 describes DC's processing components. Section 17.4.3 describes how DC uses a special class of diagram configuration schemas to avoid difficult algebra sub-proofs.

17.4.1 Diagram Configuration Schemas

The core idea of the DC model is that experts have their knowledge organized according to diagrammatic schemas which we call *diagram configuration schemas.* These are clusters of geometry facts that are associated with a single prototypical geometric image. Figures 17.3 and 17.4 show two diagram configuration schemas.

The *whole-statement* and *part-statements* attributes of a schema store the facts which are associated with the geometric image stored in the *configuration* attribute. The configuration is a prototypical configuration of points and lines which is commonly a part of geometry diagrams. In Figures 17.3 and 17.4, the configuration on the left is a prototype for any set of lines that form two triangles with a side in common. The whole-statement is the geometry statement which refers to the configuration as a whole. The part-statements refer to relationships among the

CONGRUENT-TRIANGLES-SHARED-SIDE :

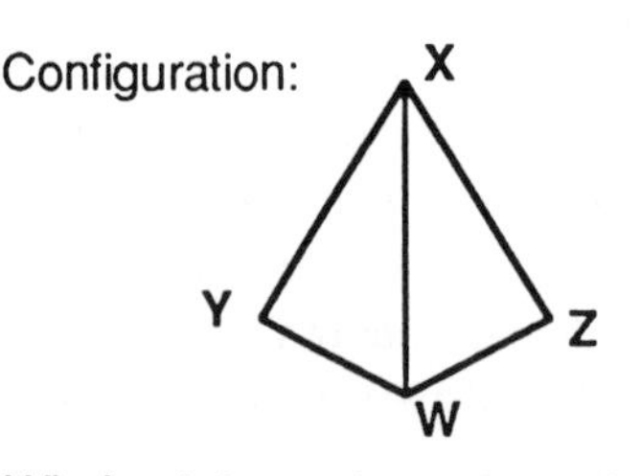

Whole-statement: $\triangle XYW \cong \triangle XZW$

Part-statements:
1. $\overline{XY} = \overline{XZ}$
2. $\overline{YW} = \overline{ZW}$
3. $\angle Y = \angle Z$
4. $\angle YXW = \angle ZXW$
5. $\angle XWY = \angle XWZ$

Ways-to-prove: {1 2} {1 4} {2 5}
{4 5} {3 4} {3 5}

Figure 17.3
First of Two Examples of Diagram Configuration Schemas. The numbers in the ways-to-prove indicate part-statements.

parts of the configuration. The whole-statement of the CONGRUENT-TRIANGLES-SHARED-SIDE schema refers to the two triangles involved while the part-statements refer to the corresponding sides and angles of these triangles. The *ways-to-prove* are used to determine whether inferences can be made about a configuration. They indicate subsets of the part-statements which are sufficient to prove the whole-statement and all of the part-statements. For example, the first way-to-prove of the CONGRUENT-TRIANGLES-SHARED-SIDE schema, {1 2}, indicates that if the part-statements AB = AC and BD = CD have been proven, the schema can be proven—i.e., all the other statements of the schema can be proven.

Our basic proposal is that planning is done in terms of these schemas rather than the statements of geometry. The problem solver tries to establish that various schemas are true of the diagram. Establishing one schema may enable establishing another. Because there are a small

PERPENDICULAR-ADJACENT-ANGLES:

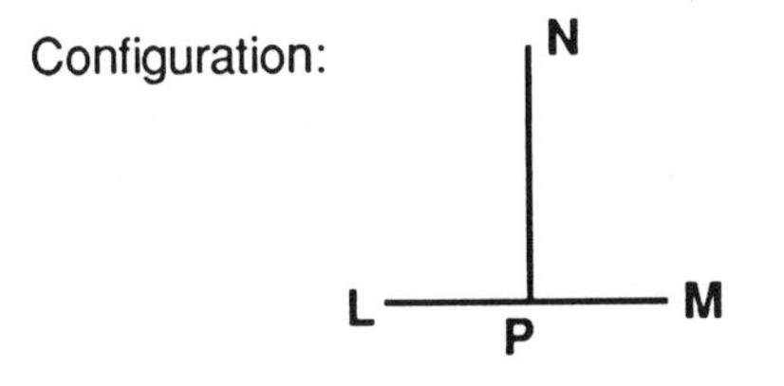

Whole-statement: $\overline{LM} \perp \overline{NP}$

Part-statements: 1. rt $\angle LPN$
2. rt $\angle MPN$
3. $\angle LPN = \angle MPN$

Ways-to-prove: {1} {2} {3}

Figure 17.4
Second of Two Examples of Diagram Configuration Schemas. The numbers in the ways-to-prove indicate part-statements.

number of schemas possible for any particular problem diagram, the search space of schemas is much smaller than the execution space.

Consider problem 3 and the expert protocol in Table 17.1. In the planning phase, the subject made four verbalizations. Of these four verbalizations, two indicate his reading and encoding of the given statements and two indicate inferences. Essentially, the subject solved the problem in two steps. In contrast, the complete execution space solution (see Figure 17.2) requires seven geometry rule applications. In other words, a problem solver who was planning in the execution space would take at least seven steps to solve this problem. DC's solution to this problem, like the subject's, is much shorter—it involves only two schemas. An instance of the PERPENDICULAR-ADJACENT-ANGLES schema can be established from the givens of the problem, while an instance of the TRIANGLE-CONGRUENCE-SHARED-SIDE schema can be established as a result. We now describe the processes DC uses to recognize and establish schemas.

17.4.2 DC's Processing Components

DC has three major processing stages:

1. *Diagram parsing* in which it identifies familiar configurations in the problem diagram and instantiates the corresponding schemas,
2. *Statement encoding* in which it comprehends given and goal statements by canonically representing them as part-statements and
3. *Schema search* in which it iteratively applies schemas in forward or backward inferences until a link between the given and goal statements is found.

Human experts integrate these processes so that they do not occur in any fixed order except to the extent that some statement encoding and diagram parsing has to be done before any schema search can begin. However, in the computer simulation each process is done to completion before the next begins. We implemented these processes as separate stages so that we could independently evaluate the role each has in reducing search relative to planning in the execution space. In turns out the diagram parsing process plays a major role as we describe below.

Diagram Parsing and Schema Instantiation. Diagram parsing is the process of recognizing configurations in geometry diagrams and instantiating the corresponding schemas. Diagram parsing consists of both a low-level component which recognizes simple geometric objects and a higher level inductive component which hypothesizes plausible diagram configurations.

The DC simulation starts with a very simple point and line representation of a problem diagram. From this representation it must recognize line segments, angles, and triangles and construct an internal representation of each. In addition, the algorithm records approximate size measures of the segments and angles it identifies.

Using the information created by this low-level object recognition process, DC looks for instances of abstract configurations. Figures 17.5 and 17.6 illustrate the diagram configurations for proof problems in a typical course up to and including the topic of triangle congruence. In some cases an image in a problem diagram may appear to be an instance of a known diagram configuration, but not actually be an instance because it is not properly constrained by the givens of a problem. On the other

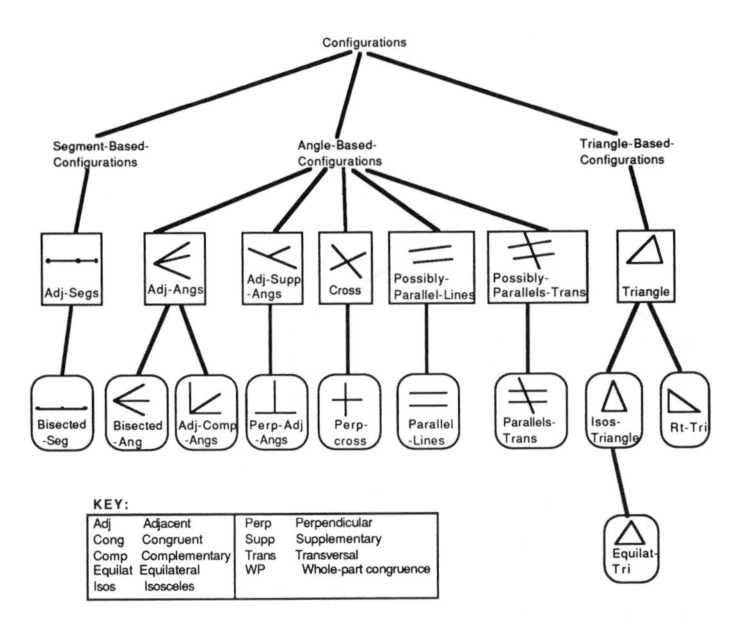

Figure 17.5
The Diagram Configurations for Geometry Up to and Including the Topic of Triangle Congruence. The configurations in rectangles are basic configurations which can be recognized immediately in problem diagrams. The other configurations are specializations of these in which certain relationships appear to hold among the parts of the configuration.

hand, some configurations do not need to be constrained by the problem givens to be a diagram configuration instance. These are called *basic configurations* and appear in the square cornered boxes in Figure 17.5.[2]

DC uses the low-level object information to recognize instances of the basic configurations. The other configurations are either specializations of the basic ones (and thus are attached below them in Figure 17.5) or specializations of pairs of basic configurations (see Figure 17.6). To recognize possible specializations, DC uses the segment and angle size approximations to check whether any of the basic configurations have the necessary properties to be specialized. For example, to recognize

[2]As you might notice from looking at some of the basic configurations, DC assumes that points which appear collinear (on the same line) in a problem diagram actually are collinear. This assumption is commonly made in high school classrooms and we told our subjects they could make it in the problems we gave them.

the ISOSCELES-TRIANGLE configuration, DC checks the triangles it has identified to see if any have two equal sides.

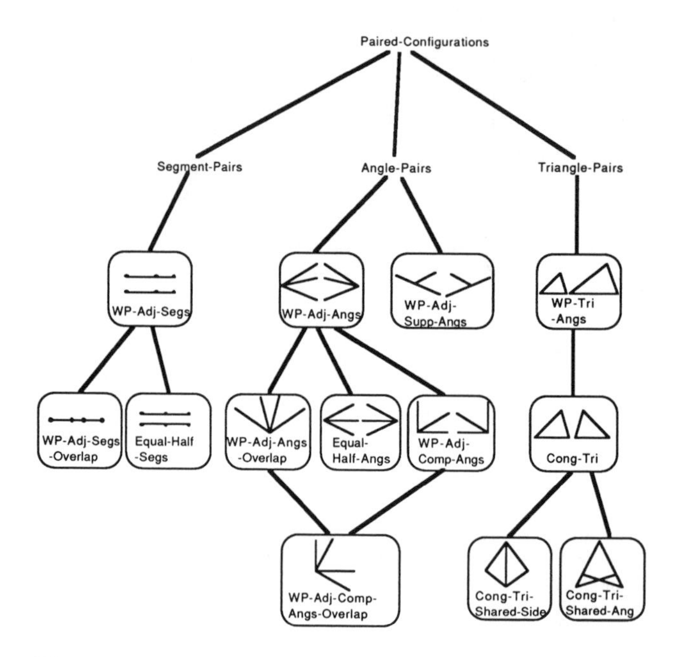

Figure 17.6
The Pairing of Basic Configurations Where Relationships Hold Among the Corresponding Parts of the Configurations Paired.

DC's diagram parsing algorithm corresponds with a very powerful visual process in humans. We make no claims that the internals of this algorithm match the internals of the corresponding human process. For instance, while it is quite likely that human perceptual processes make extensive use of symmetry in recognizing geometric images, DC makes no use of symmetry. We do claim that human experts are capable of recognizing these configurations and make extensive use of this ability in solving proof problems.

The final result of diagram parsing is a network of instantiated schemas and part-statements. Figure 17.7 illustrates this network for problem 3.

It is interesting to note that although no problem solving search is done in this first stage, in effect, most of the problem solving work is done here. The resulting network is finite and usually quite small. Searching it is fairly trivial.

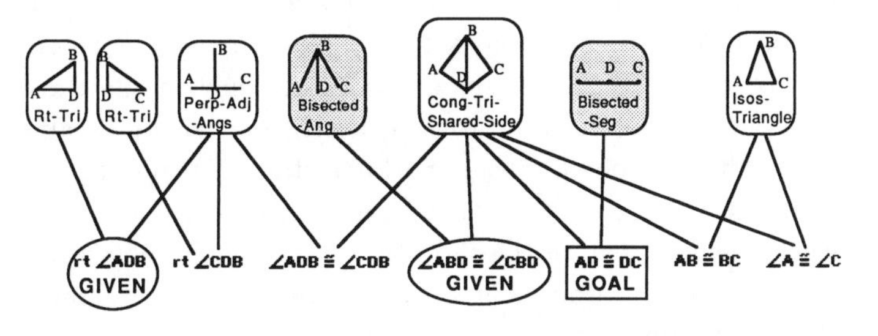

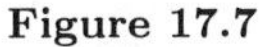
Figure 17.7
DC's Solution Space for Problem 3. The schemas DC recognizes during diagram parsing are shown in the boxes. The lines indicate the part-statements of these schemas. A solution is achieved by finding a path from the givens to the goal satisfying the constraints of the ways-to-prove slot of the schemas used.

Statement Encoding. After parsing the diagram in terms of diagram configurations, DC reads the problem given and goal statements. Statement encoding corresponds to problem solvers' comprehension of the meaning of given/goal statements. We claim that problem solvers comprehend given/goal statements in terms of part-statements. When a given/goal statement is already a part-statement, DC encodes it directly by appropriately tagging the part-statement as either "known" or "desired." However, there are two other possibilities.

First, if the given/goal statement is one of a number of alternative ways of expressing the same part-statement, it is encoded in terms of a single abstract or canonical form. For example, measure equality and congruence, as in mAB = mBC and AB $\cong$ BC, are encoded as the same part-statement. Using this abstract representation, DC avoids inferences, required in the execution space, that establish the logical equivalence of two alternative expression of the same fact.

Second, if the given/goal statement is the whole-statement of a schema, it is encoded by appropriately tagging all of the part-statements of that schema as "known" in the case of a given or "desired" in the case of a goal. For example, the second given of problem 3,BD bisects ∠ABC, is the whole-statement of a BISECTED-ANGLE schema. DC encodes it by establishing its only part-statement $\angle$ABD = $\angle$CBD as known (see Figure 17.7). Similarly, DC encodes the goal statement of problem 3 by tagging the part-statement AD = CD as desired.

Schema Search. Based on its parsing of the diagram, DC identifies a set of diagram configuration schemas which are possibly true of the problem. Its agenda then becomes to establish enough of these schemas as true so that the goal statement is established in the process. Typically, one of the ways-to-prove of a schema can be established directly from the encoded givens. So for instance, in problem 3 the PERPENDICULAR-ADJACENT-ANGLES schema can be concluded immediately. Other schemas require that additional statements be established about the diagram in order that they may be concluded. Thus, it was only after the PERPENDICULAR-ADJACENT-ANGLES schema is established in the example problem that the TRIANGLE-CONGRUENCE-SHARED-SIDE schema can be established. At this level, DC is performing a search through the space defined by its diagram schemas much like the search GTE and other previous models perform through the execution space as defined by the rules of inference of geometry. We will refer to the space DC works in as the *diagram configuration space.*

As in the execution space, a search strategy and heuristics can be employed to guide search in the diagram configuration space. At any point DC has a number of schemas which it might apply. The system has a selection heuristic to chose among these schemas. Although a more powerful heuristic could be used, we have found that because the diagram configuration space is so small, a simple heuristic is sufficient. In addition, this heuristic is consistent with our subjects who do not seem to spend much time evaluating alternatives, but rather forge ahead with the first reasonable inference that occurs to them.

Essentially, DC's selection heuristic implements a bidirectional depth first search. A schema is *applicable* if there are proven part-statements which satisfy one of the schema's ways-to-prove. It is *desired* if its whole-statement or one its part-statements are goals of backward reasoning. If a schema is both applicable and desired, then DC selects it. Otherwise, DC either makes a forward inference by selecting any applicable schema or makes a backward inference by selecting any desired schema which is one statement away from satisfying ones of its ways-to-prove.

The selection heuristic is made more efficient by only considering schemas which a quick estimate determines are potentially applicable. A schema is potentially applicable when the number of its part-statements which are proven is equal or greater than the size of the smallest way-to-prove. This estimate of applicability is much quicker to compute than checking all the ways-to-prove and it eliminates from consideration schemas which are clearly not applicable at the current moment. It also leads to an interesting prediction. Since the heuristic only estimates whether a schema is applicable, it is possible that a schema will be selected even though it is not applicable (and not desired). For example, a TRIANGLE-CONGRUENCE-SHARED-SIDE schema may be selected when two of its part-statements are known even though these part-statements do not make up a way-to-prove (e.g., because they form the insufficient angle-side-side combination). More than once we observed subjects doing just this, considering whether two triangles are congruent because they had the right number of statements but failing because they did not have the right combination of statements. In Section 17.5.2, we relate this phenomenon to an "indefinite subgoaling" phenomenon identified by Greeno (1976).

17.4.3 Avoiding Algebra in the Diagram Configuration Space

One of the places where the Geometry tutor expert (GTE) gets bogged down while attempting difficult problems is in the fruitless application of algebra inferences. Algebra expressions can be combined and manipulated in infinite variety and as a result, algebra inferences often lead problem solvers into black holes in the search space from which they may never return (see the analysis in Section 17.5.1). Thus, it is worth discussing how DC avoids the black hole of algebra.

DC avoids the algebra sub-space by having schemas which abstract away from algebra—in other words, these schemas are essentially macro-operators that make the same conclusions in one step that would require many steps to do by algebra.[3] These schemas are not ad hoc additions to remedy the difficulty with algebra sub-proofs. They correspond with

[3]While geometry textbooks have lots of theorems to skip commonly occurring steps, they do not have any theorems equivalent to the algebra schemas we are proposing (at least none of the textbooks we've seen do). We can think of two possible reasons for why they are absent. First, the utility of such theorems has been overlooked by textbook writers. We doubt that this first reason is right. Second, since these theorems are dependent on information which is implicit in the diagram but is not explicit in formal statements, they are left out because it is difficult to express them in geometry formalism.

particular geometric images and are formally no different than other diagram configuration schemas. They are instantiated as a result of diagram parsing and can be used when needed in place of difficult algebra sub-proofs. Essentially, these schemas provide a way to recognize when algebra is needed and when it is not needed. GTE does not have such a capability.

A single type of algebra schema handles most of the algebraic inferences. We call these schemas WHOLE-PART congruence schemas and they correspond with the configurations in Figure 17.6 that begin with WP. Our WHOLE-PART schemas are essentially the same as the WHOLE/PART schemas discussed in Anderson, Greeno, Kline and Neves (1981) and Greeno (1983).

A great variety of WHOLE-PART schemas can be formed by pairing any two component configurations which have corresponding parts (see Figure 17.6). However, it would be misleading to suggest that all algebra sub-proofs can be solved using some WHOLE-PART schema. For example, the geometric proof of the Pythagorean theorem requires an algebra sub-proof involving multiplication and squaring which are outside the scope of WHOLE-PART schemas. Nevertheless, the vast majority of problems in a high school curriculum that require algebra sub-proofs fall within the scope of WHOLE-PART schemas.

17.5 Evaluation of the DC Model

The purpose of this section is to discuss the strengths and limitations of the DC model. First, we describe a formal analysis of relative size of the execution space and the diagram configuration space to argue for the computational efficiency of DC. Second, we show how the DC model captures the regularity in expert step-skipping that is contrary to straight-forward abstraction and macro-operator learning approaches. Third, we provide protocol evidence for a forward reasoning preference displayed by experts on easier problems. Finally, we discuss some of the limitations of the DC model, in particular, we try to identify the task situations which stretch or break the model.

17.5.1 A Combinatoric Analysis

Comparing the problem solving effectiveness of DC with other models of geometry theorem proving is complicated by the fact that there are are multiple sources of intelligence in these models. In particular, the most important factors are 1) the problem space representation and 2) the search heuristics used. In addition to GTE, many previous models (e.g., Gelernter 1963; Goldstein 1973) search in the execution space. Variations in the problem solving effectiveness of these models can be characterized by differences in search heuristics. Since DC uses a different problem space as well as different heuristics, the task of comparison is complicated. A more tractable task is to compare the problem space representations independent of heuristics. Since search performance could be improved in both spaces by adding heuristics, an analysis of the size of the two spaces should approximate the relative effectiveness of models based on these spaces.

Method of Analysis. The relative size of the execution and diagram configuration spaces was measured by comparing the "bushiness" of a brute force forward search in each space on problem 7 in Figure 17.1. The bushiness is measured by counting the number of operators that apply at each successive "ply" of operators. The first ply is all the operators that can apply to the initial state (the givens). The second ply is all the operators that can apply to the collection of known statements created in the first ply. And so forth.

The operators we consider as part of the execution space are a collection of 27 definitions, postulates, and theorems that represent a significant share of the rules in a standard geometry curriculum up to and including rules for proving triangles congruent. To simplify this analysis somewhat some rules concerning complementary and supplementary angles were left out. The operators of the diagram configuration space are diagram configuration schemas that correspond with the same slice of the curriculum (as shown in Figures 17.5 and 17.6).

In addition to performing this analysis on the execution space and diagram configuration space, we also analyzed the size of the execution space when all the algebra and algebra-related operators are eliminated from it. The three algebra rules are the ADDITION-POSTULATE, SUBTRACTION-POSTULATE, SUBSTITUTION. In addition to these, any rules whose conclusions relate angle or segment measures need not be

Table 17.2
The Size of Three Different Problem Spaces on Problem 7. A *ply* is all the operator instantiations that apply to the known statements produced by the previous ply.

	Execution Space	Execution Space without Algebra	Diagram Configuration Space
1st ply	45	14	3
2nd ply	563	1	3
3rd ply	$> 10^5$	3	2
4th ply	$> 10^5$	1	
5th ply	$> 10^5$	2	
6th ply	$> 10^5$	6	
Total	$> 10^5$	27	8

considered since these relationships can only be acted on by algebra rules. This eliminates six more rules: DEF-MIDPOINT, DEF-BETWEENNESS, ANGLE-ADDITION, DEF-RIGHT-ANGLE, DEF-CONGRUENCE, and SUM-TRI-ANGS. We did the same analysis with this reduced rule set.

Results and Discussion. Table 17.2 indicates the results for the analysis. The general results can be summarized as follows. In the execution space, 6 plies of breadth first search are required and more than 10^6 operator applications are investigated. In the execution space without algebra 6 plies are required but only 27 operator applications are investigated. Interestingly, the size of the search space is dramatically decreased if algebra-related rules are not considered. Although this result is revealing, it doesn't suggest that we can just throw out algebra. Many problems require algebra sub-proofs in their solutions and thus, the execution space without algebra is not a workable alternative. However, the analysis indicates that algebra-related inferences can be a major source of combinatoric explosion.

Because of the larger grained operators of the diagram configuration space, only 3 plies of breadth first search and 8 operator applications are required. This space is so much smaller than the execution space that a brute force search of this space can be effective whereas domain specific heuristics are necessary to effectively search the execution space. The diagram configuration space is also significantly smaller than the execution space without algebra indicating its power is not derived solely by the algebra-avoiding WHOLE-PART schemas. In addition, whereas the execution space without algebra cannot solve problems, like problem 5 in Figure 17.1, where algebra is required, DC can solve the majority of these problems.

17.5.2 Accounting for Experts' Step-Skipping Behavior

In the process of planning a solution, our expert subjects made inferences that skipped more than 50 percent of the steps necessary for a complete solution in the execution space. In addition, we found that out subjects were skipping the same kinds of steps. In this section, we show how the diagram configuration space accounts for this regularity in step-skipping behavior.

Experimental Procedure. The data used for this analysis comes from four subjects' (B, K, J and F) verbal reports on one problem and one subject's (R) verbal reports on eight problems. Two of the single-problem subjects (B and K) were mathematics graduate students while the other two (J and F) were researchers on the Geometry tutor project. Subject R is a high school geometry teacher. All protocols were collected using the concurrent protocol methodology of Ericsson and Simon (1984) where subjects are asked to report what they are thinking as they problem solve. The four single-problem subjects were audio-taped as they entered their solutions using the interface of the Geometry tutor, while subject R was video-taped as he made pencil markings on a paper diagram and reported his solution verbally. The record of computer interactions on one hand and the video record of diagram marking and pointing on the other hand helped to resolve ambiguous verbal references like "this segment is equal to this segment."

Method of Protocol Analysis. The protocols were segmented into:

1. *Planning episodes* where subjects made inferences for the first time in the process of developing a proof sketch,
2. *Refinement episodes* where subjects refined their proof sketch by filling in skipped steps, and
3. *Execution episodes* where subjects indicated steps in their final solution.

The execution episodes of the single-problem subjects correspond with the verbalizations they made while entering steps into the Geometry tutor interface. The execution episodes of subject R, on the other hand, correspond with the verbalizations he made while reporting his final proof to the experimenter.

This particular analysis is focussed on the planning episodes. The goal of the data analysis was to identify the steps in a complete execution space solution that were mentioned by the subject during planning.[4] The execution space solution for each subject-problem pair was recorded in a proof tree diagram and each statement that the subject mentioned during planning (except the given and goal statements) was circled on this diagram. Figure 17.2 illustrates the result of this analysis for the protocol of subject R in Table 17.1.

Model Predictions. We derive predictions from DC by assuming that a statement will be mentioned for each schema application. If the schema has a whole-statement, we predict that this statement will tend to be mentioned. If it does not contain a whole-statement, e.g., like the WHOLE-PART schemas, we predict the concluding part-statement will tend to be mentioned. We predict that all other statements will tend to be skipped. This prediction entails a quite simple assumption about the verbalization of problem states, i.e., one verbalization per schema application, however, it provides a good fit to the data. Below we discuss how the the major difference between the predictions and the data might be accounted for by a slightly more complex assumption about verbalization.

Results and Discussion. In the twelve subject-problem pairs, less than half of the intermediate steps were mentioned (37/98) and more were skipped (61/98). The model predicted that 29 steps would be mentioned and 69 skipped. Tables 17.3 and 17.4 show the data for each subject-problem pair and will be discussed below (note that subject R, problem 7 is in both tables). Of the 29 steps that DC predicts will be mentioned, 23 were actually mentioned and only 6 were not. Of the 69 that DC predicts will be skipped, 55 were skipped and only

[4]The complete execution space solution for the single-problem subjects is the one they entered into the Geometry tutor interface. The multiple-problem subject R was not forced to indicate all the details of a complete execution space solution and thus, to decide what execution steps he skipped, we filled in the gaps with the shortest execution space path possible.

Table 17.3
Model-Data Fit for All Subjects Solving the Same Problem.

		Predicted Mention		Predicted Skip	
		Actual	Actual	Actual	Actual
Subject	Problem	Mention	Skip	Mention	Skip
R	7	3	0	3	2
B	7	2	0	1	3
K	7	3	0	1	6
J	7	2	0	1	3
F	7	3	0	3	9
Total		13	2	9	23

14 mentioned. A Chi square test was used to determine whether this distribution could have occurred by chance. The Chi square value ($X^2(1) = 30.3$) indicates it is unlikely that the model's fit to the data is a chance occurrence ($p < .001$). We can take a closer look at the data to see how well the result generalizes across subjects and problems, particularly since the subjects are over represented by subject R and the problems by problem 7.

Table 17.3 shows the data for all five subjects on problem 7 and indicates the model to data fit is not peculiar to subject R. A Chi square test on the column totals yields $X^2(1) = 14.1$, $p<.001$. Table 17.4 shows the data for subject R on eight problems and indicates that the results are not peculiar to problem 7. A Chi square test on the column totals yields $X^2(1) = 22.0$, $p<.001$.

If the model fit perfectly, the totals for columns two and three in the Tables would be zero. The predictions are most deviant from the data in column three—the subjects mentioned fourteen[5] steps that were predicted to be skipped. Eleven of these cases are situations where the subject must use more than one part-statement in order to prove a schema. In such situations, subjects often mention one or more of these part-statements. For example, in planning a solution to problem 3, part-statements $\angle ADB = \angle CDB$ and/or $\angle ABD = \angle CBD$ might be mentioned

[5] Adding the third column totals from Tables 17.3 and 17.4 yields seventeen. However, since subject R, problem 7 appears in both tables, we need to subtract three from seventeen to get the proper overall total of fourteen.

Table 17.4
Model-Data Fit for One Subjects Solving Eight Problems.

		Predicted Mention		Predicted Skip	
		Actual	Actual	Actual	Actual
Subject	Problem	Mention	Skip	Mention	Skip
R	1	1	2	1	1
	2	1	0	2	3
	3	2	0	0	4
	4	1	0	0	5
	5	2	0	0	8
	6	3	0	1	2
	7	3	0	3	2
	8	0	2	1	9
Total		13	4	8	34

because both are needed to prove the TRIANGLE-CONGRUENCE-SHARED-SIDE schema. To account for such situations our simple model of verbalization, namely, "one step mentioned per schema" could be elaborated to predict that extra verbalizations will tend to occur for schemas which require more than one part-statement to be proven. This more complicated model of verbalization would only provide a slightly better match to the data. While the number of misses (column 3) would be reduced by eleven, the number of false alarms (column 2) would be increased by six. The increase in false alarms results from the fact that subjects occasionally skipped part-statements the alternative model of verbalization predicts they should mention.

Other reasons why the predictions do not exactly fit the data include: 1) subjects may fail to mention an inference step for some model-unrelated reason, for example, because they momentarily forgot the experimental instruction to think aloud; 2) subjects, especially teachers, may feel inclined to explain themselves and thus, immediately report intermediate steps that support a leap of inference but were not a part of it; or 3) subjects may be at a different stage of expertise than DC by either a) being behind, having not yet acquired certain configuration schemas, or b) being ahead, having acquired larger configurations than the ones DC uses. A potential instance of (3b) may explain the 2 steps in subject R's solution to problem 8 (see Figure 17.1) that he skipped though we predicted he would mention them (see column two of Table 17.4). In this case, it appeared that the subject used a diagram configuration that combined two of DC's and thus was able to skip extra steps that the current version of DC cannot.

17.5.3 Forward Inferencing and Completion by Exhaustion

Of the eight problems subject R solved, he solved five by a purely forward search (problems 1, 3, 4, 5, 8 in Figure 17.1), one by a forward search that was guided by the goal (problem 2), and two using some backward inferences (problems 6 and 7). By pure forward search, we mean that the problem solver did all of his reasoning without using, and often without reading, the goal statement. The five purely forward solutions were on problems that tended to be easier for him in the sense that he solved them in less time. Only one of these five took longer than any of the other three.

One somewhat peculiar and interesting aspect of subject R's forward reasoning was that on a number of the simpler problems he was able to decide he had finished the proof before reading the goal. For instance, while solving problem 5 he said, "I didn't even look at the goal but I've got it." At some point in solving these problems he knows everything he can about it. As he says while solving problem 3, "we can determine anything from there" (see Table 17.1). It is as if he exhaustively searches all possible forward inferences. But, an exhaustive search of the execution space for a particular problem is unlikely given its typical vast size—particularly since algebra inferences could chain on infinitely. On the other hand, the size of the diagram configuration space for these problems is quite small. In fact, it is bounded by the number of plausible diagram configurations which appear in the problem diagram. Thus, it seems that subject R is able to stop his forward inferencing and conclude he is done when he has proven (or considered) all the plausible configurations.

Larkin, et. al. (1980a) describes physics experts as working forward on simpler problems where they are relatively sure that "solving all possible equations will lead quickly to a *full understanding* of the situation, including the particular quantity they are asked for." This description provides a good characterization of subject R if we simply replace "solving all possible equations" by "applying all possible configuration schemas."

One difference, though, is that physics equations typically correspond with one step in the solution of a physics problem, while diagram configurations correspond with multiple steps in a geometry proof. This is particularly important since the execution space of geometry is so large. Without the chunking provided by diagram configurations, it seems unlikely that a working forward strategy could work on all but the simplest geometry proof problems. Subject R's ability to purely work forward on relatively difficult problems as well as his ability to recognize he is done before reading the problem goal are further evidence for the DC model.

17.5.4 DC's Limitations

We discuss DC's limitations both in terms of how the computer simulation could be extended to be a more complete and accurate model of geometry expertise and in terms of what situations cause trouble for DC's particular problem solving approach. The computer simulation could be made more complete by adding procedures 1) to refine and execute the abstract plans DC currently creates, 2) to determine when and where constructions are necessary, 3) to integrate diagram parsing and schema search, and 4) to draw diagrams from general geometric statements.

Plan Execution. A model of plan execution would involve finding solutions, either by retrieval or by search in the execution space, to the series of short subproblems that result from planning. The majority of these subproblems are only one or two execution steps long. The longer subproblems are algebra proofs of the steps skipped by the WHOLE-PART schemas. These proofs share the same general structure and, for the most part, experts do them by retrieval. Even if the solutions to these subproblems are done from scratch, they are small enough that they can be easily solved by search in the execution space. Adding procedures for doing search in the execution space would have the additional advantage of providing a way to perform certain types of algebra inferences that do not correspond with any of DC's current diagram configurations. These inferences often involve the pairing of two different types of configurations. For example, the RIGHT-TRIANGLE and the ADJACENT-COMPLEMENTARY-ANGLES configurations (see Figure 17.5) can be paired to form an equation between the two non-right angles of the right triangle and the two adjacent complementary angles. We could supplement DC with such kinds of paired-configurations (as in Figure 17.6) or, alternatively, the execution space search component could be used to discover such pairings.

Constructions. The computer simulation could also be made more complete is by adding procedures to perform "constructions," that is, the drawing of auxiliary lines in a problem diagram to provide new inference possibilities. Currently DC is not capable of performing constructions and thus, cannot solve the class of geometry problems which require them. However, we feel that DC is particularly well-suited for adding a construction capability. The major decision points in solving proof problems which may require constructions are:

1. Deciding when a construction might be needed, and
2. Deciding what construction to introduce.

Typically, geometry systems attempt to perform constructions only when other methods appear to be failing. Since the diagram configuration space for any particular problem is relatively small compared to the execution space, DC could quickly and definitively determine when a construction is necessary by exhaustively searching this space. The task of proposing potentially useful constructions could be performed in DC by completing configurations that partially match images in the diagram.

Integrating Diagram Parsing and Schema Search. The computer simulation could be made more efficient and more accurate as a model of human problem solving by integrating the diagram parsing and schema search processes that are currently performed in separate stages. Instead of doing all of the diagram parsing ahead of time, it should only be done on demand when the system is focussed on a part of the diagram which hasn't been parsed. Initially, the encoding of the problem given and/or goal statements could provide a focus of attention on a particular part of the diagram that involves these statements. DC could parse this portion of the diagram in terms of the configurations that appear there. Later, any new part-statements proven via schema search could shift the focus of attention to other parts of the diagram which could be similarly parsed. What remains to be defined is the range of attention, that is, how much of the diagram should be parsed at one time.

Integrating the parsing and schema search would make DC more efficient in cases where the diagram contains over-specialized figures, that is, configurations that look true, but do not follow from the problem givens. In such cases, the current diagram parsing process instantiates configuration schemas that will never be used in problem solving. For example, the line GH in problem 7 turns out to be irrelevant to the solution—there is no given information that bears on it. However, since it appears parallel to line AB, the diagram parser instantiates numerous schemas that correspond with apparent relationships like $\triangle$GCK $\cong$ $\triangle$HCK, ISOS $\triangle$CGH, AB $\parallel$ GH, and GH $\perp$ CD. Without line GH the diagram contains 15 schema instances—with GH it contains 28 more. In the process of schema search these schemas are never used, so the work of instantiating them is wasted. If diagram parsing was done on demand, however, this extra work would not be necessary.

Diagram Drawing. While over-specialized problem diagrams can cause a slight amount of extra work, they do not cause DC to fail on problems. However, if the diagram is improperly drawn, that is, it does not correctly represent the problem givens, the current simulation will not be able to solve the problem. For example, if the line BD in the diagram for problem 3 did not appear perpendicular to the base, DC would not instantiate the PERPENDICULAR-ADJACENT-ANGLES schema and thus, could not solve the problem. One way to extend DC to deal with such diagrams is to allow it to consider configurations beyond those which are apparent in the diagram, like PERPENDICULAR-ADJACENT-ANGLES in the example above. An alternative involves following the standard classroom wisdom which suggests that such diagrams should be redrawn. In particular, we could extend DC to deal with inaccurate diagrams by adding a diagram drawing facility that could draw diagrams to accurately reflect a problem's givens.

17.6 Comparison with Previous Geometry Expert Systems

Geometry theorem proving models have been developed by numerous researchers, most with primarily AI concerns (Gelernter 1963; Goldstein 1973; Nevins 1975) and at least one, besides GTE, based on human data (Greeno 1978). We make comparisons with Gelernter's model because it was the first, Nevin's model because it is the most powerful system we are aware of, and GTE and Greeno's model because they were based on human data.

17.6.1 Gelernter's Geometry Theorem Proving Machine

Gelernter's model was the first AI model of geometry proof problem solving and it worked by performing a backward heuristic search in the execution space. The use of the execution space puts the model at a disadvantage that could only be overcome if the heuristics in Gelernter's model make up for the power gained by the abstract nature of the diagram configuration space. However, this is not the case. The major heuristic of Gelernter's model was to reject backward paths when they became implausible in the diagram. Since only plausible configurations are considered by DC, these backward paths that Gelernter's model rejects are not even in the diagram configuration space for a particular problem. Thus, they are rejected implicitly without ever being considered.

Gelernter made no claims about modeling the inference-by-inference behavior of human problem solvers. And even at a more descriptive level, his model's emphasis on backward reasoning is inconsistent with the opposite forward reasoning emphasis of human geometry experts. In addition to subject R's clear forward reasoning preference, a much larger proportion of the other subjects inferences were forward rather than backward.

17.6.2 Nevins' Model

Nevins (1975) presents a geometry theorem-proving program which is probably more effective and efficient than any other geometry model. His major emphasis was on structuring the problem space of geometry such that a predominantly forward reasoning strategy could be effective. He claimed that human experts engage in much more forward inferencing than backward inferencing. Although he provided no evidence and was probably reacting to the purely backward reasoning strategy of most expert systems at that time, it is interestingly that he made this claim well before empirical evidence came out verifying his intuition in physics problem solving (Larkin, et. al. 1980a), medical diagnosis (Patel and Groen 1986), and now in geometry. The success of forward inferencing in Nevins' model is made possible by the way in which he structured the problem space. Unfortunately, Nevins is not very clear about the exact structure of this problem space. The structure is embedded in the processes he describes.

However, the problem space implicit in his description is much more like the diagram configuration space than the execution space. Because the model only recognizes six predicates (LN=line, PR=parallel, PRP=possibly parallel, RT=right angle, ES=equal segment, and EA = equal angle), it is effectively working in an abstract problem space. It ignores the distinction between congruence and measure equality as well as the distinction between midpoint and bisector predicates and their corresponding equality predicates. The model makes inferences using a number of "paradigms" which are cued by certain features of the diagram and which make conclusions in the form of the predicates. These paradigms share many characteristics with diagram configuration schemas:

- They are cued by the diagram,
- They can make multiple conclusions, and
- They are often macro-operators, i.e., capable of inferences which require multiple steps in the execution space.

However, they are embedded in complex procedures within Nevins' model and are not clearly and uniformly represented like diagram configuration schemas are. Nevins' model does not use appearances in the diagram as DC does to create candidate schemas.

Although he did not present it this way, the success of Nevins' model can be considered further evidence for the computational efficacy of abstract planning in geometry. What the DC model adds is an explicit and uniform representation which 1) makes clear why Nevins' model worked and 2) makes clear how it could be extended, say, by adding diagram configurations for circles. An important side-effect of DC's explicit and uniform representation is that it is teachable (see Section 17.7.4). In addition to its computational advantages, we have provided empirical evidence that human experts solve problems like DC.

17.6.3 The Geometry Tutor Expert System

The Geometry tutor expert system (GTE), as described in Section 17.2, was designed as a model of ideal student problem solving to use as a component of an intelligent tutoring system. The system works in the execution space and uses a best-first bidirectional search strategy. To be successful in the otherwise intractable execution space, GTE uses heuristics to guide its search. These heuristics were designed to be psychologically realistic and consistent with the ACT* theory of cognition (Anderson 1983). The general idea behind heuristics in ACT* is that student problem solvers learn various contextual features that predict the relevance of an inference. These contextual features are incorporated in the left-hand sides of the production rules and, in GTE, are either features of the problem diagram, previously established statements, or goals. As an example consider the diagram of problem 7 in Figure 17.1. Although one can immediately infer GK=GK and CD=CD by the reflexive rule, only the latter is a sensible inference that good students make. According to GTE this is because good students have learned that one situation where the reflexive rule is useful is when the segment is a shared side between two triangles that might be congruent. Thus, GTE has a rule of the form:

> IF there are plausibly congruent triangles ACD and BCD,
> THEN conclude CD=CD using the reflexive rule.

GTE has a large set of such rules some of which reason forward from the givens of a problem and others which reason backward from the goal. Each rule has an aptness rating which reflects how likely it is to be useful. For instance, a variant of the rule above which tests whether there is a goal to actually prove the two triangles congruent has a higher aptness rating than the rule above which, in turn, has a higher aptness rating than a rule which simply suggests that any segment is congruent to itself. These aptness ratings correspond with production strengths in the ACT* theory.

GTE provides a reasonably good model of student problem solving and has the advantage of being embedded in a unified theory, i.e., ACT*, that provides an account of many other cognitive tasks. However, from a computational point of view, the model has the disadvantage that it often gets bogged down in fruitless search while attempting difficult problems, especially ones where algebraic inferences are required. In addition, there is no systematic way to assign aptness ratings to rules so extending the model becomes increasingly difficult. From an empirical point of view, GTE's problem solving approach does not correspond with the abstract planning approach that we observed experts using.

17.6.4 Greeno's Perdix

Greeno used verbal report data from geometry students as the basis for the design of a geometry theorem proving model called Perdix (Greeno, 1978). Like GTE, it is more accurately characterized as a model of geometry students rather than geometry experts. Unlike Nevins, Greeno's goal was not so much to build a powerful problem solving model, but rather to capture the problem solving behavior of geometry students. In relation, our goal in building DC was to capture the problem solving behavior of geometry experts so as to have a model which is not only a powerful problem solver, but also solves problems in a way that can be profitably taught to students.

Perdix used a mixture of execution space operators and more abstract macro-operator-like operators. With respect to algebraic reasoning, Perdix contained operators which are essentially the same as DC's whole-part schemas (Greeno 1983) and thus, could skip over the details of algebraic proofs. However, with respect to geometric reasoning, Perdix operators appear to have been procedural encodings of geometry rules, that is, execution space operators. In the empirical research associated with Perdix, Greeno made a couple of observations which are particularly notable in relation to DC. The first concerns the use of perceptual processing in geometric reasoning and the second concerns a useful type of non-deductive or "indefinite" reasoning that both students and experts appear to engage in.

A Physical Distance-Reducing Heuristic. The first observation is the way in which good students appear to use a visually-based heuristic to guide their selection of appropriate inferences in a certain class of "angle-chaining" problems (Greeno, 1978). These problems are common in the parallel-line lessons of geometry curricula and typically involve sets of parallel lines, for example, two sets of two parallel lines forming a parallelogram on the inside. Students are either 1) given the parallel-line relationship(s) and the measure of some angle and asked to find the measure of another angle or else 2) given only the parallel lines and asked to find a relationship between two angles. In either case, the problem usually involves finding some other angle which connects the two angles in question via the transitivity rule. Although these problems typically contain numerous angles to choose from, Greeno observed that students are fairly regular (and accurate) in their selection of this "chaining angle." They tend to pick an angle which, in the diagram, is physically between (or close to it) the two angles to be connected.

Perdix models this behavior by forming a "scanning line" between the known and desired angles in the diagram and candidate chaining angles are considered in order of their proximity to this scanning line. This scanning line method is an instance of a more general method for proposing subgoals by identifying objects that are physically between the known and desired objects. The method is based on a heuristic: an operation which reduces the physical distance between known and desired objects may also reduce the logical distance between them. Although DC has not been programmed with such a distance reducing heuristic, such a heuristic might aid DC on harder problems in identifying diagram configurations which are most likely to provide a link between known and desired configurations. The protocol data provides no evidence that experts use this heuristic, however, the problems subjects solved were not particularly demanding of such a heuristic.

Indefinite Goals. A second notable behavior that Greeno (1976) observed of geometry students is that they often engage in the setting of what he called "indefinite goals." When given a problem, like problem 5, with a goal to prove two triangles congruent, instead of attempting to prove particular corresponding parts congruent that are a part of a particular triangle congruence rule, e.g., side-angle-side, subjects attempt to prove any of the corresponding-parts statements they can. These statements are indefinite goals because they are not associated with any definite rule. DC accounts for indefinite goals as they are a natural consequence of the way in which it applies schemas in backward inferences. In DC, a schema is applied in a backward inference by making all part-statements desired. In cases where the ways-to-prove of the schema require multiple statements, the desired part-statements are indefinite goals since they were not set in order to achieve any particular subset.

A related type of reasoning is characteristic of certain types of *forward* inferencing in DC. In particular, the selection heuristic may chose to apply a TRIANGLE-CONGRUENCE-SHARED-SIDE schema in the forward direction because a sufficient number (2) of the schema's part-statements are known. This selection is indefinite in the sense that these two part-statements may not be the right ones to match any of the ways-to-prove. Geometry experts also appear to make such indefinite selections. At some point during problem 7, subjects R, B, K, and F all considered proving $\triangle ACD \cong \triangle BCD$ and/or $\triangle AKD \cong \triangle BKD$ because they had established the congruence of three corresponding parts but found that they could not since these parts formed the insufficient angle-side-side combination.

It should be noted that both the Nevin's model and Perdix (Greeno, Magone, and Chaiklin 1979) are capable of introducing constructions into the geometry diagram allowing them to solve a class of problems that DC cannot as it currently does not have a construction capability. However, as noted in Section 17.5.4, we feel that DC is particularly well-suited for adding a construction capability.

17.7 Discussion and Implications

Previous models of geometry problem solving do not provide an explanation of the abstract planning abilities of experts. Geometry experts can quickly and accurately develop an abstract proof plan that skips many of the steps required in a complete proof. We built a computer simulation of geometry expertise, DC, which models this abstract planning behavior. DC's planning is based on perceptual chunks called diagram configurations which provide a reliable index to clusters of relevant geometry facts. To establish the computational advantages of DC, we performed a problem space analysis that showed that DC is more efficient than models based on the execution space of geometry. In addition, we showed that DC's particular approach to abstract planning is much like that of human experts. Making a conservatively simple assumption about how DC would verbalize its inferences, we found that the model does a good job of accounting for what steps experts mention (and skip) while developing an abstract proof plan.

We now turn to a discussion of how these findings relate to or might inform other issues in cognitive science. In particular, we discuss: 1) how these findings bear on the controversy in the human reasoning literature (see Holland, et. al. 1986) between specific instances, mental models, schemas, and natural logic rules as the representational basis for human reasoning, 2) how these findings contribute to the study of expertise in general, 3) how these findings fit (and don't fit) within unified theories of cognition like ACT* and Soar, and finally, 4) how these findings might be applied to improve geometry instruction.

17.7.1 The Raw Material of Reasoning: Instances, Models, Schemas, or Rules

Holland, et. al. (1986) discuss four alternative theoretical views on human reasoning that have grown primarily out of the empirical research on syllogism problems and Wason's (1966) selection task. These views present different hypotheses about the nature of the basic material with which we reason. They are listed below in order from a view of reasoning knowledge as extremely specific to a view of knowledge as extremely general.

- *Specific instances*: Reasoning proceeds by recalling specific instances of past reasoning events which indicate an appropriate conclusion (see Griggs and Cox 1982).
- *Mental models*: Reasoning is performed by domain-independent comprehension procedures that construct a concrete model of the problem situation from which conclusions can be read off (Johnson-Laird, 1983; Polk and Newell 1988).
- *Pragmatic reasoning schemas*: Reasoning is performed by the application of pragmatic reasoning schemas which are abstractions of past reasoning events (Cheng and Holyoak 1985).
- *Natural logic rules*: Reasoning proceeds by the application and chaining together of abstract rules, much like the formal rules of logic, to deduce a conclusion (see Rips 1983; Braine 1978).

While the knowledge elements of the specific instance and mental model views are more concrete and declarative in nature, the knowledge elements of the pragmatic reasoning schema and natural logic rule views are more abstract and procedural. In the first two views, the knowledge elements are descriptions of concrete objects and situations in the world which must be interpreted to derive actions or conclusions. In the latter two views, the knowledge elements do not correspond to any particular situation or set of objects, but to large categories of situations and they prescribe an action to be performed or conclusion to be made in that general situation.

The question we wish to pursue is how our growing understanding of reasoning in geometry fits within the spectrum of these four alternative views of human reasoning. Geometry reasoning, as characterized by DC, is least like the natural logic rule view. DC's schemas are specific to geometry and thus, are quite unlike the general natural logic rules. On the other hand, DC's schemas are not specific enough to equate them with the specific instance view. In general, neither students nor experts solve geometry problems by simply recalling past experiences of solving them.

We are left with the two intermediate views. Because the distinction between them is somewhat subtle we describe them in more detail. The mental model approach is of intermediate generality in that it uses general language abilities to construct a model (referent) of the problem statement, but the effectiveness of this model is limited by the reasoner's specific knowledge of the language of the domain. The pragmatic reasoning schema view is intermediate in that reasoning is based on knowledge elements (schemas) which are general enough to apply to numerous problem types and domains, but are not as general as formal logic rules which are applicable in any domain. One implication of the difference between these approaches is that the mental model approach explains reasoning errors in terms of working memory failures, while the schema approach explains them in terms of negative transfer—i.e., the mapping of a schema to a situation where the schema-based inference is incorrect (Holland, et. al. 1986).

DC has similarities with both the mental model and pragmatic reasoning schema view. It is similar to the mental model approach in that it uses the problem diagram as a specific referent or model of the abstract problem statement indicated by the givens and goals. Many features of this model are usually too specific to be relevant, for example, the particular lengths of segments. However, other specifics of the model can be important as they can provide a cue to relevant inferences, for example, congruent-looking triangles can cue an inference to prove them congruent. A concrete model has the advantage of making important features or relationships clearly apparent (visible in this case) whereas they are only implicit in abstract statements. In addition, the cues from the model have the effect of allowing the problem solver to ignore lots of potentially applicable but irrelevant logical knowledge. A model building procedure like the one Johnson-Laird proposes is not necessary since the diagram provides a ready-made model.[6] According to the mental model approach, what is left for the problem solver to do is properly annotate the model and read-off the conclusion. This is essentially what we propose experts do—they annotate the diagram, on paper or in their mind's eye, by noting established relationships.

However, the annotation process is not as straight-forward as it is in other problems the mental model approach has been applied to. Rather, it involves fairly complicated logical inferences, including, for example, the checking of ways-to-prove. This inferencing requires the abstract geometric knowledge which is part of the DC schemas. This knowledge is more like pragmatic reasoning schemas in that it is applied procedurally and it appears to be acquired as abstractions of past geometry problem solving experiences.

Although the four views can be posed as competing hypotheses, it is likely that human reasoning in general contains elements of each. While the DC model lends support for the use in geometry of a combination of the mental model and pragmatic reasoning schema approaches, neither approach by itself is sufficient.

17.7.2 Contributions to the Study of Human Expertise

What's Behind Expert's Forward Reasoning Ability? One claim that has been made about human experts is that they show a greater tendency than novices (especially on easier problems) to work forward from the givens of a problem rather than backward from the goal. This result has been observed in physics word problems (Larkin, McDermott, Simon, and Simon 1980a), in classical genetics word problems (Smith and Good 1984), and in medical reasoning (Patel and Groen 1986) by comparing the problem solving behavior of experts and novices. Although the comparisons were done between different subjects, the invited inference is that as a person acquires skill in one of these domains their

[6]While many geometry proof problems given in classrooms include a diagram, it is not uncommon to state proof problems without a diagram, for example, the problem in Figure 17.2 could be stated as "prove that if the altitude of a triangle bisects the top angle, it also bisects the base." Such problems are typically solved by drawing an appropriate diagram, a concrete model of this abstract statement, and then proceeding as usual. In this case, the problem solver is constructing a mental model.

problem solving strategy will tend to shift from working backward to working forward. To observe this shift within the course of skill acquisition, Sweller, Mawer, and Ward (1983) developed a toy domain, using three equations from kinematics, where subjects could become "experts" in a relatively short period of extensive practice (77 problems). They found the expected shift as subjects worked forward on significantly more of the final problems than they did on the initial problems.

In geometry we have observed an expert (subject R) exclusively working forward on a number of the simpler problems we asked him to solve. This ability to essentially solve certain problems without looking at the goal is an ability geometry novices do not have. We would like to address the issue of how subject R and experts in general are able to successfully work forward.

It should be pointed out, first, that this shift to working forward is not characteristic of all domains of expertise. In some domains the given information is inadequate to successfully solve problems by forward search. Jeffries, Turner, Polson, and Atwood (1981) showed that expert programmers do not work forward from the problem givens (i.e., the programming language primitives), rather they work backward from the goal information (i.e., the program specifications). The shift to working forward appears to be characteristic of deductive domains, like equation chaining or proof domains, where the given information is quite rich and uncharacteristic of design domains, like programming, where the given information is poor.

In domains where working forward can be successfully performed, it should not surprise us that learners adapt toward using it more often. By working forward, problem solvers can write down inferences as they make them and relieve the memory burden of storing previous solution steps. Backward or bidirectional search, on the other hand, demands that the problem solver encode and integrate more information as well as remember intermediate goals. Sweller (1988) makes similar arguments and presents a computational model and experimental evidence to support them. The upshot is that if a learner can develop the ability to successfully work forward, she can alleviate some of the extra working memory burden required by a backward strategy.

Sweller (1988) also proposes an explanation for expert's ability to successfully work forward. He suggests that experts use *schemas* to classify problems into categories that carry implications for appropriate moves to make. He defines a schema as "a structure which allows problem solvers to recognize a problem state as belonging to a particular category of problem states that normally require particular moves." The diagram configuration schemas of the DC model fit Sweller's definition. They allow the categorization of sub-problems based on recognizing prototypical images in the problem diagram and the retrieval of the relevant sub-proof.

The key point is not so much that experts will necessarily prefer working forward. Rather, it is that as a result of the their superior skill, experts are *capable* of successfully working forward without recourse to backward reasoning. Knowledge in the form of schemas is what allows them to do so. However, schemas alone are not enough. The schemas must be large enough or the problem small enough so that they reduce the search space sufficiently for forward reasoning to be effective. We have seen how DC's schemas make the search space of even relatively difficult problems quite small, for example, the forward search space of problem 7 is only 8 schemas (see Table 17.2). Still, all of our experts did some backward reasoning on problem 7. It was only on simpler problems, like 3 and 5 with only 3 relevant schemas, that subject R performed a purely forward search.

Perceptual Chunks and Problem Solving Performance. One of the more robust results regarding expert-novice differences is the enhanced memory of experts for problem-state displays. This difference has been established in a variety of domains: chess (De Groot 1966), electronic circuits (Egan and Schwartz 1979), baseball (Voss, Vesonder, and Spilich 1980), computer programming (Jeffries, Turner, Polson, and Atwood 1981), and algebra (Sweller and Cooper, 1985). In the earliest study of this type, it was shown that chess masters can remember realistic board positions much better than chess novices can (De Groot 1966). This result does not arise from any innate perceptual or memorial advantages experts might have, rather it arises from their extensive chess experience. Experts are no better than novices at remembering boards with randomly placed pieces.

While these recall abilities are *correlated* with game playing skill, it has yet to be decisively established whether they are a *necessary* part of game playing skill or whether they are merely a side-effect of spending lots of time staring at a chess board. The theory behind the recall results is that subjects perceive the board in terms of prototypical configurations of pieces, "chunks," and that experts' chunks are made up of more pieces than those of novices (Chase and Simon 1973). Chase and Simon have suggested that experts associate appropriate chess moves with these chunks and Simon and Gilmartin (1973) have a model of chess perception. However, a model has yet to be written which is capable of both performing the recall task and playing chess. At the same time, the proposal that experts associate moves with these chunks has received criticism (Holding, 1986).

The DC model is a step towards establishing a detailed theoretical connection between perceptual chunks and problem solving performance. The diagram configurations of DC provide a ready-made theory of perceptual chunks in geometry. We have already seen that these perceptual chunks provide the basis for expert problem solving performance. It would not be difficult to model superior problem-state recall in geometry by chunking problem diagrams in terms of diagram configurations. Thus, it appears that the appropriate knowledge representation is in place in DC to model both problem-state recall and problem solving skill in geometry. Implementing a recall component and replicating the De Groot's empirical result in geometry are tasks for future research.

Turning back to chess, DC's use of diagram configurations for abstract planning might be the appropriate analogy for an integrated chess model. Rather than cueing particular moves, chunks in chess may be more effectively thought of as problem state abstractions which provide the basis for an abstract problem space in which players can plan and evaluate multiple-move strategies.

17.7.3 DC's Relation to Comprehensive Theories of Cognition

In 1972 Allen Newell gave his well known "20 questions" talk (Newell, 1973) in which he argued that to avoid spinning our wheels in cognitive science research we need to begin to integrate local hypotheses and domain models into global theories that account for cognition across a wide variety of tasks. Creating such comprehensive theories has now become a major research effort (Anderson 1983; Newell 1990; Johnson-Laird 1983; Holland, et. al. 1986). In this section we try to place DC in terms of two of these theories, ACT* (Anderson 1983) and Soar (Newell 1990). We address the issue of whether the mechanisms of problem solving and learning in these theories can account for expert geometry problem solving as modeled by DC.

Because both ACT* and Soar use a production rule representation of knowledge, our first challenge is to find a way to express DC's schemas as production rules in such a way as to not change the resulting behavioral predictions. Consider the TRIANGLE-CONGRUENCE-SHARED-SIDE schema in Figures 17.3 and 17.4. This schema can be represented as 6 production rules whose left-hand sides correspond to the 6 ways-to-prove of the schema and whose right-hand sides contain 5 actions which correspond with the 5 part-statements of the schema. A similar translation could be made to express backward schema application in terms of productions. Note that these production rules are *macro-operators* with respect to the execution space of geometry in that they have the effect of numerous execution space operators.

Is anything lost in translating schemas to productions? In terms of problem solving behavior the answer is probably no. However, another question we need to ask with respect to ACT* and Soar is whether the particular productions that correspond with DC's schemas could result from the learning mechanisms of these theories. This question is more problematic. The clusters of productions corresponding with DC's schemas organize the formal rules of geometry in a particular and efficient way. It is not clear how the production rule learning mechanisms in either ACT* or Soar could arrive at such an organized set of productions.

These theories essentially view skill acquisition as involving two phases: knowledge acquisition and knowledge tuning. In the knowledge acquisition phase, the learning system uses information about the problem domain, e.g., problem descriptions, problem constraints, example solutions, etc., to build some kind of basic problem space. In geometry, this would involve acquiring the formal rules of geometry, that is the execution space operators, through instruction and examples. In the knowledge tuning phase, the basic problem space is elaborated through problem solving practice so that the system becomes more effective and efficient. Much of the research on skill acquisition in ACT* and Soar has focussed on this second knowledge tuning phase. The basic approach of these theories to knowledge tuning is a process of reducing the number of productions required to perform a procedure— essentially both use a type of macro-operator creation mechanism in which consecutively applicable productions or operators are composed into a single production or macro-operator.[7]

There are both empirical and computational reasons to doubt that DC derives from creating macro-operators of the execution space operators. First, the step-skipping regularity we observed is an unlikely consequence of this approach. Although ACT* and Soar have some stipulations on the appropriate context in which macro-operators are formed, there is little in them that indicates which sequences of consecutively applicable productions are more likely to be composed than others. Thus, we would not expect any regularity in the kinds of steps that would be skipped in an abstract problem space of composed execution operators. However, such a regularity is exactly what we observed of subjects.

To be more precise both theories stipulate that macro-operator formation occurs within a goal structure, that is, macro-operators are formed of consecutive productions applied to achieve the same goal. Thus, the clustering of productions into macro-operators will reflect the organization of a problem solver's goals and subgoals and to the extent that this goal structure is consistent across many problems, a step-skipping regularity could emerge. However, it appears more likely that marco-operator-like knowledge in geometry is not primarily organized around goals but is organized around objects and aggregations of objects in the domain. According to this view, DC's schemas are not really macro-operators in the sense of being derived from execution operators. Rather, they derive from perceptual chunking of domain objects and they merely bare a macro-operator relation with execution space operators.

A second reason to question the macro-operator learning approach comes from evidence in the verbal reports that in the process of executing an abstract plan, subjects could not always immediately fill in the steps they had skipped during planning. For example, in problem 7 subjects would plan to prove the goal from $\angle ADC = \angle BDC$, apparently using the PERPENDICULAR-ADJACENT-ANGLES schema. During plan execution, some subjects did not immediately know how to justify the link between these two statements—they attempted an algebra proof or searched the list of available geometry rules we provided. However, if they had learned

[7]To cut off a potential confusion based the distinction in Soar between operators and productions, we would like to make clear that when we use "macro-operator" in reference to Soar, we are not referring to the combination of Soar operators into macro-operators—Soar has no direct mechanism for doing this. Rather, we are talking about the chunking of Soar productions into bigger productions.

this schema by composing execution space operators, that is, the very operators that they needed at this point, we would expect that these operators would be readily available. Since these execution operators remain necessary to execute proof plans, there is no reason why they would be forgotten in the course of skill acquisition. It appears that experts' knowledge of the macro-operator-like schemas is occasionally stronger than their knowledge of the corresponding execution operators. This evidence is inconsistent with a view of the schemas deriving from the execution operators—provided, as is the case here, that the execution operators are still necessary to solve problems.

Finally, there are computational reasons to question macro-operator explanation of step-skipping. Recall the macro-operator characterization of the TRIANGLE-CONGRUENCE-SHARED-SIDE schema given above. The collection of all such macro-operators for every schema, call it S, is a restricted subset of the space of possible macro-operators. S is restricted in two ways. First, S does not contain any of the possible macro-operators which could make inferences between statements which are whole-statements of schemas, for example, it doesn't contain an operator that could infer perpendicularity directly from triangle congruence in a problem like problem 3. Second, S does not contain any of the 2, 3, or 4 action macro-operators that would be learned on the way to a 5 action macro-operator like the one corresponding with the TRIANGLE-CONGRUENCE-SHARED-SIDE schema. To achieve DC's simplicity in search control and match to the human data, a composition mechanism would need to prevent a proliferation of unnecessary macro-operators. It is not clear how this restriction could be implemented in ACT* or Soar.

One might consider whether this restriction could be achieved within the Soar architecture by having a hierarchy of problem spaces corresponding with the desired organization. However, this approach begs the question—how would this hierarchy be learned in the first place?

17.7.4 Implications for Geometry Instruction

One of the goals of this research is to develop a second generation geometry tutoring system based on DC. The Geometry Tutor that was based on GTE has already been demonstrated as an effective alternative to homework problems improving average student performance by about one standard deviation (Anderson, Boyle, Corbett, and Lewis 1990).

We have two reasons for believing that DC might lead to an even more effective tutor. The first has to do with DC's abstract planning abilities and the second has to do with the way DC uses the problem diagram.

Tutoring Advantages of an Abstract Problem Space. One of the difficulties involved in building an intelligent tutoring system (ITS) is finding a way to communicate about the thinking that students do between their observable problem solving actions. If the grain size of the problem solving steps that the tutor allows is the same as the grain size of students' "thinking steps," then there is no problem. However, if the student and tutor are working at different grain sizes, then the tutor will be at a disadvantage in trying to diagnose student errors and provide appropriate feedback.

One of the complaints we have heard about the Geometry Tutor is that it does not provide very good global feedback. The feedback it provides is focussed locally on the *next* proof step the student might take rather than more globally at the next few steps or an overall plan. Critics had the intuition that proof ideas can be born at a more global level. Our current research on geometry experts has identified this more global level and has characterized it in terms of DC's diagram configuration schemas. In other words, skilled geometry problem solvers think at a larger grain size than the grain size at which the Geometry Tutor works. A tutor working at the smaller grain size cannot give instruction at the larger one and thus, is disabled with respect to helping students reach skilled performance. However, a tutor based on diagram configuration schemas could give instruction at the larger grain size characteristic of skilled performance. Thus, it could better aid students in reaching this level of skill.

Tutoring Advantages of a Diagram-Based Method. We are of the opinion that if you discover a clever way to solve problems in a domain, you should tell it to students. There are two caveats. First, the method must be one that is "humanly tractable." For example, although the Simplex method for linear programming is a clever way to solve certain optimization problems, it is not tractable method for humans. Second, there must be a way to communicate the method so that it takes less time and effort for students to understand it than it would for them to induce it on their own through problem solving practice.

We know that DC's problem solving method is humanly tractable because it appears to be the method human experts are using. The next question is whether we can communicate the method to students effectively. Some ITS designers have addressed the problem of communicating about planning that occurs at a more abstract level than the level at which solution steps are written or executed. Some examples of the resulting tutoring systems include Bridge (Bonar and Cunningham 1988), GIL (Reiser, et. al. 1988), and Sherlock (Lesgold, et. al. 1988). The basic approach is to develop a command language, usually menu-based and possibly graphical, which reifies this planning level.

Conveniently, we do not need to invent such a command language to reify DC's abstract problem space. Essentially, it already exists in the form of the problem diagram. What we envision is that rather than selecting an operator from a list of geometry rules as in the Geometry Tutor, students will select an operator from a list of diagram configuration icons. These icons will be the building blocks for proofs just as geometry rules were the building blocks for proofs in the Geometry Tutor.

Implications for Geometry Instruction in the Classroom. While our main focus has been on how DC can provide the basis for an improved intelligent tutoring system, our improved understanding of geometry problem solving may also have more general implications for how geometry is taught in the classroom. On one hand, the DC model is a theory of the internal thinking processes of skilled geometry problem solvers. On the other hand, it can be taken seriously as new method for doing geometry proofs which can be explicitly taught in the classroom. In addition, the organization of knowledge in DC suggests an alternative task-adapted organization of the geometry curriculum. Typical geometry curricula are organized around topics and focus on teaching the formal rules of geometry. Alternatively, a curriculum could be organized around diagram configuration schemas and have the structure in Figures 17.5 and 17.6. The formal rules, then, could be taught in context of how they are used to prove schemas. Such a task-adapted curriculum organization can help students to remember rules and access them in the appropriate situations (Eylon and Reif 1984).

Acknowledgements

Thanks to Jill Larkin, Kurt Van Lehn and Herbert Simon for insightful counsel. Thanks also to Christina Allen, Stephen Casner, Lael Schooler, editor Jim Greeno and the reviewers: Jeremy Kilpatrick, Robert Lindsay, and an anonymous cognitive psychologist for their helpful comments and advice. Portions of this work were reported at the 1989 meeting of the American Educational Research Association in San Francisco, California and at the 1989 meeting of the Cognitive Science Society in Ann Arbor, Michigan.

References

Anderson, J. R. 1983. *The Architecture of Cognition.* Cambridge, Mass.: Harvard University Press.

Anderson, J. R., Boyle, C. F., and Yost, G. 1985. The Geometry Tutor. In *Proceedings of the International Joint Conference on Artificial Intelligence.* San Mateo: Morgan Kaufmann.

Anderson, J. R., Boyle, C. F., Corbett, A., and Lewis, M. 1990. Cognitive Modeling and Intelligent Tutoring. *Artificial Intelligence.*

Anderson, J. R., Greeno, J. G., Kline, P. J., and Neves, D. M. 1981. Acquisition of Problem-solving skill. In *Cognitive Skills and their Acquisition,* ed. J. R. Anderson. Hillsdale, N.J.: Lawrence Erlbaum Associates.

Braine, M. D. S. 1978. On the Relation Between the Natural Logic of Reasoning and Standard Logic. *Psychological Review* 85: 1–21.

Bonar, J. G., and Cunningham, R. 1988. Intelligent Tutoring with Intermediate Representations. Presented at ITS–88, Montreal.

Chase, W. G., and Simon H. A. 1973. The Mind's Eye in Chess. *Visual Information Processing,* ed. W. G. Chase. New York: Academic Press.

Cheng, P. W., and Holyoak, K. J. 1985. Pragmatic Reasoning Schemas. *Cognitive Psychology* 17: 391–416.

De Groot, A. 1966. Perception and Memory Versus Thought: Some Old Ideas and Recent Findings. In *Problem Solving,* ed B. Kleinmuntz. New York: John Wiley.

Ericsson, K. A., and Simon, H. A. 1984. *Protocol Analysis: Verbal Reports as Data.* Cambridge, Mass.: The MIT Press.

Egan, D., and Schwartz, B. 1979. Chunking in Recall of Symbolic Drawings. *Memory and Cognition* 17: 147–158.

Eylon, B., and Reif, F. 1984. Effects of Knowledge Organization on Task Performance. *Cognition and Instruction* 1: 5–44.

Gelernter, H. 1963. Realization of a Geometry Theorem Proving Machine. In *Computers and Thought,* ed. E. A. Feigenbaum and J. Feldman. New York: McGraw-Hill.

Goldstein, I. 1973. Elementary Geometry Theorem Proving. Massachusetts Institute of Technology AI Memo 280.

Greeno, J. G. 1976. Indefinite Goals in Well-Structured Problems. *Psychological Review* 83: 479–491.

Greeno, J. G. 1978. A Study of Problem Solving. In *Advances in Instructional Psychology,* ed. R. Glaser. Hillsdale, N.J.: Lawrence Erlbaum Associates.

Greeno, J. G. 1983. Forms of Understanding in Mathematical Problem Solving. In *Learning and Motivation in the Classroom,* ed. S. G. Paris, G. M. Olson, and H. W. Stevenson. Hillsdale, N.J.: Lawrence Erlbaum Associates.

Greeno, J. G., Magone, M. E., and Chaiklin, S. 1979. Theory of Constructions and Set in Problem Solving. *Memory and Cognition* 7: 445–461.

Griggs, R. A., and Cox, J. R. 1982. The Elusive Thematic-Materials Effect in Wason's Selection Task. *British Journal of Psychology* 16: 94–143.

Holding, D. H. 1986. *The Psychology of Chess Skill.* Hillsdale, N.J.: Lawrence Erlbaum Associates.

Holland, J. H., Holyoak, K. J., Nisbett, R. E., and Thagard, P. R. 1986. *Induction: Processes of Inference, Learning, and Discovery.* Cambridge, Mass.: The MIT Press.

Jeffries, R., Turner, A. A., Polson, P. G., and Atwood M. E. 1981. The Processes Involved in Designing Software. In *Cognitive Skills and their Acquisition,* ed. J. R. Anderson. Hillsdale, N.J.: Lawrence Erlbaum Associates.

Johnson-Laird, P. N. 1983. *Mental Models.* Cambridge, Mass.: Harvard University Press.

Korf, R. E. 1987. Macro-Operators: A Weak Method for Learning. *Artificial Intelligence* 27: 35–77.

Larkin, J. 1988. Display-based problem solving. In *Complex Information Processing: The Impact of Herbert A. Simon,* ed. D. Klahr and K. Kotovsky. Hillsdale, NJ: Erlbaum.

Larkin, J., McDermott, J., Simon, D., and Simon, H. A. 1980a. Expert and Novice Performance in Solving Physics Problems. *Science* 208: 1335–1342.

Larkin, J., McDermott, J., Simon, D., and Simon, H. A. 1980b. Models of Competence in Solving Physics Problems. *Cognitive Science* 4: 317–348.

Larkin, J., and Simon, H. A. 1987. Why a Diagram Is (Sometimes) Worth Ten Thousand Words. *Cognitive Science* 11: 65–99.

Lesgold, A. M., Lajoie, S., Bunzo, M., and Eggan, G. 1988. Sherlock: A Coached Practice Environment for an Electronics Trouble Shooting Job. LRDC Report. Pittsburgh, Penn.: University of Pittsburgh, Learning Research and Development Center.

Nevins, A. J. 1975. Plane Geometry Theorem Proving Using Forward Chaining. *Artificial Intelligence* 6: 1–23.

Newell, A. 1990. *Unified Theories of Cognition.* Cambridge, Mass.: Harvard University Press.

Newell, A. 1973. You Can't Play 20 Questions with Nature and Win: Projective Comments on the Papers of This Symposium. In *Visual Information Processing,* ed. W. G. Chase. New York: Academic Press.

Newell, A., and Simon, H. A. 1972. *Human Problem Solving.* Englewood Cliffs, N.J.: Prentice-Hall.

Nilsson, N. J. 1980. *Principles of Artificial Intelligence.* Palo Alto: Tioga Publishing Co.

Patel, V. L., and Groen, G. J. 1986. Knowledge-Based Solution Strategies in Medical Reasoning. *Cognitive Science* 10: 91–116.

Polk, T. A., and Newell, A. 1988. Modeling Human Syllogistic Reasoning in Soar. *Program of the Tenth Annual Conference of the Cognitive Science Society.* Hillsdale, N.J.: Lawrence Erlbaum Associates.

Reiser, B. J., Friedmann, P., Gevins, J., Kimberg, D. Y., Ranney, M., and Romero, A. 1988. A Graphical Programming Language Interface for an Intelligent Lisp Tutor. *Proceedings CHI '88.*

Rips, L.J. 1983. Cognitive Processes in Propositional Reasoning. *Psychological Review* 90: 38–71.

Rosenbloom, P. S., Laird, J. E., and Newell, A. 1987. Knowledge Level Learning in Soar. In Proceedings of the Sixth National Conference on Artificial Intelligence, 499–504. Menlo Park, Calif.: American Association for Artificial Intelligence.

Sacerdoti, E. D. 1974. Planning in a Hierarchy of Abstraction Spaces. *Artificial Intelligence* 5: 115–136.

Simon, H. A., and Gilmartin, K. J. 1973. A Simulation of Memory for Chess Positions. *Cognitive Psychology* 5: 29–46.

Smith, M., and Good, R. 1984. Problem Solving and Classical Genetics: Successful Versus Unsuccessful Performance. *Journal of Research in Science Teaching* 21 895–912.

Sweller, J., Mawer, R. F., and Ward, R. W. 1983. Development of Expertise in Mathematical Problem Solving. *Journal of Experimental Psychology: General* 112: 639–661.

Sweller, J. 1988. Cognitive Load During Problem Solving: Effects on Learning. *Cognitive Science* 12: 257–285.

Sweller, J., and Cooper, G. 1985. The Use of Worked Examples as a Substitute for Problem Solving in Learning Algebra. *Cognition and Instruction* 2: 59–89.

Unruh, A., Rosenbloom, P. S., and Laird, J. E. 1987. Dynamic Abstraction Problem Solving in Soar. In *Proceedings of the AOG/AAAIC Joint Conference.* Dayton, Ohio.

Voss, J., Vesonder, G., and Spilich, G. 1980. Text Generation and Recall by High-knowledge and Low-knowledge Individuals. *Journal of Verbal Learning and Verbal Behavior* 19: 651–667.

Wason, P. C. 1966. Reasoning. *New Horizons in Psychology,* ed. B. M. Foss. Harmondsworth: Penguin.

18 Partonomies and Depictions: A Hybrid Approach

Christopher Habel, Simone Pribbenow, & Geoffrey Simmons
University of Hamburg

It is a widely-held view that cognition is based on internal representations of the world, and that reasoning can be seen as manipulation of these representations. Instead of developing and describing a formal model of internal representations and processes of reasoning, we will propose two unifying principles of successful, efficient and cognitively adequate reasoning systems, namely the *hybrid representation principle* and the *granular representation principle* (cf. Finke 1989: 141ff on "unifying principles vs. formal models").

During the last two decades, research on imagery and mental rotation has given overwhelming evidence for analog representations of spatial configurations, i.e. representations with intrinsic spatial properties (cf. Kosslyn 1980, 1994; Palmer 1978). This leads to a *principle of hybrid representation and processing,* which may be expressed as follows:[1]

> A cognitive system that reasons successfully in a general (non-restricted) real world environment is based on a hybrid architecture, which combines propositional and depictional[2] representations and processes.

The assumption of a hybrid representation system which combines propositional and depictional representations is also supported by evidence from research on comprehension and production of language (see e.g. Glenberg et al. 1987). Thus the properties of and the constraints on both depictional representations and the components processing them are determined by the modules for reasoning, visual perception and language processing (see Habel 1990, Landau and Jackendoff 1993).

[1]We argued in detail for hybrid systems in Habel (1990) and Latecki and Pribbenow (1992). In the present chapter, we don't want to discuss whether representations of objects' positions and representations of their shapes independent of their positions—i.e. representations of where and what—have to be distinguished, as Kosslyn (1987), Glasgow and Papadias (1992), Landau and Jackendoff (1993) and others assume. Our assumptions about representational formats are neutral with respect to this controversial question.

[2]By "depictional" (or pictorial, depictive,...) we refer—in the tradition of Kosslyn (1980, 1994)—to representations of an image-like character, called "depictions."

But the property of hybridicity is not sufficient to guarantee successful and efficient reasoning processes. The main obstacle is that—in many cases—large amounts of information and detail lead to inefficiency up to intractability. Hobbs' (1985) solution to this problem is to view the world at different levels of granularity; following this idea we postulate the *granular system principle* (cf. Habel 1994):

> A cognitive system reasoning successfully in a general (non-restricted) real world environment uses representations at different levels of detail (granularity). The reasoning processes primarily access information at a minimal granularity level, i.e. a level that is only as detailed as required.

The topic of this article is the use of depictive representations in reasoning about part-whole structures. In section 18.1, we present some important aspects of part-whole structures from cognitive psychology, especially the role of parts in some current theories of visual perception. Following the hybrid representation principle, we argue that current approaches to part-whole structures, which have a propositional orientation, should be augmented by a pictorial component. Furthermore, we show that hierarchical organizations of depictive representations can be seen as systems (or structures) of granularity levels, supporting the granular representation principle. The overview of perceptual and linguistic phenomena given in section 18.1 leads to a set of relevant properties of depictional representations. In section 18.2, we propose the framework of a hybrid reasoning system for the processing of part-whole-knowledge, which follows the two principles mentioned above. The depictional components of the system are constrained by the properties developed in the first part of the chapter.

18.1 Part-Whole Structures From a Cognitive Point of View

18.1.1 Partonomies: Knowledge about Part-Whole Relations

Human knowledge about the world is organized by conceptual hierarchies. In addition to the organization of kinds—*taxonomy*—which is widely investigated in AI, the organization of parts—*partonomy*—is of high importance: "Partonomies serve to separate entities into their structural components and to organize knowledge of function by components of structure." (Tversky and Hemenway 1984: 169).

The goal of partonomies is similar to the core strategy in the analysis of physical systems, especially systems of artefacts, which is "...to view the system as a whole as composed of separate components connected together. The behavior of the system can then be analyzed by studying the behavior of the component, each of which is presumably simpler than the overall system, and determining how these behaviors interact." (Davis 1990: 312).

The importance of knowledge about parts for perception, reasoning and other functions of cognitive processing is demonstated by empirical research in cognitive psychology that shows close relations to properties of human categorization systems. The two most well-known empirical effects of categorization tasks established by Rosch and her associates are the *basic level* and *typicality* effects (Rosch 1977). A number of empirical operations converge at an intermediate level in the inclusion hierarchy of taxonomies called the *basic level:* membership in basic levels categories is verified faster than membership in other categories; for the linguistic designation of objects, the names of basic level categories are preferred in neutral contexts; and so on. The typicality effect is the fact that exemplars rated as typical for a category C are more easily categorized as C's, i.e. more quickly and with fewer errors, than other exemplars.[3]

A number of findings suggest that knowledge about parts may provide a partial explanation of these findings:

- Extensive knowledge of parts is characteristic of the basic level: When asked to list attributes of concepts, most subjects produce a large number of parts as basic level attributes, fewer for subordinate and almost none as attributes for superordinate categories. Basic level categories differ from one another especially by parts, while subordinate level categories share most of their parts with the dominating basic level. On the other hand, superordinate categories such as *furniture* are generally characterized in terms of

[3]The term "category" is used in the vocabulary of cognitive psychology to denote a collection of entities regarded as equivalent in some relevant respect, and "concept" is used to denote the mental resources that underlie categorization; thus the terms distinguish an extensional and intensional notion. Our hypotheses about representations and processing are, in essence, hypotheses about the structure and processing of concepts.

their functions, rather than in terms of their parts. (Tversky and Hemenway 1984, Exper. 1-3.)

- The experiments also show a correlation between the typicality of a category member and shared parts: typical members tend to have more of the parts shared by other category members (Tversky 1990: 338).

Thus, the empirical data presented by Tversky and Hemenway suggest that in addition to the pure part-of relation of mereology,[4] cognitive systems have the two additional types of knowledge at their disposal that are essential to part-whole-structures, namely knowledge of the *spatial structure* (spatial relations among the parts, especially connection and separation) and *function* (functionality of the parts and their interactions).

In this chapter, we will focus on all three aspects and especially their interaction. It is obvious that connected parts are likely to combine their function and that separated parts—under normal conditions—do not possess directly combined functions.[5] Therefore it is necessary to augment the pure mereological system with information concerning the spatial structure of the whole as composed of its parts and information about the functions of parts and their interactions.

So far, we have only mentioned *components* as parts of objects. By components we refer—in agreement with Winston et al. (1987) and Gerstl and Pribbenow (1994)—to "parts per se," or as Gerstl and Pribbenow put it, parts that stand in a complex compositional structure making up the whole. Examples of components are the head, limbs and torso of the human body; or the seat, seat back and legs of a chair. Knowledge about the "X is a component (= componential part) of Y"-relation belongs to explicit knowledge about categories. Furthermore, it is also possible to partition an entity into other kinds of parts, which we will call *segments*

[4]The term "mereology" was introduced by the Polish mathematician Lesniewski during the first 3 decades of this century. Mereology, the formal theory of the part-of relation, was originally planned as an alternative to classical set-theory; for a detailed discussion of the mathematical and logical consequences of choosing this alternative see Lewis (1991), Simons (1987) and Eschenbach and Heydrich (1994).

[5]The detection of connections is one of the most relevant steps in the analysis of complex systems with complex behavior. For example: A car's turn signals are pairwise connected (left side-right side), as are the brake lights. An adequate partonomy has to account for these connections and therefore assume a connecting part—a cable, for example—which forms a complex part with the brake, namely the brake-light system.

(see Gerstl and Pribbenow 1994), according to spatial, functional or other criteria. Examples of segments are the *front, back, right/left side,* of an object. How does one represent information about the material of some spatial part, say the upper part of a house, if one only has knowledge about the materials of the individual components like the roof, walls, doors, and so on? To answer questions of this kind, knowledge about the components of an object and different ways of segmenting an object into parts are needed.

This means that there exist (at least) two different ways of partitioning an object: *decomposing* a complex object into its components[6] and *segmenting* an object into arbitrary parts (segments or portions) with specific features. An example for such segmentations is the partition of a house into upper and lower half, or into the parts consisting of a certain material, such as stone, wood, glass, and so on. In segmentation processes, external criteria that refer to spatial, material or functional aspects of the whole trigger the determination of the parts. These criteria are general in the sense that they can be used for all kinds of objects, whereas decomposition is specific to an object category.

Segments are constructed parts, while components are "per se"-parts belonging to the conceptual knowledge about object categories. The constructed parts can, but often do not, coincide with the object's components. It is possible to combine these two modes of partitioning, namely memory-based decomposition with constructive segmentation, e.g. by referring to the "right side of the roof of our house."

18.1.2 Partonomies in Vision and Imagery

There is strong evidence that the visual perceptual system shares its structures and processes with depictional representations. Kosslyn (1980, 1987, 1994) has proposed that certain visual subsystems are employed to process images, and that intermediate visual representations of objects that have been suggested in computational studies of object recognition (i.e. the categorization of visual stimuli) may also be applied in the generation of depictions. Theoretical research in object recognition is generally concerned with the means of processing image data (the distribution

[6]This is the part-whole decomposition, based on mereological knowledge, that is complemented by information about the spatial structure of parts, and their special function and features. This is the kind of parts with which theories of visual perception have been concerned.

of luminances projected onto the retina) so as to extract representations of objects that may be matched with stored representations of the typical properties of category members; but mental imagery may thought of as the inverse of a portion of this process (see Jackendoff 1987: 185, Finke 1989). Just as syntactic and/or semantic representations of sentences can be viewed as both the target and source of language comprehension and generation processes, respectively, so might visual representations serve as both the target of recognition processes and the source of imagination processes (see e.g. Finke 1989, Kosslyn 1994). Language and vision differ in that the images generated, unlike sentences, cannot be externalized. Moreover, the format of generated images need not be the same as that of images induced by perception, since it is probably not necessary for the purposes of depictional reasoning to generate luminance distributions over a "retinal" array; Marr's (1982) so-called $2\frac{1}{2}$-D sketch, which contains information about the depth and surface orientation of an object seen from a certain viewpoint, or Ullman's (1989) 2D contour images of an object seen from standard viewpoints, may be sufficient for the task. Therefore, when we speak of the visual system in the following, we mean the complex system responsible both for the generation and interpretation[7] of depictional representations and for the visual recognition of objects.

The study of object recognition involves the identification of the *visual invariants* characteristic of category members that may be feasibly extracted from the visual data. One of the invariants of interest is the structure of components making up an object. This is the variety of parts that has been studied closely in research on visual perception, and is most naturally associated with depictional representations.

Components are a common feature in qualitative representations of *shape* that are invariant with respect to color, texture, viewpoint and lighting conditions. Despite controversy concerning the nature of primitive shape information, there is fairly wide agreement that knowledge of an object's shape is probably structured primarily to reflect the object's componential structure. There are a number of reasons why such a strategy is advantageous:

1. The *structural relations* between parts—i.e. the relation of part

[7]By "interpretation" we refer to "inspection" as described by Kosslyn (1980, 1994) as well as to "reinterpretation" in the sense of Finke (1989: 126ff).

connectedness and the spatial locations of part joins—are invariant against changes in viewpoint and in the relative orientations of the parts (as argued by Simmons [1994]). The parts of objects in many categories are movable with respect to each other (e.g. the limbs of the human body), and hence the shape of the whole may project arbitrarily many different contours onto the retinal image. But the shapes of the parts and their points of attachment to the each other are generally very stable. Hence it seems reasonable to determine the shapes of parts in the image and the structural relations between them, to be matched against models of the part shapes and structures known to be typical for object categories.

2. There are a number of promising methods for the decomposition of a 2D image into regions that correspond to parts in 3D space. According to the principle suggested by Hoffman and Richards (1984), the image may be segmented at pairs of negative minima of principal curvature along the contour, in particular at points of concave discontinuity (see Figure 18.1). This corresponds to intuitions about part boundaries, and some of Biederman's (1987) experiments suggest that humans do indeed rely on such concavities in 2D images to recognize 3D objects.

   However, this principle is known to have a number of limitations. In particular, fluctuations of contour curvature at fine scales (perhaps due to noise) may lead to spurious negative minima. In order to cope with this problem, a number of authors (cf. Mokhtarian and Mackworth 1992) have proposed an analysis of contour curvature on multiple scales. The multiscale approach is effective in finding nonspurious curvature minima; moreover, a byproduct of the technique is that small protrusions may be detected as parts when curvature is measured on a fine scale, but not when a coarser scale is used.

   In our view, these facts—that a multiscale analysis seems necessary for reliable detection of parts in an image, and that smaller structures may or may not be detected as parts depending on the coarseness of the analysis—constitute strong arguments for the validity of the granular representation principle.

3. Since the parts known to be characteristic for object categories often form categories on their own (e.g. the category "arm" appears

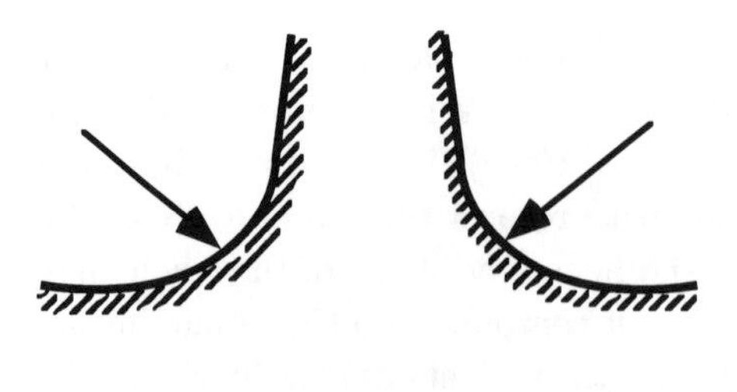

Figure 18.1
Part Boundaries May be Found in 2D Images at Pairs of Negative Minima of Principal Curvature Along the Contour (cf. Hoffman and Richards 1984).

in the partonomy of the category "human body"), structuring object knowledge in terms of parts opens the possibility of efficient cross-classification (e.g. the shape model for the category "arm" need not be repeated in the model of the shape of the human body).

For these reasons, many theories concerning knowledge of object shapes agree in their emphasis on the structural relationships of parts composing the shapes of whole objects. They disagree much more often in their approach to the shapes of parts.

We will not attempt to settle the controversy concerning the representation of part shapes, but merely reiterate our claim that shape representations functioning as the "target" of the recognition process may also serve as the starting point of imagination processes. The claim that we are interested in defending is that shape information is represented in *partonomic* structures, for the reasons given above, and that depictional representations reflect this structure. The chief advantage for depictional processes lies in the *hierarchical structure* of the partonomy, which has also some characteristics of a granularity structure (cf. section 18.1.3): The shape of a part at the next higher level may be an abstraction over the shape at the level in question, which is induced by its internal part structure at the next lower level.

Hierarchical structure is reflected in Fig. 18.2, which illustrates Marr and Nishihara's (1978) description of the shape of the human body (see also Marr 1982: 306). In their proposal, the overall description of this shape at the top level with a single generalized cylinder is highly abstract, representing nothing more than height and girth, with increasingly detailed part descriptions further down the hierarchy.

A hierarchical model makes it possible for visual object recognition to operate at an appropriate scale. As mentioned above, the detection of part boundaries calls for measurement of curvature of the contour at various scales, and may fail to detect small parts when coarser scales are used. However, it may be sufficient to recognize a human body, for example, just if the head, limbs and torso—and their relationships to each other—are recognized, without having to detect part boundaries at a scale at which fingers can be distinguished; indeed, recognition at finer scales may be unnecessarily costly and susceptible to noise. For scenes in which smaller parts are more prominent (such as a "close-up" of the hand), the lower levels of the hierarchy are more appropriate.

It is important to realize that the hierarchical models of shape proposed in the literature are of a propositional format.[8] But according to our proposal, each level of the propositional partonomy is related to an image in a depictional hierarchy with a corresponding degree of detail, precisely as Figure 18.2 suggests; thus there may be a coarse depiction of the human body consisting of six parts, and even a highly abstract one consisting of a single upright cylinder. As we argue in the next section, depictional processes have the same advantage from hierarchical models that perceptual processes enjoy: the ability to use the appropriate level of abstraction and detail needed for the task at hand.

18.1.3 Hybrid Partonomies: Levels of Granularity in Pictorial Representations

Both partonomies and the depictions associated with them are arranged according to levels of detail, which we call—in the spirit of Hobbs' seminal paper (1985)—granularity levels (Habel 1991). We will argue that the reasoning system, or more generally, the cognitive system (artificial or natural), always tries to use the "most efficient level," i.e. "least complex" level of representation that is sufficient for solving the problem in question.

In this subsection, we present linguistic arguments for usefulness of depictions associated with various granularity levels (see also Landau

[8]Therefore these representations fit nicely with Kosslyn's (1980) view that the LTM-representation format for the generation of mental images is propositional in nature.

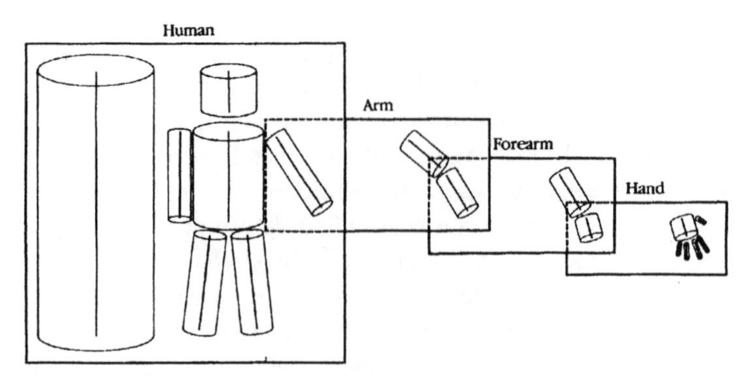

Figure 18.2
Hierarchical Model of the Shape of the Human Body. (Reprinted by permission from D. Marr and H. K. Nishihara, "Representation and recognition of the spatial organization of three-dimensional shapes," *Proc. R. Soc. London B 200*, 1978, 269–294).

and Jackendoff 1993). We assume that the representations used as a starting point for the generation of depictions may be obtained from linguistic inputs; for example, one might form of a depiction of a scene described in a text in order to be able to inspect the spatial relations that the text does not explicitly specify. Alternatively, a depiction that is already generated might be inspected to determine whether some linguistic expression applies to the state of affairs that it depicts. Thus we are interested especially in linguistic expressions whose interpretations depend on object shapes specified at various levels of granularity. We consider two classes of such expressions: the *dimensional adjectives* and *verbs of position.*

The dimensional adjectives in English include the following expressions: *long-short, wide-narrow, thick-thin, high-low, deep-shallow, tall-short.* According to the analysis of Lang (1989), dimensional adjectives specify symmetry axes of the objects described; *long* and *thick* applied to a tree trunk, for example, specify the trunk's main axis and diameter, where it is conceived as a cylindrical body. It is clear that dimensional adjectives may be used to specify axes of symmetry at any level of granularity; one can describe the height and girth of the human body even at the coarsest representation of its shape in Marr and Nishihara's hierarchical model, where it is constructed as a large upright cylinder. One may also describe limbs as *long* and a torso as *thin,* where the part in question is conceived as a simple symmetric shape and its internal struc-

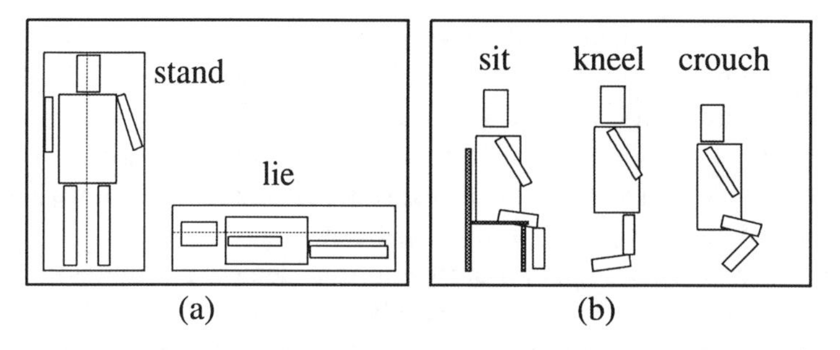

Figure 18.3
A: Level-1 Position Verbs, B: Level-2 Position Verbs

ture is irrelevant (cf. Simmons 1995). Furthermore, it can be decided which of two human bodies is taller, simply by comparing the lengths of the main axes of the level-1 cylinders, without inspecting their internal structures.

The verbs of position—with respect to humans—include the following expressions: *stand, lie, sit, kneel, crouch.* Among other things, verbs of position[9] specify a certain part configuration, as well as the orientation of the overall shape in space (relative to the gravitational vertical) and the means of support. Jackendoff (1987: 203) noticed that verbs of position specify part configurations at differing levels of granularity.

Consider a depiction such as Figure 18.3a below, in which the positions of some human beings are displayed. The components at finer granularity levels (i.e. the limbs) are aligned in such a way that a description at the coarsest level of representation, with a single axis of symmetry, is possible. Thus it is sufficient to take only that level into consideration to decide which figure is *standing* and which one is *lying*, since this distinction depends in part on whether the main axis of the object described is aligned to the local vertical (cf. Lang et al. 1991, Simmons 1995). Indeed, it would be incorrect to specify part configurations at finer levels of granularity, since the meanings of *standing* and *lying* are neutral with respect to, say, the spatial relations among the fingers.

[9]In the following, we confine the discussion to the case of "human positions." Some of the verbs listed here are not acceptable for [-animate], or even [-human] nouns; and some, such as lie, are level-2 verbs for quadrupeds. On the other hand, the conceptual lexical entry for the noun gives information about the axes (see Lang et al. 1991) at the granularity level to be considered.

However, other position predicates such as *sitting, kneeling* and *crouching* indicate a more complex internal structure and must be verified at finer levels of granularity, as Fig. 18.3b demonstrates. But again, the specification of part configurations for these positions at granularity levels that are too fine is in error, for these expressions are also neutral with respect to relations between parts at levels below the one indicated.

The linguistic evidence supports our claim that depictional representations should correspond to levels of granularity in partonomies. There are also good reasons for the use of hybrid partonomies in commonsense reasoning, and we will give a detailed example from the domain of naive physics in section 18.2.2. In the next section, we discuss the specifics of a system for reasoning about part-whole relations, the relation between structure and function, and segmentation of objects into parts that differ from the "componential" approach that was discussed in this section.

18.2 Hybrid Reasoning About Part-Whole Relations

18.2.1 A General System for Reasoning About Parts

A cognitive system able to reason about part-whole structures, i.e. to handle knowledge about parts, must allow interactions of the different types of partitioning, namely decomposition and segmentation (cf. Section 18.1). One way to enable this kind of reasoning is to provide one common basis for the different modes of partition:

A *depictorial model,* i.e. an analog, spatial model of an object can serve as a natural blackboard for different ways of segmenting that object into parts. Depictorial models, formed in the depictional representation format, have spatial as well as visual properties.[10]

In the interaction of different types of partitioning, in a depictorial model of an object one (permanent) layer represents the inherent decomposition into components, and the second (constructed) one represents a spatial segmentation into left, right, front, back, upper and lower parts. Using that model, it is possible to infer which components partly or completely belong to a certain spatial part, e.g. the front, by comput-

[10] I.e. perspective and phenomena of concealment are relevant (see Finke's 1989 discussion of the principle of *Perceptual Equivalence* and that of *Spatial Equivalence*). Since internal depictional representation are not necessarily isomorphic to the represented objects, they can have a diagrammatic character; in this case, we call them *diagrams.*

ing the components lying inside the segment of the model determined as front part.

According to the observations made so far, the basic system for reasoning about parts in a chosen domain must at least include the following facilities:

1. knowledge about the components of all the relevant objects,
2. a mechanism for computing segmentations involving external criteria, especially spatial and functional criteria,
3. a depictorial representation for the objects that serve as a blackboard for the interaction of different modes of partitioning.

Knowledge About Components Knowledge about components includes the pure (mereological) part-whole relations as well as the spatial structure of the parts, in addition to other important features such as function or material of the whole and all its parts. This may be represented in the form of concepts structured in a taxonomy. The concept of an object contains the mereological information about its components as a "has-part"-hierarchy, the *partonomy.* The spatial structure of the components is obtained by mapping the partonomy onto the depictorial model of the whole. Each entry in a partonomy, each part of the whole or part of a part, is a concept in its own right. As the case study in section 18.2.2 will show, conceptual information can be more or less complex. Some kinds of knowledge, for example concerning features like material or color, may represented as feature-value pairs, while more complex knowledge, such as knowledge about function, may take the form of rules that combine information from different sources.

An example of a taxonomy for a "city" domain is illustrated in the left half of Fig. 18.4, where "building" is a superordinate category, "house," "passage," "station" are some of the basic-level categories, and "single family house" or "duplex" are refining subordinate categories.

As mentioned in section 18.1.1 above, extensive knowledge of parts is characteristic of basic level categories (Tversky and Hemenway 1984, Tversky 1990). Tversky comments that "different subordinate categories belonging to the same basic level category ... tend to share parts and differ from one another in characteristics of their parts or in other features" while "objects belonging to different basic level categories from a single superordinate category tend to share function while having different parts." (Tversky 1990: 338).

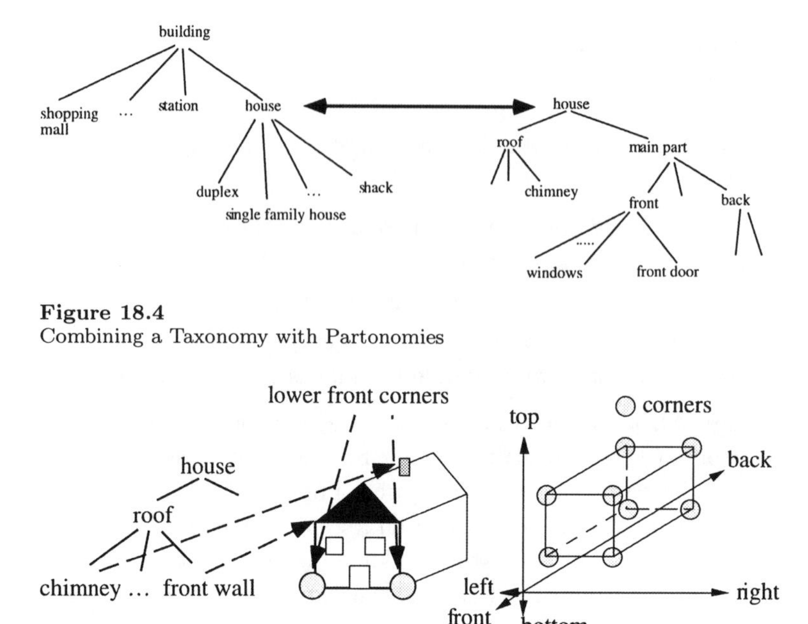

Figure 18.4
Combining a Taxonomy with Partonomies

Figure 18.5
Spatial Part Structure

The framework presented here reflects the result that there normally exists a partonomy for every basic level concept that is inherited by its subconcepts, perhaps with refinements. Concepts corresponding to superordinate categories such as furniture generally contain functional but not part knowledge. For the sake of simplicity, we assume that the partonomy of a basic concept is shared by every member of the concept, not only by the typical ones. Figure 18.4 shows the taxonomy and one of the partonomies for the "building" example.

In accordance with psychological results, we postulate a depictorial model for basic level concepts; it is used to represent the spatial part structure of a (basic level) concept by mapping the entries in the partonomy to sectors in the depiction (see Figure 18.5, left).

Mechanism for Segmentations Involving External Criteria The depictorial image also forms the basis for computing segmentations in contrast to partitions into components. Segmentations based on features like function or color use conceptual information to compute the decomposition of the whole object. For a decomposition according to material, all components sharing the same material can be grouped together to form a new complex part, which of course is characterized by reference to a specific property, e.g. "the windows and doors made of wood" in contrast to "...those made of aluminum."

Another process is used to compute spatial segments where spatial concepts and schemes are used as external criteria instead of object features. Especially important for solid physical objects is the three-dimensional scheme of a cube shown in Figure 18.5 (right), which can be used if the object or the spatial projection of the whole provides a three-dimensional form that approximates a cube[11]. The structure of a cube is used to select specific halves, sides, edges, etc. of an object.

The method for the processing of cube segments implements the external, diagrammatical scheme of the six-sided cube by procedures operating on the depictorial model of the object. Each procedure computes a different kind of segment, e.g., sides, edges, and so on. To be able to select a specific segment, e.g., the front half, the cube must be augmented by a reference system. There are different alternatives for reference systems, and the appropriate choice depends on the actual domain or application.[12] Figure 18.5 shows a cube scheme that is augmented by an intrinsic reference system. Because intrinsic reference frames are object-inherent knowledge, they form a part of the object concept.

Procedurally, the selection of a specific kind of segment from its possible extensions is done by parameters associated with the directions of the reference system. To specify a half (the *front, back,* etc.), one parameter is sufficient, while for a corner, three parameters (one vertical and two horizontal dimensions) are necessary. COR shows the procedure 'corner' and the possible parameter values. If different reference systems could be applied, an additional parameter which specifies the system must be supplied to the procedures.

```
(COR) corner(x1, x2, x3)
```

[11] "Approximation of a cube" might be decided by means of shape representation at coarse scales, as suggested in section 18.1.2. In the conceptual lexicon, the orientation-scheme appropriate for an entity is implicitly represented in the depictorial part of a concept description.

[12] The most common variants are the intrinsic or different kinds of extrinsic reference systems that are suitable for cognitive tasks, especially those that are linguistically designated, the four compass directions (*north/south, east/west*) used for geographic objects, or the (technical) internal three-dimensional systems of objects that are used in technical domains like design.

```
x1=top/bottom, x2=front/back, x3=left/right
```

In order for the segmentation procedures to be applied, a spatial representation such as a diagram of the whole is needed. An instantiated procedure selects one part of the spatial representation as the required segment. If a parameter is not specified, the procedure computes one segment for every possible instantiation of the underdetermined parameter. The selection processes vary for the different kinds of segments. For selecting a half, the process computes only a section through the center point of the object guided by the reference system; for selecting corners, gestalt aspects are taken into account to compute the pieces of the object that can be considered as corners. Figure 18.5 shows the result of the evaluation of the expression "the lower front corners of the house" or "corner(bottom, front, x)," written as procedure instantiation.

18.2.2 Case Study: Using Hybrid Partonomies for Commonsense Reasoning

Commonsense Reasoning About Physical Phenomena The case study shows the use of propositional and depictional knowledge about parts in reasoning about a thermos bottle. The emphasis of this study is on the interaction of propositional and depictional knowledge, and not on qualitative physics. Therefore, we describe only the standard view of a thermos rather than a complete model. The standard model will turn out to be sufficient to explain the following two scenes:

Imagine you are longing for a cup of hot tea. About one hour ago, you made fresh tea, poured it into your new red thermos, which you put on the kitchen table. Now you enter the kitchen again with your tea cup to fetch hot tea.

1. To your surprise, you see the stopper lying on the table beside the bottle. Who forgot to fix the stopper after pouring out tea! By chance, the tea will be cold.
2. To your dismay, the bottle is lying on the floor. You hurry to the thermos to see whether the liquid is running out, making the floor wet, or whether the stopper is fixed so nothing can leak out. After that, you check if the bottle is broken.

The kind of naive or qualitative physical reasoning involved in these two scenes based on mental models of the physical phenomena and objects in our everyday life. Such a mental model[13] of an object of everyday use incorporates mainly two kinds of knowledge:

- knowledge about the general structure of members of the object category, especially about parts and their spatial configuration (cf. the empirical results cited in section 18.1.1). This knowledge includes information about form, material, color, and other properties of objects in terms of their parts. It is appropriate for perceptual classification of objects, as mentioned in section 18.1.2, and forms the basis for functional descriptions.
- knowledge about the functionality of members of the object category defined with respect to the knowledge just described. It incorporates the description of the general functionality of objects, mostly with respect to the functionality and configuration of their parts, and the typical interaction of humans with such objects (cf. Tversky and Hemenway 1984).

In the following, we focus on the interaction of the spatial aspects of objects and their parts with the functionality of the object, abstracting from material, color and so on.

The Mental Model of a Thermos Bottle First, we look at the general structure of a thermos as given mainly by parts and their configuration. The knowledge about parts is divided between a propositional partonomy and images of the standard view of the object. The core is a partonomy expressing mereological knowledge, in which the entries are concepts themselves. Figure 18.6 shows the partonomy for our thermos; some of the leaves in the part-of tree, e.g. the handle, can be subdivided further for specific objects.[14]

The spatial configuration of these parts is reflected in depictions of a thermos bottle in standard position at different levels of granularity (see Figure 18.7). The depiction at what we call granularity level 0 is the coarsest picture and shows the thermos as seen from far away.

[13]Our notion of mental model is related to that used by Johnson-Laird (1983). But there are at least two major differences: first, we assume mental models of objects as well as of situations, and second, we give a specification of the representation format of mental models.

[14]Additionally, information about the separability of the stopper can be found both in the stopper concept as well as by means of an annotation "separable-part-of" on the link between stopper and thermos.

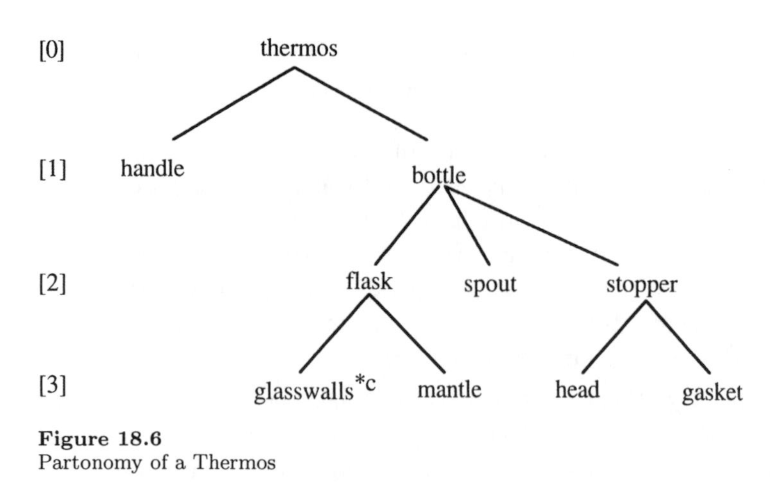

Figure 18.6
Partonomy of a Thermos

Notice that even that depiction contains enough information to decide if a bottle is standing or lying! The second figure shows level 1, which might be sufficient for the visual classification of a thermos bottle. The next two pictures show, at a more detailed granularity level (level 2), all of the visible parts (relevant for the example as presented here), and can display a fixed or a separated stopper. The entries in the propositional partonomy are linked to the corresponding parts in the depictions; the coarsest level of granularity at which a concept is depicted is indicated by a level (an integer in square brackets).[15]

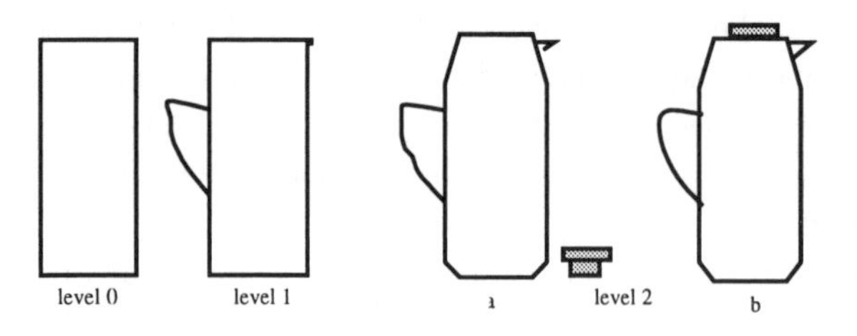

Figure 18.7
Thermos Bottle in Standard Position

So for reasoning about a thermos bottle, the partonomies and diagrams are combined with information from the part concepts. For ex-

[15]In the present chapter we neglect the problems and phenomena of parts that are concealed or otherwise not always visible. We indicate the fact that the glass walls are not visible (in level 3)—if one takes the same perspective as for level 2 —with the superscript "*c" (cf. Figure 18.6).

ample, to infer the material of the upper half of a thermos, first the segment forming the upper half must be computed in the appropriate image. This segment is inspected using the links to the partonomy to find the affected parts. The concepts of these parts now provide the information about the material.

Next, we consider the functionality of thermos bottles. We idealize our model by abstracting from nonstandard uses and temporal aspects, in order to focus on hybrid reasoning. By abstracting from time, we do not model processes such as the slow process of cooling of the contained liquid. All we propose is a static model of structure and functionality of a thermos, which can provide the basis for a process-oriented, time-dependent model.[16]

The overall functionality of a typical thermos is to keep liquids like tea or coffee hot. Under a more detailed view, there are three functionally relevant states of use for a thermos:

1. *Filling.* The bottle must be standing and the stopper unfixed. After filling in liquid, the bottle is not empty. If the preconditions are not fulfilled, then either the bottle remains empty (if it is not standing and the stopper is unfixed), or it remains in its previous condition (stopper fixed, bottle in any position).
2. *Storing Liquids.* This state can be divided further in the following two substates:[17]
3. *Providing Containment.* The bottle must be standing or the stopper must be fixed. If this state holds, a non-empty bottle remains non-empty. Otherwise, the liquid runs out, resulting in an empty bottle and an emergency. An emergency is an alarm state indicating a problem that requires immediate attention.

[16]As one of the referees mentioned: "If the time elapsed is large (say, two days), then the liquid won't be hot, regardless of whether the stopper is in place; and if the time is very short (30 seconds), then the liquid will be hot even if there is no stopper." But the static model is not an idealization only; it is also useful in commonsense reasoning. If someone enters a room and sees the thermos, she may have no information about elapsed time. Therefore, it is reasonable to use the static model in a default reasoning process. The mental model can easily be extended to bottles keeping cool liquids cool by abstracting to the function of holding the initial temperature more or less constant.

[17]Clearly, *Storing Liquids* is the state that primarily fulfills the overall function of a thermos bottle, but the other two states are no less important (since hot liquid is of no use if it cannot be made available).

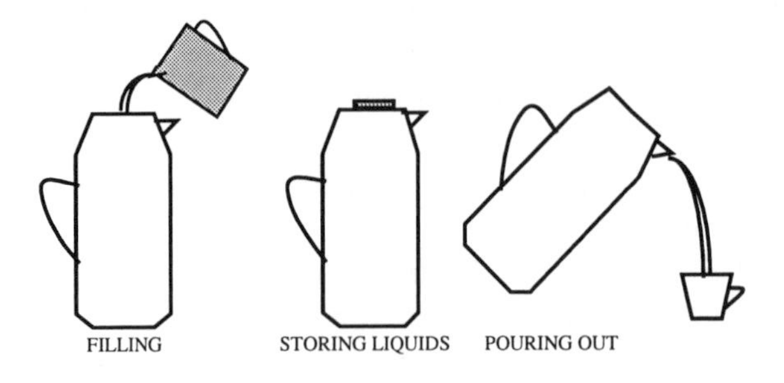

Figure 18.8
The Three States of Use of a Thermos Bottle

4. *Retaining Heat.* The stopper must be fixed. If this state holds, the contained liquid remains hot. Otherwise, it gets cold.
5. *Pouring Out.* The stopper must be unfixed and the bottle must be tilted.[18] If this state holds, the thermos can (but need not) become empty. Otherwise, the thermos behaves as in the state *Providing Containment.*

Knowledge about the states is augmented by knowledge about the initial condition of a thermos bottle, the possible transitions between the states and the actions necessary for each transition. We will ignore the transition information in the remainder of the chapter, because it is not necessary for modeling our two—static—scenes. As an initial condition, we assume that the thermos bottle is empty with fixed or unfixed stopper.

Like the general structural knowledge above, knowledge about the states just described is coded in a hybrid format. Preconditions, results and, if necessary, the causal structure of each state are defined by propositional means, e.g. by rules. The formalization refers both to the structural knowledge provided by the propositional and depictional partonomies and depictions showing the typical spatial conditions that hold in a state. The standard views shown in Figure 18.8 provide prototypical knowledge about the situations of using a thermos as described

[18]To what degree the thermos must be tilted to pour out tea depends on the amount of liquid contained, the design of the bottle, and other criteria. To model the "pouring" behavior, a more general theory including an ontology of liquids (see Hayes 1985) is necessary. On the other hand, the general situational concept of "pouring from a container" has to be instantiated with the level-0 depiction for solving this problem. We abstract from these details in the present chapter.

by the three states above. For all depictions, the finest level of granularity (level 2) is necessary in order to show the status of the stopper (fixed or unfixed).

To explain the scenes mentioned above, it is sufficient to model the overall functionality of a thermos bottle and the specific state of storing liquids. One expects a thermos bottle that has been filled to contain hot liquid if nothing has gone wrong. This expectation is formalized by the default rule `RD` with the existence of a thermos bottle as its only precondition. The phrase "if nothing has gone wrong" can be modeled according the default theory used, e.g. by the predicate ABNORMAL in the case of McCarthy's circumscriptions (McCarthy 1980) or by the M-operator in the case of Reiter's default reasoning (Reiter 1980), which we use to formalize the default condition:

```
(RD) Thermos(TH) and M[not(Empty(TH) and Hot(liquid(TH)))]
      -> not(Empty(TH) and Hot(liquid(TH))
```

`liquid` is the function which yields the content of a bottle.

The intuitive meaning of the default rule `RD` can be captured by the following English version: "IF there is a thermos bottle, and it is consistent with the system's beliefs that the bottle is not empty and that its content (the liquid in it) is hot, THEN it is appropriate to infer that the bottle is not empty and that its content is hot."

The situations that are interesting for reasoning are those in which the M-operator blocks the default rule, meaning that the thermos does not behave in the intended way. The default condition `M[p]` or "it is consistent with the system's beliefs that p" is satisfied as long as `not(p)` is not provable, and is blocked if `not(p)` is provable. That means that the proof of the default condition relies on the *absence* of knowledge.

For rule `RD` the blocking situation arises if `Empty(TH)` or `not(Hot (liquid(TH)))` can be verified. For example, the state *Pouring Out* can possibly result in `Empty(TH)`, therefore blocking the default. Another way of blocking the default condition involves problems with the two substates of *Storing Liquids.* If the preconditions of *Providing Containment* do not hold, the result is an empty bottle and an emergency (rule `R1`). If the stopper is not fixed in substate *Retaining Heat,* the contained liquid will get cold (rule `R2`).

```
(R1)  not(Standing(TH)) and not(Fixed(stopper(TH)))
```

```
      -> Empty(TH) and EMERGENCY
(R2)  not(Fixed(stopper(TH)))
      -> not(Hot(liquid(TH)))
```

`stopper` is the function which yields the stopper of a thermos.

Reasoning with Hybrid Knowledge The verification of the basic predicates `Thermos`, `Standing`, and `Fixed` can be done by visual processes, for which the image may originate either from perception or from depictional representations. The application of the predicate `Thermos` to some object, for example, may be verified by visual classification (perhaps on the granularity level 1 shown in Figure 18.7). To verify the predicate `Standing`, it must be determined whether the object's main symmetry axis is approximately aligned to the local vertical, which is done at the coarsest granularity level. In addition to visual verification at the most detailed granularity level, the predicate `Fixed` may require tactile manipulation to be verified. In any case, the visual images obtained during visual verification may be compared with images of the standard view of a state concept as described above.

Using rules, facts, and perceptual verification, there are two different ways of modeling our scenes, which both derive the same information, but perform differently. The first is the traditional theorem proving method, which as an augmentation uses visual processes to verify some predicates. The second one is an attention-driven method that uses forward inferences if a deviation from the standard case is detected by propositional or visual procedures. We present both methods by modeling the first scene mentioned above (the scene is described informally below as the "visual experience"). The intention underlying the action is to check if the thermos is not empty and if the tea contained is hot. It is formalized by goal 1, where the term `TH` refers to the specific thermos and `liquid(TH)` to the expected content of `TH`.

```
Visual experience:
  a standing thermos with stopper lying beside it
Goal 1: not(Empty(TH))and Hot(liquid(TH))
```

The goal can be verified by using the default rule `RD`.

Theorem Proving with Visual Verification The verification of the precondition of `RD` is expressed as step 1.

```
step 1: Thermos (TH) and M[Hot(liquid(TH)) and
        not(Empty(TH))]
```

The first proposition `Thermos (TH)` can be verified by a visual verification. For step 2 remains the default condition.

```
step 2: M[Hot(liquid(TH)) and not(Empty(TH))]
```

Step 3 is the result of the evaluation of the default operator `M`. The proposition `M[p]` is blocked if `not(p)` can be verified, otherwise it is satisfied. Therefore we must try to verify `not(p)`.

```
step 3: not[(Hot(liquid(TH)) and not(Empty(TH))]
```

Step 4 results from a (logical) transformation.

```
step 4: not(Hot(liquid(TH))) or Empty(TH)
```

Using rule `R2` the proposition `not(Hot(liquid(TH)))` is replaced by `not(Fixed(stopper(TH)))`.

```
step 5: not(Fixed(stopper(TH))) or Empty(TH)
```

The proposition `not(Fixed(stopper(TH)))` can be verified by a visual verification. This turns the whole formula in step 3 `TRUE`.

```
step 6: TRUE
```

With step 6, the default condition is blocked and Goal 1 cannot be proved.

One cannot decide from the fact that the goal cannot be proved whether or not there is hot tea in the thermos. One way to get a definite answer is to try to verify the negation of goal 1, which is possible by using the rule `R2`. So the finite proof states that is it not possible to get hot tea.

Attention-Driven Method In step 1, the precondition of `RD` is verified.

```
step 1: Thermos (TH) and M[Hot(liquid(TH)) and
        not(Empty(TH))]
```

The first proposition `Thermos (TH)` can be verified visually. In step 2, the default condition remains.

```
step 2: M[Hot(liquid(TH)) and not(Empty(TH))]
```

The image obtained during visual verification does not match the typical image of the state *Storing Liquids,* because the stopper is lying beside the bottle. As a result, the fact `not(Fixed(stopper(TH)))` is returned to the propositional proof procedure. In a forward proof mode, step 3 tries to evaluate this fact.

```
step 3 (Forward): not(Fixed(stopper(TH)))
```

Using rule `R2` in a forward chaining mode, the proposition `not (Fixed (stopper(TH)))` is replaced by `not(Hot(liquid(TH)))`.

```
step 4: not(Hot(liquid(TH)))
```

With step 4 the Goal 1 can be directly falsified.

The two methods result in the same inference: There is no hot tea in the thermos bottle, i.e. Goal 1 fails. In both cases, this information is ultimately derived by the observation that the stopper is not fixed. But the attention-driven method comes to that conclusion more easily. For both methods, reasoning about the overall functionality of the object takes the functionality and integration of the parts into account. For the verification of certain predicates, visual processes at different levels of granularity are necessary.

18.3 Conclusion

In this chapter we have introduced partonomies as a kind of knowledge relevant to a wide range of cognitive processes, e.g. visual classification, language processing, and reasoning about objects. The importance of knowledge about parts is based on their ability to combine purely mereological attributes with spatial and functional attributes, and on their utility in the interaction between different modes of processing.

> "Part configuration is especially important because of its role as a bridge between appearance and activity, between perception and behavior, between structure and function." (Tversky and Hemenway 1984: 188)

We use a hybrid system consisting of partonomies interacting with depictions for reasoning. Both are organized in granularity levels, and the depictions reflect the hierarchy proposed in object representations for visual processes. In the case study, we presented a reasoning process, which we call the attention-driven method, that combines knowledge about parts with depictional knowledge about the typical states that an article of daily use is involved in. By using depictional knowledge, the attention-driven method comes to a conclusion more easily than the traditional theorem proving method by detecting deviations from the standard situation.

Acknowledgements

The research described in this article was supported in part by the Doctoral Program in Cognitive Science at the University of Hamburg (funded by the German Science Foundation; Ha 1237/3) and the Center for Interdisciplinary Research (ZIF) at the University of Bielefeld. We wish to thank the members of the research group Mental Models in Discourse Processing at ZIF and the participants of the workshop on "Principles of Hybrid Systems and Reasoning" at IJCAI '93 for discussions; and Stephanie Kelter, Carola Eschenbach and two anonymous reviewers for helpful comments on the manuscript.

References

Biederman, I. 1987. Recognition-by-Components. A Theory of Human Image Understanding. *Psychological Review* 94: 115–147

Davis, E. 1990. *Representations of Commonsense Knowledge.* San Mateo, Calif: Morgan-Kaufmann

Eschenbach, C., and Heydrich, W. 1994. Classical Mereology and Restricted Domains. In: *Formal Ontology in Conceptual Analysis and Knowledge Representation,* ed. N. Guarino and R. Poli. Dordrecht: Kluwer.

Finke, R. A. 1989. *Principles in Mental Imagery.* Cambridge, Mass.: The MIT Press.

Gerstl, P., and Pribbenow, S. 1994. Midwinters, End Games, and Bodyparts: A Classification of Part-Whole Relations. In: *Formal Ontology in Conceptual Analysis and Knowledge Representation,* ed. N. Guarino and R. Poli. Dordrecht: Kluwer.

Glasgow, J., and Papadias, D. 1992. Computational Imagery. *Cognitive Science* 16: 355–394.

Glenberg, A. M.; Meyer, M.; and Lindem, K. 1987. Mental Models Contribute to Foregrounding During Text Comprehension. *Journal of Memory and Language* 26: 69–83.

Guarino, N., and Poli, R. eds. *Formal Ontology in Conceptual Analysis and Knowledge Representation.* Dordrecht: Kluwer. Forthcoming.

Habel, Ch. 1990. Propositional and Depictorial Representations of Spatial Knowledge: The Case of *Path* Concepts. In: *Natural Language and Logic: Lecture Notes in Artificial Intelligence.*, 94–117. ed. Rudi Studer. Berlin: Springer.

Habel, Ch. 1991. Hierarchical Representations of Spatial Knowledge: Aspects of Embedding and Granularity. Presented at Second International Colloquium on Cognitive Science (ICCS-91), San Sebastian.

Habel, Ch. 1994. Discreteness, Finiteness, and the Structure of Topological Spaces. In Topological Foundations of Cognitive Science, ed. C. Eschenbach; Ch. Habel; and B. Smith. Report 37, Univ. Hamburg, Doctoral Program in Cognitive Science.

Hayes, P. 1985. Naive Physics I: Ontology for Liquids. In *Formal Theories of the Commonsense World*, 71–107, ed. Jerry R. Hobbs and Robert C. Moore. Norwood, N.J.: Ablex.

Hobbs, J. R. 1985. Granularity. In *Proceedings of the Ninth International Joint Conference on Artificial Intelligence*, 432–435. San Mateo, Calif.: Morgan Kaufmann.

Hoffman, D. D., and Richards, W. A. 1984. Parts of Recognition. *Cognition* 18: 65–96

Jackendoff, R. 1987. *Consciousness and the Computational Mind.* Cambridge, Mass.: The MIT Press.

Johnson-Laird, P. N. 1983. *Mental Models.* Cambridge, England: Cambridge University Press.

Kosslyn, S. 1980. *Image and Mind.* Cambridge, Mass: Harvard University Press.

Kosslyn, S. 1987. Seeing and Imaging in the Cerebral Hemispheres: A Computational Approach. *Psychological Review* 94(2): 148–175.

Kosslyn, S. 1994. *Image and Brain.* Cambridge, Mass.: The MIT Press.

Landau, B., and Jackendoff, R. 1993. "What" and "Where" in Spatial Language and Spatial Cognition. *Behavioral and Brain Sciences* 16(2): 217–265.

Lang, E. 1989. The Semantics of Dimensional Designation of Spatial Objects. In: *Dimensional Adjectives: Grammatical Structure and Conceptual Interpretation,* ed. M. Bierwisch and E. Lang, 263–417. Berlin: Springer-Verlag.

Lang, E.; Carstensen, K.; and Simmons, G. 1991. *Modeling Spatial Knowledge on a Linguistic Basis.* Berlin: Springer-Verlag.

Latecki, L., and Pribbenow, S. 1992. On Hybrid Reasoning for Processing Spatial Expressions. In Proceedings ECAI-92, 389–393.

Lewis, D. 1991. *Parts of Classes.* Oxford: Basil Blackwell.

Marr, D. 1982. *Vision.* San Francisco: W. H. Freeman .

Marr, D., and Nishihara H. K. 1978. Representation and Recognition of the Spatial Organization of Three-Dimensional Shapes. In Proceedings of the Royal Society, Vol. B 200, 269–294.

McCarthy, J. 1980. Circumscription—A Form of Non-Monotonic Reasoning. *Artificial Intelligence* 13: 27–39.

Mokhtarian, F., and Mackworth, A. 1992. A Theory of Mutiscale, Curvature-Based Shape Representation of Planar Curves. *IEEE Trans. Pattern Analysis and Machine Intelligence* 14(8): 789–805

Palmer, S. 1978. Fundamental Aspects of Cognitive Representations. In *Cognition and Categorization,* ed. E. Rosch and B. Lloyd, 259–303. Hillsdale, N.J.: Erlbaum.

Reiter, R. 1980. A Logic for Default Reasoning. *Artificial Intelligence* 13: 81–132

Rosch, E. 1977. Human Categorization. In *Advances in Crosscultural Psychology,* ed. N. Warren, 1–49. New York: Academic Press.

Simons, P. 1987. *Parts. A Study in Ontology.* Oxford: Clarendon Press

Simmons, G. 1994. Shapes, Part Structures and Object Concepts. In ECAI-94 Workshop on Parts and Wholes: Conceptual Part-Whole Relations and Formal Mereology. Amsterdam

Simmons, G. 1995. Knowledge of Shape in Object Concepts. Ph.D. diss., Universität Hamburg. Forthcoming.

Tversky, B. 1990. Where Partonomies and Taxonomies Meet. In: *Meanings and Prototypes: Studies in Linguistic Categorization,* ed. S. L. Tsohatzidis, 334–344. New York: Routledge.

Tversky, B., and Hemenway, K. 1984. Objects, Parts, and Categories. *Journal of Experimental Psychology: General* 113: 169–193

Ullman, S. 1989. Aligning Pictorial Descriptions: An Approach to Object Recognition. *Cognitive Psychology* 12: 97–136

Winston, M. E.; Chaffin, R.; and Herrman, D. 1987. A Taxonomy of Part-Whole Relations. *Cognitive Science* 11: 417–444

IV PROBLEM SOLVING WITH DIAGRAMS

Introduction to Section IV

Problem Solving with Diagrams

Yumi Iwasaki
Stanford University

There is an old proverb in Japanese, "a hundred hearings do not equal one look." Here, "a hearing" does not refer to the act of hearing something but refers broadly to the act of acquiring information through some linguistic description, while "a look" refers to doing so through an image. The Chinese proverb "a picture is worth ten thousand words" conveys the same message though the former focuses on the mode of perception as opposed to the mode of representation.

While these are ancient proverbs, the question that Larkin and Simon asked of what it is that one gains by taking one "look" that one does not gain through hearing 100 descriptions is relatively new. Despite the broad acceptance of the sentiment expressed in these proverbs in different cultures, the main stream artificial intelligence research has mostly concentrated on use of solely symbolic means to represent and manipulate information. One could say that the main stream AI has relied only on numerous "hearings" without taking advantage of "looks." Sloman (this volume) gives a good summary of why it has been the case, not only in artificial intelligence but also in mathematical sciences in general.[1]

Intuitively, it certainly feels much easier to understand many situations by taking "one look" than by hearing an explanation. For example, given the two sentences, "A is shorter than B" and "C is longer than B," anyone can conclude that "A is shorter than C" based on the meaning of the words "shorter" and "longer." However, I can reach the same conclusion much easier and faster by looking at a drawing of three line segments properly labeled and aligned. As a student of artificial intelligence, I am

[1] In this article, I will use the term "symbolic" to mean what Sloman calls "Fregean" and what Larkin and Simon call "sentential," if only for a stylistic reason. Though I like the precision in using the term "Fregean," it is more awkward to form an adverb from "Fregean" than from "symbolic" as "symbolically." I will also use the terms "diagrammatic," "pictorial," and "visual" somewhat interchangeably to mean what Sloman calls "analogical" and what Larkin and Simon call "pictorial."

intrigued most by the questions of how a pictorial representation differs from a symbolic representation, how symbolic reasoning interacts with diagrammatic reasoning in problem solving, and, above all, how one can take advantage of pictorial representations in building efficient problem solvers.

The Role of Diagrams in Problem Solving

People often draw diagrams to solve problems. Depending on the problem, drawing an appropriate diagram is the most crucial step in the solution process. Drawing a diagram to represent the relations given in a problem often helps one gain deeper understanding of the nature of the problem. This advantage of diagrams is not limited to spatial problems, as it would be apparent if the same drawing of line segments was used to compare prices of goods instead of length of line segments in the above example.

Research has been reported in cognitive psychology as well as artificial intelligence on the roles of diagrammatic reasoning in human problem solving. Larkin and Simon discussed extensively the advantages of diagrams for facilitating inference about topological or geometric relations (this volume). They state that one important advantage of diagrammatic representation is that it makes explicit the spatial relations that might require extensive search and numerous inference steps to detect using a symbolic representation. In other words, a pictorial representation often replaces an inference problem by a recognition problem. Chandrasekaran and Narayanan (1990), Novak and Bulko (1990), Borning (1979) and others have also pointed out the usefulness of diagrams to human problem solvers as a device to aid in visualization, gedanken experiments or prediction. Novak and Bulko (1990), and Koedinger and Anderson (this volume) have explored the idea that diagrams may sometimes be used not primarily for making base-level inference, but rather to help in the selection of an appropriate method to solve a problem, i.e. as an aid in organization of cognitive activity.

Qualitative Reasoning and Diagrams

One salient characteristic of reasoning with diagrams is that it is in general qualitative. In the above example of length comparison, even if the exact lengths of the three line segments were given and the diagram drawn in the correct proportion, what could be discerned just by glancing at the diagram would still be qualitative facts such as ordering relations. People tend to use diagrams in order to obtain rough qualitative answers, while they resort to more precise means when detailed numerical answers are required. Nevertheless, qualitative analysis is essential because it allows one to understand the global characteristics without being burdened by unimportant details and to detect quickly those places that warrant further, more sophisticated analysis.

Early interests in qualitative reasoning was motivated by, among other things, the desire to formalize human knowledge about commonsense physical phenomena and eventually to give machines an inference capability about such phenomena. Some of the earliest, influential work in qualitative physics was aimed at capturing such commonsense physical knowledge with a linguistic means (as a logical theory) (Hayes 1990, Davis 1988). However, commonsense physical reasoning often involves reasoning about space and shape. It has become apparent over the years that it is very difficult to formalize human knowledge about commonsensical, spatial problems.

Forbus states that one reason for this difficulty stems from the difficulty of finding a linguistic means to qualitatively represent spatial information in a way that is not problem-specific (this volume). However, the more fundamental problem seems to be that people's reasoning process about commonsense spatial problems does not fit well the model of a reasoning process with purely symbolic representations. This view would also suggest that an architecture of a system that can solve spatial problems as well as (or in a manner similar to that of) humans should include two separate representations for pictorial and symbolic information as well as separate mechanisms for manipulation of such information. Furthermore, the solution process would involve complex interactions between the two.

The remainder of this introduction discusses work by a number of researchers on problem solving systems which use diagrams, though only a few could be included in this section because of space limitations. Many of them have two different representation forms for diagrammatic and symbolic information as well as separate inference mechanisms that manipulate each type of representations. The ways in which the diagrammatic and symbolic information interact are different from one system to another. The sections are organized according to the types of problems the systems solve. This is because diagrammatic representation forms are often very specific to the domain and the type of problems. Therefore, I expect that the ways in which diagrams are interpreted and used in the problem solving process are influenced by the nature of the domain and the problem in both overt and subtle manners.

Geometry Problem Solving

Geometry has been used by many researchers as the domain in which to study reasoning with diagrams for an obvious reason; It is the only domain in which a diagram itself (or more precisely, the spatial relations among the diagrammatic elements – lines, points, angles, etc.) is the subject of study. The article by Koedinger and Anderson in this volume provides an extensive discussion of their work and many preceding pieces of work that studied problem solving process with geometry diagrams. This section includes a paper by McDougal, which describes another system called POLYA for solving geometry problems with diagrams (this volume). The important characteristics of McDougal's work is that it focuses on the role of diagrams as a means of indexing into the memory of previously solved cases. Noting that high school geometry textbooks usually present a prototypical problem along with its complete solution followed.by a suite of practice problems that are similar to the prototype, McDougal built POLYA as a case-based reasoning system that uses features of a given diagram to retrieve the solution to a similar problem encountered in the past.

An early precursor to this idea of diagrammatic cases appeared in the work by Koedinger and Anderson, who used diagrammatic configurations to generate a restricted set of rules. The idea of using spatial features of a diagram to retrieve relevant cases is also similar to the idea of visual cases by Narayanan and Chandrasekaran (1991), although in the latter, a case also contains non-visual, domain-specific conditions. In all these pieces of work, the idea of using features of a diagram to retrieve relevant information is compelling as a model of an efficient problem solving process with diagrams precisely because human eyes are very good at perceiving non-local patterns in a scene that is not too cluttered with many unessential details.

In a slightly different vein, Lindsay uses constraint maintenance techniques to manipulate a diagrammatic representation to make inferences and test conjectures in qualitative geometric reasoning (Lindsay 1992). His goal is to demonstrate that a combination of propositional and pictorial representations offers more psychologically plausible and computationally efficient ways of reasoning about mathematical problems. He has developed a computational model of human visual reasoning in the domain of plane geometry.

Geometry diagrams have characteristics that are not shared by diagrams in any other domains. Most importantly, geometry diagrams stand for themselves. In other words, they are not abstractions of the real world or anything else that is the real object of interest. In almost every other domain, diagrams represent something other than themselves that one is trying to study. As a consequence, in any other domain one must have sufficient information about what is represented by the diagram in order to understand or to reason with it. In contrast, a geometry diagram usually includes all the information that one needs to solve the problem, and one only needs knowledge of geometry to understand and reason with the diagram. For this reason, geometry can be seen as the ideal domain in which diagrammatic reasoning process can be studied without having to worry about all the background knowledge of the domain, most of which is not represented in the diagram at all. However, the same fact also makes geometric reasoning unrepresentative of diagrammatic reasoning in general. In other domains, the interaction between the process of reasoning with the visual information in the diagram and that of reasoning with non-visual knowledge of the domain is essential to understand the whole problem solving process.

Reasoning About Static Physical Problems

One of the first pieces of work that took the diagram as an integral part of understanding and solving a problem in domains other than geometry is Novak's work on physics problem solving. His system, ISAAC, solved problems in elementary dynamics (Novak 1977). ISAAC read a problem stated in English, generated an internal geometric model of the situation, set up mathematical equations, and solved them to produce an answer. It also drew a diagram to represent the given situation based on the geometric model. Though the diagram produced was not used by ISAAC for the problem solving purpose, it was used to convey the program's internal model of the situation to demonstrate that it truly "understood" the given problem. Novak went on to explore the importance of diagrams in conveying problem statement themselves in his later work with Bulko on BEATRIX (Novak & Bulko 1990). Noting that a diagram was often used as an integral part of problem specification, they built a system called BEATRIX, which understood a physics problem stated by a combination of English text and a diagram. Novak's article in this section describes both ISAAC and BEATRIX. It also discusses various roles of diagrams in problem solving in general.

Reasoning About Dynamic Interactions Between Solid Physical Objects

Since Novak's programs only dealt with static situations in dynamics, it sufficed to draw (or parse) one diagram for a problem. However, diagrams are also useful in visualizing dynamic behavior, which requires drawing a series of diagrams or drawing and continuously modifying a diagram. The work by Funt (this volume), Forbus and his colleagues Forbus, Nielsen, and Faltings,(1991) (also this volume), Narayanan and Chandrasekaran (1991), as well as that by Iwasaki, Tessler and Law (this volume) all aim to predict qualitatively spatial behavior arising from interactions among objects. In general, qualitative kinematics is said to be much more difficult than qualitative dynamics. Forbus describes the reason for this difficulty as Poverty Conjecture, which says that there is no purely qualitative and problem-independent representation for space and shape (this volume). The reasoning mechanisms and the representations of diagrams in these pieces of work are all very different and tailored to the specific spatial problem each system deals with, but they all use both pictorial information as well as knowledge about things that are not pictorial themselves, but that dictate the visible spatial behavior.

The article in this section by Iwasaki, Tessler and Law describes their work on REDRAW-I and -II. The REDRAW systems use diagrams to determine the deformation shape of a frame structure of a building under a load. The problem is different from the problems solved by the others in that it concerns how solid objects deform as they interact as opposed to the behavior of non-deformable solid objects. Though determining the deformation shape of a frame structure is an important problem in structural engineering and precise mathematical means to obtain the solution exist, engineers' knowledge about how structures deform and how the deformation propagates under different conditions can be codified, at least qualitatively, in a fairly intuitive manner as diagram manipulation rules. Though not formally taught in classrooms, such qualitative understanding is an important part of the overall understanding of structural behavior (Brohn 1984). REDRAW-I and -II try to emulate this qualitative analysis process of frame structures by humans through manipulation of internal representations of diagrams as well as symbolic reasoning about equilibrium of forces and bending moments, and about shape.

Reasoning About Liquid and Other Deformable Objects

One of the early influential work in qualitative physics is Hayes' ontology of liquid, in which he tried to formalize commonsense reasoning about liquid (Hayes 1990). Hayes pointed out that reasoning automatically about liquid was extremely difficult. The difficulty arises from the extreme versatility of the behavior of liquid as its behavior depends on its environment much more extensively than the behaviors of solid objects do. Furthermore, humans appear to use several different ontologies to describe liquid. Hayes identified two of them as "contained-stuff ontology" and "piece-of-stuff ontology." Later, Collins and Forbus identified another, called "molecular collections ontology," which was useful in reasoning about some aspects of liquid traveling through a system (Collins & Forbus 1987).

The work by DeCuyper et al. (this volume), as well as an earlier piece of work by Gardin and Meltzer (1989), both take a very different approach to reasoning about liquid from those based on symbolic qualitative reasoning. Instead of representing a body of liquid or solid object as one object as usually done in symbolic reasoning systems, they represent both types of things as one- or two-dimensional collection of particles. Each particle represents a small piece of liquid or solid stuff. They use a two-dimensional array to represent the position of each piece and simulate the movement of each piece to predict the behavior of the collection. For simulation of movement, DeCuyper et al. apply physics laws to each cell, while Gardin and Meltzer use local rules, which govern the exchange of messages between neighboring particles. By changing the rules restricting the permissible angle between particles, Gardin and Meltzer can also simulate the behavior of solid objects, such as rods and rings, of different flexibility. Both pieces of work based on simulation with an analogical representation show a promising alternative approach to solving the problem of qualitative spatial prediction.

Reasoning About Non-Physical Problems

I have so far discussed reasoning about geometry or physical spatial phenomena, but usefulness of diagrams is not limited to physical or geometry problems. Drawing a diagram of an abstract subject often allows one to observe characteristics that are difficult to identify using any other representations. The practice of representing the behavior of a mathematical model or statistical data as a graph in order to gain a global, qualitative understanding is ubiquitous. Computer-based visualization has become a very active research area in recent years precisely because we have come to realize that, as the amount of information involved increases, it becomes more and more difficult to get the global picture without an appropriate way to visually display the information. Tabachneck and Simon showed that, even when the amount of data was not so large, the forms in which people were presented with data had significant influence on the speed and accuracy of their performance on a problem solving task (Tabachneck & Simon 1992).

Representing the behavior of an abstract, mathematical system in a diagrammatic form to enable qualitative understanding is a standard technique in dynamic systems theory. In qualitative physics, researchers such as Nishida (1991), Sacks (1990), Kalagnanam (1991), Zhao (1991), and Yip (1991) have tried to automate various parts of the process of gaining qualitative insights into the behavior of non-linear ordinary differential equation systems through the use of phase portraits. While their systems all internally represent phase portraits symbolically, the common base for their work is the paradigm in dynamic systems theory of representing data diagrammatically in order to gain qualitative understanding of complex system behavior. In particular, the system called KAM developed by Yip strongly suggests the underlying view of collections of data as diagrams, for KAM employs a technique developed in computer vision in order to classify the trajectories formed by the collection of data points produced by numerical simulation.

Conclusion

In this article, I have presented an overview of the research area on systems in which diagrams play an important role in problem understanding and solving process. As a personal perspective on the field, it reflects my long-time interests in qualitative reasoning about physical systems, and the relation between qualitative, symbolic reasoning and diagrammatic reasoning.

I believe further research in the relation between diagrammatic reasoning and symbolic reasoning will surely deepen our collective understanding of the nature of human intelligence. All the pieces of work discussed in this introduction employ pre-specified forms of diagrammatic representation. However, as there are a large number of ways to abstract a given complex situation, there are equally many ways to represent it diagrammatically. Especially, in representing non-spatial information as diagrams, it is a non-trivial but crucial task to choose an appropriate diagrammatic form. Research on automatically selecting or even devising appropriate diagrammatic forms will be an interesting direction to explore in developing more powerful and flexible diagrammatic reasoning capabilities.

References

Borning, Allan H. 1979. Thinglab–a Constraint-Oriented Simulation Laboratory. Ph.D. diss., Department of Computer Science, Stanford University.

Brohn, David 1984. *Understanding Structural Analysis.* Oxford, BSP Professional Books, Oxford, UK, 1984.

Chandrasekaran, B. and Narayanan, Hari 1990. Towards a Theory of Commonsense Vissual Reasoning. In *Foundations of Software, Technology and Theoretical Computer Science.* Berlin: Springer-Verlag, 1990.

Collins, John W. and Forbus, Kenneth D. 1987. Reasoning About Fluids Via Molecular Collections. In Proceedings of the Sixth National Conference on

Artificial Intelligence. Menlo Park, Calif.: AAAI Press.

Davis, Ernest 1988. A Logical Framework for Commonsense Predictions of Solid Object Behavior. *Artificial Intelligence in Engineering* 3(3):125–140.

Forbus, Kenneth D.; Nielsen, Paul; and Faltings, Boi 1991. Qualitative Spatial Reasoning: The Clock Project. *Artificial Intelligence* 51(1–3): 417–471.

Gardin, Francesco and Meltzer, Bernard 1989. Analogical Representation of Naive Physics. *Artificial Intelligence* 38(2):139–159.

Hayes, Patrick J. 1990. Naive Physics I: Ontology for Liquids. In *Readings in Qualitative Reasoning about Physical Systems,* ed. Daniel S. Weld and Johan deKleer. San Francisco: Morgan Kaufmann.

Kalagnanam, Jayant 1991. Qualitative Analysis of System Behavior. PhD diss., Dept. of Engineering and Public Policy, Carnegie Mellon University.

Lindsay, Robert K. 1992. Diagrammatic Reasoning by Simulation. In Reasoning with Diagrammatic Representations: Papers from the 1992 AAAI Spring Symposium. AAAI Technical Report SS-92-02.

Narayanan, Hari, and Chandrasekaran, B. 1991. Reasoning Visually about Spatial Interactions. In Proceedings of the Twelfth International Joint Conference on Artificial Intelligence, 360–365. San Francisco: Morgan Kaufmann.

Nishida, Toyoaki; Mizutani, Kenji; Kubota, Atsushi; and Doshita, Shuji 1991. Automated Phase Portrait Analysis by Integrating Qualitative and Quantitative Analysis. In Proceedings of the Ninth National Conference on Artificial Intelligence. Menlo Park, Calif.: AAAI Press.

Novak, Gordon S.1977. Representation of Knowledge in a Program for Solving Physics Problems. In Proceedings of the Fifth International Joint Conference on Artificial Intelligence, 286–291, 1977.

Novak, Gordon S. and Bulko, William C. 1990. Understanding Natural Language with Diagrams. In Proceedings of the Fifth International Joint Conference on Artificial Intelligence, 465–470. San Francisco: Morgan Kaufmann.

Novak, Gordon S. and Bulko, William C. 1992. Uses of Diagrams in Solving Physics Problems. In Reasoning with Diagrammatic Representations: Papers from the 1992 AAAI Spring Symposium. AAAI Technical Report SS-92-02.

Sacks, Elisha P. 1990. Automatic Qualitative Analysis of Dynamic Systems Using Piece-wise Linear Approximations. *Artificial Intelligence* 4(3).

Tabachneck, Hermina J. M., and Simon, Herbert A. 1992. Effect of Mode of Data Presentation on Reasoning about Economic Markets. In Reasoning with Diagrammatic Representations: Papers from the 1992 AAAI Spring Symposium. AAAI Technical Report SS-92-02, 59–64.

Yip, Kenneth M. 1991. Understanding Complex Dynamics by Visual and Symbolic Reasoning. *Artificial Intelligence* 51(1–3):179–222.

Zhao, Feng 1991. Extracting and Representing Qualitative Behaviors of Complex Systems in Phase Spaces. In Proceedings of the Twelfth International

Joint Conference on Artificial Intelligence, 1144–1149. San Francisco: Morgan Kaufmann.

19 Analogical Representations of Naive Physics

Francesco Gardin & Bernard Meltzer

19.1 Introduction

The issues of modeling common sense reasoning and the representations required for that purpose have been studied since the early days of artificial intelligence (McCarthy 1969), but the particular ones connected with our everyday knowledge of the behavior of the physical world were brought into prominence by Hayes (1979). Since his chapter, this topic has been the subject of many further research publications, a sample of some of the first and more influential being those in Bobrow (1984).

It is worth asking the question why none of these approaches even "dreamed" of using the differential equations of classical mathematical physics for their models. Let us take the case of the everyday behavior of liquids known to everybody, such as filling a glass from a bottle or spilling over a floor. Apart from the implausibility that our minds solve complicated sets of nonlinear partial differential equations in predicting or thinking about such phenomena anybody who has ever tried to solve on a computer the equations of hydrodynamics (Feynman 1963) for any but mathematically simple boundary conditions will know what an almost hopeless task it would be to model such behaviors. But there are more fundamental reasons why such an approach is quite inappropriate for the task in hand. Firstly the concepts and terms used in such representations are far removed from notions used in common sense reasoning, such as: assuming the shape of a container, being contained by, dropping, splashing, etc. Secondly, the behaviors predicted by such classical models are far more quantitatively detailed than the rough estimates that suffice for normal everyday and engineering use, and in addition it is often very difficult to extract from such "exact" solutions intuitively simple properties of the behavior.

"Too quantitatively detailed" is in fact an understatement for the representations of mathematical physics and engineering. For in general their variables and function values range over the real number continuum thus involving strictly speaking an infinite quantity of information. This surprising feature of classical natural science (surprising, that is to say, from the cognitive science point of view) emphasizes the impor-

Reprinted from *Artificial Intelligence* 38 (1989), pp. 139–159 with the permission of Elsevier Science, North-Holland Publishers, Amsterdam.

tance of the concept of "quantity space" introduced by Hayes (1979) and much used by subsequent investigators of what has come to be known as "qualitative physics," such as Kuipers (1984) and de Kleer and Brown (1984). A quantity space is simply a finite, usually totally ordered, discrete and usually small set of values a physical variable may take. For example, if we are considering the changes occurring in a body of ice being steadily heated, we might use two three-element quantity spaces: the first for temperature, namely, "less than 0°, between 0° and 100° and greater than 100°"; the second for changes of temperature consisting of "decreasing, steady and increasing." By such means a great deal of the ordinary meaningful behavior of physical and engineering systems may be understood and predicted without any reference to the real-number continuum of physical variables and their differential coefficients.

There seems little doubt that the notion of quantity space is a fundamental one, and in researches such as those cited above, it has been used to good effect to reduce the descriptions of physical variables to cognitively more sensible proportions. The typical use is to replace quantitative differential equations by their qualitative analogues, and use a kind of qualitative mathematics to deal with them.

It must be admitted however that the results of "qualitative physics" so far have not been too impressive. For instance, the formalizations of the behavior of rather simple physical systems by de Kleer and Brown (1984) and by Kuipers (1985), lead to an alarmingly large multiplicity of solutions, and the fragmentary attempts to axiomatize the behavior of liquids by Hayes (1985) and Forbus (1984)[1], which appear not to have reached the stage of implementation in programs, suggest that very large axiom systems will be needed, coming up against all the usual control problems of systems of deductive inference as well as the frame problem (McCarthy & Hayes 1969).

The researches reported below take their starting point from the consideration that the problems of cognitive implausibility and probable computational overcomplexity may well arise from the restrictiveness of the representational methods used. It is a remarkable fact that both approaches discussed above, that of classical physics and that of "qualitative reasoning," are predominantly what Sloman (1971) termed Fregean;

[1]We understand that Forbus has reported on liquid programs in articles published since this citation

the characteristic of Fregean representations is that essentially they use only one type of structure, namely the application of a function symbol to one or more argument symbols. The paradigmatic example is the language of predicate logic, but much of mathematical, computer and natural languages share this characteristic. On the other hand, much common sense thinking seems obviously to be done in terms of much richer structures usually based on our perceptions of form and movement in the physical world. In fact this appears to be the case not only for "common sense" mentation such as working out how a mechanical device functions or how a string uncoils itself, but also for abstract purposes such as using Venn diagrams for reasoning about sets and graphs for thinking about changes.

The properties of Fregean and other representations have been the subject of rather profound study by Sloman (1984), and he has identified a class of representation types which he terms "analogical"; the essential difference from the Fregean type is that objects and relations are represented not by names but by other objects and relations. Thus in a map for instance distance and directions in a territory are represented by relative distances and directions in the map. This example is instructive in a number of ways. It shows that though there may be and often is similarity of structure between the representation and what is represented, there need be no isomorphism—for example, nothing in the map may correspond to vertical dimension features or minor roads of the territory. Also representations may often be of mixed type—for example, the map may contain names of towns, rivers, etc. Analogical representation of course may, as indicated above, be used for other than spatial relationships— for example, in flow charts or Venn diagrams— but it is particularly useful for the former, as the work reported here shows.

There has been much discussion in the psychological literature of the nature of visual imagery (Kosslyn & Schwartz 1977; Shepard, R. N. 1978). The purpose of the research reported here however is not to contribute towards the solution of that problem, but to try out some ideas and experiments on the possible usefulness of analogical representations in modeling naive physics.

It was decided to concentrate on the behavior of strings in the first place, and liquids in the second place, because these seemed to us of extreme difficulty if not intractability using the other approaches. The choice of strings to start with was influenced by the reported challenge to naive physics made by Marvin Minsky (Forbus 1984) to show that "you can pull with a string but not push with it."

19.2 The Methodology Used

Two-dimensional models of the physical objects concerned took the form of sets of pixels of the two-dimensional array of a computer graphics system, so that spatial properties and relations of objects are implicit in the representation itself. The programs deal directly with these pixel sets rather than with numerical or other representations of the objects. The basic structure of the programming consists of message passing between actors; this choice of programming style was made not only because of its convenience (availability of a Symbolics 3600 LISP machine), but because of its architectural similarity to the operation of massively parallel computers (Hillis 1979) which, when they become available, would be the ones most suitable for implementing analogical representations. The issues of three-dimensional models present some special problems which will not be dealt with in this chapter.

Since in the ordinary behavior of strings and liquids, different parts of the object or mass have different motions, our representation evidently must make use of decomposition, that is, the whole mass is represented as the sum of its component parts. And since we do not know in advance at what point in the string or liquid mass this differentiation of states of motion will occur, we are compelled in our analogical representation to choose some basic grain size for the decomposition. That is to say, our model, graphically speaking, will be a configuration of identical basic elements, each of which is an aggregate of pixels, of some convenient shape, e.g. circular or square. The basic operations of the model then will be on these elementary "molecules."

Next in accordance with our intuitive notions of causality, we limit direct interactions between molecules entirely to those between spatially adjacent ones. Thus the rules of behavior will generally be local ones, whose joint operation gives rise to the global behaviors. Quite apart from the question of causality, it is probable that if we had tried to develop a system of global rules instead, it would have been overly complex both in respect of its size and of the conditions to be attached to each rule,

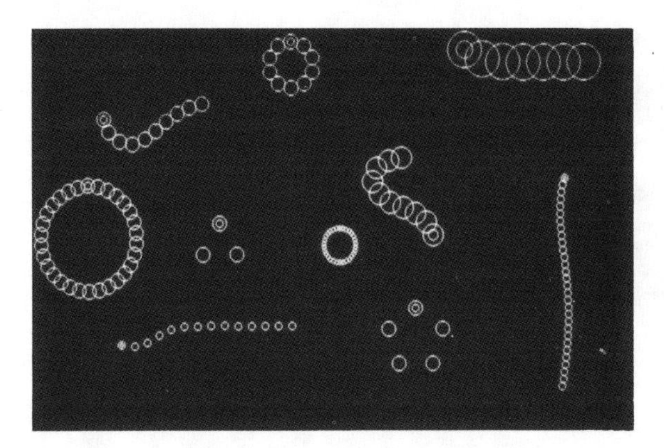

Figure 19.1
Examples of Object Models: Strings, Flexible rods, Flexible Rings.

to cope with the great variety of macroscopic behaviors possible. It is interesting that the most significant predecessor of this work, Funt's program WHISPER (Funt 1977), which was concerned with the stability of "blocks-world" structures, did not use "molecular" decomposition, but the range of behaviors that needed to be treated in such a system is exceedingly restricted: only rotations and slidings of blocks.

Overall then we see that our models consist firstly of the representation of spatial properties analogically, and, secondly, of rules of physical behavior of objects in space; these rules take the form of constraints, of very general character, such as those of causality, of noncopenetrability, of continuity, of flexibility and of liquidity. These constraints are realized by message passing between molecules, replacing in a sense the differential equations of classical physics representations.

19.3 Strings and Derived Solid Objects

In the experiment, strings were modeled (Gambardella 1985) as one-dimensional aggregates of "molecules" with exchange of messages governed only by the maintenance of the following constraints:

1. There is a fixed distance parameter (e.g. zero) between each molecule and its two neighbors, or its single neighbor in the case of the two terminal molecules (continuity).

Figure 19.2
String, flexible Rod, Rigid Bar, Held at One End and Allowed to Drop on a Fixed Surface.

2. There is a fixed angle parameter, which is an upper bound to the amount the line joining the centers of two neighboring molecules may rotate (flexibility).
3. The set intersection between the pixels of a molecule with the pixel elements of environment objects is zero (noncopenetrability). For the purpose of the present experiments it was not necessary to impose the copenetrability constraint also with other objects.
4. Forces like gravity, or wind, or viscous drag, are stored in the actor data structure of the molecule; for example, gravity as a tendency for an element to move in a certain direction a number of steps determined by a force intensity parameter (field of force)

These four constraints turn out to be sufficient to give qualitatively correct behavior of strings in a variety of situations, for example: falling in free space, falling on a floor with protuberances, being used to pull or (unsuccessfully) to push, being uncoiled, being dragged over protuberances or through narrow channels. It should be noted that some basic properties of the string are assured by the mode of representation, e.g. the conservation of length and thickness.

The freedom of choice of the parameters in the above four rules (effectable of course by a special menu on the graphics display) also permits the representation of other solid objects: The flexibility limit angle set to 180 degrees yields a string, but set to 0 degrees it gives a rigid bar, and set to angles in between it gives rods with various degrees of flexibility. A ring can be represented by joining the terminal elements of a string or rod. Figure 19.1 shows some examples. Figure 19.2 shows, respectively, a string, a flexible rod and a rigid bar, held at one end and allowed to drop on to a floor. Figure 19.3 shows a string under gravity in various environmental situations, including one under the "table" where it has been pushed against a solid object. Figure 19.4 shows the comparable behavior of a flexible rod, and Figure 19.5 that of a rigid bar. Figure 19.6 shows sequences of movements of a string, a flexible rod and a rigid bar, held at one end and falling under gravity.

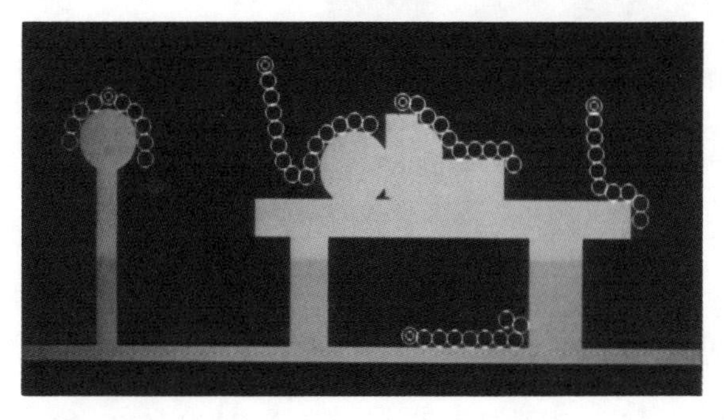

Figure 19.3
Strings under Gravity Held at Single Points, in Different Environmental Situations.

By fixing the positions of the two terminal elements of a flexible bar under gravity one obtains a catenary, and by fixing that of one internal element of a rigid bar one obtains a lever.

Figure 19.4
Flexible Rods in the Same Situations as Those of Figure 19.3.

It is interesting that although the basic representations are of inextensible objects, they can be used for representing elasticity. For example,

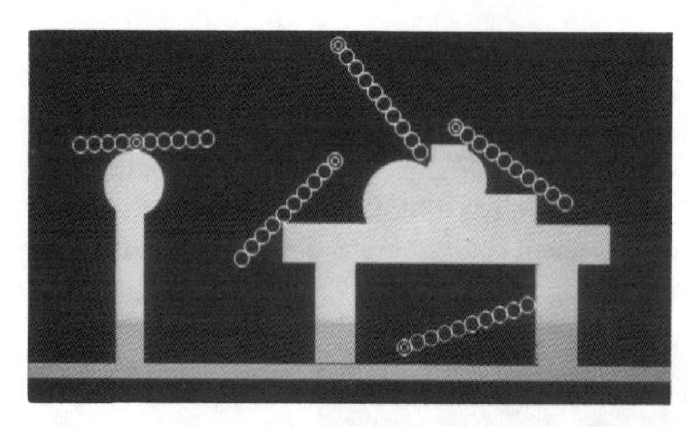

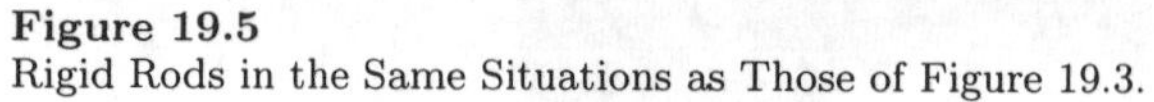

Figure 19.5
Rigid Rods in the Same Situations as Those of Figure 19.3.

Figure 19.7 shows the pulling of an elastically deformable ring through a constricting channel. This is achieved by modifying the flexibility constraint: if n is the number of base elements of the ring, the flexibility limit angle chosen is 180/ n, and this is also the preferred angle between any two neighboring elements, being decreased only if forced by the other constraints of the model.

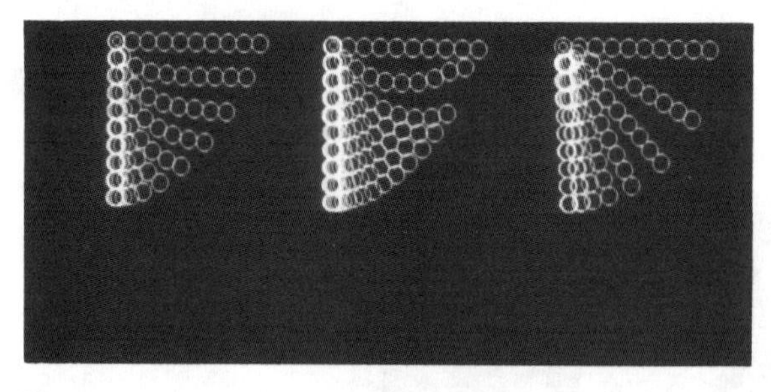

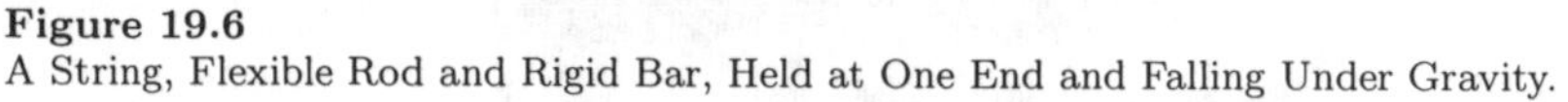

Figure 19.6
A String, Flexible Rod and Rigid Bar, Held at One End and Falling Under Gravity.

No extra difficulties are encountered in handling composite objects represented as actors. Figure 19.8 shows a lever supporting a ring on one arm and a movable rod or string attached to the other arm. Figure 19.9 shows a more complicated system composed of pulleys, lever, ring, and strings.

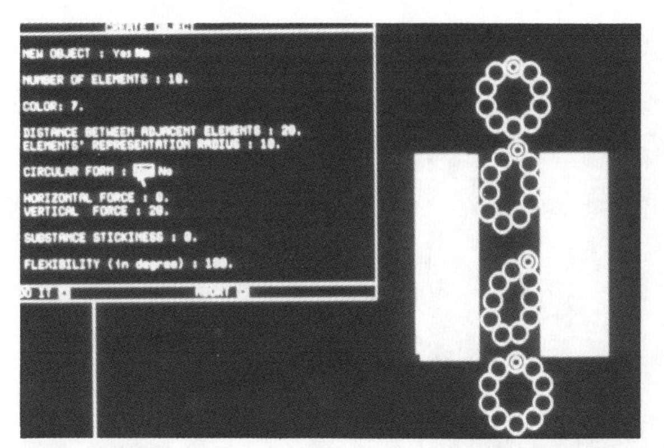

Figure 19.7
The Pulling of an Elastically Deformable Ring Through a Constricting Channel.

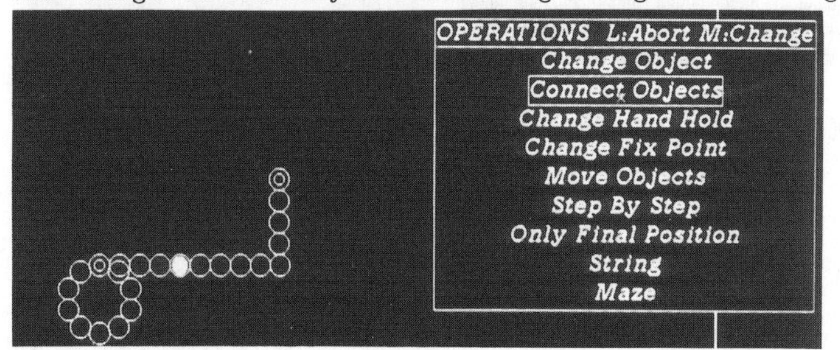

Figure 19.8
Composite Object Including a Lever.

19.4 Liquids

The simulation of liquid behavior (Stofella 1986, Gardin 1986) was effected by means of eight local rules which govern the exchange of messages between actor molecules. In the following summary of the rules we term a molecule free if the space immediately underneath it is not occupied, and constrained otherwise.

1. A molecule can change its position to a neighboring one if that one is not occupied by either another molecule or a rigid body (noncopenetrability).
2. A molecule can receive messages and pass them on to its neighbors (causal transmission).
3. A free molecule moves down until either it encounters another molecule or a rigid body; in both cases it becomes constrained

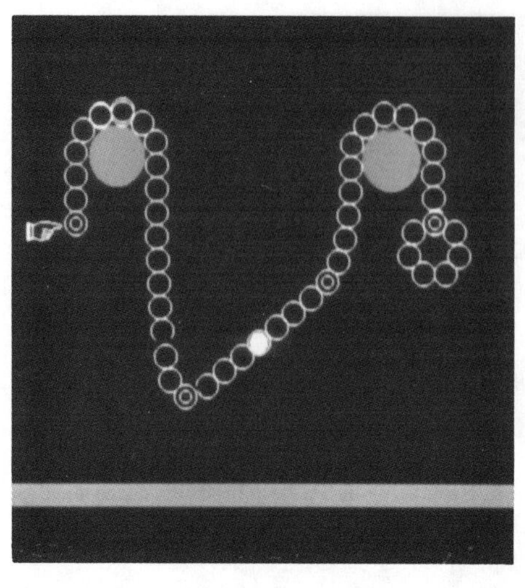

Figure 19.9
Composite Object: Moving a Ring by Means of Strings Over Pulleys and a Lever.

(gravity)

4. A constrained molecule can move in any direction only if so requested from one of its neighbors (fluidity).

5. A constrained molecule becomes free if the space underneath ceases to be occupied either by another molecule or rigid body (fluidity).

6. If a free molecule during its fall encounters a constrained molecule, before becoming constrained it will try to occupy its space (fluidity).

7. A constrained molecule which has received a request for space will try to fulfill this request by attempting to occupy another position in its neighborhood. If no space is already available it will pass on the request. If no position can be made available it will fail (fluidity).

8. No position can be occupied above the level of a free molecule which started a request for space (gravity).

The program incorporating these rules gave qualitatively correct simulations of liquid behavior in a wide variety of situations such as the filling of a container from a tap, leaking from a hole in a container, finding its own level, etc. By way of illustration Figures 19.10(a)-(f) show

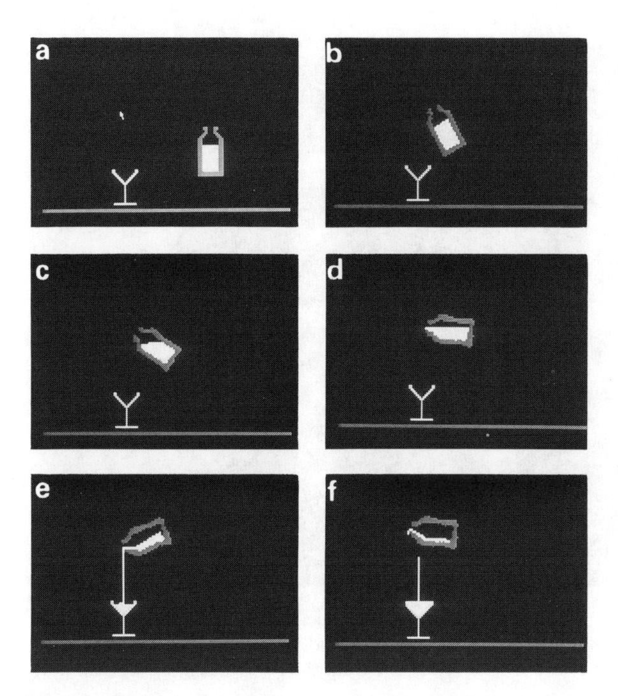

Figure 19.10
(a) Initial State: Glass Empty and Bottle Full. (b) Tilting of the Bottle Begins. (c) Tilting of the Bottle Continues. (d) Tilting of the Bottle Continues. (e) Pouring Starts. (f) Pouring Ends and the Excess Water Will Overflow from the Glass.

the filling of a glass by liquid poured from a bottle. Figures 19.11(a)-(d) show a complex of communicating vessels being filled, and subsequently leaking through a hole in a wall of a container into a larger container underneath.

The notion of "qualitatively correct" is not a precise one, being based on the judgment of the observer. However, since essentially we are concerned with modeling perceptions and knowledge of a (competent) observer about physical phenomena, such imprecision needs to be tolerated—for the present at least; in the future development of naive physics more precise concepts using Hayes' (1979) notion of quantity space may emerge.

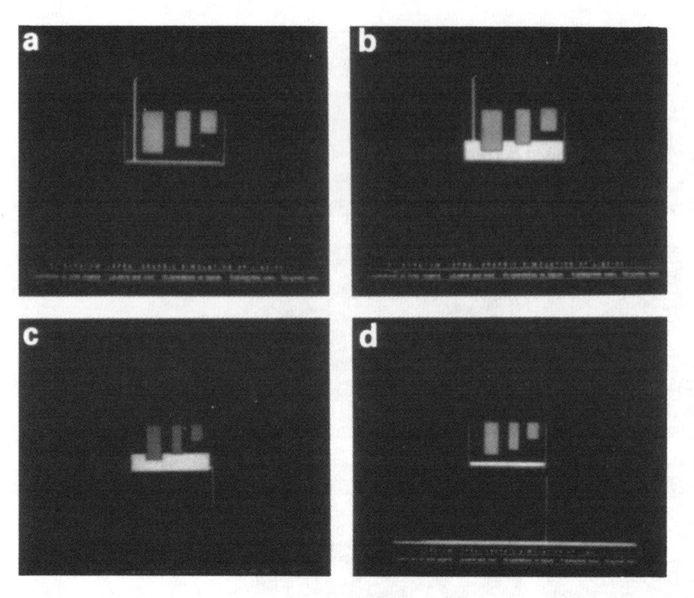

Figure 19.11
(a) A Complex of Communicating Vessels being Filled. (b) Filling Continues. (c) Leaking Through a Hole Made in the Wall of a Container. (d) Leaking Continues.

19.5 Discussion of the Simulation Programs

Only some of the issues of naive physics have been tackled so far. For instance, a rigid bar, suspended from a fixed point and allowed to fall under gravity, would not execute a pendulum motion, but come to rest in a vertical position. Similarly, the liquid program does not cover splashing. This is because we have not yet developed a satisfying model of the effects of momentum. It is an open question how far the essentially kinematical approach adopted so far can be used for dealing with such dynamical questions. (In this regard it is interesting to note that in advanced physics dynamic phenomena are often represented in kinematical, "geometric" ways; for instance, in general relativity the motion of a body is represented as a geodesic in four-dimensional space-time.) An associated open question is the degree of explicitness with which time should be represented.

Unlike programs of qualitative physics (Bobrow 1984) these programs always provide unique solutions. It might be argued that this is more apparent than real, since differences in the algorithms chosen to realize the local constraints could produce differences in behavior. For instance, in the case of the string program the precise way in which the flexibility constraint is programmed might determine whether the angle between two particular molecules of a string is, say, 60° or 70°, both being compatible with the constraint. This issue has not been studied in depth, though there is some evidence that the qualitative behavior is independent of the algorithm design for "nonpathological" situations.

Our models also automatically deal with the frame problem (McCarthy & Hayes 1969). For the effects of spatial displacements in any part of the scene represented are automatically transmitted in accordance with the reigning constraints which realize the physical rules to neighboring parts of the scene.

It was remarked in the introduction that the representations of classical (mathematical) physics involve the provision of far too much information for the purposes of naive physics, and Hayes' notion of quantity space provides a means of cutting down the "explosion" of information to a reasonable size, though we still have no guiding theory on the relationship between what we may want to know about the behavior of a physical system and the amount (as well as the nature) of the information about the system required to derive that knowledge. But there are also certain kinds of information missing in standard formalisms, but which are assumed in the use made of them.

The issue of assumed knowledge is an interesting one. In the representations of mathematical physics some of it is implicit. For instance, the fact that a body does not change its mass when moving is assured by using a constant as the symbol for its mass; or the fact that most physical phenomena have a continuous character is implied by the ubiquitous use of mathematically continuous functions (even sometimes for essentially noncontinuous events like quantum jumps!) But when one examines the application of formalisms like differential and other equations to the real world, one finds essential steps of the reasoning not represented in any way in the formalism. A simple paradigmatic example is provided by a billiard ball A moving with speed v and impacting a stationary ball B: what are the subsequent motions? If one writes down the energy and momentum equations, one obtains *two* solutions: the first brings A to rest and projects B with speed v; the second keeps B stationary while A continues with speed v. Why is the second immediately rejected? Simply because it contradicts the common sense noncopenetrability constraint (embodied in the analogical physics programs described above).

In one respect the analogical approach is identical with that of mathematical physics, namely in the use of local constraints. For local constraint is exactly what a differential equation is, and the integration of such an equation is a well-defined procedure to obtain the global from the local behavior; our graphics systems perform the corresponding "integrations" automatically by message passing. But the local constraints used in analogical naive physics are of a different character from those of classical physics. They express rather immediate "phenomenological," commonly observed characteristics of the physical world, rather than highly abstract notions such as Newton's second law. In this respect they differ also from those of most of the Fregean systems of qualitative physics so far developed. For instance, both de Kleer and Brown, and Kuipers, use abstract differential equations but ranging over quantity spaces instead of the real-number continuum. Such systems are properly characterized as being qualitative rather than naive physics.

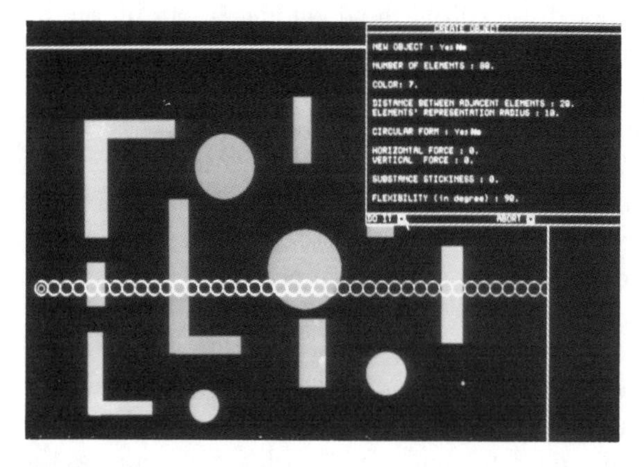

Figure 19.12
Maze Problem: Initial State of String.

19.6 Possible Uses of Analogical Representations of Naive Physics

The main purpose of our research was to show the feasibility and possible advantages of a non-Fregean approach to modeling naive physics. In this section, we shall briefly discuss issues arising as to the possible uses of such models.

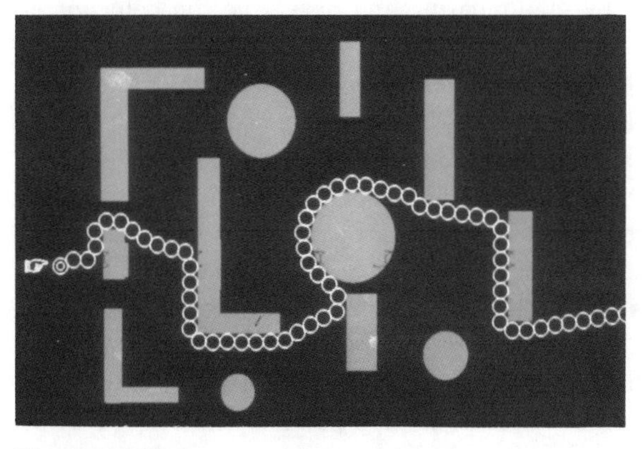

Figure 19.13
Maze Problem: Solution State of String.

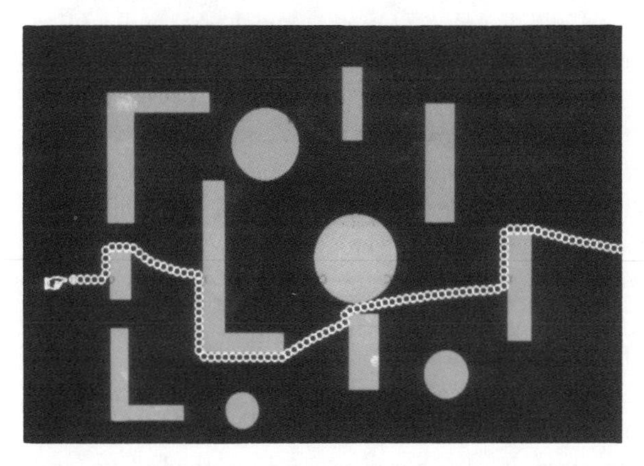

Figure 19.14
Maze Problem: Solution State with Thinner String.

Obviously, the fundamental use of a naive physics model of a range of phenomena is the same as that of ordinary physical theories, namely, prediction. The behavior of physical systems of different degrees of complexity and variability, modeled analogically, can be directly and easily observed and studied at a terminal, exploiting the use of parameter variation in the rules. Not only does this suggest applications to engineering design, but also is relevant to learning issues: for instance, in designing a production-rule expert system involving physical apparatus, if-then rules could be derived by manipulating and observing the behavior of the analogical representation for various initial conditions.

Also of interest is the possibility of using an analogical representation in the design of an autonomous reasoning or planning system. A pilot study in this area was carried out aimed at designing a "pouring program" for a hypothetical robot waiter (Taylor 1986). This program, given the analogical representation of an arbitrary collection of vessels, empty or containing liquid, first identifies and names the containers, and then, given the names A and B. say, of two of them autonomously uses A to fill B and return A to its former location. Such a program, besides the analogical simulator, requires two other components: an interpreter of what is happening in the simulation and a planner which uses a symbiotic union of simulator and interpreter. The interpreter uses a special edge function to follow the contours of the objects. This function calls a number of other functions which find all the "upward" concavities of the objects and establish which are containers, which are being filled with liquid, which have liquid flowing from them, which have liquid flowing to them, also whether liquid is flowing on a vertical or oblique surface, and whether liquid is spreading on a horizontal surface. The interpreter also supplied some predicates describing spatial relations between objects such as "left-of," "right-of," etc. The model implemented is a feedback one: the planner actuates the simulator, the state of which is periodically interpreted by the interpreter and passed back to the planner to effect any changes in the simulation that may be required. Figures 19.10(a)-(d) show the phases of an actual performance.

The algorithm which implements the model is essentially a planner with a control structure that is implicit rather then explicit as in traditional AI planning systems. It can, however, be conceived of as, and translated into, something more like a traditional planner, by being implemented as a production rule system with the following characteristics: The consequent of each production will be an action (translation, rotation) applied to the representation (e.g. "tilt container X 45° anticlockwise"); the antecedents will in general be of two types: firstly, direct predicates of the representation as supplied by the interpreter (e.g. "container X is empty"); secondly, predicates with side effects. Predicates of this last type are implemented as procedures; they exploit the specific properties of analogical representation, returning two different pieces of information: a truth value used during the antecedent verification process, and parameters used during the consequent action execution (e.g.: the rotation point predicate returns TRUE if there is a point above container B to which we can translate container A and which allows A to be rotated without touching any other container—the parameters returned are the coordinates of this point).

Besides the use of predicates with side effects, this type of planner differs from traditional ones in that it uses essentially forward instead of backward chaining, which would put a premium on the development of powerful evaluation heuristics for limiting the search space, an issue needing further research.

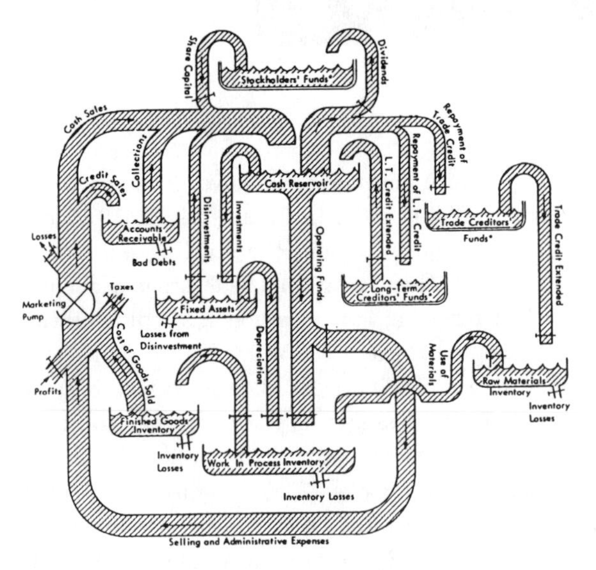

Figure 19.15
Helfert's (1982) Dynamic Funds Flow Model.

19.7 Serendipitous Applications of the Programs

Since the programs are based on such general properties of objects and substances as noncopenetrability, continuity and the most obvious properties of fluidity, it is not perhaps surprising that they find easy application to other phenomena than those for which they were devised.

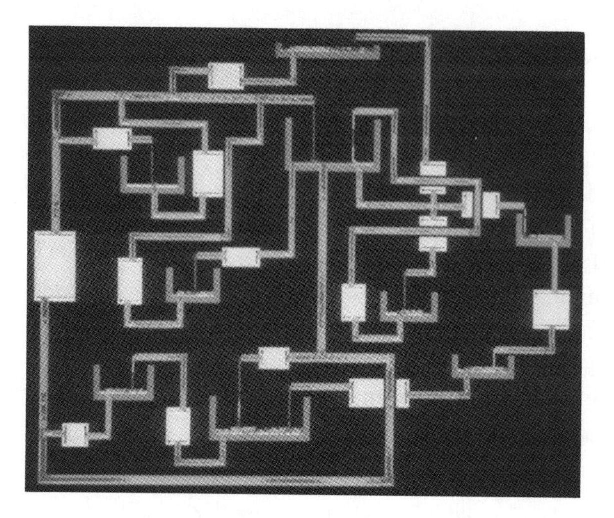

Figure 19.16
Helfert's Model Simulator.

For instance, the string program automatically solves maze problems of any degree of complexity, as illustrated in Figures 19.12, 19.13 and 19.14. All that needs to be done is to join the starting and target points by a rectilinear string, and then switch on the message exchanges between its molecules. The resulting configuration is a configuration path. It is interesting to compare the solution of Figure 19.13 with that employing a thinner string of Figure 19.14: the former because it cannot pass through as narrow passages as the latter has to find a different (and longer) path. This obviously suggests applications to the robotics problem characterized by Brooks (1981) as one of the most difficult, namely, navigation in a cluttered environment. It seems very likely also that flexible rod and rigid bar programs could be used to simulate robot arms and hands in the planning of assembly and similar tasks, as well as parts being manipulated. One could also resort to an analogical heuristic to approximate to a solution of the minimum-path maze problem: namely, let the string program operate with the maze masked by successively wider passageways directed from the starting position to the target point; the first path found would in most cases be the shortest possible.

Similarly the liquids program has been easily supplemented (Taylor 1986) for an application to economics: simulations of Helfert's dynamic

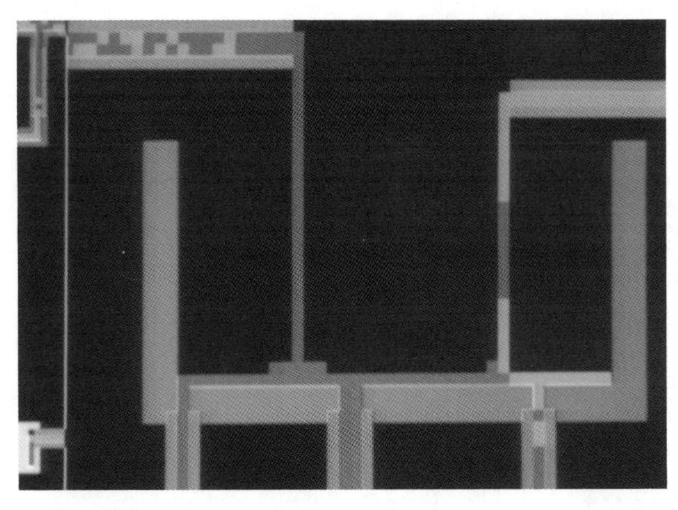

Figure 19.17
Detail of Simulation of Part of Helfert's Model: "cashreservoir."

funds flow model of a business firm (see Hart, Brazily,& Duda 1986; Helfert 1982). Figure 19.15 shows his model. Pipes, taps and pumps were added to the simulator: Figure 19.16 shows Helfert's model simulator, Figure 19.17 shows simulation of part of Helfert's model and Figure 19.18 the results of an analysis by the interpreter of the container "cash reservoir."

```
erminal 1
#<OBJ-INFORMATIONS 37163262>, an object of flavor OBJ-INFORMATIONS,
 has instance variable values:
 OBJ-NAME:               "CASH-RESERVOIR"
 CONTAINS:               NIL
 PROB-FULL:              NIL
 FILLING:                unbound
 FLOW-ON-SURFACE:        T
 FLOWING-FROM:           (#<PIPE 27014077> #<PIPE 21377322>)
 FLOWING-TO:             ((#<JUNCTION 27052252> (149 62)) (#<JUNCTION 27130624> (180 62)) (#<JUNCTION 21366574> (166 62)))
 EXPANDING:              unbound
 SPECIAL-INF:            NIL
 FIRST-COORDS:           ((166 62) (151 62) (188 42) (147 42))
 UP:                     42
 DOWN:                   64
 RIGHT:                  190
 LEFT:                   147
 CONTACTS:               (#<PIPE 27057403> #<PIPE 21366321> #<PIPE 27101251>)
 CONCAVITIES:            NIL
 PARTIALLY-INCLUDED:     NIL
 TOTALLY-INCLUDED:       NIL
```

Figure 19.18
Results of an Analysis by the Interpreter of the Container "cash-reservoir."

19.8 A New Kind of Experimental Physics

The way in which the string and liquid programs were developed suggests the paradigm of an alternative supplementary approach to traditional modes of physical investigation, that is, instead of developing theories and models and then testing them in laboratories, one combines the two activities sitting at a computer terminal, trying out different interaction rules with immediate feedback on their adequacy or validity. In just this way the four string and eight liquid rules were inducted. Possible advantages over the traditional approach include not only those of speed and convenience but also the clear and easy control of relevant variables; however, only experience will tell when and in what fields either approach is superior to the other.

References

Bobrow, D. G. 1984. *Qualitative Reasoning about Physical Systems.* Amsterdam: North-Holland.

Brooks, R. A. 1981. Symbolic Reasoning Among 3-D models and 2-D Images. *Artificial Intelligence* 17: 285–348.

de Kleer, J. and Brown, J. S. 1984. A Qualitative Physics Based on Confluences. *Artificial Intelligence* 24: 7–83.

Feynman, R. et al. 1963. *The Feynman Lectures on Physics.* Reading, Mass.: Addison-Wesley.

Forbus, K. D. 1981. Qualitative Reasoning about Physical Processes. In: Proceedings of the International Joint Conference on Artificial Intelligence, Vancouver, BC. San Francisco: Morgan Kaufmann.

Forbus, K. D. 1984. Qualitative Process Theory. *Artificial Intelligence* 24: 85–168.

Funt, B. V. 1977. WHISPER: A Problem Solving System Utilizing Diagrams and a Parallel Processing Retina. Proceedings of the International Joint Conference on Artificial Intelligence, 459–464. San Francisco: Morgan Kaufmann.

Gambardella, L. M. 1985. A Graphic Approach to Naive Physics. Master's Thesis, Department of Computer Science, Pisa University.

Gardin. F., Meltzer, B., and Stofella, P. 1986. The Analogical Representation of Liquids in Naive Physics. In: *Proceedings ECAI-86,* Brighton, England.

Hart, P. E., Brazily, A. and Duda, R. O. 1986 Qualitative Reasoning for Financial Assessments: A Prospectus. *Al Magazine* 7(1).

Hayes, P. J. 1979. The Naive Physics Manifesto. In: *Expert Systems in the Microelectronic Age,* ed. D. Michie. Edinburgh: Edinburgh University Press.

Hayes, P. J. 1985a. The Second Naive Physics Manifesto. In: *Formal Theories of the Common Sense World,* ed. J. E. Hobbs and R. C. Moore..

Hayes, P. J. 1985b. Naive Physics 1: Ontology for Liquids. In: *Formal Theories of the Common Sense World,* ed. J. E. Hobbs and R. C. Moore.

Helfert, E. A. 1982. *Techniques of Financial Analysis.* Homewood.

Hillis, D. 1979. *The Connection Machine.* Cambridge, Mass. The MIT Press.

Kosslyn, S. M., Pinker, S., Smith, G. E. and Schwartz, S. P. 1979. On the Demystification of Mental Imagery. In: *Mental Imagery.* Cambridge, Mass.: The MIT Press.

Kosslyn, S. M. and Schwartz, S .P. 1977. A Simulation of Visual Imaginery. *Cognitive Science* 1: 265–295.

Kuipers, B. 1984. Common sense Reasoning About Causality: Deriving Behavior from Structure. *Artificial Intelligence* 24: 169-203.

Kuipers, B. 1985. Qualitative Simulation of Mechanisms. Technical Report, MIT Laboratory for Computer Science, Massachusetts Institute of Technology, Cambridge Mass.

McCarthy, J. and Hayes, P. J. 1969. Some Philosophical Problems From the Standpoint of Artificial Intelligence. In: *Machine Intelligence 4,* ed. B. Meltzer and D. Michie. Edinburgh: Edinburgh University Press.

Reference Guide to Symbolics-Lisp 2: Flavors 1985. Cambridge, Mass.: Symbolics Inc.

Shepard, R. N. 1978. The Mental Image. *Am. Psychol.* 33.

Sloman, A. 1971. Interactions Between Philosophy and Artificial Intelligence: The Role of Intuition and Non-logical Reasoning In Intelligence. *Artificial Intelligence* 2: 209–225.

Sloman, A. 1984. Why We Need Many Knowledge Representation Formalisms. In: Proceedings British Computer Society Expert System Conference.

Stofella, P. 1986. Analogical Representation of Liquids in Naive Physics, Master's Thesis, Department of Computer Science, University of Milan.

Taylor, H. 1986. Development of Computational Models in Naive Physics, Master's Thesis, Department of Computer Science, University of Milan.

20 Using Diagrammatic Features to Index Plans for Geometry Theorem-Proving

Thomas F. McDougal & Kristian J. Hammond
University of Chicago

20.1 Introduction

This chapter describes POLYA, a computer program that writes proofs for high school geometry problems.

Theorem-proving has been a popular domain in which to study human problem-solving because people generally consider theorem-proving difficult and because it provides lots of problems to solve. A number of researchers in cognitive science and artificial intelligence have looked at theorem-proving in general (e.g. Newell & Simon 1956) and geometry theorem-proving in particular (Gelernter 1959, Nevins 1975, Greeno 1983, Anderson *et al.* 1985, Koedinger & Anderson 1990) in order to gain some insight into how people think.

Computer programs which proved geometry theorems have been based on a general-purpose model of theorem-proving, called *proof tree search,* in which inference rules (corresponding to the theorems, axioms, and definitions of the domain) were applied either forward from the givens, backwards from the goal, or some combination, until a path was found connecting the givens to the goal.[1] This model guaranteed that any theorem which could be proved would be proved (the *completeness* criterion), and that, as long as the rules and axioms were correct, only correct theorems could be proved (the *correctness* criterion).

Unfortunately, proof tree search is NP-complete (Cook 1971), so researchers looked for heuristics to focus search in the most promising directions. Geometry offers the possibility of using the diagram. Gelernter (1959) tested subgoal hypotheses against measurements of a coordinate diagram—if the subgoal was false, it was discarded. Greeno (1983) used the diagram to select inferences which involved objects physically close to the goal. Nevins (1975) claimed to gain efficiency by restructuring the problem space, although his program also used predicates for "possibly-parallel" and "possibly perpendicular" which could be construed as dia-

[1] A notable exception is the approach by Chou (1992), which proves or disproves geometry theorems using systems of linear equations.

grammatic. Koedinger and Anderson (1990) used diagrammatic configurations to generate a restricted set of rules.

High school geometry has an interesting feature which, in their effort to stick to general-purpose methods, these researchers have apparently ignored. Teachers and textbook authors structure the domain to make it friendly to students. To achieve this, they provide examples in the text and follow them with problems which are visually and logically similar. They extend problems from previous sections, either by extending the goal one or two steps further or by asking the student to prove something which was given before. They consistently associate patterns of givens and patterns in the diagram with particular inferences. Their goal in all this is to help the student learn to write proofs.

Case-based reasoning (Schank & Abelson 1977, Schank 1982, Kolodner 1993) is a style of problem-solving in AI designed to take advantage of exactly this kind of structure. A case-based reasoning (CBR) system reuses solutions from past problems, adapting them as necessary.

There is considerable evidence that case-based reasoning captures how people try to solve problems. Ross (1986) showed that people often refer back to previous problems when learning a new skill. Chi, Bassok, *et al.* (1989) document students' tendency to rely on examples when solving physics problems. Dosimetrists building radiation treatment plans rely on a notebook of plans for previous patients (Berger, forthcoming).

The motivation behind CBR is that retrieving and adapting solutions which have worked in the past is frequently easier than solving every problem from scratch. CBR is particularly attractive when planning from scratch is impossible, such as when the domain physics is unknown (e.g. in cooking, Hammond 1989) or when the number of preconditions one might have to consider is potentially unlimited (the *qualification problem*, McCarthy 1977), as is the case for most everyday activities. For geometry, CBR offers a way to avoid the exponential complexity of proof tree search.

POLYA applies case-based reasoning to high school geometry. It exploits the pedagogically-motivated regularity of the domain to avoid the combinatorics of constructing proofs from scratch. POLYA uses the diagram as the primary source of features for retrieving the appropriate knowledge from memory. This chapter describes the vocabulary of features POLYA uses to organize plans in memory and POLYA's architecture for extracting features from the diagram on an as-needed basis.

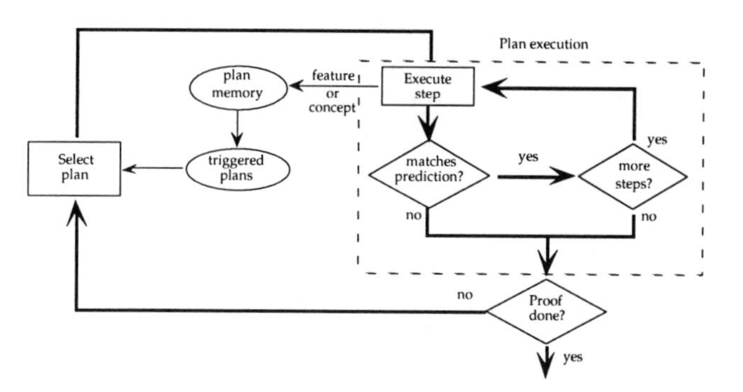

Figure 20.1
Flow of Control and Data in POLYA. POLYA selects a plan, executes it, then selects another. New plans are constantly being retrieved from memory on the basis of features generated during plan execution. Control flow is shown by the bold arrows; data flow is shown by the thin arrows.

20.2 Overview of POLYA

POLYA interleaves memory retrieval with the tasks of extracting features from the problem and writing the proof. To achieve this, POLYA's algorithm uses two loops (Figure 20.1). In the outer loop, POLYA selects a plan and passes it to the inner loop. The inner loop executes the steps in the plan and retrieves new plans from memory.

POLYA's plans serve two functions. *Search plans* gather information about the problem from the text and the diagram. That information is used to retrieve relevant *proof plans,* which actually write the proof, as well as other search plans.

Each step in a plan consists of an action and a prediction. The action might involve computing a description of some part of the diagram, conceptually associating two objects, or adding some statement to the proof. Every action generates a result which is compared against the plan step's prediction. If the result and the prediction don't match, the plan halts.

POLYA retrieves plans from memory by matching the results of actions against plan *indices* in memory. Each plan *index* is composed of one or more patterns against which the result is compared. When every pattern of an index has been matched, the plan is *triggered,* posted to a list as eligible for execution.

The inner loop halts when the plan is complete or when the result of an action fails to match the prediction. The outer loop halts when the problem is solved or when there are no triggered plans to choose from.

20.3 Examples

20.3.1 Example 1: The Easy Way

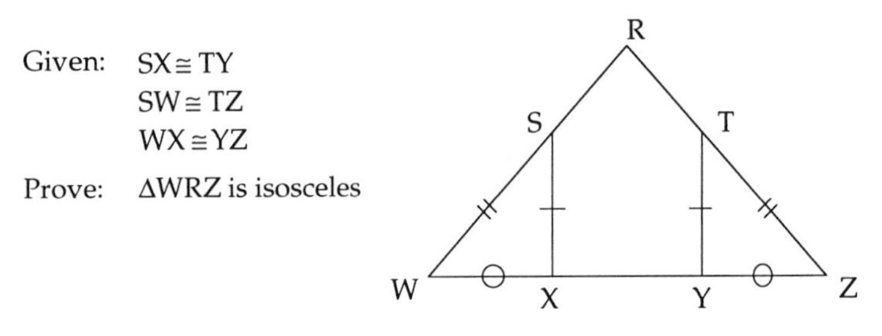

Figure 20.2
The Easy Way. POLYA solves this problem easily because it knows a solution to a similar problem.

The problem shown in Figure 20.2 is taken from a high school geometry textbook (Rhoad *et al.* 1988). What makes this problem interesting for our purposes is its similarity to several other problems in the same text, including a sample problem which precedes it, shown in Figure 20.3. This example will show how POLYA uses the diagram to index into knowledge associated with the sample problem and its solution, making the solution to Figure 20.2 easy.

POLYA starts by reading the givens and goal and computing a general description of the diagram as a whole. That description includes symmetry information and statistics about the arrangement of lines and vertices. The description of the diagram for this problem exactly matches the description of the diagram for the sample problem in Figure 20.3.

Next, POLYA locates in the diagram the objects referenced by the givens and goals, computes descriptions of them, and annotates the diagram. A statement like "WX ≅ YZ" is only useful as an index if it is accompanied by a description of the segments in the diagram.

Based on the diagram and the goal, POLYA retrieves from memory a plan based on the solution to the sample problem (Figure 20.3). This plan does two things. First, it locates in the diagram and computes descriptions of each object referenced in the earlier proof, such as angles RSX and RTY, segments SX and TY, and triangles WXS and YZT. Second, the plan establishes each step of the earlier proof as a subgoal. These subgoals will be used to select plans which seem most likely to contribute to the final proof.

Triangles WXS and ZYT correspond to two of the objects used in the earlier proof. While looking at those triangles, POLYA recognizes that they have three sides marked. That pattern triggers a plan for applying the side-side-side (SSS) theorem to prove the triangles congruent. That matches a subgoal, so POLYA runs the plan and successfully proves the triangles congruent.

Once that subgoal is proved, the remaining steps get added automatically (they have no other preconditions), and the proof is done.

A sample problem

Given: $\angle 3 \cong \angle 4$
$BX \cong AY$
$BW \cong AZ$

Prove: ΔWTZ is isosceles

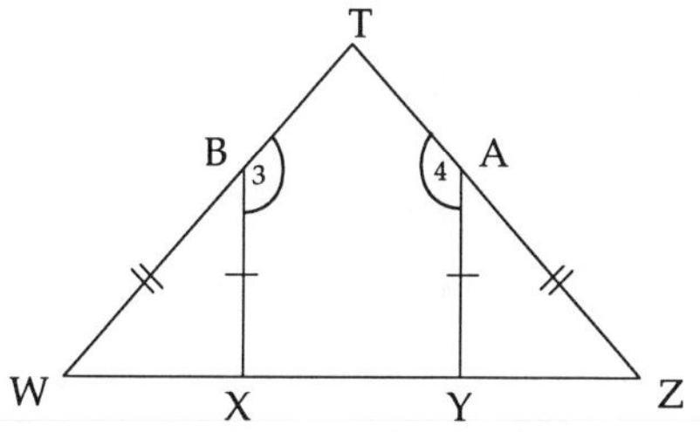

$\angle WBX$ is supp. to $\angle 3$	from diagram
$\angle ZAY$ is supp. to $\angle 4$	from diagram
$\angle WBX \cong \angle ZAY$	supps. to $\cong$ angles are $\cong$
$\Delta WBX \cong \Delta ZAY$	SAS theorem
$\angle W \cong \angle Z$	corr. parts of $\cong \Delta$ are $\cong$
ΔWTZ is isosc.	two angles $\cong$ —> isosceles

Figure 20.3
Solution to a Similar Problem. POLYA uses the solution to this sample problem to help it solve the problem in Figure 20.2.

Discussion This example shows how the diagram can be used to retrieve the solution to a previous problem, and how that solution is helpful. The solution helped POLYA decide which objects to look at (especially the corner triangles) and it completed the proof once those triangles were proved congruent.

In this case the two problems had identical diagrams. There are clear cases in which the solution to one problem could help in solving a new one even if the diagrams are merely similar rather than identical. Although POLYA's vocabulary for describing diagrams can capture significant similarities, mapping a solution from one problem to a different one is much harder when the diagrams are different. This is an area of current research.

Of course, it is not always possible to retrieve a similar problem on the basis of the diagram and the goal. POLYA then has to work harder, relying on local features to guide reasoning. The next example shows how POLYA extracts features from the diagram as part of solving the problem.

20.3.2 Example 2: The Hard Way

Example 2

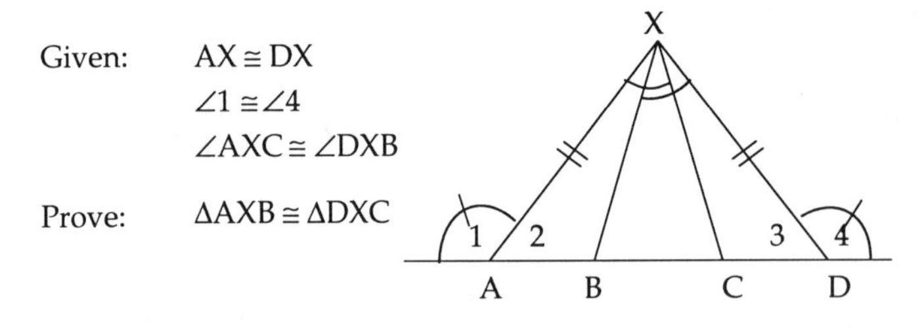

Figure 20.4
The Hard Way. POLYA solves this problem using local features to trigger specific inferences. The diagram is marked to show the given information; POLYA marks the diagram to make it easier to recognize significant patterns (e.g. the ASA triangle congruence theorem).

For the second example, POLYA will solve the problem in Figure 20.4 without the benefit of a previous case to guide its reasoning.

As before, POLYA starts by reading the givens and goal and computing a general description of the diagram as a whole. POLYA recognizes that the diagram contains an isosceles triangle and an extended baseline.[2] The fact that the triangle appears isosceles triggers a plan (which never actually runs) for examining the legs and base angles of the triangle.

[2]In fact, POLYA recognizes this as an instance of a "4-fork triangle" but, for this example, that feature is not attached to any problem-solving knowledge.

Continuing its startup routine, POLYA locates in the diagram the objects referenced by the givens and goals, and computes descriptions of them. POLYA also annotates the diagram to reflect the given information. These marks will make it easier for POLYA to recognize the applicability of certain theorems.

The description of segments AX and DX includes that they are "hinged" (non-collinear but sharing an endpoint) and that their uncommon endpoints are connected to form a triangle. The description of angles 1 and 4 includes that they are obtuse, they open up to the exterior of the figure, and they are adjacent exterior angles of a triangle. The description of angles AXC and DXB includes that they overlap. The description of the goal triangles includes that they have a common vertex and that they each have one side marked congruent (AX and DX).

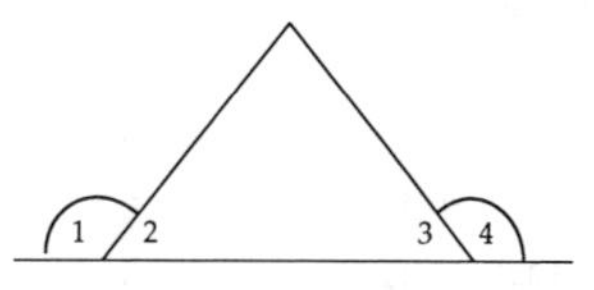

Figure 20.5
Guiding Inferences. POLYAretrieves a plan associated with this problem for inferring that angle 2 is congruent to angle 3.

The extended baseline plus the descriptions of angles 1 and 4 trigger a plan in memory associated with an earlier problem shown in Figure 20.5. That plan focuses POLYA's attention on the adjacent angles 2 and 3. It predicts (and sees) that those angles are parts of triangles. This is a common idiom in high school geometry: the problem authors have supplied a pair of congruent angles solely for the purpose of having the student infer that the adjacent angles are congruent. Any expert would quickly make that inference without worrying about how it would fit into the overall proof, and POLYA does the same. The plan adds three statements to the proof justifying that angles 2 and 3 are congruent.

From the previous observation that the goal triangles had one side marked, plus the knowledge that POLYA just proved two more angles congruent, a plan is triggered that focuses POLYA's attention again on the goal triangles. The plan predicts (and POLYA sees) that the triangles now have one angle marked in addition to the marked side. The plan focuses attention on adjacent unmarked sides AB and CD and on the unmarked angles AXB and DXC.

It sees that AB and CD are collinear, but no plans are triggered by that feature. A plan *is* triggered, however, by the angles, which are described as hinged and having a 4-fork vertex. From this description POLYA recognizes them as the non-overlapping parts of the congruent angles AXC and DXB. A plan is triggered which adds two steps to the proof to justify that the non-overlapping angles are congruent.

POLYA realizes now that the triangles are congruent by the angle-side-angle (ASA) theorem and adds that statement to the proof, completing it.

Discussion In contrast to the first example, this example looks much more like traditional theorem-proving. It does show, however, how POLYA can use features extracted from the diagram to make inferences selectively, reasoning both from the givens and the goal.

The foregoing examples illustrate how POLYA uses information about the diagram to retrieve relevant plans. In the first problem, an overall description of the diagram analogous to what a person might perceive at first glance allowed POLYA to retrieve a solution to a past problem with a similar diagram. POLYA also used a description of the corner triangles to recognize that the side-side-side theorem applied. In the second problem, POLYA retrieved plans on the basis of descriptions of three pairs of angles and the two triangles. Like any CBR system, POLYA's success depends to a large extent on the vocabulary it uses to index knowledge in memory.

20.4 Vocabulary for Memory Indexing

A case-based planner needs an indexing vocabulary which is inexpensive to compute yet highly predictive of when two problems will have similar solutions. In geometry, the primary source of predictive features is the diagram.

20.4.1 How the Problem Is Encoded

A geometry problem comprises a diagram along with a goal to be proved and a list of givens which refer to objects in the diagram. As provided to POLYA, the goal and givens are encoded in the usual way as predicates, e.g. `(congruent-segments (segment x b) (segment y a))`. The diagram is encoded as four lists: an association list linking the alphabetic labels used in the givens and goal to their corresponding (x, y) locations in the coordinate plane; a list of lines defined by the (x, y) coordinates of their endpoints; a list of marked angles comprising the (x, y) coordinates of the vertex, the orientations of the two rays, and the type of mark; and a list of marked segments comprising the endpoint coordinates of the segment and the type of mark. Here, for example, is an excerpt of the encoding of the diagram in Figure 20.3:

```
*labelled-points* = ((W . (0 0)) (X . (50 0)) ...)
*lines* = ( ((0 0) (170 0))         ; line WZ
            ((0 0) (85 100))...)    ; line WT
*angle-marks* = ( ((50 50) 4.7 0.9) . arc-mark) ...) ; angle 3
*segment-marks* = ( ((50 0) (50 50) . single-tic) ...) ; seg. BX
```

Additionally, POLYA uses the list of lines to construct a bitmap line drawing which it uses for certain computations.

The rationales for this encoding scheme are neutrality and functional convenience. For POLYA, as for a human, the diagram is an external object which must be interpreted. Thus the particular encoding is unimportant as long as it allows for the important features to be extracted and does not permit bias.

POLYA does not make any inferences directly from this coordinate information. Instead, it selectively computes symbolic descriptive *frames* of whatever objects it thinks might be important, including but not limited to segments, triangles, and pairs of angles. It is on the basis of these symbolic frames that POLYA decides how to solve the problem.

20.4.2 Recognizing the Diagram as a Whole

Problems with similar diagrams are likely to have similar solutions. To measure similarity between diagrams, POLYA uses a frame comprising statistics about the arrangement of points and lines. For example, the frame for the diagram in Figure 20.2 looks like Table 20.1.

This is the first internal representation of the diagram that POLYA uses for memory indexing. The objective of this representation is to capture important similarities and differences between diagrams while avoiding the complexities of graph matching. It captures, for example, the similarity between diagrams (a) and (b) in Figure 20.6, which have the slots noted in Table 20.2 in common. POLYA recognizes this conjunct of slot-values as an abstract concept, "maybe upright triangles share side."

Table 20.1

Slot	Value for Figure 20.2
symmetry	left/right
number of enclosed regions	3
baseline	yes
baseline-extended	no
topline	no
topline-extended	NA
left vertical line	no
right vertical line	no
symmetry line	no
cross on axis of symmetry	no
top vertices	1
bottom vertices	4
left vertices	1
right vertices	1
top-bottom linkages	2
left-right linkages	1

Table 20.2

Slot	Value for Figures 20.6 (a) and (b)
symmetry	left/right
number of enclosed regions	2
topline	no
topline-extended	NA
left vertical line	no
right vertical line	no
symmetry line	yes
cross on axis of symmetry	no
top vertices	1
bottom vertices	2
left vertices	1
right vertices	1

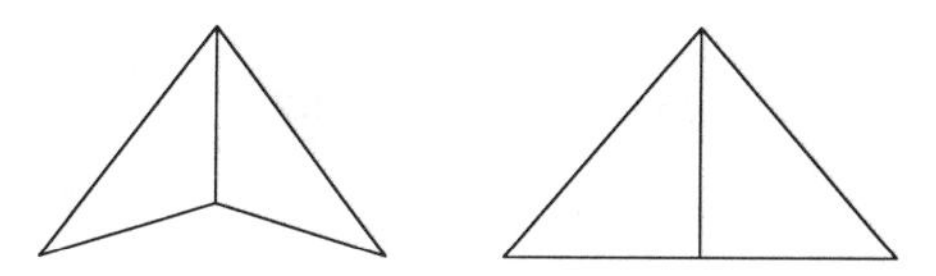

Figure 20.6
Similar Diagrams. POLYA can recognize that these two diagrams are similar.

One weakness of this representation is its sensitivity to orientation. Textbooks frequently vary problems by rotating the diagram. Currently, POLYA cannot recognize figures which are identical but rotated. Theoretically, however, it should often be possible to recognize when a familiar figure is "sideways" or "upside-down" relative to a standard orientation. POLYA could then rotate it to a standard orientation, recompute the overall description, and compare it again to diagrams in memory.

20.4.3 Local Features

Even when the diagrams are identical, two problems rarely call for exactly the same proof. To solve the problem in Figure 20.2, POLYA had to recognize that the side-side-side (SSS) theorem, rather than the side-angle-side (SAS) theorem, was called for to prove the corner triangles congruent. The SSS theorem requires congruence between three corresponding sides of the two triangles. A cheap but effective indication of this is when all three sides of the triangle have congruence marks on them. For SAS, the indicator would be two sides and one angle. The lists of marked segments and angles in the diagram make these patterns easy to compute without worrying about exact correspondences or about the placement of the marked angle between the marked sides, which can be verified by the SAS plan itself.

For triangles, therefore, POLYA determines the number of sides and angles which are marked as congruent to something else without regard to their exact placement with respect to each other. POLYA also uses the coordinate locations of the vertices to compute a description of the apparent shape of the triangle (whether it appears to be right, isosceles, equilateral, or other). The frame for the corner triangles in Figure 20.2 looks like Table 20.3.

None of these slot values can be used in the proof. This frame can only be used to retrieve from memory a plan likely to contribute to the proof. The fact that 3 sides are marked retrieves the plan for applying the SSS

Table 20.3

Slot	Value for Corner Triangles in Figure 20.2
type	right
sides marked	3
angles marked	0

Table 20.4

Slot	Value for $\angle 1$ in Figure 20.4
size	obtuse
orientation	northwest
vertex-pattern	"T"
interior-rays	0
marked?	yes
type-of-mark	tic
interior-area	0

theorem. It does not guarantee that the plan will succeed. It is effective, however, as a first-pass indication of what should be done. Checking the correspondences between the marked sides of the two triangles is handled explicitly by the plan.

In the second example (Figure 20.4), POLYA recognizes a common idiom in angles 1 and 4 and retrieves a plan to prove the congruence of angles 2 and 3. The features characteristic of that idiom are these: the congruent angles are obtuse; they open up to the outside of the diagram (and thus are not part of any polygon); the pattern of rays at their vertex is a "T"; and the adjacent (supplemental) angles are part of a triangle.

All these features except the last are easily computed for the individual angle, and are captured in the frame descriptions of angles 1 and 4. The description of angle 1 in Figure 20.4 looks like Table 20.4.

The *interior-area* slot of the angle frame contains an integer describing the space into which the angle opens.[3] Usually the angle is part of some sort of polygon, in which case the integer is a count of the number of sides (for angle 2, the interior-area slot-value is 3, because it opens up into a triangle). Zero, the slot-value here, means that the angle opens up to the exterior and is not a part of any polygon.

The *vertex-pattern* slot indicates when the angle shares a vertex with

[3]Interior area is computed with a region-flooding routine on the bitmap, a visual routine proposed by Ullman (1984).

Table 20.5

Slot	Value for ∠AXB
size	acute
orientation	southwest
vertex-pattern	"4-fork"
interior-rays	0
marked?	no
type-of-mark	NA
interior-area	3

other angles. The "T" pattern here signals a linear-pair relationship between this angle and the one adjacent to it.

The size, vertex-pattern, and interior-rays values are all used to trigger the plan which proves angles 2 and 3 congruent. The last predictive feature, viz. that the adjacent angle (∠2) is part of a triangle, is checked explicitly by the plan by computing a frame for angle 2 and verifying that the interior-area slot is 3.

The overlapping congruent angles at the top of the triangle are suggestive of another idiom, that the non-overlapping angles are congruent, but is only part of the index for a plan to prove it. What eventually triggers the plan is the description of one of the non-overlapping angles, ∠AXB, whose frame is shown in Table 20.5.

The "4-fork" vertex-pattern helps identify it as part of the same angle cluster; the fact that it has no interior-rays identifies it as one of the non-overlapping angles (the overlapping angles each had one interior ray).

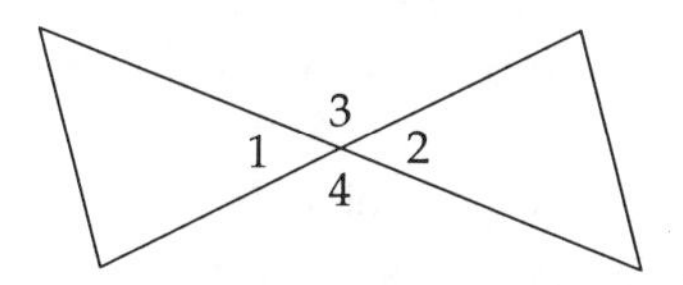

triangle-pair-vis

Slot	Value
relative-extents	bow-tie

Figure 20.7
Comparing Two Triangles. POLYA can recognize several spatial relationships between two triangles, including bow ties.

20.4.4 Comparative Features

Many other useful inferences can be made on the basis of comparisons of objects. POLYA can compare two objects to determine relative sizes, orientations, and spatial extents. The objects need not be the same;

POLYA can compare an angle and a triangle to see if the angle is part of the triangle, for example, or exterior to it. That the angles overlapped in problem 3 was one useful result of a comparison. The comparative frame for the triangles in Figure 20.7 reveals that they form a bow-tie, which would lead POLYA to conclude immediately that the vertical angles 1 and 2 are congruent (ignoring angles 3 and 4).

20.4.5 Indexing Off Abstract Concepts

In addition to the frames for diagrammatic features, POLYA also indexes some plans by abstract concepts, such as congruence or part-of relationships.

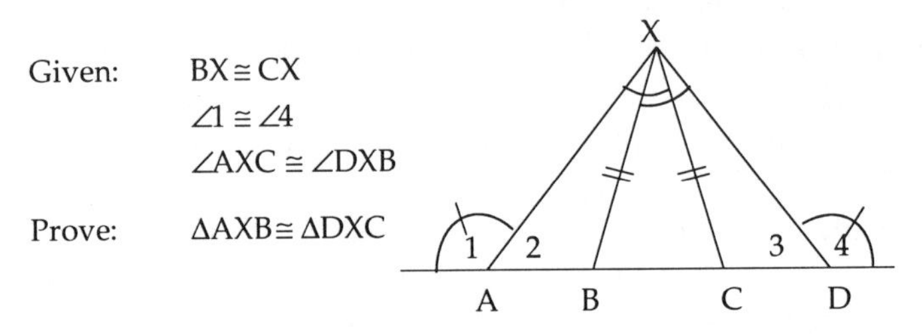

Figure 20.8
This problem differs from the problem in Figure 20.4 only by which pair of segments is given to be congruent.

Consider the problem shown in Figure 20.8. The diagram is identical to the diagram in Figure 20.4, and the problems are very nearly so. They differ only in the particular segments given to be congruent. This difference does not greatly affect the proof, except that the latter problem uses the angle-angle-side (AAS) theorem to prove the triangles congruent instead of the SAS theorem.

For POLYA to be able to distinguish between these problems it needs to recognize this difference in the givens. To extract this difference from the text alone would require checking bindings between several statements. POLYA detects the difference by situating the segments within the diagram. The way POLYA does this is by building a frame which links together the textual statement of the abstract congruence relationship, the descriptions of the two segments individually, and the spatial relationship of the two segments with respect to each other. Table 20.6 below shows how these frames differ for the problems in Figures 20.4 and 20.8.

Table 20.6

Slot	Value for Figure 4		Value for Figure 8	
relationship	congruent		congruent	
status	given		given	
seg1	slope up	; AX	slope up	; BX
	0 interior points		0 interior points	
	line=seg		line=seg	
	exterior		*not exterior*	
	...		...	
seg2	slope down	; DX	slope down	; CX
	0 interior points		0 interior points	
	line=seg		line=seg	
	exterior		*not exterior*	
	...		...	
segment-pair	equal lengths		equal lengths	
	hinged-triangle		hinged-triangle	

Table 20.7

Frame	Slot	Value for Goal in Figure 20.2
special-triangle	triangle	appears-isosceles
		no angles marked
		no sides marked
	property	isosceles
	status	goal

The difference between the frames for these two problems is in the seg1 and seg2 slots, which describe the segments as 'exterior' in one case and 'not exterior' in the other. This difference would allow POLYA to differentially index complete solutions for these two problems.

The plan for the problem in Figure 20.2 is indexed by the goal as well as by the diagram. The goal (once it has been fully instantiated in the diagram) is expressed in Table 20.7.

Frames like the one in Table 20.6 involve descriptions of several objects (two segments and one pair of segments) and are built by plans.

20.5 Parsing the Diagram on Demand

One of the challenges of working with diagrams and other spatial data is complexity. For POLYA to compute all possible descriptive frames for even a relatively simple diagram would be expensive and unnecessary. Most of the features in a given diagram are irrelevant to a particular problem. Figure 20.2 contains fourteen segments of which only eight are relevant to the proof. On the other hand, different features will be important at different times.

Even people don't see everything at once. Human vision is restricted by a limited field of view and narrow fovea.[4] There is a strong functional reason for this limitation: more sensor data requires more computational power to process it. To process a full 150 degree visual field at high resolution would require a brain weighing approximately 30,000 pounds (Eric Schwartz, personal communication to Michael Swain; see also Swain & Stricker 1993). A narrow fovea enables us to get by with a lighter brain, but the tradeoff is that we must make decisions about where to focus our gaze.

The issue is not just one of efficiency or complexity. A CBR system which pays attention to irrelevant features is likely to retrieve an irrelevant case from memory. Thus it is important that the problem-solver choose which features to compute, and it has to do this even before it knows what those features might be. The way POLYA decides what features to compute is by retrieving and executing *search plans.*

20.5.1 Search Plans

POLYA's search plans control feature extraction in the same way that the proof plans control what statements get added to the proof. A search plan is retrieved from memory on the basis of some set of features which suggest that the search plan might be useful. When the plan is selected for execution, each step in the plan generates a feature (i.e. a descriptive frame) which is passed to memory. For example, the search plan S-SIDE+ANGLE is triggered by a triangle with one side marked and one angle marked (as in the second example, Figure 20.4). It computes descriptions of the unmarked side (AB) and its symmetric counterpart (CD), and of the unmarked angle ($\angle$AXB) and its symmetric counterpart ($\angle$DXC). The purpose of this search plan is to detect some pattern which would trigger a proof plan to prove either the sides or the angles congruent.

[4]The high-resolution region of the retina, which covers only 5 degrees of the field of view.

20.5.2 Actions

Plans need to be able to specify objects in the diagram in a flexible way that is independent of the specific labels and coordinate locations of the points and lines. For example, the plan associated with the sample problem (Figure 20.3) has to be able to refer to the corner triangles in the new diagram. An interesting research problem has been to define suitable primitive operators for locating objects within the diagram.

POLYA has a vocabulary of over one hundred "actions" for locating objects of likely interest and for computing their descriptive frames from the raw coordinate data. Many of these actions are procedural versions of geometry concepts, e.g. LOOK-AT-BASE-ANGLE-1, which computes a description of one of the base angles of an isosceles triangle. Others are related to specific configurations; LOOK-AT-LINEAR-PARTNER is used to compute a description of angle 2 in Figure 20.4. The plan associated with the sample problem in Figure 20.3 uses LOOK-AT-SMALLEST-ATTACHED-TRIANGLE to get from the base angles to the corner triangles.

These primitive operators are arguably as much a part of the content of geometry as are the formal rules. When a textbook introduces new terminology, e.g. "included angle," implicit in the explanation is some procedure for finding it in a diagram. The student needs to learn that procedure or she will be unable to solve the problems that follow.

20.6 Conclusion

Teachers and textbook authors organize the high school geometry curriculum to help students learn to write proofs. The problems they ask students to solve are frequently similar to examples in the text and to other problems the student has solved before. They provide givens in certain combinations to elicit particular inferences. They use symmetry in the diagrams to help the student find and keep track of correspondences.

These properties of high school geometry render it amenable to case-based reasoning (CBR). CBR uses features in the problem to index into a memory of solutions. In geometry, the diagram is the primary source of predictive features. Extracting features from the diagram is itself a potentially expensive task, so it is important that feature extraction be part of problem-solving.

POLYA is a case-based planner that proves high school geometry theorems. It uses features in the diagram to index and retrieve plans in memory. Some of those plans are based on proofs for entire problems and are indexed by an overall description of the diagram and by the goal. Matching on such a plan usually enables POLYA to solve a problem quickly, regardless of the length of the proof. Other plans correspond to individual inferences, and are indexed by the features which *suggest* their relevance without guaranteeing it.

POLYA addresses the problem of extracting features by making that an explicit part of its task. Along with its *proof plans* for writing the proof, POLYA has *search plans* for computing descriptions of areas of likely interest in the diagram. POLYA's algorithm interleaves the processes of feature extraction and plan retrieval so that features can be extracted on an as-needed basis. Thus POLYA's architecture should be relevant to any domain in which extracting features is a difficult task.

References

Anderson, J. R., Boyle, C. F., and Yost, G. 1985. The Geometry Tutor. In Proceedings of the International Joint Conference on Artificial Intelligence. Los Angeles: International Joint Conference on Artificial Intelligence.

Berger, J. Forthcoming. *ROENTGEN: A Case-Based Reasoning System for Radiation Therapy Planning*, Ph.D. diss., Dept. of Computer Science, University of Chicago.

Chi, M. T. H., Bassok, M., Lewis, M. W., Reimann, P., and Glaser, R. 1989. Self-Explanations: How Students Study and Use Examples in Learning to Solve Problems. *Cognitive Science* 13(2): 145–182.

Chou, S. C. 1992. A Geometry Theorem Prover for Macintoshes. In *Automated Deduction–CADE-11*, 686–690. Berlin: Springer-Verlag.

Cook, S. A. 1971. The Complexity of Theorem-Proving Procedures. In Proceedings of the Third Annual ACM Conference on Theory of Computing, 151–158. New York: ACM.

Gelernter, H. 1959. Realization of a Geometry Theorem Proving Machine. In Proceedings of the International Conference on Information Processing. Paris: UNESCO.

Greeno, J. G. 1983. Forms of Understanding in Mathematical Problem Solving. In *Learning and Motivation in the Classroom,* ed. Paris, S. G., Olson, G. M., and Stevenson, H. W. Hillsdale, N.J.: Lawrence Erlbaum.

Hammond, K. 1989. *Case-Based Planning: Viewing Planning as a Memory Task.* San Diego, Calif.: Academic Press.

Koedinger, K. R. and Anderson, J. R. 1990. Abstract Planning and Perceptual Chunks: Elements of Expertise in Geometry. *Cognitive Science* 14: 511–550.

Kolodner, J., ed. 1993. *Case-Based Reasoning.* San Mateo, Calif.: Morgan Kaufmann.

McCarthy, J. 1977. Epistemological Problems of Artificial Intelligence. In Proceedings of the Fifth International Conference on Artificial Intelligence. San Francisco: Morgan Kaufmann.

McDougal, T. and Hammond, K. 1992. A Recognition Model of Geometry Theorem-Proving. In Proceedings of the Fourteenth Annual Conference of the Cognitive Science Society, 106–111. Hillsdale, N.J.: Lawrence Erlbaum.

McDougal, T. F. and Hammond, K. J. 1993. Representing and Using Procedural Knowledge to Build Geometry Proofs. In Proceedings of the Eleventh National Conference on Artificial Intelligence, 711–716. Hillsdale, N.J.: Lawrence Erlbaum.

McDougal, T. F. 1993. Using Case-Based Reasoning and Situated Activity to Write Geometry Proofs. In Proceedings of the Fifteenth Annual Conference of the Cognitive Science Society, 60–65. Cambridge, Mass.: The MIT Press.

Nevins, A. J. 1975. Plane Geometry Theorem Proving Using Forward Chaining. *Artificial Intelligence* 6.

Newell, A. and Simon, H. A. 1956. The Logic Theory Machine. *IRE Transactions on Information Theory* 2: 61–79.

Rhoad, R., Whipple, R., and Milauskas, G. 1988. *Geometry for Enjoyment and Challenge.* Evanston, Ill.: McDougal, Littell.

Ross, B. H. 1986. Remindings in Learning: Objects and Tools. In *Similarity, Analogy, and Thought,* ed. Vosniadou, S. and Ortony, A. New York: Cambridge University Press.

Schank, R. C. and Abelson, R. 1977. *Scripts, Plans, Goals and Understanding.* Hillsdale, N.J.: Lawrence Erlbaum.

Schank, R. C. 1982. *Dynamic Memory: A Theory of Reminding and Learning in Computers and People.* New York: Cambridge University Press.

Swain, M. J. and Stricker, M. A. 1993. Promising Directions in Active Vision. *International Journal of Computer Vision* 2: 109–126.

Ullman, S. 1984. Visual Routines. *Cognition* 18: 97–159.

21 Qualitative Structural Analysis through Mixed Diagrammatic and Symbolic Reasoning

Yumi Iwasaki, Shirley Tessler, & Kincho H. Law
Stanford University

21.1 Introduction

Humans often use diagrams to facilitate problem solving. In many types of problems, including but not limited to problems involving behaviors of physical objects, drawing a diagram is a natural and intuitive step in the solution process. Drawing can reveal important information that may not be explicit in a written description, and can help one gain insights into the nature of the problem. Though such use of diagrams is an integral part of human problem solving behavior, it has not received nearly as much attention in AI as symbolic reasoning has.

This chapter presents our work aimed towards understanding the role of diagrammatic reasoning in the context of solving a concrete, physical problem. The problem we chose for studying diagrammatic reasoning is the determination of the deflection shape of a building frame structure under load. We have constructed computer programs called REDRAW-I (REasoning with DRAWings) and REDRAW-II that solve this problem qualitatively using a diagram in a way similar to that of human engineers. REDRAW-I solves problems solely through manipulation of diagrams. REDRAW-II employs equations as well as diagrams, where diagrams serve as the primary vehicle to control the flow of reasoning. Our experience with these two programs show that they are in fact more helpful in gaining intuitive understanding of the behavior of frame structures as well as of how to solve this type of problems efficiently than a comparable program that reasons purely symbolically.

We chose structural analysis as the domain for studying the role of visual reasoning in problem solving because it is rich with domain-specific knowledge that has significant implications on how the diagram is manipulated and interpreted. The traditional approach to the study of structural analysis has been based, almost exclusively, on quantitative (i.e. numerical) methods. Numerical values for the loads and dimensions are needed to determine the magnitude of reactions and bending moments as well as to proportion the size of the members. Numerical analysis of structures, particularly statically indeterminate structures, requires that the size of all the structural members be specified before an analysis can be carried out. There is, however, an important step before that numerical analysis can take place: the preliminary analysis and design phase where the schematic of the structure is being defined and rough behavior of the structure is being studied. The detailed, numerical analysis is intended to be a check on the preliminary analysis and design of the structure.

Preliminary analysis requires a quite different set of techniques to determine the relationship between the load and the resulting behavior of the structure based on "qualitative," i.e. non-numerical, information. Qualitative analysis can play a significant part in the understanding of structural behavior and the overall design checking procedures, which must be constructed to ensure the correct use of computer modeling and numerical analysis programs.

This chapter is organized as follows: In the remainder of this section, we define diagrammatic reasoning and discuss its role in problem solving in general. We then discuss related work in qualitative reasoning about physical systems and reasoning with images. Before going on to describe REDRAW, we briefly review the problem of deflection of frame structures subject to load. In Section 21.2 and 21.3, we describe the architecture of the two implementations of REDRAW, REDRAW-I and -II, in detail. Section 21.4 concludes with a summary.

21.1.1 Diagrammatic Reasoning and the Roles of Diagrams in Problem Solving

The goal of symbolic or diagrammatic reasoning programs is to make inferences by manipulating and inspecting the internal representations of information. A symbolic reasoning program makes inferences through a purely descriptive representation of the knowledge of the domain and the problem itself. A diagrammatic reasoning program, on the other hand, represents at least some of the information, especially information about spatial relationships, in a more depictive form, i.e. in a form that reflects the geometric and topological structure more directly than a purely descriptive form.

We define diagrammatic representation not only in terms of the distinction between the depictive and the descriptive but also in operational terms, i.e. what types of operations on the data structure are allowed and how they are used by the program. A diagrammatic reasoning program performs at least part of its inferences using data structures with the following characteristics:

- The information represented explicitly in the data structure is the type of information that is explicit in diagrams (i.e. geometric or otherwise visual information).
- The operations that are permitted on the data structure are those that humans perform easily with diagrams. Such operations can include both visual inspection operations as well as manipulation—through either mental imagery or through actual modification of the drawing.

In contrast with diagrammatic reasoning programs, current symbolic reasoning programs use only symbolic forms of representation such as logical axioms, frames, semantic nets, etc. An important difference between a symbolic representation and a diagrammatic one is that the information represented explicitly in a symbolic program is not necessarily what is explicit in a picture. Furthermore, reasoning is performed through some inference rules, which do not necessarily reflect the types of inferences humans make with an image.

We have found that, in developing an intuitive understanding of the response of a structure under load, diagrams fulfill many of the same roles as those articulated by researchers in other fields. First, diagrams are used as "a visual language of structural behavior that can be understood with the minimum of textual comments" (Brohn 1984). The language allows the engineer to express explicitly the constraint or physical law that is relevant at each part of the proposed structure, in such a way that the constraints and some of the consequences are immediately apparent to the reader without further reasoning. Furthermore, the diagram serves as a place holder or short-term memory device by allowing the designer to sketch out the result of one deformation and then go back to see if there is a further effect or interaction that needs to be addressed. Finally, visual inspection of diagrams can serve as a means to guide the choice of a more efficient problem solving strategy when several approaches are possible.

21.1.2 Related Work

There have been some investigations on extending the methodologies developed in qualitative physics research (Iwasaki 1989, Weld and deKleer 1990) to the problem of qualitative structural analysis (Slater 1986; Fruchter, Law, and Iwasaki 1991; Roddis and Martin 1991). All of these works focused on symbolic and/or mathematical modeling of structures, rather than on emulation of the human engineer's problem solving approach. For example, we have previously built a program called QStruc to solve the same deflected shape problem described in this chapter, but using a traditional, symbolic AI approach (Fruchter, Law, and Iwasaki 1991). The program determines the qualitative values of forces, moments, and displacements in a frame structure under load. The inputs to the system are a symbolic representation of the structure in terms of its members and connections, and a load on the structure. There is no explicit representation of the shape of the structure in the program; rather, the shape is implicitly represented by the existence of such physical processes as bending, and the qualitative values (positive, negative, zero or unknown) of such parameters as displacements.

QStruc has successfully analyzed several simple two-dimensional structures, thus demonstrating the feasibility of performing qualitative analysis of structures on a computer. However, our experience with QStruc reveals that such a symbolic approach does not help an engineer to gain an intuitive understanding of the deflection process. Its solution strategy of setting up all applicable equilibrium equations and solving them reflects neither the way humans usually solve the problem nor the causal process through which the load makes the structure deform.

The cognitive architecture implemented in REDRAW is based on the ideas of Chandrasekaran and Narayanan (1992) as well as Kosslyn (1980). Chandrasekaran and Narayanan have argued that some types of reasoning are tightly coupled with perception. They proposed a visual modality-specific architecture, using a visual representation scheme consisting of symbolic representations of the purely visual aspects (shape, color, size, spatial relations) of a given situation at multiple levels of resolution. In their architecture, the visual representation is linked to an underlying analogical representation of a picture so that visual operations performed on the analogical representation are immediately reflected on the visual representation and vice versa. Their objective is "to propose a cognitive architecture underlying visual perception and mental imagery that explains analog mental imagery as well as symbolic visual representations." The idea of "perceptually grounded reasoning" is reflected in the architecture of REDRAW, which consists of symbolic and diagrammatic layers that are closely coupled.

21.1.3 The Deflection Problem of Frame Structures

Determining the qualitative deflected shape of a frame structure under load is one of the fundamental steps in analyzing and understanding the behavior of a structure. Engineers first sketch a simple, 2-D drawing of the shape of the given frame structure. Given a load on the structure, they modify the shape of the structural member under the load. They inspect the modified shape to identify the places where constraints for equilibrium and geometric compatibility conditions of the structure are violated. Those constraint violations are corrected by modifying the shape of connected structural members, propagating deflection to other parts of the structure. This process is repeated until all the constraints are satisfied. The drawing thus produced shows the final deflected shape of the frame under the given load.

Figure 21.1 illustrates an example of this type of reasoning process. (a) shows the given frame structure. Under the load indicated by the arrow, the beam $B1$ deflects in the same direction as the load as shown in (b). Since $J1$ and $J2$ are rigid joints, they must maintain a 90-degree angle. Inspecting the shape (b) shows that they are not. To make them 90 degrees, the columns $C1$ and $C2$ are rotated around the joints as shown in (c). However, since the supports of $C1$ and $C2$ do not allow displacement, the columns must be bent to keep the ends fixed in the original position as shown in (d). Furthermore, since the supports of $C1$ and $C2$ are rigid supports, the lower portion of the columns must remain perpendicular to the ground as shown in (e). Inspection of the shape (e) shows that the moment equilibrium around $J1$ is not satisfied because both members connected by $J1$ are deflected clockwise indicating that the sum of the moments around the joint is not zero, thus violating the moment equilibrium condition. The same can be said for $J2$ also. Finally, both of the end portions of $B1$ are bent upwards slightly in order to achieve moment equilibrium around $J1$ and $J2$ as shown in (f).

The above example illustrates a problem solving process that involves a pictorial representation that presents spatial information much more directly than conventional sentential representations, and uses manipulation of the representation to make inferences based on both visual and non-visual knowledge. Another important feature of this problem solving process is that the reasoning carried out is qualitative. The answer

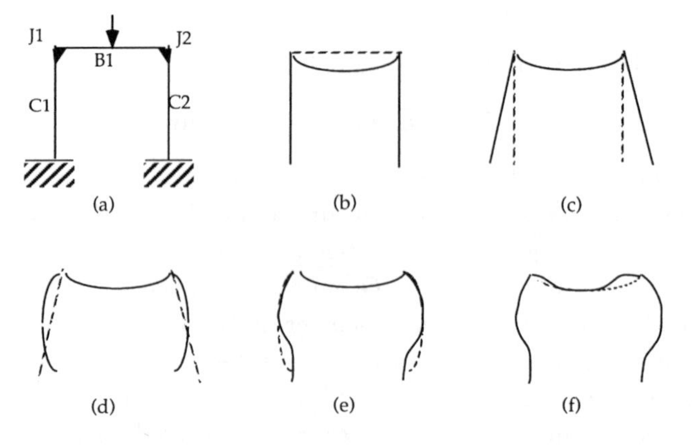

Figure 21.1
Steps in Determining the Deflected Shape

produced in this case is a picture of a deflected shape. Although the resulting picture is qualitatively consonant with the problem solution, it is not, nor does it need to be, mathematically precise or in correct proportion.

This type of problem can also be solved by a more formal, mathematical technique involving setting up equations for forces, bending moments and deflection. However, even when the more formal method is used, visualization is an indispensable first step that provides an engineer with an intuitive understanding of the behavior of the structure and enables her to recognize a good strategy for further analysis.

21.2 redraw-I

We set out to build a computer program that could reason about the deflection shape problem using diagrams just as a human engineer would. Our first implementation of such a program, REDRAW-I solves this type of deflected shape problem by directly manipulating a representation of the shape in the manner shown in Figure 21.1. Given a frame structure and a load, REDRAW-I draws a diagram of the structure and produces the underlying symbolic model in order to facilitate reasoning about non-diagrammatic concepts. Then, the program uses its structural engineering knowledge to propagate constraints on the diagram of the structure, inspecting and modifying this picture until a final shape is produced that represents a stable deflected structure under the given load as illustrated in Figure 21.1. REDRAW-I directly manipulates a representation of the shape in the same manner as depicted in the steps shown in the figure. As with the qualitative nature of human visual reasoning, the reasoning carried out by REDRAW-I is also qualitative. The answer it produces is a picture of a deflected shape.

21.2.1 System Architecture of REDRAW-I

From examining the way deflection shape problems are solved by humans, it is apparent that solving this type of problem requires not only an ability to manipulate and inspect diagrams but also substantial structural engineering knowledge. Structural engineering knowledge about the properties of various types of joints and supports is necessary to identify the constraints applicable to the state (shape) of the structure. Such knowledge is best represented and manipulated symbolically, while information about shapes is best represented as a picture. Many types of modification and inspection of the shape are also more easily carried out with a picture.

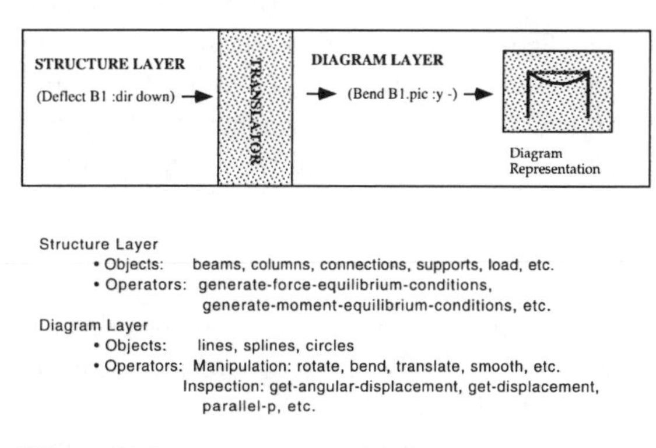

Figure 21.2
Two-Layered Architecture of REDRAW-I

The requirement for both pictorial and non-pictorial representation and reasoning suggests a layered architecture. Figure 21.2 shows the architecture of REDRAW-I schematically. REDRAW-I includes both symbolic reasoning and diagrammatic reasoning components. The former contains the symbolic representation of the structural components and the structural engineering knowledge about various types of structural members, joints, supports, and the constraints they impose on the shape.

It also includes a rule-based inference mechanism to make use of the knowledge. The diagrammatic reasoning component includes an internal representation of the two-dimensional shape of the frame structure as well as a set of operators to manipulate and inspect the shape. These operators, some of which are shown in Figure 21.2, correspond to the manipulation and inspection operations people perform frequently and easily with diagrams while solving deflected-shape problems.

The REDRAW-I system was developed using KEE[1], a Lisp-based, object-oriented knowledge engineering environment.

21.2.2 The Structure Layer

The Structure Layer contains a symbolic representation of the domain objects as well as the domain-specific knowledge. It includes non-visual information (such as that a hinged joint can rotate while a rigid joint cannot), various types of structural members, equilibrium conditions, as well as heuristic knowledge for controlling the structural analysis process. The classes of engineering objects of the domain (namely, objects representing beams, columns, supports, loads and structures) are arranged in a class-subclass hierarchy. The instances of such classes themselves contain information about its connected neighbors as well as about sub- and super-components, forming a partonomic hierarchy. Each of the symbolic objects also contains a pointer to its pictorial object counterpart.

21.2.3 The Diagram Layer

The Diagram Layer represents the two-dimensional shape of a structure. There are several operators that directly act on this representation to allow inspection as well as transformation of the shape. These operators correspond to the operations people perform easily with diagrams. The internal representation of a shape is a combination of a bitmap whose elements correspond to "points" in a picture, and a more symbolic representation where each line segment is represented by a set of x-y coordinates.

The Diagram Layer is independent of the structural engineering domain in the sense that it does not contain any structural engineering concepts. The basic objects are graphical primitives such as lines, splines

[1]KEE is a registered trademark of Intellicorp Inc.

and circles. However, the types of both manipulation and inspection operators provided for the layer do reflect the requirements of the domain. For example, the assumption that the frames consist of incompressible members made a particular set of operators necessary: the program requires a bend operator but not a stretch or compress operator. The effects of the reasoning mechanisms also depend on the specific functioning of those required operators: the bend operator creates a moderate curve rather than a complete bend that would cause the line endpoints to touch or cross, or the inspect operator may look at components connected to the component in question, but will not compare that component to any other, as it might in some other domain. The objects contain information only about their current shape and position with respect to other pictorial elements in the graphics window.

In using the diagrams to determine the deformation, the program detects only those primitive geometric properties that can be easily identified by visual inspection rather than by reasoning involving multiple steps. Such properties include whether two lines are approximately parallel and whether the angle between them is acute, obtuse or right angle. The pictures are not drawn in precise proportion. Only such information as approximate relative sizes, shapes and proximity are used to draw them.

The Diagram Layer operators affect the position of a graphical object as well as its shape by making changes to the coordinates in the object's position and the list of points depicting the objects. Making changes to these coordinate values cause the picture object to be redrawn immediately in the KEE graphics window. Picture object points can be replaced individually or by equations, and both are done in this implementation. An important point to recall is that the drawing of the curves does not need to be precise; they need only be approximately correct and "look right" to a user. The system does not need any more precision than the user would require as if the same picture is drawn on "the back of an envelope." The system needs only to know the direction and shape of the curves in order to make inferences about the shape and stability of a particular frame structure under load.

21.2.4 Linking the Structure and Diagram Layers

There is a close link between the information in the two layers. Communication between the two layers takes place by sending commands and posting constraints by the Structure Layer, which is carried out or checked by the Diagram Layer. There is a translator to mediate the communication between the two layers as shown in Figure 21.2. The system relates the representation of a particular beam in the Structure Layer to a line segment in the Diagram Layer, and the concept of deflection of a beam to an operation on a line segment to transform its shape. Likewise, the system is able to identify features of a shape (e.g. direction of bending, existence of an inflection point) and to communicate them to the Structure Layer. When the Structure Layer posts a constraint or a command, the Translator translates it into a call to a Diagram Layer operator that can directly act on the representation of the shape to manipulate or inspect it. The result is again translated back to concepts that the Structure Layer understands.

21.2.5 Example Problem Solved by REDRAW-I

We describe the problem solving process by REDRAW-I with a simple frame analysis example, shown in Figure 21.3. Figure 21.4 summarizes the communication that takes place for this example between the Structure Layer, the Diagram Layer, and the Translator, which we will denote as S, D, and T, respectively. Given the frame structure of Figure 21.3(a), with a load, $LOAD3$, placed on the middle of the beam, S sends a command, "Deflect $BEAM3$ in the same direction as the load," which T translates into an operation "Bend $BEAM3$.*pic* in the negative direction of the y-coordinate," where $BEAM3$.*pic* is the label on the line segment showing the shape of $BEAM3$. Carrying out this operation will result in the shape shown in Figure 21.3(b).

Continuing the interpretation process, S infers that since $JOINT3$ is a rigid joint, $BEAM3$ and $COL3$ must maintain the same angle, i.e. perpendicular to each other at $JOINT3$, before and after the application of the load. S issues a query to test this constraint. The query is translated into "get the angle between $BEAM3$.*pic* and $COL3$.*pic* at the ends connected by $JOINT3$.*pic*" for D. The answer, the actual angle between the two lines, is communicated to S as the answer that the constraint is not satisfied. S now issues a command to satisfy this constraint while keeping $BEAM3$ fixed, which is translated into "make the angle between $BEAM3$.*pic* and $COL3$.*pic* at $JOINT3$.*pic* be 90 degrees without modifying $BEAM3$.*pic*" for D. REDRAW-I follows the same line of reasoning for $COL4$, also. Carrying out these operations will result in the shape shown in Figure 21.3(c).

Communication between the Structure and the Diagram Layers continues until all the constraints are satisfied. The results are depicted as shown in Figures 21.3(d) and 21.3(e).

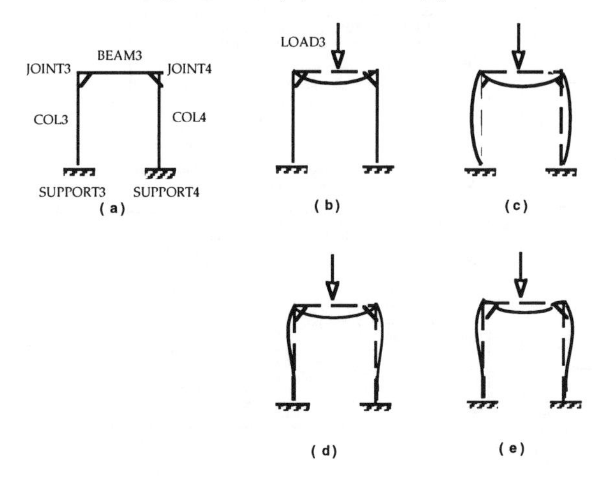

Figure 21.3
Solution Sequence by REDRAW-I—Example 1

21.2.6 Discussion

REDRAW-I successfully analyzed simple deflection shape problems. In REDRAW-I, the domain knowledge in the Structure Layer determines how the structural members are deformed one by one, and thus how the reasoning proceeds. Since the constraints in the symbolic layer implicitly contain the knowledge that deformations propagate from one component to those connected to it, examination of the diagram also proceeds from the component sustaining the original load to the components connected to it, and so forth. In addition, an issue arises concerning the necessity of a "local versus extended" examination of a component in the propagation of the deformation. A hinge joint, for example, allows rotation of the components connected to it. The effect of the hinge on two connected components is localized at the connection point. A fixed joint, on the other hand, requires an examination of the type of attachment at the other end of the component so that an appropriate constraint can be applied and the correct deformation shape be imposed. Thus a more

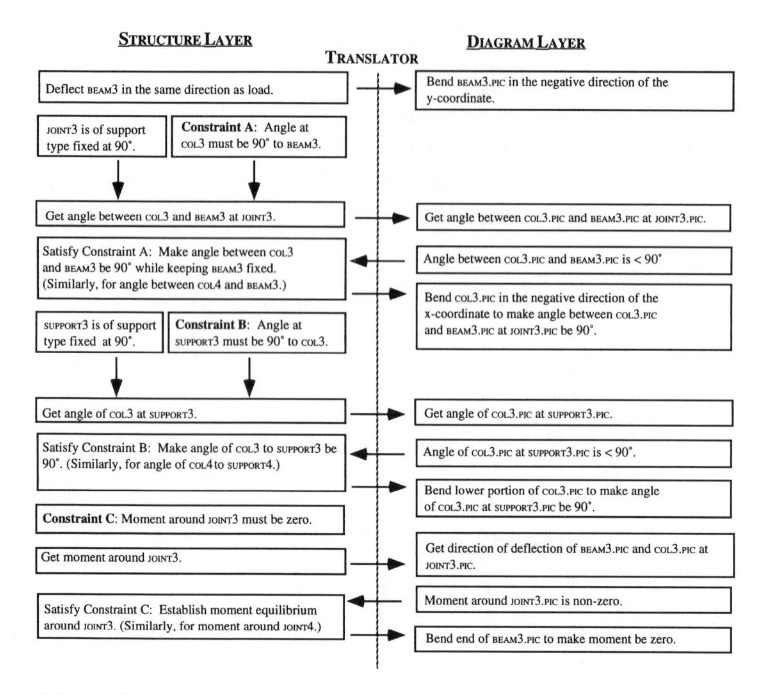

Figure 21.4
Illustration of the Inter-Layer Communication of REDRAW-I

complex or extended examination of a component must take place to correctly implement the fixed joint constraint.

REDRAW-I allows the user to concentrate on the qualitative features of the structure, without requiring the specification of details. The diagrammatic component of the system facilitates the visualization of the particular deformation problem and its likely range of solutions. To aid in this visualization, we include a "write-over" ability such that at each step after a shape transformation, the previous configuration is shown in dotted lines, just as a person might draw a deformed line over the original line rather than create a separate new drawing. Displaying the "before" and "after" shapes allows the user to visually inspect and verify the inference process that was used in the shape transformation. The explanation facility of REDRAW-I, which explains every step of the reasoning process, provides the user with further insight into the constraints imposed and the inferences made to arrive at the final stable deflected shape.

Since REDRAW-I followed a very informal analysis method, its heuristics did not work well when the structure became more complicated. The most critical shortcoming of its informal method is that it did not reason explicitly about forces and bending moments underlying the heuristics for determining how the deformation should propagate. As a result, when there were some ambiguities due to multiple rules being applicable to propagate deformation, it could not resolve the ambiguity or even reason about the real cause of such ambiguity, which would normally be due to the effects of competing forces or bending moments. Furthermore, because there was no explicit reasoning about forces and moments, one could not proceed directly from the informal analysis to a more formal analysis, which would require reasoning about those concepts. REDRAW-II, described in the next section, was implemented to address these problems, by employing a more formal analysis technique that would allow us to reason explicitly about forces, moments and the shape, while taking full advantage of diagrammatic reasoning.

21.3 REDRAW-II

REDRAW-II solves the deflection shape problem by explicitly reasoning about the forces, moments, and shape. Its analysis method better reflects the formal analysis technique employed by structural engineers, and can be used to analyze much more complex structures than REDRAW-I could in principle.

REDRAW-II differs from REDRAW-I in two main respects: First, the system's knowledge base and the reasoning mechanism make explicit the three subproblems—the force equilibrium, moment equilibrium and deflection—which the structural engineer must consider simultaneously in order to determine the final deflected shape. REDRAW-II draws and manipulates three different diagrams, a force diagram, a bending moment diagram, and a deflected shape diagram, to reason about the subproblems and display the results. In general, the three subproblems can be solved in any order, but the most efficient solution strategy depends on the problem and what information is available at any given point. A partial solution to one subproblem can be used to obtain a partial solution to another subproblem, and the solutions can be checked for mutual consistency. Secondly, the problems are not solved only through manipulating diagrams, but also through setting up equations and solving them. Finally, diagrams are used not only to solve the problems but also to make control decisions such as what force to solve for next and what equation is likely to produce an answer for a particular force.

21.3.1 System Architecture of REDRAW-II

As in REDRAW-I, REDRAW-II consists of the Diagram Layer and the Structure Layer. In REDRAW-II, the knowledge base of structural engineering knowledge in the Structure Layer is divided into two parts. One part is the set of three rule bases for rules relating to the analysis of force, moment and deflection. The relevant rule base is examined in full each time a different stage of the analysis is chosen for action. The rules express straightforward pieces of engineering knowledge which can be applied immediately to the problem at hand. Examples of such rules are "the horizontal force at a vertical roller support is zero," and "the vertical and horizontal forces at the unsupported end of cantilevered segment is zero." The other part of the Structure Layer knowledge base consists of methods for selecting an equation to formulate that is most likely to lead to a solution and methods for solving equations.

The problem solving process is represented as a set of well-defined tasks, and the system maintains queues of tasks for the three separate subproblems. This design allows the system to move back and forth among the three subproblems as relevant facts become known.

21.3.2 Example of a Problem Solved by REDRAW-II

Figure 21.5 illustrates the three sub-problems of a problem solved by REDRAW-II. Figure 21.5a shows the information that is specified about a structure to be analyzed. Figures 21.5b–21.5d show the finished results of the force, moment and deflected shape analyses. We now describe part of each of the stages of the analysis.

Focusing on the force diagram in Figure 21.5b, we are given only the vertical downward force imposed by the point load at E. In order to correctly determine the deflected shape, the system must identify all force reactions to the load and ensure that all forces are in equilibrium. The system will first examine the force rule-base for any rules that might be applicable. Finding no useful force rules, the system must set up and solve several qualitative equations to determine all of the force reactions. For example, in order to find the vertical force V_{F-A} at A, the system will set up a moment equilibrium equation about point D as

$$V_{F-E} * |BC|/2 + |BC| * V_{F-A} = 0. \tag{21.3.1}$$

Solving for V_{F-A} qualitatively, the system determines that the vertical force at A is positive (upward). A similar equation set up about A will show that the vertical force at D is also positive, allowing all forces to be in equilibrium.

For the moment diagram in Figure 21.5c, the rule-base regarding bending moments was utilized extensively. For example, the values of the bending moment at points A and D are both zero, since the specified hinged supports allow rotation of the attached column when a load is applied. This result is confirmed diagrammatically in Figure 21.5d, where the deflected shape also shows the rotation of the hinged support.

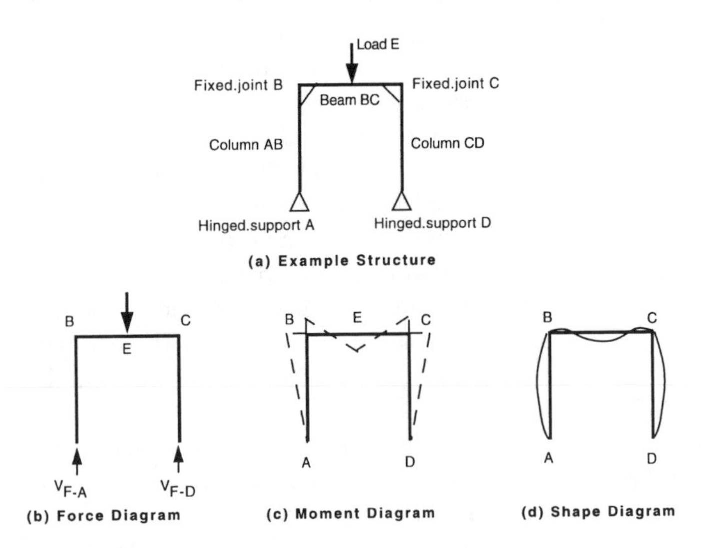

Figure 21.5
An Example of a Problem Solved by REDRAW-II

21.3.3 Discussion

REDRAW-II is able to solve the same type of deformation problems as REDRAW-I, while explicitly computing the forces and bending moments in addition to the shape. The analysis method of REDRAW-II is more formal than that of REDRAW-I. REDRAW-II explicitly reasons about the theoretical concepts of interest such as forces and moments, which underlie the determination of deformation shape but which themselves are not visual. In contrast, such knowledge was not explicit in the rules for propagating a deformation in REDRAW-I. Because REDRAW-II reasons explicitly about theoretical concepts and uses equations to reason about them, it is possible to enumerate systematically all the possible qualitative solutions when there is ambiguity and identify the causes of such ambiguity. Also, this would make it more straightforward to proceed to a more precise quantitative analysis from the results of REDRAW-II. Furthermore, the fact that REDRAW-II reasons about and generates diagrams of the forces, moments and shape makes it easier for the user as well as the system itself to check the consistency of the solutions.

Because of the more formal analysis method REDRAW-II employs, we believe that its problem solving capability is more general and also more easily extensible than REDRAW-I. With respect to the diagrammatic reasoning aspect, however, REDRAW-II relies more on symbolic reasoning to solve problems and relies less on diagrams than REDRAW-I. This is not surprising, since this type of problem is solvable in principle without any diagrammatic reasoning capability at all, as demonstrated by QStruc (Fruchter, Law, and Iwasaki 1991). The fact that diagrams was not used in REDRAW-II as extensively as it was in REDRAW-I for problem solving itself is not evidence that diagrams are useless when a more mathematical analysis method is employed. As Larkin and Simon have shown in their work, diagrams are useful for controlling the reasoning process even when a formal (mathematical) technique is used (Larkin and Simon 1987).

In REDRAW-II, the diagrammatic information is used more for control purposes than for actually solving a problem, especially for computing the forces and the bending moments. For example, forces are computed by rules in a few of the simplest cases, and by setting up and solving equations for the rest. For a given force, there are a large number of equations that can potentially produce an answer since one can formulate a force equilibrium equation and moment equilibrium equation for any subpart of the structure containing the location of the force. REDRAW-II's heuristic methods rely on diagrammatic information, such as the position of a load on the structure or the deformation of a particular member, to determine what equation is most likely to produce an answer for a particular force given the available information. REDRAW-II's ability to make such control decisions is much weaker at this point than a human engineer's partly because we have not articulated many such heuristics in a general enough form to put them into the system. Another important reason for the weakness is that the set of diagrammatic inspection operators currently implemented in REDRAW is incomplete and does not allow us to implement some heuristics, especially those requiring detection of global features of diagrams (e.g. detecting symmetry).

In implementing REDRAW-I and -II, we initially intended all the diagrammatic operators, such as bend, rotate and smooth, to be domain- and task-independent. However, it has become clear that while some operators are domain-independent, others are quite domain- and task-specific. For example, as we have mentioned in Section 21.2.3, the implementation of the "bend" operator reflects such assumptions implicit in the domain and the task as that the curvature of the bent line is large enough so that it can be clearly seen, but not so large that the structural member would appear to be broken. Also, the particular choice of inspection operators we have implemented reflect the nature of the problem we chose to work on. A more general-purpose diagrammatic reasoning layer will require a larger set of operators. The operators also need to be parameterized to work in a larger variety of situations. They must include operators for inspecting and manipulating both local and global features of a diagram and must cover the types of operations humans perform frequently and can do fairly easily with diagrams of all types.

21.4 Conclusion

We have described our work on exploring the potential of diagrammatic reasoning in a concrete problem-solving context. We have built prototype programs REDRAW-I and -II, which reason qualitatively about deflection shape problems using diagrams. They solve the problem in a more computationally efficient manner than a similar system, QStruc (Fruchter, Law, and Iwasaki 1991) in which a purely symbolic approach was taken to solve the same problem. The efficiency advantage over QStruc is due to the fact that use of diagrams allows the system to focus the solution process much better than QStruc, which blindly sets up all applicable equilibrium equations and tries to solve them. Our informal evaluation of the systems also shows that the solution process of REDRAW programs are much more instructive in helping the user to gain intuitive understanding of how a frame structure behaves under load.

REDRAW-I's informal analysis technique involving propagating deformations to other parts of the structure uses a shape diagram extensively. REDRAW-II's analysis method involves more formal, symbolic reasoning, including formulating force and moment equilibrium equations and solving them. Unlike REDRAW-I, REDRAW-II explicitly solves the three different subproblems, namely forces, bending moments and the shape. When a more formal method of solving the problem is employed, the diagram is useful for controlling the inference process.

We believe that diagrammatic reasoning has many advantages over purely symbolic reasoning in problems dealing with spatial information. The explicit representation of the geometric information greatly facilitates certain types of inferences about spatial configuration, that might require many inference steps using purely symbolic representation. Furthermore, since people do use diagrams extensively in many types of problems involving spatial information, programs that use diagrammatic representation in the similar manner will be much easier for the user to understand. For this reason, programs that are based on diagrammatic representation may also prove to be much more useful for teaching purposes.

We emphasize that REDRAW-I and-II are prototype systems that were developed primarily to explore the role of diagrammatic reasoning in problem solving in general. The primary objective is to provide a good environment for studying diagrammatic reasoning, and how that type of reasoning is integrated with symbolic reasoning for problem solving. Pursuing the objective in the context of a concrete real-world problem, namely qualitative structural analysis in this case, has allowed us to examine and model more readily the flow of pictorial and symbolic reasoning as well as to better identify the visual operators that are important in the process of reasoning with diagrams. As a result of this study, we are in a better position to identify interesting problems concerning organization of information consisting of both symbolic and pictorial components and the complexity of problem solving process that uses such information. By developing a strong understanding of the role visual reasoning plays in the problem-solving process, we hope to develop a general problem solving architecture in which diagrammatic and symbolic reasoning are tightly integrated.

21.5 Acknowledgment

This work was sponsored by the Center for Integrated Facilities Engineering and also by NSF grant IRI-9408545. It was conducted at the Knowledge Systems Laboratory at Stanford University.

References

Brohn, David 1984. *Understanding Structural Analysis.* Oxford, England: Oxford Professional Books.

Chandrasekaran, B. and Narayanan, Hari 1992. Perceptual Representation and Reasoning. In Reasoning with Diagrammatic Representations: Papers from the 1992 AAAI Spring Symposium. Technical Report SS-92-02, American Association for Artificial Intelligence, Menlo Park, Calif.

Fruchter, Renate, Law, Kincho H., and Iwasaki, Yumi 1991. Qstruc: An Approach for Qualitative Structural Analysis. In *Proceedings of the Second International Conference on the Application of Artificial Intelligence to Civil and Structural Engineering.* Civil-Comp Press.

Iwasaki, Yumi 1989. Qualitative Physics. In *The Handbook of Artificial Intelligence.* Volume 4. Reading, Mass.: Addison-Wesley.

Kosslyn, Steven M. 1980. *Image and Mind.* Cambridge, Mass.: Harvard University Press.

Larkin, Jill H. and Simon, Herbert A. 1987. Why a Diagram Is (Sometimes) Worth Ten Thousand Words. *Cognitive Science* 11.

Roddis, W. M. Kim and Martin, Jeffrey L. 1991. Qualitative Reasoning About Steel Bridge Fatigue and Fracture. In *The Fifth International Workshop on Qualitative Reasoning about Physical Systems.*

Slater, J. H. 1986. Qualitative Physics and the Prediction of Structural Behavior. In *ASCE Symposium on Expert Systems in Civil Engineering.*

Weld, Daniel S., and deKleer, Johan, eds. 1990. *Readings in Qualitative Reasoning about Physical Systems.* San Mateo, Calif.: Morgan Kaufmann.

22 A Hybrid Architecture for Modeling Liquid Behavior

J. Decuyper, D. Keymeulen & L. Steels
Vrije Universiteit Brussel

22.1 Introduction

Artificial intelligence (AI) is the scientific discipline which studies intelligent behavior and attempts to reproduce it in artificial systems. Part of this challenge consists in proposing a useful definition of intelligent behavior. So far no such definition is available but progress has been made in identifying what seems essential aspects of intelligent behavior. One such aspect is the ability to manipulate physical objects, to understand and control their behavior, and to use them in order to achieve certain goals. Humans possess this ability as may be seen from observing them at playing tennis, driving cars or simply when preparing a meal in their kitchen. The general assumption in AI is that this ability arises from the use of mental models of the physical world. Manipulating these models provides humans with common sense knowledge and allows them to predict the behavior of physical systems or to explain why a certain behavior has occurred.

Much effort has been spent over the years in order to uncover the type of mental models people have and the ways they use them to guide their behavior. In AI, most of this work has been strongly influenced by the widely accepted symbolic paradigm. According to this paradigm a mental model consists of symbols which in some way refer to entities in the physical world. With these symbols expressions may be built according to certain rules. These rules must ensure that the whole of symbols and symbolic expressions constitute a physical symbol system in the sense of Newell. Given a physical symbol system, a second set of rules may be defined that governs the manipulation of the symbolic expressions. The central assumption in the symbolic paradigm is that a set of symbolic expressions can be used to encode knowledge and that this knowledge can be used for problem solving by the lawful manipulation of the symbolic expressions. In short the symbolic paradigm proposes a symbol system as a model for people's mental models and symbol manipulation as a model for people's reasoning with their mental models.

Two distinctive approaches have emerged from the application of the symbolic paradigm to the task of modeling people's mental models of the physical world. Both these approaches are in some way related to physics and it is imperative to clearly understand this relation in order to avoid confusion. Naive physics starts from the observation that most people, from their youngest age on, are extremely dextrous in the manipulation of physical objects. Hence, their mental model must be of a very general type and need not be similar in any way to the models physicists have developed. Naive physics is an attempt to build a model for people's common sense knowledge about the physical world.

Qualitative physics starts from the observation that people who are trained in physics often rely on qualitative models which are of a different nature than the physics models. A qualitative model only captures the most prominent features of a physical system and not the details as expressed in the value of quantified variables. Despite this lack of detail qualitative models are well adapted to certain tasks such as explaining or classifying behaviors. A further observation is that people trained in physics have the capability to switch between a quantitative and a qualitative model. These observations have lead to the central challenge of qualitative physics: is it possible to take a physics (quantitative) model as input and to generate from it a qualitative model. Hence qualitative physics is an attempt at modeling the qualitative knowledge of people which is different from their physics knowledge but possibly also from their common sense knowledge.

In this chapter we are primarily interested in the limitations of the symbolic paradigm as a framework for modeling knowledge about the physical world. More specifically, we analyze naive physics as a tool for modeling knowledge about liquids. Hayes showed how a model based on first order predicate calculus could be used to infer common sense knowledge about liquids. A typical example is the prediction that liquid will flow from an open container when it is gradually tilted. However, upon close inspection it may be seen that naive physics does not quite cover all the possible behaviors. The weak spot is the representation of "shape" in naive physics which does not support inference of the influence of the shape of a container on the behavior of the liquid it contains. A similar remark holds for qualitative physics and the representations it uses. The example of rotating an open container holding liquid illustrates that liquids and the containers used to manipulate them constitute a class of physical systems for which the no-function-in-structure principle is particularly challenging. From our analysis we are led to conclude that the shape of a container cannot be represented in a symbolic model, at least not in a way that captures its importance for liquid behavior.

In order to remedy the poor representation of shape in qualitative and naive physics, we propose to use a homogeneous fine-grained representation, the prototype of which is a grid. In such a representation the influence of the shape of containers and of other spatial properties on the behavior of liquids can be taken into account provided that this behavior is itself properly encoded. The resulting model is similar in many respects to the kind of simulations which abound in computational fluid dynamics. There are however important differences both in scope and in level of detail. In our model we have traded precision for scope. We have built a simulation for liquid behavior which is not very precise but on the other hand can handle a wide set of different situations. CFD simulations usually take the opposite stance and strive to achieve high precision at the expense of generality.

The simulation we introduce does not constitute a substitute for a symbolic model. It provides a tool for modeling some aspects of liquid behavior which are difficult or impossible to handle in a symbolic model. It does not however capture *knowledge* about liquid behavior in the way a mental model supposedly does. Hence, from an AI point of view, our simulation does not contribute to understanding and modeling people's knowledge about liquids. What we do claim however is that in view of using a model for liquid behavior in a robot for example, this model cannot be purely symbolic. At least some part of it must be of a truly different nature, in our case a fine-grained simulation. This fact should not be taken as a criticism on symbolic models for it suffices to realize that people too may have different ways of controlling the manipulation of liquids. Most probably, when it comes to manipulating physical objects, the direct use of visual information, sometimes called visual thinking, may play an important role in dealing with the spatial aspects of a manipulation. In a similar way, a simulation like the one we propose, may play an essential role in a model for liquids by providing a tool for dealing with the dependence of liquid behavior on spatial aspects such as the shape of a container.

22.2 Naive Physics

In his Naive Physics Manifesto Hayes proposes to tackle the formalization of common-sense knowledge about the physical world. He motivates this exercise as an attempt to abandon toy worlds and to use a more realistic problem domain for validating artificial reasoners. Hayes chooses liquids as a first subject because liquids have some idiosyncratic properties which constitute an important challenge for formalisers. Consider for example the most basic of all properties, that of being an individual object. Liquids seem not to have the property of being individual objects for they may merge in a way which completely blurs their identity. Similarly, some properties of liquids such as their shape, are of a very volatile nature. It can change continuously during the manipulation of liquids.

In order to overcome these and other difficulties, Hayes sets up a conceptual framework which, besides liquids, also involves very basic concepts such as space, time, change, geometry and shape. He shows that within this framework it is possible to build a logical model for knowledge about liquids and to use this model to make certain predictions. These predictions are very similar to the kind of answers people produce to questions of the type: "What will happen if in this situation we do this ?" Hence, it may be concluded that the logical model of Hayes captures at least some of people's common-sense knowledge about liquids.

In this section we present an in-depth analysis of the concept of shape in naive physics. We want to show that this concept does not quite represent the shape of a real container. More precisely, the shape of a real container has a determining effect on the behavior of a real liquid and this effect cannot be accounted for in naive physics. This deficiency cannot easily be remedied by refining the naive concept of shape. We show that even if the machinery of mathematics is brought into play, no distinctive progress can be made. We conjecture that this weakness of naive physics is generic for all models of liquids that may be constructed within the framework of the symbolic paradigm. If this conjecture is correct then symbolic models alone will not suffice to enable robots to manipulate liquids.

22.2.1 The Inside of a Container.

The shape of a container determines whether liquid may flow in or out. The formalization of shape proposed in naive physics allows the characterization of containers in this respect. It is based on the concept of a piece of space such as the inside of a container, and the way it is connected with other pieces of space through common faces. Logical functions are introduced to map containers onto the space they contain. One such function is *inside()* which, when applied to a container C, returns the contained space inside C. The use of such logical primitives tends to obscure an important difficulty.

Consider for example the two containers depicted in Figure 22.1. The left one may intuitively be recognized as an open container and there is no ambiguity about its inside. The right one however presents a difficulty for it does not have a single cavity that could be called its inside. Which one of the two cavities is chosen as the inside is a subjective matter. If the container is used in the position as depicted then the smaller upward oriented cavity on the left may be considered the inside. If it can be turned around then the larger cavity is a better choice for inside.

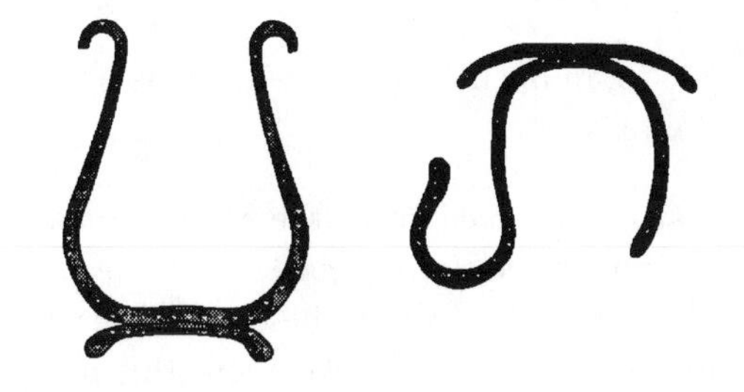

Figure 22.1
What Is the Inside of a Container?

From this example it is clear that the "inside of a container" depends on the orientation of the container. This dependence can, at least in principle, be taken into account by modifying the function *inside()* and making it depend on the function *upward()*. However, this approach is not very satisfactory for it makes "shape" and "inside" relative properties: they depend on the way a container is being used. It follows that in this line of thinking, shape and inside cannot be formalized unless also the manipulation of containers is formalized. Since there may be many different ways of manipulating containers and since each of these may affect the behavior of the liquid in the container, this approach leads to an inflation of the domain to be modeled.

The inside of a container may be made independent of its orientation by the following alternative definition: the inside of a container is a piece of space bounded by the container and which *may* hold liquid. This definition has the advantage of covering every object that can potentially be used as a container. However, it is also unsatisfactory because it connects the problem of defining the shape (inside) of a container to the problem of determining the behavior of the liquid it contains (remain in the inside). Determining the behavior of the liquid can itself not be done without sufficient knowledge about containers. From a formalisers point of view such circular dependencies are to be avoided. Hayes probably recognized this problem for he states: " I will not attempt a complete axiomatization of inside (Hayes 1985)."

22.2.2 Influence of Shape on Liquid Behavior.

The limitations of the formalization of shape are further reflected in the predictions that can be made in naive physics. Let us reconsider a problem posed by Hayes:

> What happens to the liquid in an open container when it is rotated around a horizontal axis?

The answer to this question can be inferred from the naive formal model:"At first nothing, but after a **while** *(this requires more geometry than we have developed)*, the top of the wet[1] in the cup will reach the edge of the rim ...." We want to make two remarks about this prediction. First, it does not state when the flow is going to start. In other words, no relation between the amount of rotation and the start of the flow is given. In fact all this prediction ascertains is that if the rotating is continued there will eventually be a time when the flow starts. Second, it is suggested that if a more accurate answer is needed then some more geometry could be brought into the game to provide this increased accuracy. From the point of view of designing a robot that can carry out such manipulations in a controlled way, an increased accuracy seems very desirable.

[1] "Wet" is used by Hayes to indicate the part of the inner side of a container that is in contact with the liquid

We want to show that formalizing geometry and using it to make more accurate predictions is certainly not obvious. The reason for this is that "shape" is a concept which is very hard to grasp even for geometry. In fact, for any but the most trivial shapes of containers even the full power of geometry and calculus cannot answer the simple question posed by Hayes.

Rotating a Spherical Container. Suppose a spherically shaped container holding an amount of liquid which we denote by L (Figure 22.2).

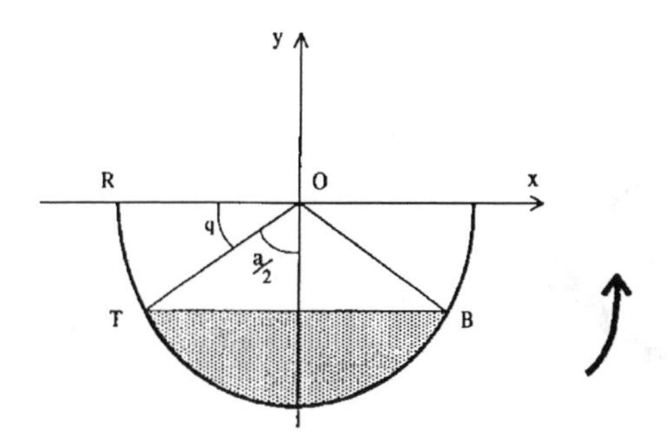

Figure 22.2
Rotating a Spherical Container Around a Horizontal Axis

For simplicity we assume the radius to be one. If this container is rotated around O, the liquid will stay in it until the edge of the rim (R) reaches the top of the liquid (T). Note that in this simplified case the liquid will always have the same shape. Therefore the maximum angle of rotation before a spill occurs equals q. The angle q is determined by the condition that the area occupied by the liquid equals the area of the sector sustained by the angle a minus the area of triangle OTB. So we have:

$$\pi\frac{a}{2\pi} - \frac{1}{2}cos\frac{a}{2}sin\frac{a}{2} = L \qquad (22.2.1)$$

After rearranging we obtain:

$$a - \frac{1}{2}sina = 2L \qquad (22.2.2)$$

Finally, the maximum angle q of rotation that we are looking for is obtained as

$$q = \frac{\pi}{2} - \frac{a}{2} \qquad (22.2.3)$$

The main difficulty here is that the equation relating a to the amount of liquid L is transcendental. Hence it is impossible to transform this equation into one of the type $a = \phi(L)$ where ϕ does not contain a. Or in other words there is no simple straightforward procedure for computing a and therefore q for a given value of L.

Rotating an Arbitrarily Shaped Container. As a second case let us look to the same problem but now for a container with a shape described by the function $y = S(x)$ (Figure 22.3). Two complications arise from this more general shape:

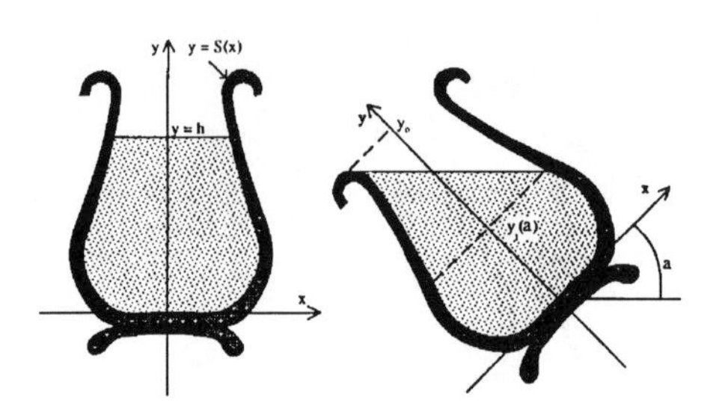

Figure 22.3
Relation Between Shape, Orientation and Level of Liquid.

- It is more difficult to determine the position of the top level of a given amount of liquid for a fixed orientation of the container.
- While the container is being rotated, the liquid in it continuously varies its shape and thus its level.

The maximum angle of rotation before a spill occurs corresponds to the position when the edge of the rim lies on the top surface of the liquid. In that position we have that the area bounded by the horizontal through the edge of the rim and the sides of the container must equal the area L. This can be expressed by the following equation:

$$\int_0^{y_1(a)} \left(\int_{x_l(y)}^{x_r(y)} dx \right) dy + \int_{y_1(a)}^{y_0} \left(\int_{x_l(y)}^{x'_r(y,a)} dx \right) dy = L \tag{22.2.4}$$

where $x'_r(y, a)$ is the abscissa of the intersection of the line through the edge of the rim making an angle $-a$ with the horizontal and the horizontal line at a height y. This equation *implicitly* determines a as a function of both the amount of liquid L and of the shape of the container. For a general shape it cannot be solved to provide an expression of the type $a = a(L, S)$.

From these two examples we conclude that bringing in geometry in order to find a quantitative relation between the angle of rotation and the time liquid starts to flow from the container does not provide a satisfactory solution. Hence the question as to *when* a liquid will start to flow from an open container cannot be answered in naive physics. It might be argued that this is not a criticism on naive physics because this type of questions cannot be answered by people using their common sense either. All, they can do is say that "after a while" a flow will start. If they are prompted to make this prediction more accurate they appear unable to do so. So in fact the lack of accuracy in the predictions of naive physics may be seen as evidence that naive physics indeed models common sense knowledge.

Rotating a Mysterious Open Container Both the previous examples were addressing the question as to *when* the liquid starts to flow. It is also possible to find containers which violate the weaker form of prediction about *if* the liquid will flow. Such a mysterious container is depicted in Figure 22.4.

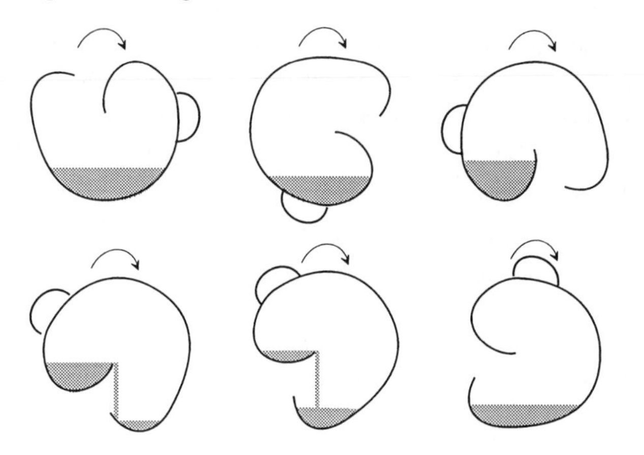

Figure 22.4
Rotating a Mysterious Container Around a Horizontal Axis

When this container is rotated to the left, the liquid will at some point start to flow out. However, when it is rotated to the right no liquid will ever flow out from it *no matter for how long the rotation is applied.* This is due to the peculiar shape of this container.

At this point the predictions of naive physics deviate from human predictions. People are capable, using their imagination and their common sense knowledge of liquids, to imagine what is going to happen with the liquid in this mysterious container. Proof of this is provided by the simple fact that we were able to come up with the container (without experimenting with any real containers and without using any sophisticated physics) and that the reader may agree with our prediction (not necessarily without using a real instance). We conjecture that the discriminating factor between a persons mental model and naive physics is the persons' visual apparatus and his memory which supports mental imagery. Taken together these tools capture the shape of a container and the effect it has on the behavior of a liquid in a way which is fundamentally different from the formal approach of naive physics. The fine-grained simulation that we present in the next section is an attempt to provide some of this visual functionality.

22.3 Hybrid Architecture for Modeling Liquids.

So far we have shown that naive physics does not provide a sufficiently powerful model for the shape of containers to allow correct inference of the behavior of liquid that is allowed to move freely in and out. We now want to make a proposal for a more powerful representation of shape. Our proposal is based on the assumption that an adequate model for liquids needs two components (Figure 22.5)

- *A symbolic modeling component.* This could be similar in many respects to naive physics and we will therefore not develop it further in this chapter.
- *A fine-grained simulative component.* This second component provides a tool to represent the shape of containers and to determine its influence on the behavior of liquids.

The fine-grained simulation is based on a discretisation of space and time. In this respect it is similar to simulations in Computational Fluid

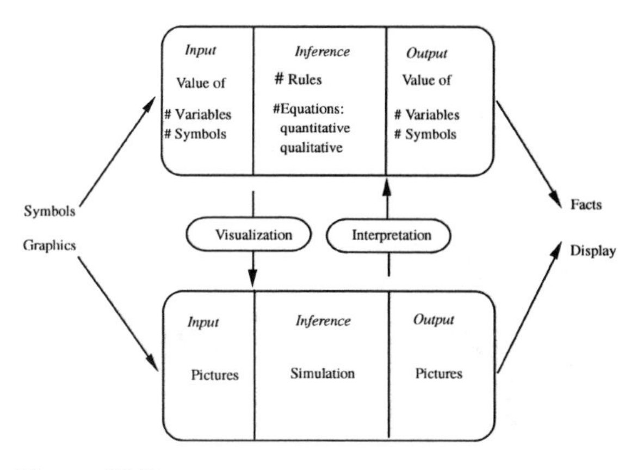

Figure 22.5
Hybrid Architecture.

Dynamics (CFD). Yet it is different. On the one hand because it only provides a very approximate outcome compared to simulations in CFD. On the other hand because our simulation does not require strong assumptions about the case to be simulated. It can handle constrained and unconstrained flow, static and dynamic situations and the transition between them.

In order to deal with such a broad scope of liquid behaviors, our simulation requires a special way to encode the physical laws. The basic construction is a dual ontology for liquids: a molecular and a continuum ontology. Both these ontologies are always used in conjunction, there is no need to switch between them according to which one is better for a particular situation. The laws of physics are adapted to this dual ontology and to the requirement that only a qualitative result is needed. Before we discuss this in more detail, we present some snapshots from two simulations which clearly illustrate the type of situations we are interested in and the qualitative nature of the phenomena resulting from the simulation. The snapshots show an array of cells where the dark ones are solid, the grey ones are liquid and the rest is air.

The first set of snapshots shows what happens to an amount of liquid that is released above a table (Figure 22.6). As expected, the liquid falls down on the table, spreads out and falls to the floor where it spreads again.

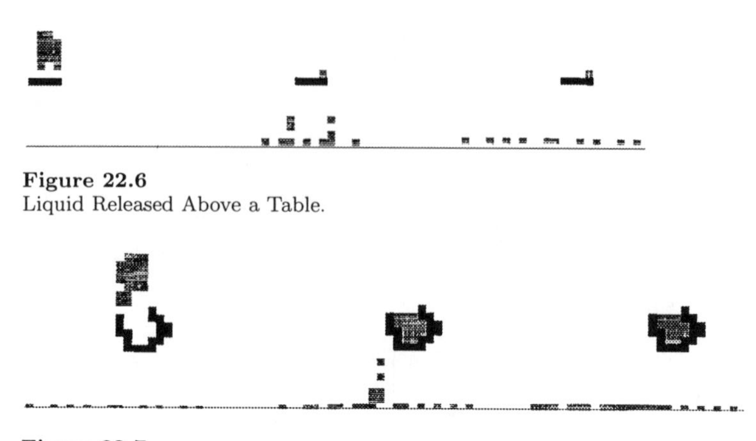

Figure 22.6
Liquid Released Above a Table.

Figure 22.7
Liquid Released Above a Container.

The second set of snapshots illustrates that an amount of liquid behaves totally different if it is released above a container instead of above a table (Figure 22.7). After falling into the container, the liquid starts to fill it up without leaving holes. If the initial amount of liquid exceeds the capacity of the container, a spill occurs. If a hole is made in the container, the liquid flows out and falls to the ground where it spreads.

From these simulations it appears that both the predictions of naive physics and the result of a simulation reveal the same phenomena of falling, wetting and spreading. There is however an important difference between predicted and simulated phenomena. The predictions are represented by symbolic expressions whereas the phenomena in the simulation are represented graphically. This distinction has important consequences for the further use of the prediction or simulation.

If the result of a simulation is to be used by a symbolic reasoner, then a conversion is needed between the graphical and the symbolic form. This conversion is similar to the visual recognition of objects in a scene and for this reason we have called it an interpretation in the hybrid model. The interpretation produces a symbolic expression for a property of the situation that is being simulated.

If on the other hand the result of a prediction must be applied to a specific situation then the symbols must be linked to the objects and phenomena in the situation. Establishing this link is in some way similar to the imagination of a situation that fits a particular description. The problem with imagination is that the result is not unique. One reason for this is that some properties like the shape of a container cannot be described accurately with symbols. We have shown with the example of a tricky cup that some shapes will and others wont comply with the predictions of naive physics. Hence, if a prediction of naive physics is applied to a specific situation then it must be validated.

Coming back to the different situations shown in the snapshots we note that the shape of containers is graphically represented as a collection of cells that make up the sides of the container. Properties such as the inside of a container or whether there is a hole in the bottom are implicit in this representation. The influence of these properties on the behavior of the liquid follows from the interaction between the liquid cells and the solid cells. The mechanism behind this is derived from the laws of physics.

22.4 Physics of the Fine-Grained Simulation of Liquids.

The prime motivation for using a fine-grained qualitative simulation of liquids is the requirement to represent the shape of containers in such a way that its influence on the behavior of a liquid can be computed. We use a 2-D grid of space cells for this purpose. Every physical situation or device is mapped onto this grid. We recognize two types of cells depending on their content:

- *Solid object cells.* This type of cells is used to represent solid objects or the solid parts of a device. It is assumed that if a cell is of type solid it is completely full of solid matter. A cell of type solid corresponds to the smallest possible solid object or the smallest possible detail in the shape of objects that can be represented.
- *Fluid cells.* Every cell which is not a solid object is considered of type fluid, where a fluid may be either a liquid or a gas (such as air) or a mixture of both.

Each cell of the grid is characterized by its type and position on the grid. The fluid cells are further charaterised by a density, pressure and velocity. [2] A solid cell has no further variables besides its type because for the time being we assume that it is always fixed in space except when moved by an external agent.

Cells and their cell variables constitute the space-bound view on liquid motion. In this view the state of a liquid is described by variables which are attached to the points in space. The value of these variables at a particular point is determined from the liquid in a small vicinity of this point. The cells in our fine-grained simulation constitute the vicinities for their centers. In a liquid in motion, the liquid content of a cell is replaced by liquid from some other neighbouring cells. As a result the value of all the variables of each cell change. The space-bound view is well adapted to describe what is going on in a liquid in motion. However turbulent this motion may be there is no need to keep track of how each part of a liquid is moving to determine the value of the variables. It suffices to consider the liquid which is in the vicinity of a point at a particular time no matter where it came from or where it is going to.

In some situations however it may be necessary to trace the motion of the liquid itself. Consider for example the situation where liquid is poured from an open container. At the beginning all of the liquid occupies a position in a restricted domain in space: the inside of the container. As the liquid starts to flow from the container this domain extends from the rim of the container downward. The space-bound-view is not very adequate to describe this phenomenon. The core of the problem are the points near the boundary of the liquid domain, i.e. the contact surface between liquid and air. The vicinity of these points may at some time be empty (air) and immediately after some liquid may have entered. Hence there must be a way to track the motion of the interface liquid-air and this is difficult in the space-bound-approach. For this type of problems physicists use a liquid-bound view. In the liquid-bound view a liquid is described by variables attached to points in the liquid. As the liquid moves these points move along and in this way the motion is tracked.

The fine-grained simulation that we have built contains both the space-bound view and the liquid-bound view. The space-bound view is represented through the cells and the cell variables. On top of this a number of liquid particles are placed and these particles can move

[2] These variables are represented by real numbers.

around over the grid of cells. It should be noted that these particles do not correspond to real molecules. Rather they represent indivisible lumps of matter of a size much smaller than the size of a cell. In order to place the particles on the grid each space cell is subdivided into a small grid of possible positions each capable of holding one particle.

The space-bound view and the liquid-bound view are both used in conjunction to implement the laws of physics. The laws we use in our model are not the discrete counterparts of the partial differential equations of continuum mechanics. Following a suggestion by Harlow we use the fundamental physical principles underlying all mechanical theories (Harlow 64). There are two of them:

- Newton's law of motion.
- Conservation of mass.

These laws have to be complemented with constitutive equations describing the particular characteristics of the different materials. For gases we use the ideal gas law which states that the pressure in a gas is a linear function of the density while for liquids we assume that they are totally incompressible. Newton's law of motion is expressed in our model in the space-bound view, i.e. via the variables that characterize the fluid in a cell. The traditional equation of conservation of mass is replaced by the assumption that all the mass is attributed to indestructible particles. During the evolution of the fluids we have only to make sure that the number of particles remains constant for the equation of conservation of mass to be fulfilled.

We will not present the technicalities of the fine-grained simulation here but we will indicate some important differences as well as some striking correspondences between our simulation and a symbolic model as exemplified by naive physics.

22.4.1 Fine-Grained Simulation Versus Knowledge Level Modeling

There are obviously many differences between the fine-grained simulation of liquids and a symbolic knowledge model for liquids, such as proposed by naive physics. We will only discuss one namely: the scale at which phenomena are represented. In the symbolic model knowledge may be obtained from the manipulation of symbols which represent distinct physical objects and formal rules which represent the behavior of these physical objects *as observed by a human.* The inference processes that are performed over these symbols mimic the way a person reasons about the objects they represent.

In a fine-grained simulation on the contrary, objects are represented as collections of small identical elements. These elements represent only tiny parts of objects, which are not recognized separately in a symbolic approach. For this reason they are more accurately called subsymbolic. The rules which govern the behavior of these subsymbolic elements do not correspond to a person's reasoning about objects. They correspond to fundamental physical principles governing the interaction between small parts of physical objects.

An important consequence of the grainsize of the simulation concerns the no-function-in-structure principle, as introduced in qualitative physics. This principle states that one should try not to make presumptions about the functioning of a device as a whole when building a model for each of its individual component. Applied to the liquid in a container, this principle requires that the model for the container should be independent of its content and likewise, the model for the liquid should be independent of the shape of the container.

The examples of containers and liquids that we have presented show that it is impossible to formalize containers and liquids independently of each other. The shape of a container has a profound influence on the liquid and vice versa, the amount of liquid determines whether a container will spill or not. Hence it is impossible to satisfy the no-function-in-structure-principle in naive physics. In the fine-grained simulation on the contrary, the laws governing the behavior of the liquid do not depend on the shape of the container. They simply express the laws of physics as applied to a tiny liquid element. Similarly, the behavior of a tiny piece of container is independent of the amount of liquid. Phenomena like overflow or complete containment result from the interaction of many liquid elements together with the tiny pieces of solid matter that make up the container. The influence of the shape of the container need not and is not explicitly modeled. The interaction between all the small elements mediates and integrates the influence of the shape of the container and guarantees a globally consistent and correct behavior. Hence it may be concluded that the fine-grained simulation provides a way to build a model for liquids that satisfies the no-function-in-structure principle.

Beside differences there are also correspondences between fine-grained simulation and naive physics. A particularly striking one concerns the ontologies used. The fine-grained qualitative simulation that we have built makes use of a space-bound view together with a liquid-bound view. It does so to achieve a large scope of possible liquid behaviors. These views correspond to the dual ontology introduced by Hayes in naive physics. In the space-bound view, space is divided into small cells which can contain liquid: these cells constitute elementary containers. Hence the space-bound view corresponds to the "contained stuff" ontology of Hayes. The difference is in the scale at which containers are represented. Hayes considers containers as objects that can be manipulated. The inside of a container is the whole space contained in it. In our simulation a container is a composite construction. Its sides are made up of small pieces: the solid cells, and its inside is composed of many small containers: the space cells that can hold liquid. This higher resolution is required to represent the influence of the shape of a container on the behavior of the liquid.

The liquid-bound view, as represented by the particles in our simulation, corresponds to Hayes' liquid individuals. The particles move around in space and can be traced individually without the need to relate them to a container. Similarly, Hayes' liquid individuals can be used to track what happens to a particular liquid when it is poured from one container into another. Again the difference between our liquid particles and Hayes' liquid individuals is one of scale. Hayes conceives a liquid individual at the scale of a recognisable amount of liquid. For example the water in a glass constitutes one individual. In our simulation this water is composed of many individuals. The higher resolution of the simulation is needed to deal with situations where a liquid is divided into several pieces for example when some water, but not all, is poured from a bottle in a glass. If the water in the bottle is considered as one individual then this individual ceases to exist at the time some of it is separated and a new individual is created. These difficulties have lead Hayes to abandon the idea of liquid individuals and to introduce containment. Only after the problems of containment became clear, did he reintroduce liquid individuals but this time coupled to the idea of histories.

There is much more that could be said about the contained-stuff versus liquid-individual ontology. From a pragmatical point of view however it is clear that both ontologies are needed to cover adequately the range of different behaviors a liquid may display. Both naive physics and our fine-grained qualitative simulation propose a way to combine the two ontologies in one model. In this respect they are different from most CFD simulations which adopt either one or the other depending on the specific situation that is being modeled. In the context of AI, where the ultimate goal is a model that can be used by an autonomous robot that manipulates liquids, any option for either one of the ontologies alone leads to severe limitations on the scope of the situations that can be dealt with.

22.4.2 Interpreting a Fine-Grained Qualitative Simulation

Complex situations involving fluid components can be simulated with a fine-grained qualitative simulation. The result is always a state characterized by the position of the particles and the velocity and pressure of the cells. A symbolic reasoner for the control of a robot cannot use such information directly. It needs to know whether there is liquid in a certain place or whether liquid is spilled if a particular container is moved in a particular way. Such knowledge can be extracted from the simulation by means of virtual sensors. We illustrate the use of virtual sensors for the task of positioning a bottle underneath a tap such that it can be filled (Figure 22.8).

The following assumptions are made:

- Bottles of different shapes and heights are allowed.
- Bottles are placed on a horizontal table and can be moved to the left or to the right by a simulated robot.
- The tap is either open or closed. When it is open it releases liquid at a constant rate.
- Spilling has to be avoided.

In order to execute this task a robot needs two possible instructions: move the bottle to the left or to the right *over a certain small distance* By repeatedly giving such instructions it is possible to make the robot position the bottle correctly.

The qualitative simulation that we have built may be used to generate

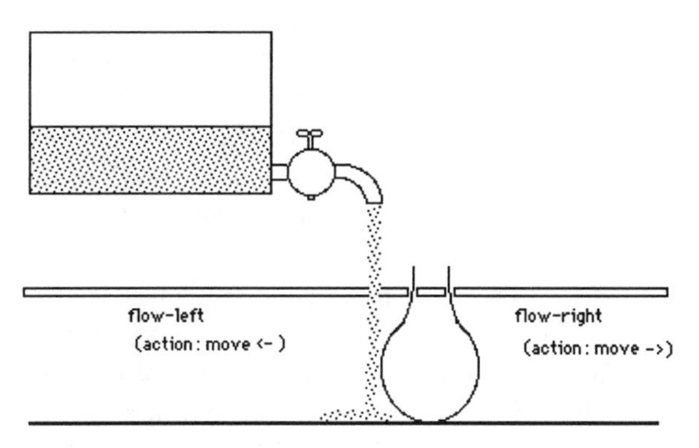

Figure 22.8
Interpreting a Fine-Grained Qualitative Simulation.

instructions for the robot that enable it to position the bottle correctly. The basic idea is that if a real bottle is correctly positioned under a tap, no liquid will end up on the floor. We carry over this idea to the simulation and install a left and right flow sensor in the simulation. If the simulated bottle is correctly positioned, both the left and right sensor will stay dry when liquid is released from the tap. If on the contrary the bottle is too much to the left, the right sensor will get wet. In that case the bottle is slowly moved to the right until no more liquid flows by the right sensor. The direction in which the bottle needs to be moved may be returned to the qualitative reasoner which can use this to issue controls to the robot.

We believe that this way of controlling a robot is in some way similar to what people do when they fill a bottle from a tap. It seems plausible that for such tasks, people rely to a large extent on their visual capabilities and the feedback from these to their muscles. It remains an open problem at which particular point reasoning is brought in and how this reasoning interacts with the vision based processes. We do not suggest that people run simulations in their head certainly not of the kind we are presenting here. Although there seems to be evidence that people can run mental movies, the true nature of these movies is still a matter of hot debate (Pylyshyn 1981, Kosslyn 1981).

What we have proposed here is a hybrid architecture that provides a *functionality* to a robot which people also possess and which cannot be reduced to a reasoning of the kind that is modeled in AI by symbol manipulation. Our fine-grained simulation together with its interpretation via sensors, complements a symbolic reasoner for those matters where people mainly rely on their vision. Such a hybrid architecture has also been used to model mental imagery as an interpretation operation on a symbolic representation (Chandrasekaran and Narayanan 1990, Narayanan and Chandrasekaran 1991).

Our hybrid architecture also fits with the metric diagram/place vocabulary proposed by Forbus to overcome the limits of symbolic qualitative representation of space (Forbus, Nielsen, and Faltings 1991; Joskowics and Sacks 1991; Faltings 1990). The spatial grid in the hybrid architecture corresponds to the metric diagram of Forbus (1992).

Acknowledgments

It is a pleasure to thank Rolf Pfeifer and Tim Smithers for many interesting in-depth discussions about AI in general and about this work in particular. The authors are also very gratefull to the reviewer who provided many constructive remarks which were very helpfull to shape some of the arguments made in this chapter. This research was partly sponsored by the ESPRIT Program P440, the IMPULS research program and the IUAP Action of the Belgian Science Ministry.

References

Chandrasekaran, B., and Narayanan, N. H. 1990. Integrating Imagery and Visual Representations. In Proceedings of the Twelfth Annual Conference of the Cognitive Science Society, Hillsdale, N.J.: Lawrence Erlbaum.

Faltings, B. 1990. Qualitative Kinematics in Mechanisms. *Artificial Intelligence* 41(1).

Forbus, K., Nielsen, P., and Faltings, B. 1991. Qualitative Spatial Reasoning: The CLOCK Project. *Artficial Intelligence* 51(1-3).

Forbus, K. 1992. Qualitative Spatial Reasoning: Framework and Frontiers. Presented at the March 1992 AAAI Spring Symposium on Diagrammatic Reasoning, Stanford, California.

Harlow, F. H. 1964. The Particle-In-Cell Computing Method in Fluid Dynamics. In *Methods in Computational Physics*, 319–343.

Hayes, P. 1985. Naive Physics I: Ontology for Liquids. In *Formal Theories of the Commonsense World.*, ed. R. Hobbs and R. Moore, 71–108. Norwood,

N.J.: Ablex Publishing.

Joskowics, L. and Sacks, E. 1991. Computational Kinematics. *Artficial Intelligence* 51(1-3).

Kosslyn, S. M. 1981. The Medium and the Message in Mental Imagery: A Theory. *Psychological Review* 88.

Narayanan, N. H. and Chandrasekaran, B. 1991. Reasoning Visually about Spatial Interactions. In *Proceedings of Twelfth International Joint Conference on Artificial Intelligence.* San Francisco: Morgan Kaufmann.

Pylyshyn, Z. W. 1981. The Imagery Debate: Analogue Media Versus Tacit Knowledge. *Psychological Review* 88.

23 Diagrams for Solving Physical Problems

Gordon S. Novak Jr.
University of Texas at Austin

23.1 Introduction

Humans often use diagrams when solving physical problems; diagrams appear in physics books and serve as a means of formal communication in engineering. Diagrams are used because physical problems require the solution of geometric subproblems, but they serve many other roles. People find it easy to interpret diagrams; this is not the case for computer programs, where vision is an unsolved problem. The challenge for AI is to give programs the ability to reason with diagrams as humans do.

This chapter describes three computer programs that use diagrams in solving physical problems. ISAAC, which understands and solves physics problems stated in English, constructs a geometric model that is equivalent to a free-body diagram for problem solving; it also constructs a diagram that serves to illustrate its understanding of the problem. BEATRIX understands physics problems specified by both English text and a diagram. The focus of this program is on understanding; the diagram and text must be understood together, and each helps to disambiguate the other. The VIP program allows a program to be specified by connections between diagrams of physical models; here, diagrams serve as a medium of communication that is natural to the user.

Section 5 discusses ways in which humans use diagrams. The final section proposes ways in which some of these uses of diagrams might be implemented in computer programs.

23.2 Geometric Reasoning in ISAAC

ISAAC (Novak 1977) solves rigid body statics problems stated in English. Figure 23.1 shows a problem that ISAAC can read, understand, and solve in less than one second. The diagram is produced from ISAAC's understanding of the English and from calculated values. A geometric model, similar to the diagram, is used in problem solving; in the geometric model most objects are reduced to lines and points.

A problem statement in natural language is not a complete description

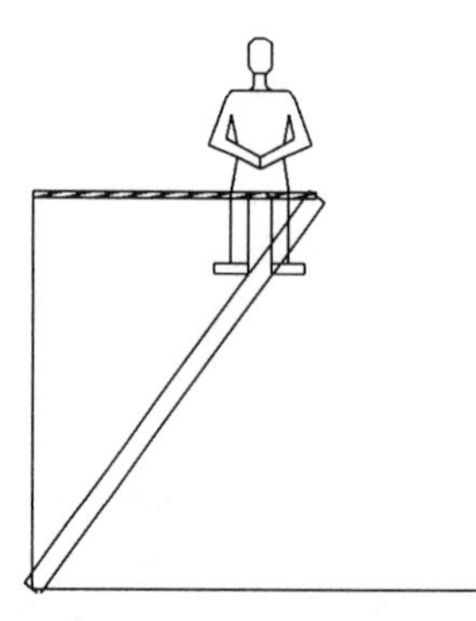

Figure 23.1
ISAAC Problem. The foot of a ladder rests against a vertical wall and on a horizontal floor. The top of the ladder is supported from the wall by a horizontal rope 30 ft long. The ladder is 50 ft long, weighs 100 lb with its center of gravity 20 ft from the foot, and a 150 lb man is 10 ft from the top. Determine the tension in the rope.

of the problem; it is only a minimal outline, requiring the reader to fill in details. To construct a geometric model sufficient for problem solving, many inferences must be made. Consider the problem statement of Figure 23.1 (van der Merwe 1961): it says "a 150 lb man *is 10 ft from the top*". The definite noun phrase *the top* denotes the top of the ladder. *10 ft from the top* must be a location on the ladder, not just any location that is 10 ft from the top of the ladder. Finally, the man *is* at this location; this must be interpreted as an attachment by contact between the feet of the man and the ladder, with the ladder supporting the man. Some of these inferences may be viewed as linguistic, but others must be based on geometric knowledge about the objects, knowledge about typical spatial relationships, and common-sense physics. ISAAC makes these inferences in several steps. A statement that an object "is" at a location on another object is interpreted as an attachment. A location relative to a point on an object is assumed to be toward the center of the object. When ISAAC writes physics equations, it finds that the ladder is supported at two points and that the man has a specified weight; it therefore assumes that the ladder supports the man. Finally, in drawing the diagram, ISAAC assumes that a person is supported at the feet.

ISAAC generates a symbolic geometric model for problem solving and a symbolic diagram model for drawing the diagram. For each type of object, ISAAC has a geometric model, including dimensions of a bounding box, names and coordinates of interesting points on the object, a program to draw a picture of the object, the name of a parameter of the object that indicates its size, and a program to estimate the size for the drawing if no size is specified.

The geometry of an individual object within a model is specified by its object geometry, the location of a reference point, the rotation of the object about the reference point, and the vector size of the object. These data are sufficient for calculation of the location of any named point on the object and for drawing it. To make a geometric or diagram model, these data must be determined for each object. The geometric and diagram models are similar, except for the following features:

1. The geometric model is a "skeleton" model, in which most objects are represented by lines or points. The diagram model requires actual sizes and points of attachment for each object.
2. The geometric model may contain symbolic variables and algebraic expressions in its coordinate values; the desired solution to a problem may be the value of a geometric variable. In the diagram, all coordinates must be numeric. The solution to the physics problem often provides numeric values for variables; when it does not, default values are assigned.

Before the diagram and geometric models are made, the model of the problem is a semantic network containing symbolic descriptions of objects, their properties, and their relationships. The diagram model is constructed from this network in the following way. In most rigid body statics problems, all of the objects are attached to each other; thus, the objects and attachments form a connected graph. A single object is chosen and assigned the coordinates `(0 0)`; the objects that are attached to it are then scaled to the appropriate size, rotated by the appropriate angle, and translated to the point of attachment to the composite model. Of course, these are vector operations on points, rather than manipulation of an image. Objects that are attached to a newly added object are then added to the diagram in the same manner.

This algorithm is sufficient if the attachments of objects form a tree structure, which is the case for most of our example problems. In the case of the ladder problem shown in Figure 23.1, however, a triangle must be solved. The triangle is detected by an *ad hoc* program that tests whether some object a is attached to an object b that is attached to c, which is attached to a. If a triangle is detected, the known parameters are abstracted and given to a triangle solver, which returns the complete set of angles and sides of the triangle. The returned parameters must then be translated back to the form needed for the definition of the object.

ISAAC's geometric model is based on analytic geometry in a single planar coordinate system. For more general application, this form of geometric model may be inadequate. Many geometric features of a physics problem may be unspecified in the problem statement. Although it would be possible to make a single, unified geometric model with symbolic values for all unspecified lengths, positions, and angles, to do so would greatly complicate the algebra. It would be better to have multiple locally precise geometries. Connections between local geometries could be topological rather than exact; exact geometries are needed only when relative distances between locations within separate local geometries are required, and such cases are unusual.

23.3 Diagram Understanding

It is difficult to describe geometry using natural language. BEATRIX (Novak and Bulko 1990, Novak and Bulko 1993) understands physics problems specified by English text and a diagram. Often neither text nor diagram is a complete description; a unified model must be produced from both. *Coreference* must be established between parts of the text and the diagram that refer to the same object or feature. Figure 23.2 shows an example understood by BEATRIX.

23.3.1 Diagram Input

BEATRIX's user interface allows diagram elements to be selected, moved, scaled, and rotated as desired; it also allows entry of text within the diagram. A symbolic description of the diagram is constructed for input to the understanding program. The diagram input consists of "neutral" components such as lines, circles, and rectangles—input that could be produced from a printed diagram by a machine vision system (Ballard and Brown 1982).

Many difficulties of understanding natural language are also present with diagrams: ambiguity of meanings of elements, ambiguity of combi-

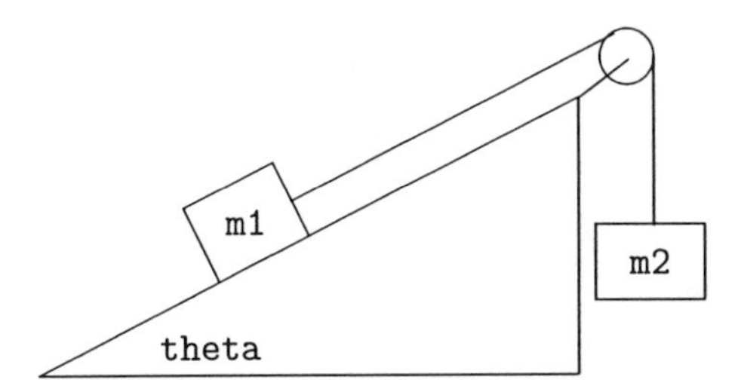

Figure 23.2
BEATRIX Example. Two masses are connected by a light string as shown in the figure. The incline and peg are smooth. Find the acceleration of the masses and the tension in the string for theta = 30 degrees and m1 = m2 = 5 kg.

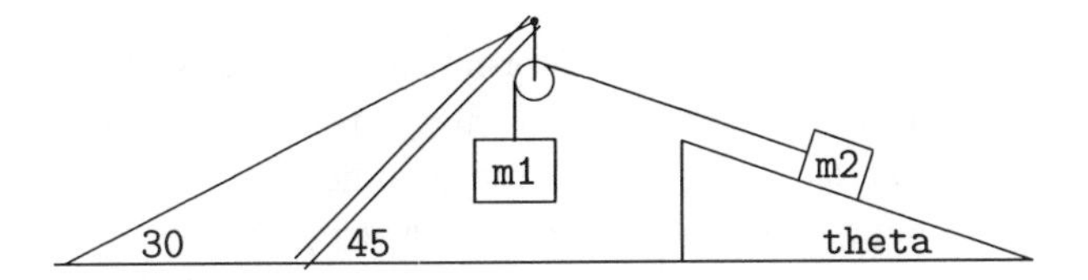

Figure 23.3
BEATRIX Example. Two masses are connected by a cable as shown in the figure. The strut is held in position by a cable. The incline is smooth, and the cable passes over a smooth peg. Find the tension in the cable for theta = 30 degrees and m1 = m2 = 20 kg. Neglect the weight of the strut.

nation of elements, and underspecification. An element such as a line is ambiguous because it might represent an edge of an object, or an object itself (*e.g.*, a cable). Lines may be combined in many ways, only a few of which are meaningful. Diagrams often omit things that can be inferred by the reader: the attachment between a rope and an object that it supports is often represented only by contact. As in speech understanding (Erman et al. 1980), ambiguity can be reduced by using several kinds of constraints:

1. An object mentioned in the text is expected to appear in the diagram.
2. As objects are identified, identifications of other objects are constrained.

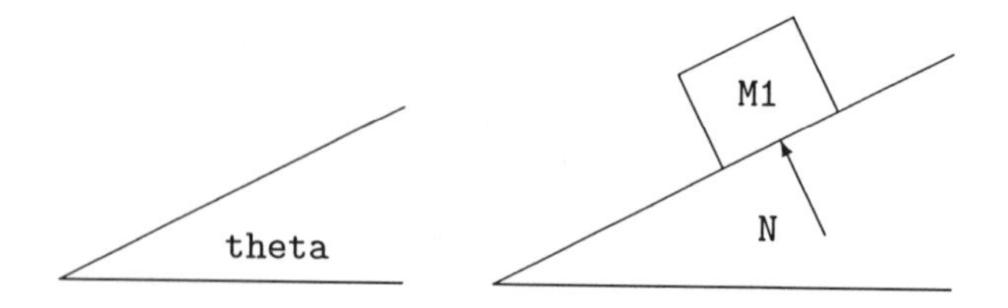

Figure 23.4
`theta` is part of angle, but `N` is not.

3. Common-sense physics provides constraints: an object is expected to be supported; a rope terminating at an object is probably attached to it.

The diagram can also reduce ambiguity in interpreting the English text.

A person reading a physics problem will alternate attention between the diagram and text. No fixed order of processing suffices for all problems, since a problem might be specified entirely by text, entirely by a diagram, or by some combination. For this reason, BEATRIX performs *co-parsing* of the two modalities, using the BB1 blackboard system (Garvey et al. 1985).

23.3.2 Diagram Parsing

The diagram input consists of points, lines, rectangles, and circles described by analytic geometry. BEATRIX performs low-level analysis of details, *e.g.* to determine whether a line is approximately tangent to a circle. The diagram is parsed by knowledge sources (KS's) that recognize special combinations of picture elements, as in a picture grammar (Fu 1974). A diagram is inherently ambiguous: it may omit objects or details, exaggerate features, or include descriptive elements that are not objects (*e.g.*, arrows used to show dimensions of objects). BEATRIX opportunistically combines related elements based on expectations of typical combinations; for example, if two lines meet at an acute angle, and there is a variable name that typically denotes an angle (such as `theta`) inside and near the vertex, then these elements will be grouped as an `angle`.

As parts of the diagram are interpreted, they trigger other KS's. For

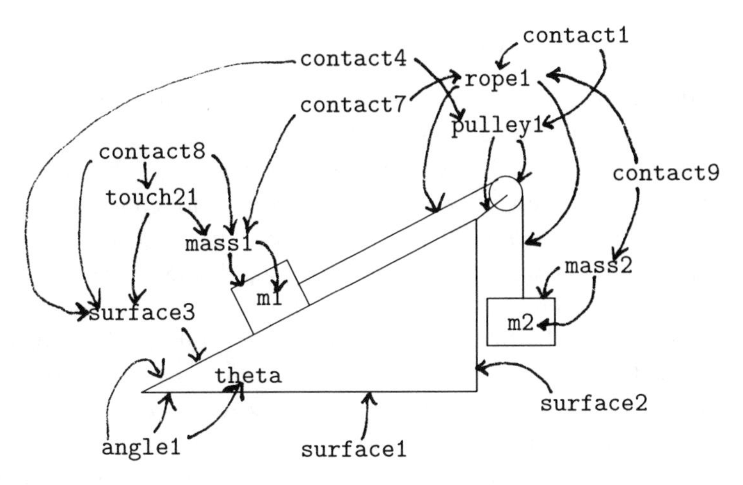

Figure 23.5
Interpretation after Diagram Parsing

example, after a small circle with a line to its center has been interpreted as a `pulley`, a KS is triggered to look for lines tangent to the pulley that represent a rope; the two lines that represent the rope are grouped into a single `rope` object, with the distal endpoints identified as its ends. This, in turn, triggers additional inferences: the ends of a rope are expected to be attached to objects or surfaces. When a KS can interpret part of the diagram, it *obviates* (removes from the execution queue) other KS's that might attempt alternative interpretations.

The diagram parsing KS's also trigger expectations for natural language processing. For example, identification of a `contact` between a mass and a surface triggers an expectation that a normal force and a coefficient of friction may be specified in the English text. Such an expectation is necessary to interpret a definite noun phrase such as "the coefficient of friction" if the `contact` appears only in the diagram.

Diagram parsing continues until no further interpretations can be made. Figure 23.5 illustrates the features that are identified by diagram parsing in an example problem; most of the `touch` relations and some `contact` relations are omitted for readability.

23.3.3 Establishing Coreference

The understanding module of BEATRIX combines the parsed English text and the parsed diagram, establishing coreference between them to produce a unified model. For example, the text might say "the coefficient of friction is 0.25", referring to a contact between a block and an inclined plane shown in the diagram. The friction value must be associated with the contact relation that was derived from the diagram. The KS's of the understanding module also make inferences based on common-sense physics. For example, BEATRIX infers that the rotation of an edge of an object is the same as that of a surface on which it rests, or that an object hanging from a rope hangs directly below it. Contact between an object and a surface is assumed to be a frictional touch contact, while contact between a rope and an object that it supports is assumed to be an attachment. Such inferences are important, since both text and diagrams often omit things that an intelligent reader can infer.

Priority ratings cause KS's with the best input data to execute first. For example, *Identify-Masses* gives itself a high rating if there is only one mass object it could match. Default KS's are triggered at a low priority to provide default values or to move objects that are mentioned in only one input modality to the unified level. Low-level KS's are triggered by the problem statement and diagram, while the higher-level KS's are triggered by the output of the low-level KS's.

23.3.4 Conclusions about Diagram Understanding

A diagram represents much more information than is shown explicitly. Understanding a diagram is not a passive process of absorbing what is plainly in the diagram, but is an active process of model construction and inference, using the diagram as an outline of the model to be constructed. ISAAC demonstrated a similar finding with English text. Brevity gives diagrams their power but also presents a challenge for diagram understanding by computer. If much of the understanding of a diagram must be inferred from the reader's knowledge, then that knowledge and the procedures to use it must be part of a diagram understanding program. It must be possible to resolve ambiguities to produce the most likely interpretation. Opportunistic identification is based not only on syntactic relationships, but also on world knowledge or common-sense physics (*e.g.*, identification of a square as a mass implies that a line coincident with the bottom of the square must be a surface, not a rope).

23.4 Problem Solving by Diagram Connections

A program called VIP (View Interactive Programming) (Novak 1994) allows a user to construct a computer program by making connections between diagrams that represent physical and geometric principles. The user can select physical laws, geometric principles, and physical constants and add them to a workspace. Connections between variable buttons in the diagrams can be made by clicking on each button with the mouse; a connection signifies that the variables are equal.

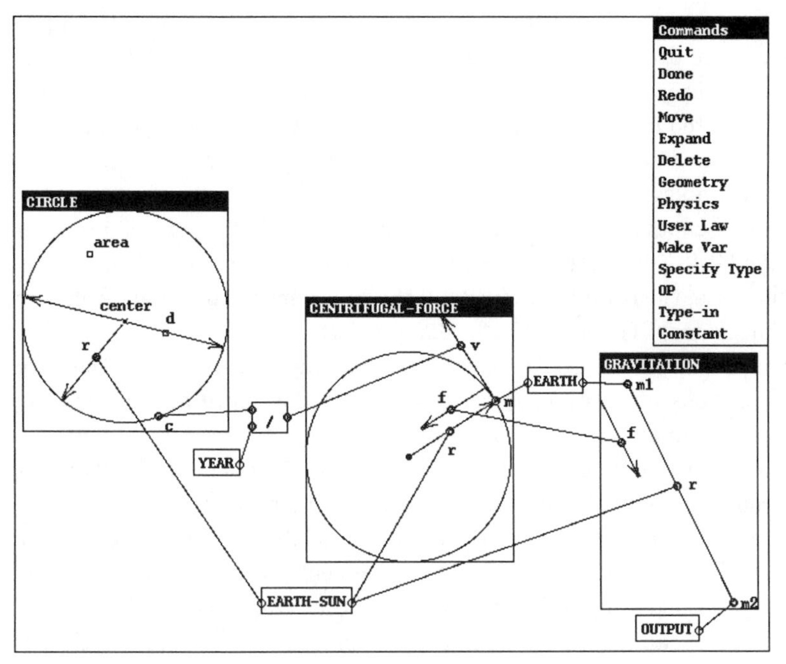

Figure 23.6
Calculating the Mass of the Sun

Figure 23.6 shows how VIP can be used to calculate the mass of the sun. The initial workspace contains only a default `output` variable. The user follows Newton's reasoning: the gravitational attraction of the earth by the sun is equal to the force required to keep the earth in its orbit.

The user selects a `gravitation` principle and a `centrifugal-force` principle from the `physics` menu and adds them to the window. The user clicks the mouse on the `f` button of each diagram, which causes a line to be drawn between them and signifies that the forces are equal. The user selects constants for the mass of the earth and the earth-sun distance and connects these to the two diagrams. The `output` box is connected to the other mass in the gravitation diagram. After these actions, only the velocity `v` of the earth in its orbit remains unspecified. This can be found by noting that the earth travels around the sun in one year. The user selects a `circle` diagram from the `geometry` menu, connects its radius to the earth-sun distance, and divides its circumference by a time constant of one year. This gives a fully specified diagram.

A program is derived from the diagram by data flow. Initially, input variables and constants are assumed to be defined. A variable that is defined is propagated into boxes to which it is connected. When a value is propagated into a box, equations associated with the box are examined to see if any can be solved. Solutions to equations produce the values of other variables, which are also propagated. When a value is propagated into the `output`, the program is complete. Compilation of this program (in the GLISP language [Novak 1983]) produces an executable program. In this case, the compiler reduces all the equations to the numeric answer (in kilograms): `(LAMBDA () 1.9660057E30)`

VIP can also be used to construct new physical principles that are combinations of existing ones; for example, the above analysis can be abstracted as an `orbital-system` principle.

VIP allows problems to be specified by correspondences of features of diagrams. Although equations and algebraic manipulation are involved, they are hidden and are performed automatically. The equations do not have to be memorized. Units of measurement are converted automatically as needed. Subproblems, such as finding the velocity of the earth in its orbit, can be solved using the system itself. Using VIP is clearly faster than doing algebra by hand; however, VIP is much easier to use if the diagrams "fit" a given problem than if they do not. For example, consider the problem:

> A block rests on a horizontal board. The board is gradually tilted upward and the block just begins to slide down the board when the angle of inclination θ is 21° ... Find the

coefficient of static friction μ_s. (van der Merwe 1961).

A diagram by a human problem solver will depict forces so that they can easily be related to the physical situation. In Figure 23.7, it is clear that the weight force can be viewed as a normal force and a force acting to move the block down the board.

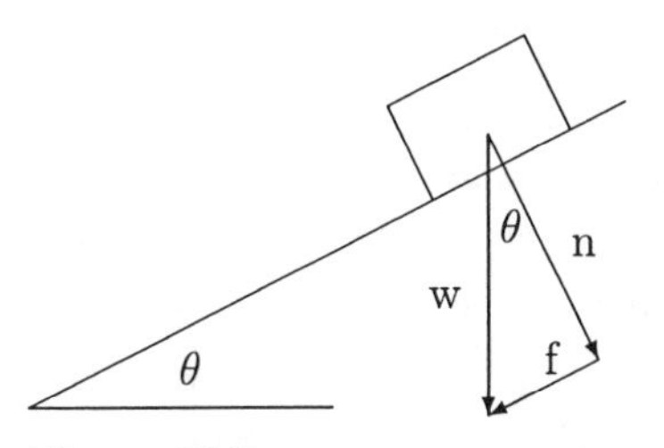

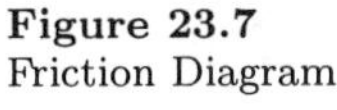
Figure 23.7
Friction Diagram

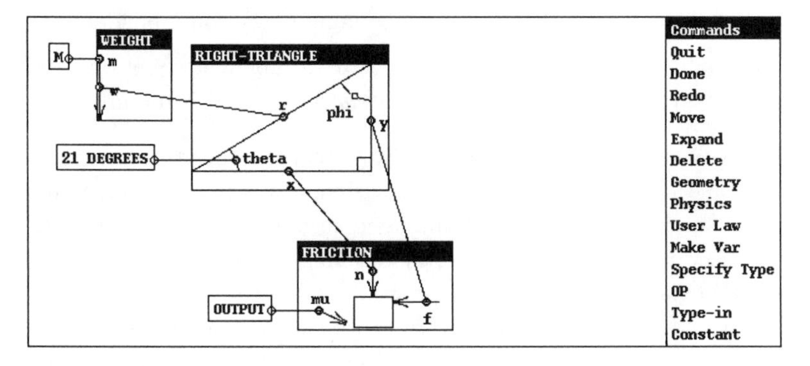

Figure 23.8
Friction Problem Using VIP

This problem can be solved using VIP, as shown in Figure 23.8. However, the correspondence between the VIP diagrams and the geometry of the problem is poor. The triangle shown in the VIP diagram is the same triangle shown in Figure 23.7, but its orientation does not match the physical situation. It is difficult for the user to determine whether `x` and `y` in the triangle diagram should respectively match `n` and `f` in the friction model, or *vice versa*; the user might have to draw a diagram on paper. Simply having diagrams is not enough: if the diagrams do not correspond well to the actual geometry of the problem, then diagrammatic inferences cannot be performed, and the diagrams will be as disconnected from the problem as a symbolic representation would be. Larkin and Simon (1987) note that in humans, a production is easily triggered only if there is a close match between stimulus conditions and its triggering conditions.

VIP would be more useful if its diagrams were more like those drawn by humans. Several improvements can be identified:

1. The orientation and size of a diagram should be variable so that the diagram can match the problem geometry. VIP should have multiple ways to draw a triangle, or better, an ability to adapt the triangle in size and orientation to parts of an existing diagram.
2. It should be possibly to overlay diagrams. In the diagram of Figure 23.6, the three diagrams shown (circle, centrifugal force, and gravitation) all refer to the same physical space. Correspondences are shown as lines between them, but it would be better to overlay these diagrams so that the corresponding parts would be identical.
3. Human problem solvers often replace variables in equations and on diagrams so that the number of variables used is minimized.

We have used VIP to develop small but realistic scientific programs (Novak 1994). Abelson *et al.* (1989) envision an automatic engineering assistant; surely such a system should use diagrams to communicate with its user. It would be interesting to try teaching physics problem solving using VIP or a similar system. This would move the focus of problem solving away from algebra and toward conceptualization of the problem by selection and instantiation of physical models. VIP could also be used to investigate the effectiveness of different kinds of diagrams for human problem solvers: experience quickly demonstrated that diagrams are much less useful if they are not isomorphic to the problem geometry.

Another research direction is machine learning of methods for analyzing problems based on correspondences selected using VIP by a physics expert. Learning of the method of application of physical principles could be a useful form of "chunking" that would allow future problems of a similar type to be solved automatically as a result of practice (Araya 1984).

23.5 Uses of Diagrams in Problem Solving

Diagrams play many roles in human problem solving. Larkin and Simon (1987) describe psychological and computational advantages of diagrammatic reasoning for human problem solvers:

1. Diagrams guide attention from one element to related elements; they reduce search because related elements are usually close together.
2. Diagrams minimize labeling: information about an element is near it.
3. Diagrams facilitate perceptual inferences and recognition of problem-solving methods that may be applicable.
4. Diagrams allow quick checks that the analysis is proceeding correctly.

This section elaborates these and other benefits of diagrams.

23.5.1 Short-term Memory

A central feature of human intelligence is limited short-term memory (Miller 1956). By writing down intermediate results, a person releases limited short-term memory for other uses. Writing and re-perceiving intermediate results is much faster and more reliable than memorizing them; pencil and paper serve a role analogous to that of a paging disk in a computer (Larkin et al. 1980). Surely diagrams also play such a role. Because people find it easy to perceive diagrams, a diagram can serve as short-term memory for intermediate geometric results. A human problem solver progressively annotates the diagram with results, making those results available by inspection when needed. Retrieval by inspection is often opportunistic, without prior planning to use the retrieved values. Indeed, one strategy for solving a problem is to perform forward reasoning, deducing geometric results that can be derived easily and adding them to the diagram, until the diagram contains the desired answer.

23.5.2 Substrate

A mental picture can serve as a "coordinate system" or geometric substrate, allowing the remainder of a problem to be described relative to

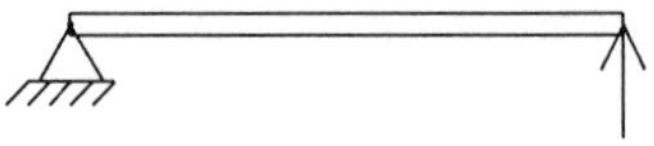

What force is required to lift one end of a pole?

Figure 23.9
Underspecified Problem

the substrate. For example,

> A car leaves point A and drives north for 6 miles ...
>
> A punter located at his 40-yard line kicks a punt at an angle of 45° to a receiver at the opposite 20-yard line ...

Since the natural language problem statement refers to geometric features of the substrate, a mental model of the substrate is required to understand such a problem.

23.5.3 Inference of Context

A difficulty faced both by humans and by AI systems is understanding an underspecified problem. Physics problems are often underspecified both geometrically and in terms of the physical principles needed for solution. A diagram can help the problem solver to infer the correct context by encouraging elaboration of elements normally associated with the diagram. An underspecified problem that is solved by ISAAC is shown in Figure 23.9.

To a person, a drawing of a horizontal pole supported only by a force at one end "looks wrong"; the exercise of drawing a free body diagram may help a human problem solver to consider all the relevant forces until the set of forces drawn on the body appears to be balanced. In this problem, ISAAC introduces (by symbolic inference) a pivot to support the other end of the pole. Physics problems often omit important geometric facts, *e.g.* that objects rest on the surface of the earth, or that walls are vertical planes that are bounded below by horizontal floors.

23.5.4 Inference by Recognition

Larkin and Simon (1987) describe "perceptual" inferences as a major advantage of the use of diagrams. While such inferences (*e.g.* the fact that vertical angles formed by intersecting lines are equal) can be made

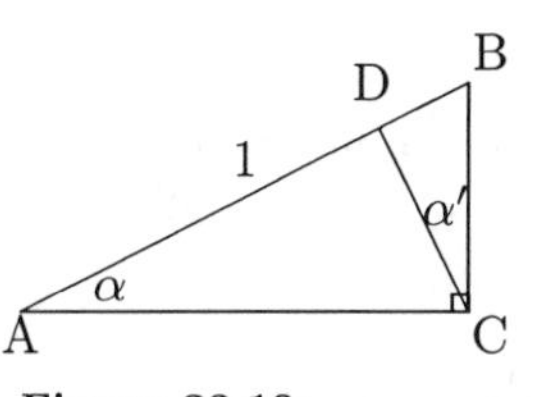

Figure 23.10
Analytic Geometry Problem

symbolically, they can be made at almost no cost by perception. Larking and Simon (1987) describe perceptual inferences that are identical to symbolic inferences that can be made formally. While perceptual inferences may suggest subproblems to be treated formally (*e.g.*, the perception that vertical angles appear to be equal may trigger the memory that this is indeed a theorem in geometry), humans often make perceptual inferences without proof or even much thought. For example, in the problem of Figure 23.2 the problem solver will make the assumption that the string is parallel to the inclined plane; this is unstated and thus *cannot* be proved.

A skilled problem solver deliberately constructs diagrams that facilitate inference by recognition. In the problem of Figure 23.10, a skilled problem solver will draw the figure so that the angle α is clearly less than 45°; this will increase the size contrast between angle α and angle ABC, facilitating recognition that the angle α' is the same as α. While this can be proved, the problem solver will probably assume that angles that appear to be equal are in fact equal.

It appears that perceptual inferences are important in other domains, even when diagrams are not used. For example, a person skilled in performing mental arithmetic can perform the mental calculation:

$$\frac{4}{.97} \cong 4.12$$

by recognizing this problem as an instance of the pattern:

$$\frac{1}{1-\epsilon} \cong 1+\epsilon \qquad \textit{where } \epsilon \textit{ is small}$$

The recognition that .97 is "almost 1" is a perceptual inference that must be made in order to trigger a production rule for this pattern. There is evidence that experts can make large numbers of such perceptual inferences, which may be an important component of their expertise.

For example, Feynman (1985) boasted (falsely) that he could compute exponentials in his head; he confounded his friends' attempts to expose his deception because he was able to recognize so many special cases that he could do every example they presented to him.

> If somebody comes along and wants to divide 1 by 1.73, you can tell them immediately that it's .577, *because you notice* that 1.73 is nearly the square root of 3, so 1/1.73 must be one-third of the square root of 3. (Feynman 1985) [emphasis added.]

People seem to be able to recognize at least the following relationships from diagrams:

1. Parallel or perpendicular lines.
2. Relative positions of objects (*e.g.* above, below, left, right).
3. Objects that are similar under translation, scaling and/or rotation.
4. Approximate equivalence of lengths, sizes, or angles.
5. Relative sizes (smaller/larger) of lines or angles.
6. Proportionality, especially division in half, of lines or angles.

Abelson *et al.* (1989) describe the use of machine vision algorithms to recognize partitions of phase space in simulations of dynamical systems. Because such a simulation produces point values rather than trajectories, partitions cannot be derived directly. However, given a large number of points, the lines can be recognized by machine vision algorithms. This is especially interesting as a case where even a computer needs a "mind's eye" to recognize the qualitative structure of a problem.

23.5.5 Diagrammatic Operators

Some inference rules seem almost to be "plastic overlays" that can be moved into position and added to a diagram. The right-hand rule of electromagnetic fields often is invoked with actual movement of the hand. The rule that "sine = opposite / hypotenuse" can be thought of as a diagrammatic operator (Figure 23.11) that can be mentally moved into position and then used to add inferences directly to a diagram.

An advantage of such diagrammatic operators is that they can be used locally by making simple mental transformations such as translation,

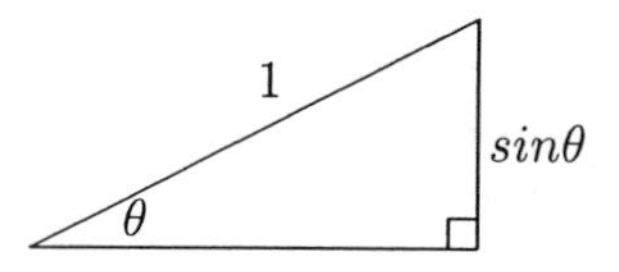

Figure 23.11
Sine Rule Overlay

rotation, and reflection to make the diagrammatic operator match the existing diagram. Intermediate results that are written on the diagram become available for subsequent use. For example, in the problem of Figure 23.10, the sine rule can be applied to the large triangle to find that $BC = sin\ \alpha$; this value can then be used with a cosine rule for the smaller triangle to find $CD = sin\ \alpha \cdot cos\ \alpha$.

23.5.6 Relating Actual Situation to Canonical Model

We have proposed (Kook 1989, Kook and Novak 1991) that the analysis of a physics problem should be represented not just as a set of equations, but as sets of correspondences between problem features and physical models. Solving a physics problem is not simply a matter of logical deduction (in which necessarily true results are derived from given premises), but a constructive process in which the given facts are elaborated by additional assumptions and physical models. In some problems, a single object will have multiple views as parts of different physical models. When represented symbolically, the correspondence sets become large and complex; a diagram can serve as a compact representation of such correspondences. Larkin and Simon (1987) note *minimizing labeling* as an advantage of diagrams. Human problem solvers also strive to minimize the number of variables used in equations. By transferring variable names from one part of a diagram to another, the same variable name can play a role in multiple physical models. A diagram may thus represent an overlaying of diagrams for physical models and actual objects.

Diagrams are often included with statements of physical laws (Gieck 1986); they presumably facilitate retrieval of the appropriate formulas from memory when a similar problem diagram is seen. In addition, the diagram facilitates matching between problem features and corresponding features of the physical model because the corresponding features appear in similar locations in each diagram. Consider the problem:

Given the gravitational constant G and the known facts about the orbit of the earth, calculate the mass of the sun.

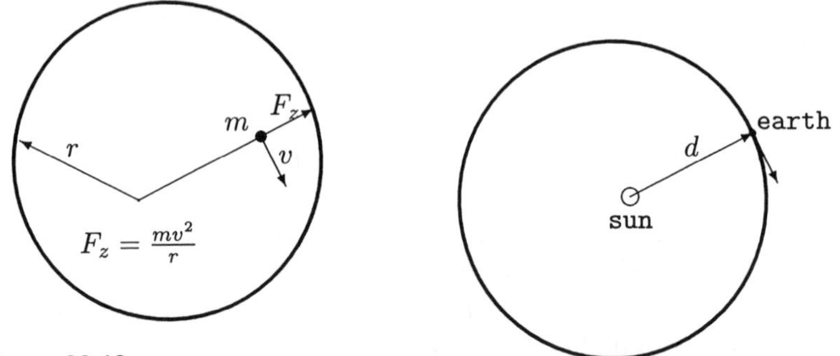

Figure 23.12
Centrifugal Force Law and Planet Problem

In Figure 23.12, the diagram on the left is as shown in Gieck (1986), while the diagram on the right is drawn to correspond to it. These diagrams immediately suggest that the sun corresponds to the center of the circle, the earth to the mass (suggesting that the earth be "coerced" to a point mass), the radius r to the earth-sun distance d, and the velocity v to the velocity of the earth (which then becomes a subproblem).

Larkin and Simon (1981) proposed the representation of problems and of physical situations as directed graphs and the use of graph-matching algorithms to find and instantiate appropriate physical models. This may be difficult, both because graph matching is computationally intractable and because missing or extra nodes prevent graphs from matching. Diagram matching may be more useful because diagrams that represent physical principles can be indexed by major features such as circular motion, which are likely to have only a few matches in a given problem. A match between a diagram and a given problem need not be exact: extra elements in the problem do not matter, and missing elements can be ignored (if not used) or taken as subproblems.

23.5.7 Making Predictions

Skilled problem solvers often use *gedanken* (thought) experiments involving actual or imagined diagrams to determine:

1. the direction of change in a system,

2. equilibrium points, bounding points or extrema,
3. connectivity, by tracing connecting paths on the diagram,
4. how a change in one quantity will affect another, and in what direction.

An excellent example is a method for determining whether a structural member of a bridge is under tension or compression: imagine the bridge collapsing with the member removed. If the member would become shorter in the collapse (Figure 23.13), it must be under compression.

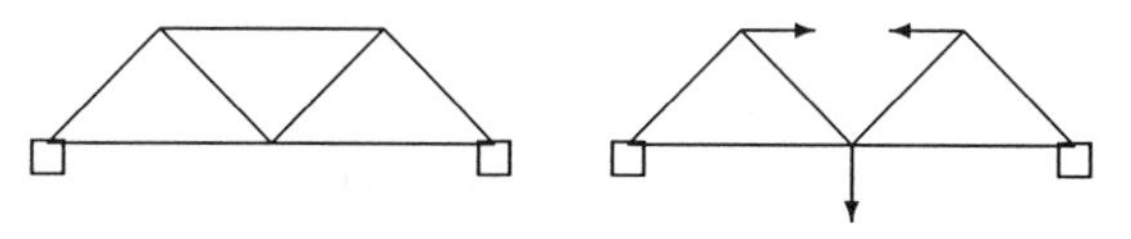

Figure 23.13
Removal of Bridge Member

23.6 Concluding Discussion

The preceding sections have described uses of diagrams in programs that solve physical problems, as well as uses of diagrams by humans. The power that diagrams give to human problem solving motivates consideration of how similar uses of diagrams could be incorporated into computer programs. The difficulty of machine perception of diagrams suggests that it would be unprofitable to try to duplicate human diagram processing directly. However, machine processing at a "sketch" level above the level of direct perception may be reasonable.

A set of basic perceptual operators, analogous to those that people use with diagrams but implemented above the pixel level of an actual diagram, might be implemented to take advantage of the strengths of the computer. A representation of geometric features such as lines, points, and circles by means of analytic geometry seems most appropriate for computer processing. Such a representation should be sufficiently accurate to determine such features as a line terminating at another line, a line tangent to a circle, parallel lines, etc.

Geometric features should be connected, bilaterally, with problem features that are represented symbolically. Sometimes geometric features represent objects, but in other cases they represent relationships (such as the earth-sun distance) or variable values. It must be possible to post values to the diagram representation; in this way, the diagram can serve the short-term memory function and allow opportunistic use of intermediate results that are "read" back from the diagram. The propagation of results by VIP is an example of posting results to a diagrammatic model.

It should be possible to group geometric objects into larger units; for example, in the bridge problem of Figure 23.13, two triangles formed from bridge members are treated as rigid bodies in visualizing how the bridge would collapse. The VIP model of the earth-sun system in Figure 23.6 shows that aspects of the geometry of the system are used in several separate models. These separate models are needed for the analysis; however, it would be better to have only a single diagram that unifies all the models rather than three diagrams with connections between them.

A library of geometric models is essential if minimally specified problems are to be understood. The statement "a ladder leans against a wall" implies the existence of a floor that supports the bottom of the ladder. It is reasonable to assume that a prototypical representation of the spatial relationships of a ladder, wall, and floor is stored; textbook problems show that a reader is assumed to have such knowledge.

Perceptual operators (*e.g.* detection of parallel lines) can operate at the analytic geometry level as special-purpose programs distinct from production rules or other symbolic analysis. "Noticing" these features can be done rapidly by special-purpose programs that perform only this function. Such noticing is a *signal-to-symbol transformation* (Nii et al. 1983) that converts analog values into symbolic values that can trigger productions. When Feynman noticed that 1.73 is almost the square root of 3, this triggered a production for problems involving a square root; 1.73 is an analog or "signal" value, while the concept of "square root" is symbolic. Noticing can direct attention to inferences based on observed relationships. For example, BEATRIX notices that two lines are tangent to a circle and infers the existence of a pulley system. Some things that are noticed can be assumed to be true, while others can trigger an attempt to prove what was noticed by more rigorous methods.

Perceptual inference also includes relating of similar models. In relating the earth-sun system to a circle, there are correspondences between the location of the sun and the center of the circle, between the earth-sun distance and the radius of the circle, etc. A stored relationship between a physical principle and a diagram could be used to relate corresponding parts of two situations that have similar diagrams. In this way, the diagrammatic representation becomes the basis for expressing the isomorphism between a problem situation and its physical model.

We have described uses of diagrams in programs that solve physics problems and have considered ways in which diagrams are used by humans. By implementing perceptual operations at a level below the operation of symbolic reasoning and by making use of correspondences between diagrams, it may be possible to gain the advantages that humans derive from diagrams for computer problem-solving systems.

Acknowledgements

This research was supported in part by the U.S. Army Research Office under contract DAAG29-84-K-0060. Computer equipment used in this research was donated by Hewlett Packard and Xerox Corporation. I thank the reviewers for their suggestions for improving the chapter.

References

Abelson, H. et al. 1989. Intelligence in Scientific Computing. *Communications of the ACM* 32(5):546–562, May.

Araya, A. 1984. Learning by Practice Using Experimentation and Generalization Techniques. Ph.D. diss., Univ. of Texas at Austin.

Ballard, D. H., and Brown, C. M. 1982. *Computer Vision.* New York: Prentice-Hall.

Erman, L. D., et al. 1980. The Hearsay-II Speech-Understanding System: Integrating Knowledge to Resolve Uncertainty. *ACM Computing Surveys* 12(2): 213–253, June.

Feynman, R. P. 1985. *Surely You're Joking, Mr. Feynman!* New York: Norton.

Fu, K. S. 1974. *Syntactic Methods in Pattern Recognition.* San Diego: Academic Press.

Garvey, A., Hewett, M., Schulman, R., and Hayes-Roth, B. 1985. BB1 User Manual. Technical Report KSL 86-60, Knowledge Systems Lab, Stanford Univ.

Gieck, K. 1986. *Engineering Formulas.* New York: McGraw-Hill.

Kook, Hyung Joon 1989. A Model-Based Representational Framework for Expert Physics Problem Solving. Ph.D. diss., Univ. of Texas at Austin, 1989. Tech. Report AI-89-103.

Kook, Hyung Joon and Novak, G. 1991. Representation of Models for Expert Problem Solving in Physics. *IEEE Trans. on Knowledge and Data Engineering*, 3(1):48-54, March.

Larkin, J., McDermott, J., Simon, D., and Simon, H. A. 1980. Expert and Novice Performance in Solving Physics Problems. *Science* 208:1335–1342, 20 June.

Larkin, J. and Simon, H. A. 1981. Learning through Growth of Skill in Mental Modeling. In Proceedings of the Cognitive Science Society.

Larkin, J. and Simon, H. A. 1987. Why a Diagram Is (Sometimes) Worth 10,000 Words. *Cognitive Science* 11:65–99.

Miller, G. A. 1956. The Magical Number Seven, Plus or Minus Two. *Psychological Review* 63:81–97.

Nii, H., Feigenbaum, E., Anton, J., and Rockmore, A. 1983. Signal-to-Symbol Transformation: HASP/SIAP Case Study. *AI Magazine* 3(2):23-35, (Spring).

Novak, G. 1976. Computer Understanding of Physics Problems Stated in Natural Language. *American Journal of Computational Linguistics*, Microfiche 53.

Novak, G. 1977. Representations of Knowledge in a Program for Solving Physics Problems. In Proceedings of the Fifth International Joint Conference on Artificial Intelligence, 286–291. San Francisco: Morgan Kaufmann.

Novak, G. 1983. GLISP: A Lisp-Based Programming System with Data Abstraction. *AI Magazine* 4(3):37–47, (Fall).

Novak, G. 1994. Generating Programs from Connections of Physical Models. In Proceedings of the Tenth Conference on Artificial Intelligence for Applications, 224–230. Los Alamitos, Calif.: IEEE Computer Society Press.

Novak, G., and Bulko, W. 1990. Understanding Natural Language with Diagrams. In Proceedings of the Eighth National Conference on Artificial Intelligence, 465–470. Menlo Park, Calif.: AAAI Press.

Novak, G., and Bulko, W. 1993. Diagrams and Text as Computer Input. *Journal of Visual Languages and Computing* 4:161–175.

van der Merwe, C. W. 1961. *Schaum's Outline of College Physics.* New York: McGraw-Hill.

Index